The Consumption
of Culture 1600–1800

Consumption and Culture in the 17th and 18th Centuries

Consumption and the World of Goods
Edited by John Brewer and Roy Porter

Early Modern Conceptions of Property
Edited by John Brewer and Susan Staves

The Consumption of Culture 1600–1800
Edited by Ann Bermingham and John Brewer

The Consumption of Culture 1600–1800

Image, Object, Text

Edited by

Ann Bermingham and John Brewer

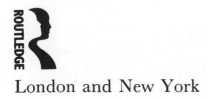

London and New York

First published 1995
by Routledge
11 New Fetter Lane, London EC4P 4EE

Simultaneously published in the USA and Canada
by Routledge
29 West 35th Street, New York, NY 10001

Typeset in Baskerville #2 by Florencetype Ltd, Stoodleigh, Devon
Printed and bound in Great Britain by TJ Press Ltd, Padstow, Cornwall

British Library Cataloguing in Publication Data
Consumption of Culture, 1600–1800: Image, Object, Text. –
(Consumption & Culture in 17th & 18th Centuries Series)
  I. Bermingham, Ann   II. Brewer, John   III. Series
  306.09032

Library of Congress Cataloguing in Publication Data
A catalogue record for this book has been requested

ISBN 0–415–12135–3

Contents

vi   Contents

Plates

Notes on Contributors

Ann Bermingham is the author of *Landscape and Ideology: The English Rustic Tradition, 1740–1860* (1986). She is a Professor of Art History at the University of California, Santa Barbara, and is presently working on a study of drawing as a social practice in Britain.

John Brewer is a Professor in the Department of History and Civilization at the European University Institute, Florence. Between 1987 and 1991 he was Director of the Clark Library and the Center for Seventeenth- and Eighteenth-Century Studies at the University of California, Los Angeles. He was the principal investigator on the research project "Culture and Consumption in the Seventeenth and Eighteenth Centuries." He is the author of *Sinews of Power* (1989) and co-editor of the two previous volumes in this series.

Thomas Crow is the author of *Painters and Public Life in Eighteenth-Century Paris* (1986) and *Emulation: Making Artists for Revolutionary France* (1995). He is Professor and Chair of History of Art at the University of Sussex.

Frank Donoghue is an Associate Professor of English at Ohio State University. He is the author of *The Fame Machine: Book Reviewing and Eighteenth-Century Literary Careers* (1995).

Robert Iliffe is a lecturer in the History of Science, Technology and Medicine at Imperial College, London. He has published a number of articles on the history of seventeenth- and eighteenth-century science and is presently completing a book on the state and the instrument-making trade in early modern London.

Lawrence E. Klein is Associate Professor of History at the University of Nevada, Las Vegas. He is the author of *The Third Earl of Shaftesbury and the Culture of Politeness* (1994) and articles on eighteenth-century cultural history.

Elizabeth Bennett Kubek completed her doctoral degree in English as the 1988–9 Susan B. Anthony Center for Women's Studies Doctoral Fellow at the University of Rochester. She is currently an Instructor in English and Textual Studies at Syracuse University. Her publications include articles on Aphra Behn and other Restoration and eighteenth-century writers.

Richard Leppert is a Professor of Comparative Studies in Discourse and Society at the University of Minnesota. His most recent books are *Music and Image: Domesticity Ideology and Socio-Cultural Formation in Eighteenth-Century England* (1989) and *The Sight of Sound: Music, Representation, and the History of the Body* (1993). He is currently finishing a book on western painting entitled *Art and the Committed Eye: Culture, Society, and the Functions of Imagery*.

Louise Lippincott is Curator of Fine Arts at the Carnegie Museum of Art, Pittsburgh. She wrote *Selling Art in Georgian London: The Rise of Arthur Pond* (1983) and is now working on an exhibition and book about the impact of artificial light on nineteenth-century art and culture.

Terry Lovell is the Director of the Center for the Study of Women and Gender at the University of Warwick. She is the author of *Pictures of Reality* (1980) and *Consuming Fiction* (1987).

Anne K. Mellor is the author of *Blake's Human Form Divine* (1974), *English Romantic Irony* (1980), *Mary Shelley: Her Life, Her Fiction, Her Monsters* (1988), and *Romanticism and Gender* (1993). She is a Professor of English at the University of California, Los Angeles. She is currently working on a study of Romantic women writers, artists, and intellectuals.

W. J. T. Mitchell is the author of *Iconology* (1986) and *Picture Theory* (1994), and the editor of *Critical Inquiry*. His recent edited books include *Art and the Public Sphere* (1993) and *Landscape and Power* (1994). He is the Gaylord Donnelley Distinguished Service Professor of Art and Literature at the University of Chicago.

Nicholas Mirzoeff is an Assistant Professor of Art History at the University of Wisconsin-Madison. He was a J. Paul Getty Postdoctoral Fellow in the History of Art in 1992–3. He is the author of *Silent Poetry: Deafness, Sign and Visual Culture in Modern France* (1995).

Mitzi Myers teaches writing and children's and adolescent literature at the University of California, Los Angeles. She has published extensively on eighteenth- and nineteenth-century women writers and historical children's literature. She is currently completing *Romancing the Family: Maria Edgeworth and the Scene of Instruction*.

Felicity A. Nussbaum is Professor of English and Women's Studies at Syracuse University. Her books include *"The Brink of All We Hate": English Satires on Women, 1660–1750* (1984) and *The Autobiographical Subject: Gender and Ideology in Eighteenth-Century England* (1989) which was co-recipient of the ASECS Gottschalk Prize. Together with Laura Brown she co-edited *The New Eighteenth Century: Theory/Politics/English Literature* (1987).

Ronald Paulson is a Professor of English and Art History at the Johns Hopkins University. He is the author of numerous studies of eighteenth- and nineteenth-century British art and literature including *Breaking and Remaking: Aesthetic Practice in England, 1700–1820* (1989), *Hogarth, I: "The Modern Moral Subject," 1697–1732* (1991), *Hogarth, II: High Art and Low, 1732–1750* (1992), and *Hogarth, III: Art and Politics, 1750–1764* (1993). *The Beautiful, Novel, and Strange: Aesthetics and Heterodoxy* is forthcoming (1995).

Peter H. Pawlowicz is an Assistant Professor of Art History at East Tennessee State University. A 1991 Clark Fellow, he is currently at work on a book about visuality and representation in eighteenth-century culture.

Paula Rea Radisich has written articles on eighteenth-century art that have appeared in the *Art Bulletin* and *Eighteenth-Century Studies*. She is an Associate Professor of Art History at Whittier College, California. She is currently completing a manuscript entitled "Painted spaces of the Enlightenment," a study of selected works by Hubert Robert.

Mary D. Sheriff is the author of *J. H. Fragonard: Art and Eroticism* (1990) and *The Exceptional Woman: Elisabeth Vigée-Lebrun and the Cultural Politics of Art*, forthcoming from the University of Chicago Press. She teaches Art History and Women's Studies at the University of North Carolina at Chapel Hill and is co-editor of *Eighteenth-Century Studies*.

Richard Sorrenson is an Assistant Professor in the Department of History and Philosophy of Science, Indiana University. He is completing a book-length manuscript on scientific instrument makers in eighteenth-century London.

Jay Tribby is an Assistant Professor of History at the University of Florida. His *Club Medici: Natural Experiment and the Making of Tuscany* is forthcoming.

James Grantham Turner is a Professor of English at the University of California, Berkeley. He has edited *Politics, Poetics and Hermeneutics in Milton's Prose* (1990) with David Loewenstein, and *Sexuality and Gender in Early Modern Europe: Institutions, Texts, Images* (1993), both from Cambridge University Press. He is the author of the *Politics of Landscape: Rural Scenery and Society in English Poetry, 1630–1660* (1979), and numerous articles on seventeenth- and eighteenth-century culture. *One Flesh: Paradisal Marriage and Sexual Relations in the Age of Milton* (1987) was reissued in 1994 in a Clarendon Paperback edition by Oxford University Press. He is currently writing two books on libertinism.

Anne M. Wagner is Chair and Professor of Modern Art at the University of California, Berkeley. The author of *Jean-Baptiste Carpeaux: Sculptor of the Second Empire* (1986), she is currently at work on the manuscript of a book to be titled *Not Made by Great Men: Sculpture and History in 19th-Century France*. The essay in this volume is part of that study. Her book *Three Artists (Three Women): Hesse, Krasner and O'Keeffe* will be published in 1996.

Don E. Wayne is a Professor of English at the University of California, San Diego. His publications include *Penshurst: The Semiotics of Place and the Poetics of History* (1984).

Kathleen Wilson, Assistant Professor of History at SUNY-Stony Brook, is the author of *The Sense of the People: Politics, Culture and Imperialism in England 1715–1785* (1995). She is currently at work on a study of theater, culture, and modernity in Georgian Britain, 1720–1820.

Preface

The papers in this volume were part of the three-year research project mounted by the Center for Seventeenth- and Eighteenth-Century Studies and the William Andrews Clark Memorial Library at UCLA on "Culture and Consumption in the Seventeenth and Eighteenth Centuries." This project was partially funded by grant no. RO 21623–88 from the Interpretive Research Division of the National Endowment of the Humanities. Additional resources came from the Dean of the Division of Humanities at UCLA, the Center and the Clark Library.

The project director, John Brewer, would like to thank not only all the scholars who took part as paper-givers and discussants but the staff of the Center and the Library whose efforts made the project possible. Ann Bermingham wishes to thank the contributors for their cooperation and Marina Romani from the Publications Department of the Center/Clark for her help in assembling the essays.

This volume is the last of three published by Routledge from the Center/Clark series. The others are John Brewer and Roy Porter (eds) *Consumption and the World of Goods* and John Brewer and Susan Staves (eds) *Early Modern Conceptions of Property*.

1

Introduction

The consumption of culture: image, object, text

Ann Bermingham

In a still life painting from the seventeenth century, the Dutch artist Willem Kalf (1616–93) depicts a sumptuous array of precious objects: a Persian carpet covering a marble-topped table; a Ming porcelain bowl; a Venetian glass flagon; a gold-worked nautilus cup; a silver tray and eating utensils (Plate 1.1). Even the foodstuffs – sugar, wine, a half-peeled lemon – are luxuries, items imported from abroad or cultivated in hothouses. Should we be tempted to suppose that "consumer society" is a recent phenomenon of the late twentieth, century, the opulence of Kalf's *pronkstilleven* should give us pause. Such images suggest that the prevailing idea that consumer society is a function of late capitalism (Debord 1967; Jameson 1991) ignores the substantial visual evidence we have from earlier periods that consumption, even conspicuous consumption, has a longer and more complex history. Our data comes not only from paintings (and indeed we should be wary of interpreting these too literally) but from the consumer objects themselves that fill our museums, antique shops, and attics and are reassembled in museum period rooms and in "living history" environments such as colonial Williamsburg. In the seventeenth century still life paintings like Kalf's were common household objects in the Netherlands. They could be bought for as little as one or two guilders or as much as six or seven (Schama 1988: 319). Dutch still life paintings are not only reflections of wealth but reflections *on* wealth by a society transformed through a rising tide of capital. They reminded their owners of the transitory nature of earthly pleasures and the vanity of their own newly acquired riches. Yet they did so in a visual language that was itself a *tour de force* of sensuosity and highly polished craftsmanship, thus intensifying the appeal of the very objects they warned against (Schama 1993: 484–5).

In eighteenth-century France Netherlandish art was esteemed and Dutch and Flemish still lifes, portraits, and landscapes were collected. This activity of buying and selling paintings is the subject of a signboard painted by Antoine Watteau (1684–1721) for the shop of his friend, the art dealer Edme–François Gersaint (Plate 1.2). The painting was one of Watteau's last works, begun six or seven months before his death in

1721. Gersaint's shop was located on the Pont de Nôtre-Dame, a place known for its concentration of artisans and dealers in art and artistic bric-à-brac. When he arrived in Paris in 1703, Watteau was first employed on the Pont de Nôtre-Dame in the workshop of a dealer in religious imagery. According to Gersaint:

> In those days, many small portraits and subjects of devotion were wholesaled to merchants in the provinces, who bought them by the dozen or even the gross. The painter for whom he [Watteau] had just begun to work was the one most in demand for this kind of painting, in which he maintained a considerable turnover. He had at times as many as a dozen miserable pupils whom he used like manual laborers. The only talent that he required of his apprentices was one for quick execution. Each one had his job: some did skies; others did heads; this one painted draperies; that one dabbed in the highlights. Finally the picture found itself finished after it had passed through the hands of the last one.[1]

Nearly twenty years separate Watteau's first experiences with the Parisian dealers and *Maîtrise* in the art shops on the bridges and *quais* of the Seine from the image he painted for his friend. Shops like the one described by Gersaint still existed, where artisans churned out clichéd images on a semi-industrialized basis for an indiscriminate provincial clientele, but there were also shops like Gersaint's own which sold paintings by recognized masters to a wealthy and urbane public.[2] Watteau shows Gersaint's shop filled with erotic mythological scenes in pastoral settings, pure landscapes, still lifes, religious images, and portraits; genres which dominated seventeenth-century Flemish painting, and to which Watteau was heir. In Gersaint's shop where this style was promoted, paintings were sold along with ormolu clocks, mirrors, and other luxury objects.

Unlike its famous seventeenth-century predecessors – Velázquez's *Las Meninas* and Vermeer's *Art of Painting* – which through the representation of paintings and mirrors play on the relationship between life and art, Watteau's scene employs these same props in a way that shifts the meaning of the painting away from an emphasis on the making of art to a reflection on its consumption. Rather than an artist's studio we have a dealer's shop, and instead of a meditation on the artist's powers of mimesis, Gersaint's signboard depicts the reception of art by an art-consuming public (Vidal 1992: 192–3). Consumption, however, is figured not simply as the exchange of money for luxury goods but as an occasion for the psychological dynamics of fantasy and narcissistic self-absorption. The woman in black, for example, absently fingers her fan and studies the landscape portion of the large oval painting while her male companion steadies himself on his walking-stick so that he can get a closer look at the area of the canvas displaying a group of naked nymphs. Each, it would seem, sees the painting differently; each, we might argue, sees a different painting. Next to them, the young woman and two gentlemen gaze at themselves in the mirror held by a shop assistant creating and seeing three distinct reflections. Thus they are shown producing their own images in the process of consuming them. In this sense, Watteau's painting suggests that what is ultimately at stake in consumption is the production of the subject through self-reflection and desire. As a meditation on the consumption of culture, Watteau's signboard provides a rich analogue for our own late modern preoccupations with issues of subjectivity, reception, and the processes of interpretation.

In addition to the visual evidence of Kalf and Watteau, the signs of an increased consumption of culture from the seventeenth century on are supported by texts in the form of diaries, household inventories, bankruptcy records, and probate wills. These records are of particular significance in Protestant countries like the Netherlands and England, which lacked highly developed institutional patronage systems, for they help to trace the flow of luxury goods to private dwellings. The abundance of this information has only begun to generate historical analyses focused on patterns of distribution and private consumption, on the reciprocal effects of supply and demand, on the social meanings and political uses of consumption, and on individual manufacturers' techniques for cultivating their clientele (de Vries 1974 and 1976; Thirsk 1978; McKendrick, Brewer, and Plumb 1982; Mukerji 1983; Campbell 1987; Weatherill 1988; Schama 1988; Shammas 1990; Brewer and Porter 1993).[3] These analyses shift the lens of economic history from the study of industrial production and the proletarianization of labor to the study of private demand and the marketing of goods. Along these lines, Neil McKendrick has argued that the early "consumer revolution" was "the necessary analog to the industrial revolution, the necessary convulsion on the demand side of the equation to match the convulsion on the supply side" (1982: 9).

Yet despite these efforts, early modern consumption is still a relatively new topic of inquiry and mapping its history remains largely preliminary. There are a number of empirical reasons for this, including the difficulty in tracking the distribution of goods in the sixteenth, seventeenth, and eighteenth centuries and tabulating their purchase and exchange, yet perhaps the most significant impediment has been the inability to conceptualize consumption in relation to early modern culture. It is perhaps no coincidence that theorists of modernism have assigned consumer society to the late twentieth century and that until recently historians of the early modern period have overlooked the evidence of a flourishing consumer culture in sixteenth-, seventeenth-, and eighteenth-century Europe. One does not look for something where one has been led to believe it does not exist. In light of this, I would like to propose that the consumption of culture's seemingly "neglected" early history has in fact been a culturally suppressed one. Suppressed by a vision of modernity which has turned largely on an economic analysis of the social organization of production, and on an ideology of modernism which has taken upon itself the task of defending "culture" against the very forms of mass consumption that we now seek to examine. In short, modernism's master narrative of culture has obscured the early history of consumption and its relationship to social and cultural forms, substituting in its place a history of culture focused on artistic production, individualism, originality, genius, aestheticism, and avant-gardism. This would help to explain why critics of postmodernism like Fredric Jameson, nostalgic for a more "authentic" culture, see consumer society as part of the superficial, schizophrenic "logic" of late capitalism (Jameson 1982; Jameson 1991). Indeed, it is only by operating outside the limits of modernism that we can see a "consumer society" that is nearly four hundred years old. This vantage point reveals cultural and social formations which by the later eighteenth century had come to represent all that a nascent modernism both needed – and needed to suppress – in order to constitute itself. Thus this volume seeks both to add to consumption's early history, and to interrogate its relation to particular modernist conceptions of culture as they came to be formulated in the seventeenth and eighteenth centuries and naturalized in the twentieth.

Such a project rests not on the assumption that "consumer society" is a homogeneous entity stretching back unchanged into the sixteenth century, but rather on the belief that just as the histories of capitalism and modernism have been assigned different periods and phases, so too the history of the consumption of culture lends itself to periodization. Diffused as it is through a wide social spectrum, this history argues for a sensitive exploration of the differences between consumers at particular times and in particular places. Rather than being seen simply as a phase of late capitalism, the consumption of culture needs to be examined as intrinsic to all phases of capitalism, even the very earliest. Such a history should not only supplement the more familiar narratives of production, but should also be used to critique them. The suppressed history of cultural consumption may help us to historicize dominant histories of modern production which mask with empirical data their deeper theoretical, moral, and aesthetic agendas. Finally, a history of the consumption of culture could reveal to us the ways in which the mass consumption of objects of commerce and high culture meet (and perhaps might be increasingly made to meet) the specific psychological and cultural needs of dynamic social groups, providing them with a sense of individual identity, social connection, and community.

Admittedly to speak of the "consumption of culture" was, until recently, to speak a kind of blasphemy. For our modern notions of culture have been constructed precisely to distinguish a unique and precious object like a painting from the mass-produced and profane commodity. While the one is an object of aesthetic veneration that transcends commerce and the ravages of time, the other is subject to both, for consumption is its *raison d'être*. As Raymond Williams has reminded us, the concept of culture as being synonymous with high art dates only from the early nineteenth century (1966; 1976). Eighteenth-century uses of the word link culture to (1) notions of husbandry and cultivation describing a general process of intellectual, spiritual, and aesthetic development, or (2) a particular way of life of a people, a group, a period, or humanity in general. According to Williams, the word "culture" begins straining towards the aesthetic in the mid-eighteenth century as a response to early industrialism, the specter of "mass" societies, and the accelerated pace of social change. After 1800 the terms "art" and "culture" become mutually reinforcing, with culture now referring not only to "the general process of intellectual, spiritual and aesthetic development" but also to the "works and practices which represent and sustain it" (Williams 1976: 91). This third use of the word culture in the nineteenth century therefore reveals a distinction between high art and other forms of creative, social, and aesthetic activity which had previously been accommodated within the term's second meaning. By the second decade of the nineteenth century, "art" and "culture" come to refer to an exclusive realm of refinement and creative genius free from the taint of commerce. It is at this time too that they take on their decided anti-bourgeois stance. The moral imperative for such a distinction between high art and low is most clearly established in Matthew Arnold's *Culture and Anarchy* (1867) where "culture" is society's only weapon against the vulgarity of "mass" or "bourgeois" culture – which is not even deemed "culture" by Arnold but "anarchy." Thus, by the middle of the nineteenth century, "culture" had evolved from a term of social inclusion to one of social exclusion.

The use of "culture" as synonymous with "art" provided the moral and political ethos for the development of an aesthetic that would continually renew itself through its resistance to more popular or mass forms of culture. The *cordon sanitaire* drawn between high art and these other forms of art and entertainment marked a line which commerce was not permitted to cross. While commerce was seen to have infected nearly every aspect of modern life, the realm of art was deemed to be free from its contagion. The anxiety to create such a space of pure aesthetics can be found in the late eighteenth and early nineteenth centuries in the writings of such theorists as Shaftesbury, Kant, and Schiller (Barrell 1986; Bourdieu 1984; Burger 1984). It was an anxiety felt particularly keenly in countries that were highly commercialized or lacked extensive patronage systems, or both. It is in terms of this *cordon sanitaire* that we might read, for instance, the founding of the Royal Academy in England (1769). The Academy was intended to dignify art and artists by giving them an education that was "liberal" rather than purely mechanical and a forum for exhibition that was not dominated by purely commercial interests and applications. Reynolds's *Discourses* to the "gentlemen" of the Academy (i.e. the students) emphasize again and again the importance of art rising above petty and socially divisive aspects of commerce in order to embrace a more grand and generalized aesthetic (Barrell 1986). The effect of the Royal Academy was to slow the highly commercial art industry which had grown up in place of extensive royal and aristocratic patronage (Lippincott 1983; Pears 1988; Solkin 1993; Pointon 1993). The Academy's attempts to gentrify, professionalize, and monopolize art practice and to tie it to royal patronage were only partially successful; their long-term effect was to contain artistic production and by the nineteenth century to inspire various revolts by younger artists against its authority.

Yet as familiar as this tale is, it is not quite the whole story, for what the *cordon sanitaire* drawn in the eighteenth century between art and commerce did was not so much to exclude commerce from art, but to mask the fact that the two were already deeply enmeshed. While we may take Reynolds at his word in the *Discourses*, we do so at our peril, for he was no wild-eyed romantic starving in a garret but a financially successful artist eminently practical about the business of portrait painting – an artist who had no compunction about aggressively marketing his works and having them reproduced in prints. Nor do we quite comprehend the British Royal Academy as an institution if we do not see that in addition to providing artists with an education and a professional status, it also provided them with an annual exhibition in which to market their wares and with a proper place to entertain aristocratic patrons and to cultivate wealthy clients. It is this entanglement of high culture with commerce that we must come to see if we are to understand the nature of both modern culture and consumption. For what seems clear is that the need to preserve art from kitsch which has been so much a part of modernist aesthetics, and which ultimately develops out of the eighteenth century's anxiety about industrialism and the commercialization of culture, has effectively obscured the fact that since the industrial revolution it has been virtually impossible to separate art and culture from the economic forces of commerce and mass consumption.

Consumption vs. production

Historians of consumption in the early modern period have used it to illuminate changing aspects of social, domestic, and economic life. As Lorna Weatherill has explained, studies of patterns of consumption reveal such things as "new drinking habits (utensils for hot drinks), new ways of behaving at table (knives and forks), decoration (pictures), acquisition of information and contacts with the wider literary world (books), the need to know time (clocks), and traditional ways of cooking and eating (pewter)" (1988: 138). We might add to this list a new concern with personal appearance (mirrors, gloves, buttons, ribbons, and other fashion apparel), a taste for amusement (novels, musical instruments, amateur art supplies, plays, concerts, and opera), an interest in science (telescopes, air pumps, orreries), and a desire for privacy (window curtains).

As this list suggests, consumption is driven largely by fashion and not economic necessity. The objects consumed were for the most part non-essentials that made life more pleasant, interesting, and comfortable. Their frivolous nature exposed them to the period's familiar cries against luxury. Critics charged that they were made from cheap materials intended to be spent and wasted and that their manufacture cost their producers almost nothing but their labor. Nevertheless, with their minimal capital costs, consumer industries were effective in employing under-used rural laborers and absorbing the extra manpower available in urban areas from population increases and immigration. Hence while they had their critics, consumer industries and the objects they produced also found support among men of business who saw labor and full employment as a social good. Toward this end the production and consumption of non-essentials could be seen as necessary to the health of the nation, for they promised to keep the indigent and the infirm usefully and gainfully employed (Thirsk 1978). Thus in addition to revealing a great deal about the texture of everyday life, the production and consumption of consumer items reveals a changing attitude towards labor, fashion, built-in obsolescence, economy, and national identity.

Extensive analyses of the social importance and political significance of consumption in early modern England have been made by Joan Thirsk and Neil McKendrick. In her study of the sixteenth and seventeenth centuries, Thirsk shows how as early as the 1540s notions of "commonweal" linked manufacture at home to employment of the poor. The production of frivolous items like buttons and pins could be morally justified by even the sternest Protestant, if such production employed a large number of other-wise indigent people (Thirsk 1978: 17). According to Thirsk "these industrial by-employments heralded the development of a consumer society that embraced not only the nobility and gentry and the substantial English yeoman, but included humble peasants, laborers, and servants as well. It gave them cash and something to spend the cash on" (1978: 8). Coupled with this development of wage-paid, cash-bearing con-sumers of all classes was the growing realization among manufacturers that home trade was as advantageous to the nation as foreign trade (Thirsk 1978: 148; McKendrick, Brewer, and Plumb 1982: 18–20). The shift then from a mercantile economy based on foreign trade and the balance of payments to an industrial one based on expanded manufacture for domestic markets and full employment is clearly mapped in Thirsk's account. While subsequent studies have questioned the amount of purchasing power available to the lower classes in the sixteenth and seventeenth centuries (Weatherill 1988: 192), they have not seriously contradicted the general picture Thirsk has drawn.

As Thirsk demonstrates, the notion of "commonweal" with its particular emphasis on the social utility of labor both justified consumption and placed a new emphasis on the labor-value of goods as opposed to their simple use-value. Yet in focusing on the social benefits of labor and employment the notion of commonweal set the terms whereby economic theories of production and technological determinism would dominate and in which consumption would be assigned a comparatively obscure role. In the eighteenth century as the wealth of nations was increasingly seen to rest on the ability to produce necessities in cost-efficient ways, the cost of labor came to be seen as critical. Adam Smith's analysis of the pin industry in which he demonstrated the cost benefits of the division of labor and the evils of the domestic system was an argument for efficiency and specialization. His attacks on mercantilist restrictions on inland and overseas commerce and his arguments for a "free market" were intended to support domestic manufacture and the consumer. Smith's arguments for free trade implied the existence of a consumer society which would benefit from increased manufacture and market competition, but he left the composition of this society and its mechanisms unspecified. Looked at from the point of view of this lacuna, one could argue that Smith simply used the vague image of a "consumer society" in order to rationalize his more highly-developed thesis about specialized labor and free trade. To pursue a theory of consumption in any detail would have presented him with a conundrum, a contradiction at the heart of capitalism: the fact that workers are also consumers. If it is in the interests of manufacturers to keep wages low in order to increase the profitability of their wares, it is also in their interests to pay their workers a sufficient wage so that as consumers they can afford to buy these wares.

If classical capitalism is weighted towards the study of production, so too are the writings of its greatest critic, Karl Marx. While he allowed that changes in social relations must be prior to technological changes (Marx 1977: 318–47), Marx saw consumption as a reciprocal yet subordinate part of production (Marx 1973: 83–111). Given that his intention was to expose the fallacies of capitalist economics, it is understandable that the major thrust of his argument is towards an analysis of labor and production. Nowhere is consumption given the intensive analysis that Marx devotes to production. Moreover, Marx's labor theory of value establishes work and not consumption as the proper form for human self-fulfillment. For Marx it is "the practical creation of an *objective world*, the *fashioning* of inorganic nature, [which] is proof that man is a conscious species-being." It is production therefore which humanizes man by allowing him to see himself as distinct from nature and as part of a larger social fabric. In producing objects therefore he "reproduces himself not only intellectually in his consciousness, but actively and actually, and he can therefore contemplate himself in a world he himself has created" (Marx 1975: 328–9). The consumption of commodities, on the other hand, becomes an activity of human alienation, fetishization, and reification. It is finally a mode of misrecognition. In the act of consumption one ceases to recognize in the commodity the social relations that produced it, seeing it instead as autonomous, mysterious, and other. Implicit in such a reading of commodities is the notion that consumption is a wholly private and isolating experience, that it is the economic logic of an unchecked radical individualism which can result only in a loss of community and in the formation of a desocialized, and thus dehumanized, self.

Marx's distrust of the commodity – his description of it as a "fetish" – is framed as a visual problem in perception. Marx writes: "the existence of things qua commodities, and the value-relation between the products of labor which stamps them as commodities, have absolutely no connection with their physical properties and with the material relations arising therefrom. There is a definite social relation between men, that assumes, in their eyes, the fantastic form of a relation between things" (1975: 72). Like the ideas of ideology which are likened by Marx to the reversed images within a camera obscura, commodities are distorted perceptions. While the false projections of ideology are "imprinted" on to the mind of the observer, commodification – in a reverse move – "stamps" the observer's fantasies on to the products of labor. The result is a perverse and primitive act of fetishization whereby the commodity becomes inappropriately valued, or – rather – overvalued. As a mode of misrecognition, fetishization disempowers observers in so far as they become driven by fantasy and alienated from their true source of political strength – their own labor.

Marx's valuation of labor as the source of human self-fulfillment has led Jean Baudrillard to argue that in this Marx was no different from other nineteenth-century thinkers – radical, liberal, and conservative – who tended to overvalue the psychic and social benefits of work and to devalue any activity, with the exception of art, that took place outside the workplace (1975). Utilitarianism, Baudrillard argues, is the basis for both political economy and its radical critique (1975: 21–51). The concept of production, so essential to capitalism, is never challenged but merely imported, hence Baudrillard claims Marxism "can never radically overcome the influence of political economy" (1975: 59). In addition to his valorization of production, Marx's tie to the intellectual formations of political economy is revealed in other aspects of his thought, such as his universalizing and essentialist notions of "Man" and "Nature," which for him, as for the political economists, exist prior to any social or cultural formations. Society and culture are the result of man's struggle to produce objects from and against nature. What Marx does not allow is that our notions of man and nature are embedded in social and cultural forms and cannot be comprehended apart from them. Hence in critiquing capitalism's celebration of the individual and of individual labor, Marx recapitulates its most essential myth in the form of his own Robinsonade, that is, a narrative in which production and culture originate with the autonomous individual. In focusing on production Marxism, like capitalism, locates the individual at the origin of production and culture. Thus Marxist thought can be linked to modernist notions of the autonomous artist struggling to produce art from common nature in a space free from the demands of the market.

For our purposes what is important to note is that Marx's notion of culture, as a product of the struggle of man against nature, subjects culture and its artifacts to the productivist and utilitarian scenarios of political economy. Moreover, it threatens to place culture as the source either of man's identity or of his alienation. For according to Marx, the objects made from nature always stand as "something alien." Their alienating effect is intensified in a factory where objects are mass produced through specialized labor and then sold as commodities. As Daniel Miller has explained, Marx's analysis of the alienating effects of the production of objects – "objectification" –

derived from Hegel's *Phenomenology*. In Hegel's thought, objectification functions as the primary means of self-knowledge, and the resulting, inevitable alienation it produces is the primary condition of existence with which man must always struggle in an attempt to feel at one with himself (1987: 42–3; see too Mitchell 1986). As Miller insightfully demonstrates, such an idea is also found in a variety of psychoanalytical analysis of childhood development. In contrast to Hegel, Marx saw alienation as the logical outcome of industrialism and the division of labor. The cure for the estrangement of the worker from the products of his own labor was the suppression of private property and the return of the means of production to him. While alienation emerges as the condition of civilization as well as industrialism, Marx does exempt art from the alienating effects of culture. Significantly, Marx's example of unalienated labor is John Milton who, he says, "produced *Paradise Lost* as a silkworm produces silk, as the activation of *his own nature*" (1977: 1044). Even though he insists that the forms of art are determined by history and social relations (1973: 101), Marx remains wedded to the idealist notion of artistic creation in which the space of artistic production is imagined apart from that of commerce and alienated labor. Thus he projected a utopian future that was a recapitulation of a prelapsarian past – a time before alienation – in the form of the romantic idea of the artist. Moreover, in emphasizing art as the natural "activation" of the artist's "own nature" Marx's representation of artistic production reproduces the notion of the artist's natural genius and originality and anticipates the modernist aesthetic of "art for art's sake." Thus the *cordon sanitaire* drawn by Kant, Schiller, and Arnold is not cut by Marx.

Like modern economics, modernist aesthetics, which has oriented the study of art around the personalities, lives, and works of individual artists, is conceptualized in terms of production. Great masters are conceived as doing battle with common nature or, alternatively, as struggling against the influence of predecessors.[4] In both scenarios the artist, if he is a great artist, exists apart from commercial life and in opposition to bourgeois culture. Thus the art for art's sake aesthetic pits the individual artist as the producer of unique objects against what Wordsworth called the "perpetual flow of trivial objects"; or in a less familiar, more radical, avant-garde mode, it allies the artist with the forms of industrialized production in order that he may transform them into the liberating media of popular consciousness.[5] In either case the artist as producer is central. Focused as it is on the artist's struggle to produce in opposition to bourgeois society, modernism's perspective on culture can never quite acknowledge the fact that the sovereign individual so deeply embedded in its aesthetic is, of course, the paradigmatic figure of bourgeois society.

Identity, emulation, and class

Rather than think in terms of individualism and the production of art, many of the chapters collected here explore the way in which the activity of consuming culture enables individuals to construct social identities. In many cases their arguments have been inspired by Jürgen Habermas's attempts to map the formation of a polite and informed public in the early modern period by examining the role of civic and public institutions, such as coffee-houses, private salons, newspapers, journals, book clubs, subscription libraries, and such cultural forms as novels and plays, in creating a social space for rational and critical debate (Habermas 1989). According to Habermas, bourgeois public opinion and class identity were formed in the cultural and social spaces of theaters, art exhibitions, and concerts. In matters of art, bourgeois public opinion believed itself to be a capable judge and hence entitled to pass judgment. Thus, Habermas notes, literary reviews and institutionalized art criticism are typical inventions of the day (Habermas 1989: 41). This same process that converted art and culture into objects for public discussion also converted them into commodities to be bought and sold (Habermas 1989: 37). The public represented in this discursive and commercial space of culture imagined itself to be polite, rational, moral, and egalitarian. In universalizing this self-image of enlightened rationality as well as its discursive and institutional formations, the bourgeoisie empowered themselves and disempowered those whom the discourse excluded or opposed. Yet no matter how many might be left out (the rural, the illiterate, the poor, the non-European, the women and children) the "public" of the bourgeois public sphere believed itself to be indeed a "public," that is to say, an inclusive body of equals. In later work, Habermas has developed and defended this image of the public sphere and its discursive formation of culture as the basis for a fully transparent society in which political consensus is attained by "communicative rationality" (Habermas 1990: 314–16). The public sphere thus forms the essential part of a larger teleological project – the history of modern democracies.

In a dialectical and dialogic relationship to the bourgeois public sphere is the private domestic sphere. It too is the result of literacy, commerce, and urbanization. Because the criticism that emerged in the literary reviews, newspapers, art, and literature of the public sphere was primarily social and aesthetic rather than political, it was oriented less towards the ancient ideals of *res publica*, and more towards the concerns of private life (Habermas 1989: 49–51). The individual and the family thus take on a new prominence and significance. Yet despite its importance, Habermas does not explore this private domestic sphere with the same kind of attention that he directs towards the formation of the public sphere. Nor does he fully examine the interaction between these two social spaces. For our purposes, the result is a somewhat lopsided account of cultural consumption and the making of a culture-consuming public. For, as many of the chapters in this volume suggest, as a retreat from the demands of public life, the domestic sphere was an important site of cultural consumption and through this process engendered its own cultural forms and practices. Moreover, given the fact that upper- and middle-class women in the early modern period were increasingly excluded from the bourgeois public sphere their role as producers and consumers of culture becomes, in Habermas's narrative, virtually invisible. Of great importance therefore to a number of contributors is the role of women in the history of consumption. While restricted to the margins of cultural production, middle-class women's supposed propensity to consume is remarked on in the literature of the time. There they often function as cautionary examples intended to warn readers of false taste and the dangers of luxury. To move beyond this narrow ideological role scripted for women by the period, and beyond Habermas's own neglect of the private sphere, is an important part of this collection's purpose.

Critics of Habermas's notions of the bourgeois public sphere and the formation of modern bourgeois culture, argue that he shares some of its universalist presumptions.

Peter Burger among others has pointed out how Habermas has ignored the breaks and discontinuities that have occurred in the cultural formations of the modern period in an attempt to create a holistic and monolithic image of modernity (1984). Others take issue with his homogeneous image of public discourse. They see him as embracing the Enlightenment's universalist conception of "Man" with the result that the differences in subject positions due to gender, sexuality, race, and social status, and the tensions and forms of cultural pluralism they generate, are ignored.[6] Thus Habermas's insightful history of modernity is seen to suffer from the same Enlightenment-induced blindness that has characterized modernity itself. An alternative to this is found in the deconstruction of Enlightenment rationalism and logocentrism and the decentering of the subject as carried out by the poststructuralist critics Jacques Derrida, Roland Barthes, and Michel Foucault. Their work is seen by some as having provided early modern studies with powerful tools with which to examine modernism's basic assumptions. As theories of modernism, they critique modernism's search for "formal structures with universal value," and – in the case of Foucault – propose in its place an "historical investigation into the events that have led us to constitute ourselves and to recognize ourselves as subjects" (Foucault 1984: 46). Enlightenment notions of autonomous, rational individualism are thus replaced with analyses of the interpellated subject.

Foucault's work overturns notions of an essential self. The modern idea of the author or artist, for instance, is seen as a "function" of social and commercial discourses that value genius and originality (Foucault 1977). Foucault's analysis of subjectivity challenges not only Enlightenment individualism but also the generally positive reading of the public sphere offered by Habermas. Rather than a source of liberation and self-discovery, public institutions with their "technologies of power" become in Foucault's eyes coercive institutions whose apparatuses of control are disguised as reason and thereby internalized by the subject. In his last works, Foucault turned from these analyses of empiricism and institutional power relations in the seventeenth and eighteenth centuries to examine "the forms and modalities of the relation to self by which the individual constitutes and recognizes himself *qua* subject" (Foucault 1985: 6). Foucault's "hermeneutics of the self" consists in a play of social codes, discourses, and systems of knowledge. The subject does not exist prior to culture and cannot be envisioned outside the processes of its own cultural becoming. Cut loose from bourgeois individualism which assumed a "normative" subject who was white, male, and middle-class, Foucault's notions of the subject coincide with contemporary feminist and multicultural explorations of identity as constructed through the play of social and cultural differences.

Useful as both Habermas's and Foucault's analyses of identity and subjectivity are, they do not quite help us to explain what it is that makes individuals want to consume culture or anything else. In attempting to answer this question many historians have been tempted to see consumption as purely a function of emulation, the universal desire to "keep up with the Joneses" (McKendrick, Brewer, and Plumb 1982: 25–30). Arguments for emulation develop from Thorstein Veblen's *Theory of the Leisure Class* (1899) and his analysis of conspicuous consumption among the *nouveaux riches* of the late nineteenth century. Far from being "universal", however, this desire, as Veblen shows, was particularly strong among a class newly liberated from labor who wished to appear "leisured." Given the class specificity of Veblen's thesis there is an obvious danger in reading it as an explanation for the consumption activities of all classes. Nevertheless, the appeal to universalize Veblen's argument is strong, for it speaks to the fact that early modern Europe was increasingly a literate and visual culture which depended on texts and images for information and which placed a new value on appearances. In this new urban and urbane commercial culture, where one engaged in public life through economic and intellectual exchange, sociability and refinement were valued as much as wealth. Wealth by itself was of no use if it could not also function in the symbolic and aesthetic realm of bourgeois sociability. The argument for emulation proposes that consumption was stimulated and managed through images of upper-class subjectivity.

Yet despite its powerful appeal, this argument has other serious limitations in addition to the one already mentioned. As an explanation for the way that both culture and the consumption of culture work, universal emulation assumes that culture flows from the top of the social pyramid downwards. Ideologically such an argument re-inforces the political view that culture is the province of the élite. In many respects this is the opinion many conservative political and social commentators of the seventeenth and eighteenth centuries themselves had of culture, and echoes of it can still be found in today's neo-conservative cult of excellence. Early modern arguments against excessive consumption and luxury among the lower classes assumed that such things as edu-cation, silk dresses, and tea-drinking were "inappropriate" to members of the working class and that they gave them ideas "above their station." The presentday argument for emulation as the key mechanism driving consumption understands consumption within the terms established in the seventeenth and eighteenth centuries. Such an argument is not capable of going beyond the period's understanding of itself in order to look at ideological stakes in its ideas about emulation and the broader historical landscape in which they emerge.

More recently Pierre Bourdieu in his analysis of contemporary French society has refined the argument of emulation into a sophisticated analysis of class differences in taste (1984). According to Bourdieu, taste is not merely a reflection of class distinctions but the instrument by which they are created and maintained. He demonstrates, for instance, how among certain classes cultural capital (the knowledge of high art and a taste for it) is valued more highly than the conspicuous display of wealth. For Bourdieu class identity is not static but dynamic and relational. As a result the consumption of culture is a function of the changing relationships between classes. The advantage of Bourdieu's analysis is that it looks at societies as dynamic and fluid, composed of groups with changing interests and desires which they continually project on to culture. If consumption is the result of social behavior then questions about its origin and meanings cannot be understood apart from their social contexts. For this reason the writings of enthographers like Bourdieu, which look at cultural meanings and recep-tions in relation to the changing needs of social groups, provide useful tools for exploring the history of consumption.[7]

The top-down model of emulation is also flawed in that it cannot accommodate situations where cultural forms seem to flow in the reverse direction. A minor example would be the extreme popularity among women of the upper classes throughout the middle decades of the eighteenth century of the straw *bergère* hat which was manufactured with a rolled brim in imitation of the milkmaid's milking bonnet. Nor does it explain the French aristocrats' fascination with the *commedia dell'arte*, and their incorporation of its

costumes and its slapstick pantomime into their private entertainments and masquerades (Crow 1985). Similarly, the remarkable popularity of Samuel Richardson's sentimental bourgeois novels among the English aristocracy, and even the composition of
chamber music for bagpipe and hurdygurdy such as Leopold Mozart's *Peasant Wedding*,
cannot be explained by this top-down model of emulation. Clearly we must refine our
understanding of aristocratic emulation or, more likely, abandon it entirely if we are to
explain these phenomena. For alongside the period's rhetoric against luxury, egalitaria-
nism and ideas of Rousseauian simplicity circulated throughout the political culture of
western Europe. It was a period, after all, when a cultural *nostalgie de la boue* enticed
queens to dress as milkmaids.

While these counter-examples of cultural forms and practices percolating up from
below might work as a corrective to the model of aristocratic emulation, they leave the
model of emulation itself intact. Moreover they continue to map the flow of cultural
forms strictly along class lines. Such class-bound models of consumption run into
trouble when they are called upon to explain commercially fabricated tastes such as
chinoiserie, or the eighteenth-century London theatergoers' love of *Macbeth* and their
dislike of *Midsummer Night's Dream* (Holland 1990), or the eighteenth-century enjoyment
of picturesque touring. Such examples suggest that our models for the consumption of
culture may include but must finally move beyond the ideas of emulation to embrace
structures of appropriation, circulation, and bricolage, and the complex workings of
aesthetics, fantasy, discipline, and sexuality. For while it is no doubt true that consumers have always used commodities and cultural artifacts to emulate their betters,
they have also used them to other ends. "Goods," Colin Campbell has pointed out,
"may be desired for their own sake rather than for any prestige which may be attached
to them" (Brewer and Porter 1993: 40). Commodities like sugar and tobacco supply
their consumers with pleasures that are obvious and immediate. In place of emulative
spending Campbell proposes that of a "character-action" model in which one identifies
the character ideals of a particular period under discussion (sensibility, aristocracy,
etc.) that might help to explain patterns of conduct in general and consumption in
particular (1987 and 1993). Of the character models available to the late eighteenth
century it was the ideal of the "bohemian" or "romantic" that most predisposed its
types to consume. The romantic creed of self-expression, Campbell believes, aligned
easily with consumption's promise of hedonistic self-gratification.

As these debates demonstrate it is impossible to understand the history of consumption without also examining our conceptions of culture, the workings of culture, and
ultimately subjectivity. In fact it has been the failure to do this which has resulted in
the purely economistic accounts of consumption which see it in a secondary role after
production or which focus on commodities rather than consumers. Moreover, we would
suggest that consumption cannot be comprehended apart from our own cultural context as well – an awareness of the predicament of "being in culture while looking at
culture" (Clifford 1988: 8). This self-consciousness alerts us to our own ideological
investments in the history we are writing. Clearly our presentday situation in which
advertising quickly incorporates avant-garde art forms, in which high art is purchased
as an investment, and in which the distinctions drawn between high and mass forms of
entertainment seem all but invisible, has forced us to question the truth-claims of
modern aesthetics. Clearly an adequate historical account of consumption and the

consumption of culture involves suspending notions of an ideal pre-consumer past in which fetishization and alienation were unknown, and along with it the vision of ourselves as inhabiting a fallen, postmodern present.

The modernist distrust of mass culture which has to a large extent both written the history of consumption and blinded us to its history rests on a tendency to think in essentialist terms about culture, class, and identity. Accordingly, culture is high and pure, classes are homogeneous and stable, and identity is unified and transparent. All of these assumptions need to be questioned if we are to write a history of consumption since the seventeenth century. Instead of seeing culture in simple productivist terms as the creation of unique objects by individuals not alienated from their labor, we need to look at the uses of culture, at the social context of cultural change and innovation, and at the solutions cultural forms propose to the social contradictions that have generated them (Barthes 1973). To do so we need a notion of culture that is less pure, one that sees culture – both high and low – as deeply embedded in society and thus fragmented, provisional, and pluralistic (Clifford 1988). We need the image of a modern culture that is, and has always been, "compromised" by economics, class, gender, race, and history, and that for particular political and economic reasons has resisted this fact. We need to understand this resistance and its instrumentality.

Rather than seeing class and identity as stable and homogeneous we need to see them as mobile, fragmented, and inventive. We need to explore the way in which individuals appropriate cultural forms to their own individual ends, as tools to construct social selves; at times to comply with and at other times to resist institutional and social coercions. We need to see cultural forms as the means through which subjects externalize themselves, transforming the anonymous products of mass production into "personal statements." Studies of contemporary social groups have revealed the way in which individuals work to negate the social anomie generated by industrialism and advertising through the practice of consumption whereby mass-produced objects are invested with personal meanings and used in ways that reestablish a sense of both individual worth and community (Hall *et al.* 1976; Hebdige 1981; Hebdige 1989). When looked at from this point of view it becomes possible to see that one of the most extraordinary aspects of mass consumption since the seventeenth century, and perhaps the thing that distinguishes the modern period from any that preceded it, is the fact that consumption has been the primary means through which individuals have participated in culture and transformed it. Consumption then should not be understood as simply a positive or a negative reality but rather as a powerful tool for social change.

The consumption of culture

The charge of this volume is to examine the consumption of cultural goods and forms – paintings, novels, music, and entertainments – in seventeenth- and eighteenth-century Europe. The project is an interdisciplinary one and draws on new work being done in sociology and anthropology on the social meanings and uses of objects, and on the problems of reception, reader response, and interpreting textual and cultural data in history and literary studies. It is the final volume in a three-volume series to develop out of the "Consumption of Culture" program held at the Clark Library at the University of California, Los Angeles, from 1989 to 1991 and like the first two volumes attempts a preliminary survey of recent approaches to the problem of consumption in the early modern period.[8] The Clark series revealed consumption to be a complex cultural organization of economic transactions, legal relations, social institutions, and ideological apparatuses that continually redrew the boundaries between social classes, between public and private life, between high art and low, and between men and women. The series illuminated a number of very difficult and very significant issues. Paramount among them is the problem of reception and audience. Our present inquiry looks upon the history of aesthetic artifacts as a history of their diverse receptions. As a result, questions about artistic or authorial intentionality and technique give way to questions about utility and meaning. Consumption shifts our attention from the artist/producer (usually male and middle-class) to others whose role in the history of culture has been less clearly articulated. Determining the audience for a particular cultural production, however, goes beyond the necessary empirical inquiry into its social composition, to embrace the broader question of how an audience comes to identify itself as a social entity (a class, a gender, a race, etc.) by consuming certain images, texts, and objects. Moreover, if we allow that consumption is to this extent an exercise in identity, we need to ask how in turn does this process give new meaning and definition to the cultural productions themselves. The whole question of a public is further complicated by the way in which culture was commercialized and packaged, for even in the seventeenth and eighteenth centuries audiences did not exist prior to cultural production; they were its effect. In other words, a culture-consuming public of the early modern period was there not so much to be tapped as to be created. Given the fact that so much has yet to be done on the nature of early modern consumer society, the ideas presented here are necessarily preliminary. Nevertheless, they show that in the seventeenth and eighteenth centuries there was no single public for art, that, in fact, there were many publics and that the ground of cultural consumption was a shifting and highly contested one.

The word "culture" is used in this volume to signify both aesthetic production and the political and socioeconomic context in which it occurred. The chapters examine a variety of cultural forms – both high and low – in terms of their appeal to certain social groups, their social and political instrumentality, and their meanings and significations. It should be noted that our working assumption has been that culture, in both senses, is not a monolithic concept. Our goal has not been to study culture so much as cultures. In order, therefore, to avoid falling into the habit of dealing with culture as an aesthetic or social unity, our approach has in many cases been to examine it from the periphery – that is, to give central place to those cultural forms and social groups (popular theater, interior decoration, women, artisans, etc.) typically defined as marginal, and to use them as points of entry to explore the diverse meanings and uses of culture as we find them strewn over the extensive social landscape of the seventeenth and eighteenth centuries. Such a focus does not neglect the more dominant modes of culture and cultural production but rather seeks to place them in relation to these other less familiar and less studied forms and practices.

Like the Clark program, the present volume implicitly invites speculation about the multifaceted relationship between culture and consumption. The contributors come from a wide range of historically oriented fields (historians of society, politics, ideas, science, literature, and the arts) and in many cases their research suggests the new proximity of interests and methods that, under the general rubric of "cultural history," has cut across areas of specialization and traditional disciplinary boundaries. While there is a confluence of topical interests, the present volume as a whole does not authorize a single reading or approach. Instead, while some authors apply theoretical perspectives developed from discourse theory, semiotics, cultural anthropology, psychoanalysis, feminism, or poststructuralism, others maintain ties to more traditional historical and critical methods of research and analysis. While widely different in their emphases and methodologies all the contributors share an interest in problematizing our ideas of such things as culture, canon, period, gender, class, the public, the private, production, and, of course, consumption.

The chapters have been grouped topically so that different points of view may be brought to bear on a single problem. The five topic areas focus on the sites, institutions, and participants in the consumption of culture. Part I, "The formation of a public," examines the problem of audience and the construction of a culture-consuming public for both literature and art. Terry Lovell discusses the role of women as consumers of literature in eighteenth-century England. The construction of reading as a gendered practice is the subject of Peter H. Pawlowicz's analysis of eighteenth-century French and British artistic and literary representations of women reading. Frank Donoghue examines the role of critical reviews in formulating modern conceptions of authorship and in developing an informed reading public. Related to these discussions of the scenes of reading and the formation of a public for literature, are the chapters that deal with painting and the way in which certain genres such as portraiture, history painting, and landscape were produced as a result of the commercial practices of artists, the wishes of connoisseurs, and the professional activities of modern scholars. These three chapters all deal in one way or another with the effect of these activities on the public meaning and consumption of painting. Louise Lippincott examines the commercialization of painting in eighteenth-century Britain and its impact on the production and consumption of portraiture and history painting. Thomas Crow discusses the working relationship between David and his pupils and its significance for the public meaning of their art. W. J. T. Mitchell probes the "discovery" of landscape as a genre of painting in the sixteenth and seventeenth centuries and its modern rediscovery by art historians as a way to frame questions of culture and representation.

Part II, "Engendering the literary canon," illuminates the ways in which literature was hierarchized, gendered, and "packaged" for a developing reading public. Canon formation is one of the most basic instruments whereby modern notions of authorship and literary quality are produced. It is through this process of selection and validation that literature is thus created and consumed. The history of canon formation in the early modern period is, as the chapters show, remarkably rich and complex. Two of the chapters deal with the canon as a function of changes in the literary marketplace. Don E. Wayne looks at Ben Jonson's literary response to the canonization and marketing of Shakespeare. Robert Iliffe analyzes how the editor of the Royal Society went about selectively constructing "Newton" by turning Newton's private letters into public texts, and by adjusting his "facts" and emending his texts to suit the tastes and beliefs of the wider reading public. Any discussion of canon formation raises the issue of the marginal status of women writers within the modern literary canon. With respect to this issue Mitzi Myers looks at the specific case of Maria Edgeworth and her marginalization by the critics of her own day who saw her as merely the mouthpiece of her famous father. And Anne K. Mellor discusses the way in which women novelists and poets of the later eighteenth century appropriated the style and clichés of the romantic tradition and transformed them into texts that spoke directly to women's experiences.

Part III, on the formation of "the modern state," groups chapters that deal with the influence of the government and politics in matters of cultural production and consumption. Several chapters focus on the way in which British nationalism and imperialism were naturalized and consumed as and through cultural objects. Felicity A. Nussbaum, for instance, explores the connection between racism and sexism in eighteenth-century Britain as inscribed in emerging notions of marriage and polygamy and as expressed in the discourses of colonialism and in sentimental novels like *Pamela*. Kathleen Wilson maps the ideological construction and consumption of empire in the popular theater of eighteenth-century Britain. Richard Sorrenson examines the creation of a clockwork universe as figured by scientific precision instruments which ordered vision, time, and space to suit the commercial needs of the British Empire. Other chapters in this section look at the way in which the state attempted to regulate the signifying powers of art and science. Jay Tribby explores scientific experiments carried out in the Medici court as a series of rhetorical strategies to secure the Medici's monopoly on culture. Anne M. Wagner's study of the fate of the statues of the kings of France during the revolution shows how the disestablishment and later reestablishment of the monarchy depended, in part, on regulating the meanings associated with representations of the king's body. Nicholas Mirzoeff sets out the modern development of sign language for the deaf ("invented" in the eighteenth century by the abbé de l'Epée, an admirer of Condillac) as, paradoxically, a way for the state to disenfranchise the deaf and to marginalize them as a culture distinct from and inferior to that of hearing and speaking subjects.

Part IV, "The social order," deals with cultural consumption and its relation to issues of class and social identity. The problems of emulation and consumption's threaten to mix classes and confuse social identities are discussed by contributors to this section. John Brewer considers the social effects of the commercialization of culture in eighteenth-century London and the attempts made to contain and discredit its influences. Lawrence E. Klein discusses the "politeness phenomena" in late seventeenth-century Britain as marked by the contradictions of a commercial culture where frugality and display, industry and sociability, diligence and dalliance were simultaneously valued. Ronald Paulson explores Hogarth's changing attitudes towards social emulation and cultural consumption evident in *The Harlot's Progress* and *Industry and Idleness* as an index of the artist's evolving political consciousness. Paula Rea Radisich unfolds the social and political meanings encoded in Hubert Robert's landscape murals made for the financier Jean-Joseph de Laborde as motivated by a desire to avoid charges of excessive opulence and luxury.

The fifth and final part, "What women want," maps the consumption of culture as it intersects with women's roles as producers and consumers of culture. Two chapters in this section deal with literary representations of the cultural and economic activities of women in seventeenth-century London. James Grantham Turner provides an account of male erotic literary fantasy which blocked and belittled female participation in urban forms of commerce in the post-Restoration period. From Turner's account of the masculine imagination we move to Elizabeth Bennett Kubek's analysis of women's own representations of urban culture at this time and of their place within it as found in women's novels of the seventeenth and eighteenth centuries. Chapters in the second portion of this section explore the position of women with regard to the production and consumption of painting and music in France and Britain. Mary D. Sheriff unfolds the gender politics of the controversy over Vigée–Lebrun's acceptance into the French Royal Academy in 1783 and explores its wider meaning for woman artists, painting practices, and the history of art. Ann Bermingham discusses the emergence of the artistically "accomplished woman" in late eighteenth-century Britain in the context of the larger cultural project of establishing the production of "high art" and its connoisseurship as masculine prerogatives. Richard Leppert's chapter sets out the gender divisions that structured the domestic performance of music in eighteenth-century Britain.

The diverse histories of consumption gathered here will compel us to see the culture of the early modern period in a new way, for they reveal a culture already formed by consumption, and one which was struggling to come to terms with this fact. What they also reveal is that if the history of consumption is to be not merely a celebration of the status quo but a progressive tool for social change, then its historical formations within the modern conditions of class, gender, and racial inequalities must be exposed and understood. We need new theories of material culture that will promote social justice not by ignoring or wishing away the evidence of consumption, but by understanding its modern history and its political instrumentality. Such intellectual work holds out the promise of a reconciliation between what have traditionally been seen as the antagonistic forces of industrialism and the needs of social groups. In short, it holds out the possibility that power may not be the exclusive prerogative of the producer, and that it can also be found dispersed among communities and embedded in their practices of everyday life.

Notes

1   Quoted in Thomas Crow, *Painters and Public Life in Eighteenth-Century Paris* (1985: 45).
2   On the subject of Watteau's public see Crow's *Painters and Public Life*. With the exception of the large *Mercury and Argus* by Jordaens in the righthand corner of the shop and the copy of the portrait of Louis XIV by Rigaud being packed in a crate the other paintings recall the work of Van Dyke, Rubens, Veronese, Snyders, and Bassano without being actual copies. See Margaret Morgan Grasselli and Pierre Rosenberg, *Watteau, 1684–1721* (Washington, DC: National Gallery of Art, 1984), p. 446 ff.
3   An excellent summary and analysis of recent studies of early modern consumption is provided by Jean-Christophe Agnew's "Consumer culture in historical perspective" (1993).
4   One finds such conceptions of the artist as early as Vasari's *Lives of the Most Eminent Painters, Sculptors and Architects*, first published in 1550 (Vasari 1957). More recently the work of formalist critics Clement Greenberg (*Art and Culture*, 1961) and Harold Bloom (*The Anxiety of Influence*, 1973) have developed theoretical positions with respect to painting and poetry oriented by what they perceive to be the stylistic and oedipal struggles of individual artists. The transformation of these critical accounts of artistic production into popular "histories" of art is best exemplified by H. W. Janson's *History of Art* (1962, 1986, 1991).
5   See, for example, the discussions of modernism's positions with respect to industrialism and

issues of social justice in Raymond Williams's *The Politics of Modernism* (1989) and Andreas Huyssen's *After the Great Divide* (1986). Clement Greenberg's seminal essay "The avant garde and kitsch" (1939) (reprinted in Greenberg 1961: 3–21) is the classic formulation of modernist, neo-Kantian idealism with its avant-gardist resistance to industrial mass culture and its association of industrial mass culture with fascism and totalitarianism.

6   See, for instance, Mark Poster's analysis of Habermas's wariness of poststructuralism in his *Critical Theory and Poststructuralism: In Search of a Context* (Ithaca, NY: Cornell University Press, 1989) and Huyssen's discussion of Habermas's attachment to the Enlightenment's "wholistic" notion of modernity in *After the Great Divide* (1986).

7   A. Appadurai, *The Social Life of Things: Commodities in Cultural Perspective* (Cambridge: Cambridge University Press, 1986); Mary Douglas and B. Isherwood, *The World of Goods* (London: Allen Lane, 1979).

8   The two previous volumes are: *Consumption and the World of Goods*, ed. John Brewer and Roy Porter (London: Routledge, 1993); *Early Modern Conceptions of Property*, ed. John Brewer and Susan Staves (London: Routledge, 1994).

Bibliography

Agnew, Jean-Christophe (1993) "Consumer culture in historical perspective," in John Brewer and Roy Porter (eds.) *Consumption and the World of Goods*, London: Routledge, pp. 19–39.

Barrell, John (1986) *The Political Theory of Painting from Reynolds to Hazlitt: "The Body of the Public,"* New Haven, CT and London: Yale University Press.

Barthes, Roland (1973) *Mythologies*, London: Paladin.

Baudrillard, Jean (1975) *The Mirror of Production*, St. Louis, MO: Telos Press.

Bloom, Harold (1973) *The Anxiety of Influence*, Oxford, London, and New York: Oxford University Press.

Bourdieu, Pierre (1984) *Distinction: A Social Critique of the Judgement of Taste*, Cambridge, MA: Harvard University Press.

Brewer, John and Porter, Roy (eds.) (1993) *Consumption and the World of Goods*, London: Routledge.

Burger, Peter (1984) *Theory of the Avant-garde*, Minneapolis, MN: University of Minnesota Press.

Campbell, Colin (1987) *The Romantic Ethic and the Spirit of Modern Consumerism*, Oxford: Oxford University Press.

—— (1993) "Understanding traditional and modern patterns of consumption in eighteenth-century England: a character-action approach", in John Brewer and Roy Porter (eds.) *Consumption and the World of Goods*, London: Routledge, pp. 40–58.

Clifford, James (1988) *The Predicament of Culture: Twentieth-Century Ethnography, Literature, and Art*, Cambridge, MA: Harvard University Press.

Crow, Thomas (1985) *Painters and Public Life in Eighteenth-Century Paris*, New Haven, CT and London: Yale University Press.

Debord, Guy (1967) *La société du spectacle*, Paris: Buchet-Chastel.

De Vries, Jan (1974) *The Dutch Rural Economy in the Golden Age, 1500–1700*, New Haven, CT: Yale University Press.

—— (1976) *The Economy of Europe in an Age of Crisis, 1600–1750*, New York: Cambridge University Press.

Foucault, Michel (1977) "What is an author?" in *Language, Counter-Memory, Practice: Selected Essays and Interviews*, ed. Donald F. Bouchard, Ithaca, NY: Cornell University Press, pp. 113–38.

—— (1984) "What is enlightenment?" in *The Foucault Reader*, ed. Paul Rabinow, New York: Pantheon Books, pp. 32–50.

—— (1985) *The Use of Pleasure: The History of Sexuality*, vol. 2, New York: Random House.

Greenberg, Clement (1961) *Art and Culture*, Boston, MA: Beacon Press.

Habermas, Jürgen (1989) *The Structural Transformation of the Public Sphere: An Inquiry into a Category of Bourgeois Society*, trans. Thomas Burger, Cambridge, MA: MIT Press.

—— (1990) *The Philosophical Discourse of Modernity*, trans. Frederick Lawrence, Cambridge, MA: MIT Press.

Hall, Stuart, *et al.* (eds.) (1976) *Resistance through Rituals*, London: Hutchinson.

Hebdige, Dick (1981) "Object as image: the Italian scooter cycle," *Block* 5: 44–64.

—— (1989) *Subculture: The Meaning of Style*, London: Methuen.

Holland, Peter (1990) "A Midsummer Night's Dream and the casting of canons," paper given at the William Andrews Clark Memorial Library, University of California, Los Angeles, Saturday, November 17, 1990.

Huyssen, Andreas (1986) *After the Great Divide: Modernism, Mass Culture and Postmodernism*, Bloomington and Indianapolis, IN: Indiana University Press.

Jameson, Fredric (1982) "Postmodernism and consumer society," in Hal Foster (ed.) *The Anti-Aesthetic: Essays on Postmodern Culture*, Port Townsend, WA: Bay Press, pp. 111–25.

—— (1991) *Postmodernism or, The Cultural Logic of Late Capitalism*, Durham, NC: Duke University Press.

Janson, H. W. (1962, 1986, 1991) *History of Art*, New York: Abrams and Prentice–Hall.

Lippincott, Louise (1983) *Selling Art in Georgian London: The Rise of Arthur Pond*, New Haven, CT and London: Yale University Press.

McKendrick, Neil, Brewer, John, and Plumb, J. H. (1982) *The Birth of a Consumer Society: The Commercialization of Eighteenth-Century England*, Bloomington, IN: Indiana University Press.

Marx, Karl (1973) *Grundrisse*, trans. Martin Nicolaus New York: Vintage.

—— (1974) *Capital*, trans. Ben Fowkes New York: Vintage.

—— (1975) *Early Writings*, trans. name to come at proof, Harmondsworth Mx: Penguin.

Miller, Daniel (1987) *Material Culture and Mass Consumption*, Oxford: Blackwell.

Mitchell, W. J. T. (1986) *Iconology: Image, Text, Ideology*, Chicago and London: University of Chicago Press.

Mukerji, Chandra (1983) *From Graven Images: Patterns of Modern Materialism*, New York: Columbia University Press.

Pears, Ian (1988) *The Discovery of Painting: The Growth of Interest in the Arts in England, 1680–1768*, New Haven, CT and London: Yale University Press.

Pointon, Marcia (1993) *Hanging the Head: Portraiture and Social Formation in Eighteenth-Century England*, New Haven, CT and London: Yale University Press.

Schama, Simon (1988) *The Embarrassment of Riches*, Berkeley, CA: University of California Press.

—— (1993) "Perishable commodities: Dutch still-life paintings and the 'Empire of things,'" in John Brewer and Roy Porter (eds) *Consumption and the World of Goods*, London: Routledge, pp. 478–88.

Shammas, Carole (1990) *The Preindustrial Consumer in England and America*, Oxford: Oxford University Press.

Solkin, David (1993) *Painting for Money*, New Haven, CT and London: Yale University Press.

Thirsk, Joan (1978) *Economic Policy and Projects: The Development of Consumer Society in Early Modern Britain*, Oxford: Clarendon Press.

Vasari, Giorgio (1957 [1550]) *Lives of the Most Eminent Painters, Sculptors and Architects*, trans. E. L. Seeley, New York: Noonday Press.

Vidal, Mary (1992) *Watteau's Painted Conversations: Art, Literature, and Talk in Seventeenth- and Eighteenth-Century France*, New Haven, CT and London: Yale University Press.

Weatherill, Lorna (1988) *Consumer Behavior and Material Culture in Britain, 1660–1760*, London: Routledge.

Williams, Raymond (1966) *Culture and Society*, New York: Harper & Row.

—— (1976) *Keywords*, Oxford: Oxford University Press.

—— (1989) *The Politics of Modernism: Against the New Conformists*, London: Verso.

Part I

The formation of a public for art and literature

2
Subjective powers?
Consumption, the reading public, and domestic woman in early eighteenth-century England

Terry Lovell

> [T]he concepts . . . from which we begin – are suddenly seen to be not concepts but problems, not analytic problems either but historical movements that are still unresolved.
>
> (Raymond Williams, *Marxism and Literature*)

In this chapter I want to explore some questions of the place of women within the emergent modern culture of the late seventeenth and early eighteenth centuries, and I want to begin by examining the three ordering concepts of the 1990–1 Clark Lecture series which provide the basis for this collection of chapters: "culture"; "consumption"; "public". All three are elusive and shifting in their connotations. Typically they present themselves in mutually defined pairs, with some slippage between them. Sometimes one partner is "silent," functioning merely to throw the other into relief. There may be a submerged third term. Two of Raymond Williams's "keywords" are there, including "culture," which he characterizes as "one of the two or three most complicated words in the English language" (Williams 1976: 76).

Williams distinguishes three major and interconnected senses of "culture":

1 the process of intellectual, spiritual, and aesthetic mental development (the "cultivation" of the self);
2 the works and practices of intellectual and especially artistic activity;
3 a particular way of life, whether of a people, period, or group.

Senses 1 and 2 are most immediately relevant to the concerns of this chapter. "Culture" as the cultivation of the intellectual and aesthetic faculties (sense 1), was commonplace by the early eighteenth century. The original horticultural metaphor is clearly visible in Locke's work on education:

> He therefore, that is about Children, should well study their Natures and Aptitudes, and see, by often trials, what turn they easily take, and what

becomes of them: observe what their Native Stock is, how it may be improved, and what it is fit for. . . . Affectation is not . . . an early Fault of Childhood, or the Product of untaught Nature; it is of that sort of Weeds, which grow not in the wild uncultivatd waste, but in Garden-Plotts, under the Negligent Hand, or Unskilfull Care of a Gardner.

(Locke 1693: 159)

Already here we can begin to see a mediating third term which gives "culture" its distinctively moral resonance: that which falls short of "culture" but cannot be attributed to nature: faulty or inadequate cultivation/education which leaves the child below its full potential as a human being. Ill-management or neglect produces not cultivated minds, but monstrosities unknown in nature. A moral component is sutured into and inseparable from the concept of culture or cultivation in this eighteenth-century usage from the start.

The idea of culture as the process of cultivation of the mental life, the formation of the inner self, was extended later to products: "works of culture." Culture in this second sense includes what Matthew Arnold in the nineteenth century was to describe as "the best that has been thought and said": works of art, of the intellect, and of the imagination. This usage, in which the moral, discriminatory aspect is especially marked, came fully into its own in the second half of the nineteenth century. The garden of culture must be scrupulously tended: "the best that has been thought and said" defended lest it is choked by the mediocre, the corrupt, the plain bad. This second concept of "culture" has always gone hand in hand with that work of identification and differentiation whose outcome would be the creation of canons: selected traditions of culture. It was an exercise in discrimination that had its roots in the eighteenth century, which was the century of nascent canon formation.

Culture, then, in both these senses, came to be defined negatively, by what was excluded, as much as by its positive attributes. "Cultivation" and culture, uses 1 and 2, were woven in the nineteenth century into a single moral and aesthetic discourse, in the tradition of cultural criticism defined and traced by Williams in *Culture and Society* (Williams 1987).

The third anthropological, usage might seem to be less implicated in this moral discourse because of its inclusiveness: it embraces every aspect of the mores, practices, habits of a people, not excluding material objects in daily use. Its catholic scope moreover legitimates a more amoral usage in discourses in which we may begin to speak of "bomb culture," or "enterprise culture," or indeed, "eighteenth-century culture" *tout court*, from pleasure gardens to poetry, without implying any moral or aesthetic judgments. While the moral overtones of the anthropological usage are harder to detect, they become visible as it is appropriated to provide a supporting frame for the other two in twentieth-century studies of modern working-class life under the impact of a commercial mass culture (Hoggart 1958). The objects of anthropology are so-called "simple societies," typically presented as functionally integrated, relatively unchanging and viable modes of life. The moral inflexion is clear when the weight of emphasis is made to fall upon the idea of a *way* of life, or in the formulation used again and again by Williams, a *whole* way of life.

In *The Uses of Literacy* Hoggart presents the cultural landscape of an older working-class community remembered from his youth in Hunslet, a working-class area of Leeds, in the 1930s: the "full, rich life" which, he argued, was being corroded in the 1950s by affluence and its manipulation by a cheap commercial culture. Williams's work, braced by a lifelong engagement with Marxism, consciously eschews nostalgia for a more satisfying imagined past, and in examining earlier cultural formations, never loses sight of the more urgent question of how the future may be shaped to create a humane socialism (Williams 1983). What Williams takes above all from the anthropological usage is perhaps an idea of *viability*: a *way* of life that is both inclusive, satisfying, and sustainable.

Williams is untouched by any of that excitement over, and celebration of, the new for its own sake that we associate with the culture of modernity. If the undertow of his work on culture does not pull us back towards an idealized, lost past, neither does it ever forget the quest for a "whole way of life": a viable, humane, and just social *order*. The term used by the character Beth in his novel *Second Generation* is "a settlement," for which she pleads in pregnancy for her unborn child, and we can see, here, the way in which "culture" lays its moral aspirations not only upon "religion, art" but also "the family and personal life" (Williams 1977: 14).

"Culture" in its adapted anthropological usage draws us towards ideas of settlement, continuity, a certain solidity; "modernity" towards restlessness, innovation, the ephemeral. When the terms are conjoined, they qualify each other. "Modernity" borrows from "culture" an accretion of approbation over and above its own indigenous connotations of progress; "culture" loses its slightly backward-looking aura of moral rectitude and stasis.

In speaking of the modern, commercialized culture which was in formation in the early eighteenth century, twentieth-century commentators are, then, applying a concept of later provenance: one which has been modernized, in an attempt to eliminate moral/aesthetic discriminatory overtones, but which trails a long history of saturation in such meanings which are remarkably difficult to exorcize.

The terms belong to a later period. But the historical problem which was to be conceptualized through nineteenth- and twentieth-century discourses of "culture" begins already to trouble participants in and commentators upon the contemporary cultural scene at the beginning of the eighteenth century. Works of art, and of the intellect and the imagination, were beginning to reach their publics through the mediation of the market: the purchase and sale of commodities. The cultural wares on offer were proliferating in number, and in a bewildering profusion of new forms, as the public for these commodities expanded, reaching as far down the social hierarchy as the means to purchase extended.

The periodical press which thrived in this commoditized culture set itself the task of taking in hand the new public (and indeed the new cultural producers and presenters) by providing instruction in the niceties of cultural taste and manners through criticism. *The Spectator* adopted a tone not of moral earnestness, but rather of urbane, avuncular good humor, in this its self-appointed task. Thus English composers and the opera-going public alike are addressed in a disquisition on the proper relationship between word and music: •

the Notes of Interrogation, or Admiration, in the *Italian* Musick (if one may so call them) which resemble their Accents in Discourse on such Occasions, are not unlike the ordinary Tones of an *English* Voice when we are angry; insomuch that I have often seen our Audiences extreamly mistaken as to what has been doing upon the Stage, and, expecting to see the Hero knock down his Messenger when he has been asking him a Question; or fancying that he quarrels with his Friend, when he only bids him Good-morrow. . . . [An] *English* Composer should not follow the *Italian* Recitative too servilely, but make use of many gentle Deviations from it, in Compliance with his own Native Language.

(Bond 1965: I, 121)

Mr. Spectator, like Isaac Bickerstaff before him, acknowledges the excesses of a burgeoning commercial culture, but is as inclined to invite laughter at its absurdities as to censure. His contemporaries, Swift and Pope, strike a more urgent note in their truly venomous satires at the expense of the dunces of modern culture: laughter is still invited, but it is far from kindly. Confidence in the power of urbane reason to defend through criticism the claims of true art and intellect is replaced by intimations of defeat and extinction in the climax of Pope's *Dunciad*:

> She comes! she comes! the sable Throne behold
> Of *Night* Primaeval, and of *Chaos* old!
> Before her, *Fancy*'s gilded clouds decay,
> And all its varying Rain-bows die away.
> *Wit* shoots in vain its momentary fires,
> The meteor drops and in a flash expires.
> As one by one, at dread Medea's strain,
> The sick'ning stars fade off th'ethereal plain;
> As Argus' eyes by Hermes' wand opprest,
> Clos'd one by one to everlasting rest;
> Thus at her felt approach, and secret might,
> *Art* after *Art* goes out, and all is Night.
> (Pope 1743: 583)

The rapid spread of a fecund, extravagant, and immensely popular commoditized culture; the profound fears over it, coupled with a horrified fascination: these mark early modern culture as surely as the rational discourses of what Habermas terms "the bourgeois public sphere" and make, I have argued elsewhere (Lovell 1987), precisely the kind of mix which is to be expected of a capitalist culture mediated both by the commodity form *and* by that mental set which Max Weber termed "the spirit of capitalism," which emerged on the historical stage through processes of class accommodation (Eagleton 1984). It is important that the label "bourgeois" not be limited to the more sober, rationalist forms of emergent cultural life. The culture of anarchic excess, ruled over by Pope's Queen of Dulness and by a capitalist Grub Street, is every bit as bourgeois, partakes as much of "the spirit of capitalism," as does the aphorism that "honesty is the best policy" or Benjamin Franklin's encomiums to thrift.

The later evolution of a post-Romantic, overtly moralizing, discriminatory concept of culture has its early roots in these historical processes of an earlier period. To attempt to make fast the boundaries, made permeable by commoditization, between "true culture" and the pit, was the new labor of Sisyphus taken up by successive generations of preachers and prophets of "culture."

Consumption belongs in the discourse of bourgeois political economy. Its conceptual partner is "production," and in the history of theorizing capitalist society, emphasis on the moment of consumption is a relatively new development. Classic Marxism is a theory of capitalist production, and it is the figure of the Weberian Protestant producer, frugal, sober, and abstemious, which has dominated classical sociology. For Marx, the power to produce was *the* generative power that distinguished human society: the appropriation of nature by labor. "Consumption" is the silent, unanalyzed, and passive partner to production in this discourse.

The idea that consumption, as well as production, may be an active and power-generating process is alien to Marxist thought, but has emerged as a major theme in recent years not only amongst liberal theorists of the sovereign consumer, the heirs of Bernard Mandeville, but also amongst those on the left who have looked increasingly to the discourses of postmodernism and poststructuralism rather than to Marxism for their theoretical resources.

Recent studies of the pre- and early history of the novel have taken place in the context of this shift of attention from production to consumption, and of the related shift of interest, under the impact of poststructuralism and postmodernism, from questions of social structure to questions of human subjectivity.

The starting-point for any contextual social history of the novel remains Ian Watt's *The Rise of the Novel* (Watt 1957). After more than thirty years of clarification, modification, and critique, the broad lines of his thesis connecting the rise of the novel with nascent capitalism and with the rise of the bourgeoisie remain intact. The story has been made more complex; problems of timing and of mediation have been addressed. But that there is a real connection of some kind has not been seriously challenged (Hunter 1990; McKeon 1987). It is good to see the resurgence of interest in this kind of cultural history, which has been out of fashion during the years which have been dominated by formalism in cultural theory. This new historicism in cultural studies is fairly eclectic in its intellectual borrowings, owing a debt in this, as in matters of more substance, to postmodernism and poststructuralism, even where it has sometimes remained within or drawn as well upon the Marxist heritage of the sociology of literature (Moretti 1987). Its preoccupations, however, have less to do with the structural relationships that link emergent capitalism and the novel, than with the relationship of the new form to the cultivation of distinctly modern forms of subjectivity in the context of capitalist consumer culture.

Although it is possible to bring Marx into alignment with certain theories of modern subjectivity (Sayer 1991) and consumption, his writings are not the most immediately obvious source for either. Marxisant sociologies of literature have ever struggled with the problem of locating literature within a form of society defined principally in terms of structural forces and relations of *production*.

Weber looks more promising at first sight, given the centrality of his concept of "status usurpation," and his interest in the subjectivity of the early Protestant entrepreneur. But while (ideal-typical) psychic processes intervene in his story of the relationship between Protestantism and capitalism, they are, precisely, processes influencing the behavior of capitalist producers, not consumers. The whole point of his famous thesis rested upon an analysis of that deeply irrational rationality which saved and accumulated, but placed a moral embargo on all unnecessary consumption. The classical tradition in sociology has given us Thorsten Veblen, but otherwise has had little to say about the dynamics of capitalist consumption in its relationship to modern forms of subjectivity (Campbell 1987).

We saw that Williams's discussion of "culture" comes to rest in an untheorized and problematic way on women and family life in the small community – the unanalyzed, taken-for-granted core of Williams's thought. Feminist scholarship over the past twenty years in literary and cultural studies has established that culture and its processes are profoundly gendered (see Moi 1985 for an overview of this body of work in feminist literary theory). The shifts of attention from production to consumption and from structure to subjectivity have opened up the field to more effective feminist intervention because the result has been to center cultural analysis at a point where gender orderings cannot be readily ignored or marginalized. Women's responsibilities for domestic consumption have long since been recognized, and modern theories of subjectivity began, after all, with Lacan's reworking of Freud, by addressing the problem of *sexed* identity.

If we focus exclusively either upon the emergence of a vibrant, if brash, culture of modernity, or upon ideal-typical constructions of the inner life of Protestant producers, or on the conservative reaction to modernity of the Augustans, we will miss the point. Capitalist culture embraces and generates both the electrifying, chaotic novelty of modernity, its impatience for the new, *and* yearning for the stability, solidity, predictability of an idealized imagined past: a *whole* and moral way of life, and a culture with the depth and resonance to order and interpret it. This particular mix is beautifully caught in Marshall Berman's analysis of Goethe's *Faust* in *All That Is Solid Melts into Air* (Berman 1982). Capitalist culture faces two ways, casting an anxious glance backwards at what is being lost, even as it embraces the new.

The third of our terms, "public" is not one of Williams's keywords, although it perhaps should have been. The term introduces a discourse that belongs in the political realm, alongside "civil society" and "the state." It is in the political or civic sense of "public" that Jürgen Habermas describes the emergence in late seventeenth- and early eighteenth-century Europe of the "bourgeois public sphere" (Habermas 1989). This sphere was constituted in England, he argued, by coffee-houses and other social forums of London, and by popular periodicals such as the *Tatler* and the *Spectator*. The last quarter of the seventeenth century had seen the emergence of the modern liberal state in the form of a constitutional monarchy and a powerful oligarchical parliament. John Locke provided the key legitimizing texts of this new form of state. In his *First Treatise of Government* he refuted decisively the arguments of Sir Robert Filmer, who had founded civil society on the authority of the patriarchal father, and in his *Second Treatise* he went on to theorize the basis in a fictional social contract of the authority of that state over its individual subjects, and the limits of that authority. Full membership of civil society for Locke being a function of the possession of property and reason, only adult male property-owners were admitted. The disenfranchised, needless to say, did not thereby escape the state's jurisdiction.

Habermas divides Locke's "civil society" into two constituent spheres: the "bourgeois public sphere" and a second private sphere about which he has notably less to say. The bourgeois public sphere provided "a forum in which private people, come together to form a public, readied themselves to compel public authority to legitimate itself before public opinion" (Habermas 1989: 25–6). It was public in the sense of being in principle open to all who were qualified to participate in its functions. These comprised the subjection to critical scrutiny of the exercise of political authority by the state; the provision of a forum for the development of reasoned public opinion; and, through the dissemination of public opinion, the molding of the conduct, manners, and taste of the general public. It was a sphere of criticism, political and cultural, and, as such, aligned itself with the moral discourse of "cultivation" as well as with human reason: with disinterested discrimination and judgment, rather than a catholic Mandevillian culture "driven by luxury, social emulation, human appetite and desire" (Brewer 1995; Ch. 18). In identifying this sphere, Habermas keeps his eyes firmly fixed upon the respectable face of bourgeois culture, that profile which it likes to present to the world and which impressed itself so forcibly upon Max Weber and classical sociology.

In addition to being "public" in the sense of being "generally accessible and available" (*Shorter OED*) the bourgeois public sphere was public in a second sense, in that it concerned itself with "matters of, or pertaining to the people as a whole" (ibid.). Richard Sennett traces the history of the term as it came to mean "a life passed outside the life of family and close friends," and the growth of places where strangers might regularly meet, such as parks, coffee-houses, theaters, pleasure grounds, etc. (Sennett 1974: 16). However, the conceptual partner to "public" is "private" and the public sphere acted, according to Habermas, as an intermediary between political authority, government, and the state on the one hand, and private and personal life on the other. Its voluble members cast a critical eye in each direction, to monitor the conduct of public affairs, but also to argue standards for personal conduct, for morality and taste, within the private sphere of the family and personal life. It was in the public sphere that the norms for the regulation of the private and the personal, and for the critical introspection of the inner self, were articulated and opened to scrutiny in an essentially public form of discourse.

Londoners participated in these forums of the bourgeois public sphere in their capacities as private, reasoning citizens and not by virtue of their social status. Habermas notes that the participating minority understood itself as "immersed within [and representative of] a more inclusive public of all private persons who – insofar as they were propertied and educated as readers, listeners and spectators – could avail themselves via the market of the objects that were subject to discussion" (Habermas 1989: 37). In the case of "the reading public" all those who had the prerequisites which gave access to reading material and who chose to exercise their ability to read were included.

Commodity literature is consumed in private. Habermas recognizes the simultaneous emergence of a "bourgeois private sphere," and it is in this discourse of separate spheres that his work touches feminist concerns most closely. Great importance has been attached in feminist theory and historiography to the separation of spheres in bourgeois society, and to the increasing restriction of women, in ideology at least, to the private domestic sphere (Davidoff and Hall 1987). The bourgeois private sphere developed in the space of domestic life and the conjugal family, and because it was the locus of early socialization, and the place where private reading occurred, it was the prime site of the early formation of those new forms of subjectivity which have occupied postmodernist and poststructuralist theorists.

To summarize: from the early modern period, culture was increasingly mediated by the market, obliged to accommodate itself to the commodity form. Within the moral and aesthetic discourses of criticism and of "cultivation" that date also from this period, the emerging rationale for those works of culture for which high critical claims were advanced, placed them in some tension with their new commoditized form. Neither profitability nor popular appeal could be their *raison d'être*. Their claims had to be grounded in their appeal to cultivated taste.

It was but a short further step to the moral discourse of Matthew Arnold, and his claims for the power of "culture" to produce "cultivation": to form, reproduce, and nourish what more than a century later he was to call "the best self": a moral actor, able to discriminate in matters of taste and judgment, one whose baser desires were firmly under control. Yet high culture was increasingly in the eighteenth century bought and sold in the marketplace, where it competed promiscuously with offerings which made less elevated claims, and whose producers and disseminators might have no scruples in appealing to more basic human desires, in the interests of profitability.

I have argued elsewhere (Lovell 1987) against Marxist functionalisms which posit a "fit," mediated by culture, between capitalism and its interpellated subjects, the selves which (mis)recognize themselves in the mirror offered up by a capitalist culture, on the grounds that capitalism has requirements which are deeply contradictory. It thrives in and stimulates a plural culture which encompasses both the forward-looking innovations of modernity and a backward-looking traditionalism which seeks to reinstate aesthetic, intellectual, and moral values perceived to be universally valid. Capitalist culture "interpellates" a split or multiple subject in a profusion of conflicting ways and we are perhaps apt to pay too much attention to its more pious utterances; its loftier cultural achievements; its more rational presentations of its collective self.

A further related point is that we may be mistaken in attempting to make too close a fit between culturally available personas and categories of persons. It is perhaps only in fictional worlds and in ideology that characters always act in character. In their day-to-day existence, and in the movements from country to town with the Season, it may be that the identities of men and women were less unidimensional than those of their fictional exemplars: a point which Amanda Vickery made very well in a paper on "Women and the world of goods" (Vickery 1993). If we set alongside Weber's abstract portrait of the ideal type of capitalist businessman the concrete sketches of the same character occupied with the task of advertising his wares that Neil McKendrick gives us (McKendrick, Brewer, and Plumb 1982), we might be excused in surmising that the subjectivity required of the capitalist producer was schizoid.

The affinity of the moderns with the energies unleashed by capitalism is evident, even if we accept recent arguments that deny any necessary connection between capitalism and modernity (Abercrombie, Hill and Turner 1986). Yet the figure summoned up by Max Weber, the sober, upright Protestant capitalist producer, has as little in common as has the Augustan critic with those moderns "who meant to start a new world from nothing. . . . New was what they desired . . . the only time that mattered was now. They were modern, they were young, they were ready" (Hunter 1990: 99). The distance between Weber's Protestant producer and the Augustan critic, on the other hand, is very great, measured by that which separates Matthew Arnold's Philistines from his scholarly bearers of sweetness and light. But classicist critics and Protestant producers shared nonetheless a belief in the existence of values having universal validity, which might inform and underwrite "a whole way of life," however far apart they were in their characterization of those values.

Weber's producer was of course male. His consort, "domestic woman," was to form herself within the bourgeois private sphere of home and family. What became known as "the ideology of domesticity," and which was associated above all in the literature with the figure of the Victorian upper-middle-class woman, was identified in the writings of early second wave feminist historians as a straitjacket imposed by patriarchy from which, in the mid-twentieth century, women still had to be liberated.

Modernist feminists have been tempted to align this emancipatory project with that other face of capitalist culture: the culture of modernity and above all, the carnivalesque street life of the modern city which, in its flux and unpredictability, was the very antithesis of the culture of domesticity. Here, it was argued, constraining identities might be lost; the boundaries of the self might prove more fluid and changeable; moral certainties might be unfixed.

In her study of the relationship of women to the culture of the city, Elizabeth Wilson argues that urban life "has emancipated women more than rural life or suburban domesticity" (Wilson 1991: 10). In her work on the eighteenth-century century masquerade, Terry Castle makes similar claims for the liberating potential of an experience which is as far removed as possible from the moral, classificatory certainties of domestic ideology. The masquerade, like the street life of the anonymous city, dissolves boundaries, challenges patriarchal structures, and offers women temporary release from "the horrific erotic repression enjoined upon respectable women by eighteenth-century culture" (Castle 1986: 44). Domestic woman might escape into the streets to taste freedom as a flâneur, or try on new identities under cover of the masquerade. Elizabeth Bennett Kubek in turn traces the manner in which the image of the eighteenth-century city was contested by women writers "who created heroines eager to experience London life," an eagerness defeated and repudiated in later works of fiction as part of an agenda for "the control of women's consumption and desires to consume" (Kubek 1995: Ch. 23).

For each of these writers the city is the locus of forbidden pleasures and "rebellious freedoms," and the association of virtuous domesticity with distaste for the city is seen as part of an ideological ring fence designed to separate passive feminine conformity from active pleasures which might breed feminist rebellion.

Nancy Armstrong draws on poststructuralism to mount a very different argument. For Armstrong there is little that is either passive or forced about the bourgeois domestic femininity of the first half of the eighteenth century. She presents "domestic woman" as the active producer of a new cultural formation which was as significant a site of class power as the business enterprise. She draws on Richardson's Pamela, the very archetype of eighteenth-century domestic woman, wholly inscribed as she was within the terms of the new domestic culture which the novel did so much to define and proselytize, and who perforce set her face against the masquerade which so thoroughly distresses and threatens her in *Pamela* II.

Armstrong's work is unusual in its insistence both that eighteenth-century domesticity was a form of power, and that the woman at its center was a power-holder rather than a prisoner. Her thesis offers a radical challenge to many of the common themes of feminist analysis: themes of the marginality of women within an alien patriarchal culture; of the opposition between that male-authored "phallogocentric" culture and a female and feminist culture-in-the-making created from the marginal spaces allotted women within that culture.

Some of these themes were present by implication in the placing of the section of the 1990–1 series of Clark lectures and workshops which dealt most directly with women and with issues of gender under the head "Consumption and Difference," where women were placed alongside "other marginal groups" as producers and consumers of culture. This association of women with the margins of social and cultural life, commonplace inside and outside feminist thought, is beginning to give way to recognition that women are, on the contrary, absolutely central in social life in general, and to the processes of the formation of a "public" for cultural consumption that are under discussion here. Indeed it is in part because women were pivotal in the creation and transmission of culture that they were such anxious objects of regulation and surveillance. This important qualification of the theme of women's marginalization within patriarchal culture may be seen emerging in the trajectory of feminist criticism since the 1970s. It began by developing a critique of the male canon and of the principles and processes of canon-making, using the concept of "patriarchal culture." It documented the exclusion of women's texts, leading on very naturally to the project of recovery and rehabilitation, and to the work of producing feminist readings and rereadings of these texts, as well as of those few which had gained a place within the canon.

Two highly influential works of gynocriticism (the reading of women's texts as *women's* texts), Elaine Showalter's *A Literature of Their Own* (Showalter 1978) and Sandra Gilbert and Susan Gubar's *The Madwoman in the Attic* (Gilbert and Gubar 1979), concentrating on women's writing in nineteenth-century England, were major sources of what came to be the early feminist literary critical consensus that writing was particularly difficult for women because the patriarchal culture within which they wrote was an alien one which moreover denied them legitimate access to the pen. In western society, Gilbert and Gubar argued, only men were licensed to generate texts, and women writers negotiated a difficult relationship between their professional identity as writers and their social identity as "proper ladies" (Poovey 1984).

Gynocriticism may take much of the credit for having stimulated the reconstruction of the history of women's writing, and for the flowering of feminist literary historical scholarship in the last fifteen years or so. But this very scholarship has had the paradoxical effect of undermining gynocriticism's major premiss. Obstacles were, it had been argued, placed in the way of women who attempted the pen, not least those internalized, psychic obstacles which brought the act of writing into conflict with norms of femininity. In a trenchant critique of gynocriticism, Toril Moi asks how it was possible on this view for women to write at all (Moi 1985). The answer can only be, with great difficulty and courage, and gynocriticism is distinctive in its tendency to present the woman writer *per se* as a species of proto-feminist heroine. But she can be so presented only so long as she remains an exceptional figure. As feminist literary scholarship has moved back into the eighteenth and seventeenth centuries, the very wealth of materials uncovered must cast doubt on the thesis of gynocriticism. Women had participated in print culture from the start (Shevelow 1989), and indeed were prolific writers prior to its inception (Ezell 1987). That there were powerful processes that ensured that women's writing was filtered out in the creation of "selective traditions" of culture is unquestionable. So, too, is the fact of the widespread participation of women as producers and consumers of print culture in early capitalism. It is the history of that participation, and not just women's texts, which has been lost from view.

A third book of feminist literary criticism which is often linked with those of Gilbert and Gubar and of Showalter, is Ellen Moers's *Literary Women* (Moers 1978). Yet while Moers is properly considered under the head of "gynocriticism" her approach was different in one significant respect. She recognized and identified some of the spaces from which it was possible for middle-class women not only to write, but to do so with authority, in nineteenth-century England and France.

The sheer bulk of writing uncovered by feminist scholarship provides confirmation that emergent bourgeois society must have contained spaces from which women were not only permitted, but actually encouraged and enjoined, to write. Reading and writing, and an active participation in culture, were essential instruments in the hands of domestic woman as she performed her allotted cultural tasks. Domestic woman, as one of her first defenders, Patricia Branca, pointed out, has been more stereotyped than studied (Branca 1975). Leonore Davidoff and Catherine Hall's massive work *Family Fortunes* has done much to make good this lack as far as Victorian England is concerned. They examined family papers, wills, and other documents in order to uncover the way in which the ideology of domesticity was actually lived, its contradictions and tensions negotiated in practice, in the daily lives and concerns of middle-class families in Birmingham and Essex between 1780 and 1850. Faced with the evidence adduced in this closely textured portrait of the women and their families with whose lives we become so caught up in this study, it is increasingly difficult to sustain the view of them as victims of an ideology which was imposed upon them or which they internalized in any simple sense. Not in circumstances of their own making it is true, they were nevertheless active participants in and producers of the meanings which gave shape to their lives.

Margaret Ezell's work on women and the family in England in the seventeenth century through literary sources is interesting in this context, especially as she is looking at the period prior to the rise of the bourgeois domestic woman, a period usually seen as one presided over by the majestic figure of the traditional patriarch (Ezell 1987). In a study that includes Dame Anne Filmer, the wife of Sir Robert Filmer, our prototypical patriarch, Ezell suggests that even the patriarch's wife exercised considerable *de facto* power and authority, legitimated by her status as second-in-command to her husband on the domestic front; that she was neither the passive victim of traditional patriarchal culture, nor yet denied a voice within it. Ezell uncovers the widespread circulation of women's writings in family networks and literary circles, and she makes a compelling case for the need to extend feminist interests beyond the most prestigious forms of literature and, above all, beyond the confines of print culture. Women's writings circulated in the seventeenth century in the form of fair MSS copies which were, she argues, clearly audience-oriented: intended to be read and discussed, which indeed they were. She adduces evidence such as the key roles that women often played in the negotiation of marriages, and even the drawing up of contracts and the determination of the disposal of wealth, to argue that women had far greater power in ordering the world of the family than is allowed for within the model of a domestic patriarchy in which the power of the father within the household matches and mirrors that of the absolute monarch over his subjects. She further supports her case by an analysis of Filmer's own writings, including a short, hitherto unpublished encomium to the virtuous wife, which is appended to her study.

Nancy Armstrong draws on poststructuralist concepts of discourse and power in mounting her analysis of bourgeois domestic woman as a power-holder (Armstrong 1987). Poststructuralism has taught us that power is not an all-or-nothing affair; that it is distributed, differentially it is true, within and by "discursive regimes"; and that those who are disadvantaged in this cultural economy may nevertheless find a greater or lesser degree of room for maneuver in the active negotiation of the terms of their own lives and the cultural meanings that attach to them. Armstrong identifies domestic fiction, dominated by women writers, as one of the most significant cultural instruments through which domestic woman made herself.

What was the authority delegated to domestic woman in emergent bourgeois society? Ellen Moers had already sketched it out in *Literary Women*, when she identified her several types of heroine: the traveling heroine; the heroine in love; the performing heroine; and above all, the educating heroine (Moers 1978). It was as possessors of immortal souls that women claimed their human and religious rights, as Richardson allows Pamela to affirm with dignity: "My *soul* is of equal importance with the soul of a princess, though in quality I am but upon a foot with the meanest slave" (Richardson 1740: 137). But it was in their responsibility for the early education and training of children that women were able most effectively to claim the right to the development of their own mental faculties. The need to educate women in the exercise of reason had to be conceded wherever the Lockean view of the mind held sway, and it is interesting to look at Locke's own work on education in this light.

Some Thoughts Concerning Education was published in 1693. His earlier *An Essay Concerning Human Understanding* (1689) had given us one of our dominant metaphors for childhood, the baby's mind as "like white paper, void of all characters, without any ideas", and with it the concomitant idea, terrifying in the responsibility it implies, that the parent and educator inscribes the child's innermost self in what she writes on this blank sheet. Such an epistemology was bound to lead to great interest in the process of human development and in control of the child's experience as the means of shaping the development of its mind: in childcare, therefore, and education, and the care and education of girls as well as boys, as future parents and educators in turn of children: those "Travellers newly arrived in a strange Country, of which they know nothing . . ."

Although the work was commissioned by Locke's friend Edward Clarke, in relation to the upbringing of his son and heir, there is in the text an indirect address to women, as mothers, nurses, governesses, teachers, which at times becomes direct. And while the child to be educated is a boy, little girls make unexpected appearances from time to time: whenever appearance, clothes, or vanity is spoken of. Thus we find, disarmingly:

> One thing the Mention of Girls brings into my Mind which must not be forgot; and that is, That your Sons *Cloths* be *never* made *strait*, especially about the

Breast. Let Nature have Scope to fashion the Body as she thinks best. She works, of her self, a great deal better, and exacter, than we can direct her. And if Women were themselves to frame the Bodies of their Children in their Wombs, as they often endeavour to mend their Shapes when they are out, we should as certainly have no perfect Children born, as we have few well-shapes that are *strait-laced*, or much tampered with.

(Locke 1693: 123)

Locke's address to women was a mixture of railery and chastisement, calculated to jolly them into rational practice. Extolling the beneficial effects of daily bathing of children in cold water, he dramatizes the anticipated response:

How fond Mothers are like to receive this Doctrine is not hard to foresee. What can it be less than to Murder their tender Babes to use them thus? What! put their Feet in cold Water in Frost and Snow, when all one can do is little enough to keep them warm?

(Locke 1693: 119)

We have indirect confirmation of this address to women in Richardson's use of the same text in Part II of *Pamela*, where he has Mr. B give Pamela Locke's treatise. She writes to him (and for us) in some forty pages her response to these doctrines, and tells Mr. B, and us, of the (modified) Lockean regime which she will institute in the upbringing of their son (Richardson 1740: 373–412). In considering the positioning of domestic woman in emergent bourgeois society, and the authority with which she was invested, it is clear that not only were women as a matter of fact a significant sector of the reading public, but that as a matter of necessity, a great deal of reading matter was addressed to women. The publications of the public sphere were oriented in considerable part towards the private, and towards the feminine.

The formation of a public, then, was a two-way process of exchange. The commodities associated with print culture, in particular the periodical, the conduct book, and, later, the early novel, stimulated and attempted not only to regulate and monitor private conduct, but to reach into and form the inner self of their "consumers", while individuals who were addressed by and recognized themselves in these commodities, in turn composed the expanding public which nourished them. Production and consumption, public and commodity, were deeply implicated in one another.

Habermas speaks of the paradox of the development of subjectivity as "the innermost core of the private self," yet "always already oriented to an *audience*" (Habermas 1989: 49). He speaks of familiar forms such as the letter, and especially the novel in letters: of "the familiarity whose vehicle was the written word, the subjectivity that had become fit to print" (51). We would expect, on this account, to find the new forms which wrote that subjectivity to be particularly subject to surveillance, and indeed we do in the history of the eighteenth-century novel, especially novels by women (Taylor 1943). But this task of surveillance was an enormous, and finally an impossible, one, because it required surveillance of the production of meaning at the point of reading as well as of writing.

Kathryn Shevelow in her work on the early periodicals in their address to "the fair sex" (Shevelow 1989) draws attention to the blurring of boundaries between writer and reader, public and private, in the *Athenian Mercury*, which "created a public discourse out of private experience" (89) in publishing its readers' letters. "The concept of reader," she writes, "and the concept of writer were conjoined; the discourse of the private became a public discourse" (Shevelow 1989: 69).

The periodicals were most certainly instrumental in the development of forms of "publication" of the private. But on the whole, they remained, so to speak, at its portals. The contents of her library are markers of the cultivated taste of the Lady Leonora in *Spectator* 37 (Bond 1965: 153) and this essay is typical of the periodicals of the bourgeois public sphere, even in their address to "the fair sex," in concerning itself with the externals of polite conduct: with what the observing spectator might divine from close inspection of the public rooms of the private house, the appearance and comportment of its actors. It did not penetrate too deeply into the ordering of the inner self, nor yet into that of private domestic life when the doors were closed on spectators, but with the front which the private self and the private sphere presented to the world in their myriad points of interface with the public. It was the novel which provided a form able to enter more fully into the inner spaces which the periodicals had begun to open up to scrutiny.

The epistolary novel offered a form in which surveillance of the reader might be attempted from within the text itself. As has often been observed (Harris 1987; Armstrong 1987), Richardson's *Pamela* II weaves the subject-matter of his extensive correspondence with the circle of women with whom he exchanged letters, into the fictional correspondence of his heroine. Richardson has Pamela enter into correspondence with Mr. B.'s sister, Lady Davers, and the letters are passed around the circle of Lady Davers's friends. They are exhaustively scrutinized, their moral and behavioral lessons debated, comments and queries being sent back in Lady Davers's letters to Pamela. For Pamela's second, and most frequent, correspondent, Polly Darnford, she keeps a journal, and these writings are in turn passed on to Pamela's parents, and back again to Polly, accumulating comment as they circulate, so that the circumstances of Pamela's initial "trials," the events and conduct of her subsequent marriage, and her ordering of her household are not only described in minute detail, but inscribed within a form which brings the debates of the public sphere regarding the proper conduct of the private, into the home, whilst opening the home, as well as private articulations of the inner self, to the critical regard of the public sphere.

Richardson used this structure of correspondence to correct what he considered to be misreadings of his work and his heroine, and to address those criticisms, made by real-life correspondents as well as by critics, to which he was most sensitive. All he had to do was to put these criticisms into the mouths (or rather the pens) of one or more of his characters, and let another meet them. Thus "the example he [Mr. B.] has set to young gentlemen of family and fortune to marry beneath them" is debated at length in this fashion (Richardson 1742: 168). Richardson has Pamela answer this charge in one set of terms – the morality and logic of seduction. Mr. B. rests his defence on another ground – the exceptional circumstance of Pamela's extraordinary beauty matched by her exemplary virtue, her understanding and accomplishments. Richardson then underscores this double defence by a second tale of attempted seduction of a servant by a gentleman – a reprise, with a difference, of Pamela's original "trials" at the hands of Mr. B. This time Pamela's own maid, Polly Barlow, is the object of Lady Davers's predatory nephew, Mr. H. (Jackey). The difference is that Polly is eagerly complicit in her own seduction, and so the case serves to justify the outcome of marriage in the one instance and not in the other (II, 185 f.). It may be noted that the form itself, the novel in letters, has the power to undermine Pamela's exemplary claims. The conventions of the epistolary form oblige her to write of a matter about which the conventions of domestic integrity demand she should keep silent.

The form used by Richardson to explore the morality of seductions across class serves, then, to underline the point made by Habermas, that the emergent private sphere, while looking inwards, and monitoring morals and manners, is "oriented to an audience": is in a sense produced in a public, communicable form. Richardson's novel in letters and the mushrooming and multi-layered correspondence within which it was in turn enfolded, is another form of that "public intimacy" in the creation of a "print community" described by Shevelow in her study of the periodicals.

In the course of this chapter I have surveyed recent thinking on the formation of a public for the consumption of a newly commoditized culture in early eighteenth-century England, emphasizing what is increasingly recognized in the literature, the profoundly gendered nature of these cultural and social processes. I have traced the ways in which feminist scholarship has reworked the figure of woman as victim of, and stranger within, an alien patriarchal culture, presenting her to herself in monstrous or angelic forms in which she recognizes herself at her peril. She has begun to be recast in a much more active role: participant in, even producer of, aspects of that culture, and a key agent in its transmission across generations. I want to close with a brief consideration of what this recasting does and does not imply.

First, it is clear that some at least of the women who negotiated rather than confronted the norms of feminine domesticity were by no means without either power or pleasure in the lives they forged for themselves within its confines. I argued in *Consuming Fiction* that bourgeois women have a distinct interest in the maintenance of class privileges and powers. Radical feminist thought has of course a strong tradition which celebrates the power of women, but these powers are primeval and universal, rooted ultimately in biology. The forms of power which are under discussion here, are institutional, historical, and differentially distributed amongst women. This placing of woman firmly within society and culture, rather than positing her either as a helpless victim or as a revolutionary from the margins, has the advantage of facilitating a more nuanced approach, both to matters of gender relations, and to questions of differences between women that have proved so deeply problematic for feminism as the voices of those who are neither white nor middle-class, neither heterosexual nor ablebodied, have begun to be heard.

Second, I want to argue that Raymond Williams's phrase "writing in society" is more useful for the understanding of the history of women's writing than the concept of "writing from the margins," whether of culture or of language itself. Writing is a social practice. It always comes from particular places, and it is addressed to particular readers. There are many positions within society and culture from which writing is not only possible, but sometimes enjoined, and some of the most significant of these are occupied by women.

Carolyn Steedman's work on working-class writing is particularly illuminating here, as she traces the ways in which the life of a radical policeman, and later a soldier, John

Pearman, with its daily routines of report-writing, facilitated the writing of a "radical soldier's tale" (Steedman 1988). The most unusual example is perhaps that of Hannah Cullwick's diaries. The position of general domestic servant, from which Hannah Cullwick wrote, was one from which writing was most certainly not expected, and her writings were as furtive and secretive as the relationship with Munby which occasioned them. Cullwick had a very particular reader in mind: Munby himself; but she served her apprenticeship in writing for Munby, to develop a broader address and a less circumscribed purpose (Stanley 1984; Davidoff 1983).

Hannah Cullwick wrote from the margins. But the middle-class women who wrote novels, journals, conduct books, and such in eighteenth-century Britain wrote, if not from the center, yet from a legitimate space within emergent modern culture.

Third, it does not follow that because many women occupied positions from which they were licensed to write, and from which, *pace* Armstrong, they exercised forms of power, and no doubt gained much pleasure, those powers and pleasures were not highly circumscribed. One of the temptations of postmodern feminisms is to rest content with the identification of active powers and pleasures in women's lives. Sabina Lovibond in her critique of postmodern feminism writes:

> The word "pleasure" . . . is apt to be brought out with a flourish, as if it clinched the case for seeing progressive or creative possibilities in something previously viewed with suspicion. . . . But . . . whoever wants to claim that conventional femininity, even at its most abject, cannot be *pleasurable* for women?
>
> (Lovibond 1989: 26–7)

The powers and pleasures identified by Armstrong and others were conditional on the acceptance of constraints that feminists might well judge to have been much too high. Certainly they may have been won on condition of eschewing feminist rebellion.

Carol Pateman's recent study (Pateman 1988) suggests that the so-called "contractual society" that emerged at the close of the seventeenth century is patriarchy transformed not overthrown: a fraternal patriarchy whose founding myth is not that of Adam and Eve, but the story reiterated by Freud of the fratricidal killing of the father by the sons, to break his monopoly of sexual access to the women of the group; and the subsequent pact which was the taboo on incest, in which the brothers gave up their rights of sexual access to "their own" women in exchange for access to the sister of another. The marriage contract does not, for Pateman, symbolize the social contract, as it does for Armstrong and also for Moretti in his analysis of the *Bildungsroman* (Moretti 1987), but rather functions to disguise the nature of the anterior sexual contract by giving it the form of an exchange freely entered into by consenting adults. The "essence" of feminism (de Lauretis 1988) lies in its commitment to social transformation, and therefore it tends towards accounts of women in society and culture which lay emphasis on constraints and inequities rather than on pleasures and powers. However, without recognition of the *investment* that women may have in given social and cultural forms, feminism will be ineffective. It will fail to persuade, and it will also fail to identify potential power-bases from which change may be initiated.

Armstrong draws heavily on Richardson's *Pamela*, which she considers (with justification) to be a key text in the formation of domestic woman. She transforms Richardson's text into something more closely resembling later domestic fictions, however, by effectively limiting it to the tale of attempted seduction which culminates in Pamela's victory over Mr. B., and their marriage. "Who does not question," she asks, "Richardson's wisdom in furnishing us with almost two hundred pages of this account" (of her ordering of Mr. B.'s household) (Armstrong 1987: 124). As the text is transformed from novel to conduct book, "No longer a form of resistance . . . the female voice flattens into that of pure ideology" (Ibid.: 125). The further sequel, *Pamela* II, is completely ignored. It is significant, however, that the funny, self-dramatizing, and slightly hysterical voice that Richardson had found for the 15-year-old Pamela in the first volume, in which she is nevertheless able so effectively to defend her right to the disposal of her own body – Locke's "Fundamental, Sacred and unalterable Law of *Self–Preservation*" (Locke 1689–90: 149) – falters and flattens precisely at the moment when she has entered the sole contract that she will ever be permitted to make, the contract of marriage. Pateman's account of the sexual contract places the last 200 pages of *Pamela* and the first part of the sequel in an interesting light. It may be seen less as an extended and transparent transmission of ideology than as its unintentional exposure. What begins to emerge is the nature of the sexual contract. Once married, as Jocelyn Harris points out, Pamela

> surrenders rights to her only property, her person. Reminded that she now runs the risk of committing " 'Laese Majestatis', a sort of 'Treason against my Liege Lord and Husband' " (334) she realises the confirmation of his power over her. Bound by her vow of obedience, Pamela may no longer resist. Whatever she thinks, she may no longer say it.
>
> (Harris 1987: 33)

Pamela loses her last Lockean struggle for control over her person: the fight she makes for the right to breast-feed her baby (Richardson 1742: 228–36). Mr. B. simply says no, and, after an unsuccessful appeal to her parents, Pamela's last act of defiance, she yields.

Bibliography

Abercrombie, N., Hill, S. and Turner, B. (1986) *Sovereign Individuals of Capitalism*, London: Allen & Unwin.
Armstrong, N. (1987) *Desire and Domestic Fiction*, New York and Oxford: Oxford University Press.
Barrett, M. (1988) *Women's Oppression Today*, London: Verso.
Berman, M. (1982) *All That Is Solid Melts into Air*, London: Verso.
Bond, D. F. (ed.) (1965) *The Spectator*, 4 vols., Oxford: Clarendon Press.
Bourdieu, P. (1984) *Distinction*, London: Routledge.
Branca, P. (1975) *Silent Sisterhood*, London: Croom Helm.
Brewer, J. (1995) " 'The most polite age and the most vicious'. Attitudes towards culture as a commodity, 1660–1800," Chapter 18 in this volume.
Campbell, C. (1987) *The Romantic Ethic and the Spirit of Modern Consumerism*, Oxford: Blackwell.
Castle, T. (1986) *Masquerade and Civilization*, London: Methuen.
Collins, A. S. (1928a) *Authorship in the Days of Johnson*, London: Routledge.
—— (1928b) *The Profession of Letters*, London: Routledge.

Davidoff, L. (1983) "Class and gender in Victorian England," in J. L. Newton, M. P. Ryan and J. R. Walkowitz (eds.) *Sex and Class in Women's History*, London: Routledge, pp. 17–71.

Davidoff, L. and Hall, C. (1987) *Family Fortunes*, London: Hutchinson.

De Lauretis, T. (1988) "The essence of the triangle, or taking the risk of essentialism seriously: feminist theory in Italy, the US and Britain," *Differences* 1, 2: 3–37.

Eagleton, T. (1984) *The Functions of Criticism*, London: Verso.

Ezell, M. (1987) *The Patriarch's Wife*, Chapel Hill, NC and London: University of North Carolina Press.

Gilbert, S. M. and Gubar, S. (1979) *The Madwoman in the Attic*, New Haven, CT and London: Yale University Press.

Greer, G. *et al.* (1989) *Kissing the Rod*, London: Virago.

Habermas, J. (1989) *The Structural Transformation of the Public Sphere*, Oxford: Polity.

Harris, J. (1987) *Samuel Richardson*, Cambridge: Cambridge University Press.

Hobby, E. (1988) *Virtue of Necessity*, London: Virago.

Hoggart, R. (1958) *The Uses of Literacy*, Harmondsworth, Mx: Penguin; originally published (1957) London: Chatto & Windus.

Hohendahl, P. U. (1982) *The Institution of Criticism*, New York: Cornell University Press.

Hunter, J. P. (1990) *Before Novels*, New York and London: Norton.

Kubek, E. B. (1995) "Women's participation in the urban culture in early modern London. Images from fiction," Chapter 23 in this volume.

Locke, J. (1689 [1975]) *An Essay Concerning Human Understanding*, ed. P. H. Nidditch, Oxford: Clarendon Press.

—— (1689–90 [1960]) *Two Treatises of Government*, ed. P. Laslett, New York: Cambridge University Press.

—— (1693 [1968]) *Some Thoughts Concerning Education*, in *The Educational Writings of John Locke*, ed. J. L. Axtell, Cambridge: Cambridge University Press.

Lovell, T. (1987) *Consuming Fiction*, London: Verso.

Lovibond, S. (1989) "Feminism and postmodernism," *New Left Review* 178: 5–28.

McKendrick, N., Brewer, J. and Plumb, J. H. (1982) *The Birth of a Consumer Society; The Commercialization of Eighteenth-Century England*, London: Europa Publications.

McKeon, M. (1987) *The Origins of the English Novel, 1600–1740*, Baltimore, MD and London: Johns Hopkins University Press.

Mitchell, J. (1974) *Psychoanalysis and Feminism*, Harmondsworth, Mx: Penguin.

Moers, E. (1978) *Literary Women*, London: Women's Press.

Moi, T. (1985) *Sexual/Textual Politics*, London: Methuen.

Moretti, F. (1987) *The Way of the World*, London: Verso.

Pateman, C. (1988) *The Sexual Contract*, Oxford: Polity.

Poovey, M. (1984) *The Proper Lady and the Woman Writer*, Chicago: University of Chicago Press.

Pope, A. (1743 [1966]) *The Dunciad*, in *Pope: Poetical Works*, ed. Herbert Davis, London: Oxford University Press.

Prior M. (ed.) (1985) *Women in English Society, 1500–1800*, London: Methuen.

Richardson, S. (1740 [1914]) *Pamela*, ed. M. Kinkead–Weekes, London: Dent.

—— (1742 [1962]) *Pamela 2*, ed. M. Kinkead–Weekes, London: Dent.

Sayer, D. (1991) *Capitalism and Modernity*, London: Routledge.

Sennett, R. (1974) *The Fall of Public Man*, Cambridge: Cambridge University Press.

Shevelow, K. (1989) *Women and Print Culture*, London: Routledge.

Showalter, E. (1978) *A Literature of Their Own*, London: Virago.

Spencer, J. (1986) *The Rise of the Woman Novelist*, Oxford: Blackwell.

Spender, D. (1986) *Mothers of the Novel*, London and New York: Pandora.

Stanley, L. (1984) "Introduction," in H. Cullwick, *The Diaries of Hannah Cullwick*, ed. and intro. L. Stanley, London: Virago.

Steedman, C. (1988) *The Radical Soldier's Tale*, London: Routledge.

Stephen, L. (1903) *English Literature and Society in the Eighteenth Century*, London: Duckworth.

Taylor, C. (1989) *Sources of the Self: The Making of Modern Identity*, Cambridge: Cambridge University Press.

Taylor, J. T. (1943) *Early Opposition to the English Novel, 1760–1830*, Morningside Heights, New York: King's Crown Press.

Vickery, A. (1993) "Women and the world of goods: a Lancashire consumer and her possessions, 1751–81," in John Brewer and Roy Porter (eds.) *Consumption and the World of Goods*, London and New York: Routledge, pp. 274–301.

Watt, I. (1957) *The Rise of the Novel*, Harmondsworth Mx: Penguin.

Williams, R. (1976) *Keywords*, Glasgow: Fontana.

—— (1977) *Marxism and Literature*, Oxford: Oxford University Press.

—— (1983) *Towards 2000*, London: Chatto & Windus.

—— (1987) *Culture and Society*, London: Hogarth.

Wilson, E. (1991) *The Sphinx in the City*, London: Virago.

3
Reading women
Text and image in eighteenth-century England

Peter H. Pawlowicz

Painting, asserted Jonathan Richardson, is "another Language" (Richardson 1725: 3). Framed by discourse, paintings in turn became discursive frames through which the audience viewed itself. Together, text and image constituted a single system of knowledge. Painting, argued Richardson, is a language that "completes" the "whole Art of communicating our Thoughts." Every picture excites "proper Sentiments and Reflections" just as "a History, a Poem, [or] a Book." Indeed they mutually "assist" one another (Richardson 1725: 2, 11). Paintings, Richardson concluded, teach us to read books and books teach us to read paintings.[1] This basic reciprocity shapes this chapter.

In the eighteenth century, new genres of writing – especially the novel – became the site of new anxieties about readers, especially women. Within the transforming phenomenon of the novel, English and French painting created new topoi. These depicted women as consumers and producers of texts, that is, as readers with the power to create stories of their own. I shall consider how images by Joshua Reynolds and Pierre–Antoine Baudouin entered the debate on the character of the novel and the role of female readers. In particular, I shall explore how they presented different constructions of women readers and the consumption of the text.

New kinds of experience, notes Raymond Williams, were the basis for the novel's "extraordinary growth and achievement." Intimate genres of writing – the journal, the autobiography, the letter – informed the novel with its "sustained analysis of a situation or a state of mind." At the end of the eighteenth century, titles rose sharply. By their simple numbers, they became a "transforming social fact" (Williams 1983: 80, 73). Early modern history defined a change in structures that generate identity. Yet while new models for the self appeared, new controls opposed them. The situation, Stephen Greenblatt insists, was "resolutely dialectical" (Greenblatt 1980: 1–2). The novel was the site of just such oppositions. Indeed, argues Elizabeth Brophy, the novel questioned how society "estimated" women and it created "believable" heroines to "emulate." In doing so, it provided women readers with new ways of being (Brophy 1991: 238, 243).

Throughout the eighteenth century, the novel remained morally suspect. One reason lay in the essence of reading, for the life of the text appealed to the constituent forces of society itself. Imitation, sympathy, and love – wrongly invoked – might betray the individual or subvert the social order. "There is," wrote John Gregory, "a universal principle of imitation among Mankind." "This," noted Edmund Burke, "forms our manners, our opinions, our lives." More importantly, it does so without "intervention of the reasoning faculty" (Burke 1978: 49). Imitation disposes each man, Gregory further noted, "to catch instantaneously" the "resemblance of any action or character that presents itself" (Gregory 1772: 101).

In 1805, Hugh Murray summed up this eighteenth-century discourse of imitation. He reduced all generic distinctions to a single trope – "imitation." "Fiction," he asserted, was the "same" as any other "kind of instruction." Their common principle was "example." Man, said Murray, was in essence "imitative." His character was "formed after that of those with whom he becomes acquainted, either by reading, or by the intercourse of life." "History," concluded Murray, "abounds with examples of men who have been betrayed into follies, and even crimes, by the indiscriminate imitation of some favorite hero" (Murray 1805: 27, 19). Thus imitation was the novel's great danger. In the fourth number of the *Rambler* (1750), Samuel Johnson explained that novels were written for "the young, the ignorant, and the idle." They were the entertainment of minds "unfurnished with ideas" and therefore "easily susceptible of impressions." Such was their "power of example" that they possessed the reader by "a kind of violence." In fact, novels might produce their effect "almost without the intervention of the will."

Contemporaries criticized Samuel Richardson's *Clarissa* on just these grounds. Richardson's image of vice – Lovelace in particular – was too attractive. The unwary might be moved to imitation. Lamented James Beattie:

> When a character, like Richardson's *Lovelace*, whom the reader ought to abominate for his crimes, is adorned with youth, beauty, eloquence, wit, and every other intellectual and bodily accomplishment, it is to be feared, that thoughtless young men may be tempted to imitate, even while they disapprove, him.
>
> (Beattie 1783: 569)

"That Richardson's Novels are written with the purest intent," intoned Vicessimus Knox, "none can deny." But, he warned, "youthful" readers attend only to the "lively description of love" and "eagerly wish to be actors in the scenes which they admire" (Knox 1789: I, 69). "Young people," judged Richard Cumberland, "are all imitation" (Cumberland 1798: 274).

Sympathies evoked by reading were no less perilous, for they might disqualify women as wives and mothers. Henry Mackenzie summarized the problem. The "principal danger" arose from a "war of duties." Novels substituted feeling for acting, for readers "open their minds to *impressions* which never have any effect upon their *conduct*." Such a divorce of emotional cause from social effect was nothing less than "depravity" (Bredvold 1962: 85). Sympathies[2] that should animate society instead lay trapped in the reader.

In particular, charged Richard Berenger, novels "cheated" women of marriage.

Ladies who would have been "good wives and good mothers" were divorced from the proper "affections of social life."[3] They were "perverted" by ideas of "romantic love" found only in "romances" (Williams 1970: 214). Berenger created a pathology of the woman novel-reader. It is the story of Clarinda, only child of a wealthy merchant. Given to the "ensnaring practice of reading novels," she rejects a proper husband because he is no "imaginary" hero. Instead his valet, Monsieur Antoine, wins her heart. Clarinda's father pays Antoine to leave her and Clarinda vows never to marry. At 55, Clarinda still prefers her novels and her dreams of Antoine to the "real blessings" of the marriage (Williams 1970: 215). Together, imitation and sympathy with their threat to marriage constituted the great danger to women readers. Critics condemned the force of imitation, the inversion of sympathy, and the false expectations of romance. In doing so, they represented the subversive female reader from outside, from the perspective of the patriarchal order that is challenged.

By contrast, Choderlos de Laclos depicted the subversive reader from within. In the *Liaisons dangereuses*, the marquise de Merteuil teaches what it means to read against the grain. A deconstructionist *avant la lettre*, she reads to disqualify traditional meanings. From their disjunction she constructs her own oppositional identity. Merteuil records the course of observation and reading by which she creates herself. "Mes principes," she declares, "sont le fruit de mes profondes réflexions; je les ai créés, et je puis dire que je suis mon ouvrage." Merteuil is unequivocally her own person. Indeed, by the age of 15, notes the marquise, "Je posédais déjà les talents auxquels la plus grande partie de nos politiques doivent leur réputation." She turns next to "le secours de la lecture." But, she warns, "ne croyez pas qu'elle fût toute du genre que vous supposez." She reads uniquely for herself.

> J'étudiai nos moeurs dans les romans; nos opinions dans les philosophes; je cherchai même dans les moralistes les plus sévères ce qu'ils exigeaient de nous, et je m'assurai ainsi de ce qu'on pouvait faire . . . et de ce qu'il fallait paraître.
>
> (Laclos 1961: 175–7)

Merteuil subverts the "natural" order of reading. Studying propriety only in order to counterfeit it, she turns the normative lessons of the text against itself. By her action, Merteuil provides a paradigm for the deconstruction of Laclos's own text.

Fiction may introduce the common reader to uncommon possibilities. Texts can be patterns for experience that as yet has no recognized form. Their narratives may provide compelling models for conduct and feeling. Such stories, argues Carolyn G. Heilbrun, teach us how to live. "These may be read, or chanted, or experienced electronically." Whatever their shape, "stories are what have formed us." And they are what we use "to make new fictions" (Heilbrun 1990: 109).

In the eighteenth century, readers shaped their lives to such fictional forms. Self-referentially, the novel depicted characters who constructed their lives like texts. Richardson's Mr. B. stole the letters that Pamela intended for her parents, then demanded to see all her writings.

> I long to see the particulars of your plot . . . for you have so beautiful a manner, that it is partly that, and partly my love for you, that has made me

desirous of reading all you write. . . . Besides, said he, there is such a pretty air of romance, as you relate them, in *your* plots, and *my* plots, that I shall be better directed in what manner to wind up the catastrophe of the pretty novel.

(Richardson 1970: I, 253)

In Laclos's *Liaisons dangereuses*, characters likewise live such "new fictions." Endeavoring to seduce the présidente de Tourvel, the vicomte de Valmont seeks to make her "une nouvelle Clarisse." To the marquise de Merteuil, Valmont's life is a kind of literature-in-the-making. Destroying Cecile Volanges, she declares to him, "sera enfin une *rouerie* de plus à mettre dans vos mémoires." The role of Cecile is to be "l'héroïne de ce nouveau roman" (Laclos 1961: 10). Mr. B., Valmont, and Merteuil shape their lives to forms of literature.

Books referenced powerful forces. In a society that demanded a high degree of conformity in women, reading defined an important site of opposition. The eighteenth-century novel was never unproblematic nor ever entirely respectable. Within the images we examine, painting encodes this ambiguity. Signifying gestures work to problematize meaning. In the space between text and reader they inscribe a dialectic of production and consumption, active and passive, masculine and feminine.

The reader I invoke is the eighteenth-century "reader, in his solitary chair" (Williams 1970: 400) – the separate, silent, print-reading individual. This is Joshua Reynolds's *Theophila Palmer Reading "Clarissa Harlowe"* (Plate 3.1). It is the portrait of his niece "Offie." Miss Palmer sits with head in hand and reading a book. Reynolds reduces the setting to essentials. It contains only the half-length figure of Miss Palmer and part of the chair in which she sits. By its insistent focus it questions both the character of the reader and the nature of reading itself.

Miss Palmer's volume of *Clarissa* exists in an easy, intimate relation to its reader. Contemporaries noted the new physical character of books – especially novels. They were, complained Vicessimus Knox, too "conveniently portable" (Knox 1789: I, 70). Generally books did get smaller. By the end of the century, there were far fewer folios and quartos than at the beginning and many more octavos and duodecimos (McKendrick *et al.* 1982: 270, n. 14). Miss Palmer reads an octavo. Grasped in one hand, Miss Palmer's book hangs by a cover. Its spine is tortured into an S. The informality of her gesture suggests an affection not only for the characters of the book, but for the physical volume itself. In Charlotte Brontë's *Shirley*, Mrs. Pryor voices the proprieties of an earlier age when she remonstrates to the heroine: "My dear, I wish you could acquire the habit of sitting to a table when you read." Miss Palmer eschews all such ceremony. Indeed, notes Sarah Fielding, "[*Clarissa*] is treated like an intimate Acquaintance by all her Readers (Fielding 1985: 15). Theophila Palmer displays the strength of this acquaintanceship. She enacts the urgent exchange between reader and text.

Stanley Fish suggests one model for this experience. He contrasts human beings "as passive and disinterested comprehenders of a knowledge external to them" with human beings "at every moment creating the experiential spaces into which personal knowledge flows" (Fish 1980: 94). Personally investing the text, Fish's active reader produces the story that others passively consume. Such reading reconfigures the essential dyad of production and consumption. Consuming the text, readers paradoxically produce it. In doing so, they not only recast the narrative but refigure the forces that shape its production. Stories that construct one kind of society may in the practice of its readers become texts for different – indeed antagonistic – personal realities. Authoring their text, active readers reproduce their unique consciousness of the world. Each new reading may thus become the text for new experience.

From the inception of the novel, readers and writers struggled to invest the printed page. Samuel Richardson complained: "It is impossible that Readers the most attentive, can always enter into the Views of the Writer." Readers inexcusably intrude – "every one putting him and herself into the Character they read, and judging of it by their own Sensations" (Richardson 1964: 316). Richardson could not trust his audience to understand his meaning and read his story. William Warner details a fascinating episode in the reception of Richardson's *Clarissa*. A struggle between author and audience, it is the public model of that private resistance to be found in every solitary reader. Responding to rumors of a tragic conclusion, Lady Bradshaw opened a debate over the proper ending of *Clarissa*. She accused Richardson: "You and others have formed . . . a Catastrophe of your own; and are . . . unwilling to part with it" (Warner 1979: 159).

Published in widely spaced installments, *Clarissa* encouraged readers to imagine their own conclusion. Many did. Infatuated with Lovelace, Lady Bradshaw invented an ending in which he reformed, then married Clarissa. To Richardson she confessed:

> If I was to die for it, I cannot help being fond of Lovelace. A sad dog! why would you make him so wicked, and yet so agreeable? He says, somewhere or other he designs being a good man, from which words I have great hopes; and, in excuse for my liking him, I must say, I have made him so, up to my heart's wish.
>
> (Warner 1979: 162)

Lady Bradshaw, Warner notes, was not alone. Colley Cibber and Henry Fielding were only the most distinguished among the engaged readers who likewise demanded a happy ending. Bradshaw's sister, Lady Echlin, in fact wrote her own alternative 166-page conclusion in which Clarissa was not raped and Lovelace died penitent (Warner 1979: 166). To superintend his text, Richardson printed a table of contents and summary of letters for the second edition. "I chose . . . to give a little Abstract of the Story, that it might be clearly seen what it was." Richardson's intent was to assure every reader's "Understanding of it, in the Way I chose" (Richardson 1964: 125).

Richardson's public struggle for meaning foregrounds the private contest of reader and writer behind his fear. In the privacy of the self, solitary readers like Miss Palmer construct a space outside authorial control. There, as did Ladies Bradshaw and Echlin, they might contest Clarissa's story. "Putting him and herself into the Character they read," they could subvert, revise, or even rewrite the author's text. Wolfgang Iser maps this process.[4] Each reader, he argues, must "find the missing link" within the vacancies of the story (Iser 1978: 196). "Contrasts and discrepancies" among norms and characters give rise to blanks. Readers fill in the spaces. Judging among characters and actions, they work to construct the meaning of the hero (Iser 1978: 196–203). Each reader must fit the shifting perspectives of narrative "into a gradually evolving pattern" (Iser 1978: 35). The work is a continuous process of assessment and adjustment. The reader must fill in the gaps, give form to what the text leaves indeterminate, and modify previous conclusions as the text gives more information. The process ends in knowledge.

In the same way, eighteenth-century critics enjoined the audience to "complete" the text.[5] Anticipating Iser, Sarah Fielding demanded that *Clarissa*'s reader "attend strictly." Richardson's novel, she insisted, is a "real Picture of human Life." As such, "The Characters must open by degrees, and the Reader's own Judgement form them from different Parts, as they display themselves according to the Incidents that arise" (Fielding 1985: 51, 35). In this "real picture" the reader must judge characters and events, and thus arrive at knowledge.

Richardson's readers actively invested the text. Their experience was vividly – even disconcertingly – "lived." In the *Gentleman's Magazine* we read: "I interrupt the unhappy Clarissa, in order to mix my tears with hers; I accost her, as if she was present with me" (Williams 1970: 247). Mrs. Montagu confessed to her daughter: "I was such an old Fool as to weep over Clarissa Harlowe like any milkmaid of sixteen" (Montagu 1965: III, 8). Sarah Fielding wrote: "Tears without Number have I shed, whilst Mr. *Belford* by his Relation has . . . made me perfectly present at her noble exalted Behaviour; nor can I hardly refrain from crying out, 'Farewell, my dear *Clarissa!*' " (Fielding 1985: 56). Readers like Fielding experienced the novel as a species of life. "Putting him and herself into the Character they read" (Richardson 1964: 316), readers placed themselves squarely in the story. Completing the text, they experienced it as actuality. For this reason we often feel, notes Iser, that as we read "we are living another life" (Iser 1978: 127).

Joshua Reynold's *Theophila Palmer* (Plate 3.1) offers one model of this sympathetic reader. Yet at the same time, it destabilizes the very model it constructs. "Enthusiastic youth," lamented Hannah More, are betrayed by novels while "imagining they indulge the noblest feelings of their nature" (More 1799: 37). That sympathy with which Miss Palmer invests the text at the same time endangers its possessor. Her body inscribes this ambiguity. Bowing her head over *Clarissa*'s pages, she literally embraces Richardson's volume. Her reading represents a powerful and equivocal sensibility. A "sympathising sensibility" and "tenderness of attachments," observed Thomas Gisbourne, are the "glory of the female sex." Yet women's "natural" "quickness of feeling" exposes them to dangers – most notably, a "familiarity with novels" (Gisbourne 1799: 23, 117). Miss Palmer's reading is the "natural" sign of her femininity. It enacts her sympathetic response to the representations of the text. But it elides with a dangerous sexuality. "Excessive sympathy" and "sentimental affection," averred Vicessimus Knox, are "but *lust in disguise*." Inspired by novels like Sterne's *Sentimental Journey* and *Tristram Shandy*, they are the ruin of "thousands" (Knox 1789: I, 70). "How much," expostulated Knox, "are divorces multiplied since Sterne!"

In a singular way, Miss Palmer shapes her own experience of Richardson's text. If we look carefully, we see that she does not actually read. When we follow the line of sight indicated by her eyes, we see that it passes over the top of the book. She sees not the printed page but her re-vision of its text. In the line of her gaze, she reconfigures the essential relation of book and reader. Miss Palmer views but as importantly re-views the text. She produces an alternative story. Though it depends on his narrative, it separates itself – literally – from Richardson's text.

What then does Miss Palmer "see"? A product of sight, imagination is invoked by the force of the sitter's gaze. What the reader "sees" is the effect of what she reads. It appears not to her physical but to her mind's eye. Man, noted Lord Kames, "can fabricate images of things that have no existence." His materials are "ideas of sight." The mechanism is "*imagination*" (Home 1769: II, 517). Indeed, the pleasures of the eye are primary. "Our first perceptions are of external objects and our first attachments are to them" (Home 1769: I, 4). The vivid representations of the text make each reader a witness to its events. Noted Kames: "I am insensibly transformed into a spectator." To read is in a manner to "lose sight" of oneself. "Forgetting himself, and forgetting that he is reading," the reader views each incident as "an eye-witness" (Home 1769: I, 93).

But seeing is a paradox. "As soon as I see," writes Maurice Merleau-Ponty, that vision is necessarily doubled with "another vision" – myself seen "as another would see me" (Merleau–Ponty 1968: 134). Similarly, David Hume observed: "We bring our own deportment and conduct frequently in review, and consider how they appear in the eyes of those who approach and regard us." Our constant habit of "surveying ourselves, as it were, in reflection" generates every social "sentiment of right and wrong" (Hume 1953: 115). Each "I" is the individual's response to the perception of others. By considering how they would appear to us in their situation, noted Adam Smith, we consider how our "passions and conduct" appear to those who view us. "We suppose ourselves the spectators of our own behavior" (A. Smith 1774: 201). Generated in the space between the individual eye and the mirror of society, the self is a reflex of the gaze. We see ourselves as others see us.

To see is necessarily to be seen – whether in society or the text. The spectator in the story encounters the full spectatorial force of its events. An "eye-witness" to its action, the reader is in turn constructed by its point of view. Viewing the story, the reader constitutes himself in the mirror of its characters – who they are, what they do, how they feel and believe. In this way, to read is necessarily to be read.

As a viewer in the story, each reader enters the spectatorial field. Laura Mulvey provides one model for viewership in the world and in the text. Founded on the binary opposition of male looking and female "to-be looked-at-ness," it equates masculine with active and feminine with passive. For Mulvey, viewing is essentially a virile act. Scopophilia – the sexual gaze – is essentially male (Mulvey 1975: 8). The male viewer/voyeur dictates the terms of spectatorship. To be a woman is to be the spectacle, the object of the male desire.

Mulvey maps the sexuality of the gaze. But more importantly, I think, she aligns relationships of looking to relations of power and it is this I want to consider. Like Mulvey, E. Ann Kaplan argues that the masculine gaze carries with it a one-way power. "Men do not simply look; their gaze carries with it the power of action and of possession which is lacking in the female gaze. Women receive and return a gaze, but cannot act upon it" (Kaplan 1983: 31). For Mulvey and Kaplan, women are the objects of sight not its initiators. Novels reproduced this state of affairs. Passive, looked-at objects of male desire in the world, women were represented as passive, looked-at objects of male desire in the text. They were heroines. As spectators in the text, women readers replicated their experience. Constructed from the point of view of the narrative and its characters, they embodied the heroine's own looked-at-ness. Indeed, Jonathan Culler posits the woman reader for whom reading is like "being watched," or being "seen as a 'girl' " (Culler 1982: 44). Constrained by the vision of the text, they read as heroines.

To read as a woman, most eighteenth-century critics found, was to read as a heroine. Young ladies, noted Condillac, "eagerly embrace" the novel's fictions. Every girl imagined "she is Angelica" – or any "heroine" – and that every man is her "Medorus" (Condillac 1971: 85). Every "female" at 18, noted Edward Mangin, "sees her picture" in the "charming and sorrowful heroine" of a novel (Margin 1805: 14). As she reads, this is what Miss Palmer sees. She herself is the charming, sorrowful heroine. For though she separates herself from Richardson's text, she cannot divorce herself from his story. While her eyes leave the page, they do not turn from the book. Her attention never wavers. Rather it subtly shifts – how subtly is a function of how closely we must look to detect its divergence. In the minute distance of this displacement we read the prepotency of Richardson's vision. Miss Palmer re-views the text but in the direction – indeed, under the direction – of the author. Reynolds's *Theophila Palmer* represents one paradigm of readerly production. Here, the reader invests the story yet is contained by the text. With paradigmatic force, Reynolds's *Theophila Palmer* represents the problematics of reading and of women readers. It encodes oppositions of consuming and producing, of readerly and authorial control, of seeing and being seen, of reading and ultimately of being read.

For the eighteenth century, Pierre-Antoine Baudouin's *Le Midi* (Plate 3.2) represented the dangerous illusion latent in all novel-reading.[6] This "discourse of desire" (Nochlin 1988: 8) proffered sexual fantasy. Baudouin represents this corollary discourse – he depicts a woman with book who unambiguously masturbates. Novels, warned Vicessimus Knox, "pollute the heart in the recesses of the closet . . . and teach all the malignity of vice in solitude" (Knox 1789: I, 70). Indeed, novels teach "the" solitary vice – masturbation. Yet the emphasis in the "solitary vice," argues Thomas Laqueur, should be less on "vice" than on "solitary." Understood as the "channeling of healthy desire back into itself," masturbation is one part of the larger eighteenth-century debate about the "possibility of human community." Here, concludes Laqueur, "Sociability, not repression, is at stake" (Laqueur 1990: 229).

At opposite extremes, Reynolds's *Theophila Palmer* and Baudouin's *Le Midi* share the same paradigm of readerly production. Each reader turns from the page but cannot separate herself from the story. Like Miss Palmer, Baudouin's reader is constructed by the terms of her spectatorship. "Seen" by the text, she becomes an object of narrative. Though she drops the book, she is part of its story. Reading – and being read – as heroine, she enacts her role as the object of desire. To a critic like Knox, she reads no different than Miss Palmer – only farther.

At multiple levels, *Le Midi* embodies Mulvey's model of the male gaze. Literally embodied in the garden bust, the power of the gaze occupies center stage. It is at once the deity of the garden and the sign of male spectatorship. Confirming its primacy, the halo of the trellis behind it confers an aura of sanctity. Looking out of the scene, the bust mirrors the male spectator looking into it. It doubles the power of his gaze. At the same time, the reader's book constructs yet another spectatorial field. Indeed, it inscribes its reader in the text. The woman reads but, more importantly, is read; and as she looks out of the picture, she is confirmed in her role by the gaze of the audience. Whether in the eyes of the bust, the spectatorship of the text, or the eyes of the viewer,

Baudouin's reader confronts the forms of her own representation. Ultimately, the garden scene recapitulates the viewing context of the print. Closed to all but the statue's view, Baudouin's garden enacts the equally private spectatorship of the print's owner. Its enclosure replicates the privacy of individual viewing experience.

Together, Reynolds's *Theophila Palmer* and Baudouin's *Le Midi* construct one paradigm of reading. Here, readers actively produce the text but are themselves inscribed within its story. Spectators within the narrative, they are constructed by its vision. Gripped by the story, their bodies are shaped by the force of its events. They read for themselves, but paradoxically they reproduce the author's text.

Joshua Reynolds's *Emilia, duchess of Leinster* (Plate 3.3) constructs a different paradigm. The duchess separates herself from her reading. Her mind and body are her own. Neither embracing the volume like Reynolds's Miss Palmer nor enacting the story like Baudouin's reader, the duchess disengages herself from the book. She holds it at a distance which is the sign of her independence. Reynolds's subject is both the duchess and the nature of reading. Books on the table and in her hand suggest the sitter's more than common literary interests. Though never published, the duchess was indeed an inveterate writer. The National Library of Ireland holds 1,770 of her letters, and for Betty Rizzo their careful preservation bespeaks the duchess's essential writerly "awareness" (Todd 1987: 145). From the scholarly folio on the table to the popular duodecimo in the hand, books suggest both the duchess's literary character and the range of her interests.

More importantly, they signal her rational mind. For his figure of the duchess, Reynolds turns to Cesare Ripa's *Iconologia*. First published in 1593, Ripa's allegorical handbook went through innumerable editions. Its influence on art until well into the eighteenth century, notes Stephen Orgel, was "incalculable" (Ripa 1976: preface). English editions appeared as late as 1777–9 and 1785. Once translated, Ronald Paulson observes, Ripa provided eighteenth-century English art with an "accepted" iconographic "lexicon" (Paulson 1975: 14).[7]

Reynolds's model for the duchess is Cesare Ripa's allegorical figure of Meditation. Her image appears in an English edition of 1709 (Plate 3.4). Meditation is

> A Woman of mature Age, and a grave, modest Aspect; sitting upon a Heap of books, in a thoughtful Posture, and a Book clos'd upon her left Knee, her Hand supporting her Head, meditating some Passage of it. . . . Her holding up her Head with her Hand, denotes the *Gravity* of her *thoughts*. . . . The Book shut, her *reflecting* upon the *Knowledge* of Things.
>
> (Ripa 1709: 51)

Like Ripa's Meditation, Reynolds's duchess sits head on hand, and on her knee is a book. Like Meditation, she represents "gravity" and "reflection." Reynolds endows the duchess with sustained and serious thought – an ability most eighteenth-century critics denied to women. Hannah More's opinion was typical. Though women possess imagination, she wrote, "they seem not to possess in an equal measure the faculty of . . . deep and patient thinking" (More 1799: II, 27). Using Ripa's "lexicon," Reynolds confers upon the musing duchess the gravity of Meditation herself.

But Reynolds refigures Ripa's trope (Plate 3.4). In Ripa, Meditation looks inward; her gaze is contained. She is passive and "reflective" – enframed both by the text she reads and by the image that contains her. In Reynolds, the duchess breaks this confinement. The text cannot contain her reading, nor can the frame contain her gaze. The duchess opposes the closure of control. She projects herself beyond the boundaries of textual inscription and the limits of the painting's frame. The duchess shuts her book and replaces its representations with her own. Writer that she is, she authors a new text. Behind the duchess we see a landscape in a window. She looks away. Metonymically – the gaze of the sitter/our view of the landscape – the window suggests an object of sight. Yet we cannot know what the duchess "sees." Like the view through the window, it must remain partial, fragmented, inchoate. Within the public space of Reynolds's portrait, it is the sign of a private self-constructed sphere. Looking beyond the book, the duchess constructs a critical space from which to re-view both its text and the structures it imposes.

Reynolds's painting doubles the spectatorial field. It represents the containment both of text and canvas. Unlike Baudouin's reader, the duchess breaks their closure. Within the painting, she turns from the audience. While she cannot abolish the specular power that constructs her, she can deflect it. Withholding herself from its gaze, the duchess embodies an alternative spectatorial force. Her vision excavates a private space within the painting analogous to the personal power she exercises within the text. In a way that Reynolds's Miss Palmer and Baudouin's reader cannot, she sees for herself.

Occupying the text, Miss Palmer and Baudouin's reader generate an experience beyond the page. Yet at the same time, they are constructed by the stories they read. Eye-witnesses within the narrative, they become constituents of its spectatorial field. In contrast, the duchess of Leinster refutes the vision of the text and its power to construct her. Together, these three images enact a dialogue of representation and resistance. Within their contending visions, eighteenth-century women are read and newly seek to read themselves.

Notes

1 Indeed, Roland Barthes argues the difficulties of construing any system of images independently of language (Barthes 1968: 11).
2 John Mullan explores these ideas in a chapter devoted to sympathy and the production of society (Mullan 1988: 18–56).
   Numerous eighteenth-century writers confronted the problem: John and Anna Laetitia Aikin, "An enquiry into those kinds of distress which excite agreeable sensations," (1773) (Williams 1970: 288–9); Henry Mackenzie, *The Lounger* XX (1785) (Bredvold 1962: 85); Thomas Monroe, *Olla Podrida* XIV (23 June 1787) (Williams 1970: 350); *Analytical Review* (1 July 1788) (Williams 1970: 355–6); Hannah More, *Strictures on the Modern System of Female Education* (More 1799: II, 123–6); Edward Mangin, *An Essay on Light Reading* (Mangin 1805: 101–2). Together, they outlined a model of the anti-social reader.
   Both Ioan Williams (ed.) *Novel and Romance 1700–1800* (Williams 1970) and John Tinnon Taylor, *Early Opposition to the English Novel* (Taylor 1943) provide substantial surveys of contemporary reaction to the novel. I rely heavily on their findings.
3 Critics consistently pointed out the novel's threat to love and marriage: Richard Berenger, *The World* 79 (Thursday, July 4, 1754) (Williams 1970: 214–15); William Woodfall, review of *De l'Homme, et de la femme, considérés physiquement dans l'état du mariage* [1772], *Monthly Review* XLVII (July 1773) (Williams 1970: 279); Vicessimus Knox, *Essays Moral and Literary* (Knox 1789: II, 19); Richard Cumberland, *The Observer* (Cumberland 1798: I, 271); Clara Reve, *The*

Progress of Romance (Reve 1785: II, 78); Maria Edgeworth, *Practical Education*, 2 vols., 1798, I: 332–3; II: 296–7 (Hill 1984: 60–1); Edward Mangin, *An Essay on Light Reading* (Mangin 1805: 13–14; 16–20).

4   Jonathan Culler provides a comprehensive survey of contemporary reading theory (Culler 1982: 31–83).

5   David Bartine considers mid-eighteenth-century rhetorical handbooks by John Mason, *An Essay on Elocution and Pronunciation* (1748) and Thomas Sheridan, *A Course of Lectures on Elocution* (1762). They, like Iser, question the "stability" of the text and suggest the "reader, not the author," determines meaning (Bartine 1989: 72, 83).

6   Baudouin's image exists in another version, a small attractive gouache in the Paris Musée des arts décoratifs. Here, the subject is aestheticized almost beyond recognition. As Philippe Huisman observes, "licentious details" disappear in its "perfect delineation" (Huisman 1969: 44). Roger Chartier, however, rightly insists on the pornographic character of the image (Chartier 1989: 147).

7   Ronald Paulson explores this provocative interplay of verbal and visual paradigms in his *Emblem and Expression* (Paulson 1975: 35–47). I am indebted to his model.

Bibliography

Addison, J. and Steele, R. (1965) *The Spectator*, ed. D. F. Bond, Oxford: Clarendon Press.

Barthes, R. (1968) *Elements of Semiology*, New York: Hill & Wang.

Bartine, D. (1989) *Early English Reading Theory: Origins of Current Debates*, Columbia, SC: University of South Carolina Press.

Beattie, J. (1783) *On Fable and Romance* in *Dissertations Moral and Critical*, London: W. Strahan.

Blair, H. (1783) "On fictitious history," in *Lectures on Rhetoric and Poetry*, London: W. Strahan.

Bredvold, L. I. (1962) *The Natural History of Sensibility*, Detroit, MI: Wayne State University Press.

Brophy, E. B. (1991) *Women's Lives and the Eighteenth-Century English Novel*, Tampa, FL: University of South Florida Press.

Burke, E. (1978) *A Philosophical Enquiry into the Origin of our Ideas of the Sublime and Beautiful*, ed. James T. Boulton, London: Routledge & Kegan Paul.

Chartier, R. (1989) "The practical impact of writing," in *A History of Private Life*, Vol. III, ed. R. Chartier *et al.*, Cambridge, MA: Harvard University Press, pp. 111–59.

Condillac, E. B. de (1971 [1761]) *An Essay on the Origin of Human Knowledge*, trans. Thomas Nugent, London: Nourse; reprinted Gainesville, FL: Scholars' Facsimiles & Reprints.

Culler, J. (1982) *On Deconstruction*, Ithaca, NY: Cornell University Press.

Cumberland, R. (1798) *The Observer*, 5th edn., London: Dilly.

Fielding, S. (1985) *Remarks on Clarissa*, intro. Peter Sabor, Los Angeles, CA: Clark Library, University of California Press, 1985.

Fish, S. (1980) *Is There a Text in this Class?* Cambridge, MA: Harvard University Press.

Gisbourne, T. (1799) *An Inquiry into the Duties of the Female Sex*, London: Cadell & Davies.

Greenblatt, S. (1980) *Renaissance Self-Fashioning*, Chicago: University of Chicago Press.

Gregory, J. (1772) *A Comparative View of the State and Faculties of Man, with Those of the Animal World*, 5th edn., London: J. Dodsley.

Heilbrun, C. G. (1990) "What was Penelope unweaving?" in *Hamlet's Mother and Other Women*, New York: Columbia University Press, pp. 103–11.

Hill, B. (1984) *Eighteenth-Century Women: An Anthology*, London: Allen & Unwin.

Home, H., Lord Kames (1769) *Elements of Criticism*, 4th edn., London: S. Kincaid & J. Bell; Edinburgh: A Millar and T. Caddell.

Huisman, P. (1969) *French Watercolors of the Eighteenth Century*, New York: Viking.

Hume, D. (1953) *An Enquiry Concerning the Principles of Morals*, La Salle, IL: Open Court.

Iser, W. (1978) *The Act of Reading: A Theory of Reader Response*, Baltimore, MD: Johns Hopkins University Press.

Kaplan, E. A. (1983) *Women and Film: Both Sides of the Mirror*, London: Methuen.

Knox, V. (1789 [1778]) *Essays Moral and Literary*, 5th edn., 2 vols., London: Charles Dilley.

Laclos, C. de (1961) *Les Liaisons dangereuses*, ed. Y. Le Hir, Paris: Garnier Frères.

Laqueur, T. (1990) *Making Sex*, Cambridge, MA: Harvard University Press.

McKendrick, N., Brewer, J., and Plumb, J. H. (1982) *The Birth of a Consumer Society: The Commercialization of Eighteenth-Century England*, London: Europa Publications.

Mangin, E. (1805) *An Essay on Light Reading*, London: Carpenter.

Merleau–Ponty, M. (1968) *The Visible and the Invisible*, trans. Alphonso Lingis, Evanston, IL: Northwestern University Press.

Montagu, M. W. (1965) *The Complete Letters of Lady Mary Wortley Montagu*, ed. R. Halsband, 3 vols., Oxford: Clarendon Press.

More, H. (1799) *Strictures on the Modern System of Female Education*, 2 vols., London: Cadell & Davies.

Mullan, J. (1988) *Sentiment and Sociability. The Language of Feeling in the Eighteenth-Century*, Oxford: Clarendon Press.

Mulvey, L. (1975) "Visual pleasure and narrative cinema," *Screen* 16: 6–18.

Murray, H. (1805) *The Morality of Fiction: Or, An Inquiry into the Tendency of Fictitious Narratives*, Edinburgh: Mundell & Son; reprinted (1972) Folcroft, PA: Folcroft Library Editions.

Nochlin, L. (1988) *"Women, Art, and Power" and Other Essays*, New York: Harper & Row.

Paulson, R. (1975) *Emblem and Expression*, Cambridge, MA: Harvard University Press.

Priestley, J. (1965) *A Course of Lectures on Oratory and Criticism*, eds V. Bevilacqua and R. Murphy, Carbondale, IL: Southern Illinois University Press.

Reve, C. (1785) *The Progress of Romance, through Times, Countries, and Manners*, Colchester, Essex; reprinted (1930) New York: Facsimile Text Society.

Richardson, J. (1725) *Essay on the Theory of Painting*, 2nd edn., London: Bettesworth.

Richardson, S. (1964) *Selected Letters of Samuel Richardson*, ed. John Carroll, Oxford: Clarendon Press.

—— (1970) *The Novels of Samuel Richardson*, 19 vols., New York: AMS Press.

Ripa, C. (1709) *Iconologia: or, Moral Emblems by Caesare Ripa*, ed. Pierce Tempest, London: Motte.

—— (1976) *Iconologia*, pref. Stephen Orgel, New York: Garland.

Slattery, W. C. (ed.) (1969) *The Richardson-Stinstra "Correspondence" and Stinstra's "Prefaces" to Clarissa*, Carbondale, IL: Southern Illinois University Press.

Smith, A. (1774) *The Theory of Moral Sentiments*, 4th edn., London: Strahan.

Taylor, J. T. (1943) *Early Opposition to the English Novel. Popular Reaction from 1760 to 1830*, Morningside Heights, New York: King's Crown Press.

Todd, J. (ed.) (1987) *A Dictionary of British and American Women Writers 1660–1800*, Totowa, NJ: Rowman & Littlefield.

Warner, W. B. (1979) *Reading "Clarissa." The Struggles of Interpretation*, New Haven, CT: Yale University Press.

Williams, I. (ed.) (1970) *Novel and Romance 1700–1800. A Documentary Record*, London: Routledge & Kegan Paul.

Williams, R. (1983) *Writing in History*, London: Verso.

4
Colonizing readers
Review criticism and the formation of a reading public

Frank Donoghue

The word "critic" receives a significantly peculiar treatment in Samuel Johnson's *Dictionary* (1755). His primary definition of the word is "a man skilled in the art of judging of literature; a man able to distinguish the faults and beauties of writing," but his illustrations are the following three quotations:

> This settles truer ideas in men's minds of several things, whereof we read the names in ancient authors, than all the large and laborious arguments of *criticks*. (Locke)

> *Criticks* I saw, that other names deface,
> And fix their own with labour in their place. (Pope)

> Where an author has many beauties consistent with virtue, piety, and truth, let not little *criticks* exalt themselves, and shower down their ill-nature. (Watts)
>
> (Johnson 1967)

All three examples are pejorative in exactly the same way: they imply that the real definition of "critic" is "a man who *pretends* to be skilled in the art of judging of literature," and who does so in order to usurp a cultural authority that rightly belongs to authors. The discrepancy between Johnson's examples and the neutral definition to which they supposedly attest reveals a rupture, a locus of conflict in the field of mid-eighteenth-century literature. It posits a huge gap between the ideal and the actual, and implies that no "true" critics exist in 1755, for the definition of the word remains, in Johnson's mind, fundamentally unresolved.

Another slightly earlier definition points to the same problem in a very different way. In the introductory chapter to Book 8 of *The History of Tom Jones* (1749), Henry Fielding defines the word "critic" as follows: "By this word here, and in most other parts of our work, we mean every reader in the world" (Fielding 1975: 396). Fielding's definition is willfully idiosyncratic: by making "every reader in the world" a critic, Fielding radically democratizes the term, erasing the conventional discrimination between critic and common reader, denying the special skill and training by which his audience would recognize a critic as a privileged judge of letters. Like Johnson, Fielding wishes, without explicitly announcing his desire, to disempower those of his contemporaries who claim to possess special qualifications that define them as critics. Johnson implies that critics are charlatans; Fielding, that critics are no different from any other readers. Both authors are clearly concerned, though, that critics present a danger to the literary system because they threaten to encroach upon a conceptual space big enough for authors and readers alone.

The near-uniform hostility of authors towards critics that prevailed at mid-century dissipated dramatically over the course of the next two or three generations, however, giving way by the early nineteenth century to a set of relations in which critics were at least grudgingly accepted as legitimate intermediaries between authors and readers. It is my contention that this transformation is intimately connected with the founding of the *Monthly Review* (in 1749) and the *Critical Review* (in 1756). These journals were devoted exclusively to reviewing all contemporary publications, and they conceived of the practice and aims of reviewing in terms very different from their predecessors. The nearly immediate and tremendous success of the *Monthly*, the *Critical*, and their descendants is one of the great unexplained phenomena of eighteenth-century letters. By the end of the 1760s, both journals had steady circulations of between two and three thousand (despite the failure of every previous attempt along these lines in England) (Basker 1988: 172–3). By 1767, the *Monthly* and the *Critical* were significant enough to merit discussion in the famous interview between Johnson and George III, even though Johnson had just twelve years earlier disparaged critics in general in the *Dictionary* (Boswell 1980: 383). In 1778, Frances Burney dedicated her first novel, *Evelina*, to the editors of these two Reviews. And by 1812, Lord Byron, anxiously awaiting news of the reception of the first two cantos of *Childe Harold's Pilgrimage*, referred to the editors of the influential *Edinburgh* and *Quarterly Reviews* as "monarch-makers in poetry and prose" (Marchand 1974: III, 209).

The rise of the Review to the position of cultural authority that Byron imputed to the *Edinburgh* and the *Quarterly* was a process at once rhetorical and material. The early reviewers' attempts, in the pages of their journals, to pass judgment on current publications were met with scores of hostile pamphlets from outraged authors. But circumscribing this textual battlefield were the consuming habits of thousands of readers whose desires ultimately drove the publishing industry. For, through their critical pronouncements, the reviewers sought to create hierarchies of taste and mold habits of reading that they hoped would influence the book purchases of individuals and circulating libraries. This chapter returns to the early years of the *Monthly* and the *Critical* to examine some of the factors that inform this complex process, the foundations and consequences of the Reviews' struggle to acquire cultural authority during the second half of the eighteenth century.

The chief obstacle to specifying exactly the role played by the Reviews in the literary culture of their day is that, except for the journals themselves and authors' attacks on them, we have little concrete information about what the Reviews aimed to do, or how well they succeeded. The work done for the *Monthly* and the *Critical* was anonymous, and the reviewers never spoke out or entered the limelight, except in rare celebrated cases, such as the conviction of Tobias Smollett, editor of the *Critical*, for libeling

Admiral Knowles (Knapp 1963: 230–2). The *Monthly* commenced with only a brief advertisement, and remained reticent about its aims throughout the rest of the century. The *Critical* had more definite, explicitly stated plans, but, as I will argue later, drastically (and silently) modified them, leaving the modern-day reader with only a vague sense of how that Review continued to perceive itself. Aside from their own perspectives, we see the *Critical* and the *Monthly* almost exclusively through the eyes of authors whose books were reviewed unfavorably, and who then retaliated in print. Thus we must work at all times with the terms of idiosyncratic, polemical relationships between individual authors and "the reviewer," made almost monolithic by his anonymity and institutional bearing.

The issue of anonymous reviews (the practice of both the *Monthly* and the *Critical*) is particularly intriguing because it is the principal means by which these journals constructed themselves as institutions. London's literary society was presumably so close-knit that the identities of reviewers, particularly, could not remain concealed. Both Reviews maintained an informal staff of experts, many of them prominent authors themselves, in various important fields – literature, science, music, history. The list of independent contributors to either the *Monthly*, the *Critical*, or both, includes Samuel Johnson, David Hume, Oliver Goldsmith, the music historian Charles Burney, and the famous surgeon John Hunter. Moreover, the *Critical* was widely known to have distributed many of its assignments among three of its editors, Smollett, John Armstrong, and Thomas Franklin, all of whom were important men of letters (Basker 1988: 45). Reviewers and authors were, in other words, drawn from the same pool. But even if the notion of an anonymous review was in the main a fiction, it was one that authors under review nevertheless respected with remarkable regularity. In correspondence, authors tend to refer to the *Monthly* and the *Critical as* institutions. The act of consulting the Reviews is a common episode in mid- and later eighteenth-century literary biography, memoirs, and letters, and the authors of the notices (if they were known) are rarely mentioned. The following examples are representative:

> This morning the *Critical Review* on our *Letters between the Hon. Erskine and James Boswell* came out, and in great form did we read it. They did not use us with candour, but they were less abusive than we imagined they might be. (James Boswell, 1763)
>
> (Pottle 1950: 271)

> Pray send to Sheffield for the last *Monthly Review*; there is a deal of stuff about us and Mr. Colman. (Letter from Thomas Gray to William Mason, 1760)
>
> (Gosse 1884: IV, 57)

> My first publication, "Village Memoirs," (1761) was praised by the *Critical* and *Monthly* Reviewers, who were unwilling, perhaps, to discourage a young beginner.
>
> (Craddock 1828: 43)

Laurence Sterne, whose relationship with both Reviews was more involved and tempestuous than that of any of his contemporaries, never named his reviewers. Nor did Oliver Goldsmith, who directly engaged critics of his plays during the 1760s and early

1770s. Goldsmith had written for both the *Monthly* and the *Critical*, and certainly would have been familiar with the workings of these journals and their contributors. There were, of course, celebrated attacks that were more specific, such as Joseph Shebbeare's *The Occasional Critic*, and Charles Churchill's *Apology*, both directed at the *Critical*. But even in these cases, the author's dissatisfaction with a particular review article, or with the journal's policies, or with a member of its staff (Shebbeare had a long-standing rivalry with Smollett) was always blended with expressions of resentment towards the office of critic *in general*. Thus, authors under review were in a sense complicit in preserving the artificial separation between themselves and that other collection of writers who staffed the Reviews.

Given these obstacles and complications, it seems to me that we can recognize the central place of review criticism at the source of institutional cultural authority only if we contextualize the *Monthly* and *Critical* in ways that illuminate review criticism's attempts to define authorship and reading protocols for the mid-eighteenth century. This exploration entails situating the *Monthly* and the *Critical* in the context of already existing critical conventions and practices in English periodicals. We must also assess the rhetoric of professionalism by which the reviewers sought to legitimate their journals. Finally, we need to speculate on what Tony Bennett has called the "reading formations" that inform each Review's enterprise.[1] The founders of the *Monthly* and the *Critical*, had decidedly contrasting political biases, and these are, I will argue, reflected to some extent in their differing conceptions of reading as a social practice. All of these complex forces are in play in every issue of the *Monthly* and the *Critical*, and they are resolved in a wide variety of ways. The second half of my chapter will examine one such resolution in prefaces to two early volumes of the *Critical*, one which appeared in 1761 (vol. 11), after the journal had been in existence for five years, the other in 1765 (vol. 19).[2] These prefaces, which function as manifestos of their early work, illustrate the *Critical*'s first attempts to work out its relationship with authors and with the English reading public.

The mid-century reviewing mode seems to have derived chiefly from two sources: the abstract journals that began to appear in the middle of the seventeenth century (the most highly respected of which was Denis de Sallo's *Journal des Savants*), and the popular essays of Addison and Steele, published during the years 1709–14. But this ancestry does not account for the success of the *Monthly* and the *Critical*. Nor, indeed, does the history of book-reviewing in England during the first half of the century. The Reviews published between 1700 and 1749 were all short-lived, a fact usually taken as a sign of a weak and precarious demand for books. The bookseller Michael de La Roche started three abstract journals, none of which ran for more than four years: *Memoirs of Literature* (1710–14); *New Memoirs of Literature* (1725–7); and *The Literary Journal*, a quarterly publication that ran for only a few issues in 1730–1. Perhaps the most successful of these early Reviews, though it chiefly treated classic authors, was *The Present State of the Republic of Letters*, edited by Andrew Reid, which ran from 1728 to 1736 (Graham 1930: 200).

Just before mid-century, however, a flurry of changes in the conventions of reviewing and in the planning of Review journals occurred, marking, I believe, a vital turning-point in the English literary trade's perception of its public. A chronology of this activity suggests a remarkable similarity among the projects being undertaken.

December 1748: several members of a literary club gathered around Edward Cave, editor of the *Gentleman's Magazine*, began planning a journal that would "give an impartial account of *every* work published, in a 12d. monthly pamphlet" to be called the *Monthly Review* (Carlson 1938: 115). The plans never materialized.

February 1749: a group of professional writers under the direction of the bookseller Ralph Griffiths (and completely unconnected with Cave) produced the first issue of their journal, also titled the *Monthly Review*, the first English periodical devoted exclusively to reviewing.

March 1751: the *Gentleman's Magazine*, which had, since its inception in 1731, simply listed in each issue books published during the previous month, began to include descriptive commentary in that list, a move that was most likely a compromise on Cave's original plan. Since the *Gentleman's* had the largest circulation of any English magazine (roughly 3,000 copies a month were sold in 1746), this change reached a great many readers (Basker 1988: 170).

December 1755: within one week of each other, advertisements appeared for two more journals devoted solely to reviewing – the *Critical Review*, founded by Tobias Smollett, and the *Literary Magazine*, founded by Samuel Johnson. Smollett's Review went on to become the foremost competitor of the *Monthly*, while Johnson's, compiled entirely by himself, failed in 1758.

January 1762: the *London Magazine*, chief competitor of the *Gentleman's*, began offering brief reviews in its own monthly register of newly published books. It too had previously only listed them.

It is not an exaggeration to say that this sweeping reconception of the practice of reviewing affected virtually everyone in the English reading public – these were the most popular magazines of the time, printed in very large numbers with each copy reaching several readers. Although a few scholars have recognized the suddenness and scope of this transformation, no one has adequately explained its significance. Rather, critics from A. S. Collins in *Authorship in the Days of Doctor Johnson* (1927) to Alvin Kernan in *Printing Technology, Letters, and Samuel Johnson* (1987), have constructed a standard story that contextualizes the change by locating it in a larger process, the democratization of reading. That story, in short, is that Review journals and magazines which began reviewing books were answering a fast-developing need in the literary marketplace. By mid-century even the most literate readers could no longer keep up with the profusion of printed matter available to them. They were drowning in a newly born but rapidly growing information culture. More inexperienced readers, by the same token, were thrown into a situation in which they could not possibly make intelligent choices – there was simply too much from which to choose. A passage from Samuel Johnson's private notebooks epitomizes this need. Boswell relates that:

> In one of his little memorandum-books I find the following hints for his intended Review or Literary Journal: "*The Annals of Literature, foreign as well as domestick*. Imitate LeClerk – Bayle – Barbeyrac. Infelicity of Journals in England. Works of the Learned. We cannot take in all."
>
> (Boswell 1980: 203)

The assumptions underlying this standard story need to be brought to light and evaluated, since they have spawned several examples of a naively progressive literary history of eighteenth-century England. It presents the expansion of the reading public in the eighteenth century as an inevitable, "natural" process, uninformed by ideological concerns and undaunted by conservative opposition. As Michael Warner has argued, the fundamental premiss of this progressive account – that print technology "has an ontological status prior to culture" – is impossible, and must be set aside before we can examine the relationship of print to enlightenment culture (Warner 1990: 7).

I wish to argue that the emergence of review criticism is part of a much more complex narrative of cultural change, one that galvanized various definitions, then in circulation, of reading and readers alike. The *Monthly* and its rival, the *Critical*, are informed by competing ideologies of reading whose histories reach back to the earliest days of mass-produced printed matter. To state the conflict simply, reading in the early modern period was chiefly perceived either as a politically neutral means of acquiring information, or, quite to the contrary, as a way of consolidating and strengthening discriminations of social class. The *Monthly* and the *Critical*, initially at least, occupied opposing sides of this schism.

Reading conceived as an exploring process emerges out of what N. H. Keeble has labeled "the literary culture of nonconformity." As Keeble points out, the influence of the Dissenting or Nonconformist tradition on English literary culture has long been underestimated. Throughout the seventeenth century, Dissenting authors such as John Bunyan and Richard Baxter suited their evangelism perfectly to a newly expanding print medium. They endorsed reading for everyone as a means to conversion, and they published their work in unprecedented volume: there were, all told, twenty-two seventeenth-century editions of *Pilgrim's Progress*, a total of some 30,000 copies; and 20,000 copies of Baxter's *Call to the Unconverted* were printed in the year it was published, 1658. It too had reached a twenty-third edition by 1685, the later editions accounting for an additional 25,000 copies (Keeble 1987: 128). These authors minimized the value of formal doctrine, the classical tradition, and traditional programs of study, and espoused instead the pursuit of a kind of pure learning. As Bunyan claimed: "I have not writ out of a venture, nor borrowed my Doctrine from Libraries. I depend upon the sayings of no man: I found it in the Scriptures of Truth, among the true sayings of God" (Keeble 1987: 157). Baxter sums up this process in one of his *Dying Thoughts*: "We must go on to learn as long as we live" (Keeble 1987: 161).

This Nonconformist ideology of reading persisted into the eighteenth century, where it informs much Whig political writing. It anticipates or demands a specific kind of review criticism, the chief aim of which is to supply a comprehensive account of, and abundant information about, new books in print. The *Monthly Review* was committed to this aim: its founder and editor, Ralph Griffiths, was a Dissenter himself, who saw his journal primarily as something that would "be serviceable to such as would choose to have some idea of a book before they lay out their money or time on it" (*Monthly* 1 (1749): i), a goal he planned to reach by providing a "compendious account" of new publications. This premiss was later largely abandoned, I will argue, as competitive pressure from the *Critical Review* (beginning in 1756) pushed the *Monthly* into more and more opinionated articles, but it was nevertheless initially underwritten by specific democratic assumptions about the social function of reading.

The conception of reading as a means of gaining information that should ideally be available to all was strenuously opposed, however, by those who saw reading as an activity that clarifies social hierarchy. In the theories of social entropy that circulated throughout the century (but reached a fever pitch in the 1750s) reading could be seen as an agency of refinement, a process that would correct and sustain the cultural disposition of a gentleman "of candour and taste." This ideology of reading often found a place, as I will later show, in conservative attacks on luxury and the degeneration of English values, treatises that addressed the threat to traditional class divisions posed by "the moneyed men" (the phrase is from Bolingbroke's *Idea of a Patriot King* [1749]) and the increasing possibilities for upward social mobility. For conservatives such as John Brown, Henry Fielding (in his later years), and Tobias Smollett, reading was definitely not for everyone, but rather served an exclusive, civilizing purpose. The uncontrolled spread of reading was perceived as a threat that needed to be aggressively contained.[3]

Such conservatives demanded a review criticism of their own, one whose differences from the *Monthly*'s practices are immediately evident. The *Critical Review* served as the most prominent vehicle for this set of assumptions about the relationship between reading and social hierarchy. It was organized by a self-proclaimed "society of Gentlemen," and was originally envisioned by its founder, Smollett, as part of an extensive learned society (as was Johnson's *Literary Magazine*). Smollett's political leanings were conservative – while editor of the *Critical* he contracted to write a weekly sheet, *The Briton*, in defense of the Bute ministry. He seemed to perceive the society of gentlemen as a kind of institutional community of the cultural elite, and aimed in his journal to police the boundaries between classes. For example, the *Critical*, as John Sekora observes, "criticized the charity schools . . . for placing too much emphasis on reading and writing and not enough on 'labour and industry' " (Sekora 1977: 166). Most importantly, the Review committed itself to what it envisioned as the systematic exercise of critical judgment. Its writers promised, in an early preface, "to exert their best endeavours for the regulation of taste and the honour of criticism" (*Critical* 9 (1760): preface). The notion that there is an intrinsic, aristocratic merit to criticism ("honour") and that their task involved correcting or civilizing the tastes of the reading public, combine to epitomize the *Critical*'s sense of its purpose and to differentiate it from the *Monthly*'s more populist aims.

This delineation of the respective reading formations of the *Monthly* and the *Critical* requires a couple of important qualifications. First, because of the sheer number of voices contributing to both Reviews, it is difficult to make a compelling case for the firmness of the ideological differences I have described. Nor do I mean to claim a cause-and-effect relationship between a Dissenting ideology and the *Monthly*, or a conservative ideology and the *Critical*. These political predispositions obviously predate the Reviews, as does the perceived need for review criticism and the "genre" of the review article. Secondly, and more importantly, the *Monthly*'s conception of reviewing after its rival was founded becomes less clear. After 1756, that is, more opinion finds its way into *Monthly* articles, and *Monthly* reviewers begin speaking directly (and critically) to authors and readers. In its first years of operation, the editors of the *Monthly* were extremely cautious about imposing their judgments on their readers, and corrected against their possible influence by characterizing the extracts that they reproduced as a means of allowing the readers to make up their own minds. The typical formulation of this attempt to maintain a neutral balance was to say, for example: "That our readers may not think we have passed too severe and unjust a censure upon this work, we shall present them with a few extracts . . ." (*Monthly* 5 (1751): 65), or "but that we may not be said to have anticipated the opinions of our readers, we shall lay before them . . . some extracts, whereby they may be enabled to form a judgment" of their own (*Monthly* 10 (1754): 31). This defensiveness, this concern that their reviews might be presumptuous, followed from the *Monthly*'s original aim as stated in several early articles, and epitomized in the journal's comments on Richardson's *Sir Charles Grandison*. Stating that "the intention of this Review is *information* rather than *decision*" (original emphasis), the reviewer declines to intervene in the popular discussion of the novel (*Monthly* 10 (1754): 70–1).

Not long after the founding of the *Critical*, however, the *Monthly*'s general tone changed distinctly. Slipping into many of their reviews are the new assumptions that bad writing is an aspect of more widespread social ills, and that it is the Review's duty to resist this decline by, in effect, telling its audience what it should and should not read. There are, for example, disdainful references to "the Genius of Romance . . . drooping among us" (*Monthly* 24 (1761): 415), "a nation absorbed in luxury" (*Monthly* 24 (1761): 260), and, perhaps most tellingly, "these novel-scrawling times, when footmen and servant-maids are the authors, as well as, occasionally, the heroes and heroines of their own most elegant memoirs" (*Monthly* 21 (1758): 441). This attitude, steeped in distinctions based on social class, which the *Critical* had adopted from its outset, derides a large part of either Review's readers, a move that in pre-*Critical* days the *Monthly* was so reluctant to make.

More significantly, *Monthly* articles after 1756 begin to discriminate among reading practices, creating hierarchies among its audience by assessing the habits and tastes of different kinds of readers. A review of a posthumously published collection of poems by Thomas Parnell (which the reviewer believes are spurious) draws an opposition between "the hasty Reader," who will accept the poems as authentic, and "those who are curious and critical," and hence will not be fooled (*Monthly* 19 (1758): 380). A broader and more elaborate distinction occurs in a notice about George Colman's *The Jealous Wife*, in which the writer tries to justify a negative review of the very popular play:

> When Pliny was dissatisfied with the Judgment of his Critical Friends, to whom he submitted his compositions, he used to say, *Ad Populum provoco*. In all cases, whatever, the last resort is undoubtedly to the people, from whose decree no appeal can be made to any superior tribunal. Nevertheless, there are instances in which we may venture to appeal from the people to themselves.
>
> (*Monthly* 24 (1761): 181–2)

The reviewer resorts to casuistry in an effort to overcome anxieties that follow from the *Monthly*'s original conception of itself. He delivers an unmistakably anti-populist review of the play, but does not want to admit it. The inconceivable notion of appealing "from the people to themselves" is hardly convincing, but is representative of the ambivalence often found in *Monthly* articles as that journal's rhetoric became absorbed into that of the *Critical*. Though important ideological distinctions remained – the *Monthly*, for example, continued to express more liberal views on religion and especially politics – the two journals increasingly managed the difficult triangular relationship between themselves, authors, and readers in the same way. Thus, though the prefaces that I will examine next are from the *Critical*, it is possible to draw conclusions from them that apply equally to both journals. Indeed, they come to characterize their place in literary culture in the same terms largely as a result of their rivalry.

If we ask why this congruity developed, I believe that we must look to the crude polemics that mark the early rivalry between the *Monthly* and the *Critical* for an answer. After the *Critical*, in 1756, began challenging the *Monthly*'s virtual monopoly on review criticism, Ralph Griffiths and Tobias Smollett each tried to discredit the other's journal. Their colorful, if ridiculous, rhetoric forms the basis of later misconceptions about the level of seriousness and sophistication in eighteenth-century popular criticism. One exchange in particular has come to stand as an emblem of their primitive conflicts. It was first cited in John Forster's *Life and Adventures of Oliver Goldsmith* in 1848, and quickly became a commonplace in nineteenth- and even twentieth-century arguments that the early reviewers were hacks. Griffiths asserts:

> The Monthly Review is not written by physicians without practice, authors without learning, men without decency, gentlemen without manners, and critics without judgment.

And Smollett responds:

> The Critical Review is not written by a parcel of obscure hirelings, under the restraint of a bookseller and his wife, who presumes to revise, alter, and amend the articles occasionally. The principal writers in the Critical Review are unconnected with booksellers, unawed by old women, and independent of each other.
>
> (Forster 1848: II, 79–80)

Bombastic exchanges such as this, however, paradoxically generated the essential criteria for professional standards as both editors understood them. The content of this attack and counter-attack, considered apart from its inflated rhetoric, allows us to deduce a great deal of information about the emergent profession of reviewing.

The exchange between Griffiths and Smollett identifies either straightforwardly, by negation, or by implication the characteristics that define their enterprise. Each editor begins by observing that the other is not a reviewer by profession, but has rather turned to reviewing after mismanaging his original line of work. Griffiths tells us that Smollett is, after all, a physician, who apparently edits the *Critical* because he is unable to maintain a medical practice. But if Smollett is an amateur reviewer, Griffiths is worse. Smollett identifies him as a bookseller, an accusation that carries two different negative associations. First, Smollett is implying that Griffiths runs the *Monthly* as though it were a shop: treating his writers not like gentlemen, but like tradesmen, and presuming to alter their work as he would alter the work of a printer. (Indeed, Smollett suggests, they may deserve nothing better, since they are in fact "hirelings.") Moreover, Griffiths runs a poor shop, one in which his wife is constantly allowed to interfere. Worse still, Griffiths's real profession as a bookseller will inevitably force him into conflicts of interest that ought to disqualify him as a literary arbiter. He cannot judge impartially books from which he hopes to profit.

But the force of the emerging category of professional remains difficult to assess in this exchange. The term is never mentioned, even though the notion of being a reviewer by profession is precisely what is being debated. In addition, the competitors draw a sharp division between professional and mercenary considerations – Smollett, in fact, makes that issue the centerpiece of his attack on Griffiths. The result is extremely complex: we find an exaggerated version of the professional rhetoric of our own day, more zealous in severing connections between social function and material reward, more sanctimonious in mystifying both by means of a vocabulary of refinement ("decency," "manners").[4] But this rhetoric is coupled with a basic uncertainty about the definition and social value of professionals.

One thing at least becomes clear if we look at this exchange and others like it during the years 1756–60: the foundation of the *Monthly* in 1749 did not in and of itself signal the beginning of professional popular criticism, for the *Monthly* first promised to "venture no farther into criticism than necessity required" (*Monthly* 1 (1749): 72). Rather, the anxious rivalry between the two that began seven years later initiated a struggle that was conducted through the use of a rhetoric of professionalism even as both parties sought to define the profession of reviewing. The rapid development of the Reviews to a position of prominence on the literary scene resulted chiefly from a dialectic made possible by the establishment of the *Critical* in 1756, after which the professional qualifications of popular critics became the subject of an intense open debate. The contest between the two journals raised the issue of critical authority in a clearly professional context, and the two journals came to characterize their place in literary culture in the same terms largely as a result of their rivalry.

Many questions remain about the professional standards and the ethic of reading that both Reviews attempted to impart to their readers, and I would like now to turn to two prefaces from the early years of the *Critical* as the most cogent means of addressing them. Generally though, the habit of discriminating between elite and untutored readers – the "critical and curious" as opposed to the "hasty" reader – practiced by the *Critical* from its inception and soon after adopted by the *Monthly*, set the stage for some potentially embarrassing problems. This characterization of their reading audience put the Reviews in the uncomfortable position of having to wait for attempts at its reform to take effect. And, indeed, as the years passed, large numbers of readers showed no signs of heeding the Reviews' disparagement of many kinds of "bad" writing, particularly novels. But the multitude of unregenerate readers were inseparable from the authors and booksellers who catered to their desires. This combination – readers, authors, and booksellers all indifferent to the reviewers' exhortations – presented an alarming prospect for both Griffiths and Smollett, since it seemed to demonstrate the futility of their efforts to intervene in the literary market. It appeared, in other words, to confirm Johnson's and Fielding's definitions of "critic" as ineffectual interloper. Predictably, the most energetic response to this problem came from the *Critical*, which was perhaps more thoroughly committed to the refinement of English reading tastes. But the prefaces from the *Critical*, though they defend that journal specifically, also defend the enterprise of reviewing generally against the possibility of its being written out of literary culture.

The *Critical* begins its defense by treating authors and readers as mutually exclusive entities, as though readers could not also be authors, and vice versa. This represents a conceptual difference from reigning notions of the seventeenth century when, as Sartre puts it, "the reader, if not strictly identical with the writer, was a potential writer" (Sartre 1949: 87).[5] The Reviews tend, as I will show, to avoid extensively characterizing their readers, but they are in a sense compelled to specify either positive or negative opinions about authors.[6] Yet the prefaces suggest that the editors of the *Critical* are hostile towards both, that they are aware of the artificiality of separating authors from readers, and that in part they attack authors because they cannot safely attack the more serious source of their alarm, the emerging English reading public, whose tastes, they feared, might prove to be both unsophisticated and uncontrollable.

In both prefaces, authors are first figured as the military enemies of the reviewers, and then, even more unsympathetically, as animals. In the 1761 preface, the editors describe the *Critical* as having "sustained all the complicated assaults of dulness, whose name is Legion," and pursue this metaphor by claiming that "dulness, tho' formidable in her own strength, is not the only adversary that hath taken the field against the Critical Review," listing as well "the rage of jealousy, the fury of disappointment, the malevolence of envy, the heat of misapprehension, and the resentment of overweaning merit." The second preface (1765) imagines an imperial struggle, with the editors of the *Critical* as governors of a "province" that is "perhaps the most ungrateful and difficult in the republic of letters," and hostile authors as a "formidable and busy band" of natives.

The image of authors as equal adversaries or hostile natives quickly degenerates in both prefaces, however, into images of authors as pests. In the 1761 preface, authors are compared to "the insects of a summer's day" that "have buzzed, and stung, and stunk and expired." The 1765 preface unites the two metaphors – author as combatant and author as vermin – into a single grotesquely formulated vow:

> Armed thus with integrity and independency, they [the editors of the *Critical*] are determined to proceed in the paths of candour and conscience; regardless of those porcupines who, irritated through disappointment, dart their fretful quills at the writings or persons of the Reviewers, who fear them no more than Pyrrhus did the weapon of Priam, which fell upon his buckler – *Imbelle sine ictu*.[7]

The shift in characterization from author as soldier to author as pest is not mere rhetorical flourish, chiefly because it implies a change from deliberate opposition to unthinking havoc. By comparing authors with insects or porcupines, the editors of the Review wish to characterize them as mindlessly hostile, and implicitly to dismiss the more threatening notion that those authors might be organized and purposeful. That second possibility is more threatening because it would confirm a legitimate pluralistic conception of taste. The *Critical* instead grounded its authority in the possibility of a catholic, monistic taste in reading, and construed lack of unanimity in the public's opinions about books as a failure of education. Thus, contentious authors could be most safely dismissed as unlearned, irrational mavericks – or, in the extreme, as pests. Were it acknowledged, however, that those authors spoke from a specifiable position, that they had rational cultural dispositions of their own, the *Critical* would have had to concede that the first principle of its project of reform was open to debate.[8] The unfocused resentment that the Reviews imputed to bad authors was, they believed, ultimately manageable, but cogent opposition would not be.

These descriptions of authors are evidence of the *Critical*'s struggle to find a way to legitimate its authority. The prefaces patch together two very different rhetorics, bringing each to bear upon their adversaries in the literary culture. The first is the anti-Grub-Street invective employed by Swift and Pope during the 1720s and 1730s.[9] The personification of dulness, and dehumanizing metaphors for authors, had become clichés by 1760, but could still be used to invoke the authority wielded by the powerful writers of an earlier generation, and to historicize the reviewer–author relationship by aligning it with Swift and Pope's triumphs over their detractors. But the comparison with Swift and Pope is ironically self-reflexive, for Swift's and Pope's defenses of the integrity of authorship frequently involved attacks on critics of their own day. The *Critical*'s attempt to occupy a Popean position in the literary society of mid-century is undercut by the lasting currency of the *Dunciad*'s representation of the very office that the reviewers occupy. The other, wholly positive rhetoric is part of the emergent professionalism that, I argue, was produced in part through the rivalry between the two Reviews. Through normative values such as "integrity and independency," "candour and conscience," the reviewers attempt to define a distinctly corporate kind of authority, different from the personal integrity championed by Swift and Pope, and calculated to be effective in the more expansive, thoroughly professionalized literary environment of the later eighteenth century.

The central place of authors characterized as hostile in these prefaces suggests that the place of review criticism in literary culture was dynamically unresolved. More significant, though, is that in 1765, after only nine years of operation, the *Critical*'s editors appear exasperated by the failures of these strategies to overcome growing suspicions that they were relatively powerless over literary production. Their frustration is nowhere more evident than in the choice (in the 1765 preface) of the beleaguered colonial governor as a metaphor for their own situation. That metaphor, in which the editors imagine themselves as the governor of an "ungrateful and difficult" province, plagued by a "formidable and busy band" of authors, alludes to the volatile state of affairs in the American colonies during the 1760s. The Proclamation of 1763 returned St. Pierre and Miquelon to France, and Cuba and the Philippines to Spain, in exchange, respectively, for Canada and Florida, both undeveloped and potentially hostile tracts of land that would, many thought, prove far too difficult to colonize profitably. Moreover, the Great Indian Uprising during the same year, which threatened British outposts throughout the western frontier, immediately underscored the apparent dubiousness of the Proclamation's terms.

The resulting controversy over management of the colonies unleashed an enormous number of opposition pamphlets that pointed out the folly of the government's policy and set the stage for more extreme statements, such as the infamous issue no. 45 of the *North Briton*, in which John Wilkes accused the Bute ministry of treason. The swarm of charges that England had foolishly overextended itself makes the pro-ministerial *Critical*'s identification with colonial governors deeply problematic, though in a curious way it is quite appropriate as well.[10] Laurence Henry Gipson in *The Triumphant Empire* describes the predicament of the typical governor in terms that would have been very familiar to the reviewers:

> In reality, the power of a royal governor was not nearly so impressive as an
> enumeration of his powers would indicate. . . . If he were to maintain bearable

relations with the inhabitants of the colony, he could not be forgetful of their interests, which might not be compatible with the free exercise of many of his powers. . . . At best his situation at all times was one of great delicacy in guarding, on the one hand, against a summary recall from his superiors at home for neglect of his office and, on the other, against the development of an opposition within his province that might leave him helpless to perform his duties.

(Gipson 1954: IX, 17–18)

Like a governor in the colonies, the editors of the *Critical* felt themselves in 1765 to be caught in a thankless mediating position, between a clear (though self-appointed) set of duties and the incorrigible practices of authors. Like the anti-Grub-Street rhetoric, this ambiguous metaphorical alignment with the colonial governor ultimately calls attention to the Review's own inadequacy, by asserting its authority only as an appeal for help.

The *Critical*'s efforts to anchor its authority in the field of literature were not directed at authors alone, however, and I contend that readers ultimately constituted a far more "formidable and busy" opposition to reviewers. Vocal and identifiable, authors presented a tangible threat that could be met head-on in the arena provided by the Review itself. Readers, however, were another matter – the everpresent material foundation of the Reviews' existence, they were nevertheless always silent. The editors of the *Critical* could speculate on the identity of these readers, but never engaged them in the medium of print. Indeed, neither the *Critical* nor the *Monthly* followed the lead of the earlier *Gentleman's Magazine* (founded in 1731), which seemed to imagine a far more fluid relationship between itself and its readers. The *Gentleman's* gradually expanded from its omnibus format to characterize many of its feature articles as "original correspondence" (even if much of this material was in fact written by the editors). Its radically democratic motto, "*E Pluribus Unum*," sharply differentiated its concerns from the Reviews' attempts to police the boundaries between reviewer, author, and reader. The absence of textual exchanges between readers and reviewers in the *Critical* and the *Monthly* does not mean, however, that the Reviews' readership was an enigma. On the contrary, as I will suggest, readers were capable of expressing their desires very powerfully *as consumers* of literature. Thus, the reviewers could contain or rebut the articulated opposition of authors, but the unwritten, material opposition of readers filled them with a sense of frustration at their own powerlessness – a frustration they could conveniently vent only at authors.

The *Critical*'s chief recourse in the face of this resentment was to incorporate its dissatisfaction with what it perceived as wayward reading practices into a comprehensive social critique. The journal resituated its exasperation with readers and the books that they purchased within a general campaign against luxury and the corruption of taste. All the public's undisciplined or unprincipled desires in reading posed a threat, the *Critical* theorized, to the cultural and moral stability of the nation. The terms of this position were, in fact, quite powerful throughout the eighteenth century. John Sekora identifies luxury as "the greatest single social issue and the greatest single commonplace" of the mid-eighteenth century, and notes that the British Museum and the London School of Economics possess more than 460 books and pamphlets on the subject from the years 1721–71, most of them overwhelmingly against luxury (Sekora 1977: 66, 75). Writers for the *Critical* consistently make their review articles part of this larger polemic.[11] Luxury served as a bogeyman – it allowed the editors of the *Critical* to justify their fear of failure by suggesting that everyone should be afraid. Rather than castigating readers directly, they attacked bad taste as a symptom of luxury, and constantly reasserted the principles on which they believed writing ought to be predicated. As the 1765 preface reveals, however, such assertions were by no means guaranteed to succeed, and for all their attempts to neutralize popular opinion by embedding it in a rationalized and abstract critique, the unmanageable tastes of the general public remained a constant source of concern to the editors of the *Critical*.

Perhaps the best illustration of the acuteness of this fear is the journal's treatment of the most famous attack on luxury written during mid-century, John Brown's *Estimate of the Manners and Principles of the Times* (1757). The *Estimate* epitomized the ferment that I have touched upon here: the first volume ran through seven authorized and pirated editions in 1757 alone, and as Sekora points out, it is immediately distinguishable from contemporary works on the subject by the "breadth and particularity of Brown's indictment" (Sekora 1977: 93). One might expect such a treatise to be right in line with the philosophy that informs the *Critical*, but the journal instead said that the *Estimate* should be deplored and repudiated, not so much because of its argument, but because of its appeal to anarchical, mass emotions. This discrepancy, puzzling as it seems at first glance, goes to the heart of the subtle but potentially volatile tensions that mark the relationship between reviewer and reader. The very popularity of the *Estimate* is enough to make it seem dangerous to the Review's editors, and they take that popularity to be a more persuasive argument than anything Brown has to say *against* anarchic public opinion. The *Critical*'s fear of the public is, in other words, more urgent than Brown's, and the editors seem compelled by that fear to take an even more radically reactionary stance than Brown himself took.

If we turn, however, from this abstract critique to the *Critical*'s direct characterizations of its readers, and of the reviewer–reader relationship, the problems and the rhetoric become far more nuanced. The difficulties arise chiefly, I think, out of a conflict inherent in the reviewers' project. In order to succeed in one sense, the *Monthly* and *Critical* reviewers had to present their journals *as books*, as saleable commodities competing with the productions of other writers for the patronage of a finite assortment of readers. Yet, at the same time, the reviewers had to present themselves as *above* the literary marketplace – offering a disinterested perspective on all other kinds of published writing, in order to police the reading practices of the very audience they wished to attract. Thus, in 1761, the editors of the *Critical* thank a neutral and undifferentiated "public," but express the hope that their work will be agreeable to the more particular "reader of ingenuity and candour." They acknowledge that they owe their success to the favor of that larger public, yet promise to "continue to exert their best endeavours for the regulation of taste," that is, paradoxically, to remake the audience that has so far supported them. The *Critical Review* hoped, in other words, to deny the possibility that the reading public on which it depended may have been unreformable – that the reader who buys the *Critical* may have had no wish to become "the reader of ingenuity and candour."

In fact, though, this very danger was realized in the early 1760s, forcing the editors to acknowledge, in the preface of 1765, insoluble problems in the relationship between reviewer and reader. They note in that preface that, since George III's accession to the throne (1760), "political writings have engrossed the attention of the public of England more than they have done at any time since the Revolution," and that they, "the Critical Reviewers, according to the plan of their undertaking and their constant practice, could not help reviewing political as they did other works." But this practice laid them open to charges of partiality, and they thus found themselves accused of taking part, on the government's side, in the controversy. These charges *were* well founded – Smollett's allegiance to the ministry was well known, and his politics continued to inform the journal even after his departure as editor in 1763. Because of its stated commmitment to impartiality, the *Critical* obviously could not admit to biases, political or otherwise. But the means by which its editors deny their pro-ministerial slant is a curious abdication of responsibility, a tacit, reluctant deferral to the reading public:

> It happens, however, as the most indifferent bystanders may observe, that the papers and pamphlets against any administration, are brought up with much greater avidity than those written in its defense; and consequently the opposition writers are, of late, more numerous than those for the government, as well as more indecent, more shallow, and more incorrect, because the bulk of them write only for the profit of their publications; and therefore the Reviewers have, perhaps, censured a greater number of antiministerial than of ministerial productions.
>
> (*Critical* (1765): preface [n.p.])

Having committed themselves to making a comprehensive account of contemporary writing, they now find themselves compelled by their own rules to review a barrage of pamphlets that they would almost certainly like to ignore. An occasional single work they could choose not to review, but not a flood of books written on the same subject or in the same style. A trend in literary production such as the glut of anti-ministerial pamphlets of the early 1760s demonstrated, by its sheer volume, the limitations of the Reviews' control over English readers. Nor are these pamphlets a unique case: the tone of exasperation that we find in the 1765 preface is echoed in the many reviews of sentimental novels, romances, and scurrilous pamphlets on non-political topics (such as the literature that sprang up around *Tristram Shandy* during the 1760s).[12]

The history of the *Critical*'s responses to novels, in particular, mirrors the progressive discouragement that led to the 1765 preface. Early articles present novels as "innocent amusement," and even apologize for reviewing them negatively.[13] But in later articles (from about 1760) reviewers seem exasperated by the productions of "the common herd of novelists,"[14] which they see as indistinguishable from one another. A review of *The History of Mr. Byron and Miss Greville* archly summarizes the standard plot:

> As usual, the hero and heroine are all perfection, in person, sentiment, morals, and conduct; and of course they are persecuted by their ill-fated stars, and the inflexibility of parental opposition. However, they at length come together, and are necessarily then at the very pinnacle of felicity.
>
> (*Critical* 16 (1763): 217)

Reviewers also begin to move from attacks on the novels to broader social critique, such as an article which speaks of the "youth of the present age" as "corrupted by romances" (*Critical* 23 (1767): 210). An article about yet another product of booksellers, John and Francis Noble's "novel *manufactory*," quickly becomes a comprehensive indictment of a cycle of production and consumption that the reviewer feels has spun out of control:

> The booksellers, those pimps of literature, take care every winter to procure a sufficient quantity of tales, memoirs, and romances for the entertainment of their customers, many of whom, not capable of distinguishing between good and bad, are mighty well satisfied with whatever is provided for them: as their female readers in particular have generally most voracious appetites, and are not overly delicate in their choice of food, every thing that is new will go down. The circulating librarians, therefore, whose very beings depend on amusements of this kind, set their authors to work regularly every season, and, without the least grain of compassion for us poor Reviewers, who are obliged to read their performances, pester the public with their periodical nonsense.
>
> (*Critical* 16 (1763): 449)

The tone of exasperation anticipates the preface of 1765. It registers the same complaint in a more elaborate way, describing a literary system modeled on prostitution, with booksellers as pimps, authors as their prostitutes, and circulating libraries as brothels of a kind that facilitates this disreputable kind of reading. The analogy between prostitution and literary production is by no means original, but it is given a distinctive inflection here, where the reviewer uses it to deflect the blame for the glut of bad books away from consuming readers. These readers are described first as indiscriminate customers and unwitting victims. Then, in an intriguing reversal of gender roles, they are figured in particular as women with voracious appetites. Appetite itself is unconscious and is implicitly placed in opposition to taste, the deliberate and informed selection of food. At the end of this chain of commercial dependencies are "us poor Reviewers," a kind of literary vice squad rendered helpless by a system in which producers and consumers alike are complicit. It is significant that both in this particular review and in the preface of 1765, the editors of the *Critical* are careful to represent abuses in the literary system in metaphors that mitigate the responsibility of readers. The standard analogy in which appetite predominates over taste makes the reader's affinity for bad books appear involuntary, while the ingenious analogy of prostitution implies that the reader is manipulated into bad choices by the criminal element in the bookselling industry. But these excuses for readers excuse the reviewers as well, since they complicate what would otherwise be indisputable evidence of their failure to influence the public's consumption of literature.

I should add that the treatment of novels in the *Monthly* took an almost identical turn. One reviewer, for example, voices his exasperation at the publication of a sequel to a novel, *The Man of Honour; or the History of Harry Waters*, that the journal had earlier disparaged:

> Vain were the hopes we expressed, on reading the first of these stupid volumes, that we should never be troubled with any more of them. The public, or the

circulating libraries, have formed a different judgment of the merit of this work; and lo! the sequel is before us.

(*Monthly* 48 (1773): 71)

The notion that the "different judgment" about *Harry Waters* is formed by "the public, or the circulating libraries," bears a clear similarity to the *Critical*'s analogy of booksellers as pimps. The reviewer seems to shift, in mid-sentence, from blaming the public directly for the appearance of another bad novel, to blaming the institution of circulating libraries – as if circulating libraries could exist independently of consumer demand.

In *Women and Print Culture*, Kathryn Shevelow makes the important point that any periodical's representation of its audience is a "textual *projection* – sometimes idealized, frequently ideological – whose constitution and influence is distinct from any empirical account of its actual readers" (Shevelow 1989: 32). This distinction entailed a special dilemma for the Reviews, whose aim was, in effect, to make their textual projection into reality, to turn all subscribers into versions of the ideal reader. The friction between the *Critical* and its readership which I have described arose from the journal's growing exasperation with thousands of particular readers who showed no signs of cooperating with the Review's program of reform. Both the *Critical* and the *Monthly* were able to articulate one version of the eighteenth century's ideal reading practices, but were unable to enforce them in a way that affected the publishing industry.

The discrepancy between ideal and actual readers engages the workings of taste itself, which is always uncomfortably self-reflexive: taste is an aesthetic judgment that is passed on one's ability to make aesthetic judgments. Claiming the right to prescribe or judge the judgments of others became more and more difficult to justify as the eighteenth century's debate about taste escalated. Though a great many philosophers (perhaps Kames [Home] and Gerard addressed the issues most directly) agreed that there were empirical standards of taste, no one could adequately articulate them, and the plurality of theories served only to undercut each of them. The Reviews, first the *Critical* and then the *Monthly*, entered the scene at the peak of this philosophical dialogue, and they occupied a far more conservative position than any of their interlocutors. Rather than trying to demonstrate an empirical standard of taste in reading, the reviewers preferred to assume that self-evident standards were already in place, that these tendencies and norms in reading were shared by an elite subset of the book-buying public, and that they could eventually be conveyed to everyone else. But they overestimated both the size of that subset and their own ability to reform the judgment of the rest of the public.

If the *Critical Review* so plainly failed in its attempts to police the reading habits of the English public, and if the idea of normalizing that public's tastes was so resolutely reactionary, then it seems that we need to reinvestigate the "function" of this very successful kind of popular criticism. We need to account on the one hand for the continued survival both of the *Critical*'s and of the *Monthly*'s attempts to establish a universal standard of taste, and on the other for the fashions that resulted, for example, in countless romances. We need to ask, in other words, why the conservative rationale from which review criticism sprang was not dislodged by the nascent *laissez-faire* consumer culture with which it seems so much at odds.

In perhaps the most provocative discussion of what Neil McKendrick, John Brewer, and J. H. Plumb have identified as the "consumer revolution," Colin Campbell describes what he calls "modern autonomous imaginative hedonism," which instills an inexhaustible array of desires in the English public of the eighteenth century. He describes the "key to the understanding of modern consumerism" as the recognition of "longing as a permanent mode, with the concomitant sense of dissatisfaction with 'what is' and a yearning for 'something better'" (Campbell 1987: 90). I suggest that one central, though paradoxical, aspect of that longing was the desire for a means of assessing those very wants themselves. Perhaps nowhere was that need more acutely felt than in the field of literature. The period 1650 to 1750, as Plumb has described, saw books transformed from "semi-precious objects . . . carefully and beautifully bound," and read largely by the affluent, to plentiful, everyday objects within the purchasing reach of the bourgeoisie (McKendrick *et al.* 1982: 268). The Reviews answered a crucial need not merely by claiming to offer, hypothetically, an impartial and independent judgment about books, but by offering the consumers of those books an orderly and comprehensible way of participating in the literary culture of their day.

The success of the *Monthly* and the *Critical* is perhaps most dependent on the fact that in 1760 (as well as today), reading a Review and abiding by its recommendations were two very different and not necessarily related activities, even though the two usually go hand in hand. Indeed, it is no exaggeration to say that in the modern era the complexity of the act of reading has been severely underestimated. As books became more widely available and affordable, and as literacy became more widespread, reading became an activity at once more commonplace and more taken for granted. This development, a function of the new consumer society, unfolded at such a rapid pace that one could mistakenly come to assume that reading books was and is a cultural practice with a single meaning. It is easy to recognize that differences in social class, educational background, and gender would very likely make for different preferences in books (the cliché among reviewers that the typical reader of novels is female is but one example). But too little attention has been paid to the corresponding differences in *how* the representatives of these social groups read what they read. The meaning of reading, so to speak, can be almost anything. It can be a coerced deference to dominant ideological interests, in which "I can read" means "I know how to behave" (Grivel 1985: 160). But reading can also be what Michel deCerteau describes as a pervasive "poaching," an endless series of particular subversions of the official texts of the social elite. Reading, for deCerteau, is ideally "reading underneath scriptural imperialism" (deCerteau 1984: 168). It is crucial to keep in mind, however, that the notion of the reading process as a symbol of one's place in the cultural spectrum is possible only in a society where reading itself has been commodified. The beginnings of book-reviewing mark an important stage in this development, for they indicate that not just books but the ways of reading them have become so numerous and varied that someone (the reviewers) must regulate them. The idea of institutionally ordered reading practices is at once the urgent goal and the impossible hope of the early Reviews. They approach their goal only in that the act of regularly reading or subscribing to a book review indicates a sophisticated and comprehensive level of consumer awareness; it is an attempt at intellectual self-definition in relation to the ideal reader implied by the journal. But the act of reading one or more books at a reviewer's suggestion, and recognizing the correctness of his assessment, is at best merely a coincidental function of that larger ambition, if it is even that – and therein lies the certain failure of the *Monthly*'s and *Critical*'s ambition. The desire to peruse the whole range of printed matter available for purchase in a given month is nevertheless a vital step in the history of the consumption of culture. The determinants of that desire will always remain elusive, but their existence is confirmed dramatically by the very emergence of the *Monthly* and the *Critical*.

Notes

1 Tony Bennett defines a reading formation as "a set of discursive and intertextual determinations that organize and animate the practice of reading, connecting texts and readers in specific relations to one another by constituting readers as reading subjects of particular types and texts as objects-to-be-read in particular ways" (1958: 7).

2 Basker cites Philip J. Klukoff (1967: 418–19), as presenting "convincing evidence" that the first preface was written by Smollett (1988: 261). The 1765 preface remains unattributed.

3 For analogous developments in the history of painting, see John Barrell (1986: 1–68).

4 For a discussion of vocabulary as an aspect of professional credentials, see JoAnne Brown (1986: 33–51).

5 Discussing the situation of writing in France in the seventeenth and eighteenth centuries, Sartre goes on to speculate that the division between author and reader is a function of romanticism's positing of a mass audience: "a revolution analogous to romanticism is not conceivable in this period [the seventeenth century] because there would have to have been the concurrence of an indecisive mass, which one surprises, overwhelms, and suddenly animates by revealing to it ideas or feelings, of which it was ignorant, and which, lacking firm convictions, constantly requires being ravished and fecundated" (1949: 88).

6 There are occasional exceptions. The reviewer of *The Adventures of Miss Beverly* refrains from wholly blaming the author for writing a bad novel, and instead steps back to take the more generous, if patronizing, view that "this publication is evidently fabricated in the cave of Poverty," for "nothing but the necessity of the author's writing *something* could have produced it" (*Critical* 26 (1768): 209).

7 The allusion is to Priam's "weak and helpless spear" in the *Aeneid*, Book II, 544. The analogy seems an odd one to draw, since Pyrrhus is, of course, the villain in this episode, and kills the aged Priam in cold blood.

8 Terry Eagleton observes that this is a characteristic irony of Enlightenment criticism: "while its appeal to standards of universal reason signifies a resistance to absolutism, the critical gesture itself is typically conservative and corrective, revising and adjusting particular phenomena to its implacable model of discourse" (1984: 12).

9 Familiar examples can be found throughout Pope's "Essay on criticism" and his *Dunciad*, and in Swift's "The progress of poetry," "Advice to Grub-Street verse writers," "Directions for a birth-day song," and "On poetry: a rhapsody."

10 The *Critical*'s response to the pamphlets I discuss later was consistent with this metaphor. *Critical* 16 (1763): 184, 231, 234, 267; 17 (1764): 63, are all programmatically in favor of government policy. The most extraordinary example is an October 1763 review of the collected papers of *The North Briton*. A polemical *tour de force*, the article first places the *North Briton* in a long tradition of opposition papers (*Mist's Journal*, *Fog's Journal*, *Common Sense*, *The True Briton*, *The Craftsman*, and *Old England*), condemning each in turn, then justifies the entire list by an appeal to neutrality that typifies the new professional rhetoric I have been describing:

> Upon the whole, we hope we shall be acquitted by every candid and judicious reader, in the account we have given of those celebrated papers, from every

imputation of rancour or party, but above all of resentment. What we mean is, to present to the public, in a cool hour of recollection, a Review of those objects, which, when they first made their appearance, presented themselves to many through the mediums of party and presupposition.

(*Critical* 17 (1764): 285)

Even as early as June 1764, however, the *Critical* began to show a sensitivity to the complexities of imperial government. Reviewing *The Administration of the Colonies* (the thesis of which was that if the Crown could not establish its right to govern, the American colonists should be allowed to govern themselves), the writer for the *Critical* disagrees very respectfully, conceding at several points to the pamphleteer (*Critical* 17 (1764): 281–4). The editors' identification with the difficulties of the colonial governor is all the more poignant in light of a notice such as this.

11   Sekora lists the following examples: *Critical* 2 (1756): 451–2; 4 (1757): 219–20; 5 (1758): 290; 9 (1760): 263; 10 (1760): 42; and 17 (1765): 395.

12   For example, more than twenty imitations of *Tristram Shandy* appeared during 1760 alone. See Lewis P. Curtis (1935: 107–8), and Arthur H. Cash (1986: 366–7).

13   The term "innocent amusement" is from *Critical* 8 (1759): 458. One example of an apology for a negative review of a novel is *Critical* 2 (1756): 140.

14   The "common herd of novelists" are disparaged in *Critical* 21 (1766): 440. Other expressions of impatience with the sameness of novels occur in *Critical* 28 (1769): 257, which describes one novel as circulating library "furniture"; also, *Critical* 29 (1770): 43, 294, and *Critical* 34 (1772): 472.

Bibliography

Barrell, J. (1986) *A Political Theory of Painting from Reynolds to Hazlitt*, New Haven, CT: Yale University Press.

Basker, J. G. (1988) *Tobias Smollett, Critic and Journalist*, Newark, DE: University of Delaware Press.

Bennett, T. (1985) "Texts in history: the determinations of readings and their texts," *MMLA* 18: 1–16.

Boswell, J. (1980) *Life of Johnson*, New York: Oxford University Press.

Bourdieu, P. (1984) *Distinction: A Social Critique of the Judgment of Taste*, trans. Richard Nice, Cambridge, MA: Harvard University Press.

Brown, J. (1986) "Professional language: words that succeed," *Radical History Review* 34: 33–51.

Burney, Frances (1982) *Evelina*, London: Oxford University Press.

Campbell, C. (1987) *The Romantic Ethic and the Spirit of Modern Consumerism*, New York: Blackwell.

Carlson, C. (1938) "Edward Cave's club, and its project for a literary review," *Philological Quarterly* 17: 115–120.

Cash, A. (1986) *Laurence Sterne, The Later Years*, London: Methuen.

Christensen, J. (1987) *Practicing Enlightenment: Hume and the Formation of a Literary Career*, Madison, WI: University of Wisconsin Press.

Collins, A. S. (1927) *Authorship in the Days of Doctor Johnson*, London: Robert Holden.

Craddock, J. (1828) *Literary and Miscellaneous Memoirs*, London: J. B. Nichols.

Curtis, L. (1935) *Letters of Laurence Sterne*, Oxford: Clarendon Press.

DeCerteau, M. (1984) *The Practice of Everyday Life*, trans. Stephen Randall, Berkeley, CA: University of California Press.

Eagleton, T. (1984) *The Function of Criticism from "The Spectator" to Post-Structuralism*, London: Verso.

Fielding, H. (1975) *The History of Tom Jones, A Foundling*, ed. Martin Battestin, Middletown, CT: Wesleyan University Press.

Forster, J. (1848) *The Life and Adventures of Oliver Goldsmith*, London: Bradbury & Evans.

Gerard, A. (1963) *An Essay on Taste* (a facsimile reprint), ed. W. J. Hipple, Jr., Gainsville, FL: University of Florida Press.

Gilmore, T. (ed.) (1972) *Early Eighteenth-Century Essays on Taste*, Delmar, NY: Scholar Facsimiles and Reprints.

Gipson, L. (1954) *The Triumphant Empire: The British Empire before the American Revolution*, Vol. 9, New York: Knopf.

Gosse, E. (1884) *The Works of Thomas Gray*, New York: Macmillan.

Graham, W. (1926) *The Beginnings of the English Literary Periodicals*, Oxford: Clarendon Press.

Grant, D. (1956) *Poetical Works of Charles Churchill*, Oxford: Clarendon Press.

Grivel, C. (1985) "The society of texts: a meditation on media in 13 points", trans. Michael Jurich, *Sociocriticism* 1: 153–78.

Helgerson, R. (1983) *Self-Crowned Laureates: Spenser, Jonson, Milton, and the Literary System*, Berkeley, CA: University of California Press.

Home, H., Lord Kames (1762) *Elements of Criticism*, London: A. Millar.

Hooker, E. N. (1934) "The discussion of taste, from 1750–1770, and the new trends in literary criticism," *PMLA* 49: 577–92.

Johnson, S. (1967) *Dictionary of the English Language*, New York: AMS Press reprint.

Jones, C. (1942) *Smollett Studies*, Berkeley, CA: University of California Press.

Keeble, N. H. (1987) *The Literary Culture of Nonconformity in Later Seventeenth-Century England*, Leicester: Leicester University Press.

Kernan, A. (1987) *Printing Technology, Letters, and Samuel Johnson*, Princeton, NJ: Princeton University Press.

Klancher, J. (1987) *The Making of English Reading Audiences, 1790–1832*, Madison, WI: University of Wisconsin Press.

Klukoff, P. (1967) "A Smollett attribution in the *Critical Review*," *Notes and Queries*, n.s., 14: 418–19.

Knapp, L. (1963) *Tobias Smollett, Doctor of Men and Manners*, New York: Russell & Russell

Larson, M. (1977) *The Rise of Professionalism*, Berkeley, CA: University of California Press.

Leenhardt, J. (1985) "Savoir lire or some socio-historical modalities of reading," trans. Daniel Russell, *Sociocriticism* 1: 139–52.

McKendrick, N., Brewer, J., and Plumb, J. H. (1982) *The Birth of a Consumer Society: The Commercialization of Eighteenth-Century England*, Bloomington, IN: Indiana University Press.

Marchand, L. (1974) *Byron's Letters and Journals*, Cambridge, MA: Bellknap Press.

Pottle, F. (1950) *Boswell's London Journal*, New York: McGraw–Hill.

Sartre, J. (1949) *What Is Literature?*, trans. Bernard Frechtman, New York: Philosophical Library.

Sekora, J. (1977) *Luxury: The Concept in Western Thought, Eden to Smollett*, Baltimore, MD: Johns Hopkins University Press.

Shevelow, K. (1989) *Women and Print Culture: The Construction of Femininity in the Early Periodical*, New York and London: Routledge.

Spector, R. (1966) *English Literary Periodicals and the Climate of Opinion During the Seven Years' War*, The Hague: Mouton.

Sterne, L. (1965) *The Life and Opinions of Tristram Shandy*, ed. Ian Watt, Boston, MA: Houghton Mifflin.

Sullivan, A. (ed.) (1983) *British Literary Magazines*, Westport, CT: Greenwood Press.

Warner, M. (1990) *The Letters of the Republic: Publication and the Public Sphere in Eighteenth-Century America*, Cambridge, MA: Harvard University Press.

Wilensky, H. (1964) "The professionalization of everyone?," *American Journal of Sociology* 70: 137–58.

5

Expanding on portraiture
The market, the public, and the hierarchy of genres in eighteenth-century Britain

Louise Lippincott

In eighteenth-century Britain portrait painting thrived, history painting struggled. Explanations of the phenomenon have always relied on the theoretical connections between history painting and public virtue, portraiture and private interest (Barrell 1986). How could an art as idealistic, altruistic, and noble as history painting survive in an age increasingly committed to commerce, consumption, and private life? How could the portrait with its connotations of luxury, privacy, and individualism, do less than flourish? One may blame the state for its detachment, the aristocracy for its ignorance, the bourgeois public for its debased tastes, the Academy for its exclusiveness, the entrepreneurs for their pursuit of pure profit, or the artists for their moral and technical failings. But was a taste for portraiture truly an indication of loss of public virtue and the rise of capitalist enterprise? Was the fall of history painting a logical consequence of the "rise of the bourgeoisie" and the private citizen? Yes; but not in the relationships of cause and effect to which we are accustomed. It is possible to argue that a taste for portraiture expressed an individual's sense of social and civic responsibility, while buying history paintings comprised one of the depravities of commercial capitalism as understood in the eighteenth century.[1] One would then conclude that the British public, far from succumbing to the seductions of commercialism in the fine arts, virtuously adhered to traditional images of honor and heroism. Unfortunately for academic theory, such images were portraits.

In this chapter I will examine the "life" of eighteenth-century paintings first as commodities, then as property. How did these objects fare in the marketplace, and what happened to them after they found a buyer? I wish to focus on such transactions because they pinpoint in a new way some of the problems history painters faced, as well as issues that still bedevil art and cultural historians today. The principal questions then and now were and are: who would support history painting in eighteenth-century Britain, why would they do it, and how? Despite well-established theories on how the state, the Church, and the public *ought* to respond to the genre, in point of fact the absence of a solid native school of history painters rendered the question academic until the founding of the Royal Academy made it an urgent reality.[2] How were the genre's public and market to be discovered, formed, and defined? To what extent did these two groups overlap or relate? Most of the evidence about the character of the public and market for art was and is fragmented and anecdotal. Perceptions were, and are, skewed by theoretical and critical arguments, spectacular individual examples of success and failure, and the obscurity of general trends.

Concrete information about the reception of history paintings comes from records of transactions involving them as well as from published and unpublished criticism. Sales to patrons, auctions, income from print sales, costs of engravers, bankruptcy of entrepreneurs, were matters of consuming interest to the art world, of course. Information about them is abundant in artists' correspondence, diaries, account books, and other private sources. However, significant information of this type was increasingly available to a broader eighteenth-century public as well, thanks to newspaper reporting and advertising, literary and gossip magazines, pamphlets, brochures, and the very informative captions on reproductive engravings. Caricatures drawn and published by artists and printsellers and hung in shop windows brought the latest art world controversies out on to the street (Penny 1986: 364–71). As a result of the expansion of the reading public and the ephemeral press, the whole business of art, and in particular this new business of history painting, appeared less and less a matter of private transaction and more and more a matter of polite public curiosity. The commercial fates of these novel paintings were in many cases as notable and newsworthy as their aesthetic merits; and the entanglement of art and commerce in public perceptions of the historical genre produced some surprising and unintended consequences.

Comparing the "lives" of history and portrait paintings reveals important differences in the ways these objects were produced, marketed, and consumed. In fact, one can detect a hierarchy of genres established by the marketplace which reverses the moral economy of academic theory. The drudging portrait painters who yearned for an ideal Great Style and the grand narrative composition are familiar figures. But in evaluating their complaints, we have overlooked the fact that in terms of the marketplace, their portraits occupied the moral high ground. The much-envied history painter succeeded as an exponent of civic virtue to the extent that he could expand on the genre of portraiture; the successful history painting "lived" as closely as possible the market life of a portrait.

Let us begin with the market life, that is, the process of production, sale, and ownership, of a narrative history painting in the second half of the eighteenth century (Plate 5.1). It was difficult and expensive. History paintings were supposed to be large, due to their pretensions as public art, and they contained a multitude of figures, since they usually represented historically significant public actions. Designing the composition could therefore be a lengthy process requiring the preparation of composition drawings, detailed studies, travel, presentation designs for the approval of the patron (if any), then revisions, and repetition of the process until artist and patron were satisfied. To execute the final design, the artist required a large space for his canvas, models, props, supplies, and assistants, all of which had to be paid for more or less on the spot. Immured in his painting room, the artist was faced with the monumental task of finishing an enormous canvas. Execution of important compositions could consume many years and costs could often rise unpredictably over the duration. In the meantime, the painter faced the loss of other potentially prestigious or lucrative jobs. Moreover, there was the tremendous risk that this single venture might fail artistically and/or commercially. In some cases, the artist's reward for his work was only the intangible satisfaction of completing the most difficult and prestigious type of subject despite numerous obstacles. From the point of view of the producer, history paintings were enormous gambles.

This was also true from the viewpoint of any prospective purchaser. Commissioning a history painting was fraught with difficulties and dangers. In eighteenth-century Britain, history painting was a recently imported concept closely linked with the absolutist state and the Roman Catholic Church. Its best-known practitioners were French or Italian. In its traditional Baroque form it represented anathema to an eighteenth-century aesthetic dominated by considerations of artifice, sensation, individualism, and privacy.[3] Acknowledged native-born masters of history painting in late eighteenth-century Britain were few and the two most important were actually Americans. With the exception of the prolific Benjamin West, they were apt to be slow and could easily be expensive. Selecting a subject and evaluating a composition was an agonizing experience. So many of the traditional baroque themes failed to address the concerns of a Protestant state with a parliamentary form of government, or they even seemed antithetical to them. Inventing or discovering new subjects required some imagination and research and the difficult task of communicating the idea to the artist. Settling on a price for an unseen or unique product to be completed at some unspecified future date could be even more unnerving.

More important, why should anyone want or need to own a history painting? If the purpose of viewing history paintings was to heighten one's public spirit, this could be achieved by visiting a painter's studio or exhibition, pronouncing on the work, offering encouragement of the verbal kind, and departing in a state of high moral virtue. The powerful could even eliminate the inconvenience of travel by requesting that the painting be sent to them for examination. Capital investment was not necessary, so that the only immediate benefits went to the footmen and porters carting (unsold) paintings around London's West End (Pye 1845: 229–30). A prospective owner might also be discouraged by the fact that this very public art looked out of place in most domestic settings. History paintings were large, difficult, and at times violent in subject. In any case a pressing desire to display *exempla* of moral rectitude on the walls could be more easily and economically satisfied with the purchase of a suitable old master painting, reproductive engraving, or painted copy. These alternatives probably served most buyers' purposes better, because subjects and sentiments were more easily recognized, the risks of making a bizarre mistake greatly reduced, and prices standardized and controlled by the large competitive markets established in the print-selling and auction trades.

Not surprisingly, commissions for history paintings were exceedingly rare in a nation where state patronage of the arts was limited and institutional patronage sporadic. Only Benjamin West, enjoying a salary of about £1,500 from the king, could be said to have earned a steady income from history painting. His nearest rival, John Singleton Copley, resolved optimistically to paint history only on commission, but was soon forced into more uncertain ventures to keep in work. Commissioned works were usually paid for with a deposit of half the agreed-upon sum at the onset of the project, with the remainder to be paid on its completion. The painter gambled on finishing the work quickly and efficiently enough to ensure some profit at the end; the patron gambled that the artist would finish within the budget allotted to him. Often neither side won, and lawsuits such as the lengthy battle between Copley, the Corporation of London, and John Boydell over Copley's ambitious *Siege of Gibraltar* could result (Prown 1966: 322–36). Squabbles over ownership of the reproduction rights often accompanied such disagreements, since each party hoped to make up losses through print sales.

Many history paintings were undertaken without a true patron or commission. Embarking on a long-term, expensive project without hope of salary or sometimes even expenses, the painter expected to recoup through sales of tickets to the work's public exhibition (more expenses for rental of tent or exhibition room, advertising and printing of programs), sale of the work itself (unlikely), sale of publication rights (safe but relatively low profit), sale of engravings after the composition (large investment in payment to the engraver and further delay in realizing a profit), or sale of future work to patrons attracted by the initial one. The desperate might undertake a lottery, as Hogarth had done with his *Sigismunda* (in his case to unload the painting and publicize the plight of history painting in England). Each of these strategies exposed the painter to special dangers. Public exhibition, at first glance both a civic-minded and an economically sensible expedient, presented a peculiar peril. The Royal Academy frowned on member or would-be member artists displaying their work outside its galleries. Because the Academy maintained and disbursed the only pension fund available to painters, and only to its own members, exclusion from the group meant loss of the only economic safety-net available. (Ironically, the Academy funded the pensions with income from ticket sales to its own exhibitions which was not shared out to the exhibitions' participants [Pye 1845: 10–11].) One other potential disaster threatened such long-term projects. A subject selected with an eye to commercial exploitation in one decade might not please by the time it reached completion in the next. Copley, for example, began *Charles I Requesting from Parliament the Five Impeached Members* in 1782 (Plate 5.2), when the success of its companion piece, *Death of the Earl of Chatham*, was still fresh in the public mind. Unfortunately he completed it in 1795, after the Terror had instilled widespread distaste for themes of parliamentary rebellion and regicide. Not surprisingly the public exhibition was a disappointment despite a visit from the monarch.[4]

History painting appealed primarily to artists and patrons with ready capital, a taste for speculation, and a high desire for public recognition. For these reasons as well as for its theoretical and philosophical pretensions, history painting was unlikely to attract the patronage of women, one of the fastest-growing and most influential segments of the British art market. Even so, immense profits awaited the perceptive, diligent, or fortunate promoter, but bankruptcy was a far more common, at times even inevitable, outcome of an ambitious project. Painters rarely possessed much in the way of capital, and few were speculators, but many risked their time, skill, and slim resources in pursuit of reputation. Beginners might produce history paintings as "loss leaders," like West's unsold classical subject carried around London to no immediate profit. It fulfilled its purposes by announcing the arrival of an ambitious new painter in the city, and in West's case it did lead to notoriety, commissions, fame, and success. Probably the most depressing example of such a project is James Barry's mural for the Society of

Arts – seven years' work on *The Progress of Human Culture*, for which he earned only expenses and which brought nothing in the way of future projects. Established artists were lured into such ventures by the challenge of the genre, the desire for glory, and some speculative ambitions. Financially secure, they could support their efforts at history painting by work in other genres (notably portraiture), they could afford to pay a good engraver for the reproductive print, and they could afford to wait (years, if necessary) for the profits from its sales. Subscription sales, in which print-buyers made down payments for their purchases, helped cover engraving expenses. Failure was less devastating if the painter had a solid reputation and clientele in other areas.

History paintings sold best to the art world's big speculators, the printsellers. In fact, engravers and printsellers were among the most prominent commissioners and promoters of history painting in Britain. John Boydell is the leading example of support for and exploitation of history painting, and Boydell's success, riches, and rewards for his commercial acumen and civic-mindedness are legendary in the history of British art. Enriched by sales of cheaply engraved landscape views, he made his greatest profits from selling engravings of history paintings successfully exhibited at the Royal Academy in the 1770s. In many cases he bought only the right to reproduce the painting, but the scale of his earnings far exceeded the relatively small scope of his investment. His profit margins can be discerned from the record of one of his greatest successes, *The Death of General Wolfe*, painted by Benjamin West and engraved by William Woollett. West painted the subject on speculation, finally selling it to Lord Grosvenor for a price rumored to be between £400 and £600 (von Erffa and Staley 1986: 211–13). Boydell may have bought the rights from either the artist or the painting's owner; on an investment of at most a few hundred pounds, he earned £15,000 from the print (Bruntjen, 1985: 36). Significantly, the Shakespeare Gallery, into which Boydell had sunk substantial sums by commissioning paintings himself, ended in financial failure. However, during its heyday it spawned commercially motivated galleries and "Museums" of historical and literary paintings in imitation. Ticket sales provided immediate income for the entrepreneur; in some cases publishing ventures were also launched, or the works of art on display might also be up for sale, sometimes on consignment from private owners. The high philosophical and cultural value assigned to history paintings by the academic hierarchy of genres enabled the entrepreneurial exhibitors to claim that they were performing a public service by displaying such art to paying audiences (Lippincott 1987: 44–6). The teachings of theory, far from elevating the genre, sold it.

Speculating in history paintings was in some way comparable to gambling on the stock market. There was the initial investment of substantial capital on an untried invention of specialized genius. There was the division of risk and profits into shares divided between inventor (painter), entrepreneur (printseller), manufacturer (engraver), and other investors (sometimes including the owner of the painting). There was the public launching of the finished product and the agonized wait for public response, followed in short order by fame and riches or bankruptcy and obscurity. There was also the perception on the part of the public that, as with stock speculations, private interests were manipulating concerns of public or national importance for their own gain. Because of the visibly commercial exploitation of history painting, it was easy to associate this artistic genre with other novel capitalistic ventures in public entertainment, from fly-by-night museums to Vauxhall Gardens (which was actually decorated with subject paintings by Hogarth, Hayman, and others).

Even after a history painting survived the initial burst of exploitation, it remained a tainted object. If the artist retained ownership of the original, it generally appeared again on the market, if only at the auction of his property after his death. Similarly, a printseller's collection, such as Boydell's Shakespeare Gallery, would be put up for sale to mitigate financial difficulties (the Shakespeare Gallery was lotteried, then auctioned) or liquidate the business. Private art collections (excluding portraits) seem to have been treated as personal rather than family property and were disposed of accordingly. They often went up for sale at the owner's death unless the heirs shared their deceased relative's taste in art. They could also be consigned anonymously to auction sales or commercial "museums." Many of these events occasioned grandiloquent claims and extensive advertisement, only to end in ignominy and low prices. Thus the cycle of sale and exploitation repeated itself over the lifetime of the object.

That the highest form of art should be dependent on the grubby speculations of merchants and undertakers aroused the ire of every thinking artist, theorist, and connoisseur of the era. The situation violated the most fundamental tenet of history painting: the ostensibly disinterested motivation of the parties involved in its production and appreciation (Barrell 1986: 49). And that these images of timeless virtue and immortal heroism could be the subject of notoriety, fall out of fashion, and fail at exhibition or auction, undermined the claims to sovereignty of the genre and the Academy that promoted it. Production or private ownership of a history painting in late eighteenth-century Britain connoted not discriminating taste and altruistic nobility, but capitalistic speculation, personal ambition, and private venality (see Plate 5.3). Citizens of the republic of taste might admire the theoretical pretensions of the genre, study examples in exhibitions, and own them in replica, but the original works of art were in many ways shopworn and suspect. The exploitation of history painting illustrated the new, commercially spawned corruptions of public values to which eighteenth-century Britain seemed increasingly vulnerable (Sekora 1977: 110–31; Barrell 1986: 38, 65).

In contrast, the market life of portraits appeared enviably safe, simple, and virtuous (although the lives of their makers were not). Portrait painters complained that much of their work was drudgery, but few could resist the security and prosperity that could be gained by even modest skills (Pointon 1984: 187–205). Most portraits were small, single-figure compositions focusing on the head, torso, and hands of the sitter. Because materials were portable, a portrait painter could work anywhere: his lodgings or home, or the home of his sitter. Sizes of portraits were more or less standard, and it was possible to buy appropriately sized canvases, stretchers, and frames with relative ease. The model was paying for the opportunity to sit. Costumes and props were supplied by the sitter or could be improvised from one or two stock pieces of furniture and some lengths of fabric. Special backgrounds could be copied from engravings. Compositions were simple and could be endlessly repeated, thus obviating the need for elaborate preparatory drawings. Some portrait painters kept on view in their studios a repertory of standard poses, costumes, and props from which a sitter made his selection. In the most prolific practices, short cuts were common; the master painted the head and hands of his sitter on the canvas, while figure, drapery, and background were added by an assistant later. Skilled drapery painters haunted London and could be hired by the job or the month. Thus it was possible to execute portraits easily and efficiently despite the short-term volatility of the market, which was heavily influenced by the London Season and a relatively high percentage of female patrons.[5]

Since production of most portraits was more a matter of routine than invention, they were also far easier to budget and complete than history paintings. Output might be hampered by a rush of fashion-mad patrons, but the availability of cheap, skilled labor enabled the painter to adjust to increases in demand. An established master had the luxury of picking and choosing his clients, and could – within limits – resist their more extravagant demands. (If demand declined, on the other hand, a painter could easily pack up his materials and embark on a provincial tour, a standard method of finding new business, reducing expenses, and building up a clientele.) Although interest in an individual's work might fluctuate, demand for portraits in general in eighteenth century Britain remained high. Few portraitists worked on speculation, although an occasional good likeness of a current celebrity or hero helped to keep one's reputation fresh in the eyes of the public. (As ever, the initial investment of time and money was less than for a history painting.) Reasonably talented portraitists could count on finding patrons somewhere, so that their particular professional challenge consisted in finding the most prestigious sitters, winning the most challenging commissions (full-length and group portraits), and charging the highest prices. The successful portraitist had to be socially skilled, remarkably well organized, and artistically talented; Reynolds still stands out today because his artistic skills matched or exceeded the other two prerequisites; Gainsborough moved to Bath because his talent outweighed his willingness to court sitters or run a large workshop. By and large, portraits were manufactured in an environment formed by stiff competition, division of labor, standardized product, and standardized prices. Lacking in opportunities for the exercise of genius, invention, expression, and learning – from the producer's viewpoint – the profession of portraiture deserved its relatively low rank in the hierarchy of genres.

Buying a portrait was also routine for the patron, and in most cases the task was a pleasant one. British art from the time of Queen Elizabeth had been dominated by portraiture. Portraits abounded in public buildings, in private homes, in prints ranging from fine engravings to scurrilous caricatures, and in books as frontispieces and illustrations. They were familiar, and since the standard criterion of success consisted in their likeness to the sitter, judgment of quality required good eyesight and common sense rather than a liberal education in history, literature, and aesthetics. For this reason portraiture was considered an appropriate aesthetic interest for women, not only as sitters but also as painters or patrons. Selection of an appropriate artist, pose, costume, and setting could be as satisfying to the psyche as a session in front of some magically flattering mirror. Portraits might also be easily invested with meaning by the addition of props ranging from the standard (such as a ship for a sea captain, or a book for a scholar) to the intensely personal (such as papers, maps, or jewelry) (Bennett). For the shy, ugly, and unfashionable beings who must have viewed the whole process with shame and horror, there was no convenient alternative – one's portrait could not be found at auction. Yet posing might even be pleasant, since visits to the portrait painter were a recognized social pastime enlivened by conversation and gossip. Because the portraitist needed his sitter only for the face and hands, most sittings ended before their novelty wore off. Often portraits were finished within a year of commission, making the genre one of the speediest in its presentation of the end product. Payment was also relatively uncontroversial. Fees were fixed according to standard conditions: the size of the canvas, the number of hands to be included, the complexity of the accessories (extra for representations of horses or servants), and the rank of the portraitist. Surprises were rare.

If the product was predictable and unthreatening, its purposes were also clearly defined and publicly acceptable. While a sitter might be criticized for some excess of vanity if his or her portrait violated local standards of decorum, to sit for one in itself rarely inspired comment. The act of commissioning or sitting for a portrait was first and foremost one of commemoration (Scholl 1984: 42–3). A man might sit on the occasion of leaving Eton, departing for the Grand Tour, coming into his inheritance, marrying, or acquiring a significant new property, office, or title. Women sat at the time of their marriage, before the birth of a child, or in celebration of widowhood. Parents increasingly commissioned portraits of children, reflecting their expanding role in family life. It is remarkable how few sitters paid for their own portraits; many posed to oblige parents, relatives, and friends. One commentator noted that in England portraits were common and popular as gifts (Rouquet c. 1755: 45). Thus, even the most private commissions fulfilled important social functions by maintaining family relations and sealing ties of friendship. Given the importance of family and friends in Britain's political, social, and economic life, portraits in their commemorative and gift guises also played very important public roles. A roomful of family portraits, by evoking the assemblages of likenesses accumulated by families in ancient Rome, could allude to traditions of public service and historic distinction. (Reynolds's portraits of sitters in a sort of generic classical dress may have recalled such Roman portrait galleries even more explicitly than they referred to the conventions of his grand style.) Portraits of a family's important patrons or political heroes hung in the hall, portraits of divines and poets graced the library, portraits of friends and relatives hung in private chambers. At the highest level, every ambassador carried to his post one or more portraits of the monarch, and the gift of such a portrait could initiate or finalize complicated diplomatic negotiations, hard political bargains, or the subtle movement of influence. The portrait painter to the king and portraitists of the powerful and influential seem to have worked at industrial rates to supply these public stamps of recognition, alliance, and gratitude. Significantly, the important books on British history published during the eighteenth century were structured around and illustrated by portraits, not narrative scenes.[6] These books in turn gave rise to the practice of collecting portrait prints to serve as markers and memorials of the nation's historic past. Giving, owning, displaying, caricaturing, defacing, and disposing of portraits were acts of public import. Selling the family portraits symbolized the dissolution of the family. In eighteenth-century Britain portraits fulfilled the moral and civic roles that academic theory envisioned for history painting.[7] They recorded history, heroes, virtue, and friendship. They taught morality, enforced loyalty, and represented tradition. They spoke forcefully to a public which, by dint of more than two centuries of conditioning, understood, it would seem instinctively, their meanings and purpose.

Portraits were also immune to the flamboyant extremes of the speculative market. The number of practitioners ensured that competition would keep prices down, quality up, and service reliable.[8] Subsequent to their manufacture, portraits existed outside the commercial market, belonging instead to what might be called a traditional or gift economy (Douglas and Isherwood 1979: 57–9; Hyde 1983: xiv, 13, 37–45, 56). Since the initial purchase transaction was trivial, routine, and socially useful, it was not considered commercially motivated. Since the image subsequently changed hands by gift or inheritance rather than by public sale, it remained uncorrupted by speculations on its market value. Most portraits were executed on commission, and profitably, so artists rarely sent them to public exhibitions other than those at the Royal Academy, which were, of course, nonprofit. Usually they were transported to the owner's home and displayed there, far removed from any commercial taint. For the publicity-conscious, reproductive prints rather than the original painting served to make the image/sitter known. Painters usually commissioned prints of their best work in order to enhance their reputation and find more jobs. A few sitters commissioned prints of their portraits even at the risk of exposing themselves to accusations of inordinate vanity or unseemly public ambition. However, many permitted artists or printsellers to perform the dirty deed, or they commissioned a print, distributed the images among their friends, and cancelled the plate to prevent further (presumably profit-oriented) publication (Penny 1986: 190, 230). Portrait prints could and did bring prestige, employment, and social advantage, but they rarely earned any of the interested parties much immediate income. Serious speculation on the scale associated with history painting occurred primarily with celebrity portraits, where the private interests of artist, sitter, entrepreneur, and audience all happily coincided.

Nor did portraits make great splashes at public sale. Their commemorative and affective purposes made them difficult to part with, and most lost whatever value or interest they might retain over time when they were removed from their specific social context. Consequently they rarely fetched much money. They also endured in the home because they could be adjusted to changes in the style of interior decoration with relatively greater ease than history paintings (whose complex compositions resisted alteration). Old family portraits were less apt to be sold than rearranged on the walls, cut down, enlarged, reframed, and labeled with the name of the sitter for the benefit of future generations. Most became associated with a family house, furniture, and heir-looms, passing from one owner to another by inheritance rather than sale. In such a context, the identity of the subject took precedence over that of the artist, which was apt to be confused or forgotten, further reducing the chances that the image would be sold speculatively.

In eighteenth-century Britain, the competing roles and hierarchical positions assigned to the two genres by academic theory and the art market contrived to make history painting morally and economically dangerous, and portraiture respectable and safe. There are few indications that the British public found the situation disturbing. Change – principally the elevation of history painting within the market hierarchy (and consequently the moral one) of the consuming public – therefore became the responsibility of artists and a small circle of critics and connoisseurs. Artists' and connoisseurs' efforts to form or re-form their public are well documented and well known.[9] (The question of whether or not a public for art existed at all in Britain before about 1720 is still an open one. I would hazard a guess that for most forms of painting except history a large but not especially distinguished public had existed since the Restoration.[10])

Theoretical treatises from Shaftesbury to Reynolds insisted on the primacy of historical, literary, and even – apologetically – religious subject-matter, and the founding of the Royal Academy institutionalized this academic doctrine. Every effort was made to eliminate speculative involvement in history painting and maximize its exposure to an elite buying public. The Academy promulgated the theory of history painting in its presidents' discourses; it discouraged speculative exhibitions within its own walls and elsewhere; and it sought financial security for its members by maintaining a pension fund. Printsellers and engravers were excluded from full membership and entrance fees charged for the annual exhibitions reduced the attendance of undesirables. The short-term effects of these policies were, of course, disastrous. Far from creating a new public for art, they seemed instead to redefine within dangerously narrow limits a broad-based audience that already existed. The elite public posited by theory and sought by the Academy, if it existed at all, was slow or largely unwilling to assert leadership in the market. Consequently, the Academy's attack on speculation made history painting riskier than ever. After 1768 history painters faced an unattractive choice between financial disaster or professional ostracism. Outraged engravers and printsellers accused the academicians of seeking monopoly control, dropping the history painters' moral position to a new low. The entrepreneurs' efforts to set up competing operations were remarkably successful.

More important in the short run were painters' pragmatic attempts to reform their product to accommodate both the interests of private patrons and the dictates of their own genius. Reynolds's portraits in the grand style are the best-known case of an expansion of the genre to meet the new pretensions. "Fancy portraits" also extended it into new realms of meaning. The flowering of group portraiture in general during the era may have occurred because of artists' new-found willingness to attempt elaborate, multi-figure, and in some cases allegorical compositions resembling histories in all but name. The fact that such portraits were commissioned, and each figure was paid for (not the case in history painting), made the risks of the task measurably easier to accept. From both the patron's and the painter's point of view, these expansions of the portrait genre beyond the usual limitations of the single likeness offered the most conservative route to higher ambition.

At the riskier end of the trade, history painters profited by borrowing some of the important attributes of portraiture. Many of the most successful history paintings included portraits of living persons and might almost be considered to be elaborate individual or group portraits. Copley's *Watson and the Shark* (Plate 5.1) and West's *Death of General Wolfe* were early and important examples of this merging of the genres, which gave rise to that peculiarly British invention, history painting in modern dress.[11] One might term these paintings "action portraits" with equal justification. With *Watson and the Shark*, history and portraiture merged with inspiring inventiveness. The work was commissioned by Watson himself – as a portrait might have been – and it commemorated an event in his life, in this case his rescue from a shark attack in the harbor of Havana – as a portrait might have done. Successfully exhibited at the Royal Academy, it remained in the sitter's possession until his death, when it was bequeathed to the Royal Hospital as an instance of private virtue and public service.

The commemorative aspects of portraiture come to the fore in these modern-dress subjects. The deaths of some heroes, Wolfe, Chatham, Peirson, Nelson, and the victories of others, Duncan and Rooke, seemed tailor-made for historical compositions designed to include the usual commemorative likenesses. In the case of the *Death of General Wolfe*, the portrait of an expiring secular hero replaces the crucified Christ in a traditional Lamentation composition. Painted speculatively like the celebrity portraits and pure history paintings from which they depended, these monuments to public celebrities often found private buyers as well as an enthusiastic audience for reproductive prints, provided they appeared within public memory of the personages and events they celebrated. Moreover, if the artist could persuade the event's participants to pose for his composition, he often earned related portrait commissions or a reputation as a portraitist on the side.

Given these developments, tailoring the subject to suit the patron – unavoidable in portraiture – began to happen with increasing frequency in pure history paintings. The artist might be anticipating public response, as in the cases of the big commemorative subjects, or gratifying the private wishes of a commissioning patron. Joseph Wright, for example, sought subjects of historic or national significance that would appeal to the particular interests of his Midlands clients. Echoes of the commemorative aspects of portraiture are also discernible. For the potter Josiah Wedgwood, Wright painted the famous *Corinthian Maid* commemorating the discovery of modeling and the legendary antique origins of Wedgwood's industry (Plate 5.4). Its pendant of *Penelope Unravelling Her Web*, showing the wife of Odysseus undoing her work on the shroud of her father-in-law, complements the *Maid* with its reference to spinning (the other important Midlands industry) and its theme of feminine loyalty to absent men (Plate 5.5). Significantly, each woman is engaged in the production of a commemorative object, and the Maid's is a portrait. Themes of industry, national pride (the rebirth of the arts on British soil), and domestic virtue dominate these two popular images that influenced later allegorical images of Britannia (Plate 5.6). Wright's emphasis on female-oriented subject-matter may reflect an attempt to adjust history painting to the tastes and interests of women, increasingly prominent as students and patrons of art.[12] They must also have exerted considerable influence in more vaguely defined roles as tastemakers. His alterations of both the *Corinthian Maid* and *Penelope* to meet the demands of female modesty indicate the importance attached to this segment of the domestic audience by Wedgwood at least (who was among the first of Britain's entrepreneurs to successfully cultivate that market).

Wright also altered his production methods. Most of his histories destined for private sale are relatively small, corresponding in size to his small full-length or standard three-quarter-length (50 × 40 ins.) portraits. They fit well into decorative schemes and standard-size frames. The number of figures is reduced and their interactions simplified to streamline and cheapen the design and execution phases of his project. In some cases Wright reduced his literary subjects to single figures – portraits – in paintings such as *Edwin, from Dr. Beattie's Minstrel* and *Maria, from Sterne, a Companion to the Picture of Edwin*. Such reductions in scale, complexity, and grandeur of subject did much to improve the marketability of history, which, at the lower end of the scale, flirted dangerously with genre and book illustration.

By favoring themes drawn from national history, current events, and English literature, history painters enhanced their works' accessibility and acceptability to the general public. Unblemished by the taint of absolutism or Roman Catholicism, scenes from Chaucer, Shakespeare, Pope, Sterne, historical chronicles, and the daily press competed successfully with old master subjects for the attention of serious collectors and house furnishers. By 1800 history painting had become a viable profession for artists and relatively uncontroversial for consumers. However, the lightweight productions of Smirke, Westall, and Stothard, set against the frustrations of Fuseli and Blake, illustrate how far the genre had to fall in order to triumph in the portrait-dominated market. History painting was rescued from its predicament less by formation of a new public than by redefinition of its "traditional" capitalist supporters. Nineteenth-century associations between private enterprise and public benefit ended the conflicts between market and theory that had bedevilled the history painters of the eighteenth century. By the middle of the nineteenth century extensive patronage from great industrialists and entrepreneurs for serious historical painting could be perceived publicly as a sign of the genre's true ascendancy. The traditional merging of interests of the ambitious painter and the public-minded patron was finally achieved.

Notes

This chapter originated as a contribution to the workshop on "Consumption and the Formation of a Public" organized by the UCLA Center for 17th- and 18th-Century Studies as part of a series of workshops and lectures on "The Consumption of Culture: Word, Image, and Object in the 17th and 18th Centuries." I am grateful to John Brewer and Ann Bermingham for the opportunity to participate, as well as for their comments and the observations of other participants on the paper itself.

1   For discussion of the possibility of discerning historical meaning in the act of purchasing a commodity, see Campbell (1990).
2   The question of how eighteenth-century artists or public actually understood academic theory has never been carefully addressed. Were the works of de Piles, Shaftesbury, Richardson, and others read closely, and if so, by whom? How important were other sources of theoretical knowledge, such as pamphlets, magazine essays, and biographical dictionaries of artists? At what level of discourse did politics become a factor? André Rouquet observed in c. 1755 that English art patrons argued the merits of their favorite painters as hotly as they debated the characters of their politicians; this association between art and politics is at once simpler and potentially more interesting than the political content or interpretation of theory itself (Rouquet, c. 1755: 42–3).
3   This was true not only in England, but also France, where the decline, indeed crisis, of patronage for history painting has been documented by Crow (1985).
4   Prown (1966: II, 345–6). Prown ascribes the painting's failure with the public to its "pedantic nature," and it is certainly one of Copley's less appealing works in the historical genre. Nevertheless, its subject cannot have increased its attractiveness to the public.
5   For example, among Arthur Pond's female patrons (19 percent of all patrons), more than 60 percent bought portraits, and less than 20 percent provided repeat business (Lippincott 1983: 66–8).
6   For example, Thomas Birch, *The Heads of Illustrious Persons of Great Britain, engraven by Mr. Houbraken, and Mr. Vertue with their Lives and characters* (1743).
7   Thus when we consider eighteenth-century images of public-spirited virtue, Hogarth's *Captain Coram* comes immediately to mind; history paintings do not. Even theatrical portraits played these roles (West 1991: 225–49).
8   Lorna Weatherill has suggested that middle-ranking people in England spent their surplus resources upgrading and expanding their holdings of objects for routine use instead of

making isolated conspicuous expenditures on large-scale purchases (Weatherill 1988: 64–5, 111). If such is the case, the regulated and moderate prices of portraits relative to history paintings would make the former the obvious economic choice, as well as the obvious cultural one.

9   Lipking (1970); Barrell (1986: *passim*). British art theory, especially as expressed in Reynolds's discourses, is notoriously inconsistent. These inconsistencies have been explained in terms of the theorist's intellectual development, or attempts to speak to a changing audience. It is not yet clear to what extent the topics and issues addressed by Reynolds in particular might have been determined or influenced by current events in the London art world. While the *Discourses* stand as an important work of literature and theory, it must not be forgotten that they formed only part of Reynolds's (and the Academy's) broader, active program of aesthetic, social, and market reform. To what extent did Reynolds value pragmatic, reform-oriented goals in relation to theoretical consistency? Can the *Discourses*, however variable in themselves, be subsumed within a larger institutional effort to effect change?

10 For work on the problem to date, see Pears (1988) and Lippincott (1983: 55–75). See Lippincott (1990) for the possibility of different types of audiences for history and other forms of painting. Weatherill (1988) indicates that a taste for "pictures" (including maps, prints, portraits, broadsides, etc.) was established in middle-class London households by 1715 and was expanding rapidly into the provinces a decade later (p. 31).

11 The term was first used by Edgar Wind, in "The revolution of history painting," *Journal of the Warburg Institute* 2 (1938–9): 116–27.

12 I am indebted to Ann Bermingham's discussion of women, drawing, Wright of Derby, and the arts (especially in Bermingham 1992).

Bibliography

Barrell, J. (1986) *The Political Theory of Painting from Reynolds to Hazlitt: "The Body of the Public"*, New Haven, CT and London: Yale University Press.

Bennett, S. M. (1992) "A Muse of Art in the Huntington Collection," in Guilland Sutherland (ed.) *British Art 1740–1820 Essays in Honor of Robert R. Wark*, San Marino, CA: The Huntington, pp. 57–80.

Bermingham, A. (1992) "The origin of painting and the end of art: Wright of Derby's *Corinthian Maid*," in John Barrell (ed.) *Painting and the Politics of Culture*, Oxford: Oxford University Press, pp. 135–66.

Birch, T. (1743) *The Heads of Illustrious Persons of Great Britain, engraven by Mr. Houbraken, and Mr. Vertue, with their Lives and characters*, London: John and Paul Knapton.

Bruntjen, S. (1985) *John Boydell, 1719–1804. A Study of Art Patronage and Publishing in Georgian London*, New York and London: Garland Publishing.

Campbell, C. (1990) "Character and consumption: an historical action theory approach to the understanding of consumer behaviour," *Culture and History* 7: 37–48.

Crow, T. (1985) *Painters and Public Life in Eighteenth-Century Paris*, New Haven, CT and London: Yale University Press.

Douglas, M. and Isherwood, B. (1979) *The World of Goods: Towards an Anthropology of Consumption*, New York: Basic Books.

Hyde, L. (1983) *The Gift. Imagination and the Erotic Life of Property*, New York: Random House.

Lipking, L. (1970) *The Ordering of the Arts in Eighteenth-Century England*, Princeton, NJ: Princeton University Press.

Lippincott, L. (1983) *Selling Art in Georgian London: The Rise of Arthur Pond*, New Haven, CT and London: Yale University Press.

—— (1987) "John Boydell, printseller and patron," *Blake Quarterly* 21, 1: 44–6.

—— (1990) Review of Pears (1988), *Burlington Magazine* 132: 580.

Pears, I. (1988) *The Discovery of Painting. The Growth of Interest in the Arts in England 1680–1768*, New Haven, CT and London: Yale University Press.

Penny, N. (ed.) (1986) *Reynolds*, London: Royal Academy of Arts.

Pointon, M. (1984) "Portrait painting as a business enterprise in London in the 1780s," *Art History* 7, 2: 187–205.

Prown, J. (1966) *John Singleton Copley*, 2 vols., Cambridge, MA: Harvard University Press.

Pye, J. (1845) *The Patronage of British Art*, London: Longman, Brown, Green, & Longman.

Rouquet, A. (*c*. 1755) *The Present State of the Arts in England*, London; reprinted (1970) London: Cornmarket Press.

Scholl, S. (1984) *Death and the Humanities*, Lewisburg, PA: Bucknell University Press.

Sekora, J. (1977) *Luxury: The Concept in Western Thought, Eden to Smollett*, Baltimore, MD and London: Johns Hopkins University Press.

von Erffa, H. and Staley, A. (1986) *The Paintings of Benjamin West*, New Haven, CT and London: Yale University Press.

Weatherill, L. (1988) *Consumer Behaviour and Material Culture in Britain 1660–1760*, London and New York: Routledge.

West, S. (1991) "Thomas Lawrence's 'half-history' portraits and the politics of theatre," *Art History* 14, 2: 225–49.

Wind, E. (1938–9) "The revolution of history painting," *Journal of the Warburg Institute* 2: 116–27.

6
The abandoned hero
The decline of state authority in the direction of French painting as seen in the career of one exemplary theme, 1777–89

Thomas Crow

Over the decade or so preceding the outbreak of the French Revolution, state activity in funding large-scale, public works of art underwent a dramatic increase in intensity. With the accession of Louis XVI in 1774 came a new chief administrator of the arts who was determined to make an immediate mark on what had been for some time a neglected area of official cultural policy. From 1777 forward, each of the great public Salon exhibitions in the Louvre would be provided with a substantial number of grand narrative paintings on morally elevated themes. It was a conscious and ambitious effort to match the standard of patronage associated with the reign of Louis XIV and the cultural policies of Colbert.

This dramatic revival also had an immediate effect on smaller works which were not produced to any official commission but were conceived with an eye to attracting such support. It was in this artistic penumbra of state initiatives that one of the dominant themes of pre-Revolutionary art was first established. The theme in question was the virtuous and persecuted exile, and initially it was embodied in representations of the blind Belisarius. In 1767 Jean-François Marmontel had published his novel *Bélisaire*, in which the deposed commander of Justinian's armies assumes the voice of a perfected Enlightenment thinker and exemplary public servant (Marmontel 1968: III). Despite the emperor's having charged him, falsely, with treason and ordered that he be blinded and dispossessed, Belisarius remains loyal to the interests of his sovereign and the state. In lengthy monologues, Marmontel's character denounces the social evils that his creator believed were eroding the vitality of the French monarchy: official religious intolerance, a parasitical nobility, the reign of luxury over civic virtue, and the domination of favoritism over merit. Eventually the sanity of his message induces the mighty again to seek out his counsel: Justinian comes in secret, in the company of his heir-apparent Tiberius, to listen to his ever-faithful general, who can no longer see him.

It was a series of contingent political events that put the image of Belisarius at the center of official art patronage in France. D'Angiviller had assumed office as friend and ally to the Minister of Finance and head of government, A.-R.-J. Turgot. Their common outlook had led both to come to the defense of Marmontel's *Bélisaire* when its advocacy of religious toleration had brought on censure by the clerics of the Sorbonne (Renwick 1974: *passim*). Once in office, both famously embarked on reformist programs: the latter to introduce a new rationality to the economy and administration of the state; the former to create a systematic program to encourage the celebration of civic virtue in historical painting. Turgot's attempt to apply principles of economic science to the grain trade produced inflation and shortages, which in turn provoked violent resistance that quickly forced him from office. In the view of his supporters, the new arts director among them, intriguers at court and in the Parlement of Paris had taken scandalous advantage of the ignorance of the mobs to disgrace France's best hope for enlightened leadership.

D'Angiviller did not, however, follow Turgot into exile from power. His responsibilities were minor by comparison, and he had the advantage of a long and close relationship with the young monarch (he had once been responsible for supervising the education of the royal grandchildren, the future Louis XVI among them). François–André Vincent was the first of an ambitious new generation of painters to sense the special resonance that Marmontel's hero would possess for d'Angiviller, who was balancing his competing loyalties to the king and to his deposed friend and ally. For the public Salon exhibition of 1777, he produced a canvas (Plate 6.1) on the theme of the blind Belisarius, reduced to begging, as he is recognized by a soldier who had once served under him. To underscore the theme of tutelary wisdom, Vincent painted a pendant picture on the theme of Socrates admonishing Alcibiades (Plate 6.2). Two of the artist's principal rivals for official approval and public acclaim, Pierre Peyron and Jacques-Louis David, followed suit with Belisarius paintings, the former in 1779 (Plate 6.3), the latter in 1781 (Plate 6.4).

Their iconography of Belisarius centers on his legendary humbling to the condition of helpless and homeless wanderer. From preparatory studies to final paintings, one can observe a steady weakening of the figure in terms of its physical and emotional forcefulness (Crow 1985: 198–209). It was, after all, important that Belisarius not be taken as the focus of antagonistic revenge against the ruling order, however unjust its treatment of him. He is shown to be equally ignored by a fickle urban populace; only among obedient peasants (Peyron's version) does he find any comfort. This exile must be taken as an object of pity and sentimental regret, his misery and its contrast with an exalted former state constituting a mute appeal for a renewal of lapsed royal benevolence – and nothing more incendiary. Peyron's version was commissioned by the French ambassador to the Vatican, himself a cardinal (Rosenberg and van de Sandt 1983: 290); d'Angiviller for his part was so impressed with David's large-scale rendition of the theme that he commissioned a smaller copy of the canvas for his personal collection (Michel 1983: 161–6).

For all of its initial vitality, this was nevertheless a self-limiting iconographic program, based as it was on the flattery of a small group of state functionaries, salving their loss of power in symbols of rejected virtue. By 1783, two years after David's *Belisarius* had given him his first public success, official direction of subject-matter virtually ended. Vocal critics in the press had begun decrying dictated themes for painters as a despotic violation of the necessary liberty of the arts. D'Angiviller seems to have lost the energy to resist both royal indifference and journalistic hostility to his leadership. State support for large historical canvases went on as before, but he ceased any effort to impose coherent direction from above (Jobert 1981: 7–8).

Nevertheless both the cash and the spirit of moral improvement that d'Angiviller had brought to the production of ambitious narrative painting permanently changed the conditions of art-making and the perceived nature of the artist's vocation. The studio of David in particular quickly constructed itself into a kind of ideal artistic republic, one in which even higher standards of virtue and public-mindedness would prevail. The undiminished monetary support from the state freed David from dependence on private commissions. That crucial appearance of disinterestedness, more than its more limited reality, gave him the opportunity to seize the leadership recently ceded by d'Angiviller. The artist's admirers, and the students who joined his studio, believed that the way was open for a modern French painter to act as had the artists of the Greeks, who (so it was argued) were granted creative liberty and thus were inspired to express the ideals of their communities in perfected physical form.

This new *élan* and communitarian ethic, however, ultimately had the effect of reinstating the figure of the dejected or defiant outcast, rejected by his fellows, at the heart of ambitious French painting. That development was generated out of the never-ending tension between egalitarian and hierarchical practices in the life of the studio: the exile becoming the very emblem of this conflict.

One telling anecdote can serve as an opening illustration. A young student of irregular background named Philippe-Auguste Hennequin had been among the very first to opt for David's camp. Slight and youthful in appearance, he arrived in time to serve, by his account, as the model for the begging boy between the extended arms of Belisarius (Hennequin 1933: 57). To the degree that this honor betokened special closeness to the master, Hennequin was the object of two kinds of revenge, one symbolic and one quite painfully real, at the hands of his colleagues. The 19-year-old Jean Germain Drouais joined the studio in the following year and promptly put his precocious talent to work on a painting of the *Prodigal Son*, embraced by a Belisarius-like father, whose welcome prompts the jealousy of brothers whose loyalty was longer-established (Plate 6.5). Drouais's advanced technical and conceptual skills, amply in evidence in this demanding, multi-figured composition, were beyond those of Hennequin and the rest of the pupils. If there is a note of triumph in the painting, the rapid elimination of his rival had borne it out. Hennequin had already been forced from the studio, the apparent victim of a malicious trick by another student, Jean-Baptiste Wicar, whereby David came to believe him guilty of theft (Hennequin 1933: 58 ff.; Beaucamp 1939: 40–1).

In the years prior to 1785, Drouais, more than his master, cast himself as the reincarnation of antique virtue in the arts. The death in 1775 of his father, the wealthy society portraitist François-Hubert Drouais, had thrust him into a precocious independence that took him far beyond his comfortable family milieu. With his exceptional freedom and fortune, he chose to fashion an ascetic life in which privilege counted as little as possible (Suard 1806: 273–84). Though he was blessed, witnesses tell us, with wealth, good looks, musical talent, and social magnetism, he rejected all their benefits for a ceaseless devotion to his art: "I will be a painter, and I will need all of my life to become one" was his reported credo (Anonymous 1788).

The extremism of that devotion demanded that he make himself a voluntary outcast from the society that had given him access to his vocation. He neglected his health by working beyond normal endurance, painting all day and drawing into the night. To evade the intervention of his worried family, he hid in his studio, answering the door only at a prearranged knock to receive his frugal meals. Once, when prevailed upon by friends to go out in fashionable society, he is said to have dressed with greater elegance than was his normal habit. But on taking one last look in the mirror, he calmly took up scissors and cut away the curls "which the wigmaker had fashioned with so much skill." Thus crippled socially, he could return to his habitual simple dress and to his work with no further distractions (Anonymous 1788). This mutilation of the social self to enforce dedication to painting is something one more readily associates with a legend concerning Géricault more than thirty years later, who was imagined to have shaved his head during his work on the *Raft of the Medusa* in order to make himself similarly unacceptable in society (Chenique 1991: 281–2). But Drouais's priority here indicates that there was nothing necessarily "romantic" about that gesture: in the context of the particular ideological pressures faced by ambitious young artists in the 1780s, such a gesture would have made sense as a conspicuous refusal of privilege and favoritism. In his first competition for the *Grand Prix de Rome* in 1783, he exhibited the same kind of coldly destructive fury on behalf of an ideal. When his entry, on the subject of *The Resurrection of the Son of the Widow of Naim* (Musée Tessé, Le Mans), disappointed him, he sliced into the canvas and brought the torn pieces to David (David 1973: 157).

Drouais's formation occurred during a period when the example of Greece and Rome – above all, Greece – had become significantly more compelling for him than it had been for his master. There was a degree of intensity in the veneration of the ancients that had been unknown a decade before. David, as we learn from his well-known autobiographical statements, had yet to fall under the spell of the antique before his first sojourn in Rome (David 1973: 157). There ought to be no surprise in this, in that during the early 1770s the spell was weaker than we sometimes imagine. The rigorous and chastened vision of antiquity advanced by Winckelmann had not immediately taken hold in France. It did not achieve its strongest force until the 1780s when it ceased to be a matter of antiquarian or aesthetic interest alone.[1] Imitation of the ancients came to be understood – in a way that is true to the spirit of Winckelmann's text – to mean emulation of a whole way of life, one in which the artist was a selfless representative of a democratic and egalitarian society (Winckelmann 1781: II, 15–20). The perfection of ancient sculpture was a small window left to us through which a lost, better form of community might be glimpsed. The object of imitation was not cold marble alone, it was the liberated imagination and social conscience deposited in the marble (Carmontelle 1781: 36; Anonymous 1782: 66–7: Anonymous 1787: 14–15).

The sharpened distinction between Greece and Rome, which had been advanced most authoritatively by Winckelmann, was used in this period to link social hierarchy and artistic decline. The decadence of Roman painting, the German antiquarian had argued, followed from the employment of liberated slaves as artists (Winckelmann 1781: II, 342). Servitude was the enemy of artistic achievement; once acquired, servile and ignoble habits could not be shed. In modern times, the despotic hierarchy of the official art system, along with the degenerate taste of private patrons, meant that the great majority of artists were blocked from the education and economic independence necessary to emulate the free-born ancients (Anonymous 1782: 66–7: Anonymous 1787: 14–15). If that were not enough, the artisan-class background of most recruits to the profession, their early apprenticeship and arrested formal education, left even the best-intentioned without the requisite inner resources to match the Greeks and provide stirring models of virtue for their fellow citizens.

The rise of this line of thinking led to two linked and self-cancelling conclusions: independence from patronage and favoritism was 1) an essential prerequisite to great artistic achievement and 2) a nearly impossible goal in modern society – that is, until the Davidians changed the rules. And in terms of the charged mythology of antique art, Drouais was the most fascinating figure among them. His image was mediated by French classicism far less than was David's; his very being seemed at one with Raphael and the exemplary artists of ancient Greece.

The challenge to established authority contained in Drouais's growing personal myth surfaced forcefully in the events surrounding the competition for the *Grand Prix de Rome* in 1784. The events of the exhibition and judgment of the entries were reported with unusual interest by the reporter for the clandestine journal *Les Mémoires secrets*. In a report written prior to the announcement of the results, he singled out Drouais's painting (*Christ and the Canaanite Woman*, Plate 6. 6) for extraordinary praise as "above all competition." The artist, as the journalist went on to enthuse,

> is only 20 years old. He already enjoys an independent fortune of 20,000 *livres* per year and so he works only for his talent and for the love of glory. This noble spur along with the great gifts with which nature has endowed him will take him a very long way indeed.[2]

The stress on Drouais's inherited wealth and social position indicates that more was at stake here than precocious technical competence. Because of his freedom from any need for official favor or private patronage, Drouais was free to work, as the ancient Greeks had done, for *la gloire* alone. This was the condition both for his artistic superiority and a tense separation from the normal channels of encouragement. In the midst of his praise of Drouais, this writer pauses to state that the director and *les anciens* were opposed to him. When this statement proved wrong the very next day, the desire on the part of Drouais's admirers that he be a martyr to official disfavor only intensified. It was widely reported in the press that his victory in the competition prompted the audacious proposal from the floor that he be made an *agréé* of the Academy on the spot, in advance of his training in Rome and without the formal presentation of a *morceau d'agrément* (Michel 1981: 201). Entirely predictably, the proposal was dismissed, which allowed one journalist later to lament: "They appealed to rules and customs; they failed, by a servile submission to these customs, to these rules, to provide a great example to artists and a great object of emulation to students."[3]

This outrage might seem misplaced when one considers that its beneficiary was just over 20 years old and probably had only two completed canvases to his credit – both set subjects from the Bible. A *Grand Prix* for a young artist normally affirmed the institutional framework that made his achievement possible; Drouais's was constructed in the press as a victory over the system. The exemplary qualities to be found in art were now seen to belong to the painter as much as (and in Drouais's case more than) to what he painted. Though the critic tries to make an indisputable case for the painting, the *émulation* that Drouais offered his contemporaries proceeded primarily from his person, from the gifts of fortune that underwrote his talent. And these gifts, the conditions of his virtue, meant that antagonism and misunderstanding would be his lot.

Drouais had been marked as an exception, by himself and by his admirers, in a state system that placed a premium on conformity and obedience. Being distant from Paris did not in fact weaken the reach of administrative control from Paris; it rather intensified and concentrated the application of discipline to be resisted. The Paris Salons with their heavily subsidized displays of history painting were the public side of d'Angiviller's reforms; its internal force was directed most of all towards the prize-winners housed in the Palazzo Mancini in Rome. On his accession to office, d'Angiviller quickly came to believe that discipline and order in the Rome Academy had declined to a shocking level, and he dispatched Joseph–Marie Vien to Rome as the new director in 1775 with a mandate to clean house. The two of them issued a detailed set of regulations that sought to control the studies and the personal lives of the students to the maximum degree possible (Montaiglon and Guiffrey 1887–1912: XIII, 158). Every minute of the day was accounted for: students were to rise at five in the morning, attend prayer "with attention and modesty required," and descend at six for the day's two-hour session with the live model. After breakfast, there were courses in anatomy and perspective, with the possibility of copying elsewhere in Rome – though wandering far was curtailed by required attendance at the midday meal. The rest of the day was similarly parceled out, with bed-check at ten in winter and eleven in summer. Along with this control over time and movement, extreme plainness of dress was ordained. Indeed the royal funds to which d'Angiviller insisted the students be limited would not permit much more.

Even before Drouais succeeded in winning the *Grand Prix de Rome*, both master and pupil had signalled their intention to evade this regime. David was determined to preempt the supervisory role of the Academy's director in Rome by accompanying his pupil and remaining with him for the first year (David 1983: 174). The two had already arranged for their travel to Italy before the results were announced and effectively declared themselves independent of the state by financing the journey from their own resources (Anonymous 1791: 56). Once there, they worked closely together to complete the *Oath of the Horatii between the Hands of Their Father* (Plate 6.7), the painting that would secure David's preeminence among the artists of his generation, not only in France but in the rest of Europe as well (Péron 1838: 33 ff.). This kept Drouais away from the Academy for protracted periods.

Shortly after David's return to Paris in the latter part of 1785, the director of the Rome Academy, Lagrenée the elder, wrote to Paris in frustration that the young artist would not submit his work to academic supervision or account for his time (Montaiglon and Guiffrey 1887–1912: XV, 50). When faced with the next standard requirement, that he do his old master copy for the king, he once again defied his official masters. Lagrenée made the following report to Paris:

> Drouais asks if, in place of the copy that he is required to make for the king's collection, you wish that he do an original picture, which would belong to the

king and which would represent all of the fruits of his studies in Rome, because he swears to me that he had never copied in his life and that it was a martyrdom for him to copy anything but nature.[4]

The Rome director passed the request along with guarded sympathy, noting also the general discontent among the students for both requirements: "it is not always those who make the most beautiful academic studies," he observed in grudging agreement, "who afterwards make the most beautiful paintings."[5]

D'Angiviller, however, was having none of it; discipline would prevail:

> We cannot observe without distress that the youth of today, more confident than ever, seem to announce that it is better informed about the means of acquiring talent than were the most celebrated men who have come before. . . . These gentlemen must persuade themselves that they are not the masters, that, far from being fit to try their own wings, they still need to study and that they can follow no better course, despite their repugnance, than to follow the rules which have been laid down for good reason. If some among them find it too exacting to conform, they can master the art of leaving the Academy. I will find it easy to replace them.[6]

Drouais's bravado had in recent weeks troubled the Director-General in other ways. He had stepped in, though unarmed, to rescue one of the Academy's servants from two attackers with knives (J.-L.-J. David 1880: 38–40). The servant went away unharmed, and one of the attackers was arrested. Threats from the family of the arrested man, however, led to serious fears for Drouais's well-being, and the artist himself carried pistols for some weeks. This courting of physical danger was accompanied by a heedless abuse of his body through lack of rest and general neglect of his health – no light matter in as pestilential an environment as eighteenth-century Rome. The pursuit of perfection in painting was bound up with putting oneself at risk – from authority, from injury, and from disease.

On account of this tendency to extreme personal witnessing of virtue, Drouais came to represent, for his master as well as for the world, an exemplary integration of art and life. In this light, one senses more than ever the depth of David's famous lament after the death of his pupil from smallpox in 1788: "I have lost my emulation" (*Mercure de France*: 40). David, during this time, was playing a waiting game, enjoying a life in fashionable society, and avoiding any insistence on the hard line in virtue. But Drouais had already begun to construct an identity that would reproduce the zeal of the young Horatii. Though he was passionately devoted to his master, who was plainly his anchor in a fatherless world, the renown he had gained was not purely a matter of reflected glory. But virtue, however relentlessly pursued, was never going to be a substitute for tested experience. David's triumph in 1785 would mean that an enlightened transformation of artistic practice no longer remained in the realm of abstract possibility. Drouais was left behind in Rome to ponder his future while David returned to Paris with the *Horatii* rolled and ready. No one foresaw its impact more clearly than the bereft pupil. It was more a challenge to him than it was to the complacent history painters of Paris. Lest his identity collapse, he was virtually compelled to match it in practice – and at some level surpass it.

The subject of his grandly scaled canvas, *Marius at Minturnae* (Plate 6.8), was the Roman general and consul Caius Marius, to whose life Plutarch devotes a lengthy account. The finished painting depicts the decisive moment in an episode near the end of that life. Having been proscribed by the Senate, the aged Marius, wandering alone and abandoned, has been captured near the town of Minturnae and placed under arrest. At first, in deference to Rome, the town votes his execution, but, as Plutarch relates,

> No one of the citizens would undertake the task, so a horseman, either a Gaul or a Cimbrian (for the story is told both ways), took a sword and went into the room where Marius was. Now, that part of the room where Marius happened to be lying had not a very good light, but was gloomy, and we are told that to the soldier the eyes of Marius seemed to shoot out a strong flame, and that a loud voice issued from the shadows saying: "Man, dost thou dare to slay Caius Marius?" At once, then, the Barbarian fled from the room.
>
> (Plutarch 1920: 572–3)

Having prevailed at this crucial moment, Marius, as the past savior of Italy on the battlefield, wins the sympathy of the local people and is allowed his freedom.

The painting, out of necessity, had to perpetuate Drouais's existing role as David's purer, uncompromised self. It extended the aesthetic of the *Horatii* – the dialectical sharpness, abrupt transitions, self-aggrandizing utterance, and single-minded stress on pride and inflexibility in the mores of ancient Rome – to a degree that eliminated even David's small allowances for prevailing taste. *Marius* matched the *Horatii* in scale as well as in stylistic rhetoric, the two contending figures being life-sized. A young student in Rome had of course no business undertaking a narrative canvas of this ambition, one clearly intended for the public arena in Paris. He worked in secret, neglecting his obligatory student work in order to throw himself into a project beyond his years and his station.

In thematic terms, Drouais's vehicle for his tribute and answer to the *Horatii* involved a return to David's starting-point, the aged exile from civic life. Like Belisarius, Marius wanders alone and abandoned, an abject figure cast out by the society he had once protected in victorious campaigns against barbarian invaders: at one point he is recognized and given refuge by a farmer who had known him in his former greatness, as is Belisarius in Marmontel's novel (Marmontel 1968; III, 221–5).

Yet this same Marius, in nearly every other respect, is the inversion of this positive patriarch. As vividly characterized in Plutarch, he was a figure motivated by uncontrollable rage, greed, and irrational ambition, whose defects of character helped plunge the Roman republic into terminal civil war. The outcome of his display of inner character at Minturnae is that he raises an army, returns to Rome, and in retribution subjects the population to a reign of indiscriminate executions (and he is so depicted in a forceful drawing, probably from the early 1790s, by another of David's pupils, François Gérard [Louvre, Paris]). His revenge, however, brings him no relief from his constant fears and tortured instability of mind; increasingly anxiety-ridden and delusional, he drinks himself to death.

The strong iconographic parallels with Belisarius only underscore the stark differences between the two Roman generals. Marius is even capable of exaggerating his poverty and dejection in order to deceive his enemies into underestimating his strength. Inflexible nobility of bearing and behavior is utterly foreign to his character. In relation to the *Horatii*, the inversion on the symbolic level is just as complete. The power and civic authority of the older male no longer pass to the youth who stands in the position of the sons of Horatius. Instead, that force paralyzes the younger man and stops his performing a legal duty that would have prevented future atrocities and enormous suffering for the city of Rome.

To reverse the significance of David's example in this way was no easy task for Drouais, and the development of the painting reveals a painful awareness of its inherent contradictions. An earlier drawing of the complete composition depicts Marius as a well-favored, bearded elder, very like the old Horatius in appearance and expression (Plate 6.9). So does the sheet containing individual studies of both figures – presumably the culmination of a series of experiments – on which David wrote, "Ne changez rien. Voilà le bon" (Plate 6.10). But the oil sketch and a compositional drawing squared for transfer (Plate 6.11) show a strikingly different face, stripped of the beard with its connotations of paternal venerability, revealed as distorted and ugly to the point of bestiality. This face, in its extreme vehemence, comes close to caricature, but it is truer to the narrative than the stern but handsome countenance that, in a last reversal, Drouais restores on the canvas. That other face, it seems, could not coexist with the formal order of the *Horatii*.

The positive transformation of Marius's features allows Drouais to recognize and express a devotion that overcomes the fear and rivalry in their situation, the darker side of which emerged in the rejected studies. But at the same time the fear and rivalry will not stay suppressed. They are figured most of all in the cloak with which the young Cimbrian shields his face. That gesture was not present in the first study; it enters the compositional process as a barrier against the monstrous Marius, but remains when the face of the hero reverts to the canon of nobility. And Drouais uses it to turn his painting diametrically against its model in the *Horatii*. David's heroes are engaged in rapt attention to the tense point of contact between them. The vision of the spectator is vicariously engaged with the same intensity. But when that same spectator puts himself in the place of either protagonist in the *Marius*, the effect is blindness and isolation. Neither actor can see the other. The false face of Marius is one that Drouais refuses to contemplate; he will accept it, even love it, but at the same time puts an abyss, a cancellation of vision, between it and himself. The conflict between generations is affirmed and denied in the same moment.

Writing later to David on his difficulty in finding a new subject, Drouais plainly stated his dilemma:

> I have found many fine ones, but they are all either ones you have planned or ones you have done. On the one hand, I should not and would not honorably take on a subject that you should do, and if I do one that is analogous to one of yours, I will be mocked. . . . Tell me, what should I do? The finest subjects arouse me as much as they do you.[7]

He would, before his death in 1788, offer a resolution to these fears, but not in a multi-figured composition that contended directly with David's example. He would return instead to the genre of the academic nude and to the theme of the outcast, now in the starkest possible terms. The subject he chose was *Philoctetes on Lemnos* (Plate 6.12). That choice provided a complex narrative tradition for a single figure that was likewise in a state of torment. The heart of the story of course is the wound suffered by the warrior Philoctetes as he is sailing with the Greek army to Troy. The bite of a sacred snake is the cause of his injury, and the result is an agonizing wound that will not heal. His endless cries of anguish and the stench of the wound lead his companions, led by Odysseus, to leave him behind on a deserted island. There he is able to survive for ten years because, as the friend of Heracles, he had been given the bow and arrows of the hero, weapons which never miss their target. An old prophecy had foretold that those arrows would be needed to defeat the Trojans. After the death of Achilles, his son Neoptolemos, accompanied by Odysseus, returns to Lemnos to fetch the arrows, with their owner or without him.

Drouais's canvas provides clear tokens of the story's basic elements: the rocky cave on the barren shore where Philoctetes makes his home; the weapons with relief decoration depicting the exploits of Heracles; the dead bird which is both food and the source of a fan to soothe in some small measure the fire of his wound. But the essential drama is drawn into the figure, which is divided internally against itself. The ageing face is modeled after the antique bust then believed to be the portrait of Homer. This choice does several things at once: it evokes the archaic literary source of the Trojan cycle itself and underscores by association the spare, elemental formal quality Drouais is seeking; it uses Homer's blindness as a displacement of Philoctetes's affliction – "In his parch'd eyes the deep sunk tears express poetry / his endless misery, his dire distress," went the epigram of Glaucus on a lost painting of the outcast by Parrhasius (Webb 1760: 162); it is further a visual equivalent for the key moment in the tragedy when the mounting pain, finally overcoming the hero's manful ability to bear it, drives him into a swoon; and it stands finally for age and its inroads on the body as contrasted with the markedly more youthful treatment of the rest of the figure, which bespeaks a vigorous early middle age. The disfigurement of the body is not shown but rather is signaled by inanimate substitutes: the picturesquely rendered wing and unraveling bandage. Drouais, further, crossed the legs of the figure, altering the open sitting position favored in earlier renditions of the hero, such as Antonio Lombardo's Renaissance prototype in relief sculpture (the Victoria and Albert, London) and James Barry's related composition of 1770 in Bologna (Pinacoteca Nazionale). The sculptural association of the resulting pose recalls the quintessentially youthful *Thorn-Puller*, accentuating the division of age within the figure by means of an art-historical coding opposed to that of the *Homer* (Michel 1985: 18). There is an ironic effect in this as well, calling attention to the enormous difference in magnitude between the two injuries and thus, by the inadequacy of the reference, suggesting any comparison with his agony to be impossible.

The pain suffered by Philoctetes is above all the means by which his heroism is made manifest; it consists in accepting endless suffering rather than submitting to a base compromise with a duplicitous and unheroic enemy (as Odysseus appears in the tragedy by Sophocles). But more than this, it is the means by which the heroism of the young protagonist Neoptolemos, having been thrown into question in the middle of the play, is restored at the climax of the action. Witnessing the older man's pain and his admirable bearing of it brings the son of Achilles back to his true nature; the trusting Philoctetes has handed his weapons to Neoptolemos at the point when he is just about to lose consciousness, but in the end, the latter abandons his part in Odysseus' scheme which would despoil the suffering man by deception, and gives them back. Thus it is crucial that Drouais has turned the figure – in contrast to an earlier drawing – to confront the viewer directly. This confrontation with his pain, in which we stand vicariously in the place of Neoptolemos, deepens the meaning of the picture in two ways: one is in its intervention in an aesthetic debate, the other is in its working-through of the inner dilemmas of Drouais's sense of vocation and self.

In the first instance, Drouais is addressing the issue of what it meant to be true to the ancients less through the politicized conception of antique virtue operating in Paris and more through close reflection on his text and its central place in Lessing's critique of Winckelmann (Michel 1985: 17). In *Laocoön*, the former had taken issue with the assumption that the heroes of antique literature must, like their counterparts in the visual arts, maintain a physical composure in the face of even the greatest suffering. Yes, Lessing concedes, in sculpture the essential beauty of the figure will be compromised by any distortion of the features or contortion of the limbs, but he cites Sophocles' *Philoctetes* as his central example of a hero who must manifest suffering to the most extreme degree, to the point that he comes close to abandoning his humanity. He advances a number of arguments for this expressive excess based on good Aristotelian presuppositions, culminating in its crucial function in the recognition and reversal undergone by the younger of the two heroes: "Had Philoctetes been the master of his pain," Lessing states simply, "he would have confirmed Neoptolemos in his subterfuge" (Lessing 1965: 86). Virgil's Laocoön screams as well; the difference between Sophocles' hero and the Laocoön group is not between kinds of heroes but between their proper representation in two different media (Lessing 1965: 74).

Lessing's sophisticated passage of criticism is not simply a dictum about the spheres of the arts; it is bound up with close attention to the tragedy represented. Drouais makes a similar move between the formal and the thematic, each aspect reinforcing the other. There is one instant in the tragedy in which its hero is silent yet aware of his pain at its maximum necessity – when he has surrendered his bow and arrows at the brink of unconsciousness and a temporary refuge from agony. Drouais does not depict the moment literally, but its elements are all in place: Philoctetes for the moment in a pose of monumental calm, his consciousness retreating inward, his weapons out of his grasp.

The painting becomes one of the silence of Philoctetes when that was precisely the point at issue between Winckelmann and Lessing. It advances its own argument about the expressive limits of the visual arts; it counters Lessing in its way by discovering means to recover that noisy hero for visual representation without imposing a restraint upon him that is unnatural for the character. And that solution is one with psychological resonances for the artist as well. Like the *Marius*, it is about the decisive encounter between an imposing older man and a young soldier. Neoptolemos is, while absent from the painting, more of a presence than the Cimbrian assassin had been because 1) he has a history and heroic stature, and 2) he can see; he stands where we do, and his seeing is the condition of our viewing the painting at all – and vice versa. Moreover Neoptolemos, who has lost a remote and furiously martial father whose prowess he cannot match, here finds another whom he can pity and who will pass on the instruments of power to the next generation. At the moment when the weapons of Heracles change hands, Philoctetes addresses him as his child.

As Drouais stood before his Philoctetes, he thus contemplated an exemplary older male whose predicament allowed a younger protagonist scope for choice and action. He had returned full circle to the image of reconciliation present in his precocious *Prodigal Son* of 1782, countering the unassimilable aspects of the story of Marius that had caused him so much indecision and inner conflict: both heroes had been cast out and left to their fate, but where the events at Minturnae restored Marius to murderous revenge, Neoptolemos's part in removing Philoctetes from Lemnos restored the suffering hero to his place in the civilized social order (albeit at Troy's expense) and himself to his father's legacy.

He had sought and largely succeeded in finding a way out of his particular impasse through a deeply meditated engagement with antique texts and the fashioning of pictorial strategies adequate to their complexities of meaning. But such matters did not reenter the public sphere of discourse in the French capital. It is telling that Drouais's last painting would languish in Rome, dismissed as unfinished, when the more obviously energetic yet more problematic *Marius* would make the young painter's reputation in Paris (Goethe 1967: XI, 519). His admirers appeared to see the work of both master and pupil as a relatively undifferentiated corpus of antique virtue, and only the rare antagonistic critics were able to register the moral ambivalences present in it (Anonymous 1791: 57). When the *Marius* was put on display in Paris in February 1787, Thomas Jefferson joined the stream of enthusiastic spectators: "It fixed me like a statue a quarter of an hour, or half an hour," he wrote, "I do not know which, for I lost all ideas of time, even the consciousness of my existence" (Jefferson 1955: XI, 187). The taut, nervous intensity of the painting, which is in part a result of its unresolvable contradictions of meaning, temporarily banished rational reflection from at least one spectator otherwise eminently capable of it.

Public acclaim, it seems, rendered moot any probing questions into the thematic complexity and ambiguity of the work. Questions of history, moral philosophy, and political action that properly belonged to the public sphere of discussion and debate over contemporary art were increasingly becoming matters of importance within a narrowing circle of private reflection and communication between intimates. Drouais's actual circumstances of exile – separation from Paris and the studio that was his home, alienation from the Academy in Rome, longing for the presence of his mentor and *alter ego* – were the matter of his new, unseen painting. Its strength is that, despite these circumstances, it did not retreat into sentimental autobiography. This signalled something larger, a separation of the most advanced historical painting from the active arena of public life which had sustained it over the decade before. The exile of this strain of stoic classicism within French art was to be more or less permanent.[8]

Notes

1   Extracts from Winckelmann's *Gedanken über die Nachahmung des greicheschen Werke in der Melerei und Bildhauerkunst* were available in French translation by 1756; a mediocre translation of *Geschichte der Kunst des Altertums* was published in 1766, to which the author himself publicly

objected. A second and superior translation of the *Geschichte der Kunst des Altertums* appeared in 1781 as *L'Histoire de l'art dans l'Antiquité*, translated by Michel Huber (Leipzig). It received a lengthy, favorable review in the *Mercure de France* (January 11 and January 18, 1783), which included Winckelmann's famous description of the Belvedere Apollo and called attention to Winckelmann's struggles against poverty and his lowly birth. J.-C. Poncelin de la Roche–Tilhac, *Chef-d'oeuvres de l'Antiquité sur les Beaux-Arts* (Paris: 1784), pp. 113–14, contains an almost literal translation of the Belvedere Apollo passage. The second edition of J. J. de Lalande's widely read *Voyage d'un Français en Italie* (Paris: 1786) contained inserted excerpts from Winckelmann's work: once again the description of the Belvedere Apollo along with those of the Antinous and the Belvedere Torso. For a discussion of these texts and a detailed summary of the passage of Winckelmann's works and ideas into the French language in this early period, see Edouard Pommier, "Winckelmann et la vision de l'antiquité dans la France des Lumières et de la Révolution," *Revue de l'Art* 83 (1989): 9–10.

2   *Mémoires secrets* XXVI (August 27, 1784): 199–200:

> Quoique tous ces tableaux soient en général bien fait, un d'eux a paru l'emporter infiniment sur les autres et être au-dessus de toute concurrence. . . . L'auteur de ce tâbleau si vanté et si digne d'être est M. Drouais.
>
> Il n'a que vingt ans, il jouit déjà de 20 mille livres de rentes et ce n'est que par une passion pour son talent et par l'amour de la gloire qu'il travaille. Il ne peut qu'aller très loin avec ce noble aiguillon et les heureuses dispositions dont la nature l'a doué.

3   Mercure de France (June 7, 1788): 38: "On réclame les règles et les usages; on manqua, par une soumission servile à ces usages, à ces règles, à donner un grand exemple aux Artistes, et un grand sujet d'émulation aux Elèves."

4   Montaiglon and Guiffrey, *Correspondance des Directeurs* (September 6, 1786): XV, 101:

> Le s^r *Drouais* demande si, en place de la copie qu'il est obligé de faire pour le Roi, vous voulez qu'il fasse un tableau original, qui apartiendra au Roi et qui serait le fruit de toutes ses études de Rome, car il m'a avoué qu'il n'avait jamais copié de sa vie et que c'etait pour lui une martire que copier toute autre chose que la nature.

5   Ibid.: XV, 100: "ce n'a pas toujours été ceux qui ont fait les plus belles académies qui, ensuite, ont fait les plus belles tableaux."

6   Ibid.: XV, 105–6:

> On ne peut voir sans peine aujourd'hui que la jeunesse, plus confiante que jamais, semble annoncer qu'elle en sait davantage sur les moyens d'acquérir les talents qu'en savaient les hommes les plus célèbres qui l'ont précédé. . . . Ces Messieurs doivent se persuader qu'ils ne sont pas les maîtres, que, loin d'être en état de voler de leurs propres ailes, ils ont encore besoin d'étudier, et qu'ils ne peuvent mieux faire, malgré leur répugnance, que de suivre les règles qui ont été établies avec pleine connaissance de cause. Si, parmi eux, quelques-uns trouvent trop dur de s'y conformer, ils sont les maîtres de quitter l'Académie. Je trouverai facilement moyen de les remplacer.

7   J.-L.-J. David, *Le Peintre Louis David* (1880: 44–5):

> J'en ai trouvé beaucoup de beaux, mais les uns sont des sujets que vous avez faits. D'un côté, je ne dois pas et n'aurais garde pour mon honneur de faire un sujet que vous devez faire, et si j'en fais un qui ait de l'analogie avec ce que vous avez fait, on se moquera de moi. J'avais presque tout à fait composé le moment où les Tarquins viennent visiter Lucrèce, mais je l'ai abondonnée pour cette dernière raison. Dites-moi, que dois-je faire? Les plus beaux sujets, quoique difficiles, me chatouillent autant que vous.

8   The discussion in the present chapter is expanded in T. Crow, *Emulation: Making Artists for Revolutionary France* (New Haven, CT and London: Yale University Press, 1995).

Bibliography

Anonymous (1782) *Sur la Peinture. Ouvrage succinct qui peut éclairer les artistes sur la fin originelle de l'art et aider les citoyens dans l'idée qu'ils doivent se faire de son état actuel en France*, The Hague.

—— (1787) *L'Ami des Artistes au Salon par M. L'A. R.*, Paris.

—— (1788) *Journal de Paris* (April 28, 1788).

—— (1791) *Lettres analitiques, critiques et philosophiques sur les tableaux du Salon*, Paris.

Beaucamp, Fernand (1939) *Le Peintre lillois Jean–Baptiste Wicar (1762–1834) son oeuvre et son temps*, Lille.

[Carmontelle, Louis de] (1781) *La Patte de Velours*, London.

Chenique, Bruno (1991) "Géricault: Une Vie," in Régis Michel and Sylvain Laveissière (eds.) *Géricault*, Paris: Réunion des Musées Nationaux, Vol. I, pp. 281–2.

Crow, Thomas (1985) *Painters and Public Life in Eighteenth-Century Paris*, New Haven, CT and London: Yale University Press.

David, Jacques–Louis (1973) Manuscript autobiography in D. and G. Wildenstein (eds.) *Documents complementaires au catalogue de l'oeuvre de Louis David*, Paris.

—— (1983) Manuscript autobiography in Philippe Bordes, *Le Serment de Jeu de Paume de Jacques–Louis David: Le Peintre, son milieu et son temps de 1789 à 1792*, Paris: Réunion des Musées Nationaux.

David, J.-L.-J. (1880) *Le peintre Louis David, 1748–1825: souvenirs et documents inédits*, Paris.

Goethe, Johann Wolfgang von (1967) *Goethes Werke*, ed. E. von Einem and E. Trunz, Hamburg.

Hennequin, Philippe–Auguste (1933) *Un peintre sous la Révolution et l'Empire: Mémoires de Ph.-A. Hennequin écrits par lui-même*, Paris.

Jefferson, Thomas (1955) *The Papers of Thomas Jefferson*, ed. J. P. Boyd, Princeton, NJ: Princeton University Press.

Jobert, Berthélémy (1987) "The 'Travaux d'encouragement': an aspect of official arts policy in France under Louis XVI," *Oxford Art Journal* 10, 1: 3–14.

Lessing, Gotthold Ephraim (1965) *Laokoon*, ed. D. Reich, Oxford.

Marmontel, Jean–François (1968) *Oeuvres complètes*, Geneva.

Mercure de France (June 7, 1788).

Michel, Régis (1981) "Jean-Germain Drouais et Rome," in Académie de France à Rome, *David et Rome*, Rome: De Lucca.

—— (1983) "David: *Bélisaire*," in Marie-Catherine Sahut and Nathalie Volle, *Diderot et l'Art de Boucher à David*, Paris, Réunion des Musées Nationaux, pp. 161–6.

—— (1985) "Drouais, Rome, David," in Patrick Ramade and Régis Michel, *Jean–Germain Drouais*, Rennes: Musée des Beaux–Arts.

Montaiglon, A. de and Guiffrey, J. J. (1887–1912) *Correspondance des directeurs de l'Académie de France à Rome*, Paris.

Péron, Alexandre (1838) *Examen du Tableau du Serment des Horaces peint par David, suivi d'une Notice historique du tableau, lus à la Société des Beaux–Arts*, Paris.

Plutarch (1920) *Plutarch's Lives*, trans. B. Perrin, London: Loeb Classical Library.

Renwick, John (1974) "Marmontel, Voltaire, and the Bélisaire affair" issue, *Studies in Voltaire and the Eighteenth Century* 121.

Rosenberg, Pierre and van de Sandt, Udolpho (1983) *Pierre Peyron 1744–1814*, Paris: Arthena.

Suard, J.-B.-A. (1806) "Eloge de M. Drouais, élève de l'Académie royale de peinture," in J.-B.-A. Suard, *Mélanges de la littérature*. Vol. III, Paris.

Webb, Daniel (1760) *An Inquiry into the Beauty of Painting*, London.

Winckelmann, Johann–Joachim (1781) *L'histoire de l'art dans l'antiquité*, trans M. Huber, Leipzig.

7

Gombrich and the rise of landscape

W. J. T. Mitchell

The following chapter is part of a larger project called "Imperial landscape" that attempts to theorize the problem of landscape on a global scale. Such a totalizing project is, while highly problematic, not completely unprecedented. Recent work in geography (Jay Appleton's *The Experience of Landscape* [1975], Denis Cosgrove's "The idea of landscape" [1984], Yi–Fu Tuan's *Topophilia* [1974]) and sociology (Dean MacCannell's *The Tourist* [1976]) has taken up this traditional subject with a new comprehensiveness. Within art history, by contrast, the totalizing tradition which runs from Ruskin to Kenneth Clark's *Landscape into Art* (1976) has been supplanted by more narrowly focused studies which tend to remain within national boundaries and examine in detail the economic and social function of landscape painting. The most exciting recent work on landscape in art history has, in my view, developed out of the British Marxist tradition, building on E. P. Thompson, Raymond Williams, and John Berger.[1] John Barrell's *The Dark Side of the Landscape* (1980) and Ann Bermingham's *Landscape and Ideology* (1986) have taken the idealizing and aestheticizing account of British landscape bequeathed to us by Kenneth Clark and the picturesque tradition, and decisively overturned it in favour of a much more detailed, historically nuanced political and ideological critique.[2]

This critique has taught us a great deal about the particular cultural politics of landscape in eighteenth-century England, but at the same time it has not yet moved on to challenge the global theorizing of landscape that remains embedded in the discourse of art history.[3] This chapter is an attempt to do just that. I have argued in "Imperial landscape"[4] that this discourse is built on three main claims: (1) the "westernness" of landscape, its peculiar status as a European invention that contrasts radically (in what is called its "pure form") with representations of nature in non-western cultures; (2) the "modernity" of landscape, as a revolutionary invention that can be precisely located and dated in a specific moment (usually the sixteenth century) and was previously unknown, either in antiquity or the Middle Ages; (3) the "visual-pictorial" essence of landscape as, at one and the same time, a mode of seeing and a mode of painting, a way of perceiving and a way of representing. In its radical form, this permits the claim that not merely landscape *painting*, but the visual perception of landscape, is a revolutionary historical discovery of the European Renaissance that marks, in Ruskin's words, "the simple fact that we are, in some strange way, different from all the great races that existed before us."[5] ("Imperial landscape," in Mitchell 1994).

All three of these postulates depend upon an even more fundamental axiom, that there is something known as "pure landscape," a representation or perception of nature "for its own sake."[6] In art-historical terms, pure landscape is a painting in which natural scenery is depicted with no adulteration of narrative, allegory, drama, or other textual elements; ideally, in its purest form, pure landscape is even free of any human figures that might suggest an interpretable situation, a readable scenario beyond the pure display of natural forms for their own sake.[7] The art-historical account of landscape is a kind of quest-romance in which pure landscape is the grail to be obtained after numerous trials. Paintings are assessed in terms of their place in this quest, and considerable importance is attached to being the "first" instance of pure landscape. The teleology of landscape merges quite readily, it should be obvious, with the teleology of modernism outlined above. The search for pure landscape is finally the same as the search for pure painting, painting whose meaning and value are not located outside the picture, in any text or function the picture might have. Pure landscape, like pure painting, is unreadable as a text, and unusable as a rhetorical or ritual object.

Unlike pure painting, however, pure landscape has a specific role to play in what might be called the "natural history" of modernity. Another way to formulate the postulate of landscape's "visual/pictorial" status is to note the ambiguity of the term "landscape" as a name for a specific genre of painting, on the one hand, and for what might be called a "medium," on the other.

Understood as a medium, landscape clearly transcends painting. The study of landscape as a medium would have to include physical landscaping, gardening, the shaping and interpretation of a "built" (or "found") environment, the favoring of specific sites, natural or artificial, for heightened perceptual attention, the patterns of travel, migration, and settlement in relation to typical or prototypical sites of cultural value. Landscape as a medium is the proper subject, not just of art history, but of geography, anthropology, sociology, and (not least) literary history, in the study not only of writing about landscape, but of landscape as itself a kind of writing.

Understood as a genre, on the other hand, the question of landscape tends to reduce itself to an issue in philology and art history in which all roads lead to the Renaissance. The history of words tells us that a new term entered European languages in the sixteenth century; the history of art provides the reference for this term by tracing the emergence of a new genre of easel painting that emphasizes the importance of natural settings or "backgrounds" to an unprecedented degree. It is this generic form of painted landscape that is the focus of the discourse of modernity, westernness, and visuality I have outlined, a genre which, in a marvel of inversion, manages to install itself as a general model for the whole medium of which it is merely one small part. I label the result of this inversion "imperial landscape," suggesting by that term not only that the genre of landscape painting that emerges in western Europe is deeply involved with the rise of the western empires, but that the conceptual inversion by which a local, regional, or national "genre" is extracted from a globally disseminated medium and inflated into a universal and natural sign is a fundamental gesture in the discourse of imperialism. The crucial moment in the genre-centered account of landscape, in other words, is the moment when the Eurocentric narrative of the "rise of landscape painting" is generalized as a master-narrative for a parallel "rise of landscape" in the world at large.

Two qualifications need to be entered immediately. First, I am not arguing that the art-historical story of the rise of landscape painting is false. The canonical account of the emergence of a new genre of painting emerging in northern Europe in the sixteenth century is, so far as I am able to judge, in line with too many "facts" to be utterly wrong. My critique is aimed at the discourse in which the facts are constituted, in which their meaning and historical significance are extrapolated and universalized. A second qualification: in associating this universalizing process with imperialism, I do not mean to say that landscape painting is simply "caused by," or "complicit with," or a "tool of," imperialism. What I mean to suggest is that imperialism has been the *non-dit* of art-historical accounts of landscape, and that the various economic and aesthetic explanations that have been given for the "rise of landscape" might be put in a new light by consideration of this fact.

My beginning-point, however, is not with a frontal assault on the issue of imperialism, but with an internal critique of what is arguably the most complex and influential art-historical account of landscape as a genre, Ernst Gombrich's "The Renaissance theory of art and the rise of landscape." First published in 1953, this essay has shaped the research of at least three generations of scholarship on the history of landscape painting, and its influence has spread even more widely into landscape research in garden history, sociology, and geography.

Gombrich's argument about landscape begins *in medias res*, as it were, not with an examination of first principles or definitions of landscape, but with an intervention in an ongoing argument within art history. "Westernness" – the uniqueness of "pure landscape" as a European invention – is taken for granted. What is at issue is the "novelty" of European landscape "in the modern sense" (Gombrich 1966: 108), the historical location and explanation of the "rise of landscape" in the sixteenth century. Gombrich's argument consists of three main claims:

1   the rise of landscape was a revolutionary event in the history of art, not a gradual evolutionary process;
2   the revolution is fundamentally driven by artistic theory, not artistic practice;
3   a revolution in perception – the aesthetic response to natural landscape – is a product of the new genre of art, which is itself a product of the new theory.

It should be clear that these claims are practically identical with the general position on landscape that I have attributed to the discipline of art history as a whole. They give that position a specificity and a kind of radical clarity, however, that one rarely finds in studies of this or that landscape painter or movement. Gombrich's essay is "canonical" in at least two senses: it establishes the narrative and discursive patterns that govern a whole body of research, serving as a text that can only be supplemented and elaborated, never read with a critical eye; it fixes the canonical examples in the genealogy of an artistic genre, inviting the art historian to work backwards within that genealogy to uncover new moments of origin, and forward to discover the telos or goal of the genre in some absolutely exemplary realization. In what follows, I would like to combine exposition and critique of this canonical operation, showing how Gombrich's concept of landscape is constructed, why the history it generates must be incoherent, and why, despite this incoherence, it manages to remain persuasive and canonical. I will also try to indicate what sort of history of landscape might take its place.

1   Landscape as revolution

Gombrich confronts the prevailing "stylistic" art-historical account of the rise of landscape with what he calls an "institutional" approach. According to the stylistic account, landscape "developed gradually" out of religious and historical painting, leaving the distinction between "landscape background" and "landscape as 'an absolute and entire Art' . . . perhaps . . . a little blurred" (Gombrich 1966: 107). Against this blurred gradualist account Gombrich offers a story of landscape as a radical departure, a revolutionary break in the history of art:

> of all the "*genres*" which the sixteenth-century "specialists" began to cultivate in the North, landscape painting is clearly the most revolutionary.
>
> (Gombrich 1966: 108)

What exactly is the character of this revolution? Gombrich cites the seventeenth-century English miniature painter Edward Norgate, who looks back on the rise of landscape painting from the vantage of a century's distance. Norgate provides Gombrich with evidence that "landscape painting was felt to be a real discovery," figured in the familiar contrast between ancients and moderns:

> it doth not appear that the antients made any other Accompt or use of it but as a servant to their other peeces, to illustrate or sett of their Historicall painting by filling up the empty Corners, or void places of Figures and story, with some fragment of Landscape. . . . But to reduce this part of painting to an absolute and intire Art, and to confine a man's industry for the tearme of his Life to this onely, is as I conceave an Invencon of these latters times.
>
> (Norgate, quoted in Gombrich 1966: 107)

The only text in which Gombrich's "revolution" appears is written a hundred years after the fact, in a manuscript that remained unpublished until 1949, four years before Gombrich's own essay.[8] The "revolution" Gombrich is describing was a remarkably quiet and minor one, involving little more than the emergence of a new kind of speciality in artistic production. The empirical evidence for Gombrich's revolution (and against the gradualist argument from "evolution") is simply that "after the middle of the sixteenth century, landscape became an acknowledged subject for both paintings and prints." This "institutional" or "market" account of a new artistic commodity is the only substantial feature to Gombrich's revolution. Why, then, the hyperbolic rhetoric of revolution? Even more puzzling: why, given the urge to characterize the rise of landscape as a revolution, does Gombrich not develop the figurative language of reversed power relations in Norgate's text to support his claim? Norgate describes landscape as a practice which was formerly a "servant" in the painterly economy, but which now has become "an absolute and intire Art," worthy of the attention of a specialist like the Dutchman Paulo Brill, "a very rare Master in that Art" (Norgate, quoted in Gombrich 1966: 42). Perhaps this characterization of the rise of landscape as a transformation of servant into master goes unremarked because Norgate immediately complicates it with a reversal, suggesting that the new mastery is also a kind of servitude that "confine[s] a man's industry for the tearme of his Life."

An even more remarkable detail in Norgate's account which Gombrich cites but leaves unremarked is the religious status of landscape, "of all kinds of painting the most innocent, and which the Divill himself could never accuse of Idolatry" (Norgate, in Gombrich 1966: 44). The "innocence" of landscape gives a specific doctrinal inflection to the notion of "purity" we have already encountered. Landscape is innocent because its lack of figures, narrative, or textual content keeps it non-committal on religious matters; no human or animal figure dominates the composition sufficiently to become an object of devotion or worship. Landscape, Norgate (or Gombrich) might have gone on to say, is the perfect genre for the iconoclastic Protestant cultures of northern Europe during the Reformation. Why does it not occur to Gombrich to connect the revolutionary rise of landscape to a revolution in religious imagery when his own example, indeed his own quotation, begins by making this connection?

The answer, I think, is that Gombrich's revolutionary landscape is systematically insulated from changing power relations in religion or politics,[9] and is located instead in a cloistered space identified with aesthetic consumption and display – the collector's cabinet. Gombrich provides an exemplary scene of this revolution by showing us a painting, formerly attributed to Hans Jordaens III, entitled *A Collector's Cabinet* (now dated in 1620, painter unknown; Plate 7.1). He treats this painting as a window into the art world of the seventeenth century noting that "in the interiors of art shops and collectors' 'cabinets' painted by Jan Breughel or H. Jordaens 'pure' landscapes are part of the regular stock in trade." But Gombrich's hasty glance through this window leaves a number of questions unresolved. Which paintings in the collector's cabinet count as "pure landscapes"? And (assuming we can pick out the pure landscapes) what in the painting suggests that they occupy a revolutionary position in the array of genres? It seems clear that, even if we could decide which paintings to call "pure landscapes" (and Gombrich will later argue that this is not something we can know just by looking at a picture), the painting provides no indication that landscape is a special innovation, much less a "revolutionary genre." On the contrary, landscape is represented in all its subgenres and gradations, ranging from background to history to main subject: in the upper center of the *Cabinet* a sublime Alpine vista abuts a Dutch marine painting, which adjoins an Italianate pastoral. The overwhelming impression of this array of images is of a space in which genres are juxtaposed in relations of arbitrary adjacency, subordinated to an order of encyclopedic comprehensiveness.[10]

At the same time as this order enlists notions of generic distinctness to give its ensemble of images the aura of representativity, samples of "all the kinds," it simultaneously suggests a blurring of genres, an incorporation of them all into a canonical system of the visible and picturable, a realm which surrounds a subregion of readability and literariness. The two sides of *The Collector's Cabinet* dramatize this interchange between the visual and the verbal, dividing the scene into two groups, one involved in reading and conversation under the aegis of Minerva, goddess of wisdom, the other engaged in the viewing of pictures under the image of Venus, goddess of the senses. This image of the relation between the visual and the textual, the *mundus sensibilis* and the *mundus intelligibilis*, clearly privileges the visual and pictorial. The witty emblematic touch of the monkey on the window-sill suggests that the "real" landscape out the collector's window is also a representation, a mockery of visual reality that is no more real than the paintings on the walls, or the collector's cabinet pictured here.

The truly revolutionary image in Gombrich's example, then, is not the "pure land-scape" (whichever one it is) hanging on the collector's wall, but the painting of the cabinet itself, the "metapicture," as it were, in which landscape is located. This anonymous work is dated *c.* 1620, about the time that the radically new genre of collector's cabinet paintings appeared in Antwerp. It is not, as my allegorical reading suggests, a window onto the seventeenth-century art world, but a highly contrived *musée imaginaire*, a fantasy of an art world as an aristocratic center of an encyclopedic, metropolitan culture, synthesizing learning and sensuality, commerce and the love of art. The reality was rather more mundane and problematic. Antwerp was the leading art center of Europe, the banking center of the Spanish Empire, but it was also the crossroads of the Counter-Reformation, a principal site of struggle between emergent northern Protestant nationalism, the residual fantasies of the Holy Roman Empire, and the very real threat of the Spanish Empire. Most Antwerp collectors were burghers, not aristocrats, and the record of inventories suggests that their collections could not have looked this way either. This becomes quite evident when one compares a few examples of collectors' cabinets and realizes that the same paintings seem to show up in all of them. Far from being a revolutionary genre, landscape is, as Gombrich himself puts it, just another "part of the stock in trade." A hint of this world of exchange inside the illusion of aristocratic potlatch is the figure with the open purse at the table touching the slip of paper – a receipt or letter of credit? Perhaps this is really a scene of satirical mockery (as the monkey emblem suggests), a vision of burghers disguised as aristoc-rats, playing a scene of commerce in the costumes of gift-giving and *noblesse oblige*.[11]

The more one presses Gombrich's attempt to document the "sudden appearance" of landscape in western painting, the more it seems to slip back into the gradualism of the stylistic account, a supplementation of that account by economics and a history of art theory. When Gombrich comes to the role of theory in his revolution, he will concede that "a radical change in the very concept of art could not, and did not, develop overnight" (Gombrich 1966: 110). The "revolution," it would seem, is more like a rhetorical gesture within the discourse of art history, an attempt to re-orient that discourse around the poles of art-collecting, art markets, and aesthetic theory, and to enliven it with a progressive narrative punctuated by radical innovations and revolu-tionary advances.

The real stakes of the argument, then, are disciplinary. Gombrich offers a program within which research might make progress in reconstructing a history that is itself shaped by a progressive narrative. The year before his landscape essay was published, Gombrich had presented a paper on "The Renaissance conception of artistic progress and its consequences" at the 1952 Amsterdam Congress on the History of Art. Gombrich opens by acknowledging that the concept of progress in art is the subject of considerable skepticism. He immediately renounces any claim to deal with the question in a theoretical way: "I do not want to ask whether there is such a thing as artistic progress or not" (Gombrich 1966: 1). Instead, he says, "my question is a historical one" that concerns the "effect" of the Renaissance "belief" in the "idea of progress." The effect, unsurprisingly, turns out to be progressive, not so much in its "psychological effect" on young, ambitious artists, but in creating "a new institutional framework for art" (Gombrich 1966: 3). This is, of course, the very same institutional framework that makes possible the emergence of landscape painting, the "most revolutionary" of the Renaissance genres.

Despite his disclaimer, then, Gombrich certainly does want to claim that there is such a thing as artistic progress. Not that there always was progress in art. At a certain point in time (the Renaissance) a "conception" of progress was born – a conception of conception, we might say. This conception had "consequences" in the real world: it induced a series of historical changes that could be described only as progressive. The idea of progress begets the reality of progress. Before the idea of progress held sway – in the Middle Ages, for instance – progress could not occur. Art was merely a craft or trade, repeating traditional formulas. In the Renaissance, by contrast, art is progressive, driven by an ideal: "the artist," says Gombrich, "had not only to think of his commission but of his mission. This mission was to add to the glory of the age through the progress of art" (Gombrich 1966: 3).

Landscape, then, as the "most revolutionary" genre, is the epitome of the progressive model of art, which spins out recursively to structure the history of art. I hope it is clear now why Gombrich needs the revolutionary rhetoric of landscape's "sudden appearance" in the sixteenth century, and why that revolutionary moment must vanish whenever he tries to locate it precisely. Modernism must be allowed to tell its own story in its own way, as a revolutionary moment always about to be or always already passed. Its story of art must posit a precise revolutionary moment that dissolves, on closer inspection, into a protracted quest romance for the grail of the "absolute and intire art." In short, the failure of Gombrich's attempt to precisely locate the landscape revolution in history is exactly what makes it successful as a model of the "long revolution," the emergence of modernity. What we need to examine next is the precise mechanism of that modernity, the way Gombrich figures the role of theory, practice, and economic exchange in the rise of landscape.

2 Landscape and modernity

Gombrich's claim is that the novelty of European landscape must be seen in terms of a dialectic between a northern productive practice (landscape paintings are first *made* in Germany, Flanders, and the Netherlands), and a southern theory of pictorial consumption (landscape paintings are first *seen*, *bought*, and *named* in the south): "It is in Venice, not in Antwerp, that the term 'a landscape' is first applied to any individual painting." While the painters of Antwerp "were far advanced in the development of landscape backgrounds . . . there is no evidence that the collectors of Antwerp had an eye or a word for the novelty" (Gombrich 1966: 109). Southern theorists and consumers are clearly the dominant factors in this cultural exchange, a dominance that Gombrich illustrates dramatically with two canonical examples. Dürer's topographical watercolors may look like "pure landscapes," and to the stylistic approach "Dürer was one of the world's great landscape painters" (Plate 7.2); yet for Gombrich's institutional theory of landscape, Dürer "never took the step into the institution of landscape painting. He probably regarded his famous topographical watercolors as studies which he could not sell for honest money" (Gombrich 1966: 108). Giorgione's *Tempesta* (Plate 7.3), another canonical "first" in the progress towards pure landscape, achieves its status only in the inventory of the Italian connoisseur Marc Antonio Michiel. Nothing could illustrate more decisively the dominance of theory over practice, market over production, the verbal label over the pictorial object: Dürer's landscape study only "appears" to be a pure landscape from the standpoint of a false history based in an evolutionary sequence of paintings; from an institutional perspective it scarcely exists (at least at the time of its production) because it lies outside the circuit of exchange. Giorgione's *Tempesta* only appears to be a recondite allegorical invention with a landscape background; to the institutional approach it is first and foremost a *paesetto*, a "small landscape."

Now there are a number of obvious internal objections we could raise to Gombrich's account at this point. His claim that the first labeling of paintings as landscapes occurs in Venice in 1521 has been put in doubt by subsequent scholarship. It now appears that the earliest record of this usage is in a contract drawn up in the Netherlands in 1490 (Gibson 1989: 53). Evidently a sense of market lingo, if not of theoretical discourse, had made its way to the north rather earlier than Gombrich supposed. One might also quibble about the examples. While Dürer "probably" regarded his studies as unmarketable, it does not follow that he had no "eye or word" for them as landscapes. Gombrich himself notes that Dürer applied the phrase "the good landscape painter" to his contemporary Joachim Patinir. The example of Giorgione's *Tempesta*, finally, is perhaps the most paradoxical, for this is a painting that was almost certainly not *produced* as "a landscape" in any generic or purist sense of the word. Most of the recent scholarship on this work has been devoted to deciphering the lost allegory that was encoded in it from the first.

But these objections are, in several senses, beside the point. The challenge is not to "correct" Gombrich's account of the originating moment in landscape by substituting another date or another artist. The idea is to challenge the whole discourse of origins and progress driven by a unilinear sequence of causes and effects. In its place, I suggest, we need to construct a set of dialectical histories produced by multiple determinations, critical histories that attend to the sort of narratives Gombrich offers us but continually deconstruct their claims to origin and progress. In such a critical history the positioning of Giorgione's *Tempesta* as a "first" landscape does not cease to be a fact. But it is now seen as a fact produced by a certain kind of erasure, amnesia, and misrecognition. In this account, *Tempesta* is no longer anomalous, but quite typical of the fate of numerous allegorical and historical paintings under modernism. It exemplifies the way in which the practice of generic labeling and commodification simultaneously produces a new value in an object and erases a previous value. So far as the specific history of landscape as a genre is concerned, it may give us some insight into the general problematic of landscape and memory. What, we might ask, if landscape were to be thought of, not so much as a representation of a "memorable" scene in nature, but as a mechanism for *forgetting* or *erasing* history? Certainly, the transformation of *Tempesta* into "a landscape" involves a double forgetting – of the painting's original genre (allegory) and thus of even the possibility of remembering the meaning of that allegory, since the generic relabeling erases the need for interpretation. A similar set of questions would arise with Dürer's *aquarelles*, the central one being: in what sort of frame, against what background, would it make sense to write on this drawing, "This is not a landscape"?

The answer, for Gombrich, is: just outside the frame of a new form of subjectivity emerging in the sixteenth century. Gombrich thinks that Dürer could not see or name his *aquarelles* as landscapes because he could not "sell them for honest money" as commodities under this name. By the mid-sixteenth century, however, this situation had changed, and Dürer's drawings could, in principle, be seen as landscapes whether they ever were in fact or not. More likely they were sold under a rather different, but related, generic label: as "Dürers," signature products of the hand of genius.[12] This does not mean that Gombrich is offering an economic or (despite his opening remarks) an "institutional" history of art in any materialist sense. The root cause of the new perception is not the market, but a new conception of art: "the first condition" for "a demand" for landscape paintings is an "aesthetic attitude . . . which prizes works of art for the sake of their artistic achievement rather than for their function and subject-matter" (Gombrich 1966: 110). Landscape's tendency to erase subject-matter and liturgical or rhetorical function is simply one of the features that makes it a "growth" commodity in a market of this sort. The mainspring of Gombrich's history, then, is not the market, the institution, or the material practices of painting, but the beholder's "attitudes," and especially the theories of art, the "conceptions" that give "rise" to those attitudes: "the classical theory had created an atmosphere in which the products of Northern realism appeared in an entirely new and possibly unintended light" (Gombrich 1966: 112).

3 Painting and vision

If the ultimate cause of the rise of landscape lies in the spectator, however, it is not in the gaze of an "innocent eye" on the beauties of nature: "the idea of natural beauty as an inspiration of art," says Gombrich, "is . . . a very dangerous over-simplification. Perhaps it even reverses the actual process by which man discovers the beauty of nature. We call a scenery 'picturesque' . . . if it reminds us of paintings we have seen" (Gombrich 1966: 117). "Similarly . . . the discovery of Alpine scenery does not precede but follows the spread of prints and paintings with mountain panoramas. . . . Thus, while it is usual to represent the 'discovery of the world' as the underlying motive for the development of landscape painting, we are almost tempted to reverse the formula and assert the priority of landscape painting over landscape 'feeling' " (Gombrich 1966: 118). With these gestures towards the picturesque priority of painting over vision, Gombrich seems to have pulled off another paradoxical reversal of field, for it is hard to see how landscape painting can take priority over landscape perception, when paintings themselves could not be seen as landscapes until the sixteenth century. It looks as if Gombrich is caught in a very tiny and vicious circle, governed by a "chicken and egg" relation between painting and vision.

But Gombrich has his escape from this binary cycle, and it lies in the third term which has been hovering over his text throughout – the notion of "theory," the expression of an ungrounded (and disembodied) "mind" which introduces new conceptions into the world. An appeal to theory releases him from the account of landscape in terms of *either* vision *or* painting, and releases him from the paradox he is "almost tempted" to commit: "there is no need to press this argument to its paradoxical extreme. All that matters in this context is that this movement in a 'deductive' direction from artistic theory to artistic practice, from artistic practice to artistic feeling, does in fact deserve to be taken into account" (Gombrich 1966: 118).

What is this "theory," and what would it mean to take it into account? We have already seen two of its main principles in what Gombrich reconstructs as the general theory of art in the Renaissance: the progressive notion of art as oriented towards a "mission" rather than a "commission"; the notion of artistic achievement for "its own sake" rather than for "function and subject-matter." The texts specific to landscape theory that Gombrich offers are from Alberti and Leonardo. Alberti associates landscape painting with therapeutic "psychological effects," the power to relieve fever, to overcome sleeplessness, and "to restore the tired spirits of the man of affairs" (Gombrich 1966: 111, 114). Leonardo praises landscape by associating it with the godlike power of the artist to create a whole world, "first in his mind" and then with "his hands."

Now it does seem a bit odd to dignify these remarks with the label of "theories" (Gombrich even calls Leonardo's remarks "the first complete aesthetic theory of landscape painting"); they are really just fragmentary and commonplace notions in the art discourse of the fifteenth century. But Gombrich needs something more than a set of commonplaces as the mainspring of his history, and nothing less than a full-blown theory will do. The theory, after all, cannot merely "precede" the practice of landscape painting as scattered hints or "pre-texts" that might, along with the classical precedents of Pliny and Vitruvius, be used to rationalize and justify an emerging practice. The theory has to engender the practice, the way Leonardo's "idea in the mind" precedes work with the hands. The theory, moreover, has to create a revolution in art that is perfectly epitomized by the revolution in landscape painting. No matter if the character of that revolution is evanescent, incoherent, and self-contradictory. Gombrich will one minute argue that the new art is released from any "function," the next minute cite Alberti's remarks on its therapeutic function. He will talk as if the ideal mission of "art for its own sake" has superseded the mere "trade or craft" of art for a "commission," and then characterize the emergence of the new art in terms of direct appeals to the marketplace. He will argue that theory has priority over practice and that painting has priority over vision, and then admit that "such questions of priority cannot be settled empirically" (Gombrich 1966: 117). The only remaining questions are, what other histories are erased by this non-empirical, theory-driven history?, and why?

4 The empire of theory

One way to focus these questions is to reread Gombrich's account of landscape as a geographical and geopolitical narrative. I noted at the outset that Gombrich takes for granted the unique "westernness" of landscape. His way of doing this is to construct the process of landscape's emergence exclusively as an exchange between northern and southern Europe. But Gombrich rejects the straightforward explanation based on geographical determinism offered by Paolo Pino in 1548: "The Northerners show a special gift for painting landscapes because they portray the scenery of their own homeland, which offers the most suitable motifs by virtue of its wildness, while we Italians live in the garden of the world, which is more delightful to behold in reality than in a painting" (Gombrich 1966: 116). Gombrich has to reject this account because it suggests a direct (as opposed to "arduous") relation between perception and representation, puts vision before painting, and (most important) locates cultural agency in artistic practice rather than theory.

But Gombrich does not simply abandon the traditional notion of geographical division of labor; he adapts it to a model of a unified European economy. The relation of north to south is refigured as an exchange between producers and consumers, practice and theory, the manual and the intellectual arts: "Northerners are famous for their good landscape painting because they have their brains in their hands, while Italians, who have them in their heads, paint mythologies and histories" (Gombrich 1966: 115). This exchange replicates the formal exchange of places that constitutes the emergence of landscape as a genre. Landscape is the background or *parergon* of history painting, a mere servant or accessory to the main subject in the traditional hierarchy of values. The *parergon* is the border, frame, or "margin" of the painting, that which lies outside the center, at the edge of its true significance and content.[13] The same relationship holds for northern and southern Europe, practice and theory. The south is figured in Gombrich's map of Europe as the center, the "head" of the body, the site of metropolitan culture. The north is figured as the outer border or "margin" of European culture, the site of provinciality, instrumentality, mere unreflective production. Far from being an original invention of northern European painting, landscape is merely the response to a "demand" that "was the gift presented by the Renaissance South to the Gothic North" (Gombrich 1966: 110).

Gombrich is quick to insist that "there is more" in the relationship of southern theory and northern practice than "mere resignation to an inferior position. The idea that each nation and each school of art should do what it can do best is symptomatic of a complete change in the notion of art" (Grombrich 1966: 115). Gombrich thus recuperates Pino's notion of geographical determination and cultural nationalism. Landscape can be seen as an expression of national pride, the uniqueness of a "land" and its people, and as a response to an international "world economy" centered in the metropolitan cultures of the south. The "division of labor" in medieval artistic production had been merely "practical," aimed at "speeding up the work on a given commission" (Gombrich 1966: 117). "Now the division of labor no longer applies to a concrete painting but to Art as such. It is to Art as an abstract idea that each nation should make its contribution where it is best equipped to do so." The hegemony of southern theory over northern practice is thus preserved and extended from the art of landscape painting (as the "gift" from the south to the north) to "Art as such." It would not be much of a step to extend Gombrich's argument and suggest that "nationalism as such" is the most potent "gift" given by the south to the north. The nations of northern Europe where landscape painting first "rises" – Germany, Flanders, the Netherlands –

owe the south not only the ideas of landscape and of "Art as such," but the very idea of their existence as independent nations.

The figures of free economic exchange and unilateral "gift-giving" that govern Gombrich's picture of the rise of European landscape depend upon a singularly rosy picture of European political relations in the sixteenth century, almost as rosy as the scene of his "revolution" in *The Collector's Cabinet*. This picture would surely darken if it took account of things like the Eighty Years' War, the political assertiveness of Germany under the Holy Roman Empire, the ambitions of the Spanish Empire, and the forging of an independent republic in the Netherlands. Gombrich's tracing of all agency in his history to Italian Renaissance theory is a kind of art-historical echo of the argument made by the Chancellor of the Holy Roman Empire under Charles V, that "political control over Italy . . . meant the dominant position in Europe and the world." From the perspective of a political history of the sixteenth century, the rise of the three major schools of landscape painting in Antwerp, the Danube region, and the Netherlands might take on a more militant and embattled tonality, might in fact be pictured in relation to protracted struggles for religious and political independence.

Gombrich rejects this narrative, not directly, but under the cover of his dismissal of the gradualist "stylistic" account of the rise of landscape painting. The most influential version of the gradualist account is by Max Friedlander, whose work Gombrich criticizes for failing to explain the "sudden appearance" of the Danube school, and for failing "to do justice" to the novelty of the genre. Friedlander wrote his classic studies of Flemish and Dutch painting as an exile and émigré in Utrecht, after being forced from his position as director of the Kaiser Friedrich Museum in Berlin in 1933.[14] His understanding of sixteenth-century landscape is heavily inflected by his emigration to a major site of resistance to twentieth-century European imperialism. His account of Brueghel's originality in genre and landscape, for instance, is couched in just such a rhetoric of resistance: "Despite the presence of popular genre-like everyday themes in Brueghel's work, we feel a latent heroic strength. His productivity falls in the time of Gravella and Alba, when the Inquisition, foreign overlordship, religious intolerance, oppression and misery goaded people to secret resistance and fomented the struggle for freedom" (Gombrich 1966: 88). Gombrich's story of landscape is both a misreading and an inversion of Friedlander, representing his predecessor's political account as merely "stylistic," and reversing the power relations so that political struggle becomes aristocratic gift-giving. Here is Friedlander's account in his own words:

> About 1620 this struggle had been decided in all essentials. The northern States had secured independence, religious freedom and a life under their own law. The visual arts no longer create triumphant symbols, are not heroic. The great event is not reflected that way at all in painting. The Dutch soul has roused itself and wards off everything foreign with quiet self-confidence. Protestantism holds its own against the "universal" Church, the Germanic element against the southern, the bourgeoisie against autocracy, simplicity against pomp, painting against drawing. The cut makes a deep mark in the history of the landscape picture.
>
> (Friedlander 1963: 88–9)

We need not buy into the essentialist rhetoric of "Dutch souls" and "Germanic elements" to see that Friedlander's account is somewhat richer than the placid story of gradual stylistic development that Gombrich foists upon him. Gombrich's account of the rise of European landscape, written after the Second World War, is couched in what might be called the rhetoric of the Marshall Plan and NATO, envisioning a pan-European economic recovery, looking towards the goal of a Common Market.[15] Friedlander's story of landscape grows out of the direct experience of fascism with its "triumphant" and "heroic" symbols and its occupying armies. One story of landscape proceeds by the rapid dissemination of a "modern" idea through an international marketplace; the other traces a protracted struggle for national identity and independence. The economic account projects a painless "revolution" in painting that will produce an art history based mainly in patronage studies leavened by what Gombrich calls "theory"; the political account projects a complex and diverse set of strategies of resistance and collaboration.

It is probably obvious that I find Friedlander's account more compelling as a starting-point than Gombrich's. I am not suggesting, however, that Gombrich's version can be forgotten or ignored, but that it must be read as a specific kind of constructed history that systematically repressed a previous history, allowing the forgetting of a whole body of knowledge and directing research away from that knowledge. My final question, then, is what happens if we start, not so much from Friedlander's assumptions, as from a reading of art-historical discourse that tries to overcome the sort of amnesia that Gombrich's influence has bequeathed to us.

One thing that immediately follows, I would suggest, is that the rise of landscape in Europe during the sixteenth century ceases to be a monolithic "thing" located in a totalized "north" and springing from an equally unitary "south." The "rise of European landscape" may occur in roughly the same time-frame in three different places (the Danube, Antwerp, and the Netherlands), but it does not do so in relation to a single source of "theory" or consumer demand, nor are the motives of its production reducible to any single notion of "pure landscape" or "nature for its own sake." In the Danube region, for instance, Larry Silver's recent work has shown us that the motifs of wild men and satyrs in wooded landscapes, far from being unreadable, are oriented towards a resurgent German nationalism encouraged by the Emperor Maximilian I and the mythologies of the Holy Roman Empire. The "world landscapes" of Patinir and the Flemish painters, with their mountain top prospects and cartographic perspectives, become explicable in relation to Antwerp's position as the banking center for the Spanish Empire.[16] And the "unreadability" of Dutch landscapes of the seventeenth century becomes readable, as Ann Adams's recent work demonstrates, as a strategy for the articulation of private, bourgeois identity within an emergent public sphere.[17]

Perhaps the most important conceptual result of decentering Gombrich's history of landscape is the demolition of the notion of "pure landscape," devoid of textuality, history, allegory, or readability of any sort.[18] Landscape (and painting more generally) is never pure, never an "absolute and entire art" except as part of the rhetoric that might accompany a strategy of resistance to some previous notion of "impurity" or readability. Finally, landscape in a post-Gombrichian history might break out of its privileged status as a stalking-horse for modernism, and open out into a program of research that recognized the insularity, the historical specificity and relativity of

European landscape in relation to the diversity of human responses to and reshapings of the environment. The European "rise of landscape" would no longer be tellable as the story of the "first" discovery of "nature for its own sake." Or rather, that story would be retold in quotation marks, as one of the constitutive myths by which the history of art collaborates in selling the naturalness and universality of a long, unfinished revolution.

Notes

1   Thompson's *The Making of the English Working Class* (1963) established much of the foundation for a class analysis of landscape perception and consumption in nineteenth-century England. Raymond Williams's *The Country and the City* (1973) continues to be the basic text for the social history of the English pastoral ideal. John Berger's brief remarks on landscape painting and property in *Ways of Seeing* (1972) provided the initial provocation for a whole series of revisionist accounts of British landscape.

2   See also the important collection of essays edited by Simon Pugh, *Reading Landscape: Country/ City/Capital* (1990). Other significant revisionist accounts of landscape are provided by Ronald Paulson, *Literary Landscape: Turner and Constable* (1982), and Carole Fabricant, "Binding and dressing Nature's loose tresses: the ideology of Augustan landscape design" (1979).

3   John Berger, for instance, repeats all the commonplaces about the "first pure landscapes" appearing in the seventeenth century that will be in question in the following pages, and the authority of Gombrich's master-narrative of the "rise of landscape" remains unchallenged in Simon Pugh's *Reading Landscape*.

4   In *Landscape and Power*, ed. W. J. T. Mitchell (1994). The western, Eurocentric, and modernist framework of art-historical accounts of landscape comes to seem less natural and inevitable, I argue, when seen in relation to landscape as an issue in colonial encounters. Recent work by landscape scholars in New Zealand, Australia, and South Africa is doing a great deal to unsettle the centrality of the British tradition in particular. See, for instance, Krim Benterrak, Stephen Muecke, and Paddy Roe, *Reading the Country: Introduction to Nomadology* (1984).

5   John Ruskin, "The novelty of landscape," in Bermingham (1986: 21).

6   See the entry on "Landscape painting" in *The Oxford Companion to Art* for a compendium of these commonplaces. It is notable in this context that John Berger's relentlessly economic and ideological treatment of oil painting seems to run into a snag when it comes to landscape: "Landscape," he says, "of all the categories of oil painting, is the one to which our argument applies least. . . . The first pure landscapes – painted in Holland in the seventeenth century – answered no direct social need. . . . Landscape painting was, from its inception, a relatively independent activity" (Berger 1972: 104–5).

7   Landscape in this "pure" sense might be thought of as the obverse of still life, "the great anti-Albertian genre" in Norman Bryson's words. If still life feasts on the intimacy of tactile objects, the closed-in space of the body, its reach and gestures, landscape delights in the "sovereign prospect of the eye," an infinite field whose "jewel" is the vanishing-point (Bryson 1990: 71). Both genres involve the "removal of the human body" (Bryson 1990: 60) and the elimination of narrative – but not the elimination of meaning. On the question of the human body as sign in landscape painting, see John Dixon Hunt, *The Figure in the Landscape* (1976).

8   See Edward Norgate, *Miniatura, or the Art of Limning*. Norgate continues to be cited in histories of landscape with a ritualistic frequency and authority as the first witness to the "rise" of landscape. See, for instance, Pugh (1990: 3) and Walter Gibson (1989: 3).

9   Cf. Berger's claim that "the first pure landscapes . . . answered no direct social need" (Berger 1972: 105).

10   My discussion here is heavily indebted to Zirka Zaremba Filipczak's excellent book, *Picturing

Art in Antwerp, 1550–1700 (1987), the most comprehensive treatment of the collector's cabinet genre that we have. My thanks to Anne Jensen Adams for bringing this book to my attention.

11 Filipczak notes an intriguing fact, however: "there is only one reference to a gallery painting in the published records of Antwerp dealers" (Filipczak 1987: 61). It appears that these paintings not only were in general circulation on the art market, but were "probably ordered by the collectors themselves, who, however, did not always keep the works they had commissioned but instead occasionally passed them on as gifts. A number of gallery paintings of fictional collections were likewise acquired as gifts." Could it be that these images not only portray scenes of *noblesse oblige*, but are themselves objects of potlatch?

12 It is certain that Dürer rapidly became a "name" whose signature was worth its weight in gold. See Francis Haskell, *Patrons and Painters* (1980: 98), on the trading of Dürer for Raphael. The collector in question thinks that two Raphaels would be worth an entire collection of "Alberto Dürer and other German masters," but it is notable that Dürer has already become a singular commodity in his own right.

13 See Jacques Derrida, "Parergon," in *La vérité en peinture* (1978).

14 See Jakob Rosenberg, "Friedlander and the Berlin museums" (March 1959). I am grateful to Linda Seidel for bringing this article to my attention.

15 It is ironic, in this context, that the first proposal for a common European currency came from the Italian humanist Gattinara during the reign of the Emperor Charles V. See Koenigsberger, Mosse, and Bowler (1968: 236).

16 Walter Gibson's *"Mirror of the Earth": The World Landscape in Sixteenth-Century Flemish Painting* (1989) provides the starting-point for such an interpretation, despite his own orientation towards a Gombrichian account of the rise of landscape. Gibson's book opens with familiar claims about the "momentous step" entailed in the development of landscape "as an independent category in art," and even quotes the very same passages from Alberti and Norgate that Gombrich does (Gibson 1989: xix, 3).

17 See Adams, "Citizenship and identity: competing identities in seventeenth-century Dutch landscape," in *Landscape and Power* (Mitchell 1994).

18 The continued sway of this notion of "pure painting" understood as an evacuation of textuality is notable even in a relatively sophisticated treatment of northern art like Svetlana Alpers's *The Art of Describing* (1983). Alpers continues to accept Gombrich's reigning categories, postulating a "specifically visual, as contrasted with a textual, culture" (Alpers 1983: xxiv) that produces pictures concerned with "describing the world seen rather than as imitation of significant human actions" (Ibid.: xxv). These oppositions are then mapped on to the difference between south and north, Italy and the Netherlands, to reconstruct "not the history of Dutch art, but the Dutch *visual culture*" (Alpers 1983: xxv). The candor of this renunciation of history is based, in turn, in an even more radical extrapolation of Gombrich's theory of artistic progress: "no history on the developmental model" can be written about Dutch art, because "the art did not constitute itself as a progressive tradition. For art to have a history in this Italian sense is the exception, not the rule" (Alpers 1983: xxv). If Gombrich thought there was no progress in art before the Italian Renaissance, Alpers thinks there is no progress afterwards! And if no progress, no history: just a description of an "art of describing," of "what persists and is sustaining, not what is changing, in culture." Alpers's idea that history is only narrative, only progressive, only developmental (in contrast to descriptive stasis) is a cloven fiction as fundamental as her reliance on Gombrich's binary oppositions of north and south.

Bibliography

Alpers, Svetlana (1983) *The Art of Describing: Dutch Art in the Seventeenth Century*, Chicago: University of Chicago Press.
Appleton, Jay (1975) *The Experience of Landscape*, London: John Wiley.

118   W. J. T. Mitchell

Barrell, John (1980) *The Dark Side of the Landscape: The Rural Poor in English Painting, 1730–1840*, Cambridge: Cambridge University Press.

Benterrak, Krim, Muecke, Stephen, and Roe, Paddy (1984) *Reading the Country: Introduction to Nomadology*, Australia: Freemantle Arts Centre Press.

Berger, John (1972) *Ways of Seeing*, London: Penguin and BBC.

Bermingham, Ann (1986) *Landscape and Ideology: The English Rustic Tradition, 1740–1860*, Berkeley, CA: University of California Press.

Bryson, Norman (1990) *Looking at the Overlooked: Four Essays on Still Life Painting*, Cambridge, MA: Harvard University Press.

Clark, Kenneth (1976) *Landscape into Art*, 2nd edn., New York: Harper & Row.

Cosgrove, Denis E. (1984) *Social Formation and Symbolic Landscape*, London: Croom Helm.

Derrida, Jacques (1978) *La vérité en peinture*, Paris: Flammarion.

Fabricant, Carole (1979) "Binding and dressing Nature's loose tresses: the ideology of Augustan landscape design," *Studies in Eighteenth-Century Culture* 8: 109–35.

Filipczak, Zirka Zaremba (1987) *Picturing Art in Antwerp, 1550–1700*, Princeton, NJ: Princeton University Press.

Friedlander, Max J. (1963 [1947]) *Landscape/Portrait/Still-life*, trans. R. F. C. Hull, New York: Schocken; first published as *Essays über die Landschaftsmalerei und andere Bilgattungen*, The Hague.

Gibson, Walter (1989) *"Mirror of the Earth": The World Landscape in Sixteenth-Century Flemish Painting*, Princeton, NJ: Princeton University Press.

Gombrich, E. H. (1966) *Norm and Form: Studies in the Art of the Renaissance*, Chicago: University of Chicago Press; the essay "The Renaissance theory of art and the rise of landscape," included in this collection, was originally published as "Renaissance artistic theory and the development of landscape painting," *Gazette des Beaux-Arts*, 6ᵉ période, XLI (1953): 335–60.

Haskell, Francis (1980) *Patrons and Painters*, New Haven, CT: Yale University Press.

Hunt, John Dixon (1976) *The Figure in the Landscape: Poetry, Painting, and Gardening During the Eighteenth Century*, Baltimore, MD: Johns Hopkins University Press.

Koenigsberger, H. G., Mosse, George L., and Bowler, G. Q. (1968) *Europe in the Sixteenth Century*, New York: Longman.

MacCannell, Dean (1976) *The Tourist: A New Theory of the Leisure Class*, New York: Schocken.

Mitchell, W. J. T. (ed.) (1994) *Landscape and Power*, Chicago: University of Chicago Press.

Norgate, Edward (1949) *Miniatura, or the Art of Limning*, ed. Martin Hardie, Oxford: Oxford University Press.

Osborne, Harold (ed.) (1970) *The Oxford Companion to Art*, Oxford: Oxford University Press.

Paulson, Ronald (1982) *Literary Landscape: Turner and Constable*, New Haven, CT: Yale University Press.

Pugh, Simon (ed.) (1990) *Reading Landscape: Country/City/Capital*, Manchester: Manchester University Press.

Rosenberg, Jakob (March 1959) "Friedlander and the Berlin museums," *Burlington Magazine* 101, 672: 83–5.

Silver, Larry (1983) "Forest primeval: Albrecht Altdorfer and the German wilderness landscape," *Simiolus* 13, 1: 4–43.

Thompson, E. P. (1963) *The Making of the English Working Class*, New York: Pantheon.

Tuan, Yi-Fu (1974) *Topophilia: A Study of Environmental Perception, Attitudes, and Values*, Englewood Cliffs, NJ: Prentice–Hall.

Williams, Raymond (1973) *The Country and the City*, London: Chatto & Windus.

Part II

Engendering the literary canon

8
British Romanticism, gender, and three women artists

Anne K. Mellor

In the opening decades of the nineteenth century, women dominated the production and the consumption of literature in England. The success of the circulating or lending libraries, which spread rapidly throughout England in the late eighteenth century, meant that hitherto prohibitively expensive books were now available to a new and ever-growing readership, a readership composed in large part of increasingly literate and leisured upper- and middle-class women who preferred to read literature, and especially novels, written by women. The tabulation of the contents of the ten leading circulating libraries in London in 1800 compiled by the London Statistical Society suggests that the bulk of both the subscribers and the writers for these libraries was female.[1] Three-quarters of the 2,000 books in circulation were either "Fashionable Novels, well known" (439 volumes) or "Novels of the lowest character, being chiefly imitations of Fashionable Novels" (1,008 volumes). Two additional categories also appealed primarily to women readers: "Romances" (76 volumes) and "Novels by Miss Edgeworth, and Moral and Religious Novels" (49 volumes). Even a cursory survey of the literary reviews of the period suggests that by 1830 there were over 200 living women writers who could boast at least one novel to their name, while the most prolific novelist of the period by far, as Mitzi Myers has observed, was "A Lady."[2] Moreover, the most popular novelists of the period 1800–20 were women: Maria Edgeworth, Elizabeth Hamilton, Amelia Opie, Mary Brunton, Jane and Anna Maria Porter, and Sydney Owenson, to whom must be added the names of only two men, Walter Scott and Thomas Surr (Jones 1986: 3–6). Women were also a powerful presence in the production of poetry – Stuart Curran has identified 339 women poets publishing in England between 1760 and 1830 in addition to 82 anonymous female poets (1990: 1–42). The leading dramatist of the day was a woman (Joanna Baillie). And Mary Robinson in her *Thoughts on the Condition of Women* (1799) lists over two dozen prominent female literary critics (Anna Barbauld and Clara Reeve, most notably), essayists, historians, biographers, translators and classical scholars.[3]

What happens to our interpretations of Romanticism if we focus our attention not on the canonical poets (Wordsworth, Coleridge, Blake, Byron, Keats, Percy Shelley) or novelist (Walter Scott) but on the women writers who produced more than half of the literature published in England between 1780 and 1830? Or on the women artists who flourished in this period? I recently argued in my *Romanticism and Gender* (1993) that a paradigm shift in our conceptual understanding of British literary Romanticism occurs when we give equal weight to the thought and writing of the women of the period. After describing this paradigm shift, I wish to examine in this context the work of the three leading women artists of the British Romantic period – Angelica Kauffman, Maria Cosway, and Mary Moser.

Over the last three decades critics have offered various interpretations of British Romanticism as a cultural movement – and for the moment let me focus on *literary* Romanticism. Some have described Romanticism as a commitment to imagination, vision, and transcendence, as did Meyer Abrams, Harold Bloom, and John Beer. Some have seen it as a questioning, even a systematic demystification, of the very possibility of a semiotically unmediated vision, as have Geoffrey Hartman, Paul de Man, and a host of other critics. Others have defined it as an ideology located in specific political and social events, as urged by Carl Woodring, Jerome McGann, John Barrell, and the school of new historical Romanticists inspired by their work. Many have concluded that it is a complex configuration derived from all of these recent critical approaches. But all these critics have based their constructions of British Romanticism exclusively upon the works of male writers (Wordsworth, Coleridge, Blake, Byron, Shelley, Keats, Scott) and artists (Constable, Turner, Gainsborough, Morland, Blake, Fuseli, Martin) – their descriptions of "Romanticism" are thus unwittingly gender-biased.

When we look at the corpus of female-authored literature in the Romantic period, we find a focus on very different issues from those which concerned these canonical male writers and artists.[4] Decades of further research will be necessary before we can accurately map this new literary terrain, the *terra incognita* of women's literary Romanticism. While I have time here to survey only the significant differences between the thematic concerns, formal practices, and ideological positionings of *male* and *female* Romantic writers, there are wide variations *between* these women writers as well – ranging from the conservative Evangelical acceptance of a patriarchal Christianity endorsed by Hannah More to the systematic denunciation of the evils of patriarchy found in the writings of Wollstonecraft, Mary Robinson, Mary Hays, and many others.

Let me briefly summarize the most immediately obvious contours of what I have called "feminine Romanticism" (since I wish to preserve for this female-authored corpus both the historical and the political connotations of the term "Romanticism"). The women writers of the Romantic period for the most part forswore the concern of their male peers with the capacities of the creative imagination, with the limitations of language, with the possibility of transcendence or apocalyptic vision, with the development of an autonomous self, with political (as opposed to social) revolution, with the role of the creative artist as a political leader or religious savior. Instead, women Romantic writers, both conservative and radical, celebrated neither the achievements of genius nor the spontaneous overflow of powerful feelings but rather the workings of the rational mind, a mind relocated – in a gesture of revolutionary gender implications – in the female as well as the male body.

Following Mary Wollstonecraft's call in *A Vindication of the Rights of Woman* in 1792 for "a REVOLUTION in female manners," they insisted that women should be educated in the same ways and towards the same goals as men and that women were as capable as men of thinking rationally and of acting virtuously. They endorsed Wollstonecraft's argument that the ideal marriage is one based, not on sexual passion, but on mutual respect, self-esteem, affection and compatibility. Their novels and poetry repeatedly celebrate marriages of equality and *rational love*. For the most part, they contested what Jane Spencer has called the eighteenth-century "didactic tradition" of "reformed heroines" (Spencer 1986: 140–80) – the female *Bildungsroman* in which the heroine develops under the mentorship of her lover-teacher from fallible youth into a mature acceptance of the status quo and her role of dutiful wife, the plot of Eliza Haywood's *History of Miss Betsy Thoughtless* (1751) and Frances Burney's *Evelina* (1778). Instead, the women writers influenced by Wollstonecraft's revolutionary feminine Romanticism put forth a powerful critique of this hegemonic domestic ideology. Their novels, poetry, and plays subtly condemned the contemporary construction of masculinity, the flaws in intelligence and moral virtue inherent in patriarchy as demonstrated by their male characters.

Equally important, they insisted upon the dangers of Romantic love and excessive sensibility, and of the errors and human suffering produced by an imprudent reliance upon the creative imagination, in the lives of *both* men and women. To Hannah More's conservative argument that the rational woman, however powerful as an educator and moral guardian at home, should uphold the doctrine of the separate spheres and acknowledge the superiority of her husband in the public realm,[5] they responded with a revolutionary criticism of patriarchal authority in both the public and the private spheres, with a demand for genuinely egalitarian marriages, and with an insistence that the domestic affections alone can provide a valid basis for public as well as private virtues and happiness. In effect, they argued that good government begins at home, and that rational women – as the educators of children and the cultural preservers of moral norms – are best qualified to identify the most effective models of political organization for the public realm.

Maria Edgeworth's *Belinda* (London, 1801) offers a textbook example of this new feminine Romantic ideology. Belinda Portman, an attractive young woman of sound sense, wide reading, prudence, personal modesty, and a capacity for loyalty and enduring affections, is the new woman who will replace Pope's "fairest of mortals" as the envy of her age. Rejecting the marriage proposals of both Mr. Vincent, a talented young West Indian but a compulsive gambler, and – with more reluctance – Clarence Hervey, a charming, intelligent, wealthy but misguided young man who has made the mistake of following Rousseau and trying to create out of an adopted ward his own Sophie, Belinda finally succeeds in establishing a marriage of equality and compatibility by educating Clarence Hervey until he has arrived at the sound judgment she already possesses.

This plot – in which women subtly educate men – is repeatedly retold in women's novels of the Romantic period, in Susan Ferrier's *Marriage* (1818), in Helen Maria Williams's *Julia* (1790), in Lady Morgan's *The Wild Irish Girl* (1806), but perhaps nowhere so subtly and vividly as in Jane Austen's fiction. Austen endorsed a value system firmly grounded on a belief in both women's and men's capacity for intellectual and moral growth, in the desirability of egalitarian marriages based on rational love and mutual esteem, and in the prototype of domestic affection and responsibility as the paradigm for national and international political relations. As Claudia Johnson and Alison Sulloway have recently and persuasively argued, Austen's fiction is that of a *moderate* feminist, solidly progressive in its measured examinations both of the failures of the patriarchy and the landed gentry and of the potential for moral and intellectual equality between the sexes.

Jane Austen's novels are above all novels of female education, novels in which an intelligent but ignorant girl learns to perceive the world more accurately, to understand more fully the ethical complexity of human nature and society, and to gain confidence in the wisdom of her own judgment. Emma Woodhouse – Jane Austen's fantasy figure of unrestricted female power, benevolence, and authority[6] – must still recognize how unfairly she has criticized Jane Fairfax, how insensitively she has manipulated Harriet Smith, how her vanity and pride have led her to misjudge both Robert Martin and Frank Churchill, and how cruelly she has insulted Miss Bates, before she can justify her claim to be the "first in Highbury" and demonstrate that she is the equal in intelligence and good breeding – and the superior in generosity – of Mr. Knightley. Above all, Emma must curb her Romantic imagination, must cease being an "imaginist" like Cowper before his fire in *The Task*, "Myself creating what I saw,"[7] and learn to perceive others more correctly and compassionately, before she can fully emerge as Jane Austen's ideal woman, one who exercises both rational judgment and responsible authority and thus deserves to be the ruler of both Hartfield and Donwell Abbey.

The ideology of feminine Romanticism insisted upon the innate rational and moral equality of men and women. At the same time, Romantic women writers suggested an alternative way of understanding the human self, of constructing subjectivity. William Wordsworth, in *The Prelude*, represented the growth of a poet's mind as the achievement of a self that is unified, unique, enduring, capable of initiating activity, and above all aware of itself as a self. This Wordsworthian self, the hero of his epic autobiography, has been taken by intellectual historians, theorists of autobiography, and deconstructive critics alike to represent *the* Romantic self, a self that Foucault identified with the historical emergence of the individual who participates both in social contract theory and in bourgeois capitalism, that "every Man" who, in Locke's famous formulation, "has a *Property* in his own *Person*."[8]

This Wordsworthian or modern self is, however, as Marlon Ross, Richard Onorato, and others have shown,[9] a specifically *male* self, one that follows an oedipal model of development, that grounds its achievements on masculine tropes of heroic quest and conquest, and that linguistically realizes its claim to be the *universal* human self only by suppressing the somatic or bodily dimensions of its own being. Thus Wordsworth can finally portray his self as a Kantian transcendental ego, pure mind or reason, standing as a *spectator ab extra*, a detached observer, both of Nature – the scene spread before his feet at the top of Mount Snowdon that becomes the "perfect image of a mighty [male] Mind" – and of his own life.

> Anon I rose
> As if on wings, and saw beneath me stretched
> Vast prospect of the world which I had been,
> And was; and hence this song, which like a lark

> I have protracted, in the unwearied heavens
> Singing.
>> (*The Prelude*, 1805: XIII, 377–82) ·

Deliberately denying his corporeality, even his mortality, the Wordsworthian "mind of man" finally

> becomes
> A thousand times more beautiful than the earth
> On which he dwells, above this frame of things
> (Which, 'mid all revolutions in the hopes
> And fears of men, doth still remain unchanged)
> In beauty exalted, as it is itself
> Of substance and of fabric more divine.
>> (*The Prelude*, 1805: XIII, 446–52)

Precarious indeed is this unique, unitary, transcendental subjectivity, for Wordsworth's sublime self-assurance is rendered possible, as many critics have observed,[10] only by the arduous repression of the Other in all its forms: of the mother, of Dorothy, of other people, of history, of nature, of "unknown modes of being," of that gap or "vacancy" which divides his present writing self from his past identity. To sustain such a divine intellect, Wordsworth must first silence a Nature he typically genders female, then spiritually rape her (as in "*Nutting*"), then colonize and finally completely possess her. By the end of *The Prelude*, female Nature is not only a thousand times less beautiful than the mind of man but has even become his "Brother" (XIII, 89), thus losing her gendered Otherness. I have already discussed at length, both in my *Romanticism and Gender* (1993) and in my *Mary Shelley: Her Life, Her Fiction, Her Monsters* (1988) the poetic and cultural consequences of this masculine Romantic poetic attempt, in *The Prelude*, *Frankenstein*, and elsewhere, to speak *for* female Nature, the ways in which a repressed Nature or female returns to haunt and punish the hubristic male. Here I wish to show that other ways of constructing subjectivity, of representing the self, than that chosen by William Wordsworth were available in the discourse of the Romantic period.

Reading Dorothy Wordsworth's Alfoxden and Grasmere journals, we find a very different concept of self from the egotistical sublime proposed in her brother's poetry. Her most succinct statement of this alternative mode of identity, critics agree, occurs in her poem "Floating island at Hawkshead, an incident in the schemes of Nature."

> Harmonious Powers with Nature work
> On sky, earth, river, lake, and sea:
> Sunshine and storm, whirlwind and breeze
> All in one duteous task agree.
>
> Once did I see a slip of earth,
> By throbbing waves long undermined,
> Loosed from its hold; – *how* no one knew
> But all might see it float, obedient to the wind.

Might see it, from the verdant shore
Dissevered float upon the Lake,
Float, with its crest of trees adorned
On which the warbling birds their pastime take.

Food, shelter, safety there they find:
There berries ripen, flowerets bloom:
There insects live their lives – and die:
A peopled *world* it is; – in size a tiny room.

And thus through many seasons' space
This little Island may survive
But Nature, though we mark her not,
Will take away – may cease to give.

Perchance when you are wandering forth
Upon some vacant sunny day
Without an object, hope, or fear,
Thither your eyes may turn – the Isle is passed away.

Buried beneath the glittering Lake!
Its place no longer to be found,
Yet the lost fragments shall remain,
To fertilize some other ground.[11]

Having assumed "one duteous task" in which all "harmonious powers," including human life, "agree" with Nature, the poem presents a floating island loosed from its hold, passively moved by the wind. And yet this fluid, constantly shifting, circumscribed island is a "peopled *world*" where birds, insects, flowers all find food, shelter, safety, then death. A domesticated world – "in size a tiny room" – the island survives till Nature takes it away, till it is "buried." Yet even then its "fragments" remain to "fertilize some other ground."

This poem constitutes Dorothy's most mature response to her brother's concept of the self. In *The Prelude*, William had denounced his youthful life at Cambridge University in these terms:

Rotted as by a charm, my life became
A floating island, an amphibious thing,
Unsound, of spongy texture, yet withal,
Not wanting a fair face of water-weeds
And pleasant flowers.
            (*The Prelude*, 1805: III, 339–44)

In contrast, Dorothy's poem affirms a floating island life or self that is interactive, absorptive, constantly changing, and domestic – it can be contained within a tiny room. It is a self that produces and supports other lives – warbling birds, blooming flowers, a "crest of trees" – a self that provides food, shelter, safety for others. It is a self that is sometimes visible, sometimes not, a self that can appear and disappear in a moment, a self that is constructed in part – but only in part – by the gaze of others.

"*I* see" it but some day "you" may not. It is a self that is profoundly connected to its environment, to those "harmonious powers" of sunshine and storm, of nature and human society, that surround, direct, even consume it. Above all, this is a self that is *embodied*, that is composed of organic fragments that literally fertilize the ground. Significantly, it is a self that *does not name itself as a self*; the metaphor of the floating island as a life or self is one that has to be intertextually transferred from her brother's poem.

Susan Levin first noted the degree to which Dorothy Wordsworth's floating island self conforms to one model (among several possible models) of feminine identity (Levin 1987: 5), that proposed by our contemporary Self-in-Relation school of psychology derived from British objects-relations theory by Nancy Chodorow, Jean Baker Miller, and Carol Gilligan. Dorothy's sense of self is fluid, relational, exhibiting the permeable ego boundaries Chodorow attributed to the social construction of the feminine gender in those western cultures in which females are assigned the role of primary infant caregiver, of mother. Like many female autobiographers who preceded her – like Margaret Cavendish, Margery Kempe, Julian of Norwich, and Anne Bradstreet – Dorothy Wordsworth constructed her identity "by way of alterity," in relation to a significant other, whether a man, a woman, God, nature or the community.[12] Many female women writers of the Romantic period – Joanna Baillie, Maria Edgeworth, Susan Ferrier, Mary Shelley, and Helen Maria Williams, among others – endorsed this commitment to a construction of subjectivity based on alterity.

Such a commitment carried both ethical and political consequences. These women writers based their moral systems on what Carol Gilligan has taught us to call an ethic of care, which insists on the priority of the rights and needs of the interrelated group – the family or the community – over those of the individual in both moral and political decision-making. They opposed the revolutionary Jacobin politics based on the rights of the common man urged by Rousseau and Thomas Paine, by the young Wordsworth and Coleridge, by Blake, Godwin, and Percy Shelley. Instead, the women writers of the Romantic era offered an alternative program of social progress and reform, one grounded on the trope of the family-politic, on the idea of a nation-state that evolves gradually and rationally under the mutual care and guidance of both mother and father.

Although they occasionally invoked Edmund Burke's concept of the organic development both of the human mind and of the body-politic under benevolent parental control as the model of a successful human community, they radically revised Burke's patriarchal gender politics by insisting on the equal authority of the mother as the guide and guardian of civic responsibility. As Mary Wollstonecraft argued in her *Vindication of the Rights of Men* (1790), political authority should be based on the paradigm of the egalitarian family, on that "first source of civilization," namely, "natural parental affection, that makes no difference between child and child, but what reason justifies by pointing out superior merit" (Wollstonecraft 1960: 46). Only by meeting equally the needs of all the members of the body-politic can a just society be constructed. As Mary Shelley articulated this political position in *Frankenstein*,

> if no man allowed any pursuit whatsoever to interfere with the tranquillity of
> his domestic affections, Greece had not been enslaved; Caesar would have

spared his country; America would have been discovered more gradually; and the empires of Mexico and Peru had not been destroyed.

(Shelley 1982: 51)

Inherent in this feminine Romantic political ideology is a commitment to the equality of the sexes and the incalculable value of each family member. The oldest son is no better – nor worse – than the youngest daughter; both are to be cherished equally. At the level of sexual politics, the trope of the family-politic entails a democracy in which women and men have equal rights and responsibilities. At the level of economic organization, it entails a social program of the distribution of goods and services based on needs rather than on rights, similar to the socialist/feminist program recently outlined by Nancy Fraser in her *Unruly Practices: Power, Discourse and Gender in Contemporary Social Theory* (1989). Advocating gradual rather than violent social change, Romantic women writers insisted that the values of domesticity – of such private virtues as sympathy, generosity, tolerance, devoted care, and a commitment to the preservation of familial affections – should become the guiding program for all *public* action.

Women Romantic writers grounded their notion of community – the family-politic – on a concept of Nature or the physical world very different from that promoted by their male colleagues. Male Romantic writers and artists, following Burke's *Philosophical Inquiry into the Origin of Our Ideas of the Sublime and the Beautiful* (1757), tended to identify threatening landscapes with the (masculine) sublime, sensuously alluring landscapes with the (feminine) beautiful. The sublime thus became associated with an experience of masculine empowerment, the beautiful with a contrasting experience of maternal nurturance, erotic love, and physical relaxation. In its life-threatening aspects, Nature was the punishing father, but a father who could, in the oedipal dynamic traced by Thomas Weiskel in *The Romantic Sublime*, be overcome; in its life-enhancing or procreative aspects, Nature was the devoted mother.

Women writers reacted in three distinct ways to this cultural engendering of Nature or the landscape. One group of writers, familiar to us as the authors of Gothic fiction, accepted Burke's identification of the sublime with the experience of masculine empowerment, but they explicitly equated this masculine sublime with patriarchal tyranny. Ann Radcliffe, for instance, located the exercise of life-threatening violence, not in a Nature she gendered as female, but rather *within the household*, in the patriarchal transgression – usually represented as the threat of father-daughter incest – that in her novels is everywhere most monstrous and most ordinary. At the same time she located in external Nature, in the landscapes she borrowed directly from Salvator Rosa, the acknowledged master of the sublime landscape painting, the experience of *female* empowerment for her besieged heroines. Surveying a Rosa landscape from the turret of her prison, Ellena in *The Italian* is exalted: "her soul, refreshed by the views it afforded, would acquire strength to bear her, with equanimity, thro' the persecutions that might await her" (Radcliffe 1981: 90–1).

In contrast, writers like Susan Ferrier, Sydney Owenson (Lady Morgan) and Helen Maria Williams who grew up surrounded by the mountainous landscapes of the sublime, in Scotland, Ireland, or Wales, defined such landscapes as *home scenery*, the locus of blissful childhood memories in a Nature that they imaged as a loving mother or sister. In their novels, most notably Ferrier's *Destiny* (1831) or Morgan's *The Wild Irish Girl*, Nature is represented as a *female friend* with whom they share their most intimate experiences and with whom they cooperate in the daily business of life, to the mutual advantage of each. For this tradition of women writers, the experience of the sublime is never – as it almost always is for their male peers – a solitary one. If alone, the female protagonist of their works feels comforted, even addressed by, female Nature, with whom she communes in words or song. Most often, their female protagonists immediately share their experience of the sublimity of female Nature and the heightened sensibility it stimulates with another person, usually a cherished lover. Thus the female sublime, in a novel like *The Wild Irish Girl*, produces an experience of *communion* between two different people, that very "sympathy" or *domesticated sublimity* which Morgan hails on the last page of her novel as the essence of "reason and humanity" (Morgan 1986: 255).

If, on the other hand, a woman writer entirely embraced Burke's identification of the category of the beautiful with the female sex, as did the poet Letitia Elizabeth Landon, her work – consciously or unconsciously – revealed the life-threatening dimensions within this hegemonic construction of the woman as the object of beauty, the recipient but never the owner of the connoisseur's gaze. Following Burke's construction of the beautiful as that which is delicate, smooth, soft, enervating, and above all melancholy, Landon's poetry obsessively retells the narrative of female love as a narrative of love offered, a love sustained with devotion, but a love that is always lost or rejected: her female protagonists inevitably love men who finally abandon them. I have discussed Landon's poetry at length in this context in my *Romanticism and Gender* (Ch. 6); here I have space only to point out that Landon, by commodifying her poetry and her portraits as purchasable icons of female love and beauty, sacrificed both her identity (her autobiographical tale, based on the already conventional plot of the neglected "Female Genius," of a life of "Sorrow, Beauty, Love, and Death" (Landon 1837: 312), was a complete fabrication) and, literally, her life. Forced at 38 into marriage in order to preserve an already questioned reputation for virginal purity, she emigrated to West Africa where she soon died.

Summing up, the ideology of feminine literary Romanticism was based on a subjectivity that claimed both the mind (rationality) and the body as constitutive dimensions, yet a subjectivity that was constructed in relation to other subjectivities, a self that typically located its identity within a larger human nexus, whether the family or the neighboring community. Taking the family as the grounding trope of social organization, feminine Romanticism opposed violent military revolutions, especially the French Revolution, in favor of gradual or evolutionary reform under benevolent parental guidance, a "natural" process of evolution they learned from the botanical and biological researches of Erasmus Darwin. This involved a commitment to an ethic of care (as opposed to an ethic of individual justice), an ethic that takes as its highest value the insuring that, in any conflict, no one should be hurt. In this context, Nature becomes not so much a source of divine creative power to be appropriated by the poet, more a female friend or sister with needs and capacities, one who both provides support and requires cultivation, with whose life-giving powers one willingly cooperates. In this feminine Romantic ideology, moral reform both of the individual and of the family-politic is achieved, not by utopian imaginative vision, but by the communal exercise of reason, tolerance, and the domestic affections that can embrace even the alien Other (including Frankenstein's monster).

Contesting the hegemonic construction of gender, the doctrine of the separate spheres and the cult of female beauty subscribed to by Letitia Landon, feminine Romanticism insisted on the equal value and rational capacities of women. Although Romantic women writers differed on how women could best employ their rationality, and hence on how ideal femininity should be constructed, they all resisted a construction of gender that deprived women both of an education and of cultural authority. Finally, feminine Romanticism found its appropriate mode of linguistic expression in specific genres: in the novel which enables the author to represent in the vernacular a human community whose multiple relationships extend over time, in the comic or tragic drama which focuses on family conflicts and resolutions, and in those poetic genres (the sonnet, the ballad, the shorter lyric) which celebrate the value of the quotidian,[13] of daily domestic and social involvements.

Turning now to the three best-known women artists of the Romantic era in Britain, the two women elected as founding members of the Royal Academy of Art in 1768, Angelica Kauffman and Mary Moser, and the gifted Maria Cosway (who gave up her career at the command of her husband, the artist Richard Cosway), I would like to suggest that these women artists can best be understood within the context of the feminine Romanticism promoted by their sister writers. The most talented and prolific of these three women painters, Angelica Kauffman confidently constructed in her numerous self-portraits (the incomplete catalog of her works compiled by Manners and Williamson lists over twenty-five self-portraits, as well as several fancy pictures and group portraits in which she includes herself) a subjectivity that is both rational and physically embodied. She invariably represents herself as a fully empowered, mentally alert, creative artist, with drawing pencil, paintbrush, or harp (she was also a gifted musician). She gazes forthrightly at the viewer, eschewing the demure downcast eyes of Letitia Landon's portraits.

In contrast to portraits of the female artist by men who, following Joseph Wright of Derby's *The Corinthian Maid* (1783–4; Plate 5.4), depict the female artist as one who merely *copies* the outlines and works of male artists and models,[14] Kauffman asserts her capacity for original thought. She also rejects the image of the accomplished upper-class lady as the Muse of Art put forth by Gainsborough in his portrait of *Penelope, Viscountess Ligonier* (1770) or by Reynolds in his portrait of *Anne Hussey Delaval, Lady Stanhope* (1765).[15] In both these works, the lady with pencil or brush in hand is a Muse of Art who inspires male artists but does not herself produce masterpieces. Instead, Kauffman portrays herself as a creative genius, exercising originality, professional craftsmanship, and rational choice, as when she occupies the position of Hercules choosing between Vice and Virtue in her *Angelica Choosing between Music and Painting* (1796).

Kauffman's portraits of other women also emphasize the rational capabilities of her subjects, frequently depicting them as readers, with book in hand – as in her portraits of Lady Henderson of Fordel, of Dorothy Holroyd, of Margaret, countess of Lucan, and of Mary Joanna Cutts Revett. Where possible, she assigns them the further attributes of the mental creator. Mary "Perdita" Robinson, with scroll in hand, is titled "The British Sappho." The sculptor, the Honourable Ann Damer, wears a crown of laurel.

Mrs. Mary Townshend is completing a highly skilled and elaborate piece of needle-work. And in one of her most aesthetically successful portraits, painted in glowing blues, whites, and reds, Kauffman represents Miss Cornelia Knight (City of Manchester Art Gallery; Plate 8.1) as *both* a writer and an artist. Knight's published book, *Marcus Flaminius*, lies on the table beside her, while she sits, pencil in hand, drawing a model for a public monument to celebrate Nelson's first naval victory. Scrolled pages of her compositions lie before her. Cornelia Knight is Angelica Kauffman's representation of the ideal woman as learned bluestocking and cultural leader. Significantly, Kauffman had originally painted a bust of Athena – the goddess both of wisdom and of the independent polis – on Knight's belt-buckle, but had then changed it willingly, at Knight's request, to a bust of herself,[16] thus implicitly affirming her female self-representation as a cultural and political authority.

For Angelica Kauffman, there is no conflict between the rational woman and the mother. The countess of Galloway is represented as an educator, teaching her daughter how to draw. And in a daring iconic shift, Kauffman represents herself as a "nursing artist," her drawing pad and pencil held to her breast in the position of a nursing infant, in her 1784 self-portrait now in the Munich Bayerische Staats-gemaldesammlungen. Kauffman's females are women who choose to be involved in relationships with others. Where she typically portrays her male sitters as isolated figures, accompanied by the tools of their trade, she represents her female sitters as actively interacting with other living things, whether animals (the Honourable Caroline Curzon holds a bird) or flowers (as in her portraits of Mrs. Samuel Whitbread and Ann Seymour Damer) or, most often, a family member, either a sister (as in her portrait of the duchess of Devonshire and Lady Duncannon) or a child (as in her portraits of Mrs. Rushout and her daughter, the marchioness of Townshend and her son, the duchess of Brunswick and her child, the Lady Elizabeth Hervey and her daughter, or the marchioness of Lothian and her son). Kauffman thus subtly suggests that the subjectivity of her female sitters is a relational one, one that actively engages them in a sympathetic correspondence with the surrounding world.

Kauffman's history paintings assert both her claim to cultural authority and her sexual politics, her "revolution in female manners." These paintings insist upon the equality of women with men and upon the superiority of the domestic affections. Her claim to sexual equality was recognized, if not endorsed, by her male peers. Emphasizing her attempt to elevate her women characters to heroic heights, Henry Fuseli sourly commented:

> The male and female characters of Angelica never vary in form, feature, or expression from the favourite ideal in her own mind. Her heroes are all the man to whom she thought she could have submitted, though him, perhaps, she never found. Her heroines are herself, and while suavity of countenance, and alluring graces shall be able to divert the general eye from the sterner demands of character and expression, can never fail to please.[17]

Fuseli, however resentfully (Kauffman had rejected his sexual overtures and usurped his role as foremost interpreter to England of continental history painting), correctly perceived beneath their surface charm the deeper argument of Kauffman's construc-tions of female subjectivity, the representation of woman as the equal of man in moral character and determination. The poet Peter Pindar also understood Kauffman's feminist politics, but saw them as an attempt to enfeeble men rather than to empower women; as he wrote sarcastically in his "Lyric Ode to Royal Academicians" (1794):

> Angelica my plaudits gains –
> Her art so sweetly canvas stains! –
> Her Dames so Grecian! give me such delight!
> But were she married to such gentle Males
> As figure in her painted tales –
> I fear she'd find a stupid wedding night.
>
> (Pindar 1794: I, 45)

Working in the highest genre of eighteenth-century art, history painting, Kauffman asserted both her ability to compete with the leading male history painters of the day (West, Hamilton, Barry) and her independence from their subject-matter. Forswearing images of male heroism located in military victories or defeats, past or present, she offered a different definition of heroism as the triumph of the domestic affections. In her *Hector Taking Leave of Andromache* (Plate 8.2) Hector is portrayed not as a military hero but as Andromache's devoted husband. As Albert Boime has perceptively commented, Kauffman here transforms Hector

> from the stalwart hero who rejects the entreaties of his wife to a wistful juvenile who wears his helmet uneasily. Kauffman's emphasis is on Andromache's tender gesture and the nurse who cradles the child in her arms. The picture tells less about masculine courage than about domestic concerns which Hector repudiates.
>
> (Boime 1787: 112–13)

In contrast, Gavin Hamilton's *Hector's Farewell to Andromache* clearly suggests that the emotional bonds of family love must be given up for the good of the state – Hector is there depicted with helmet and horse, towering above his fellow warriors, the savior of the besieged Trojans beyond him, while Andromache kneels before him, offering up her son for a farewell blessing that could also be read as a premonitory sacrifice. Similarly, Gavin Hamilton in his multiply peopled, staged tableau of *Andromache Bewailing the Death of Hector* (Plate 8.3) emphasized the tragic and universally mourned death of the masculine hero laid out on his bier. In contrast, Kauffman in her *Andromache Weeping over the Body of Hector* (Plate 8.4) stressed the equally tragic grief of two women and a child who, surrounding the urn (Hector does not even appear in Kauffman's image), are as much the victims of battles as the warriors who die in them.

Focusing her history paintings on women, either by placing them at the center of the painting or by lighting them more brightly than the men,[18] Kauffman repeatedly portrays the capacity of feminine love to defeat masculine aggression, as when the Amazonian Imbaca prevents Tremor from continuing to fight, in *The Power of Love* (1773), based on Book 6 of Ossian's *Fingal*; or the triumph of the domestic affections, as when Eleonora risks her life to save her husband, in *Eleanora sucking the Venom out of the Wound of Edward I, her Royal Consort, received from a Poisoned Dagger by an Assassin in Palestine* (1780). Other paintings celebrate female love for its fidelity even unto death, as in her *Cleopatra adorning the Tomb of Mark Antony* (1770) or *Dido invoking the Gods before mounting the Funeral Pyre* (1777). Frequently invoking classical events, Angelica Kauffman subverts their ideological significance away from a glorification of military prowess to a glorification of domestic love: Cornelia is shown exhibiting her small sons as her "jewels" rather than as the mother of victorious fighters (in *Cornelia, Mother of the Gracchi*, 1785), while Achilles is shown, not in the triumph of battle, but rather in emotional agony (in *The Despair of Achilles on being informed by Antilochus of the Death of Patroclus*, 1775 and again in 1789). Kauffman thus contests her culture's hegemonic definition of the woman as "the one who loves" by suggesting that love is the highest activity to which a man, too, can aspire, a point she makes again in *Paris and Helen* (1773); in *Damon and Musidora* (1782); in *Bacchus and Ariadne* (1764); and most globally, in her allegorical *Science resting in the Arms of Peace* (1780).

While celebrating the triumph of domestic love over military aggression, Kauffman nonetheless insisted that love – especially for women – must be guided by reason. In her version of Jane Austen's *Sense and Sensibility*, a series of allegorical paintings depicting a young woman torn between passionate love and common sense, Kauffman painted only one instance of *Beauty Yielded to Love, Quitted by Prudence* (1782) but several of the reverse, *Beauty Tempted by Love, Counselled by Prudence* (1778, 1780, 1783).

Maria Cosway also celebrated the rationality of women in her best work: in her version of a Hogarthian *Rake's Progress* entitled *The Progress of Female Virtue and the Progress of Female Dissipation* (London, 1800); in her illustrations for William Ackerman's edition of "Perdita" Robinson's *Poems* (London, 1803); and in her portraits of the duchess of Devonshire and of Mrs. Fitzherbert. All these works demonstrate a sustained effort to redefine the female character. Exhibited at the Royal Academy in 1782, Maria Cosway's portrait of the duchess of Devonshire as Diana descending from the heavens offered a new construction of femininity. Her image is based on Spenser's description of Britomart in *The Faerie Queene* at the moment when Britomart, the embodiment of Amazonian British courage and devoted love, first lifts her visor, allowing "her goodly visage to appere" like the light of the moon:

> As when faire *Cynthia*, in darkesome night,
> Is in a noyous cloud enveloped,
> Where she may find the substaunce thin and light,
> Breakes forth her silver beames, and her bright hed
> Discovers to the world discomfited.
>   (Book 3, Canto 1, Stanza 43)

Maria Cosway portrays the duchess in wildly swirling robes, crowned with a crescent tiara, hurling herself down upon the earth. Her arms are spread – the left forward and down, the right up and back – in a commanding gesture that separates the bright clouds, revealing the darkness behind her. Her gesture echoes traditional images of God separating the light from the dark; assigned to a woman, it seemed almost blasphemous to Cosway's audience, at the very least, as Horace Walpole commented, "extravagant."[19] But to my eyes it is an image of female power and unrestrained authority, of woman as the embodiment of both purity and sexual fertility (as the voluptuous contours and ample, almost entirely exposed, white breasts of the duchess suggest), of woman as the one who divides light from darkness, virtue from vice.

This construction of woman as capable of both rational and moral choice also underlies Maria Cosway's portraits of Mrs. Fitzherbert, in which Mrs. Fitzherbert mediates nature and culture – she is seated outdoors in a pastoral landscape, fondling her dog with her left hand, while peering intently into a book held just before her eyes – and of Princess Amelia, in which the princess insistently holds forth to the spectator a page of her own creative work. Cosway presents this conception of the rational woman more programmatically in her parallel progresses of female virtue and female dissipation. Cosway's canvas is confined to an entirely domesticated, middle-class world. Here Cosway may have been influenced by Mary Wollstonecraft who, both in her pedagogical conduct book for the daughters of the gentry and professional middle classes, *Original Stories from Real Life* (1788, with illustrations by William Blake), and in her *Vindication of the Rights of Woman* (1792), insisted on portraying the ideal woman as an average middle-class wife and mother:

> Let fancy now present a woman with a tolerable understanding, for *I do not wish to leave the line of mediocrity*, whose constitution, strengthened by exercise, has allowed her body to acquire its full vigour; her mind, at the same time gradually expanding itself to comprehend the moral duties of life, and in what human virtue and dignity consist.
>
> Formed thus by the discharge of the relative duties of her station, she marries from affection, without losing sight of prudence, and looking beyond matrimonial felicity, she secures her husband's respect before it is necessary to exert mean arts to please him and feed a dying flame, which nature doomed to expire when the object became familiar, when friendship and forbearance take the place of a more ardent affection. – This is the natural death of love, and domestic peace is not destroyed by struggles to prevent its extinction. I also suppose the husband to be virtuous; or she is still more in want of independent principles.
>
> Fate, however breaks this tie. – She is left a widow, perhaps, without a sufficient provision; but she is not desolate! . . . I think I see her surrounded by her children, reaping the reward of her care. The intelligent eye meets hers, whilst health and innocence smile on their chubby cheeks, and as they grow up the cares of life are lessened by their grateful attention. She lives to see the virtues which she endeavoured to plant on principles, fixed into habits, to see her children attain a strength of character sufficient to enable them to endure adversity without forgetting their mother's example.
>
> The task of life thus fulfilled, she calmly waits for the sleep of death, and rising from the grave, may say – Behold, thou gavest me a talent – and here are five talents.[20]

Cosway too insists on the intelligence, the domestic affections, and the moral virtue of her ideal woman. In the first plate she represents her as a Christian mother teaching her infant daughter to pray; in the second, as an educator teaching her to read "the moral tale." In the third plate, the growing girl then demonstrates her strength of character and Christian generosity by giving "her mite" to the poor "Blind Child."

In the image which interests me most in this series, the young woman is next represented as an artist, seated with her sketch-book, looking out the window at a wooded landscape, while a completed painting stands on the easel behind her (Plate 8.5). The caption for this design reads:

> While Nature's beauties her free lines pourtray,
> She knows not that she's fairer far than they.

At the surface level, Cosway is emphasizing the modesty (as well as the beauty) of her ideal woman.

But this image suggests another, and more revolutionary, reading. Cosway's ideal woman is an artist, and one who, unlike the Corinthian Maid, does not *copy* the works of men but rather draws directly from Nature. And what she sees in Nature is what we see on her easel, a painting which portrays, so far as I can make it out, a woman, presumably a mother, bending over a rounded, helmet-like basket or bassinet, which rests beside her on a bench. (Such personifications of Nature occur frequently in Cosway's work, from the moon as the duchess of Devonshire to the cloudy night as Melancholy, in *Female by the Sea, repelling the Spirit of Melancholy* in the Whitworth Art Gallery, Manchester, and were of course common in the poetry and art of her time.) Like Lady Morgan and Ann Radcliffe, Maria Cosway here domesticates the sublime, writing the forest landscape outside her window as Mother Nature caring for her beloved child. Cosway both endorses a reading of Nature as female, as the mother, and at the same time defines the female artistic process as a legitimate participation in a natural rhythm of generational production. Moreover, were this female artist to stand up, she would tower above the easel behind her: for Cosway, the woman artist is a giant, mediating between nature and culture without the visual interposition of a male mentor or male-authored art.

As the fusion of the best in both nature and culture, Cosway's ideal female then in Plate V marries a youth who looks no older or wiser than she. Significantly, this is the only time that a man appears in these designs, and he assumes a position of equality with the young woman. Our bride then becomes a mother. The last three designs present her first with an infant nursing at her breast (Plate VI), then as a mother surrounded by three children ("the blessings of her happy home," Plate VII), and finally as a grandmother with three grandchildren. The absence of men from all but one of these designs suggests that Maria Cosway's ideal woman, like Wollstonecraft's widow, has become the sole bearer of both natural fertility and cultural authority, teaching boys and girls alike to value the domestic affections as the embodiment of religious and political virtue.

In contrast, the dissipated female is one who undermines the family-politic and the harmony of the domestic world. She is badly educated by her mother, given toys rather than rational and religious instruction, taught only to become the object of the gaze. In Plate II she dresses up before the mirror; in Plate IV (Plate 8.6), she looks at herself in the mirror even as she fingers her harp. She learns only the female "accomplishments" of harp-playing and dancing (the latter, in Plate III, from a Fuseli-like woman of fashion who forces both her own and her pupil's body into unnatural contortions: "She's tam'd and tortur'd into foreign graces, / To sport her pretty face at public places"). This vain, self-regarding female enters marriage, in Plate V, with *no* visible husband: she is accompanied to a Temple of Hymen which rests precariously on soft clouds only by three cupids who carry her frivolous feathers and jewels. We next see her at her toilette, elaborately coiffed and costumed and be-hatted (Plate VI), then abandoning her weeping children to attend a society ball (Plate VII), and finally as an elderly "grey Dowager" spending all her time with another old dowager at tea, cards, snuff, and malicious gossip. Cosway's didactic message is clear: women have the power to construct their own lives. Cosway may here confine the lives of her women characters to the domestic sphere, but like Hannah More she insists that women have the capacity for rational and moral choice, and are individually responsible for their own lives, for the decision to enact a life of Christian benevolence or a life of personal ostentation and social waste.

That Maria Cosway knew what was at stake in such social waste is evidenced in her illustrations for her friend Mary "Perdita" Robinson's poems in 1803. Here she looks beyond the domestic walls of the private sphere. She contrasts the enervated idleness of an aristocratic woman's "Winter Day" (Plate I) and her self-indulgent fashion mongering at "The Milliner" (Plate IX) with the extreme suffering experienced by the rural poor: by the beggar woman mourning her child dead of starvation and cold in "Death on the Heath" (Plate II) and by the dying woman unable to suckle her infant as her husband flees in despair in "Poverty" (Plate VIII). Here Cosway endorses Robinson's arguments in her *Thoughts on the Condition of Women, and on the injustice of Mental Subordination* (1799), that women must be educated, that they have the moral and intellectual capacity to choose a life of virtue, and, finally, that their Christian charity can actively alleviate the sufferings of the poor.

The second female founding member of the Royal Academy was Mary Moser, the daughter of the Keeper of the Collection, George Moser. That neither Kauffman nor Moser was considered a "full" member of the Royal Academy is clear in the group portrait of *The Academicians of the Royal Academy* painted by Johann Zoffany in 1771. While all the male members of the Royal Academy are portrayed in full, engaging in active contemplation of a nude male model being posed by George Moser, Angelica Kauffman and Mary Moser appear only as half-portraits hung in frames upon the wall *behind* the model: this because women were excluded from the presence of naked men.

In order to understand the possible significance of the work of Mary Moser, we must look at her paintings of flowers through the lens of one of the leading female poets of the day, Charlotte Smith. In her most famous poem, "Beachy Head," published in London in 1807, Smith clarified the significance of flowers for her contemporaries. Flowers had long been associated with the female sex – both nominally and metaphorically – and the amorous *langage des fleurs* popular in Renaissance literature had survived into the nineteenth century, as had their Christian symbolism.[21] But Smith's poem suggests a different way of reading the language of flowers, one that Moser may also have had in mind. "Beachy Head" is a lengthy but subtle attack on the evils of English imperialism, on the slave trade, on commerce, on the unjust class system, on the artifice and waste of upper-class British society. In contrast to this perversely "cultivated" England, Smith offers an alternative political and moral ideology, a vision of an organic, natural England rooted in the soil of rural villages and fields, a life of simplicity, domestic affections, and good "fellowship," one that she associates with the "cottage garden" and "upland shepherd" home of her Surrey childhood. As Smith expounds:

The cottage garden: most for use design'd,
Yet not of beauty destitute. The vine
Mantles the little casement; yet the briar
Drops fragrant dew among the July flowers;
And pansies rayed, and freak'd and mottled pinks
Grow among balm, and rosemary and rue:
There honeysuckles flaunt, and roses blow
Almost uncultured: some with dark green leaves
Contrast their flowers of pure unsullied white:
Others, like velvet robes of regal state
Of richest crimson, while in thorny moss
Enshrined and cradled, the most lovely, wear
The hues of beauty's glowing cheek. . . .

An early worshipper of Nature's shrine,
I loved her rudest scenes – warrens, and heaths,
And yellow commons, and birch-shaded hollows,
And hedge rows, bordering unfrequented lanes
Bowered with wild roses, and the clasping woodbine
Where purple tassels of the tangling vetch[22]
With bittersweet, and bryony inweave,[23]
And the dew fills the silver bindweed's cups –[24]
I loved to trace the brooks whose humid banks
Nourish the harebell, and the freckled pagil;[25]
And stroll among o'ershadowing woods of beech,
Lending in Summer, from the heats of noon
A whispering shade; while haply there reclines
Some pensive lover of uncultur'd flowers,
Who, from the stumps with bright green mosses clad,
Plucks the wood sorrel,[26] with its light thin leaves,
Heart-shaped, and triply folded; and its root
Creeping like beaded coral; or who there
Gathers, the copse's pride, anemones,
With rays like golden studs on ivory laid
Most delicate: but touch'd with purple clouds,
Fit crown for April's fair but changeful brow.
("Beachy Head," ll. 300–12, 319–40)

Smith insists that the native virtues of England lie in her "uncultivated" flowers, in a cooperative interaction between humanity and Nature that leads to useful agricultural production. Attacking the exploitation of both the poor and the land by British capitalist interests, she offers a moral program grounded in "uncultur'd" flowers, native-grown, unforced, organic.

Moreover, her extensive footnotes, which I have deliberately included, insist upon her botanical learning, her ability to cite the correct Latin names of each particular specimen. Smith thus lays claim to a scientific competence long denied to women, asserting her ability to participate in a botanical discourse that had hitherto been considered the exclusive domain of male scientists and that had greatly expanded in the eighteenth century under the new classificatory systems introduced by Linnaeus and the innovative research into the evolution of both plants and animals published by Erasmus Darwin in his long poem, *The Botanic Garden: The Economy of Vegetation* and *The Loves of the Plants* (London, Vol. II appearing first, in 1789, with Vol. I following in 1791). Implicitly invoking Darwin, Smith here affirms a political program of natural, gradual evolution rather than the military battles and conquests she observes from her post on Beachy Head, looking across the Channel at France.

If it is plausible to view Mary Moser's flower paintings in the context of the discourse on botany and natural history developed in England in the eighteenth century, they may have more significance than has hitherto been recognized. In the examples of her work I have seen, it is notable that she chooses to paint *native* rather than recently imported exotic flowers: the lily of the valley, the English rose, the peony, the iris, the daisy, the morning glory (convolvulus), the bear's-ear (auricula), the stock, the tulip, the poppy. These are all English garden flowers, grown in England since the sixteenth century and most of them mentioned by Shakespeare. In one painting, in the Victoria and Albert Museum, she places her flowers in a vase, but allows them to spill out (in a rococo composition derived from Jan van Huysum and the tradition of Netherlandish flower painting); in another, in the Spooner Collection, the flowers are strewn on the ground, as though spontaneously dropped in front of the viewer. In a third, in the Broughton Collection, she adds English fruit (apples and grapes) and butterflies. Is Mary Moser suggesting, as Charlotte Smith had done, that a natural, organic England – and a natural Englishwoman – is preferable to a highly sophisticated, artificial one?

Like the Dutch and Flemish painters upon whom she drew, Moser insists on the minute differences and particularities of her flowers, rendering each in careful detail (see Plate 8.7). Like Smith, she thus suggests that Nature is both infinitely various and stubbornly resistant to any attempt to unify, harmonize, or confine her within such limited aesthetic categories as the sublime, the beautiful, or the picturesque, those categories imposed upon English landscape by such male writers and painters as Burke, Gilpin, Coleridge, Wordsworth, Gainsborough, Constable, and Turner. For Moser, as for Smith, Nature remains insistently Other – to be reverently appreciated and cooperatively used, but not to be possessed or systematized.

If my readings of the works of Kauffman, Cosway, and Moser are defensible, it would seem that these British women painters, like their sister writers, shared a feminine Romanticism deeply at odds with the Romantic ideology propounded by the leading male writers and painters of the day. I should clarify that the "feminine Romanticism" I have been describing is not based on biological sex but on the cultural construction of gender; men as well as women could work within the discourse of this feminine ideology – as did the poet John Keats when he embraced a non-egoistic construction of subjectivity in his concept of "negative capability" and the painter Thomas Stothard when he, like Kauffman, emphasized the "sentimental" values of the domestic affections over scenes of classical heroism in his history paintings. Needless to say, the ideology of "feminine Romanticism" and the works of Romantic women writers and artists have been largely erased from the western cultural canon of "Romanticism" – an erasure produced in large part by the homoerotic investments of the dons (most notably Walter Pater and Edmund Gosse) who first constructed the academic canon of

English literature at Oxford University in the 1890s and reinforced by the celebration of alienated, ironic masculinity found in the Modernist movement's response to two world wars. This erasure has impoverished both our understanding of the cultural past and our regard for the achievements of Romantic women artists and writers. In the future we will need to take the work of these women into account whenever we speak of Romanticism as a literary or artistic movement, both in order to acknowledge the ways in which "British Romanticism" or "the Romantic movement" as we have traditionally understood it is an exclusively *masculine* phenomenon, and to recognize that their feminine Romanticism grounded on rationality, a relational subjectivity, and an ethic of care demonstrates the ideological *continuity* between the artistic cultures of the eighteenth-century Enlightenment and the high Victorianism of George Eliot, Dickens, Ruskin, and Millais.

Notes

1   Altick 1957: 217–18. Coral Ann Howells's comments on Lane's Minerva Press, one of the most successful circulating libraries (1978: 80–2) further document that women were the major contributors to these libraries, as well as the primary subscribers. Paul Hunter (1990: 69–75) argues for the increasing literacy of women in the eighteenth century and points out that at least half of the popular "Guides for Youth" or conduct books were addressed to female readers (265–6).

2   Myers 1989: 122. The major role of women in literary publication in the early nineteenth century in England is also supported by the data concerning Macmillan's publishing house collected by Gaye Tuchman in *Edging Women Out* (1989).

3   Mary ("Perdita") Robinson concludes her *Thoughts on the Condition of Women, and on the injustice of Mental Subordination* (1799) with a list of thirty-nine eminent living women writers and artists. She further insists that "the best novels that have been written, since those of Smollett, Richardson, and Fielding, have been produced by women: and their pages have not only been embellished with the interesting events of domestic life, portrayed with all the elegance of phraseology, and all the refinement of sentiment, but with forcible and eloquent, political, theological and philosophical reasoning" (1799: 95).

4   In my *Romanticism and Gender* (1993) I selected as representative of this enormous body of female literary production only twenty or so women writers acknowledged at the time or later to be the most influential, gifted, or widely read: Jane Austen, Joanna Baillie, Anna Laetitia Barbauld, Mary Brunton, Frances Burney, Maria Edgeworth, Susan Ferrier, Mary Hays, Felicia Hemans, Letitia Landon, Hannah More, Amelia Opie, Sydney Owenson (Lady Morgan), Ann Radcliffe, Mary Robinson, Mary Shelley, Charlotte Smith, Jane Taylor, Helen Maria Williams, Mary Wollstonecraft, and Dorothy Wordsworth.

5   Elizabeth Kowaleski-Wallace (1991) argues persuasively for the conservative tendencies of Hannah More but fails to recognize the degree to which the claim for female rationality put forth by both More and Edgeworth in itself carried revolutionary implications for the construction of gender in the Romantic period.

6   Here I am endorsing Claudia Johnson's persuasive interpretation of *Emma* in her *Jane Austen – Women, Politics and the Novel*, Ch. 6, and rejecting the more traditional view of Emma as, in Susan Morgan's overly extreme formulation, "the most flawed of Austen's heroines" (1980: 77).

7   Jane Austen, *Emma* (1966: 331, 340). These lines, quoted by Jane Austen from William Cowper's *The Task*, Book IV, are the inspiration for Coleridge's celebration of the freely associating and unifying Romantic imagination in his "Frost at Midnight." Austen, in opposition to Coleridge, identifies the liberated imagination with the errors of perception to which Emma and others (here, possibly, Mr. Knightley) are prone.

8   Carole Pateman has demonstrated the way in which the individual assumed capable of entering into the social contract in both classical and modern social contract theory is exclusively male, in *The Sexual Contract* (1988); John Locke's equation of the individual with the ownership of his own capacities, attributes, and physical body occurs in his *Two Treatises of Government* (1967: II, 27). In his inquiry into "the archeology of knowledge" initiated in *Les Mots et les choses* (1966), translated as *The Order of Things*) (1970), Michel Foucault defined the late eighteenth century as a pivotal moment in the evolution of the idea of the self, the beginning of an episteme in which the individual has a new sense "of something taking place in himself, often at an unconscious level, in his subjectivity, in his values, that traverses the whole of his action in the world" (82–3).

9   On the masculine, specifically oedipal construction of William Wordsworth's subjectivity, see Marlon B. Ross, *The Contours of Masculine Desire – Romanticism and the Rise of Women's Poetry* (1989); Richard J. Onorato, *The Character of the Poet – Wordsworth in The Prelude* (1971); and my *Romanticism and Gender* (1993: 148–52).

10 For discussion of the way Wordsworth precariously represses the Other, see Susan J. Wolfson, *The Questioning Presence: Wordsworth, Keats, and the Interrogative Mode in Romantic Poetry* (1986) and Mary Jacobus, *Romanticism, Writing and Sexual Difference – Essays on The Prelude* (1990).

11 The collected poems of Dorothy Wordsworth are reprinted in Susan Levin's *Dorothy Wordsworth and Romanticism* (1987): Appendix One, pp. 175–237 (207–9).

12 Mary Mason has analyzed the "evolution and delineation of an identity by way of alterity" in the writings of Cavendish, Julian, Kempe, and Bradstreet in "The other voice: autobiographies of women writers" (1988: 19–44).

13 Stuart Curran has emphasized the concern of Romantic women poets with the representation of the "quotidian," in "The 'I' altered" (1988: 185–207).

14 Ann Bermingham has discussed the significance of the widespread trope of the Corinthian Maid as the prototype of the female artist in the eighteenth century, in "The origin of painting and the ends of art: Wright of Derby's Corinthian Maid," *Painting and the Politics of Culture*, ed. John Barrell (forthcoming).

15 Shelley M. Bennett has analyzed the transformation of the accomplished woman as sketcher into the woman as Muse of Art in the work of Gainsborough, Reynolds, and other French and English painters, in "A Muse of Art in the Huntington Collection" (1992).

16 Lady Knight's journal description of the composition of and changes made in her daughter's portrait by Angelica Kauffman is quoted in the catalogue for *Exhibition of Paintings by Angelica Kauffman* (1955: 19).

17 Henry Fuseli's description of the work of Angelica Kauffman is quoted in the catalogue for the Kenwood *Exhibition of Paintings by Angelica Kauffman* (1955: 3).

18 Albert Boime also emphasizes the centrality of women and of the value of the family to Angelica Kauffman's art (1987: 113–15). He quotes William Beckford's perceptive letter to Sir William Hamilton – "As for Angelica, she is my Idol; so say everything that can be said in my name, and tell her how I long to see Telemachus's Papa and all the noble Family" – and concludes that Kauffman "managed to create an appealing environment of domesticated, playful, erotic deities for lords and ladies who looked upon them as their antique counterparts" (Ibid.: 115) and thus both identified with and became a commercial product of the upper classes who patronized her.

19 Horace Walpole's comment is quoted by John Walker, in "Maria Cosway: an undervalued artist" (1986: 324, Appendix).

20 Wollstonecraft, *A Vindication of the Rights of Woman* (1988: 51). Wollstonecraft's biblical allusion is to Matthew 25. 15–28.

21 For a summary of the traditional symbolism of flowers, especially as located in Dutch and Flemish flower painting of the sixteenth to nineteenth centuries, see Sam Segal, *Flowers and Nature – Netherlandish Flower Painting of Four Centuries* (1990).

22 Vetch: *Vicia sylvatrica* (C. Smith note).

23 Bittersweet: *Solanum dulcamara*; Bryony: *Bryonia alba* (C. Smith note).

24 Bindweed: *Convolvulus sepium* (C. Smith note).

25   Harebell: *Hyacinthus non scriptus*; Pagil: *Primula veris* (C. Smith note).
26   Sorrel: *Oxalis acetosella* (C. Smith note).

Bibliography

Altick, Richard D. (1957) *The English Common Reader: A Social History of the Mass Reading Public 1800–1900*, Chicago: University of Chicago Press.

Austen, Jane (1966 [1816]) *Emma*, Harmondsworth, Mx: Penguin; reprinted 1983.

Bennett, Shelley M. (1992) "A Muse of Art in the Huntington Collection," in *British Art, 1740–1820: Essays in Honor of Robert R. Wark*, ed. Gilland Sutherland, San Marino, CA: Huntington Library, pp. 57–80.

Bermingham, Ann (1992) "The origin of painting and the ends of art: Wright of Derby's Corinthian Maid," in *Painting and the Politics of Culture*, ed. John Barrell, Oxford: Oxford University Press.

Boime, Albert (1987) *Art in an Age of Revolution*, Chicago and London: University of Chicago Press.

Chodorow, Nancy (1974) *The Reproduction of Mothering: Psychoanalysis and the Sociology of Gender*, Berkeley, CA: University of California Press.

Curran, Stuart (1988) "The 'I' altered," in *Romanticism and Feminism*, ed. Anne K. Mellor, Bloomington, IN: Indiana University Press, pp. 185–207.

—— (1990) *A Textbase of Women's Writing in English, 1330–1830: Bibliography of British Women Poets, 1760–1830*, available from the Brown University Women Writers Project or from the author.

Foucault, Michel (1970 [1966]) *The Order of Things: An Archaeology of the Human Sciences*, trans. A.M. Sheridan Smith, New York: Random House.

—— (1980) *Michel Foucault: The Will to Truth*, New York: Methuen.

Fraser, Nancy (1989) *Unruly Practices: Power, Discourse and Gender in Contemporary Social Theory*, Minneapolis, MN: University of Minnesota Press.

Gilligan, Carol (1982) *In a Different Voice: Psychological Theory and Women's Development*, Cambridge, MA: Harvard University Press.

Howells, Coral Ann (1978) *Love, Mystery, and Misery: Feeling in Gothic Fiction*, London: Athlone Press.

Hunter, J. Paul (1990) *Before Novels: The Cultural Contexts of Eighteenth-Century English Fiction*, New York: W. W. Norton.

Jacobus, Mary (1990) *Romanticism, Writing and Sexual Difference: Essays on The Prelude*, New York: Oxford University Press.

Johnson, Claudia L. (1988) *Jane Austen: Women, Politics, and the Novel*, Chicago: University of Chicago Press.

Jones, Ann H. (1986) *Ideas and Innovations: Best Sellers of Jane Austen's Age*, New York: AMS Press.

Kauffman, Angelica (1955) *Exhibition of Paintings by Angelica Kauffman*, the Iveagh Bequest, Kenwood, May–September 1955, London, London County Council.

Kowaleski-Wallace, Elizabeth (1991) *Their Father's Daughters: Hannah More, Maria Edgeworth, and Patriarchal Complicity*, New York and Oxford: Oxford University Press.

Landon, Letitia Elizabeth [L. E. L.] (1837) *Traits and Trials of Early Life*, London: Henry Colburn.

Levin, Susan (1987) *Dorothy Wordsworth and Romanticism*, New Brunswick, NJ: Rutgers University Press.

Locke, John (1967 [1690]) *Two Treatises of Government*, ed. P. Laslett, 2nd edn, Cambridge: Cambridge University Press.

Manners, Victoria and Williamson, G. C. (1924) *Angelica Kauffmann, R. A.*, London: John Lane.

Mason, Mary (1988) "The other voice: autobiographies of women writers," in *Life/Lines: Theorizing Women's Autobiography*, ed. Bella Brodzki and Celeste Schenck, Ithaca, NJ: Cornell University Press, pp. 19–44.

Mellor, Anne K. (1988) *Mary Shelley: Her Life, Her Fiction, Her Monsters*, New York and London: Methuen/Routledge, Chapman & Hall.

—— (1993) *Romanticism and Gender*, New York: Routledge, Chapman & Hall.

Miller, Jean Baker (1976) *Toward a New Psychology of Women*, Boston, MA: Beacon Press.

Morgan, Lady [Sydney Owenson] (1986 [1806]) *The Wild Irish Girl*, London: Pandora Books.

Morgan, Susan (1980) *In the Meantime: Character and Perception in Jane Austen's Fiction*, Chicago: University of Chicago Press.

Myers, Mitzi (1989) "Sensibility and the 'walk of reason' – Mary Wollstonecraft's literary reviews as cultural critique," in Syndy McMillen Conger (ed.) *Sensibility in Transformation – Creative Resistance to Sentiment from the Augustans to the Romantics*, Rutherford, NJ: Fairleigh Dickinson University, pp. 120–44.

Onorato, Richard J. (1971) *The Character of the Poet: Wordsworth in The Prelude*, Princeton, NJ: Princeton University Press.

Pateman, Carole (1988) *The Sexual Contract*, Cambridge: Polity Press.

Pindar, Peter (1794) *The Works of Peter Pindar, Esquire*, ed. J. Wolcot, 2 vols., London.

Radcliffe, Ann (1981 [1797]) *The Italian*, Oxford: Oxford University Press.

Robinson, Mary [Perdita] (1799) *Thoughts on the Condition of Women, and on the injustice of Mental Subordination*, 2nd edn., London.

Ross, Marlon B. (1989) *The Contours of Masculine Desire: Romanticism and the Rise of Women's Poetry*, New York: Oxford University Press.

Segal, Sam (1990) *Flowers and Nature: Netherlandish Flower Painting of Four Centuries*, The Hague: SDU Publishers.

Shelley, Mary (1982 [1818]) *Frankenstein, or The Modern Prometheus* (the 1818 text), ed. James Rieger, Chicago: University of Chicago Press.

Smith, Charlotte (1807) *Beachy Head: with Other Poems*, London: J. Johnson.

Spencer, Jane (1986) *The Rise of the Woman Novelist: From Aphra Behn to Jane Austen*, Oxford: Blackwell.

Sulloway, Alison G. (1989) *Jane Austen and the Province of Womanhood*, Philadelphia, PA: University of Pennsylvania Press.

Tuchman, Gaye, with Fortina, Nina (1989) *Edging Women Out: Victorian Novelists, Publishers and Social Change*, New Haven, CT: Yale University Press.

Walker, John (1986) "Maria Cosway: an undervalued artist," *Apollo Magazine* CXXIII (May): 318–24.

Weiskel, Thomas (1976) *The Romantic Sublime: Studies in the Structure and Psychology of Transcendence*, Baltimore, MD: Johns Hopkins University Press; reprinted 1986.

Wolfson, Susan J. (1986) *The Questioning Presence: Wordsworth, Keats, and the Interrogative Mode in Romantic Poetry*, Ithaca, NY: Cornell University Press.

Wollstonecraft, Mary (1960 [1790]) *A Vindication of the Rights of Men* (London), facsimile edn. with introduction by Eleanor Louise Nicholes, Gainesville, FL: Scolar Facsimiles & Reprints.

—— (1988 [1792]) *A Vindication of the Rights of Woman*, ed. Carol H. Poston, 2nd edn., New York: Norton Critical Editions; first published 1975.

Wordsworth, Dorothy (1987) *The Collected Poems of Dorothy Wordsworth*, reprinted in Susan Levin, *Dorothy Wordsworth and Romanticism*, New Branswick, NJ: Rutgers University Press, Appendix One.

9

The "exchange of letters"
Early modern contradictions and postmodern conundrums

Don E. Wayne

It is no accident that Marx should have begun with an analysis of commodities when, in the two great works of his mature period, he set out to portray capitalist society in its totality and to lay bare its fundamental nature.

(Georg Lukacs, *History and Class Consciousness*)

What do you lack? What is't you buy? What do you lack?

(The stock phrase of Elizabethan shopkeepers and peddlers, and a refrain in Ben Jonson's *Bartholomew Fair*)

In the latter part of 1990, when this chapter took its first form as a paper for a William Andrews Clark Library colloquium series on "Consumption in Early Modern Europe," I began by remarking on the euphoria then current in the west after the collapse of most of the eastern European states in what used to be called the Soviet bloc. I noted the complacency of some western commentators who rejoiced in the imagined spectacle of "democracy" opening eastern Europe to the free market, as though nature itself had finally been liberated from a fallen condition, and who gleefully asserted that Marx was finally proven wrong. Now that the Soviet Union has disintegrated it would seem an even less propitious moment to invoke Marx. Yet it is significant that while these most recent events may have reinforced the euphoria and complacency of the more myopic free-marketeers, other western observers, no less committed to free-market ideology, express anxiety and ambivalence about what may follow upon the breakup of the Soviet Union. They worry not only about the disposition of Soviet nuclear stockpiles, but also about the cost to the west of extending the dreams of the free market and the consumer society to the east. Meanwhile, in the USA within the same time period we have seen the lightning quick passage of that other euphoric moment called "Desert Storm" (a naturalist updating of the nineteenth-century providential euphemism "manifest destiny"); and in its place we hear the ominous term "depression" displacing "recession" in the American media for the first time in decades. Such has been the pace of the collapse of Soviet communism, and such the pace at which the free market's cynical reason can generate and short-circuit euphoria.

Despite the most recent events, indeed perhaps because of them, I remain skeptical of the ease with which Marx has been dismissed. Without wishing to reinvent a debate concerning the predictive value of Marxist theory, I do want to raise the issue of whether the analytical and critical component of Marx's work is easily abandoned at the very moment when capitalism appears least able to legitimate itself in terms that are anything other than cynical. It is striking that many conservative intellectuals, classical liberal humanists, and postmodern radical cultural critics alike proclaim the bankruptcy of Marxist historical and critical analysis precisely at a time when the economic has assumed such an unmediated presence in our own culture. Twenty years ago, when I entered graduate school, efforts to deal with the material bases of literary production were dismissed contemptuously by even my most liberal professors as "vulgar economic determinism." Today, the socioeconomic is widely thematized, not only in scholarship identified under the rubric of "cultural studies," but also in literary studies proper, particularly in that loosely structured movement sometimes called "new historicism," sometimes "cultural poetics" (both terms strike me as euphemisms for what is more like an approach to cultural history that acknowledges, however cautiously, a relationship between literature and political economy). The tendency is evident in work on the literature of all periods, but I shall limit my comments to the particular case of "early modern studies" (that this phrase has begun to displace "Renaissance studies" in current usage is itself indicative of a growing distrust of nostalgic and idealist categories; "early modern" may entail a residual caution with respect to economistic explanations, but it does strike me as marking an inclination towards a more materialist cultural history and theory). Whether the theme is literal, as in recent studies of print technology, theater, and the market (Newton 1982; Murray 1983; Loewenstein 1985; Agnew 1986; Newman 1989), or figurative, as in the prevalence of terms like "circulation," "exchange," "negotiation," and "cultural capital" in Stephen Greenblatt's brilliant but puzzlingly evasive *Shakespearean Negotiations* (1988),[1] the presence of the economic in current literary critical discourse inverts earlier norms of literary history. Though often masked by the more Nietzschean or Foucauldian term "power," the economic is foregrounded in literary studies today in ways that were unthinkable a generation ago.

I cannot speak of the field of history, but in English literary studies it is only very recently that conferences and publications devoted to the "literary marketplace" or to the origins of "literary consumption" would be considered within the normative discourse of the discipline. Obviously, this is no accident; the presence of the economic can hardly be resisted in the domain of cultural history when cultural historians find themselves caught up in that same cultural logic driven by commodity fetishism that Fredric Jameson describes with respect to the aesthetics of postmodernism. Central to this description is the observation that in the kind of society that developed in the West after the Second World War (variously termed consumer society, postindustrial society, multinational capitalism, society of the spectacle, media society) art is increasingly unable to resist the commodity form:

What has happened is that aesthetic production today has become integrated into commodity production generally: the frantic economic urgency of producing fresh waves of ever more novel-seeming goods (from clothing to airplanes), at ever greater rates of turnover, now assigns an increasingly essential structural function and position to aesthetic innovation and experimentation. Such economic necessities then find recognition in the institutional support of all kinds available for the newer art, from foundations and grants to museums and other forms of patronage.

(Jameson 1984: 56)

Now it seems to me that a corollary of this development is the inability of any postmodern theoretical or historical aesthetics – deconstruction, new historicism, cultural poetics, for example – to ignore the relationship under capitalism between high culture and commodity exchange (nor, for that matter, is it easy for such a critical practice to ignore its own exchange-value within the market for cultural criticism that is now institutionalized in the American academy). That such a relationship existed in inchoate form long before the invention of a "postmodern" aesthetic will be the argument of this chapter. That a literary public had to be constituted as a society of consumers before it could be represented ideologically as a community of readers will be a central feature of this argument.

My work as a literary critic has focused primarily on the plays and poems of Ben Jonson. One of the themes of my writing on Jonson has been the contradictory way in which his texts satirize emergent capitalism and yet register the complicity of culture – more specifically, poetry and drama – in the process of early capitalist development. My early interest in Jonson developed from an appreciation of the way his plays represent the subjective effects of the market society that was then emerging in England, and from what I saw as a quality of disequilibrium in his writing. I came to view this textual disequilibrium as an expression of the social situation in which Jonson found himself, a situation fraught with contradictions. The patronage system required that he engage in flattery. Jonson persistently claimed to be free of such obligation to praise even as he performed it. Moreover, while a servant of courtiers and kings, Jonson also wrote occasionally for the public playhouses. His status therefore involved a double dependency; and yet, as Peter Stallybrass and Allon White argue, against both the authority of his patrons and the demands of popular theater audiences, Jonson tried to define a new role in which authority was invested in authorship itself (Stallybrass and White 1986: 77).

Now what has interested me about Jonson is that conflict and contradiction always seem to get in the way of the claims he makes for the independent status of the author. Indeed the figure of authorship which he defended was finally legitimated not by the reputation he achieved himself but by the reputation he helped create for Shakespeare, a subject to which I will return in a moment. In the England of Jonson and Shakespeare's time, the Reformation and the early stages of capitalist development had already eroded an ideology based on the sense of a community whose spontaneous adherence to a universal and eternal moral code could be taken for granted. As in the domain of jurisprudence, so in the new domain of "literature," authority could not be presumed to derive from eternal and transcendental law. In the case of secular law, it is increasingly the contract and the exchange-value of goods and services mediated by the contract that are seen as the basis of order and authority in society.[2]

Jonson's play *Bartholomew Fair* registers this transition from an ideology based on status to one based on contract. In the Induction to the play a contract is literally presented between the author and the audience at the Hope theater on the Bankside. The agreement stipulates "that every man here exercise his own judgment, and not censure by contagion, or upon trust, from another's voice or face that sits by him." The satire becomes crankier as the rest of the agreement is read. The Reformation doctrine of "free will" is given parodic acknowledgment with reference to the audience's capacity for judgment; moral and aesthetic value are reduced to a universal equivalent in money:

> It is further agreed that every person here have his or her free-will of censure, to like or dislike at their own charge, the author having now departed with his right: it shall be lawful for any man to judge his six pen'orth, his twelve pen'orth, so to his eighteen pence, two shillings, half a crown, to the value of his place; provided always his place get not above his wit . . . marry, if he drop but sixpence at the door, and will censure a crown's worth, it is thought there is no conscience or justice in that.
>
> (Induction, ll. 76–86)

Stallybrass and White note that one party to the contract, the audience, is divided into separate classes: "the patricians, who are themselves divided into 'the curious and the envious' and 'the favouring and judicious', are set against the plebeians with their 'grounded judgments and understandings' " (Stallybrass and White 1986: 69). But Jonson's satirical device also constitutes an acknowledgment, however grudgingly, of the growing power of audiences in the public theaters, and an appeal that they judge the scene with the same independence of mind the author imagines himself to have used in creating it. Stallybrass and White rightly stress the contradiction between Jonson's temporary obligation to the largely plebeian audience of the public theater and his insistence on a more exalted role for the poet, one uncontaminated by the theater and the market. They also read the play as subverting the very notion of contract, a point on which we probably disagree inasmuch as I have argued that it is, finally, a version of the social contract that provides the comic denouement. This is not the place to debate the point with respect to *Bartholomew Fair*. What I wish to emphasize is that the contamination of moral and poetic value by exchange-value is not adequately contained by Jonson's antitheatrical posture.

There is no question that Jonson sought to construct through his poetry, and even through his works for the stage, an image of a literate community led by a poet combining the roles of high priest and chief magistrate, and charged with the moral responsibility for social order. *Judgment* is the key word in this project, and judgment would be arrived at only through attentiveness to language. Hence, Jonson's preoccupation – in marked contrast to Shakespeare – with the way in which his works were printed; hence, the frequent distinction in the prefatory matter of printed texts between the aural and the visual: "Words, above action; matter, above words" (Prologue to *Cynthia's Revels*); between readers and spectators; and the finer distinctions between readers and understanders (*The Alchemist*, 1612 Q; see also, *Epigrams*: 1), or the reader in ordinary and the reader extraordinary (*Catiline*, 1616 F₁). *Volpone*, the play by which Jonson is best known to twentieth-century audiences, opens with a prefatory epistle to "the Most Noble and Most Equal Sisters, the Two Famous Universities," Oxford and Cambridge, where the play was presented after its initial performance by Shakespeare's company at the Globe in 1606. The feminine-gendered universities are described as "most learned Arbitresses" of the masculine poet's art, but it is the poet himself who is arbiter of nature: "He . . . that comes forth the interpreter and arbiter of nature, a teacher of things divine no less than human, a master in manners . . . [who] can alone, or with a few, effect the business of mankind . . ." Distinguishing himself from other playwrights who would "make themselves a name with the multitude," Jonson claims in this play to be constituting a new, literate audience and to "have labored for their instruction and amendment, to reduce not only the ancient forms, but manners of the scene: the easiness, the propriety, and last, the doctrine, which is the principal end of poesie, to inform men in the best reason of living" (Jonson 1962: 28, 31–2).

Among the rival authors with whom Jonson scorned to be identified was Thomas Dekker, the playwright and pamphleteer. Yet Dekker himself would shortly make his own satirical jibe not only at the playwrights but at the audiences of the public playhouse: "The theatre is your poets' Royal Exchange upon which their Muses – that are now turned merchants – meeting, barter away that light commodity of words for a lighter ware than words – plaudits and the breath of the great beast [the masses] which, like the threatenings of two cowards, vanish all into air "(Dekker 1967: 98).[3] Dekker employs "exchange" in a relatively recent sense of the term (see the *Oxford English Dictionary*), denoting a marketplace for the transaction of business. The first such place in London was built by Sir Thomas Gresham and given the official name "Royal Exchange" by Elizabeth I in 1566. A second commercial center, called the "New Exchange" or "Britain's Burse," was financed by Robert Cecil and built in the Strand in the same year in which Dekker's pamphlet was published. Jonson, too, makes frequent topical reference to the London exchanges, most often in passages that satirize the rampant acquisitiveness of the time. But there is at least one instance where Jonson employs the term "exchange" in a manner comparable to Dekker's; that is, with respect to his own profession.

The passage in question – and the source of my title for this chapter – occurs in a commendatory poem written for the second volume of William Browne's *Britannia's Pastorals* (1616):

> Some men, of books or friends not speaking right,
>   May hurt them more with praise, than foes with spite.
> But I have seen thy work, and I know thee:
>   And, if thou list thyself, what thou canst be.
> For though but early in these paths thou tread,
>   I find thee write most worthy to be read.
> It must be thine own judgment, yet, that sends
>   This thy worth forth: that judgment mine commends.
> And where the most read books on authors' fames,
>   Or, like our money-brokers, take up names

> On credit, and are cozened, see that thou
> > By offering not more sureties than enow
> Hold thine own worth unbroke: which is so good
> > Upon the exchange of letters, as I would
> More of our writers would, like thee, not swell
> > With the *how much* they set forth, but the *how well*.[4]
>
> > > > > > (*H & S*: VIII, 386)

Now this is surprising. Dekker had used the figure of the Exchange with respect to the theater. Jonson uses it with respect to the pastoral poet. Dekker's usage is satirical. Jonson, the arch-satirist of his generation, the scourge of poetasters, the self-proclaimed master poet whose aim it was "to dissociate the professional writer from the clamor of the marketplace and to install his works in the studies of the gentry and the libraries of the universities" (Stallybrass and White 1986: 76), here employs the phrase "exchange of letters" without apparent irony. The poem's effect is achieved by the epigrammatic wit that culminates in the last line's distinction between value estimated in terms of quantity and value in terms of quality. But the central figure throughout is that of exchange-value in a literary market. The reference to "money-brokers" is satirical. In contrast, Browne's work is complimented by the assertion of intrinsic worth which requires no broker.

But the compliment is compromised by the occasion: i.e. this is a commendatory verse, printed along with others as a prefix to Browne's poems. Such prefatory verses had become conventional as a form of advertising in the relatively new booksellers' trade, and by 1616 Jonson's fame was sufficient to make his name a selling-point to the emerging community of readers. The poem acknowledges this function even as it disclaims it: ". . . where the most read books on authors' fames, . . . thou / By offering not more sureties than enow / Hold thine own worth unbroke." Complimenting Browne for his moderation and judgment in prefacing his work with only a few but well-chosen "sureties" (another economic figure applied to poetry), Jonson compliments himself, calling attention to the value of his own commendatory verses in the literary marketplace. The absence of any overt irony in the phrase "exchange of letters" is contradicted by the contextual irony of the poem's function.

Jonson performed this function on a number of occasions. It was one of the ways in which he sought to influence the creation of an enlightened literary public in England. Best known of his commendatory poems are the two that appeared in the front matter of the Shakespeare First Folio of 1623, the longer of which canonized Shakespeare as the poet who "was not of an age, but for all time!" Jonson's own *Works* had been printed in a far more elegant folio in 1616 containing not only plays but court masques and two collections of poems, including *Epigrams* to which Jonson pointedly referred, professing the high seriousness of his endeavors, as "the ripest of my studies." Despite seeing the work of his early and middle years printed in such a glorious edition, Jonson was destined, as Jonas Barish has wryly remarked, "to be dragged captive [through literary history] behind the triumphal chariot of Shakespeare worship" (Barish 1963: 1). But to this must be added the irony that it was Jonson himself who instituted the mode of Shakespeare worship to which the literary public became accustomed over the next four centuries, and to that extent the triumph was partially his (cf. *H & S*: II, 378:

"It [the longer of Jonson's two poems on Shakespeare] is rather a song of triumph than an elegy").

Leah Marcus opens her book *Puzzling Shakespeare* with a discussion of the front matter of the Shakespeare First Folio. In Marcus's analysis, Jonson's poem opposite the Droeshout portrait, and the longer dedicatory poem that follows, is the principal means by which an image of the transcendental Bard as head of a timeless canon of great English authors was enunciated in the early seventeenth century. The first poem, "To the reader," negates the possibility of discovering the "real" Shakespeare in the artist's portrait on the facing page. The reader is instructed to "looke / Not on his Picture, but his Booke." Marcus comments that "at a time when English writers were asserting unprecedented autonomy and mastery over their own work through allegorical frontispieces, admonitory prefaces, overt and covert declarations of intent, Jonson's poem abolishes Shakespeare as an entity apart from his writings. What the author may have intended becomes void as a category because there is no space at all between the man and his work" (Marcus 1988: 19; cf. Greg 1955: 449–55; and, especially, de Grazia's important discussion of the prefatory matter to the First Folio which elaborates on Marcus, but also differs with respect to the function of the Droeshout portrait [de Grazia 1991: 14–48]). One is tempted to conclude from Marcus's analysis that the "author-function," in Foucault's well-known phrase (Foucault 1977: 113–38), is constituted in English literary history principally by means of this elision of the man and the book in the figure of Shakespeare as drawn not by Droeshout but by Jonson. Marcus's ingenious reading of the pictorial and rhetorical anomalies of the First Folio turns on two major emergent phenomena, that of authorship in the modern sense and that of a literary public: "There was a tension, often quite explicit [in such folio volumes] . . . between the intellectual elitism claimed for authorship and the broader appeal required if authorship were to prosper in the marketplace" (Marcus 1988: 21). Compared with the title-pages of other folios (including that which graced Jonson's own *Works* of 1616) the relative plainness of the title-page to the Shakespeare First Folio has the effect of denying elitism and inviting a more general readership.

However, the design and organization of the front matter to the Shakespeare First Folio serves not only as invitation. It is *advertisement* – both in the sense, conventional by the time, of a notice to the reader concerning a book's contents (see *OED* entry, sense #4), and in a sense not yet current, but already anticipated in the rhetoric of such prefatory matter, of publicity and marketing strategy. Marcus's analysis is focused on the construction of the "transcendent Bard" as the basis of a more general ideology of authorship and canon. But the volume is also an early instance of the contradiction between, on the one hand, the great author's book as vehicle of cultural and moral authority and, on the other, the book as commodity. The book's status as commodity is acknowledged in the prefatory note "To the great Variety of Readers" which appears over the signatures of John Heminge and Henrie Condell, two leading members of Shakespeare's company who claim to have collected the plays for this memorial volume: "the fate of all Bookes depends upon your capacities: and not of your heads alone, but of your purses."[5] At the same time, it is characteristic of Jonson to assume the task of asserting the book's cultural and moral authority. The longer of Jonson's commendatory poems has the effect of placing Shakespeare in a transcendent realm, a realm signified by the word printed in full capitals in the poem's title – "To the memory of my beloved, The AUTHOR, Mr. William Shakespeare, And what he hath left us."

Everything about Jonson's career suggests that the role he assigns to Shakespeare in this poem is one he desired for himself. The opening lines hardly disguise that desire:

> To draw no envy (Shakespeare) on thy name,
>   Am I thus ample to thy book and fame . . .

Such disavowal is typically Jonsonian, betraying the ambivalence that always marked Jonson's references to even the most admired of his competitors. But Shakespeare had now been seven years in the grave, and Jonson could afford to restrain the sense of rivalry that animated his allusions to the older playwright while the latter still lived. More importantly, the fact that this was a memorial volume enabled Jonson to appropriate Shakespeare's name for his project of mythologizing the office of Poet. Earlier in his career, Jonson had performed a similar (and similarly ambivalent) apotheosis of Sir Philip Sidney (Wayne 1990: 228, 233). But by 1623 the courtly amateur was being displaced by the professional author in the literary system, the economy of aristocratic patronage was beginning to give way to a more open literary market, and with the broader potential readership came a need for a representative English pantheon that was not restricted by class. Jonson now places Shakespeare at the head of this pantheon:

> My Shakespeare, rise; I will not lodge thee by
> Chaucer, or Spenser, or bid Beaumont lie
> A little further, to make thee a room:
> Thou art a monument, without a tomb,
> And art alive still, while thy book doth live,
> And we have wits to read, and praise to give.
>
> (11. 19–24)

References follow to Lyly, Kyd, and Marlowe among English authors. Of these, Beaumont was of the highest social rank, descended from an old family, but a family of professional lawyers. Sidney is not even mentioned.

As Marcus points out, it is not so much by opposing nature to art as in naturalizing and idealizing Art itself, that Jonson represents Shakespeare's apotheosis. Indeed, Jonson's highest praise of Shakespeare is the sort of praise he sought for himself:

> For though the poet's matter nature be,
>   His art doth give the fashion . . .
> For a good poet's made, as well as born;
> And such wert thou. Look how the father's face
>   Lives in his issue: even so, the race
> Of Shakespeare's mind and manners brightly shines
>   In his well-turned and true-filed lines.
>
> (11. 57–8, 64–8)

This sets Jonson somewhat at odds with the immediately preceding text in the First Folio, the address "To the great Variety of Readers," signed by Heminge and Condell, which helped inaugurate the tradition of Shakespeare as the quintessential natural genius: "Who, as he was a happie imitator of Nature, was a most gentle expresser of it. His mind and hand went together: And what he thought, he uttered with that easinesse, that wee have scarce received from him a blot in his papers."

But in other respects, the notice to the readers attributed to Heminge and Condell reads as though it could have been written by Jonson himself. Indeed, a number of scholars have asserted as much.[6] Certainly the first paragraph is striking in its close resemblance to the Induction to *Bartholomew Fair*:

> ### To the great Variety of Readers
>
> From the most able, to him that can but spell: There you are number'd. We had rather you were weighd. Especially when the fate of all Bookes depends upon your capacities: and not of your heads alone, but of your purses. Well! It is now publique, & you wil stand for your priviledges wee know: to read, and censure. Do so, but buy it first. That doth best commend a Booke, the Stationer saies. Then, how odde soever your braines be, or your wisedomes, make your licence the same, and spare not. Judge your sixe-pen'orth, your shillings worth, your five shillings worth at a time, or higher, so you rise to the just rates, and welcome. But what ever you do, Buy.

Even if Jonson did not actually write these lines, those who did were alluding to his authority. But that the text of Jonson which lends authority to Heminge and Condell's address to "The great Variety of Readers" should be the Induction to *Bartholomew Fair* is stunning in its irony. Jonson's authority in the two dedicatory poems depends on the laureate status he had claimed in the 1607 epistle to *Volpone*, and to an extent had achieved by 1623. By contrast, *Bartholomew Fair* is of all Jonson's plays the one, according to Richard Helgerson, "that most persistently questions the bases of [Jonson's] laureate self-presentation" (Helgerson 1983: 164). Jonson's presence in the address to the readers (whether as Heminge and Condell's ghost writer or merely by allusion) implicates him in the contradictory status of the project. As in Jonson's poem on William Browne's pastorals, here in the front matter of the Shakespeare First Folio the emerging literary system's function as part of an emerging system of commodity exchange (i.e. a mode of production in which consumption must be encouraged through advertising) is disclosed despite the transcendent roles assigned to Art and to the AUTHOR.

One symptom of this commodification of literature is the fact that the word "broker" has a long history as a pejorative for pirate printers and plagiarizers. In such contexts, the term is sometimes associated with pandering. It appears in that sense in the printer John Day's address to the reader of the second edition (*c*. 1570) of Sackville and Norton's *Gorboduc*, one of the earliest English tragedies, where Day castigates the unauthorized printer of an earlier "exceedingly corrupted" quarto (Sackville and Norton 1970: 4–5). In other words, "broker" tends to be used in early printed editions of English plays and poems to call the readership's attention to a violation of the author's and the authorized printer's proprietary right. At the same time, such terminology evokes the violation or sale of a woman's body, an image that Wendy Wall describes as "a pervasive cultural phenomenon in which texts were ushered into the public eye in a titillating fashion" (Wall 1989: 36). Jonson employs the term satirically in a number of places, including the poem on Browne's pastorals quoted above and the epigram "On poet-ape" ("Whose works are e'en the frippery of wit, / From brocage is become so bold a thief, / As we, the robbed, leave rage, and pity it"). I know of no instance where Jonson employs the term "broker" in any positive way, certainly not with respect to the office of poet. On the contrary, following the ancient example of Horace and the more recent example of Sidney in the *Defence of Poesy*, Jonson styled himself as a sort of secular priest whose function it was to exalt English poetry and to establish the criteria for an English literary canon. But in Jonson's practice the image of the poet-priest becomes contaminated by that of the broker, and never did he play this composite role better than in the Shakespeare First Folio.

In his later years Jonson's anxiety with respect to audiences and readers seems to have shifted somewhat. His earlier writings consider public audiences and common readers with surly disdain. The main anxiety, in addition to that expressed towards rival authors, concerns his relationship with patrons. He worries in print about the obligation to praise without "smelling parasite" ("To my muse," *Epigrams* 65, 1. 14). In the later writings the anxiety begins to include a wider readership for his work, partly because of the steady growth in numbers of readers outside the court circle and partly because Jonson's position at court was weaker after James I's death in 1625 (*H & S*: I, 89–93). The extreme self-consciousness of Jonson's late plays can be attributed to the inescapable fact of the poet's dependence on the emerging market system he had for so long treated satirically. Dryden referred to these later plays as Jonson's "dotages," and that judgment resounded with authority for nearly three hundred years. But recent commentators have argued that, far from being the effects of mental or moral exhaustion, these plays manifest an experimentalism no less energetic than that which characterized Jonson's early and middle comedies.

The first of these late plays, *The Staple of News*, was written not long after Jonson had played his part in the production and promotion of the Shakespeare First Folio. Performed by the King's Men in 1626, *The Staple of News* marked the end of a ten-year hiatus during which Jonson had written for the court but had produced nothing for the playhouses, public or private. As with other plays in the Jonson canon, *The Staple of News* is often linked to the tradition of the morality play. But it also constitutes an odd conjunction of the characteristic features of city comedy with the allegorical method that Jonson had developed in his court masques. Indeed, whole passages in *The Staple of News* are lifted from two masques which Jonson had composed earlier, *News from the New World* (1620) and *Neptune's Triumph* (1624). *The Staple of News* can be read as an experiment in genre, appropriating the device of the antimasque (a sequence involving grotesque characters usually played by professionals, and serving as a foil for the masque proper in which courtiers played the parts) for more extended use in a play written for the mixed audience of the Blackfriars. A central figure, and the chief object of the gaze of others in the scene, is the lady Aurelia Clara Pecunia Do-all, Infanta of the Mines. "She is / The talk o'the time, th'adventure o'the age!" (I.vi.63–4).[7] She appears with a retinue of attendants whose names are drawn from legal discourse, and particularly from the law pertaining to real property and contracts: her ladies-in-waiting are named Mortgage, Statute, Band (i.e. Bond), Wax; her secretary and gentleman-usher is named Broker.

Portions of the action are set in a News Office, a topical reference to the recent opening of the first news bureau in England. While the satire on newsmongering exaggerates the degree to which news was invented to suit the contemporary appetite for gossip, it is nonetheless significant as an early representation of a business in which information is a commodity. The master of the Staple of News is Cymbal, a name which Herford and Simpson attribute to the "sounding brass and tinkling cymbal" of the Bible (I Corinthians 13.1) but which also derives from a Greek word with the connotation of hollowness. Cymbal stands for an orientation to language that is the diametric opposite of what Jonson had sought earlier to represent through the figure of The AUTHOR, Mr. William Shakespeare, the substantial literary monument worthy of reproduction in print. The difference is signaled by Cymbal's attitude to the medium of print: "We not forbid that any News be made, / But that it be printed; for when News is printed, / It leaves Sir to be News" (I.v.47–9). Cymbal goes on to assert that news from his office "shall come from the Mint . . . Fresh and new stamp'd, / With the Office-Seal, Staple Commodity" (I.v.62–3). The words serve Jonson's satirical intent, but they also register the incipiency of an age in which "news" would come to epitomize consumerism and commodity culture.

The mixing of high and low genres is especially evident in the middle acts of the play. Act III takes place in the staple and includes a scene in which Cymbal engages in an absurd parody of courtly love while trying to win the lady Pecunia away from the prodigal heir Penniboy Junior. Act IV is situated in a tavern room called, ironically, Apollo, the name of the celebrated tavern room where Jonson himself purportedly held forth regularly as the "father" of a group of younger writers who called themselves the Tribe of Ben (*H & S*: I, 85). When Penniboy Junior hosts a dinner in Apollo in Pecunia's honor, the poetaster Madrigal sings her praise in a sarabande that parodies Jonson's own vocation in the courts of James and Charles Stuart:

> *Madrigal*:
> As bright as is the Sun her sire,
> Or Earth, her mother, in her best attire,
> Or Mint, the midwife, with her fire,
> Comes forth her grace! . . .
> She makes good cheer, she keeps full boards,
> She holds a fair of knights and lords,
> A market of all offices
> And shops of honour more or less.
> (IV.ii.95–8, 113–16)

The effect is of an embourgeoisement of the masque form, a comment, perhaps, on the embourgeoisement of nobility in the recently ended reign of James I. Shortly after Madrigal's song, the play's moral commentator, Penniboy Canter (his given and allegorical name is Frank), a beggar who will eventually disclose his true identity as the father Penniboy Junior had presumed dead, describes the society we have witnessed to this point in the play. His words again evoke the antimasque:

> *Penniboy Canter* [aside]:
> Look, look, how all their eyes
> Dance i' their heads (observe) scatter'd with lust

At sight o' their brave idol! How they are tickl'd
With a light air, the bawdy sarabande!
They are a kind of dancing engines all,
And set by nature, thus to run alone
To every sound! All things within, without them,
Move, but their brain, and that stands still! Mere monsters,
Here in a chamber, of most subtle feet!

(IV.ii.134–42)

Though the language is moralistic and obsessively anti-erotic, it manages to convey a striking early image of what Marx, Weber, Lukacs, and social theorists of the Frankfurt school would later describe as the reification of subjectivity that occurs when commodity exchange comes to dominate social relationships and when the circulation of social energy is expressed as the circulation of money (Marx 1973: 163–4; Weber 1978: 636–7; Lukacs 1971: 83–110; Horkheimer and Adorno 1972: 37). Indeed, most of Jonson's plays can be seen as an early depiction of the phenomenon of reification.[8]

Jonson's resolution of the action in *The Staple of News* is a weak compromise between the satire of reification as an effect of the cash nexus in a market economy and the celebration of conventional bourgeois ideals of thrift, industry, the circulation and reproduction of capital linked to the theme of marriage, the family, and domestic harmony. "Trust" is identified by Anne Barton as a crucial term that helps mediate this compromise. Barton remarks on the frequency of the word in the last act of the play. She writes that "sentences like [the lawyer] Picklock's 'No matter, Sir, trust you unto my *Trust*' (V.i.108) deliberately confound an impersonal legal document with the kind of delicate human relationship the law was originally designed to protect but now, more frequently, betrays" (Barton 1984: 251). While the observation is helpful, I do not share Barton's conclusion that Jonson successfully resolves the dilemma. The antithetical abuses of money – extravagance in the figure of the prodigal Penniboy Junior, and miserliness in the figure of the usurer Penniboy Senior (also called Richer Penniboy) who is Pecunia's guardian – are exposed as equally destructive. After a number of further turns in the plot, Penniboy Junior, whose wasteful ways cost him his inheritance at the end of Act IV, repents and is restored to his fortune. Penniboy Senior is also reformed and given a brief lecture on the new contractual order of things by his brother Penniboy Canter who explains that the prodigal will now be freely contracted to the lady. And the lady Pecunia, herself freed from the usurious constraints of her uncle Richer Penniboy, and from the danger of promiscuous circulation suggested earlier in the tavern dinner scene, will now be bound to Penniboy Junior in marriage, a figure in this context for the legitimate circulation and reproduction of money:

Penniboy Canter:
            Nay, Pecunia herself
Is come to free him fairly and discharge
All ties but those of love unto her person,
To use her like a friend, not like a slave
Or like an idol. Superstition
Doth violate the deity it worships

No less than scorn doth. And believe it, brother,
   The use of things is all, and not the store.
                     (V.vi.19–26)

The passage is interesting for the way in which it collapses exchange-value into use-value, and for the equivalence it draws between a reified form of human relations (money) and the conjugal relation signified here by the word "friend" which stands as a mean between "slave" and "idol."[9] Pecunia repeats the equation in the final words of the play, responding to Penniboy Junior's wish that the spectators "may, as I, enjoy Pecunia":

Pecunia:
And so Pecunia herself doth wish,
That she may still be aid unto their uses,
Not slave unto their pleasures or a tyrant
Over their fair desires, but teach them all
The golden mean.
                     (V.vi.60–4)

The notion that a wife, like money, is a medium of exchange in an orderly society is conventional. I would suggest, however, that there is a third term in Jonson's equation, though one that remains hidden in the play's conclusion, the term "knowledge". After all, the context here is a play whose title and early scenes focus not only on the exchange of women and of money but on the exchange of information, albeit information in the vulgar form of news that is little more than gossip.

But *The Staple of News* also betrays anxiety about the status of that form of information more properly termed knowledge or truth over which the poet in Jonson's conception presides. Jonson's employment of the trope of "use" here and of a wife as the proper emblem of "use" is worth comparing with a similar passage in Bacon's *Advancement of Learning*, published about twenty years earlier in 1605:

> For men have entered into a desire of learning and knowledge, sometimes upon a natural curiosity and inquisitive appetite; sometimes to entertain their minds with variety and delight; sometimes for ornament and reputation; sometimes to enable them to victory of wit and contradiction; and most times for lucre and profession; and seldom sincerely to give a true account of their gift of reason to the benefit and use of men. . . . Howbeit, I do not mean, when I speak of use and action, that end before-mentioned of the applying of knowledge to lucre and profession. . . . Neither is my meaning, as was spoken of Socrates, to call philosophy down from heaven to converse upon the earth; that is, to leave natural philosophy aside, and to apply knowledge only to manners and policy. But as both heaven and earth do conspire and contribute to the use and benefit of man; so the end ought to be, from both philosophies to separate and reject vain speculations and whatsoever is empty and void, and to preserve and augment whatsoever is solid and fruitful, that knowledge may not be as a courtesan, for pleasure and vanity only, or as a bond-woman, to acquire and gain to her master's use, but as a spouse, for generation, fruit, and comfort.
>   (*Works* 1859: III, 294–5)

The tropological connection between these texts is evident: woman is figured negatively as "courtesan" (Jonson's "idol") and as "bond-woman" (Jonson's "slave"), and affirmatively as "spouse" (Jonson's "friend"). Also prominent in each text is the word "use." But the passage from Bacon is especially revealing because of the contradictory senses in which the term is employed. "Use" occurs four times, a signal of its importance as a qualifier of "knowledge," first in the positive phrase "to the benefit and use of men," which is reiterated twice more, then finally in a negative sense "as a bondwoman, to acquire and gain to her master's use." Bacon could have employed the traditional Augustinian distinction between "use" and "abuse" (St. Augustine, *On Christian Doctrine*, I, Ch. 4, ed. Schaff, 1887: 523). Instead, he allows the ambiguity of the single term "use" to resonate retrospectively across the entire passage once the negative connotation has appeared in the penultimate phrase. This juxtaposition of positive and negative senses of "use" in the same passage is symptomatic of an ideological dilemma that the passage does not successfully resolve, a dilemma Bacon and his contemporaries inherited from the later medieval Church which had to generate legalistic circumventions of its own prohibitions against usury and against the ownership of property by some religious orders. Indeed, the latter of these prohibitions gave rise in the twelfth century to the legal device of the "use" which developed into that of the "trust" (Berman 1983: 235).[10] When Anne Barton notes that Jonson is playing ironically on the word "trust" in *The Staple of News*, she is acknowledging only one side of the play's ideological crux. For the absence of irony in the play's invocation of the term "use" – ("the use of things is all") – marks a distinction without a difference. In Bacon's text the association of one kind of use with generation and fruit appears to be an allusion to the doctrine of *usufruct* which in medieval law licensed a form of interest in land owned by another, as distinct from the Church's interdiction on usury. Knowledge properly understood is like a wife, a commodity for the usufruct and enjoyment of a good husband in this life, but a property belonging ultimately to God. The distinction between normative and excessive "use," between knowledge as socially redeeming truth and knowledge as commodity, is somewhat ambiguous in Bacon's programmatic utilitarianism, though not as ambiguous as it is in Jonson.

Predictably, Jonson resorts to prologues and to a printed note "To the readers" in attempting to distinguish between the sort of information peddled by Cymbal and the poetic truth of his own text. A "Prologue for the Stage" urges the audience "for your own sakes . . . to hear, not see, a play," and, provisionally, treats with respect the audience's potential for judgment:

> Great noble wits, be good unto yourselves
> And make a difference 'twixt poetic elves
> And poets.

> (11. 19–21)

There follows a "Prologue for the Court" which, characteristically, praises by invidious comparison with the playhouse audience. The play is offered to the king and the court

> as a rite
> To scholars, that can judge and fair report

> The sense they hear above the vulgar sort
> Of nutcrackers, that only come for sight.
>
> (11. 5–8)

The distinction between dramatic poetry and spectacle is a Jonsonian convention. In this play Jonson dramatizes the distinction through the ingenious device of having four "Gossips" seated on the stage who arraign the play and the poet in the intermeans between acts. They are described as "four gentlewomen ladylike attired" and are named Gossip Mirth, Gossip Tattle, Gossip Expectation, and Gossip Censure. They constitute an ignorant chorus and are a further extension of Jonson's use of a conventional figure, the talking woman as a threat to moral and social order, which Karen Newman has discussed with respect to Jonson's earlier play *Epicoene*. Newman links "the discourses which managed and produced femininity in the late sixteenth and early seventeenth centuries" to contemporary ambivalence about commodity exchange and consumption. "The talking woman is everywhere equated with a voracious sexuality that in turn abets her avid consumerism: scolds were regularly accused of both extravagance and adultery" (Newman 1989: 506–7). If talk in women functions as a displacement of the general anxiety about consumption in the new market society, then the feminine Gossips of *The Staple of News* can be understood to function as a screen for masculine authorial anxiety about audience and reader consumption of play texts.

While the Gossips open the play and appear before each act, they are banished from the resolution. Yet foolish as their judgments may be, they are palpable representations of the sort of pressure Jonson could not help but feel from audiences, especially after his long absence from the stage. That pressure involves the demand for something "new," a demand which is perhaps reflected ironically in the title of this play and of its successor, *The New Inn* (1629).[11] In *The Staple of News*, the "Prologue for the Court" calls attention to this irony:

> Wherein, although our title, sir, be *News*.
>   We yet adventure here to tell you none,
> But show you common follies.
>
> (11. 9–11)

But the addition of a note "To The Readers" for the printed text of 1631 suggests once again that Jonson was forced to respond to the urgent pressure for novelty. This conjecture is reinforced by the fact that Jonson's address "To The Readers" does not appear in the usual place at the front of the printed text but intrudes on the body of the play, coming immediately after the Gossips' intermean at the end of Act II:

To The Readers

In this following Act, the Office is open'd and show'n to the Prodigal and his Princess Pecunia, wherein the allegory and purpose of the author hath hitherto been wholly mistaken, and so sinister an interpretation been made as if the souls of most of the spectators had liv'd in the eyes and ears of these ridiculous gossips that tattle between the Acts. But he prays you thus to mend it. To consider the news here vented to be none of his news or any reasonable man's, but news made like the time's news (a weekly cheat to draw money) and could not be fitter reprehended than in raising this ridiculous Office of the Staple.

It is as though Jonson's satirical strategy in the theater and at court had backfired, as though the demand for novelty had been intensified in audiences by the Gossips' commentary in stage performances of the play. The necessity to regulate his readers' response by interrupting the play – an extraordinary controlling mechanism even for Jonson – bespeaks a fear of being unable to contain the effects of misreadings pronounced by characters of his own making. The Gossips, though objects of satire, reflect the degree to which Caroline audiences and readers of play texts were beginning to take on an active and demanding role in establishing the canons of taste in the theater.[12]

Throughout his career, Jonson worried about compromising his high ideal of the poet as a kind of supreme magistrate of moral philosophy. In poems composed as early as 1600 he frets about his dependency on patronage, offering obligatory praise while denying that he is so obliged; in later years this anxiety is compounded by the pressure of audiences and readers who are knowledgeable about the stage repertoire and are emboldened by their growing sense of power as consumers in a literary marketplace. As one who had necessarily engaged in flattery of undeserving patrons, and in the promotion of other poets' and playwrights' reputations, most notably Shakespeare's in 1623, Jonson's self-consciousness in *The Staple of News* suggests an uneasy sense that his own social role bordered uncomfortably, in kind if not in degree, on the roles of such characters in his plays as the flattering poetaster Madrigal or the secretary to the Lady Pecunia, so aptly named Broker.

Joel Fineman has argued that Shakespeare's sonnets culminate in and revise the project of a Renaissance literature of praise in which, finally, a new mode of literary subjectivity was constructed. This newly constituted poetic subjectivity which experiences its ego ideal as other or as absent, and which Fineman describes as an "identity of ruptured identification," becomes the basis of a psychological interiority that will have authority in literature from Shakespeare's time to our own (Fineman 1986: 25). Fineman's analysis, couched in Lacanian and phenomenological language, has historical validity as well. In Shakespeare, the pathos of modern alienated subjectivity finds its most articulate early exponent. If that is indeed the case, then what we see in Ben Jonson is a drama of a different kind, a drama in which interiority and depth are subordinated to the depiction of an exterior social surface fragmented by the logic of commodity fetishism. This representation has not compelled the sort of imaginative engagement elicited by the Shakespearean texts which have produced for generations of readers the sense of a deep, personal interiority harboring an elusive, ideal self. Shakespeare has never ceased to be legible to the modern reader because the ruptured, alienated subject constructed through his poems and plays is a subject with which modern readers could identify – or with which readers were trained to identify by Shakespeare's critics, beginning with Jonson in 1623.[13]

In Jonson's own poetry and plays the authorial subject bravely, if ponderously, asserts its wholeness, its integrity, its "centered self" (Greene 1970), which it must ultimately and ironically validate by association with the patriarchal authority of canonical poetry in the person of the AUTHOR, Mr. William Shakespeare. Yet what the Jonsonian subject describes as *its* other, as the mode of being from which it struggles to distinguish itself, is a condition not of alienation but of fragmentation. That condition did not become the basis of a canonical literary figure for modern subjectivity. Literature became institutionalized and consumable in proportion to the degree to which it could be taken up and circulated as an index of the universal. In Jonson's plays and poems the overwhelming image is of a society and of subjects that are fragmented; if there is a site of alienation, it is the author's own subjectivity which cannot legitimate its claim to independence, cannot justify its status of impartial and critical observer because it is logically committed to recognizing its complicity in what it observes. The reader is invited to become reflective and to share the author's judgment, but that means also sharing the author's alienation. In contrast to this structure of the author–reader relationship is a structure articulated in the texts of Shakespeare. Here alienation is thematized and dramatized while the authorial subject is not easily located.

We can thus rewrite Keats's well-known formula of "negative capability"[14] as the governing rule of modern literary subjectivity: that AUTHOR is most widely circulated who is least visible. In this sense, I agree with Marcus's argument that local interpretation and topicality, i.e. historical specificity, must be suppressed for the realization of bardic transcendence. But I would add that Greenblatt's figure of "cultural capital" must also be recognized as a factor here, though I admit to employing the figure with somewhat different emphasis. The AUTHOR, Mr. William Shakespeare, is the cultural capital of English Literature. It is principally through Shakespeare that Literature is founded and that the readership it serves becomes the sort of community that Jonson sought to constitute and to consecrate in his role as the English Horace. Ironically, that community is formally constituted as a society of consumers, though its function would be to provide intellectual and affective compensation for the hegemonic ethos of consumption that would eventually characterize the logic of capitalist development.

To the extent that figures of fragmentation do appear in early modern literature, they are perhaps only now beginning to be legible as a result of the fragmentation of the subject in our own time.[15] I am not suggesting that Jonson's texts constitute some sort of prototypical postmodern representation of the crisis in bourgeois subjectivity. On the contrary, he *is* very much of an age. His texts depict the social consequences of commodity fetishism at a very early stage of capitalist development and forecast the way in which efforts to ground knowledge, morality, and social order are destabilized by the unpredictable expediencies of a market economy. Jonson was far more pious than Shakespeare in propagating the secular faith in literary art. It is Jonson who writes "the father's face / Lives in his issue." But the father is Shakespeare, and in the canon that he engendered generations of readers would experience the self as the redolent trace of a lost plenitude of Being located somewhere deep within the individual. In our own time, when it becomes less and less possible to rely on the notion of a centered self or even an alienated self as a bulwark against the destabilizing and reifying effects of the consumer society, Jonson's depiction of social fragmentation perhaps takes on a mimetic relevance that it lacked for earlier generations in the Romantic and modern periods.

I have employed the term "irony" frequently in this chapter, though I trust not in the same sense in which irony has functioned as a watchword of literary criticism in the past. For literary critics writing today the fact that the commodity aspect of literature should be acknowledged at the very time when the mode of production that exalted Literature proclaims itself triumphant, is supremely ironic. That the literary community no longer denies its origins as part of an emergent market system, that the literary profession and professionalism are now at the center of discussion and debate among literary professors, that we hold colloquia and publish volumes such as the present one dealing with the history of culture as commodity, are all indices of an ironic situation in the academic market that resembles the moment when the literary market first came into being, a moment when the ideology of the Author and of a community of readers had not yet become the quintessential imaginary representation of a relation of production and consumption.

A final, topical notes

The Clark Library paper that formed the basis of this chapter was completed in mid-January 1991, during breaks from watching CNN reporters describe in ecstatic and aesthetic terms the launching of US Cruise missiles from warships in the Persian Gulf. Over computerized video-monitored images of laser-guided bombs destroying their targets, the voice of one reporter, breathless with adoration, spoke of the "beautiful night vision" of the Stealth Bomber. While this immediate context seemed remote from my concerns with the intersection in early modern culture of two emergent systems of communication and consumption, "news" and Literature, I felt nevertheless a bizarre conjunction between my topic and the way literate media commentators tallied the day's destruction and moralized on its legitimacy. The feeling remained somewhat vague until January 18, when the op-ed page of the *Los Angeles Times* carried a column by George Will with the following:

> Indeed, the war's longest reverberation may be from the fact of Arab participation in the studied punishment of an Arab nation whose crime is transgressing values enunciated most clearly by the United States, the symbol of Western political values and of cultural modernity. Iraq's fate in the fighting will demonstrate redundantly that militarism is not an alternative to political modernization. In the modern age, military proficiency is increasingly a function of scientific, cultural and commercial modernity. . . . The hope is that this war will be the thin end of a large wedge, sufficient to pry parts of Arabia into participation in the modernity that is capable of such technological prowess and moral purpose.
>
> (p. B7)

Regardless of one's feelings concerning the legitimacy of US policy in the Gulf, the effortlessness with which this statement glides from the claim of commercial hegemony and military proficiency to the claim of cultural superiority might give one reason to pause and reflect. Will's cultural arrogance barely conceals the truth about "modernity" adumbrated in the early modern and disclosed again in the postmodern: that is, the fact that in the system for which "modernity" is a euphemism, culture is inextricably bound up with commercial and technological domination.

In the centuries between Shakespeare's time and our own, high culture served to mediate between commercial and technological development and subjective experience. During these four hundred years, conventionally schematized into the periods of Enlightenment, Romanticism, and Modernism, literature represented subjectivity in ways that gave priority first to reason, then to imagination and affective response, and finally to form. Among the distinguishing features of postmodernism is the tendency to do away with this mediatory function for culture, to represent culture and even subjectivity itself as commodities. I do not mean to suggest that George Will necessarily believes in this equation of postmodern culture with commodity fetishism; but I do think his language betrays his commitment to a dominant culture that can no longer confidently express its values as distinct from value in marketing terms.

Notes

1   By "evasive" I mean that Greenblatt acknowledges the relationship between literature and commerce in Shakespeare's England, but that he proceeds to aestheticize and mythologize that relationship. In his opening chapter, the circulation of capital is revealed as an essential facet of Shakespearean drama; but this relationship is then reveiled by a discourse that essentializes the economic metaphors it employs ("cultural transaction," "cultural capital," etc.). The effect is a rather curious new version of Shakespeare's transcendence in which the Bard is now a monument to that conflation of the aesthetic and the economic that constitutes the postmodern version of the Sublime. Perhaps that effect is inevitable when postmodern criticism, with its tendency to aestheticize commodity relations, is brought to bear on early modern culture, a culture in which the division between secular art and the commodity form was not yet fully articulated. If indeed the conflation of aesthetic and economic categories is an expression of our own historical moment, as differentiated from earlier moments that produced the Romantic version of the sublime, and modernist formalism, then it seems to me that a critical practice calling itself a "new historicism" must attempt to account for the conditions that produced that difference. One can admire Greenblatt's redefinition of the energy and intensity that characterize Shakespearean drama without necessarily finding adequate his explanation of how he arrived at this redefinition. This critique, admittedly all too brief, is made notwithstanding my admiration for Greenblatt's work and my sympathy with his defense of a new historicism in the last essay of his subsequent book, *Learning to Curse: Essays in Early Modern Culture* (1990). In that essay Greenblatt replies to some of his earlier critics. I do not believe he addresses the fundamental issue I raise here concerning the economic metaphors of *Shakespearean Negotiations*. It is striking, moreover, that while he eschews an older historicism characterized by "veneration of the past or of tradition," and while he continues to employ the economic categories of "negotiation and exchange," the very title of his essay, "Resonance and Wonder," suggests a desire to reinstate the *aura* of the work of art which, in Benjamin's well-known formulation, is lost in the technological consumer society. As I suggest in what follows, the *aura* of the literary text is a historically specific effect produced in the reader/subject by a textual strategy for naturalizing and idealizing Art and for the apotheosis of the Author, an effect epitomized in the Shakespeare First Folio.

2   For a more thorough discussion of the relationship between early seventeenth-century changes in the English law of contract and representations of social order in the drama, see Wayne (1982); cf. Agnew (1986: 67–8, 82).

3   Similarly, James Shirley's prologue to a play called *The Toy* advises the theater audience: "so we are in this wits Market, furnish'd with all ware, / But please your selves, and buy what you like best, / Some cheap commodities mingle with the rest" (Shirley 1970: 45).

4   *Ben Jonson*, ed. C. H. Herford, Percy Simpson, and Evelyn Simpson (1925–52: VIII, 386), with spelling modernized. References to Herford, Simpson, and Simpson's critical commentary are given in parentheses in the text, hereafter cited as *H & S*.

5   References to the Shakespeare First Folio here and in what follows are cited from *The Norton Facsimile* (Shakespeare 1968).

6   Herford and the Simpsons devote several pages (*H & S*: XI, 141–4) to disputing the

detailed argument of the eighteenth-century Shakespearean editor George Steevens. Their rejection of Steevens's evidence is not, to my mind, conclusive.

7   Ben Jonson, *The Staple of News* (1975). Further line references in the text are to this edition.

8   In this respect, it would be a mistake to accept L. C. Knights's well-known explanation of Jonson's comedy of humors under the simple category of "tradition," that is, as the nostalgic evocation of a medieval "anti-acquisitive attitude" (Knights 1937). Instead, I view these plays as among the earliest manifestations in English literature of the subjectivity effects produced by a developed system of commodity exchange. Far from being traditional, the solution proposed by these plays to the dislocative effects of the emerging market society is a dramatized model of what seventeenth-century political theorists would formulate as the social contract (Wayne 1982). As Agnew has shown, contract evolved as a device to control representation and misrepresentation in the market society; the model for Hobbes's "master trope of representation" was the theatre (Agnew 1986: 57–61, 102). And in C. B. Macpherson's analysis, the ultimate form that representation takes in Hobbes's social and political theory is the reified form of the commodity: "Transfers of power are assumed to be so usual that there is a market in power. A man's power is treated as a commodity, regular dealings in which establish market prices" (Macpherson 1962: 37).

9   This passage and the climax of the play's comic action may also allude to the debate in pamphlets and tracts of the 1620s over purported causes and proposed remedies of the depressed English economy, a debate that revolved around the East India trade (for which see Supple 1959: Ch. 9; Hutchison 1988: 6–7, 21–3, 83). Regardless of their differences, contributors to the debate were in general agreement that the fundamental problem was a shortage of money: "The want of money," wrote Gerard Malynes in *The Maintenance of Free Trade* (1622), "is the first cause of the decay of trade, for without money commodities are out of request" (quoted in Hutchison 1988: 21). Thomas Culpeper's *A Tract against Usury* (1621) called for the freeing of money for trade through government control of interest rates, a position shared by Bacon in his essay "Of usury" (1625). Thomas Mun's *England's Treasure by Foreign Trade*, first published in 1664 but written and possibly circulated in the 1620s, argued against government prohibitions on the export of money and specie. Mun was an officer of the East India Company, the interests of which he defended in attempting to undermine the bullionist and protectionist restraints advocated in more conventional mercantilist doctrine. As Patricia Fumerton points out, "it was Mun . . . who [among the pamphleteers] best understood the commodification of money" (Fumerton 1991: 180). And, one might add, it was Jonson among playwrights!

10   The English concept of the trust was derived historically from the concept of the "use," which was known and used throughout Europe from the twelfth century on, and which was developed in England in the Chancellor's court in the fourteenth and fifteenth centuries. . . . The "use" (like the later English "trust") presupposed three parties: a donor, a donee, and a beneficiary. The donee took the gift as a trustee for the beneficiary. Normally, however, property given to an ecclesiastical corporation was owned by the corporation; *it* was the donee. Nevertheless, it was also a beneficiary. If its officers had power to possess, use, and dispose of the corporation's property, they were required to exercise such power as its "trustees." That is still the rule of English company law as well as of American corporation law. It was, and is, also the rule of the canon law of the Roman Catholic Church.
(Berman, 1983: 239)

11 On Jonson's refusal to accommodate himself to the new tastes of Caroline theater audiences, see Michael Hattaway's introduction to his edition of *The New Inn* (1984).

12 On the growing sophistication of audiences, the purchasing of playbooks, and the general establishment of a "flourishing literary world" around the Caroline theaters see Butler, (1984: Ch. 6).

13 Nancy Armstrong has shown how by the mid-nineteenth century such training was thematized in novels where political and historical information was rewritten as psychological information. Armstrong describes a "scene of reading" in Charlotte Brontë's *Shirley* (1849),

where, in a domestic setting, a middle-class woman (Caroline Helstone) guides a middle-class man (Robert Moore) in reading aloud from *Coriolanus*. Caroline instructs Robert to "discover by the feeling the reading will give you at once how high and how low you are." Armstrong comments: "Even as it constitutes Shakespearean drama as a written text . . . this scene of reading turns writing into the record of and basis for speech. The written Shakespeare has taken the place of gossip. More important than that, the written word, when spoken, becomes the direct expression of emotions that exist prior to any speech act and that arise, so it appears, from pre-verbal sources within the self. Brought to life as a modern form of subjectivity, Shakespeare becomes the means of reproducing the same form of subjectivity within the reader" (Armstrong, 1987: 216). The reading of literature is here validated over parlor games and gossip as a worthwhile leisure activity; what is more, the vehicle of such validation is the representation of interpretive power as a feminine prerogative, a role that developed as an idealized aspect of feminine domesticity in the two centuries that followed Jonson's satiric placement of the Gossips on stage to mock the author of *The Staple of News*.

14   In a letter to his brothers George and Thomas composed in December 1817, Keats writes: "several things dovetailed in my mind, and at once it struck me, what quality went to form a Man of Achievement especially in Literature and which Shakespeare possessed so enormously – I mean Negative Capability, that is when man is capable of being in uncertainties, Mysteries, doubts, without any irritable reaching after fact and reason. . . . This pursued through volumes would perhaps take us no further than this, that with a great poet the sense of Beauty overcomes every other consideration, or rather obliterates all consideration" (Gittings 1987: 43).

15   A number of recent cultural critics argue that the frantic pace of commodity production and consumption has so fractured the bourgeois ego that we now observe through the culture of "postmodernism" a shift from alienation to fragmentation of the subject. See, for example, Jameson (1984) and Dews (1987).

Bibliography

Agnew, Jean–Christophe (1986) *Worlds Apart: The Market and the Theatre in Anglo-American Thought, 1550–1750*, Cambridge: Cambridge University Press.

Armstrong, Nancy (1987) *Desire and Domestic Fiction: A Political History of the Novel*, Oxford: Oxford University Press.

Augustine St., *On Christian Doctrine*, trans. J. F. Shaw (1887) in Philip Schaff (ed.) *A Select Library of the Nicene and Post-Nicene Fathers of the Christian Church*, Vol. II, New York: Scribner's.

Bacon, Francis (1859 [1605]) *Of the Proficience and Advancement of Learning*, in *The Works of Francis Bacon*, Vol. 3, ed. James Spedding, Robert Leslie Ellis, and Douglas Denon Heath, London: Longman.

Barish, Jonas A. (1963) "Introduction" to *Ben Jonson: A Collection of Critical Essays*, ed. Jonas A. Barish, Englewood Cliffs, NJ: Prentice-Hall, pp. 1–3.

Barton, Anne (1984) *Ben Jonson, Dramatist*, Cambridge: Cambridge University Press.

Berman, Harold J. (1983) *Law and Revolution: The Formation of the Western Legal Tradition*, Cambridge, MA: Harvard University Press.

Butler, Martin (1984) *Theatre and Crisis 1632–1642*, Cambridge: Cambridge University Press.

De Grazia, Margreta (1991) *Shakespeare Verbatim: The Reproduction of Authenticity and the 1790 Apparatus*, Oxford: Clarendon Press.

Dekker, Thomas (1967 [1609]) *The Gull's Horn-Book*, in E. D. Pendry (ed.) *Thomas Dekker*, Stratford-upon-Avon Library 4, London: Edward Arnold.

Dews, Peter (1987) *Logics of Disintegration: Post-Structuralist Thought and the Claims of Critical Theory*, London: Verso.

Fineman, Joel (1986) *Shakespeare's Perjured Eye: The Invention of Poetic Subjectivity in the Sonnets*, Berkeley, CA: University of California Press.

Foucault, Michel (1977) *Language, Counter-Memory, Practice: Selected Essays and Interviews*. ed. Donald F. Bouchard, Ithaca, NY: Cornell University Press.

Fumerton, Patricia (1991) *Cultural Aesthetics: Renaissance Literature and the Practice of Social Ornament*, Chicago: University of Chicago Press.

Gittings, Robert (ed.) (1987) *Letters of John Keats: A Selection Edited by Robert Gittings*, Oxford: Oxford University Press.

Greenblatt, Stephen (1988) *Shakespearean Negotiations: The Circulation of Social Energy in Renaissance England*, Oxford: Clarendon Press.

—— (1990) *Learning to Curse: Essays in Early Modern Culture*, New York and London: Routledge.

Greene, Thomas M. (1970) "Ben Jonson and the centered self," *SEL* 10: 325–48.

Greg, W. W. (1955) *The Shakespeare First Folio: Its Bibliographical and Textual History*, Oxford: Clarendon Press.

Hattaway, Michael (1984 [1631]) "Introduction" to Ben Jonson, *The New Inn*, ed. Michael Hattaway, Manchester: Manchester University Press.

Helgerson, Richard (1983) *Self-Crowned Laureates: Spenser, Jonson, Milton and the Literary System*, Berkeley, CA: University of California Press.

Herford, C. H., Simpson, Percy, and Simpson, Evelyn (eds.) (1925–52) *Ben Jonson*, 11 vols., Oxford: Clarendon Press; cited in text as *H & S*.

Horkheimer, Max and Adorno, Theodor W. (1972) *Dialectic of Enlightenment*, trans. John Cumming, New York: Herder & Herder.

Hutchison, Terence (1988) *Before Adam Smith: The Emergence of Political Economy, 1662–1776*, Oxford: Blackwell.

Jameson, Fredric (1984) "Postmodernism, or The cultural logic of late capitalism," *New Left Review* 146: 53–92.

Jonson, Ben (1962 [1607]) *Volpone*, ed. Alvin B. Kernan, New Haven, CT: Yale University Press.

—— (1963 [1614]) *Bartholomew Fair*, ed. Eugene M. Waith, New Haven, CT: Yale University Press.

—— (1975 [1626]) *The Staple of News*, ed. Devra Rowland Kifer, Lincoln, NB: University of Nebraska Press.

Knights, L. C. (1937) *Drama and Society in the Age of Jonson*, London: Chatto & Windus.

Loewenstein, Joseph (1985) "The script in the marketplace," *Representations* 12: 101–14.

Lukacs, Georg (1971) *History and Class Consciousness*, London: Merlin Press.

Macpherson, C. B. (1962) *The Political Theory of Possessive Individualism: Hobbes to Locke*, Oxford: Oxford University Press.

Marcus, Leah S. (1988) *Puzzling Shakespeare: Local Reading and Its Discontents*, Berkeley; CA: University of California Press.

Marx, Karl (1973) *Grundrisse*, trans. Martin Nicolaus, Harmondsworth, MX: Penguin.

Murray, Timothy (1983) "From foul sheets to legitimate model: antitheater, text, Ben Jonson," *NLH* 3: 641–64.

Newman, Karen (1989) "City talk: women and commodification in Jonson's *Epicoene*," *ELH* 56: 503–18.

Newton, Richard C. (1982) "Jonson and the (re-)invention of the book," in Claude J. Summers, and Ted–Larry Pebworth (eds) *Classic and Cavalier: Essays on Jonson and the Sons of Ben*, Pittsburgh, PA: University of Pittsburgh Press.

Sackville, Thomas and Norton, Thomas (1970 [1562]) *Gorboduc: or, Ferrex and Porrex*, ed. Irby B. Cauthen, Jr., Lincoln, NB: University of Nebraska Press.

Shakespeare, William (1968 [1623]) *The Norton Facsimile: The First Folio of Shakespeare*, ed. Charlton Hinman, New York: W. W. Norton.

Shirley, James (1970 [1646]) *Narcissus, or The Self-Lover*, in *James Shirley, Poems 1646*, facsimile edn., Menston, Yorks: Scolar Press.

Stallybrass, Peter and White, Allon (1986) *The Politics of Transgression*, Ithaca, NY: Cornell University Press.

Supple, B. E. (1959) *Commercial Crisis and Change in England, 1600–1642*, Cambridge: Cambridge University Press.

Wall, Wendy (1989) "Disclosures in print: the 'violent Enlargement' of the Renaissance voyeuristic text," *SEL* 29: 35–59.

Wayne, Don E. (1982) " 'Drama and society in the age of Jonson': an alternative view,"
Renaissance Drama n.s., 13: 103–29; reprinted in Mary Beth Rose (ed.) (1990) *Renaissance
Drama as Cultural History: Essays from Renaissance Drama, 1977–1987*, Evanston, IL:
Northwestern University Press, pp. 3–29.

—— (1990) "Jonson's Sidney: legacy and legitimation in *The Forrest*," in M. J. B. Allen, Dominic
Baker–Smith, and Arthur F. Kinney, with Margaret M. Sullivan, (eds.) *Sir Philip Sidney's
Achievements*, New York: AMS Press, pp. 227–50.

Weber, Max (1978) "The market: its impersonality and ethic (fragment)," in Max Weber,
Economy and Society: An Outline of Interpretive Sociology, ed. Guenther Roth and Claus Wittich,
vol. 1, Berkeley, CA: University of California Press, pp. 635–40.

10
Author-mongering
The "editor" between producer and consumer

Robert Iliffe

> With the increasing extension of the press, which kept placing new political, religious, scientific, professional, and local organs before the readers, an increasing number of readers became writers [and] it began with the daily press opening to its readers space for "letters to the editor." . . . As expert, which he had to become willy-nilly in an extremely specialized work process, even if only in some minor respect, the reader gains access to authorship.[1]

On August 2, 1712, the *British Mercury* complained of "the furious Itch of Novelty" and the "Immoderate Appetite of Intelligence" which now characterized all levels of society and which had led to "*that inundation of* Post-Men, Post-Boys, Evening Posts, Supplements, Daily Courants, and Protestant Post-Boys, *amounting to twenty-one every week*." Readers of these relatively ephemeral publications were well aware of this phenomenon, while the substantial growth of the paper pulping industry after the repeal of the Licensing Act in 1695 represents a significant physical index of the massive increase in this material. Consumers also bought more refined literature in unprecedented numbers, and their financial power allowed them to own much of the vast output of both ancient and modern classics. The producers of this literature – the growing numbers of booksellers, authors, translators, and editors – were attuned to the effects which these publications were supposed to have on their readers. Samuel Johnson remarked that "to increase the value of his copies," Dryden had often accompanied his work with a preface of criticism, "a kind of learning then almost new in the English language . . . which he was able to distribute copiously as occasions arose." He added that by "these dissertations the publick judgement must have been much improved," but Swift recalled that Dryden "regretted the success of his own instructions, and found his readers made suddenly too skillful to be easily satisfied." Yet even in the Restoration period, contemporaries had been concerned about the deleterious social effect which the many editions of classical authors would have on the standing of these authors, and Roger L'Estrange complained of "the selling of translations so dog cheap [that] every nasty groom and roguey lackey is grown familiar with Homer, Virgil and Ovid." These changes to both the tastes of the readers and the social status of the authors were integral parts of the literary culture of early eighteenth-century England, and authors who had lived on the shelves of universities were now to be found in the homes of Augustan consumers. In 1765, Joseph Priestley could accurately describe the kind of social transformation that had taken place in the previous century: "The politeness of the times has brought the learned and the unlearned into more familiar intercourse than they had together before. . . . Criticism, which was formerly the great business of a scholar's life, is now become the amusement of a leisure hour."[2]

A few translators and editors of texts such as Pope and Dryden possessed a reputation of their own, and they were explicit about the extent to which they had imposed upon their "authors" through having translated them or by having turned their work into modern poetry. Having a contemporary "name," their editions could well be described as Dryden's *Virgil*, or Pope's *Homer*. Yet there were countless other editions and translations of authors, and the status of these nameless editors and translators was by no means clear-cut. How much credit were they to get? Even those with a well-established name, such as Dryden and Pope, were prone to attack for related reasons. Was Dryden's *Virgil* really Virgil? Or Pope's *Homer* Homer? In the case of the thousands of nameless "editors" who edited classical texts for commercial or political purposes, or who edited newspapers and journals, the same question arose. Were they in any sense "authors" of these texts, that is, were they to be given *credit* similar to that given to the authors they helped publish? Or were they simply drudges, whose hard but lowly work was as yet not sufficient to give them a name or a social status?

While some scholars have asserted that the appearance of the editor was an integral part of the change in print culture of this period, the nature of this role has been little studied. Since it is the editor who literally "gives out" the work, this appears to be a major omission. In this chapter, I look at some different versions of this role that existed in the past: the fictive editor in the epistolary novel, the editor of the periodical and the natural philosophy journal, and the editor of the ancient and modern text. In the first case, the correspondence related by the epistolary novel was governed by a nameless editor, who interceded on behalf of the reader to produce a readable and exciting text. I suggest that this device was credible by the time Richardson produced *Pamela* and *Clarissa* in the 1740s because the reading public was familiar with the role of the editor in the formats of newspaper and journal, and because it was a device which was closely linked to other literary techniques such as those used by Defoe and Swift. I compare these editorial interventions with those of the first editor of the *Philosophical Transactions*, Henry Oldenburg, whose correspondence offers substantial evidence of the nature of his work in bringing together letters from all over the world on to the printed pages of the *Transactions*. I contrast the way in which Oldenburg tried to make a name and an identity for Isaac Newton through publication in the *Transactions*, with the means by which "editors" like Richard Bentley and Lewis Theobald fought with the Scriblerians and the so-called Christ Church wits over the proper techniques, decorum, social status, and identity of the editor of the works of both ancients and moderns. In both these cases, I suggest that the manifestation of the "editor" was intimately bound up with the appearance of the "author," and should be taken into account in the history of the latter.[3]

The roles and functions of those individuals designated by their contemporaries as "editors" were connected by virtue of their ability to make "names" for their authors and construct public "identities" for them. They were supposed to be trustworthy managers of the transit of private and personal material into the public sphere, and I explore the means by which both real and fictitious editors seemed to exercise control over these regions. Finally, I look at the ways in which various editing techniques were used by booksellers and editors in the formation of canons at the beginning of the eighteenth century. Historians have lately begun to appreciate the importance of booksellers in the complex picture of the appearance of "literature" in the eighteenth century, and the production of journals and special "editions" of authors' works were largely the result of an alliance between authors, editors, and these booksellers. Editorial techniques and strategies, allied to a skillful manipulation of the market, endowed certain texts with an authoritative status. To approach this issue, I look at the appearance of what has been called "print culture" in the early eighteenth century.[4]

Editor-functions

Following the work of such scholars as Elizabeth Eisenstein, the social and technological relations making up the printed text have loomed large in explanations of the social and literary transformations that took place in Augustan England. For instance, in a bold analysis which draws upon Eisenstein's account of the active agency of the printing press as a force for effecting cultural change, Alvin Kernan isolates what he calls the "primary tendencies of print logic" such as "multiplicity," "systematization," and "fixity." The "distinctive marks of canon-making" all appear at the beginning of the eighteenth century: "the apocrypha of Grub-Street hackwriting, the increase of legitimating criticism, [and] the enormous growth in the activity of editing literary texts." He suggests that the invincible replicability offered by print triumphed over the "cathedral atmosphere" of rare books libraries; while every manuscript was inevitably different, only a printed text was capable of being accurate and the "stigma of print" that was initially felt in the more aristocratic culture of "letters" was ultimately overcome. Kernan identifies many of the key parts to this story, yet two parallel explanatory schemes run through his book. On the one hand, he remarks that "it was the need of print for copy that created writers," while on the other he claims that "the hack-writers . . . make it obvious that the social construction of a new print-based system of letters was not a technologically determined process."[5]

As a means towards resolving this tension, one might look more closely at some of the narrative techniques and texts being forged in the mythologically squalid places where most of the hacks plied their trade. In a recent treatment of this issue, Kathryn Shevelow has looked at the ways in which early periodicals turned out women, literally.[6] She looks at the processes of inclusion and exclusion that went into making saleable copies of such significant periodicals as the *Athenian Mercury* and the *Athenian Oracle*, and explores the topology of this construction. Women were naturalized as necessarily possessing certain qualities and this was also accompanied and circumscribed by a specific *place* in which women were to exist, along with a leisure *time* in which to read. Shevelow shows how this notion of the ideal gentlewoman with a surfeit of time for self-improvement was constructed and then swiftly incorporated by its purveyors into the literature of this period. A number of courtesy manuals now affirmed that letter-writing as well as reading was a virtuous pastime for ladies. Letters – correspondence – were private, and so were not supposed to threaten the public, male realm. Shevelow draws attention to the capacity of certain periodicals to circumvent this privacy and allow women to see themselves in public. For example, John Dunton's *Athenian Mercury* (and later, the *Ladies' Mercury*) "represented women as writing subjects in an unprecedented way." Such periodicals concertinaed the social and geographical spaces of epistolary converse so that a writer could quickly see her own anonymous (and possibly doctored) letter on the printed page. Letters were often printed in the form of a question-and-answer session, or with the editor doubling as a confessor; indeed, by being so openly confessional they rivalled the vogue for biographies of factual and fictional criminals. Shevelow notes that the "authority residing in the representation of feminine experience was of course always situated in relation to the greater authority exercised by the editorial pronouncements."[7]

This dramatic presence of the editorial voice and of the potential audience contribution to the printed text was immediately visible to contemporaries, and it could be a powerful tool for subversion. Tom Brown's *London Mercury* (which appeared in 1692) made the important point that the *Athenian Mercury* was a leveling text; it was dangerous because all and sundry appeared together in the same place, often with no markers for the reader to distinguish between the social hierarchy of the contributors. To critics of these works, the editor was a major threat because he had absolute control over the content of the letters. Yet the editor's identity was also a source of fascination, and "real" editors made great play in testing the fictive device of their *alter ego* to its limits. Hence the occasional intervention, as in *Spectators* 271, 442, and 542, where Steele (442) and Addison informed the readers that the editor did not "always publish the letter itself," and in the *Review* of October 4, 1711, where Defoe denied that the "editor" had written letters to himself. There was a multiplicity of responses to this genre. One might be thrilled if one recognized one's self displayed in print (although there was a tradition of anonymity in the *Mercury*), or be titillated at seeing authentic "immodest" experiences expressed in public. Many of the latter could barely be published for a wider audience in any other form, but here they could be opened up to the gaze of the reader. One could even be led to think that the letters were false; then the game was to try to identify the "real" editor. In this way, a new community of (mainly urban) consumers continuously renewed itself, in and around a series of easily available texts.[8]

The device of the editor was closely related to similar narrative techniques that were being developed elsewhere. It guaranteed the credibility of the correspondence in the epistolary novel, just as the "narrator" in works like those of Daniel Defoe vouched for the authenticity of the facts described within his texts. Defoe borrowed credit-making devices such as "witnesses" from sources like Robert Boyle to establish the "matters of fact" that he (often anonymously) reported, and he recommended that the social world should be subject to the same reporting techniques as the natural. Other stories, such as those of apparitions of the dead, he branded as "fictions" and "cheats." Yet his strategy could be turned against him, and in 1715 he complained of the pirates who had taken his books and even his "Name," which "had been hackney'd about the Street by the Hawkers, and about the Coffee Houses by the Politicians, at such a rate, as no

Patience could bear." Contemporaries noted that he was "truly Master of forging a story and imposing it on the World for Truth" and by the end of the nineteenth century he had earned the reputation of being "a truly great liar, perhaps the greatest that ever lived."[9] Defoe might circumvent the problems of anonymity by turning his stories into morally instructive narratives, but according to contemporary conventions, this did not preclude their being "histories." His *A Journal of the Plague Year* (published in 1722) was presented as history and was initially perceived as such, and the narrative voice was endowed with the same power as the fictitious editor of the journal. Other works, which the modern audience retrospectively takes to be early versions of the "novel", invoked the authoritative voice of the impartial narrator to underpin the credibility of the tale. In the "autobiographical" *Moll Flanders*, the author's "Preface" claims that Moll's manuscript had been changed considerably to leave out "some of the vicious part of her Life, which cou'd not be modestly told . . . the Copy, which came first to Hand, having been written in Language more like one still in *Newgate*." There were yet other sources for Defoe's craft, and he had learned his trade compiling histories and editing texts like the pro-government *Review* for Harley.[10] A host of other writers such as John Toland (who edited political texts and histories for Tonson and Harley) eked out an existence anonymously "editing" political biographies and histories. Yet as I explain later on in this chapter, anonymity was obviously a problem for anyone who wanted public credit as an author or editor.[11]

The nameless "editor" appeared to be in an excellent position to vet and publish the authentic and morally instructive private letters of Augustan England. The *device* of the editor, emplotted along with the "author" and "reader" in the newspaper, journal, or epistolary novel, was transformed into one of the most important techniques for controlling this realm and making it public. Whatever the supposed status of the printed word in this period, the manuscript letter had immense power as a purveyor of private information which could escape the public eye.[12] This was recognized by the authorities; a great deal of personal correspondence in Restoration England had been deemed subversive, and the state was forced to assert a degree of control over the circulation of letters. In the 1680s, when there were a number of real and fictitious plots against the lives of royals and government officials, radicals like John Locke devised ways of coding information in letters, employing the device of "canting." An extraordinary effort was made by the English government to detect these letters and their authors. As Richard Ashcraft has shown, mail was systematically intercepted and opened by their agents, and London was said to contain those who had "tricks to open letters more skillfully than anywhere in the world." In turn each side attempted to plant false letters and documents.[13]

Consumers in the early eighteenth century wanted to buy and see private correspondence, and booksellers were not slow to capitalize on this genteel vogue for printed letters. The "Unspeakable" Edmund Curll advertised for authentic examples of them – both sides of the correspondence – and, not to be outdone, so did John Dunton, while in 1725 there appeared Lillie's edition of the *Original and Genuine Letters to the Tatler and Spectator*. Ever careful to ensure that his letters were preserved for posterity, Alexander Pope lamented that once a bookseller announced his intention to publish one's letters, "you have not only Theft to fear, but Forgery. . . . Any domestick or servant, who can snatch a letter from your pocket or cabinet, is encouraged to that vile practice." But despite Pope's concern over securing a proper status for his own correspondence, Curll finally gained the rights to it and renamed his shop "The Pope's Head" to commemorate his triumph. Pope's lament shows that if authentic letters were unobtainable, then their fictional counterparts would do. A number of writers turned to the relatively new genre of the epistolary novel, which in its various forms has been estimated to have comprised nearly a fifth of eighteenth-century fiction. A group of female authors wrote plays for the social space of the theatre before embarking on this kind of enterprise, and their experience was significant for developing the skills required to compose the epistolary novel. Such tales appeared to be the "authentic" account and staging of the sentiments of the letter-writers' souls; here, little or nothing seemed to exist outside the seemingly spontaneous and pure (but actually heavily disciplined) area of the correspondence, aside from references to the vagaries of the postal service or to the act of letter-writing itself. In turn, the genre of letter-writing manuals was consolidated and refined. It was precisely this type of work that was produced by the printer Samuel Richardson, and his experience in composing letters formed an essential resource for his popular epistolary novels.[14]

While there was a long tradition of epistolary novels preceding *Pamela* and *Clarissa*, the appearance of newspapers and *Spectator/Tatler*-type productions had served to sophisticate the growing readership and shape the taste of consumers of such books. When *Pamela* appeared in November 1740 it was an immediate bestseller. Written by Richardson in the midst of composing his *Familiar Letters on Important Occasions* (1741), it telescoped sexual and cultural politics into the structure of a journal of letters composed by a servant girl. Using a technique that was crucial to the narrative structure, the "History" of the letters was organized by an "editor" who reassured the reader that the letters had a deep moral purpose. In later editions, Richardson would refine Pamela's discourse (as in removing most of the dialect in her voice), to make her more of a lady, and to dignify the novel in general. Yet by 1740, *Pamela* was not a radically new or astonishing production. Day argues that its success was in no small way due to a combination of Richardson's advertising and promotional strategies, the puffs that it was given by influential friends, its bulk, and its "warm scenes" and moral preaching. On the other hand, contemporaries *did* believe that Richardson had achieved a dramatic *tour de force*. As Mrs. Donnellan wrote to Richardson in September 1750: "the epistolary style is yours, 'tis speaking, 'tis painting."[15] As the author of the text, Richardson was seen by his contemporaries to exert a remarkable control over his heroines. This was perhaps heightened by the fact that his second work, *Clarissa*, was published in installments. Just as Pamela is condemned to marry Mr. B. despite her ill use at his hands, so Richardson (particularly in the correspondence with Lady Bradshaigh) in his lengthy creation of *Clarissa* was captured by readers and correspondents in the act of executioner. Although "Belfour" (Lady Bradshaigh) warned Richardson on October 10, 1748 that she "was afraid of hating you, if you alter not your scheme," Richardson invoked literary fate and had Clarissa killed off.[16]

Despite his protestations that these texts were intended as moral instruction by example, Richardson was attacked for the voyeuristic nature of his work. His friend George Henry Cheyne invoked St. Paul to tell him: "It is a shame for you to speak of those things that are done by you in secret," while Fielding parodied this world and the position of the editor in *Shamela*, a text in which characters compose letters in absurd situations and which begins with "A letter to the Editor from Himself." The situations of writing and reading had been an integral part of Richardson's text, as were the multifarious ways in which Pamela's private spaces were violated. At one point in the story, the textually pregnant Pamela is forced to clothe herself in her papers: "I begin to be afraid my Writings may be discover'd; for they grow large! I stitch them hitherto in my Under-coat, next my Linen." The "editor" also had control over these places and allowed the relation of these experiences to extend to an "extravagant prolixity." Horace Walpole remarked that his novels were "pictures of high life as conceived by a bookseller," while the poet William Shenstone claimed that *Clarissa* was "needlessly spun out . . . which he could scarce have done had he not been a *Printer* as well as an Author. . . . Nothing but *Fact* could authorise so much particularity, and indeed not that: but in a court of Justice." Richardson and his readers were acutely aware of the spatial implications of the text, and Diderot remarked that Richardson had "written for the solitary, who [could] be moved to tears in silence." This reading experience was supposed to be a private matter between the letter-writer and the reader, unlike the very public matter of reading newspapers in coffee-houses.[17]

This topological exchange was studiously crafted, and Richardson incorporated insights from his own correspondents into his narratives. He asked them to leave a margin "at sides, top and bottom" so that he could inscribe his own marginalia, and he asked them to scour their own letters for intimate comments on personal matters that might "provide him material for his work in progress." Lady Bradshaigh, for example, was asked for the comments she had made in the margins of her copies of *Pamela* and *Clarissa*. The very form of the letter in the novel was also crucial to the goal of the printer-author, and Watt points out that Richardson printed Clarissa's "jumble of poetical fragments at varying angles on the page in imitation of her original demented doodlings." For strategic purposes, Richardson did not want anything of *himself* in the finished text, and he claimed that the author of the "instantaneous descriptions" of the letters (i.e. Richardson) was "screened behind the umbrage of the editor's character."[18]

The device of a nameless organizer of these letters who yet made a minimum of intervention in the text was essential for the plot to succeed. The "editor" had to be trusted and accepted by readers as a reliable purveyor of the original text but this technique could succeed only if there was a well-developed notion of the role of the editor in the production of newspapers and journals. Real editors led much more active if fragile existences than their fictional counterparts, although like them they had to be trustworthy and work "off" the page. Editors and printers of material deemed to be politically or morally subversive were repeatedly threatened by government raids, and Joseph Streater, the printer of the *Principia Mathematica*, was prosecuted for printing pornography more than once after 1687. Editors were always suspect as they were in a crucial position to oversee the selection of elements of handwritten material and then make it suitable for publication. In the following section, I examine the basis of this editorial power to construct author and text by looking at the ways in which Henry Oldenburg managed Isaac Newton's problems of publication, ownership, and authorship in the late seventeenth-century Royal Society.

Names

Amongst the group of noblemen, clergy, naturalists, experimenters, astronomers, and natural philosophers which made up the early Royal Society, the question concerning the extent to which an author could be said to *own* the results of his labor was a key component in ordering its business. In this closed (but nominally open) community, a series of codes of behavior and conventions were constructed which were supposed to provide solutions to these problems and thus to give proper credit to the labors of individual members. When the *Philosophical Transactions* began publication in 1665, its "editor" Henry Oldenburg was chiefly responsible for managing the economy of this credit and he played an integral part in deciding whether credit should be conferred on or withheld from letter-reports that were knowledge-candidates. The Royal Society functioned as a repository for reports of monsters, observations, and experiments from all over the known world, and, as the king's property, it had the right to embellish texts with its own imprimatur. Correspondence was crucial to this enterprise and letters in the form of stylized reports or narratives – "papers" – made up the bulk of the *Philosophical Transactions*. Oldenburg had almost total control over the content of this text and to a large extent it was his own creation and property. As he put it to a correspondent, "please be careful not to ascribe the *Philosophical Transactions* to the Royal Society, since they are edited and published by me alone, as the Secretary."[19]

In finding a niche for himself in this community, he had to tread a fine line between different personae. He was editor of the *Transactions* and Secretary of the Royal Society, while he was also a member of the Society in a "personal" capacity. The assumption of these different identities was a trick at which he was adept. As editor, he frequently had to intervene in the texts that he published in the *Philosophical Transactions*, but these forays could leave no evidence that he had been there. Oldenburg was recognized by contemporaries as being good at what he did; the Royal Society's reputation declined dramatically after 1677 when Oldenburg died, and had done so again by 1687 when Tancred Robinson (one of the Society's Secretaries) warned Hans Sloane in Jamaica that the Society was in danger of discontinuing because "there [was] not one correspondent in being." To an overwhelming extent, the Society *was* its correspondence, and this was controlled between 1660 and 1677 by Oldenburg.[20]

A report submitted to the Society could not usually be accepted on its own, but required some other mark of its credibility. This came in the form of testimony from a member of the Society, from a gentleman, or from someone who was "known" to a member. As stipulated in Thomas Sprat's *History of the Royal Society* of 1667, and epitomized by the work of Robert Boyle, the ideal report was to be expressed in such a way that an ordinary reader could see and understand it as well as believe that the action that the report described had actually been carried out. The report was credible if there was no ostensible basis for thinking that its relator was prejudiced, and Boyle suggested that reports and illustrations submitted to the Society should be composed in such detail that the reader was effectively witnessing the instrument or object itself.[21] The credibility of a report and the social status and trustworthiness of the relator were therefore intimately linked. If there was a dispute within the Society, its central authorities could mediate by offering equal credit to inventors and discoverers, or, as in a priority dispute over the sighting of an astronomical object (the comet of 1664/5), by postulating the existence of two objects. This credit system relied on the notion that gentlemen were unproblematic relayers of truth, but if one were not yet a fully accredited member of this system, then your word might not be believed and one's testimony would then have to be bolstered by someone who had a reputable *name*. Problems associated with this feature of the Society's "philosophical commerce" were common. For example, in 1664 William Hann neglected to sign his relation of the dissection of a double-headed child; Oldenburg told Robert Boyle that he was "sorry [Hann] did not put his name to the account he gave of the operation; and we must contrive some way or other to have it yet done, for the more authenticness of the relation, now it is to be recorded by a Royal Society of severe philosophers." As a prospective natural philosopher, it was essential that one had the identity of a gentleman and thus a *good* name so that one's word was believed. In civilized debate, men were to be "reasoned," not forced, out of their opinions, and correspondents were invited to direct their criticisms at things, not persons. As Secretary of the Society, and editor of the *Transactions*, Oldenburg's brief was to manage this socio-nomenclature.[22]

While Boyle was based in Oxford in the 1660s, Oldenburg took care of much of his business in London. He had overall control in managing the publication of Boyle's texts, but this was fraught with difficulties. From the middle of this period, Oldenburg and Boyle saw themselves as jointly threatened by hordes of literary pirates who wanted to claim their work for themselves, or who were hiring hacks to translate their texts into other languages. In November 1664, Oldenburg had to tell Boyle that his bookseller was keeping Boyle's papers "unexposed to ye eye of ye Philosophicall Robber." By August of the following year, Boyle was becoming worried that Dutch competitors would preempt the projected Oldenburg edition of his *Origin of Formes and Qualities*, and that "Divers of ye Expts wch possibly will appear new and somew^t, curious, may be wth or w^{th}out a little variation, adopted & divulged by others." Later, Boyle was sufficiently fazed by the thought of piracy to tell Oldenburg that he would have to send his "matters of fact . . . maimed and unfinished, as they come to hand, to the press." Finally, he grew concerned that the "more subtile" plagiarists would give subsequent editions of their pirated texts the same date as the real first editions and smuggle stolen experiments behind this smokescreen.[23] In the course of such debates, the Royal Society created much stricter regulations for ensuring intellectual property and for the surveillance of entry and conduct. A significant event occurred in October 1674 when attendance at its meetings was restricted to certain members who were forbidden from discussing the nature of these meetings outside the Society's walls. Oldenburg had been locked up in the Tower in 1667 for charges relating to spying, and, sensitized to questions of secrecy, he was a key participant in this decision. By the 1670s, he was at the focal point of the most sophisticated exchange of information about the natural world then in existence.[24]

In a significant sense, many members of English society in Restoration England could not appear in "public." Steven Shapin has demonstrated this with Boyle's "technicians"; although Boyle rarely sullied himself with "hands-on" work, it was "under" his name that his works appeared. Likewise, the names of Boyle's "technicians" tended to be mentioned in his manuscript notes only if there was a mishap such as an accident or explosion in his laboratory. When it came to publication, Boyle apparently had little contact with printers or suchlike, and this matter was almost entirely carried out by Oldenburg who organized the dissemination of Boyle's texts and liaised with the printers and booksellers amongst whom, he warned Boyle, there was a "kind of conjuration, and a very mystical one." Printers, and the servants and operators who acted as the early modern equivalent of the technician, did not possess sufficient standing to be given credit as authors of the texts they had helped to produce. One needed a "name" to publish in the *Transactions*, and the case of Hann cited earlier shows that here anonymity was a dangerous publishing strategy; the reader could not then readily judge the credibility of the "matters of fact" that the anonymous works (like alchemical texts) contained. If the reports of noblemen like Boyle were basically indisputable, this was not the case for those of an indeterminate social status such as the draper Anton Leeuwenhoek and Isaac Newton, the Lucasian Professor of Mathematics at Cambridge. In order for his name to appear in public at all, Newton needed, sought, and received, an immense amount of management and support from Oldenburg.[25]

Newton's major publishing strategy paradoxically revolved around the quest for anonymity and solitude. These conventions were common in many areas but, for the reasons given, were deemed inappropriate for the Royal Society. Hence "making" Newton's name so that Newton could appear as an author in public was to be the key problem for Newton and Oldenburg in the forum of the Royal Society. From the very beginning of his career, Newton courted the privacy of Trinity College at Cambridge. He told the first Lucasian Professor, Isaac Barrow, that he wished to remain anonymous when Barrow revealed some of his mathematics to John Collins in 1669; Newton himself told Collins that he had leave to publish his solution to an annuity problem provided "it bee wthout my name to it." There was nothing "desirable in acquiring and maintaining . . . publick esteeme"; this was what he "cheifly studied to decline."[26]

Asked to complete his revisions for Kinckhuysen's *Algebra*, he totally flabbergasted Collins when he once again requested anonymity and Collins replied, "why you should desire to have your name unmentioned I see not." When he later made contact with the Royal Society via Barrow, he again asked that his identity be withheld. This time, however, Oldenburg suggested that his telescope and its inventor's name be recorded in the Society's Register Book to prevent it from being "snatched away . . . by pretending bystanders." Newton parried with the claim that he was "surprised to see so much care taken about securing an invention to mee, of wch I have hitherto had so little value," as without the Society's "patronizing . . . [it would] have still remained in private as it hath already done some years." At the end of a following letter he casually announced that he had a theory of light upon which the design of the telescope was based, and that he would send it if he had the time. But Newton had been irrevocably seduced into the public arena, and his ensuing paper on light and colors was read to the Society in February 1671/2. In this letter he cited no named witnesses to his work but argued that light was a "body" and that white light was a heterogeneous aggregate of its color-making component rays. As proof, he constructed an "Experimentum Crucis" and claimed that the doctrine he asserted was "mathematicall" and based on "certain" principles. It was these claims which were distressing to many of his readers, and which involved him in controversy.[27]

The dispute with Robert Hooke that followed this paper was stage-managed by Oldenburg, and there is other evidence from the 1660s that he actively encouraged similar exchanges.[28] The observations that Newton had made in his paper had been, as Oldenburg put it in his letter of thanks, almost the only "entertainment" that the Fellows had experienced recently, and he was not about to let Newton retreat into his Cambridge chamber. Newton was now introduced to many of the conventions that governed the publication of work in the Society. After the printing of his work in the *Philosophical Transactions*, Newton was asked to compose a response to his critics. Oldenburg suggested that in his reply

> ye names of the objectors, especially if they desire it be so, be omitted, and their objections only urged: since those of ye R. Society ought to aime at nothing, but the discovery of truth, and ye improvement of knowledge, and not at the prostitution of persons for their misapprehensions or mistakes.[29]

In fact, Oldenburg had already been forced to alter and delete much of Newton's initial paper before it was fit to be printed.[30] Newton replied that he was "not at all concerned whether Objections be printed wth or wthout ye Objectors names," but two weeks later he claimed that he did not "understand [Oldenburg's] desire of leaving out Mr. Hooks name because the contents would discover their author." Newton now announced that he wished to "withdraw" from the Society because he had been "cut short of that fredome of communication [he] had hoped to enjoy." Nevertheless, he informed Oldenburg that Hooke "should have obliged [him] by a private letter" and Hooke was coerced into writing an apologetic note to a senior member of the Society claiming that he would indeed appreciate "a private correspondence" with Newton, and that his letter "had never been intended for Mr. Newton's perusal."[31]

To his dismay, Newton's theory was not met with the acquiescence that he expected, and he again stated that he would withdraw from public life. By not accepting the "matters of fact" which he was relating, his detractors were not accepting his word and so were calling his "good" name into question. Yet, by all of the usual conventions of the Society's correspondence, his critics – such as the Jesuits at Liège – were not behaving in an untoward or unorthodox manner. According to the received etiquette, they were entitled to ask for a witness to the experiments of the relatively unknown Lucasian Professor, or indeed for any evidence that he had carried out the work which he claimed he had performed. Later, the question arose as to whether the "weight," or "number," of experiments counted for making credit. While Newton stressed the importance of the single *crucial* experiment against Boyle's insistence that a number of *witnessed* experiments increased the probability of the effect being related, he was duty-bound to provide some witnesses to his work at Cambridge. Yet he was unable to produce them.[32]

When he contacted Oldenburg, Newton repeatedly asked him to mollify any expressions which might appear to be "personall," and Oldenburg complied with these requests. He was often obliged to make much more serious alterations to Newton's texts. In effect, he was Newton's patron in London, and Newton used him as such. When Newton again tried to withdraw from the Society in March 1672/3, Oldenburg reassured him that the "general body" of the Society "esteemed and loved" him. At some point in 1675, Newton changed his tactics completely. Since his Jesuit adversaries were simply denying his word, he asked Oldenburg for some help in identifying some witnesses to an experiment he had performed in London in early 1675, but Oldenburg could not remember who they were.[33]

Desperate for sufficient recognition to end these disputes, Newton sent a "Hypothesis" concerning the nature of light to Oldenburg in December 1675, along with a series of "Observations" on the same matter. Once more, a problem with Hooke arose, this time explicitly couched in terms of intellectual property. Newton suggested that, in private conversation, Hooke had "accommodated his Hypothesis to [Newton's] suggestion of colours" but Hooke took umbrage and claimed that the theft was the other way round. Oldenburg passed this information back to Newton who countered by telling him to delete from the printed version of his "Hypothesis" a section in which Newton had named "Hooke" as being a co-discoverer of diffraction. He composed a vicious letter in which he painted Hooke as a philosophical magpie who had merely "modified" those parts of Descartes' work which he had not stolen. In turn, Hooke responded by showing the members of his newly formed "Philosophicall Clubb" exactly where from Hooke's *Micrographia* Newton had pilfered Hooke's own notion of the "aether." Three weeks later, Newton was still raging at Hooke and he thanked Oldenburg – whom he called his "representative" in London – for passing on the news of Hooke's "mistakes." Nevertheless, by the end of this letter, he had adopted a different line and now suggested that his problems with Hooke had resulted from a "misapprehension." Having attempted to cite Hooke and his friend Abraham Hill as witnesses to his own experiments, he now added that Oldenburg should "leave out w^t I mention of [them], or at least put letters for their names: for I believe they had rather not be mentioned." Ten days later Hooke offered to "correspond [with Newton] about such matters by private letter," referring to Oldenburg's "sinister practices" in misrepresenting him. Finally, Newton acknowledged Hooke's offer of a private correspondence on the grounds that "what's done before many witnesses is seldome wthout some further concern then that for truth, but what passes between friends in private usually deserves ye name of consultation rather then contest."[34]

In this ostensibly "public" culture, the physical act of citing someone's name when one's criticisms were supposed to be directed at their "doctrines," or of striking out (as Newton did Hooke's name in the manuscript of his *Principia*) a rival's name, was replete with significance. The phenomena of citation and eponymity conferred property rights on a colleague and citing an ally meant that as far as you were concerned, that person was entitled to the work that went under his name. This set up networks of credit dependency; if your work was attacked, you could appeal to the authority of someone whose work you had cited as an ally. Newton's inability to achieve this sort of good credit, I would suggest, is the fundamental feature of his relations with the Royal Society in the 1670s and 1680s. This is what Oldenburg was trying to do for Newton whenever he helped Newton rewrite or suppress his material. Newton was totally dependent on Oldenburg, and when Oldenburg died in 1677, Newton finally did withdraw to the Fens. As editor of the *Philosophical Transactions*, Oldenburg was therefore in a pivotal position to oversee this exchange of credit. In one sense, he was a respected curator of the space enclosed by the *Philosophical Transactions* and, to a large extent, he controlled the social topology of that space. It was ultimately his decision to place reports of monsters alongside narratives of vacuum experiments, and he had to ensure that these narratives were credible by attaching a name to the report so that it would have the requisite *authority*.

In the Royal Society, whoever could successfully manage his name and identity was king, as was whoever controlled the public credibility of his targets. In cultures distinct from the Society, there were other conventions. For example, the Scriblerians drew from a very similar tradition of authorship to that of Newton and derided the techniques and hard labors which scholarly translators and editors of ancient texts proclaimed as the foundation of authority for their productions. Pope professed what Mack has described as the "aristocratic attitude" towards writing, which entailed protestations that he wrote only for pleasure and was detached from the sordid demands of the vulgar literary trade, and this ethos is clearly visible in the attempt by Thomas Gray to get Dodsley to publish anonymously his "Elegy written in a country churchyard." Gray asked Walpole to let Dodsley print the poem "without my name . . . [and] if he would add a Line or two to say it came into his Hands by Accident, I should like it better." Here, anonymity was a necessity, and striving after an authorial name was a vulgar and tawdry exercise. As Swift put it in describing the productions of Grub Street:

> Poems read without a Name
> We justly praise or justly blame . . .
> But if you Blab, you are undone
> Consider what a Risk you Run
> You lose your credit all at once;
> The Town will mark you for a Dunce.

At the outset of his public career, Pope was very quickly made aware of these issues. In 1712 he told Steele that if he had known that Steele was going to connect his name to a public text, he would have expressed himself with "more modesty and diffidence." Even earlier, he told Wycherly that "This modern custom of appearing in Miscellanies, is very useful to the Poets, who, like other thieves, escape by getting into a Crowd, and herd together like *Banditti*, safe only in the multitude." He used this image nearly twenty years later, when discussing duncing tactics with John Arbuthnot. Pope suggested that they "name names" in their correspondence, as "'tis only by hunting One or Two from the Herd that any Examples can be made."[35]

The Scriblerian project revolved around their ability publicly to manipulate the identities of themselves and their adversaries by means of distorting the names of their targets. In a significant letter to Pope (of July 16, 1728), Swift discussed this in regard to the format of the forthcoming *Dunciad Variorum*. The letter shows how carefully their barbs were aimed and their audiences primed; Swift asked whether the quarto edition would "come out anonymously as published by the Commentator, with all his pomp of Prefaces &c., and among complaints of spurious editions?" He then suggested that Pope's scholarly apparatus

> be very large, in what relates to the persons concern'd; for I have long observed that 20 miles from London no body understands hints, initial letters, or town facts and passages; and in a few years not even those who live in

London. . . . I insist, you must have your Asterisks fill'd up with some real names of real Dunces.

As with the case of the Royal Society, the further that one moved away spatially and temporally from the locus of control – London – the more that the power of one's credit system and hence that of one's texts dissipated. In the world of Scriblerus, to be named was to be a Dunce. From the safety of their lair, anonymous authors might poke abuse at those who misused power and who deployed illegal techniques to gain credit for themselves and their work. They could do this by denying their opponent's identity or by subverting or inverting it. Those who "edited" the works of Great Men and who thereby tried to arrogate an excessive name and reputation for themselves were fair game for their wit, and the editing strategies of Richard Bentley provided ample ammunition for their attacks. Bentley attempted to apply classical editing techniques to the interpretation of texts which, in terms of textual authority, implied an almost equal amount of editorial and authorial credit. In this new social role, the editor as author purported to bring the authentic "author" to the public, and to gain credit on that basis. The Scriblerians objected to Bentley's manner, technique, and social class. Above all, they objected to what and therefore who Bentley was.[36]

Identities

Unlike the experience of editing newspapers and magazines, the editing of ancient texts had a long history and possessed a deeply entrenched tradition of hermeneutic techniques and interpretive rules. It has recently been argued that medieval scholars had a much more discriminating view of the past than had previously been believed; there was no obvious break between medieval "accumulation" and Renaissance criticism, and distinguishing "true" from "false" texts was an integral part of the earlier culture.[37] Editors from the fifteenth century onward who published editions of Greek and Latin authors were thus relying on an established genre of criticism in which manuscripts and texts were compared with each other according to a sophisticated set of rules. These rules were based on the practices of the lawcourts and were thus quasi-judicial; a text could provide "testimony" about the status of another text, and, if this was the case, then it was said to be a "witness" to the other text. This process relied to a large extent on the accumulative authority of "older" texts. Without the benefit of radio-carbon dating, critics would inspect the "internal testimony" of a work to judge how much evidence it gave about another text. If, for example, a manuscript did not comment on a particular passage in another text the interpreter felt justified in assuming that the other text was later, especially if there were independent grounds for believing that it *should* have been mentioned.[38]

Since the basis of this system was derived from the language and practice of the lawcourts, so-called authors of various texts – whether these authors were ancient or modern – were routinely "tried" by these critics for their veracity and (moral) probity. By the beginning of the seventeenth century, any respectable "edition" of a canonical text was expected to contain an elaborate scaffolding of these authorities, and this could be presented to the reader in various ways depending upon the "confidence" that each editor had in a specific "reading." Some texts, such as the *Hermetica*, were accepted as genuine only to be later gradually removed from the canon. In this culture, apparently unassailable proofs of forgery could always be circumvented in principle. For example, Isaac Casaubon and others argued that the *Hermetica* were post-Christian forgeries, yet this did not prevent later authors such as Ralph Cudworth from circularly suggesting that, despite the fact that they were forgeries, they were composed by authors who had a very keen notion of the real Hermetic truths.[39]

Textual criticism of Scripture was particularly sensitive, and different denominations had their own authoritative versions of the Bible.[40] Nevertheless, the basic principle of this kind of investigation was the same as that of establishing a faithful reading of a non-scriptural text; authority rested in the oldest and best-documented manuscripts.[41] Modern authorities were mixed on the page with ancient authorities, and editors balanced the relative testimonies of these authorities and the "sense" of the text against that of the age of the manuscript. By the end of the seventeenth century there was an international effort to excavate the readings of these ancient manuscripts, but in biblical criticism such programs were recognized as intensely dangerous. It was hard to accept that an opponent had disinterestedly judged the relative testimony of the manuscripts if in fact they contained unpalatable readings. On top of this, the textual researches of Richard Simon and the genome-like project of John Mill at Oxford to identify *all* the known variant readings of the New Testament posed a real threat to traditional (and particularly Protestant) accounts of scriptural testimony. It was at this point that the young classical scholar Richard Bentley entered the fray.[42]

Bentley has been passed down to posterity with a dual identity. In the annals of classical scholarship, he stands out as England's finest textual scholar, the tyro who burst upon the world in his *Epistola ad Millium* of 1691 with the "completely unknown fact that *synapheia* prevails in Greek anapaestic systems right through to the catalexis." In literary history, he stands out as the ridiculous "critic" lampooned in the *Tale of a Tub* and the *Dunciad* and the author of the absurd edition of *Paradise Lost* (1732) in which a talentless editor was invoked by Bentley to account for the supposed faults in Milton's text.[43] A number of scholars are now reexamining Bentley's intellectual milieu. Although he edited a number of classical texts in the eighteenth century, he was already well known in the mid-1690s thanks to his *Letter to Mill* of 1691 and his Boyle Lectures of 1692. By the late 1690s he was a major figure in one of the most significant intellectual circles of the day, a group which included Evelyn, Pepys, Newton, and Locke. However, it was not this which made his name and gained him his repute, but rather his attack on Sir William Temple, and his performance in the debate over the relative merits of the ancients and moderns.[44]

The project upon which Bentley and other such editors were engaged was the descendant of the strand of the humanist historical enterprise in which a text was subjected to a judicial extraction of truth, and the interpretive techniques associated with editing were based on the practices developed by medieval lawyers and on the topology of the courtroom. Bentley was steeped in this practice, and used its technical apparatus to investigate any text on which he could lay his hands. In the wake of William Wotton's (1694) attack on Temple's revised *Essay on Ancient and Modern Learning*, a group at Christ Church College, Oxford decided to defend Temple and his view of the merit of Aesop's *Fables* and the *Epistles of Phalaris*. Led by the Honourable

Charles Boyle, these men sought out the Phalaris manuscript in the king's library, of which Bentley was at this time the chief librarian. A comedy of errors ensued, the result of which was that Bentley was attacked in Boyle's *Epistles of Phalaris* of 1695 for not allowing Boyle ("out of his singular humanity") sufficient time to peruse the manuscript. Bentley responded in 1697 with his *Dissertation on the Epistles of Phalaris*. It was a simple matter for Bentley to show that the epistles were not mentioned by any writer before the tenth century and that their language contained phrases taken from authors who clearly postdated Christ. He explicitly set out to "try" Phalaris, and inconsistencies and infelicities in the text were treated as "confession."[45]

The mainly Tory "wits" (the work was mostly composed by Francis Atterbury) responded the following year, as did Swift, although his *A Tale of a Tub* did not appear until 1704. These authors lampooned Bentley's techniques by suggesting that the work could not have been composed by Bentley; "critics" were described as "a sort of Inferiour and Subaltern Officers [who] go for Scholars among all the Little Men," while Bentley was criticized for having had the temerity both to correct Sir William Temple and to speak rudely to the Honourable Charles Boyle. As Boyle put it, "anybody would easily guesse that [Bentley] is not a Man of Business . . . but a mere Library-Keeper." He was a "Tailor-Critic" and "full of himself," a nobody who was even "ungrateful to his sources," which, in any case, he had plagiarized. He was heavily browbeaten for inventing "a new language, neither that of the Learned, nor that of his Country," and readers were warned that Bentley's "new words" would be "hissed off the stage." Temple supported the production and criticized Bentley's "foulmouthed raillery," adding that he had "no mind to enter the lists with such a Mean, *Dull*, Unmannerly Pedant."[46] In the *Battle of the Books*, Swift attacked Bentley's conduct as being that of one who was "deformed [and] inhumane . . . Courts have taught thee ill Manners, and polite Conversation has finished thee a Pedant." The charges of pedantry and lack of "wit" stuck to Bentley, and his overwhelming response of 1699 only drew more fire from writers like William King and Francis Atterbury, who concluded ironically that "Emendators and various readings are much more intoxicating than good sense and fine writing; Manners, Propriety and Wit raise you but one step above common Mortals, but Words, Phrases and Derivations give you a seat among the Stars!"[47]

The attacks on Bentley's approach by the "wits" therefore constituted a social comment on his unbecoming conduct as a hermeneut. Nevertheless, his trademark was a device which was commonly employed by other scholars, namely the so-called "conjectural emendation," a means by which a "dubious" reading in a text would be replaced by one which "made more sense." Bentley placed a high authority on his ability to discern the "sense" of a text, and in the "Preface" to his *Horace*, conjecture was treated as being as important a source of criticism as the testimony of ancient manuscripts. In fact, he virtually dispensed with the notion of the "received text," and his *Horace* contained nearly 800 new "readings." For example, in the story of the fox caught in the granary, Bentley ignored the significance in the tale of the fox's proverbial cunning and emphasized instead that a fox would not eat grain. He therefore put forward the emendation of "*nitedula*" (field-mouse) for "*vulpecula*" (fox). Unsurprisingly, these methods met with fierce criticism, and in LeClerc's *Judgement and Censure of Dr. Bentley's Horace*, this "overconfident" treatment of the text was reproached as "boundlessly rash." Critics tended to assume that the authors they studied always "wrote up to the utmost vigour of Property and Elegance," but according to LeClerc, editing was not supported by "mathematical evidence." The same criticism was made in the *Dunciad*; not only did "critics" assume "that an Author could never fail to use the *best word* on every occasion"; they also believed that they could "not chuse but know *which that is*."[48]

Bentley became famous for his almost pathological propensity to "emend." When he sought to act as editor to the second edition of Newton's *Principia*, Newton grew hostile when Bentley began to "emend" his *magnum opus* and the bulk of the work was quickly passed on to someone else. In a marked departure from his previous technique, Bentley was careful to reverse his usual treatment of the respective authority of "common-sense" emendation and manuscript testimony when he set out to produce an authentic version of the Greek New Testament. But the question remained as to *which* manuscripts to privilege as authoritative; contrary to the impression given by the work of privilege as not every Greek manuscript was relevant and "there will scarce be two Hundred out of so many Thousands [Various Readings] that can deserve the least consideration." At the last moment, he capitulated before his habit and claimed: "If the Author has any thing to suggest towards a Change of the Text, not supported by any Copies now extant; he will offer it separate in his Prolegomena."[49]

Alongside examples of emendatory skill, expositors like Bentley wove stories about how such corruptions occurred. Inattentive or corrupt scribes took most of the blame, although an earlier editor might also be guilty. In 1732 Bentley stunned his opponents into stupefaction with a long critique of how Milton's "editor" had ruined *Paradise Lost*. Admirers like Lewis Theobald noted that Bentley was only doing the sort of analysis that was common in classical scholarship, suggesting that it had not been Bentley's intention that every conjecture should be a restoration of the text, but it was "to shew the world, that if Milton did not write as He would have him, he ought to have wrote so," and that it was clearly more his intention to "pare off the Excrescencies . . . than to restore corrupted passages." However, he also told Warburton that he was "sorry that he has now dabbl'd in a Province, where even the Ladies are prepared to laugh at, and confute him."[50] *Milton's Paradise Lost* was lambasted for ill-manners to Milton, although in fact Bentley blamed an "editor" for unintentionally or even deliberately perverting the text after the blind author had dictated his thoughts: "This suppos'd Fiend (call'd in these notes the Editor) knowing Milton's bad Circumstances . . . thought he had a fit Opportunity to foist into the Book several of his own Verse. . . . This trick has been too frequently plaid; but especially in works published after an Author's Death." In his assessment of the "editor's" work, Bentley felt that he could sense the very process of composition. In one superb note to the line "He cover'd, but his robe / "Uncover'd more" in Book Nine (a section in which Bentley himself had so far intervened uncharacteristically little), he suddenly noted that "The Editor, of whom we have heard nothing for more than twenty Pages, grew quite impatient of staying longer; and seems to have thrown this line in at mere Random . . . what could the man design by it? Adam had no robe yet, and without one how could he *cover*? Nonsense outragious!"[51]

As the Christ Church wits and LeClerc had noted, it was this tendency of the editor to insinuate himself into the text that was so obviously "impolite." This was why discussion of Bentley's work always referred to his dubious moral authority and "confident" reputation; Bentley put so much of himself into the text that the text was all "Bentley," and his commentaries had nothing to do with the author who had ostensibly been the object of study. This was the hubris which Mallet reckoned to consist of "to *Milton* lending sense, to *Horace* wit / He makes 'em write what never Poet writ," and which Pope parodied in his Bentleian note to Book Four of the *Dunciad*: "Correct it therefore repugnantibus omnibus (even tho' the Author himself should oppugn) in all the impressions which have been or shall be made of his works." The "microscope of wit," the "critic Eye," would "petrify a Genius to a Dunce." Yet, in spite of the criticisms leveled at Bentley's work, the editorial process itself ran the risk of minimizing the authority and presence of the original author to the point where he became reduced to a mere author-function. In satirizing the fashionable debate over the merits of the ancients, Swift warned the reader of the *Battle of the Books* that when "Virgil" was mentioned, "we are not to understand the Person of a famous Poet, call'd by that Name, but only certain sheets of Paper, bound up in Leather, containing in Print, the Works of the said Poet."[52]

Some of the very people who ridiculed the techniques of editors like Bentley were sucked into the business of editing the works of "modern" authors, and entrepreneurs sought to give these the aura and authority of distant ancients through the very act of producing complete editions of their works. Booksellers like Jacob Tonson Sr. recognized that there was a great untapped (and unformed) demand for the "authentic" collections of more modern poets and authors, and he pioneered the publication of the works of Milton and Dryden in the 1680s and 1690s. In addition to this, the Tonsons published every major edition of Shakespeare from Rowe in 1709 to Johnson in 1765. They made these collections widely available and gained a formidable reputation and status in the process. In 1696 Tonson was told that the time would come when "'twill be as impossible to think of Virgil without Mr. Dryden as of either without Mr. Tonson," although in February of that year Dryden had told him that he found "all of your Trade are sharpers, and you more than others." Pope remarked in 1709 that Tonson "[created] Poets, as Kings sometimes do Knights, not for honour, but for money," and when Tonson set up a rival version to Pope's *Homer* of 1714, he called him "a great Turk in poesy, who can bear no brother to the throne."[53] By this time Tonson wielded immense power, and had been the prime instigator in the creation and wording of the Copyright Act of 1710.[54]

Complete editions served to distance the author from the Augustan consumer in such a way that the author's abilities became transcendent, and the author – no longer a mere mortal – was thus endowed with a timeless aura and reputation. How could this be reconciled with the more conversational relationship which the critics of editors like Bentley proposed as the model relationship between editor and author? Pope, who despised the judicial textual process which put the author on trial, proposed a more gentlemanly ethos for the role of editor. This was a much more *polite* encounter with the author, and in the advertisements for his own editions he claimed that he would offer authoritative texts *without* indulging in the techniques connected to the relentless pursuit for authenticity which customary "editing" demanded. Nevertheless, the whole business of editing depressed him and he complained of his fall "first from a pretending Poet to a Critick, then to a low Translator, lastly to a meer Publisher." He told a number of correspondents in the early 1720s that he would not be indulging in conjectural emendation in his forthcoming edition of *Shakespeare*, while throughout the 1710s and 1720s he produced a number of major editions of moderns and ancients, all of which involved a great deal of work either seeking subscriptions in taverns or, as in the case of *Shakespeare*, staying up late "wrapt up in dull Critical Learning [with] the Headake every Evening" with fellow compositors at Twickenham. When the last volume of his *Shakespeare* appeared in 1725, it was prefaced by the statement that he had "discharg'd the dull duty of an Editor to my best judgment, with more labour than I expect thanks."[55]

As Pope might have expected, it was not well received by the "Editor-Critics." Lewis Theobald was moved to compose a response the following year which earned him the wrath of Pope and the appearance of a mangled version of his name in the *Dunciad*. Aided by Warburton (who attacked Pope's edition anonymously but later defected to his cause in 1738), Theobald published his own edition of *Shakespeare* in 1733, a work in which he accused Pope of barely condescending to collate any old copies of Shakespeare's works at all. Pope had "seldom corrected the text but to its Injury; he attack'd [Shakespeare] like an unholy *Slaughterman*, and [had] not lopped off the *Errors*, but the *Poet*." Warburton himself offered a Tonson *Shakespeare* to the world in 1745, the last of the major pre-Johnsonian "Shakespeares."[56]

Invisible men

Who owned the rights to Shakespeare? Whose Shakespeare was the authentic Bard? In the commercial world of early eighteenth-century publishing these matters were now inextricably linked, and the issues were resolved by deploying rival interpretive techniques to seize control of and then remake names and identities. Up to the beginning of the seventeenth century, the contests over the authentic interpretation of ancient texts and the identity of their authorship and authority had been fought between scholar-editors. In the following decades, a new and equally competitive market-driven breed of workers deployed similar techniques to produce the definitive texts of more recent authors, and authenticity was now a commodity which could be bought and sold. In the case of Shakespeare, it was still essential to get the oldest copies of his plays, and it was still useful, as now, to offer opinions on how and why the texts had been corrupted. Pope suggested that the first published versions of Shakespeare's works were "stolen and surreptitious copies, maimed and deformed by the frauds and stealths of injurious imposters," and he even advertised in newspapers for the early folios and quartos. Successive editions of Shakespeare's works boasted of having had access to the oldest copies, and calls for old editions to be brought to the publisher were made in the newspapers whenever a new edition was set afoot. In Johnson's *Proposals for Printing . . . the Dramatick Works of William Shakespeare* of 1756, the prospective editor argued that Shakespeare had now "assumed the dignity of an ancient." Of modern attempts to use conjecture in order to provide the public with an acceptable text, he wrote: "The laborious collator at some unlucky moment frolicks in conjecture"; while some conjectures "had all the joy and all the pride of invention," such criticism had been "of great use in the learned world." Nevertheless, it was his "settled principle, that the reading of the ancient books is probably true," and that these readings were not to be changed for the sake of "elegance, perspecuity, or mere improvement of the sense." "Print" had not demolished the authority of the manuscript, and the printed texts in the three cultures which I have examined in this chapter actually *required* letters, ancient manuscripts, and their representations to vouch for their own authority and authenticity. Despite what Benjamin calls the consuming desire to bring authors " 'closer' spatially and humanly," editors and publishers had to insert a delicate textual balance – of proximity and distance, and of authenticity and reproduction – into the homes of the public.[57]

Where editors of *Homer* or *Shakespeare* had brought all ancient authorities into the contemporary dock for trial, Johnson reminded his readers that this very process – the judicial display of the power of the canonical edition – allowed the editor to control the relative "distance" of the original author from the eighteenth-century reader. What was needed was balance between the author as man and as a source of authority for the text at hand. The power of the space encompassed by the textual apparatus was its ability to bring all authorities into the same place so that they could be "tried" against each other and allow the final interpretation to take place. On the other hand, editors were also supposed to adopt a less adversarial and more respectful approach to their authors. If carried out properly, the editing process occasionally produced strange effects, such as that of "[leaving] Homer with fewer unintelligible passages than Chaucer," but it did not exonerate the editor from employing certain accepted conven-tions. So just as Pope and others denied that Bentley's *Milton* was about Milton, the same criticism could be made of Pope's *Homer* – translated "first in English, secondly in Rhyme, thirdly not from the Original, but fourthly from a French Translation, and that in Prose by a Woman too." "How the Devil," concluded the author (Bentley's nephew), "should it be Homer?"[58]

Thanks to a series of changing economic and social relations, the material and social communities of booksellers, readers, editors, and authors spewed out growing numbers of newsletters, journals, novels, and editions. In the commercial world of print culture, editors demanded some kind of recompense for their work and responsibilities, but they had to try to receive public recognition without being accused of usurping the credit due to those whose names and identities they made. The Scriblerians despised what they took to be the vulgar power of this new material world, and reckoned that no amount of learning would turn an ill-mannered hack or a drudge into an editor fit to comment on the great authors. Their satirical assaults implied that editors like Bentley and Theobald, who lacked any refinement in "taste" or "wit," were lackeys with no proprietorial rights to their works. In the same way, Newton found that the private, conversational mode which he posed as the ideal ethos for a philosophical common-wealth was completely inappropriate for the competitive public information market whose credit allocation was arranged by the editor of the *Philosophical Transactions*.

Despite Priestley's confident assertion regarding the more "familiar" relationship between the "learned and unlearned," authors in Augustan England could only with great difficulty get close enough to their invisible readers for the conversational ethos to survive. The booksellers Defoe called the "Master Manufacturers" needed and created a new breed of middlemen to pass on manuscript work and thus make it suitable for the audience whose tastes and interests they hoped to fashion. Hazlitt later remarked that many editors were "scrubs, mere drudges, newspaper-puffs: others are bullies or quacks." Others, he went on, "are nothing at all – they have the name; and receive a salary for it!" For all his exertions in the late seventeenth and eighteenth centuries, there were powerful interests which sought to deny authorial credit to the editor. Perhaps, like the author (and despite exceptions like Pope), his "dull" work still left him only a minion serving the interests of the bookseller and the reader.[59]

Notes

1   W. Benjamin, *Illuminations*, ed. and intro. H. Arendt (New York: Schocken, 1969), p. 232.

2   L'Estrange's observation is cited in R. A. Day, *Told in Letters: Epistolary Fiction before Richardson* (Ann Arbor, MI: University of Michigan Press, 1966), p. 69; see also Johnson, "Life of Dryden," in G. B. Hill (ed.) *The Lives of the English Poets*, 3 vols. (Oxford: 1905), Vol. I, p. 366; J. Priestley, *An Essay on a Course of Liberal Education for Civil and Active Life* (London: 1765), pp. 22–3. See also R. Astbury, "The renewal of the Licensing Act in 1693 and its lapse in 1695," *Library*, 5th series, 33 (1978): 296–322; C. J. Mitchell, "The spread and fluctuation of eighteenth-century printing," *Studies on Voltaire and the Eighteenth Century* 230 (1985): 305–61; A. Kernan, *Samuel Johnson and the Impact of Print*, (Princeton, NJ: Princeton University Press, 1989), pp. 74 and 89. For nineteenth-century editing, see J. H. Wiener (ed.) *Innovators and Preachers: The Role of the Editor in Victorian England* (Westport, CT: Greenwood Press, 1985) and R. Porter, W. Bynum, and S. Lock (eds.) *The History of Medical Journalism* (London: Routledge, 1992). Jeremy Black points out that there is very little information on the "selecting process" of the eighteenth century since transactions between editor, printer, and owner were "primarily verbal." See Black, *The English Press in the Eighteenth Century* (London: Croom Helm, 1987), pp. 35, 38, 42. Printers and publishers like Dodsley had some degree of editorial control and occasionally did the work now reserved for proof-readers and editors. See P. Simpson, *Proof Reading in the Sixteenth, Seventeenth and Eighteenth Centuries* (Oxford: Oxford University Press, 1970), and K. T. Winkler, "The forces of the market and the London newspaper in the first half of the eighteenth century," *Journal of Newspaper and Periodical History* 4 (1988): 22–35 (22 and 26–7).

3   Cf. Kernan, *Samuel Johnson and the Impact of Print*. See also M. Woodmansee, "The 'genius' and the copyright: economic and legal conditions of the emergence of the 'author,' " *Eighteenth-Century Studies* 17 (1984): 425–48; and M. Rose, "The author as proprietor: *Donaldson* vs. *Becket* and the genealogy of modern authorship," *Representations* 23 (1988): 51–85, who argues that the modern author is the construction of eighteenth-century London booksellers who "[created] him as a weapon in their struggle with the booksellers of the provinces"; Ibid: 56.

4   See G. Walters, "The booksellers in 1759 and 1774: the battle for literary property," *Library*, 5th series, 29: (1974): 287–304; J. Feather, "The publishers and the pirates. British copyright law in theory and practice, 1710–1775," *Publishing History* 22 (1987): 5–32; T. F. Bonnell, "Bookselling and canon-making: trade rivalry over the English poets, 1776–1783," *Studies in Eighteenth-Century Culture* 19 (1983): 53–69 (esp. 54, 57–63; and J. Chandler, "The Pope controversy: Romantic poets and the English canon," in R. Von Hallberg (ed.) *Canons* (Chicago: Chicago University Press, 1984), pp. 197–226.

5   E. Eisenstein, *The Printing Press as an Agent of Change: Communications and Cultural Transformations in Early Modern Europe*, 2 vols. (Cambridge: Cambridge University Press, 1979); Kernan, *Samuel Johnson and the Impact of Print*, pp. 74, 87, and 158–72; (esp. p. 161).

6   K. Shevelow, *Women and Print Culture: The Construction of Feminity in the Early Periodical* (London: Routledge & Kegan Paul, 1989). For related views, see R. Perry, *Women, Letters, and the Novel* (New York: AMS Press, 1980), esp. pp. 63–91, and N. Armstrong, *Desire and Domestic Fiction: A Political History of the Novel* (Oxford: Oxford University Press, 1987).

7   Shevelow, *Women and Print Culture*, pp. 10, 61, 79–80. For the genre of the criminal biography, see L. B. Faller, *Turned to Account: The Forms and Functions of Criminal Biography in Late Seventeenth- and Early Eighteenth-Century England* (Cambridge: Cambridge University Press,

1987). Daniel Miller offers a sophisticated account of this material reappropriation in *Material Culture and Mass Consumption* (Oxford: Blackwell, 1991); see also C. Campbell, *The Romantic Ethic and the Spirit of Modern Consumerism* (Oxford: Blackwell, 1987).

8   Shevelow, *Women and Print Culture*, pp. 45–6. London was a market with an excellent postal service which readily facilitated the speedy appearance of letters in print (and their return to the consumer). Ian Watt relates urbanization to increased possibilities for seclusion and privacy in *The Rise of the Novel* (London: Chatto & Windus, 1957), esp. Ch. 6. See also F. J. Fisher, "The development of London as a centre of conspicuous consumption," *Transactions of the Royal Historical Society*, 4th series, XXX (1948): 37–50; and N. McKendrick, J. Brewer, and J. H. Plumb, *The Birth of a Consumer Society: The Commercialization of Eighteenth-Century England* (London: Hutchinson, 1983). Anne Howe remarks: "London, I am persuaded, is the place of all others, to be private in," in S. Richardson, *Clarissa: or, The History of a Young Lady: Comprehending the Most Important Concerns of Private Life, and Particularly Showing the Distress that May Attend the Misconduct Both of Parents and Children, in Relation to Marriage*, ed. A. Ross (Harmondsworth, Mx: Penguin, 1985), p. 1018.

9   S. Schaffer, "Daniel Defoe and the worlds of credit," in J. Christie and S. Shuttleworth (eds.) *Nature Transfigured: Science and Literature, 1700–1900* (Manchester: Manchester University Press, 1989), pp. 13–44 (esp. pp. 16, 20, 37); D. Defoe, *An Appeal to Honour and Justice* (London: 1715), in J. T. Boulton (ed.) *Selected Writings of Daniel Defoe* (London: Cambridge University Press, 1975), p. 189; *Weekly Journal* (November 1718) quoted in M. Novak, *Realism, Myth and History in Defoe's Fiction* (Lincoln, NB: University of Nebraska Press, 1983), p. 17; Watt, *Rise of the Novel*, p. 93, quoting William Minto, *Daniel Defoe* (London: 1887), p. 169.

10 R. Mayer, "The reception of the *Journal of the Plague Year* and the nexus of fiction and history in the novel," ELH 57 (1990): 529–56 (532–4); D. Defoe, *The Fortunes and Misfortunes of the Famous Moll Flanders, &c. . . .*, ed. E. H. Kelly (London: Norton, 1973), p. 3. See also G. M. Sill, *Defoe and the Idea of Fiction* (Newark, NJ: University of Delaware Press, 1983); L. Davis, *Factual Fictions: The Origins of the English Novel* (New York: Columbia University Press, 1983), p. 157; M. McKeon, *The Origins of the English Novel, 1600–1740* (Baltimore, MD: Johns Hopkins University Press, 1988); and J. A. Downie, *Harley and the Press: Propaganda and Public Opinion in the Age of Swift and Defoe* (Cambridge: Cambridge University Press, 1979), p. 15. John Tinkler argues persuasively that "novels were a logical extension of rhetorical history [and] inventing dialogues and speeches was a standard part of the historian's craft," in "Humanist history and the English novel in the eighteenth century," *Studies in Philology* 85 (1988): 510–27 (524–5).

11 For Toland's editing prowess, see B. Worden's edition of Ludlow's *"A Voyce From the Watch Tower": Pt. 5, 1660–1662*, Camden 4th series, Vol. 21 (London: Royal Historical Society, 1978), pp. 17–60, and in particular, J. A. I. Champion, *The Pillars of Priestcraft Shaken: The Church of England and Its Enemies, 1660–1730* (Cambridge: Cambridge University Press, 1992), Ch. 7.

12 See Pat Rogers, *The Augustan Vision* (London: Weidenfeld & Nicolson, 1974), pp. 146 ff., and Watt, *Rise of the Novel*, pp. 188–90.

13 Richard Ashcraft, *Revolutionary Politics & Locke's Two Treatises of Government* (Princeton, NJ: Princeton University Press, 1986), pp. 342–3 and 383 ff.

14 G. Birkbeck Hill (ed.) *Lives of the English Poets* (Oxford: Clarendon, 1905), Vol. III, p. 207; Day, *Told in Letters*, pp. 48, 50–5, 61, 146–7 (for the first entirely epistolary novels in English); Watt, *Rise of the Novel*, pp. 196–201; N. Würzbach, *The Novel in Letters: Epistolary Fiction in the Early English Novel, 1678–1740* (London: Routledge & Kegan Paul, 1969), pp. ix, xii, xx–xxi, 25; G. Sherburn (ed.) *The Correspondence of Alexander Pope*, 5 vols. (Oxford: Clarendon Press, 1956), Vol. I, pp. xxxix–xl; and L. S. Kauffman, *Discourses of Desire: Gender, Genre, and Epistolary Fictions* (Ithaca, NY: Cornell University Press, 1986), esp. pp. 120–6. For letter-writing manuals, see R. Chartier, "Distinction et divulgation: la civilité et ses livres," in R. Chartier, *Lectures et lecteurs dans la France d'Ancien Régime* (Paris: Seuil, 1987), pp. 45–86. McKeon offers a fine account of the (conventional) self-reflexive features of Richardson's *Pamela* in his *Origins of the English Novel*, p. 358. For Pope's duel with Curll, see P. Rogers, "The case of Pope vs. Curll," *Library*, 5th series, 27 (1972): 326–31, and

J. McLaverty, "The first printing and publication of Pope's letters," *Library*, 6th series, 2 (1980): 264–80.

15 T. C. Duncan Eaves and B. D. Kimpel, *Samuel Richardson: A Biography* (Oxford: Oxford University Press, 1971), Ch. 10, and p. 145 for Richardson's efforts to protect these letters as his own property; P. Gaskell, *From Writer to Reader: Studies in Editorial Method* (Oxford: Clarendon Press, 1978), pp. 65 ff.; Day, *Told in Letters*, p. 207; A. L. Barbauld (ed.) *Correspondence of Samuel Richardson. Selected from the Original Manuscripts*, 6 vols. (London: 1804), Vol. IV, p. 32. *Pamela* was based on a true story Richardson had heard a number of years earlier which he had incorporated into his *Familiar Letters*; see Richardson to Aaron Hill, January 1741, in J. Carroll (ed.) *Selected Letters of Samuel Richardson* (Oxford: Clarendon Press, 1964), pp. 39–41.

16 For a good discussion of this, see Kauffman, *Discourses of Desire*, pp. 120–8. In S. Richardson, *Pamela, Or Virtue Rewarded*, ed. Duncan Eaves and Ben D. Kimpel (Boston, MA: Houghton Mifflin, 1971), the "editor" makes brief interventions at pp. 89–94 and 408–12.

17 The remark from Cheyne to Richardson and Shenstone's comment on *Clarissa* are quoted in Watt, *Rise of the Novel*, pp. 201 and 57; cf. also W. S. Lewis (ed.) *Correspondence of Horace Walpole*, 48 vols. (New Haven, CT: Yale University Press, 1937–83), Vol. XXXV, p. 244. *Pamela's* textual dressing is related in Richardson, *Pamela*, ed. Eaves and Kimpel, p. 120; Diderot's remark is quoted in Day, "Speech acts, orality, and the epistolary novel," *The Eighteenth Century* 21 (1980): 187–97 (188), from his "éloge de Richardson" of 1761, in *Oeuvres Aesthetiques*, ed. P. Vernière (Paris: Garnier, 1968), p. 34. The responses to *Pamela* are examined in B. Kriessman, *Pamela–Shamela: A Study of the Criticisms, Burlesques, Parodies and Adaptations of Richardson's "Pamela"* (Lincoln, NB: University of Nebraska Press, 1960). For a good account of the close economic ties between the proprietors of coffee-houses ("Coffee-men") and the owners of newspapers, see M. Harris, *London Newspapers in the Age of Walpole: A Study of the Origins of the Modern English Press* (Cranbury, NJ: Associated University Press, 1987), esp. pp. 30–1.

18 H. Anderson, P. B. Daghlian, and I. Ehrenpreis (eds.) *The Familiar Letter in the Eighteenth Century* (Lawrence, KS: University of Kansas Press, 1966), pp. 74–5; Kauffman, *Discourses of Desire*, p. 128; Watt, *Rise of the Novel*, p. 198. For discussions of related questions of space and privacy, see S. Varey, *Space and the Eighteenth Century Novel* (Cambridge: Cambridge University Press, 1990), esp. pp. 141–7 and 184–8; W. Ray, *Story and History: Narrative Authority and Social Identity in the Eighteenth-Century French and English Novel* (Oxford: Blackwell, 1990), pp. 133–57; T. Castle, *"Clarissa"'s Ciphers* (Ithaca, NY: Cornell University Press, 1982); R. Folkenflik, "A room of Pamela's own," *ELH* 39 (1972): 585–96, and C. M. Gillis, *The Paradox of Privacy: Epistolary Form in "Clarissa"*, (Gainesville, FL: Florida University Press, 1984).

19 A. R. Hall and M. B. Hall (eds.) *The Correspondence of Henry Oldenburg*, 15 vols. (Vols. I–IX, Madison and Milwaukee, WI: University of Wisconsin Press; Vols. X–XI, London: Mansell; Vols. XII–XV, London and Philadelphia, PA: Taylor & Francis: 1965–86; hereafter *OC*), Vol. X, p. 570.

20 Waller to Sloane, BL Sloane Ms. 4036 fol. 30.

21 S. Shapin and S. Schaffer, *Leviathan and the Air-Pump: Hobbes, Boyle, and the Experimental Life* (Princeton, NJ: Princeton University Press, 1986), pp. 55–79.

22 Oldenburg to Boyle, November 17, 1664, in T. Birch (ed.) *The Works of the Honourable Robert Boyle*, 6 vols. (London: 1772), Vol. VI, p. 176.

23 Oldenburg to Boyle, November 3, 1664, *OC*, Vol. II, p. 283; Boyle to Oldenburg, August 6, 1665, *OC*, Vol. II, pp. 453–4; Vol. IV, pp. 98–9. See also Adrian Johns, " 'Wisdom in the concourse': natural philosophy and the history of the book in early modern England" (PhD thesis, University of Cambridge, 1992), esp. Ch. 4.

24 For intellectual property disputes in the early Royal Society, see R. Iliffe, " 'In the warehouse': privacy, property and priority in the early Royal Society," *History of Science* 30 (1992): 29–68.

25 See Shapin and Schaffer, *Leviathan and the Air-Pump*, pp. 70–2, and in particular S. Shapin, "The invisible technician," *American Scientist* 77 (1989): 554–63. Mayer, "Reception," shows

that the status of Defoe's *Plague Year* as fact or fiction was dramatically affected (but by no means settled) by the fixing of Defoe's authorship of the text in the 1770s; cf. Ibid., pp. 534–5.

26 Barrow to Collins, August 20, 1669 and Newton to Collins, February 18, 1669/70, in *The Correspondence of Isaac Newton*, 7 vols, ed. H. W. Turnbull, L. Tilling, A. Prag, and A. Hall (Cambridge: Cambridge University Press, 1959–81; hereafter *NC*), Vol. I, pp. 14–15 and 27.

27 Newton to Collins, July 11, 1670; Collins to Newton, July 13, 1670; Oldenburg to Newton, January 2, 1671/2; Newton to Oldenburg, January 6, January 18, and February 6, 1671/2; *NC*, Vol. I, pp. 31, 33, 73, 79, 82, 92–102. For another account of the rhetorical strategies involved in composing letters, see J. R. Henderson, "Erasmus on the art of letter-writing," in J. J. Murphy (ed.) *Renaissance Eloquence: Studies in the Theory and Practice of Renaissance Rhetoric* (Berkeley and Los Angeles, CA: University of California Press, 1983), pp. 331–55.

28 For example, see Oldenburg's translation for Hooke of a letter from Auzout on the effectiveness of different sorts of eyepieces in August 1665. In the margins of this he made such comments as "You must rally with him again," "A handsom sting again will be necessary," and "Here you may toss railleries with him"; *OC*, Vol. II, p. 474.

29 Oldenburg to Newton, May 2, 1672, *NC*, Vol. I, p. 151.

30 See *NC*, Vol. I, pp. 105–6 notes 19, 20, 22, 24, 33, 36, 37, 39, for changes by Newton and Oldenburg. Newton was apparently unaware that the most significant change had been made; cf. Ibid., n. 19.

31 Newton to Oldenburg, May 4, and May 21, 1672; Newton to Collins, May 25, 1672; Newton to Oldenburg, June 11, 1672; Hooke to ?, c. June 20, 1672: *NC*, Vol. I, pp. 154–5, 159–60, 161, 171, 193.

32 Newton to Oldenburg, September 21, 1672, *NC*, Vol. I, p. 237.

33 Newton to Oldenburg, November 13, 1675; *NC*, Vol. I, pp. 358–9.

34 Newton to Oldenburg, December 7, December 14, and December 21, 1675; Oldenburg to Newton, December 30, 1675 (now lost); Newton to Oldenburg, January 10, 1675/6; Oldenburg to Newton, January 15, 1675/6 (now lost); Hooke to Newton, January 20, 1675/6 and Newton to Hooke, February 5, 1675/6: *NC*, Vol. I, pp. 363, 392–3, 405–6, 406 n. 1, 408–9, 411, 411 n. 1, 416–17.

35 M. Mack, *Alexander Pope: A Life* (New Haven, CT: Yale University Press, 1986), p. 110; Gray to Walpole, February 11, 1751, in Kernan, *Samuel Johnson and the Impact of Print*, pp. 64–5; Swift, "On poetry: a rhapsody," pp. 129–30 and 135–8; Pope to Steele, November 29, 1712, in R. Blanchard (ed.) *The Correspondence of Richard Steele* (Oxford: Oxford University Press, 1941), p. 65; Pope to Wycherley, May 20, 1709 and Pope to Arbuthnot, see Sherburn (ed.) *Pope Correspondence*, Vol. I, pp. 60–1 and Vol. III, pp. 417 and 423. For an account of the different attitudes adopted in reading named or anonymous texts, see Johnson, *Rambler* 23.

36 Sherburn (ed.) *Pope Correspondence*, Vol. II, pp. 504–5; Pope, *Epistle to Dr. Arbuthnot*, 1. 164.

37 A. Grafton, "Higher criticism ancient and modern: the lamentable deaths of Hermes and the sibyls," *Warburg Institute, Surveys and Texts*, XVI, *The Uses of Greek and Latin: Historical Essays* (London: Warburg Institute, 1988), pp. 155–70; J. F. D'Amico, *Theory and Practice in Renaissance Textual Criticism: Beatus Rhenanus between Conjecture and History* (Berkeley, CA: University of California Press, 1988), and especially G. Constable, "Forgery and plagiarism in the Middle Ages," *Archiv für Diplomatik* 29 (1983): 1–41. For other general histories of classical scholarship, see U. von Wilamowitz–Moellendorff, *History of Classical Scholarship*, trans. A. Harris, ed. with intro. and notes by H. Lloyd–Jones (London: Duckworth, 1982); L. D. Reynolds and N. G. Wilson, *Scribes and Scholars: A Guide to the Transmission of Greek and Latin Literature* (Oxford: Clarendon Press, 1991), esp. pp. 164–241; E. J. Kenney, *The Classical Text: Aspects of Editing in the Age of the Printed Book* (Berkeley, CA: University of California Press, 1974) and C. O. Brink, *English Classical Scholarship: Historical Reflections on Bentley, Porson and Housman* (Oxford: Oxford University Press, 1985).

38 See, for example, W. Schwarz, *Principles and Problems of Biblical Translation: Some Reformation Controversies and their Background* (Cambridge: Cambridge University Press, 1955); G. Reedy, *The Bible and Reason: Anglicans and Scripture in Seventeenth-Century England* (Philadelphia, PA:

University of Pennsylvania Press, 1985); M. O'R. Boyle, *Rhetoric and Reform: Erasmus' Civil Dispute with Luther* (Cambridge, MA: Harvard University Press, 1983); A. J. Minnis, *Mediaeval Theory of Authorship: Scholastic Literary Attitudes in the Later Middle Ages* (Aldershot, Hants: Scolar Press, 1988) and J. F. Tinkler, "The splitting of humanism: Bentley, Swift, and the *Battle of the Books*," *Journal of the History of Ideas* 49 (1988): 453–72.

39 See A. Grafton, "Protestant vs. prophet: Isaac Casaubon on Hermes Trismegistus," *Journal of the Warburg and Courtauld Institutes* 46 (1983): 78–93.

40 See J. O. Newman, "The world made print: Luther's 1522 New Testament in an age of mechanical reproduction," *Representations* 11 (1985): 95–133.

41 Kenney, *The Classical Text*, p. 101 n. 3, argues that the New Testament critic has problems regarding origins, authorship, and local textual states "generally foreign to the critic of classical and patristic texts," in addition to uncertainties surrounding the "complexity of [its] transmissional process" due to the large number of mss. of the Greek text. Reliance on the oldest text as the most authoritative text is now dismissed as a pernicious error in textual editing.

42 For these researches, see Reedy, *The Bible and Reason*, pp. 101–4. Intensive study in these areas was too close to Socinianism, and, indeed, anti-Trinitarians expended great effort in these areas. See H. J. McLachlan, *Socinianism in Seventeenth-Century England* (Oxford University Press, 1951). Newton composed a remarkable essay in September and November 1690 on the "corruption" of the Trinitarian passages 1 John 5.7 and 1 Timothy 3.16. He passed this on to Locke for publication but suppressed it at the last moment. Newton was also a significant contributor to the Millian enterprise.

43 Cf. Wilamowitz–Moellendorf, *History of Classical Scholarship*, p. 79. The major account of Bentley's work is still that of James Henry Monk, *The Life of Richard Bentley D.D.*, 2 vols. (London: 1833); for modern assessments see Tinkler, "Splitting of humanism"; R. E. Bourdette, "To Milton lending sense: Richard Bentley and *Paradise Lost*," *Milton Quarterly* 14 (1980): 37–49, and J. Levine, "Bentley's Milton: philology and criticism in eighteenth-century England," *Journal of the History of Ideas* 50 (1989): 549–67.

44 Bentley's *Epistola ad Joannem Millium* was appended to *Joannes Antiocheni cognomento Malelae Historia Cronica* (Oxford: 1691).

45 See J. Levine, *The Battle of the Books. History and Literature in the Augustan Age* (London: Cornell University Press, 1991), pp. 49–52; Brink, *English Classical Scholarship*, pp. 50–7; Monk, *Life of Richard Bentley*, Vol. II, pp. 139–41, 149. The revised edition of Temple's *Essay* appeared in 1692.

46 Monk, *Life of Richard Bentley*, Vol. II, p. 109; R. Boyle, *Dr. Bentley's Dissertations on the Epistles of Phalaris and the Fables of Aesop Examin'd* (London: 1698), pp. 91–2, 99, 185; R. Boyle, *A Short Account of Dr. Bentley's Humanity* (London: 1699), p. 140. There is now a good analysis of this dispute in Levine, *Battle of the Books*, pp. 59–77, who makes the point that "for many the quarrel was reduced to an exercise in decorum"; Ibid., p. 67, and cf. pp. 108–9. See also John Arbuthnot's *Account of the State of Learning in the Empire of Lilliput. Together with The History and Character of BULLUM the Emperor's Library-Keeper* of 1728, who tells of how BULLUM (Bentley), "whenever he felt himself affronted . . . immediately slung a great Book at his Adversary, and if he could, fell'd him to the Earth" (Ibid., pp. 24–5). For the mainly Whig circle of which Bentley was a significant part, see M. Jacob, *The Newtonians and the English Revolution, 1689–1720* (Hassocks, Sx: Harvester Press, 1976).

47 Cf. Monk, *Life of Richard Bentley*, p. 123; William King, *Dialogues of the Dead Relating to the Present Controversy Concerning the Epistles of Phalaris* (London: 1699); Anon. (Atterbury), *A Short Review of the Controversy between Mr. Boyle and Dr. Bentley with Suitable Reflections upon It. And the Dr's Advantageous Character of Himself given at length. Recommended to the serious perusal of such as propose to be Considered for their Fairness, Modesty, and good Temper in Writing* (London: 1701); Levine, *Battle of the Books*, pp. 67–115 (109). For the social meaning of "pedantry" in this period, see S. Shapin, " 'A scholar and a gentleman': the problematic identity of the scientific practitioner in early modern England," *History of Science* 29 (1991): 279–327. For the different connotations of "wit" and "sense," see W. Lee Ustick and H. Hudson, "Wit, 'mixt wit,' and the bee in amber," *Harvard Library Bulletin* 8 (1935): 103–30; R. M. Krapp,

"Class analysis of a literary controversy: wit and sense in seventeenth-century English literature," *Science and Society* 10 (1946): 80–92, and E. N. Hooker, "Pope on wit: the Essay on Criticism," in *The Seventeenth Century* (Stanford, CA: 1951), pp. 225–46.

48 Reynolds and Wilson, *Scribes and Scholars*, p. 186; LeClerc, "Judgement," pp. 6–7, 12–13, 16 (cf. Kenney, *The Classical Text*, pp. 68–72); Pope, *Dunciad*, note to Book 2 in Pope, *Poetical Works*, ed. P. Rogers (Oxford: Oxford University Press, 1989), p. 495.

49 *Dr. Bentley's Proposals for Printing a New Edition of the Greek Testament, and St. Hierom's Latin Version* (London: 1721), pp. 8–9.

50 Levine, *Battle of the Books*, pp. 567–8; D. Nichol–Smith (ed.) *Eighteenth–Century Essays on Shakespeare* (Oxford: Clarendon Press, 1963), p. 75; Theobald to Warburton, October 30, 1731 and March 21, 1732 in R. F. Jones, *Lewis Theobald* pp. 278–9, 299–301.

51 *Milton's Paradise Lost*, pp. 302–3; Book Nine, l. 1058. Bentley informed the reader that he himself had "made the Notes extempore, and put them to the Press as soon as made." By Book Twelve he claimed that, like the editor, he was "now weary and fatigu'd"; Ibid., "Preface" and p. 380.

52 Cf. David Mallet's *Of Verbal Criticism: A Letter to Mr. Pope, Occasioned by Theobald's Shakespeare, and Bentley's Milton* (London: 1733), ll. 127–40 (esp. 135–6); Pope, *Dunciad*, ed. Rogers, Book 4, ll. 234, 264; J. Swift, "The bookseller to the reader," in R. A. Greenberg and W. A. Piper (eds.) *The Writings of Jonathan Swift* (New York: Norton, 1973), p. 374.

53 Kennett to Tonson, September 30, 1696, cited in K. M. Lynch, *Jacob Tonson, Kit-Kat Publisher* (Knoxville, TN: Tennessee University Press, 1971), p. 119. See also H. M. Geduld, *Prince of Publishers: A Study of the Work and Career of Jacob Tonson* (Bloomington, IN: Indiana University Press, 1969), esp. p. 73, and G. F. Papali, *Jacob Tonson, Publisher: His Life and Work (1656–1736)* (Tonson, NZ: 1968), pp. 43 and 61. For the critical reception of Shakespeare in the eighteenth century see J. Bate, *Shakespearian Constitutions: Politics, Theatre, Criticism, 1730–1830* (Oxford: Clarendon Press, 1989); P. Seary, *Lewis Theobald and the Editing of Shakespeare* (Oxford: Oxford University Press, 1990) and A. Sherbo, *The Birth of Shakespeare Studies* (place to come: publisher to come, dare?). The Tonsons bought up rights to the Shakespeare plays in 1707; cf. Geduld, pp. 134–5. Tonson had owned the copyright to *Paradise Lost* since 1690 and possessed Milton's manuscript, and his nephew was one of the publishers of Bentley's edition of 1732; Ibid., p. 118. When he read it, Tonson Sr. was sufficiently outraged to urge Pope to "lash the detractor of the divine Milton." Pope's response was the outstanding "Sober advice from Horace," perhaps his best burlesque of Bentley's style. Pope (anonymously) claimed to print the poem "Together with the ORIGINAL TEXT, as restored by the Revd R. Bentley, Doctor of Divinity." For an excellent account of this, see F. Stack, *Pope and Horace. Studies in Imitation* (Cambridge: Cambridge University Press, 1985), pp. 78–91 (esp. pp. 84–5, 90–1).

54 H. Ransom, *The First Copyright Statute: An Essay on "An Act for the Encouragement of Learning, 1710"* (Austin, TX: University of Texas Press, 1956), pp. 57 and 90; Feather, "Publishers and Pirates," pp. 5–13 and T. Belanger, "Tonson, Wellington, and the Shakespeare copyrights," in R. W. Hunt, I. G. Philip, and R. J. Roberts (eds.) *Studies in the Book Trade in Honour of Graham Pollard* (Oxford: Clarendon, 1975), pp. 195–209. The Act of 1710 recognized that there was a legal right to publish a copy which was a piece of *property*, yet immediately after this Act and again in 1731–2 when pre-1710 copyrights were due to expire, shares in the copy of the works of "modern" authors like Milton and Shakespeare were traded for rising prices, as if, in effect, the Act had made little or no difference. For the resolution of the issue over the relative rights to copy of authors and booksellers, see Rose, "The author as proprietor" and Feather "Publishers and Pirates," esp. pp. 17–25.

55 Sherburn (ed.) *Pope Correspondence* Vol. II, pp. 141–2. Cf. P. Rogers, "Pope and his subscribers," *Publishing History* 3 (1978): 7–36 (esp. 8–19); J. R. Sutherland, "The dull duty of an editor," *Review of English Studies* 21 (1945): 202–15; J. Levine, "The battle of the books and the shield of Achilles," *Eighteenth–Century Life* 9 (1984–5): 33–61 (esp. 44–7) and Levine, *Battle of the Books*, esp. pp. 552–6.

56   See T. R. Lounsbury, *The First Editors of Shakespeare, (Pope and Theobald)* (London: 1906); Levine, *Battle of the Books*, pp. 226–32. In 1730, the Tonsons were concerned about the imminent termination of their "copy" on Shakespeare, which was twenty-one years from the 1710 Copyright Act. Theobald approached a group of anti-Tonsonian publishers who offered him a substantial amount for the work. When he heard of this, Jacob Tonson Jr. offered to double whatever the others had suggested, a move which Theobald accepted. The publication of the work caused much friction between Tonson Jr. and Pope; for a good discussion of this incident, see Geduld, *Prince of Publishers*, pp. 140–6; for Warburton's edition, cf. A. Sherbo, "Warburton and the 1745 *Shakespeare*," *Journal of English and German Philology* 51 (1952): 71–82.

57   A. Sherbo (ed.) *The Yale Edition of the Works of Samuel Johnson*, (New Haven, CT: Yale University Press, 1968–), Vol. VII, pp. 101 and 106; Levine, *Battle of the Books*, p. 227; Benjamin, *Illuminations*, pp. 221, 223, 243 n. 5, 244 n. 6.

58   Ibid., p. 110; T. Bentley, *A Letter to Mr. Pope Occasioned by Sober Advice from Horace* (London: 1735), p. 14. Conyers Middleton praised Warburton for displaying "the Orthodoxy of Mr. Pope's Principles," in the latter's 1751 edition of Pope's works, but added: "like the old commentators on his *Homer*, [you] will be thought perhaps in some places, to have provided a meaning for him, that he himself never dreamt of. However, if you did not find him a Philosopher, you will perhaps make him one . . ."; cited in E. F. Knapp, "Community property: the case for Warburton's 1751 edition of Pope," *Studies in English Literature* 26 (1986): 455–68 (458).

59   Hazlitt, "On editors," in P. P. Howe (ed.), *Complete Works of Hazlitt* (London: 1913), p. 461.

11
Shot from canons; or, Maria Edgeworth and the cultural production and consumption of the late eighteenth-century woman writer

Mitzi Myers

There is a security and sense of reality in studying from life which the most inventive imagination can never attain.

(Maria Edgeworth, August 7, 1813, quoted in R. Grey 1909: 253)

Maria was remembered by her companions [at school] for her entertaining stories . . . among those of her originals she recollected only one which was specially applauded: of an adventurer who had a mask made of the dried skin taken from a dead man's face, which he put on when he wished to be disguised, and kept buried at the foot of a tree.

(Edgeworth 1867: I, 10)

Samuel Rogers's "most solid remark was on literary women: 'How strange it is that while we men are modestly content to amuse by our writings, women must be didactic. . . . Miss Edgeworth is a schoolmistress in her tales.' "

(January 6, 1834, quoted in Robinson 1938: I, 436)

Had Maria Edgeworth (1768–1849) never existed, perhaps Jane Austen scholarship might have invented her. After all, she makes such a convenient didactic foil for the supremely artistic and impeccably canonical Austen, just as the ugly stepsisters set off Cinderella's perfections.[1] Then again, maybe not. Jocelyn Harris's recent study of Austen's sources and reading thoughtfully analyzes such male notables as Locke, Richardson, Shakespeare, and Chaucer at length, yet discusses no late-eighteenth-century female novelists whatever – though Austen's own letters and novels pay frequent tribute to the writing women of her day. The "only a novel" section of *Northanger Abbey* (1818) is the most explicit, but, as another survey of Austen's books observes, the novels are filled with oblique retellings of women's fictions now obscure but undoubtedly influential for Austen's work (Doody 1986: 347–63). Simultaneously serious and ironic, Austen's defense of the novel as a genre in *Northanger Abbey*'s chapter

5 cites Frances Burney's *Cecilia* and *Camilla* and Edgeworth's *Belinda* to exemplify those maligned "performances which have only genius, wit, and taste to recommend them . . . in which the greatest powers of the mind are displayed, in which the most thorough knowledge of human nature, the happiest delineation of its varieties, the liveliest effusions of wit and humour are conveyed to the world in the best chosen language" (1959b: 37–8).[2] Not long ago, Burney would have been a likely candidate for the other ugly stepsister, but several revisionist studies have lately released her from the "courtesy novel" corset that so long pinched her fiction and her readers' perceptions of it.[3]

Edgeworth, surely the most important and most successful British woman novelist of the early nineteenth century, has had no such luck (I add "British" because of Madame de Staël).[4] She was a bestseller after Burney faded, she was a household name long before her contemporary Austen was widely read (much less elevated to the pantheon of ironists erected by ahistorical New Criticism), and she was paid generous tribute by Sir Walter Scott, whose staggering popularity and recuperation of the novel's respectability were in large part enabled by Edgeworth's pioneering.[5] Scott's acknowledgment is usually read as referring merely to Edgeworth's naturalistic Irish dialect and empathic avoidance of stereotyped characters, but in fact he recognizes the politics implicit in her familiarizing an English audience with Irish ways: her contribution towards a reformed British cultural identity.[6] In a series of articles in the *Edinburgh Review*, the often acerbic Francis Jeffrey similarly takes her work seriously, according it the highest praise for its literary innovations and its culturally reconstructive aims. His assessment of her second series of *Tales of Fashionable Life* (1812) is typical:

> The writings of Miss Edgeworth exhibit so singular an union of sober sense and inexhaustible invention . . . so just an estimate both of the real sources of enjoyment, and of the illusions by which they are so often obstructed, that it cannot be thought wonderful that we should separate her from the ordinary manufacturers of novels, and speak of her Tales as works of more serious importance than much of the true history and solemn philosophy that comes daily under our inspection. . . . she has combined more solid instruction with more universal entertainment, and given more practical lessons of wisdom, with less tediousness and less pretension, than any other writer with whom we are acquainted. . . . With the consciousness of such rare qualifications, we do think it required no ordinary degree of fortitude to withstand the temptation of being the flattering delineator of fashionable manners, instead of their enlightened corrector; and to prefer the chance of amending the age in which she lived, to the certainty of enjoying its applause.
>
> (Jeffrey 1812: 100–1, 103)

It is indicative of twentieth-century attitudes towards the "didactic" that a 1979 critic should assume Jeffrey's reiterated praise of Edgeworth's reforming morality must be "ironical" (Voss–Clesly 1979: I, 85 n.). It is not. The issue for the *Edinburgh*, as for Edgeworth and many other writers, was what shape the embourgeoisement of English society should take: fashionable emulation or civic morality, profligacy and dissipation versus culture, virtue, and industry. "Fashion" is an extraordinarily charged word in this period, resonant with political and modernist anxieties; it is a trope for a way of living, not just clothes.[7] In his chapter on "Classical economics and the middle classes," the *Edinburgh*'s analyst John Clive details the journal's ethos: "the world of fashion was . . . that world from which corruption could spread through the whole body of the people" (1957: 144). Gender, of course, traverses Jeffrey's cultural concerns, as his enthusiastic embrace of the manly Waverley novels indicates. But the gendered thinking that shapes this period's literary production and consumption does not bifurcate as tidily as some recent reception studies would have it.[8]

Although Edgeworth's first productions were too early for the great nineteenth-century journals, the *Edinburgh* and the *Quarterly Review* (its political opposite number) notice all her later work extensively and often more perceptively than subsequent literary historians. Since both periodicals, like nineteenth-century culture at large, define "literature" much more broadly than has been customary in twentieth-century academia, their coverage of Edgeworth is especially significant, for fiction was rather seldom reviewed.[9] Marking Edgeworth's transatlantic reputation and her significance for the stature of the woman writer, the American Joseph Story proclaims in his Phi Beta Kappa Address of 1826, "A new path is thus open for female exertion. . . . Man no longer aspires to an exclusive dominion in authorship. . . . Who : . . does not contemplate with enthusiasm . . . the fine character painting, the practical instructions of Miss Edgeworth, the great KNOWN, standing . . . by the side of the great UNKNOWN [Scott]?" (1826: 17). In fact, Edgeworth exerted enormous influence on adult American fiction as well as on children's books, though the tradition of women writers she shaped was marginalized as the academic American literary canon took shape. Widely respected by her peers and successors, Edgeworth was also widely read; letters and memoirs regularly remark on her work. Nineteenth-century tributes could be multiplied for pages; Edgeworth was taken not just as an agreeable writer, but as a social thinker of considerable profundity.

Unlike Mary Wollstonecraft, whose stormy private life (exposed by her grieving widower William Godwin in 1798) undercut her rational theorizing and rendered her a publicly suspect feminist model for generations, Edgeworth managed to be culturally reformist and pro-woman and also personally irreproachable. She took woman's rationality as indisputable and specialized in portraits of female ascendancy, discussed political and economic matters at length (even representing conversations between men alone), and escaped with only occasional bruises for her secularism and her refusal to pander to sensibility and sensationalism. Yet however much critics at the turn of the century enjoyed carping at the novel as a gendered genre, stereotypically sentimental like the sex which monopolized it, they were nevertheless sometimes a bit taken aback when they actually encountered the rational woman writer they had long professed to desire. After a perceptive and highly flattering analysis of Edgeworthian realism, for example, the *Quarterly*'s reviewers admit, "To our shame . . . we always think her most agreeable when she deviates a little from her rigid realities, and concedes to the corrupted taste of her readers some petty sprinkling of romantic feeling and extraordinary incident" (Stephen and Gifford 1809: 147).[10] Edgeworth's want of sentimentalism and religious rhetoric became more of a reputational liability as Romantic and Evangelical ideologies took root and as nineteenth-century emotional grammar reinflected the feminine as the feeling. As "Christopher North" expresses emergent attitudes in *Blackwood's* "Noctes Ambrosianae" series, "there is always a fund of romance at the bottom of every true woman's heart. Who has tried to stifle and suppress that element more carefully and pertinaciously – and yet who has drawn, in spite of herself, more genuine tears than the authoress of Simple Susan?" And his conversant "Tickler" heartily concurs, "Aye, who indeed! But *she's* up to any thing" ("North" [J. G. Lockhart] 1831: 533). (Like Sir Walter Scott, the interlocutors are adult admirers of one of Edgeworth's most famous children's tales, for this period's readers did not yet bracket off the juvenile from the adult, popular fiction from the high-art novel, or moral concerns from aesthetic forms.)[11]

Often ideologically and formally adventurous, Edgeworth's literary production was also astonishingly copious, diverse, and virtually coextensive with her long life. (She began writing in her early teens and published her last fiction the year before her death in her eighties.) Besides stacks of juvenile and adult tales, her output includes educational writing for every age and class from the toddler to the newly literate worker to the male professional, biography, varied essays on language and culture, and a staggering number of letters. Even after her reputation as a novelist for adults began to fade, her children's fiction stayed in print well into this century, and her reformist pedagogy attracted admiring progressives who hailed her as their forerunner. Without diminishing Jane Austen's achievement or deploring the voluminous scholarship generated since F. R. Leavis enshrined Austen as "the inaugurator of the great tradition of the English novel" and Lionel Trilling discovered that she "first represented the specifically modern personality and the culture in which it had its being," one can't help asking whatever happened to the nineteenth century's "great Maria" (Leavis 1963: 7; Trilling 1959: 228)?[12] How is it that the predecessor Scott and Austen themselves acknowledge so generously has received no canonical inscription remotely commensurate with the reputation she achieved in her own day? Whether we look at modern histories of children's literature, education, women's writing, or the novel proper, Edgeworth gets little space and grudging praise, and the account will almost certainly be marred by glaring factual errors and post-Romantic literary judgments that have pressed particularly hard on Edgeworth's rational and extraordinarily referential art. Despite the revisionism in adult Romantic studies, pre-Wordsworthian writing for children and young adults is still in thrall to fairyland and Romantic ideology; works realistic or rational, domestic or female, are patronizingly dismissed. Despite Edgeworth's obvious relevance, she finds no place in recent studies of the eighteenth-century feminist mind or of bestsellers in Jane Austen's age either (Browne 1987; Jones 1986).[13]

Much more complexly than I have room to indicate here, Edgeworth's erasure interrogates the process of canon formation, including that of the emergent feminist alternative canon. Edgeworth was not "Romantic" enough to fit the paradigm of periodization that eventually became our way of making sense of the Revolutionary decades. She was especially unfortunate in arriving so shortly before the Wizard of the North, whose eclipse of all previous fiction is partially eclipsed for us in turn. A reviewer of the collected novels remarks in 1831, for example, that "the present century has no name in its annals of more enviable distinction than that of Walter Scott; the victories of Napoleon were not so wide, nor his monuments so likely to endure," a wry reminder that canons are human constructs serving specific historical needs. Epitomizing the "fine imagination," Scott allowed his readers to fill out idealized character sketches with their own fancy and to lose themselves in the grand sweep of past events, imagining themselves patriotically loyal while daydreaming of treason, as William Hazlitt dryly remarks (Peabody 1831: 386; Hazlitt 1964: 231). In an 1834 critique of Edgeworth's art that produced a lengthy and revealing response from the author, Colonel Matthew Stewart (the philosopher Dugald Stewart's son) contrasts Scott's bold general outlines and Romantic masculinity with Edgeworth's tethering the reader to time, place, and scrupulous moral choice, a vernacular realism he feels allows insufficient escape from the problematics of everyday life. Constructing fiction as imaginative release, he also questions whether what we read really has any influence on who we are. Edgeworth concedes that she might be "too Dutch too minute," favoring "acute observation of individuals" and "diligent accumulation of particulars" in representation, but she was stung at "his believing that [fiction] has seldom or ever any effect on the conduct or character of human creatures."[14] She never lost her respect for fiction's power to configure the reader's subjectivity, and her educational investigations made her especially alert to the experiential modes and cultural practices through which the self is constituted and connected to its milieu.

If Edgeworth was not enough of the imaginatively ennobling "poet and orator" to compete with the Scott mania, she was not feminine or Christian enough to suit the later nineteenth century either, as Jane Austen could be made to be (Everett 1823: 385).[15] Nor is Edgeworth's art so readily available to the deracinating and decontextualizing moves that mapped Austen on to the heights of literary greatness in our century, a valorization of the apparently ahistorical only recently – and contradictorily – challenged by such critics as Marilyn Butler (1975), Julia Prewitt Brown (1979), Warren Roberts (1979), Margaret Kirkham (1983), Mary Evans (1987), Nancy Armstrong (1987), Claudia L. Johnson (1988), James Thompson (1988), Alison G. Sulloway (1989), and Jan Fergus (1991), as well as less specialized feminist studies like Sandra M. Gilbert and Susan Gubar's (1979), Judith Lowder Newton's (1981), and Mary Poovey's (1984), or more general Romantic inquiries like Clifford Siskin's (1988). Even now, the issue of Austen's cultural involvement is hotly charged, those who read her polemically as Tory or radical, Romantic or modern, jostling those who would leave her disengaged and serene, transcendently above the fray: 1989 and 1991 Modern Language Association sessions relevant to the topic spilled their standing-room-only audiences far into the convention halls.[16] Crammed with ideas and information, footnotes and allusions, Edgeworth's fiction was far tougher for earlier twentieth-century critics to etherealize and universalize – and not just because what canonical toehold she has is specifically local: that of her period's token Irish regionalist. Her writing assumes the reader's intelligence and appetite for knowledge and anecdote (a favorite authorial word). It insists on its location, on a real world that it relates to and seeks to change, and on its locution, on unabashedly having something to say and saying it in lively dialogue. It does not seek refuge in feminine staples like scenery or sensibility, it is not wholly engrossed by the vicissitudes of love, and it does not mind occasional plot violations of the naturalistic conventions it scrupulously adheres to in character and language if a seemingly improbable narrative line unravels constructions of reality the tale wants us to rethink.

Writing to Mrs. Dugald Stewart, John William Ward, later earl of Dudley, reviewer of *Patronage* (1814) for the *Quarterly*, illustrates the emergent distinction between the ways the two women have been read: "I have only just finished Miss Edgeworth, and am lost in wonder and delight. How the deuce she contrives to know London life so well – for I never heard of her on this side of the water. She deserves all Jeffrey has said of her." But Ward is still more taken by the feminine charms of *Mansfield Park* (1814): "I am a great admirer of the two other works by the same author. [Austen published anonymously; Edgeworth did not.] She has not so much fine humour as your friend Miss Edgeworth, but she is more skilful in contriving a story, she has a great deal more feeling, and she never plagues you with any chemistry, mechanics, or political economy, which are all excellent things in their way, but vile, cold-hearted trash in a novel, and, I piously hope, all of old Edgeworth's putting in. By the bye, I heard some time ago that the wretch was ill. Heaven grant that he may soon pop off" (1905: 170, 250). If Edgeworth's novels reach beyond the standard young lady's entrance into the world plot, if they are as interested in public matters as in courtship and marriage, it must be the father's doing. Though not the first, Ward's is an early example of the myth of paternal ventriloquism that still determines Edgeworth studies, as well as a predictor of the Victorianizing and aestheticizing of Austen. It is worth remembering that Richard Whately, whose 1821 essay in the *Quarterly* is often cited in Austen criticism as a landmark, was archbishop of Dublin and that one of his reasons for preferring Austen's art to Edgeworth's is that "Miss Austin [*sic*] has the merit (in our judgment most essential) of being evidently a Christian writer" (1821: 359; rpt. in Southam 1968: 95).[17]

Though she praises Austen highly on occasion, Edgeworth with her more overtly intellectual viewpoint could also find the younger author a bit insipid. She concurs with the scientific writer Jane Marcet's judgment on Austen's last novels in 1818: "that one grows tired at last of milk and water even tho the water be pure and the milk sweet" (Häusermann 1952: 90). The *New Monthly Magazine*'s reflections "On the female literature of the present age" in a two-part 1820 survey are similarly worth noticing; odd as we may find the assessment of Austen, it is typical of the period. Praising Edgeworth for her shrewd and witty realism and her knowing raillery of fashionable manners, "T." also worries over her determined avoidance of the spiritual. Brilliantly depicting the classes and stages of "human life, she never seems to regard it as the infancy of an eternal being." More soulful and passionate than Edgeworth, Sydney Owenson is all tempestuous female heart, so that "we turn from the dazzling brilliancy of Lady Morgan's works to repose on the soft green of Miss Austen's sweet and unambitious creations. . . . There is a moral tenderness pervading them all." Austen's "serious yet gentle" mind disposes her audience to "pensive musing, and tranquillizes every discordant emotion" – just the sort of fictional Valium requisite for the reader exhausted by Edgeworth's inability to stop thinking or Morgan's inability to stop theatricalizing (274, 637). The diversities of the *New Monthly*'s assessments challenge the mapping of "female literature" as a unified textual field. But the many flourishing women writers "T." surveys (along with their eighteenth-century predecessors) are largely erased from modern mainstream narratives of the literary past, typically replaced by Jane Austen as the foundational figure of women's literary achievement, the first as well as the best. It comes as no surprise to find George Moore pronouncing Austen the "inventor of a new medium of literary expression . . . the inventor of the formula whereby domestic life may be described" early in this century (1926: 45), but assertions of originary power still regularly punctuate Austen studies, including much current feminist criticism.[18]

The same processes of canon deformation and tokenization obtain in French literature, where the dominant masterpiece model also assumes that privileged works somehow simultaneously exemplify and transcend their historical moment.[19]

Far removed from her period's "war of ideas" till late in this century, Austen loomed canonically larger and larger in its mid-years for her ironies and ambivalences, her seeming transcendence of her particular historical moment. A formally impeccable artist and profound moral thinker of international importance, she was also (like Shakespeare) a writer for Everyman and Everywoman.[20] Publishing on Edgeworth in 1950, P. H. Newby simultaneously confirms his subject's larger scope and mythologizes Austen's art and accessibility to the common reader, who "looks for pleasures that are more immediate than the realisation that whereas Jane Austen was so much the better novelist Maria Edgeworth may be the more important. For whereas Jane Austen surveyed with the eye of a realist ground that had already been tilled, and brought it to perfection, Maria struck out and subdued stretches of new territory, the psychology of children, the dignified and humorous mind of the peasant, the resolute mind of a woman of affairs, and she supplied an impetus for the writing of all regional fiction" (1950: 93–4). (Should the common Janeite nevertheless require assistance with Austen's submerged eighteenth-century provenance, two Austen companions, numerous guidebooks, and two separate Jane Austen societies, as well as biographies and shelves of more academic studies, continue to accumulate.) Austen's body of work was small, in print, and amenable to the mid-twentieth-century's psychic and critical needs. Like that of many other important contemporaries (male as well as female), Edgeworth's sprawled across genres and transgressed academic periodization, neither readily available physically nor easily uprootable from its intellectual context.[21] Her effects often come from an intricate pastiche of allusions or from subtly writing against the grain of her culture's conventions. When she insists on terming *Belinda* (1801) and other works "tales," for example, she is not being a prude, but making an ambitious claim for her fiction's philosophical and moral significance as opposed to what contemporary reviewers recurrently call ordinary novel manufactory – the commodification of unchallenging amusement.[22]

If Austen could be constructed as universal Woman Writer (a handy counterweight to the six Great Men who came to represent the Romantic period, as well as the initiator of the classic realist novel), Edgeworth was marginalized as mother of the regional novel at the expense of all her other achievements because of her first adult fiction, *Castle Rackrent* (1800), and other Irish tales. By the nineteenth century's end, William Butler Yeats presages the best that has conventionally been said for her in the literary histories that shape canons and curricula: "the one serious novelist coming from the upper class in Ireland, and the most finished and famous produced by any class there, is undoubtedly Miss Edgeworth" (1891: 27).[23] As the initiator of a provincial prose genre, Edgeworth has been peripheral to transcendental Romantic verse and the mainstream fictional masterpiece as well.[24] Her non-Irish work has often been dismissed as secondhand and derivative, not the artless transcription of actual experience that her stories about her homeland could be naively supposed. When not simply ignored as trivial and paraliterary, her educational and juvenile writings count against her, signs of her dull didacticism as opposed to Austen's elegant ethics; despite canonization's imbrication with instructional policy and practice at every level, serious educational interests typically compromise the aesthetic product. Appropriating Newby's image – the colonial trope that permutes through Edgeworth studies – Walter Allen's assessment in his very popular 1954 history of the novel opens with resounding praise, finding 1800 a date of the "first importance" in world fiction because of *Castle Rackrent*. Edgeworth "occupied new territory for the novel." Before her, everything but London had been general and conventional, but she not only "gave fiction a local habitation and a name": she dramatized the relation between place and populace (1954: 107–8).

Allen and Newby might have added that she also vocalized those new territories, giving a multitude of voices to subjectivities previously unspoken, the child's as well as the peasant's. Resident in Ireland since 1782 and fascinated by colonial customs, mentality, and especially language, Edgeworth produced her first adult novel, *Castle Rackrent*, by what she describes as a transcribing of the colonized voice, being the medium through which Thady spoke while she simply wrote down what he said: a disclaimer of her skills in sophisticated and ironic mimicry which need be taken no more seriously than other authorial mythologies of automatic writing. Significantly, Edgeworth's are strikingly talky fictions, veritable textbook examples of heteroglossia in which every tongue has its say, and dialogue is the operative mode, the didactic message problematized by the dialogic medium. Virtually every dialect, idiom, and linguistic nuance of every available class, race, and nationality (including the liveliest representation of the juvenile voice to date) can be found somewhere in an Edgeworth novel. Yet Allen concludes by throwing out virtually all of Edgeworth's work unexamined, with the regretful dismissal that has become ritualistic in considerations of her production: "Miss Edgeworth was essentially a didactic writer. . . . Fiction was an aid to education. . . . [her] theories of human nature and right behavior trip her up as a novelist. This is most apparent in her English novels. In the Irish ones she is writing much more of what she knows at first hand, writing with her eye on the object. . . . her educational preoccupations spoil her" (1954: 112). (As readers of eighteenth-century conduct books will recognize, the notion that a woman so unfortunate as to have any ideas had best hide them dies hard.)

Edgeworth's diminution from mainstream author to Ango-Irish colonialist and didactic educator derives partly from extrinsic factors like the narrowing and aestheticizing of what counts as "literature," but also from the critical logistics intrinsic to narrativizing a complex career. Although her prose popularized the schema of contextualized character formation over time as insistently as Wordsworth's poetry, the when, how, and what of her own literary production offer no easy developmental paradigm. She published an enormous body of work around the turn of the century, beginning with children's stories and educational writing, moving on to pioneering adolescent fiction, and then adult novels – and her production of the 1790s set a high standard to maintain, not a bumbling start to transcend. She returned over and over to kinds of writing she had begun earlier, producing successive sequels to early children's stories over many years, never abandoning the juvenile for "mature" genres. Several of her most serious and significant adult works began as juvenile productions, and for Edgeworth as for other women and progressive thinkers, educative genres often function as personal and cultural narratives, subversions of the publicly unsayable in innocuous guise. The last tale she published was for young people; although she felt Ireland's situation no longer amenable to adult fiction, *Orlandino* (1848) is an Irish story structured by colonialism and community, a genealogy and imaginative resolution of orphanage, estrangement, and famine. Subtly allusive to cultural politics and her own personal history, her books are also interreferential. Thematically, *Belinda*, her second tale for grownups, invites comparison with the last adult fiction she published over thirty years later, which reworks similar issues of gender and generation, the relation of child and adult, within a very different political and personal context. Few critics could agree with Edgeworth's most recent literary biographer's dismissal of her first two novels as mere apprentice work; certainly *Castle Rackrent* draws the most readers and critics (Butler 1972). If it is hard to produce a predictable critical story of progress or decline, it is equally hard to box off Edgeworth's juvenile from her adult work, her Irish from her English fiction. Though that is how literary histories and even specialized studies awkwardly package her, her seemingly heterogeneous literary production is remarkably consistent in its concerns and strategies, whether for child or adult, whether early or late: the focus on character and community, the romancing of pedagogy and the family, the vividly realistic dialogue and informative details, the playfulness with referentiality and conventions, the intellectual curiosity that emerges in literary allusion as well as sociocultural fact and footnote.

In tales for schoolchild and statesman alike, Edgeworth impresses for the surprisingly flexible ways the child–adult relationship so central to her psychobiography figures in her work and for her sophisticated strategies of making domestic instances represent larger issues. Her interreferential and intertextual fiction is crosshatched with multivalent allusions and parallels. It is a representational fiction that repeatedly, almost obsessively, incorporates the real, its pages punctuated with everything from recipes for humane rabbit traps and records of West Indian slave torture to transmutations of actual people and familial anecdotes. Edgeworth loves to write "taken from fact," and the close reader of her life, letters, and work is as startled by her skill in making capital of the smallest events of her everyday life as by the breadth of her reading. Despite Ward's aside, she does not foreground chemistry (like Jane Marcet) or political economy (like Harriet Martineau), but she does converse with, rewrite, and parody a wealth of authors from Aristotle and Tasso to eighteenth-century travel writers and literary notables, British (Pope, Addison, George Lyttelton, Richard Cumberland, Johnson, Gibbon, Richardson, Henry and Sarah Fielding, Charlotte Lennox, Burney, Wollstonecraft, Elizabeth Inchbald, Anna Letitia Barbauld, John Moore, Thomas and Anna Seward, the duchess of Devonshire, Erasmus Darwin, Thomas Day, George Crabbe, Lady Morgan, Scott), and continental (Voltaire, Rousseau, Marmontel, Saint–Pierre, Berquin, Genlis, de Staël, Jeanne Isabelle de Montolieu, Kotzebue), to name but a few. But the densely textured referentiality of Edgeworth's realistic moral tales also has a fairy-tale layering. As much utopian as it is pragmatic, her representational mode also repeatedly, almost obsessively, enacts private and public fantasies – reformist and revisionary plots of human happiness which most often involve fetishizing the family. Although the opening epigraphs of this chapter seemingly align with warring notions of fiction, a no-nonsense realism and an unembarrassed romanticism, both narrative impulses coexist in Edgeworth's work; both are central to her ambitious tales.

It would not be easy to make for this fiction the sanitized aesthetic artifact case that has so often been made for Austen's novels, since Edgeworth's tales are undeniably contingent, obviously historically conditioned by gendered, generic, and generational concerns. Orderly, yet dense with personal and cultural reference, Edgeworth's family romances can be read homologously, as at once answers to psychic, educational, and communal dilemmas. To Edgeworth's narrative techniques of displacement may be added her interest in the displacements of personal and cultural identity. This predilection for the homeless and unhoused – colonials, émigrés, absentees, orphans – functions as the reality principle of Edgeworth's family fantasy, for, most notably, her writing is characterized by its compulsive hovering over and quite overt politicizing of the family as prototype of community and a reformed British cultural identity.[25] The themes of colonialism and community, of marginality and inclusion, which interweave through the history of Edgeworth's literary reputation and the textualizations of her life, also interpenetrate her work: if colonialism is the precondition, community is always the answer. It has recently been argued that biblical parallels are inappropriate, that *literary* canonicity really implies resonant participation in a culture's critical colloquy; this malleable canonicity needs multivalent works amenable to interminable exegesis, works that continually reveal "unexpected significances" to stave off canonical limbo (W. Harris 1991: 112). If canons are constructed of sophisticated readings instead of etherealized texts and if, as Barbara Herrnstein Smith argues, the values we grant texts are contingent rather than determinate, it is no heresy to suggest that other women writers might share Austen's multivalence had their work's complexities been the focus of equally loving explication and ongoing critical dialogue (1984, 1987). What is repeatedly treated and taught attains a cultural valence not necessarily commensurate with demonstrable textual mutivalence.

But Edgeworth's marginal canonicity, her status as a colonial property, really depends less on the body of her writing than on her own body. Physically child-sized, she was often effaced by her father in public appearances during her life. And, however important the vagaries of historical happenstance or the difficulties of critical management, it is Maria's position as Edgeworth *fille* that still determines discussion of her work. More than a century and a half after his death, Richard Lovell Edgeworth is as vigorously alive in literary history as he was in life, diverting to himself the lion's share of what attention Maria's writing receives. Ironically, the more Maria's art occasions critical interest, the more that interest is deflected to the drama of her history as daddy's girl. The nineteenth century produced a colorful array of anecdotes about Richard Lovell and his eldest daughter (by the first and least loved of his four wives). His energy and egotism vexed outsiders, who could not understand his daughter's or his family's devotion. Lord Byron and Joanna Baillie, a sister author who became a friend, strikingly depict the family visit to London in 1813, when Maria was the successor to Byron's 1812 triumph. Looking back from 1820, Byron dismisses the father as "bad – in taste and tact & decent breeding. . . . I thought him a very tiresome coarse old Irish half and half Gentleman and her a pleasant reserved old woman – with a *pencil* under her petticoat – however – undisturbed in it's [sic] operation by the vicinity of that anatomical part of female humanity – which would have rendered the taking notes neutral or partial in any other she animal above a Cow. – That sort of woman seem to think themselves perfect because they can't get covered." Like many of Edgeworth's reviewers and critics, Byron finds the proximity of the woman's sex and the rational pen disturbing, but his attention is similarly deflected from the daughter's private phallic usurpation to the spectacle of the father's self-display. Byron's journal for January 19, 1821 calls Richard Lovell "active, brisk, and endless. . . . intelligent, vehement, vivacious, and full of life," noting the London unpopularity of Edgeworth *père* and the joke about a subscription to send him back to Ireland. "The fact was – everybody cared more about *her*. She was a nice little unassuming 'Jeanie Deans'-looking bodie' . . . and if not handsome, certainly not ill-looking. Her conversation was as quiet as herself. One would never have guessed she could write *her name*; whereas her father talked, not as if he could write nothing else, but as if nothing else was worth writing." Byron's jaded remembrance may seem to reflect no more than his own aristocratic and misogynist *grossièretés* – though he could also profess intimidation at the intelligence and wit of Maria's writing and wish he could wed one of her heroines – but he was neither the first nor the last outsider to pronounce Maria's father a "bore – the worst of bores – a boisterous Bore" (Marchand 1977: VI 217–18; 1978: VIII, 29–30; 1979: IX, 33).[26]

Joanna Baillie relates to Sir Walter Scott English society's eagerness to meet Maria Edgeworth, so tiny that, as the novelist herself said, the crowd literally "closed over her." The dramatist found Maria "frank, animated, sensible, and amusing," so "confiding and affectionate" that she won Baillie's heart. More charitable than most, Baillie also records the father's proclivity for center stage. Shy in youth, Maria had found her tongue as she gained authorial confidence, eventually becoming as well known for her conversational powers as her own Lady Delacour and Lady Davenant.[27] By 1813, when father and daughter began to talk at once, "she as often gets the better as he." Baillie thought him a "strange mortal," tactless and conceited, "yet his daughter is so strongly attached to him that I am sure he must have some real good in him . . . I have taken a goodwill to him in spite of fashion, and maintain that if he would just speak one half of what he speaks he would be a very agreeable man" (July 1, 1813, Scott 1894: I, 299–300).

Richard Lovell Edgeworth's autobiography documents his liveliness, his anecdotal skills, his pride in himself, his family, and his scientific accomplishments, and his marital and instructional adventures – four wives and twenty-two children, so that the family was an ongoing educational laboratory – in vivid and startlingly frank prose, quite different from the stiff little prefaces to Maria's work he sometimes produced. (The liveliest introductions, like other work signed by him, were actually written by his daughter.) He insisted that Maria finish and publish the memoir after his death, so the second volume is hers, a completion of Richard Lovell's life which is also her autobiographical narrative of his relation to her and to her work: *Memoirs of Richard Lovell Edgeworth, Esq. Begun by Himself and Concluded by His Daughter, Maria Edgeworth* (1820). Maria's continuation foregrounds and mythologizes what shrewd reader and rumor already surmised, that hers were texts self-consciously written under the sign of the child; though it is "true," it is also a literary account, a daughter's memory, and an educational romance not at all easy to interpret. The story that she wants to tell is of collaboration – of her father's generosity in throwing out ideas, of his careful verbal corrections, of their literary partnership in educational writing. What she cannot fully narrate is the extent to which the collaboration was a creation of the writing, a literary production that brought her desire into being. Within the context of her loveless early years, her literary production enables emotional literacy; it is a story of writing's power rather than its impoverishment. Following the 1867 private printing of *A Memoir of Maria Edgeworth, with a Selection from Her Letters by the Late Mrs. Edgeworth* and of Augustus J. C. Hare's 1894 partial publication of that correspondence, a number of literary biographies turned their attention to her life, passing summary (and occasionally astute) judgments and perpetuating each other's errors about her actual writing, many of which have to do with Richard Lovell's ruinous intervention.[28] Ironically, the women writers who sought to free Maria from her father's influence damaged her reputation in the numerous academic surveys emerging to explain English literary history. Maria Edgeworth the successful woman writer was embalmed as Richard Lovell's daughter, daddy's girl. And there she remains, a colonized property rather than a canonical participant.

The standard approach in considering Edgeworth, even by her advocates, is to look for two things: the moral purpose and the father's influence, the two almost invariably linked. Edmund Gosse and George Sampson typify the obstructionist case for the paternal legacy. Gosse finds *Castle Rackrent* "perhaps the best of her writings, because the least interfered with; most of her books had to undergo the revision and general tinkering of her conceited and pedantic father" (1904: IV, 94). *The Concise Cambridge History of English Literature* pronounces that "her father . . . affected his daughter's work very much for the worse, by the admixture of purpose and preachment which he either induced her to make or intruded on his own account" and that she "was devoted to her father, who ruthlessly used her, as if she had no right to a life of her own" (Sampson 1961: 610). Edgeworth has been unlucky not only in the literary histories' winnowing, but also in the way that specialized studies insistently narrativize her life at the expense of her literary production, the drama of her daughterhood occluding the drama in her texts. For example, because she wishes to efface popular depreciation of the father, Marilyn Butler's massive 1972 literary biography is organized in terms of "Apprenticeship," "Partnership," and "Independence," the last of which includes sections on "Living without her Father" and "Writing without her Father." Absolving Richard Lovell of damaging interference, Butler portrays a didactic daughter enabled by the father's broader experience, who turns aside from her "pretty stories & novellettes" to embrace the manly sociological realism that is her true claim on our attention, a paternal depreciation of Edgeworth's more obviously gendered fictions that has been persistently reinscribed in considerations of her work from her first reviewers on (1972: 209). Bolstered by unpublished papers and in essence recapitulating the family narrative of the benevolent father that Maria Edgeworth herself devoted much energy to constructing, Butler's enthusiasm for Richard Lovell – more arresting in her account than his child – and for his salutary contribution to his daughter's oeuvre has enlivened patriarchal fixations instead of resolving them. Claire Tomalin's biography of Mary Wollstonecraft illustrates how Butler's work can be misread and twisted, justifying a selective quotation from Edgeworth that eviscerates her wit and rationalism to "an insistence that women's lives must be envisaged in terms of restraint and endurance." Offering a troublingly debilitated and Victorianized summation of Edgeworth's thinking and family life, Tomalin then gives Butler credit for her "excellent account" (1974: 244 n.).

Although the canon is popularly thought of as battered, Edgeworth's status has not really benefited very much so far, not even when, as is rarely the case, her work is addressed by feminist critics (Topliss 1981; Spender 1986; Kowaleski–Wallace 1988, 1991). Ideologically wanting with respect to Wollstonecraft, she is aesthetically deficient compared with Austen, who gets good marks for subversion as well as style. Despite *The Madwoman in the Attic*'s privileging of Charlotte Brontë, for example, even Sandra M. Gilbert and Susan Gubar's Austen has a spunk denied Edgeworth, subsumed in their account as archetypal daddy's girl and permanent child. Indeed, eighteenth-century and earlier women writers have not fared especially well in canon reformation. Unless they can be glamorized as rebels like Aphra Behn and Mary Wollstonecraft, they are unlikely to make it to the reading list; despite their clout with contemporaries and their importance to women's history, Hannah More and Sarah Trimmer are dubious candidates. The continual recycling of Austen, the necessity for reckoning with her by uncovering her feminism or Romanticism or modernism, testifies that much apparent canon change is just interpretive change, that much historicism validates a claim still perceived as timeless and unassailable, as Julia Prewitt Brown's review essay on "The feminist depreciation of Austen: a polemical reading" demonstrates. Brown, author of a protofeminist reading locating Austen's marriage plots within an emergent cult of the family, deplores feminist interrogation of Austen's romantic resolutions as much on the high ground of "aesthetic perfection" as on the argument that marital choices encode significant social power. "What more need be said," she asks rhetorically, "of a mind" that could engage a children's classic on equal terms with Austen (1990: 303).[29]

If Brown exemplifies the conservationism inherent in making the past new, "Jane Austen and the masturbating girl," Eve Kosofsky Sedgwick's 1991 article in *Critical Inquiry*, offers an outré example of contemporizing the classic. Who could resist so engaging a title? Sedgwick's montage of Marianne Dashwood and the little girl who just couldn't keep her hand from between her legs certainly makes for arresting reading, especially conjoined with "Why there's no sex in Jane Austen," Susan Morgan's contribution to the ongoing discussion of the Austen heroine and her place in literary history. For Morgan, Austen is the modernist foremother, who "metamorphosed the idea of the virgin heroine" (1989: 23). For Sedgwick, "Austen criticism is notable mostly not just for its timidity and banality but for its unresting exaction of the spectacle of a Girl Being Taught a Lesson," a pedagogically abjected figure who is also "Jane Austen" in the hands of her punitive explicators, her text a mere fossilized relic of the "now-subtracted autoerotic spectacle": Austen's masturbatory sensibility effaced by repressive sense.[30] "How can it have taken this long," Sedgwick wonders, "to see that when Colonel Brandon and Marianne finally get together, their first granddaughter will be Lesbia Brandon?" (1991: 833–6). But no matter how their argumentative agendas conflict, Sedgwick and Morgan coincide in demonstrating once again that nothing sells like sex and Jane Austen, that savvy literary criticism need not worry too much about Austen's forebears.

Just as naturalistic conventions or Mary Poovey's "proper lady" can be discovered in Austen's text and projected on to her contemporaries as normative and evaluative, so we can be sure that a desiring Austen will loom larger than life, a big name wielding power (or perhaps a vibrator) that mysteriously elevates her beyond the humdrum specifics and literary traditions in which her lesser contemporaries are mired. Whether Austen's influence is idolized or Benthamized (as in, for example, the disciplinary semiotics Nancy Armstrong finds to be the Victorian legacy of Austen's literacy), her continually mutating canonicity maps her on to the past in a determining quasi-causal relationship at odds with her actual reception history, though of course accomplished under the rubric of historicism (1987: Ch. 3).[31] Eternally reinvented like Madonna, Austen is an icon, a multivalent "spirit of the age," the female presence omitted from Hazlitt's exemplary pantheon of great men. Realistically, not many earlier women writers (who tend to be white and elite) are likely to achieve canonicity via revised academic syllabuses when formerly neglected, more culturally diverse literatures also solicit representation – or even via period specialties perhaps, for speedy publication and name-brand subjects matter.[32] Canons evolve, but they perdure; like studies of writing and actual teaching, books on "minor" figures and genres are unlikely to propel the critic to academic superstardom. Still, one hopes that lots of scholars will undergo the archival drudgery to correct the record before a new feminist canon is produced and consumed, before the serried ranks of newly gendered anthologies proclaim: here is how women wrote; here are all the women who matter. Maria Edgeworth as permanent child – overly impressionable and father-fixated, Maria Edgeworth as didactic schoolmistress – overly rational and obsessed with pedagogy: if we reanimated the dried masks, what literary adventurer would we find?

Notes

1   Perhaps I should call this Chapter "Yes, I love Jane Austen too, but . . ." to emphasize that it should not be misconstrued as an attack on Austen's claims to canonical inscription or on all those industrious critics who have done so much to elucidate her work. My point is, rather, that no matter how much we value Austen, we need a recuperative scholarship that inquires why she has been singled out as the Romantic period's exemplary woman writer and how the literary landscape might differ had other female territory been tilled as extensively as Austen's fiction.

2   Although it was published posthumously, *Northanger Abbey* originated many years before. Austen also writes to Anna Austen, "I have made up my mind to like no Novels really, but Miss Edgeworth's, Yours & my own" (September 28, 1814; Austen 1959a: 405).

3   Joyce Hemlow's 1950 essay on "Fanny Burney and the courtesy books" shaped modern attitudes towards Burney and the novel of manners. Among the most impressive recent Burney studies are Margaret Anne Doody's biography (1988) and the analyses of Kristina Straub (1987) and Julia Epstein (1989); slighter studies by D. D. Devlin and Judy Simons appeared in 1987. Epstein's final section in *The Iron Pen* surveys Burney's "Critical afterlife," but the contemporary efflorescence of interest in Burney promises a much more glamorous conclusion to the dismissive commonplaces there recorded. A few years back, for instance, an entire issue of a major scholarly journal devoted to one Burney novel alone would have been unthinkable (see the July 1991 "Special *Evelina* Issue" of *Eighteenth-Century Fiction*). Since all Burney's novels are in print for the first time since the early nineteenth century, she is now available for teaching and the ongoing critical reconstitution that confers cultural value.

4   I am going to contravene accepted practice by using "Edgeworth" for Maria; where confusion might result, I will use the first names of father and daughter. Although Harriet Kramer Linkin's 1991 survey of "The current canon in British Romantics studies" reveals that some teachers are attempting to expand the canon, it also underscores the continued privileging of the masculine and the poetic in early-nineteenth-century period studies. Austen is a staple of novel surveys, but only familiarly named women get much taught in

Romantics courses: Mary Shelley and Dorothy Wordsworth (who did not publish in her own day). Edgeworth and other women writers widely popular at that time very seldom get included.

5 In occulting the name and date of the work under review, Michael Munday's attempt to reanimate early nineteenth-century commentary on fiction obscures Edgeworth's (and other "didactic" women's roles) in transforming critical discourse. In casting his narrative as a progress towards Romantic aesthetics, "works of more pure imagination," he smooths messy examples into modern canonical values (1982: 214).

6 Scott acknowledges his debt in Chapter 72 of *Waverley* (1814) and still more fully in the 1829 General Preface to the series, where he remarks that Edgeworth "may be truly said to have done more towards completing the Union than perhaps all the legislative enactments by which it has been followed up" (1972: 493, 523). The two became friends, exchanging visits and many letters.

7 The ground-breaking study of this larger "fashion"'s emergence is, of course, N. McKendrick, J. Brewer, and J. H. Plumb's 1982 *The Birth of a Consumer Society: The Commercialization of Eighteenth-Century England.*

8 See, for example, I. Ferris's 1991 gendered segmentation of the literary marketplace in *The Achievement of Literary Authority: Gender, History, and the Waverley Novels.*

9 Recent considerations of "literature"'s emergence include the work of L. Gossman (1990), A. Kernan (1987), and D. L. Patey (1988). Part 1, "History of Literature," in Gossman's *Between History and Literature* (1990) reprints his important 1982 essay, "Literature and education."

10 This review of the first series of *Tales of Fashionable Life* is remarkable for its conflation of intelligent praise and religious bias (Stephen and Gifford 1809: 148–9). William Gifford inserted the attack on Edgeworth's secularism, and John Murray tried to make amends via later reviewers for having used her "very scurvily" (Shine and Shine 1949: 8, 31). For Gifford, as for more overtly denominational critics, Edgeworth's Enlightenment morality was insufficiently pious and spiritual. John Foster's article on the same volumes for the *Eclectic Review* similarly berates her for writing without reference of a "judgment to come," though "for predominant good sense, knowledge of the world, discrimination of character, truth in the delineation of manners, and spirited dialogue, it is hardly possible to praise [her work] too much" (1856: I, 426–7).

11 "Christopher North" usually stands for John Wilson, but this number of the "Noctes" is by John Gibson Lockhart, who shortly thereafter negotiated the sale of Edgeworth's last adult novel for a remarkably high price and also reviewed it in the *Quarterly.*

12 The phrase, one among many of Sir Walter Scott's tributes, is used as the title of Elisabeth Inglis-Jones's 1959 Edgeworth biography. The Leavises had of course been promulgating their notions of Austen for decades before the publication of *The Great Tradition.*

13 Jane Rendall's 1985 study of modern feminism's origins is unusual in its brief inclusion of Edgeworth and its positive depiction of the relation between mothering and education in the period's thought.

14 The sequence of letters (Bodleian MS. Eng. lett. c 721) is curtailed to one of Edgeworth's responses in the *Memoir*, September 6, 1834 (Edgeworth 1867: III, 144–60), an important letter still further reduced in Hare (1894: II, 248–55). The final quotation comes from a manuscript letter to Edgeworth's favorite sister, Fanny Edgeworth Wilson, August 21, 1834. Butler (1972: 260–3) uses the letters to bolster her claims for Edgeworth's sociological art. Stewart in her account comes across as a more astute critic than Edgeworth herself, for Butler discusses neither Stewart's blatant Romantic bias nor his faulting Edgeworth for not ranging human nature according to his father's classificatory system. Edgeworth's response as a realist novelist was that human beings are idiosyncratic and inconsistent, contravening the noble "unity" of Romantic art and philosophical categorizing Stewart valorizes.

15 The *North American Review*'s account of Scott mania ends with a noteworthy assessment of Edgeworth's stature: "she is the author of works not to be forgotten; of works which can never lose their standard value as 'English classics,' " even though "it is true, that all classes and orders of readers have agreed to like Scott's novels, more unanimously than any thing

was ever liked before . . . a reception more wide, more prompt, more superstitiously fond, than could be believed possible, were it not known to be real" (Everett 1823: 389).

16   In a sharp turnabout from past readings of Austen the pure artist disengaged from messy revolutionary realities, Austen's fictions are currently being mined by historians like Oliver MacDonagh (1991). Her novels are similarly appropriated for their anthropological insights into social structure (Handler and Segal 1990). Yet the "historical" Austen MacDonagh delivers is innocent of the feminist consciousness that many recent critics foreground, demonstrating once again the novelist's amenability to divergent interpretations.

17   Like Ward, Whately is also uncomfortable with the sheer amount of information in *Patronage*, as well as with Edgeworth's ruptures of naturalistic plotting. B. C. Southam's rather slim *Jane Austen: The Critical Heritage* is, as the editor points out, short on "critical illumination": "the birth and growth of Jane Austen's critical reputation was a dull and long-drawn-out affair" (1968: 1). From the perspective of canon formation, Southam's anthology is invaluable, for it documents the extent to which Austen's stellar status is a twentieth-century phenomenon. Three articles on Jane Austen criticism in *The Jane Austen Companion*, ed. J. D. Grey, A. W. Litz, and B. Southam, offer a developmental overview of Austen's canonization (1986: 93–117).

18   For a sociological appraisal of women's demotion in the literary hierarchy, see Gaye Tuchman's *Edging Women Out: Victorian Novelists, Publishers, and Social Change* (1989). Typical examples of the foundational premiss in Austen studies include Kate Fulbrook's belief that Austen "begins the mainstream of fiction" (1987: 56) and Susan Morgan's that she was the first to decenter the courtship plot (1989: Ch. 2). Bracketing the secular Edgeworth with the devout Hannah More and Jane West, Barbara Horwitz finds all previous educators "sternly conservative politically and highly orthodox theologically," so that Austen wins laurels for radical pedagogy as well as aesthetic perfection (1989: 182). In fact, Edgeworth's educational tracts were often faulted for their progressivism and irreligion.

19   See "The Politics of Tradition: Placing Women in French Literature" issue, ed. J. Dejean and N. K. Miller, of *Yale French Studies* 75 (1988), especially Miller's essay on "Men's reading, women's writing: gender and the rise of the novel."

20   Despite the dissenting grumpiness about her alleged nasty tongue and narrow limits that marks some modern criticism, Austen's central positioning in the history of western ethical thinking in Alasdair MacIntyre's *After Virtue* is thoroughly representative of the respect her work has been accorded (1981: 169–74, 222–6). Although he actually says little about her (or any other woman writer), Ian Watt similarly underlines her "eminence in the tradition of the English novel" for her "successful resolution" of Richardson's and Fielding's differing narrative methods (1962: 296). For F. R. Leavis, her formal perfection is cognate with her "moral significance": "Without her intense moral preoccupation she wouldn't have been a great novelist" (1963: 7).

21   "Canon" and "period," Frank Kermode suggests, are evaluative packaging operations for managing historical deposits, with period characteristics assuming archetypal force (1987: 115, 121). The replacement of the heterogeneous literature produced in the decades around 1800 with Romantic masculine poetry is exemplary. Stuart Curran of the University of Pennsylvania has identified over 600 women poets of the late eighteenth and early nineteenth centuries, most hitherto unnoted; for a brief overview of these poets, see his essay (1988) in Anne K. Mellor's *Romanticism and Feminism*. Since many women did not publish their work, as Margaret J. M. Ezell notes, and many published anonymously, numerous women writers in other periods and genres may also have been left unpackaged (1990).

22   Nineteenth-century publishers' catalogues of titles offer a dizzying array of generic names for fiction, calling into question tidy accounts of the novel's evolutionary supremacy.

23   Yeats's commentary is riddled with factual errors, yet his artistic assessment still rings true. Almost a century later, Edgeworth is once again being rediscovered as a major Irish writer; see, for example, the anthology of essays edited by Cóilín Owens (1987) and the studies by Thomas Flanagan (1959), Patrick Rafroidi (1972, rpt. 1980) John Cronin (1980), Anthony Cronin (1982), A. Norman Jeffares (1982), Tom Dunne (1984), W. J. McCormack, (1985), Barry Sloan (1987), James M. Cahalan (1988), and Ann Owens Weekes (1990). Weekes

is especially notable for positioning Edgeworth at the start of the uncharted tradition of Irish *women* writers. Oddly, Weekes does not include Sydney Owenson, Lady Morgan, whose Irish "romance" interweaves with Edgeworth's Irish "realism" in the early years of the nineteenth century; both women and their generic mixes contribute significantly to the reconstitution of British cultural identity.

24 Since what David Perkins (1990) describes as "The construction of 'the Romantic movement' as a literary classification" contributed to Edgeworth's marginality, it is pleasant to find Romanticists beginning to grant her parity: see Gene W. Ruoff's "1800 and the future of the novel: William Wordsworth, Maria Edgeworth, and the vagaries of literary history" (1987) in K. R. Johnson and G. W. Ruoff's *The Age of William Wordsworth*.

25 The literature considering the transformations in manners and morals, family patterns, and national identity during the revolutionary decades is enormous, even before the woman writer's particular contribution is factored in. Some relevant studies include Benedict Anderson (1983), Nancy Armstrong (1987), Leonore Davidoff and Catherine Hall (1987), Muriel Jaeger (1956), Maurice J. Quinlan (1941, rpt. 1965), Gerald Newman (1987), and Raphael Samuel (1989). My 1982 paper includes numerous references on the turn of the century's reform or ruin polemic.

26 Byron's letters and journals are sprinkled with references to Edgeworth and her work (e.g. Marchand 1973: II, 199; 1974: III, 44, 48).

27 Visitors to Edgeworthstown were enthusiastic about the participatory family society; if the father talked the most, all the children were included in everything, M.-A. Pictet records of his 1801 visit. He describes his first impression of Maria for the readers of the *Bibliothèque britannique* (an influential journal which popularized Edgeworthian educational theories and fiction abroad): "des yeux presque toujours baissés; l'air profondément modeste et réservé" (1802: 102). Maria always enjoyed disconcerting those who expected a stately bluestocking and was certainly aware of her father's failings, as Charles Kendal Bushe notes in 1810: "He talks a great deal and very pleasantly and loves to exhibit and perhaps obtrude what he wou'd be so justifiably vain of (his daughter and her works) if you did not trace that pride to his predominant Egotism, and see that he admires her because she is *his* child, and her works because they are *his* Grand Children. . . . Miss Edgeworth is for nothing more remarkable than for the total absence of vanity. She seems to have studied her father's foibles for two purposes, to avoid them and never to appear to see them" (in Somerville and Ross 1925: 49–50).

28 Jack Stillinger's 1991 *Multiple Authorship and the Myth of Solitary Genius* usefully problematizes the Romantic notion of unitary authorship submerged in such accounts. There is no manuscript evidence for the kinds of intervention often ascribed to Richard Lovell, but there is, as Stillinger demonstrates, much evidence for varied collaborative procedures among all kinds of writers.

29 For a less polemic view of feminist Austen from a scholar who stands for her conservative humanism, see Alastair M. Duckworth's 1991 "Review: Jane Austen and the construction of a progressive author." In a curious choice for a feminist critic, Brown cites Carol Iannone's "Feminism vs. literature" (1988) in support of literary taste; George F. Will's 1991 championing of Iannone demonstrates the paranoia unleashed by "literary politics." Relevant books putting actual canon changes in perspective include Herbert Lindenberger on Stanford (1990: Chs. 6 and 7) and Carey Kaplan and Ellen Cronan Rose on feminism, the academy, and the common reader (1990).

30 Sedgwick feels that "A lot of Austen criticism sounds hilariously like the leering schoolprospectuses or governess-manifestoes brandished like so many birch rods in Victorian sadomasochistic pornography" (1991: 833). Should masturbation prove too tame for the jaded Austen connoisseur, Glenda A. Hudson's 1992 *Sibling Love and Incest in Jane Austen's Fiction* promises a different glamor.

31 E.g., "In helping to establish the semiotic organization of nineteenth century [*sic*] England . . . the novel helped to create the conditions theorized by Bentham. . . . With a kind of selfawareness rivaled . . . only by Jeremy Bentham, Austen proposes a form of authority – a form of political authority – that works through literacy rather than through traditional

juridical means to maintain social relations" (Armstrong 1987: 156–7). The difficulties involved in writing literary history in a postmodern age are explored by Brook Thomas, *The New Historicism and Other Old-Fashioned Topics* (1991), and David Perkins, *Is Literary History Possible?* (1992).

32 The current remarkable popularity of Madonna herself as a topic for scholarly papers and conferences speaks to the same professional yen for the popular and the timely.

Bibliography

Allen, W. (1954) *The English Novel: A Short Critical History*, New York: E. P. Dutton.

Anderson, B. (1983) *Imagined Communities: Reflections on the Origin and Spread of Nationalism*, London: Verso.

Armstrong, N. (1987) *Desire and Domestic Fiction: A Political History of the Novel*, New York and Oxford: Oxford University Press.

Austen, J. (1959a) *Jane Austen's Letters to Her Sister Cassandra and Others*, ed. R. W. Chapman, 2nd edn., London: Oxford University Press.

—— (1959b [1818]) *Northanger Abbey and Persuasion*, Vol. 5 of *The Novels of Jane Austen*, ed. R. W. Chapman, 3rd edn., 5 vols., London: Oxford University Press.

Brown, J. P. (1979) *Jane Austen's Novels: Social Change and Literary Form*, Cambridge, MA and London: Harvard University Press.

—— (1990) "Review essay: The feminist depreciation of Austen: a polemical reading," *Novel* 23: 301–13.

Browne, A. (1987) *The Eighteenth-Century Feminist Mind*, Detroit, MI: Wayne State University Press.

Butler, M. (1975) *Jane Austen and the War of Ideas*, Oxford: Clarendon Press; reprinted 1987.

—— (1972) *Maria Edgeworth: A Literary Biography*, Oxford: Clarendon Press.

Cahalan, J. M. (1988) *The Irish Novel: A Critical History*, Boston, MA: Twayne.

Clive, J. (1957) *Scotch Reviewers: The "Edinburgh Review", 1802–1815*, London: Faber & Faber.

Cronin, A. (1982) "Maria Edgeworth: the unlikely precursor," in *Heritage Now: Irish Literature in the English Language*, Dingle, Ireland: Brandon Book Publishers, pp. 17–29.

Cronin, J. (1980) *The Anglo-Irish Novel*, Vol. 1, *The Nineteenth Century*, Totowa, N J: Barnes & Noble.

Curran, S. (1988) "Romantic poetry: the I altered," in *Romanticism and Feminism*, ed. Anne K. Mellor, Bloomington and Indianapolis, IN: Indiana University Press, pp. 185–207.

Davidoff, L. and Hall, C. (1987) *Family Fortunes: Men and Women of the English Middle Class, 1780–1850*, London: Hutchinson.

Dejean, J. and Miller, N. K. (eds.) (1988) "The Politics of Tradition: Placing Women in French Literature" issue, *Yale French Studies* 75.

Devlin, D. D. (1987) *The Novels and Journals of Fanny Burney*, New York: St. Martin's Press.

Doody, M. A. (1986) "Jane Austen's reading," in *The Jane Austen Companion*, with *A Dictionary of Jane Austen's Life and Works* by H. A. Bok, ed. J. D. Grey, A. W. Litz, and B. Southam, New York: Macmillan, pp. 347–63.

—— (1988) *Frances Burney: The Life in the Works*, New Brunswick, NJ: Rutgers University Press.

Duckworth, A. M. (1991) "Review: Jane Austen and the construction of a progressive author," *College English* 53: 77–90.

Dunne, T. (1984) *Maria Edgeworth and the Colonial Mind*, O'Donnell Lecture 26, Cork, Ireland: University College.

Edgeworth, M. (1867) *A Memoir of Maria Edgeworth, with a Selection from Her Letters by the Late Mrs. [Frances] Edgeworth*, ed. by her children, 3 vols., London: privately printed Joseph Masters and Son.

Edgeworth, R. L. and Edgeworth, M. (1820) *Memoirs of Richard Lovell Edgeworth, Esq. Begun by Himself and Concluded by His Daughter, Maria Edgeworth*, 2 vols., London: R. Hunter and Baldwin, Cradock, and Joy.

Epstein, J. (1989) *The Iron Pen: Frances Burney and the Politics of Women's Writing*, Madison, WI: University of Wisconsin Press.

Evans, M. (1987) *Jane Austen and the State*, London and New York: Tavistock Publications.

[Everett, E.] (1823) Review of *The Works of Maria Edgeworth*, *North American Review* 17: 383–9.

Ezell, M. J. M. (1990) "The myth of Judith Shakespeare: creating the canon of women's literature," *New Literary History* 21: 579–92.

Fergus, J. (1991) *Jane Austen: A Literary Life*, New York: St. Martin's Press.

Ferris, I. (1991) *The Achievement of Literary Authority: Gender, History, and the Waverley Novels*, Ithaca, NY and London: Cornell University Press.

Flanagan, T. (1959) *The Irish Novelists 1800–1850*, New York: Columbia University Press.

Foster, J. (1856) "The morality of works of fiction," review of *Tales of Fashionable Life*, by M. Edgeworth, 1810 edn. [vols. 1–3], in *Critical Essays Contributed to the Eclectic Review*, ed. J. E. Ryland, 2 vols., London: Henry G. Bohn, Vol. 1, pp. 417–28.

Fulbrook, K. (1987) "Jane Austen and the comic negative," in *Women Reading Women's Writing*, ed. S. Roe, Brighton, Sx: Harvester Press, pp. 39–57.

Gilbert, S. M. and Gubar, S. (1979) *The Madwoman in the Attic: The Woman Writer and the Nineteenth-Century Literary Imagination*, New Haven, CT and London: Yale University Press.

Gosse, E. (1904) *English Literature: An Illustrated Record*, 4 vols., Vol. 4, New York: Grosset & Dunlap.

Gossman, L. (1990) *Between History and Literature*, Cambridge, MA: Harvard University Press.

Grey, J. D., Litz, A. W., and Southam, B. (eds.) (1986) *The Jane Austen Companion*, with *A Dictionary of Jane Austen's Life and Works* by H. A. Bok, New York: Macmillan.

Grey, R. (1909) "Maria Edgeworth and Etienne Dumont," *Dublin Review* 145: 239–65.

Handler, R. and Segal, D. (1990) *Jane Austen and the Fiction of Culture: An Essay on the Narration of Social Realities*, Tucson, AZ: University of Arizona Press.

Hare, A. J. C. (ed.) (1894) *The Life and Letters of Maria Edgeworth*, 2 vols., London: Edward Arnold.

Harris, J. (1989) *Jane Austen's Art of Memory*, Cambridge: Cambridge University Press.

Harris, W. V. (1991) "Canonicity," *PMLA* 106: 110–21.

Häusermann, H. W. (1952) *The Genevese Background: Studies of Shelley, Francis Danby, Maria Edgeworth, Ruskin, Meredith, and Joseph Conrad in Geneva (with Hitherto Unpublished Letters)*, London: Routledge & Kegan Paul.

Hazlitt, W. (1964) "Sir Walter Scott," in *Lectures on the English Poets and the Spirit of the Age: or Contemporary Portraits*, intro. C. M. Maclean, Everyman's Library, London: Dent; New York: Dutton, pp. 223–34.

Hemlow, J. (1950) "Fanny Burney and the courtesy books," *PMLA* 65: 732–61.

Horwitz, B. (1989) "Lady Susan: the wicked mother in Jane Austen's work," in *Jane Austen's Beginnings: The Juvenilia and "Lady Susan,"* ed. J. D. Grey, Ann Arbor, MI and London: UMI Research Press, pp. 181–91.

Hudson, G. A. (1992) *Sibling Love and Incest in Jane Austen's Fiction*, New York: St. Martin's Press.

Iannone, C. (1988) "Feminism vs. literature," *Commentary* 86: 49–53.

Inglis-Jones, E. (1959) *The Great Maria: A Portrait of Maria Edgeworth*, London: Faber & Faber.

Jaeger, M. (1956) *Before Victoria*, London: Chatto & Windus.

Jeffares, A. N. (1982) *Anglo-Irish Literature*, Macmillan History of Literature, Dublin: Gill & Macmillan.

[Jeffrey, F.] (1812) Review of *Tales of Fashionable Life*, Vols. 4–6, by M. Edgeworth, *Edinburgh Review* 20: 100–26.

Johnson, C. L. (1988) *Jane Austen: Women, Politics, and the Novel*, Chicago and London: University of Chicago Press.

Jones, A. H. (1986) *Ideas and Innovations: Best-Sellers of Jane Austen's Age*, New York: AMS Press.

Kaplan, C. and Rose, E. C. (1990) *The Canon and the Common Reader*, Knoxville, TN: University of Tennessee Press.

Kermode, F. (1987) *History and Value*, the Clarendon Lectures and the Northcliffe Lectures 1987, Oxford: Clarendon Press.

Kernan, A. (1987) *Samuel Johnson and the Impact of Print*, Princeton, NJ: Princeton University Press.

Kirkham, M. (1983) *Jane Austen, Feminism, and Fiction*, Brighton, Sx: Harvester Press; Totowa, NJ: Barnes & Noble.

Kowaleski-Wallace, E. (1988) "Home economics: domestic ideology in Maria Edgeworth's *Belinda*," *The Eighteenth Century: Theory and Interpretation* 29: 242–62.

—— (1991) *Their Fathers' Daughters: Hannah More, Maria Edgeworth, and Patriarchal Complicity*, New York and Oxford: Oxford University Press.

Leavis, F. R. (1963) *The Great Tradition: George Eliot, Henry James, Joseph Conrad*, New York: New York University Press.

Lindenberger, H. (1990) *The History in Literature: On Value, Genre, Institutions*, New York: Columbia University Press.

Linkin, H. K. (1991) "The current canon in British Romantics studies," *College English* 53: 548–70.

McCormack, W. J. (1985) *Ascendancy and Tradition in Anglo-Irish Literary History from 1789 to 1939*, Oxford: Clarendon Press, pp. 97–122.

MacDonagh, O. (1991) *Jane Austen: Real and Imagined Worlds*, New Haven, CT and London: Yale University Press.

MacIntyre, A. (1981) *After Virtue: A Study in Moral Theory*, Notre Dame, IN: University of Notre Dame Press.

McKendrick, N., Brewer, J., and Plumb, J. H. (1982) *The Birth of a Consumer Society: The Commercialization of Eighteenth-Century England*, Bloomington, IN: Indiana University Press.

Marchand, L. A. (ed.) (1973) *Byron's Letters and Journals*, Vol. 2, 1810–12, *"Famous In My Time,"* London: John Murray.

—— (ed.) (1974) *Byron's Letters and Journals*, Vol. 3, 1813–14, *"Alas! The Love of Women!"* London: John Murray.

—— (ed.) (1977) *Byron's Letters and Journals*, Vol. 7, 1820, *"Between Two Worlds,"* Cambridge, MA: Belknap Press of Harvard University Press.

—— (ed.) (1978) *Byron's Letters and Journals*, Vol. 8, 1821, *"Born for Opposition,"* Cambridge, MA: Belknap Press of Harvard University Press.

—— (ed.) (1979) *Byron's Letters and Journals*, Vol. 9, 1821–2, *"In the Wind's Eye,"* Cambridge, MA: Belknap Press of Harvard University Press.

McCormack, W. J. (1985) *Ascendancy and Tradition in Anglo–Irish Literary History from 1789 to 1939*, Oxford: Clarendon Press, pp. 97–122.

Miller, N. K. (1988) "Men's reading, women's writing: gender and the rise of the novel," *"The Politics of Tradition: Placing Women in French Literature"* issue ed. J. Dejean and N. K. Miller, *Yale French Studies* 75: 40–55.

Moore, G. (1926) *Avowals*, New York: Boni & Liveright.

Morgan, S. (1989) *Sisters in Time: Imagining Gender in Nineteenth-Century British Fiction*, New York and Oxford: Oxford University Press.

Munday, M. (1982) "The novel and its critics in the early nineteenth century," *Studies in Philology* 79: 205–26.

Myers, M. (1982) "Reform or ruin: 'A revolution in female manners,' " in *Studies in Eighteenth-Century Culture*, ed. Harry C. Payne, Madison, WI: University of Wisconsin Press, 11: 119–216.

Newby, P. H. (1950) *Maria Edgeworth*, English Novelists series, London: Arthur Barker.

Newman, G. (1987) *The Rise of English Nationalism, A Cultural History 1740–1830*, New York: St. Martin's Press.

Newton, J. L. (1981) *Women, Power, and Subversion: Social Strategies in British Fiction, 1778–1860*, Athens, GA: University of Georgia Press.

"North, Christopher" [Lockhart, J. G.] (1831) "Noctes Ambrosianae: No. 58," *Blackwood's Edinburgh Magazine* 30: 531–64.

"On the female literature of the present age," (1820) *New Monthly Magazine* 13: 271–5, 633–8.

Owens, C. (ed.) (1987) *Family Chronicles: Maria Edgeworth's "Castle Rackrent,"* the Appraisal Series, Dublin: Wolfhound Press.

Patey, D. L. (1988) "The eighteenth century invents the canon," *Modern Language Studies* 18: 17–37.

[Peabody, W. B. O.] (1831) Review of the *Waverley Novels*, by W. Scott, *North American Review* 32: 386–421.

Perkins, D. (1990) "The construction of 'the Romantic movement' as a literary classification," *Nineteenth-Century Literature* 45: 129–43.

—— (1992) *Is Literary History Possible?*, Baltimore, MD and London: Johns Hopkins University Press.

Pictet, M.-A. (1802) "Letter VII" *Bibliothèque britannique* 19: 77–108.

Poovey, M. (1984) *The Proper Lady and the Woman Writer: Ideology as Style in the Works of Mary Wollstonecraft, Mary Shelley, and Jane Austen*, Chicago and London: University of Chicago Press.

Quinlan, M. J. (1941) *Victorian Prelude: A History of English Manners 1700–1830*, Hamden, CT: Archon Books; reprinted 1965.

Rafroidi, P. (1972) *Irish Literature in English: The Romantic Period (1789–1950)*, Gerrards Cross, Bucks: Colin Smythe; reprinted 1980.

Rendall, J. (1985) *The Origins of Modern Feminism: Women in Britain, France, and the United States 1780–1860*, London: Macmillan.

Roberts, W. (1979) *Jane Austen and the French Revolution*, New York: St. Martin's Press.

Robinson, H. C. (1938) *Henry Crabb Robinson on Books and Their Writers*, ed. E. J. Morley, 3 vols., London: J. M. Dent.

Ruoff, G. W. (1987) "1800 and the future of the novel: William Wordsworth, Maria Edgeworth, and the vagaries of literary History," in *The Age of William Wordsworth: Critical Essays on the Romantic Tradition*, ed. K. R. Johnson and G. W. Ruoff, New Brunswick, NJ and London: Rutgers University Press, pp. 291–314.

Sampson, G. (1961) *The Concise Cambridge History of English Literature*, 2nd edn., Cambridge: Cambridge University Press.

Samuel, R. (ed.) (1989) *Patriotism: The Making and Unmaking of British National Identity*, Vol. 1, *History and Politics*, History Workshop series, London and New York: Routledge.

Scott, Sir Walter (1894) *Familiar Letters of Sir Walter Scott*, ed. D. D[ouglas], 2 vols., Boston MA:, Houghton Mifflin.

—— (1972) *Waverley*, ed. Andrew Hook, Harmondsworth, Mx: Penguin.

Sedgwick, E. K. (1991) "Jane Austen and the masturbating girl," *Critical Inquiry* 17: 818–37.

Shine, H. and Shine, H. C. (1949) *The Quarterly Review under Gifford: Identification of Contributors 1809–24*, Chapel Hill, NC: University of North Carolina Press.

Simons, J. (1987) *Fanny Burney*, Women Writers series, Totowa, NJ: Barnes & Noble.

Siskin, C. (1988) *The Historicity of Romantic Discourse*, New York and Oxford: Oxford University Press.

Sloan, B. (1987) *The Pioneers of Anglo-Irish Fiction 1800–1850*, Irish Literary Studies 21, Totowa, NJ: Barnes & Noble.

Smith, B. H. (1984) "Contingencies of value," in *Canons*, ed. R. von Hallberg, Chicago and London: University of Chicago Press, pp. 5–39.

—— (1987) "Value/evaluation," *South Atlantic Quarterly* 86: 445–55.

Somerville, E. A. O. and Ross, M. (1925) *Irish Memories*, London: Longman, Green.

Southam, B. C. (ed.) (1968) *Jane Austen: The Critical Heritage*, London: Routledge & Kegan Paul; New York: Barnes & Noble.

"Special *Evelina* Issue" (July 1991) *Eighteenth-Century Fiction* 3, 4.

Spender, Dale (1986) *Mothers of the Novel: 100 Good Women Writers before Jane Austen*, London and New York: Pandora Press, pp. 270–300.

[Stephen, H. J. and Gifford, W.] (1809) Review of *Tales of Fashionable Life*, vols. 1–3, by M. Edgeworth, *Quarterly Review* 2: 146–54.

Stillinger, J. (1991) *Multiple Authorship and the Myth of Solitary Genius*, New York and Oxford: Oxford University Press.

Story, J. (1826) *A Discourse Pronounced before the Phi Beta Kappa Society*, Boston, MA: Hilliard, Gray, Little, & Wilkins.

Straub, K. (1987) *Divided Fictions: Fanny Burney and Feminine Strategy*, Lexington, KY: United Press of Kentucky.

Sulloway, A. G. (1989) *Jane Austen and the Province of Womanhood*, Philadelphia, PA: University of Pennsylvania Press.

Thomas, B. (1991) *The New Historicism and Other Old-Fashioned Topics*, Princeton, NJ: Princeton University Press.

Thompson, J. (1988) *Between Self and World: The Novels of Jane Austen*, University Park, PA and London: Pennsylvania State University Press.

Tomalin, C. (1974) *The Life and Death of Mary Wollstonecraft*, New York and London: Harcourt Brace Jovanovich.

Topliss, I. (1981) "Mary Wollstonecraft and Maria Edgeworth's modern ladies" *Études Irlandaises* 6: 13–31.

Trilling, L. (1959) *The Opposing Self: Nine Essays in Criticism*, New York: Viking Press.

Tuchman, G. with Fortin, N. E. (1989) *Edging Women Out: Victorian Novelists, Publishers, and Social Change*, New Haven, CT and London: Yale University Press.

Voss–Clesly, P. (1979) *Tendencies of Character Depiction in the Domestic Novels of Burney, Edgeworth, and Austen: A Consideration of Subjective and Objective World*, Salzburg Studies in English Literature 95, 3 vols., Salzburg, Austria: Universität Salzburg.

Ward, J. W. (1905) *Letters to "Ivy" from the First Earl of Dudley*, ed. S. H. Romilly, London: Longman, Green.

Watt, I. (1962) *The Rise of the Novel: Studies in Defoe, Richardson, and Fielding*, Berkeley and Los Angeles, CA: University of California Press.

Weekes, A. O. (1990) *Irish Women Writers: An Uncharted Tradition*, Lexington, KY: University Press of Kentucky.

[Whately, R.] (1821) "Modern novels," review of *Northanger Abbey* and *Persuasion*, by J. Austen, *Quarterly Review* 24: 352–76.

Will, G. F. (1991) "Literary politics," *Newsweek* (April 22): 72.

Yeats, W. B. (1891) Introduction, *Representative Irish Tales*, ed. M. H. Thuente, Atlantic Highlands, NJ: Humanities Press; reprinted 1979.

Part III

Consumption and the modern state

12
Polygamy, *Pamela*, and the prerogative of empire

Felicity A. Nussbaum

Nay, don't give us India. That puts me in mind of Montesquieu, who is really a fellow of genius too in many respects; whenever he wants to support a strange opinion, he quotes you the practice of Japan or of some other distant country, of which he knows nothing. To support polygamy, he tells you of the island of Formosa, where there are ten women born for one man. He had to suppose another island, where there are ten men born for one woman, and so make a marriage between them.

(Samuel Johnson in Boswell's *The Journal of
a Tour of the Hebrides* [1785])

I

"Africa is indeed coming into fashion," Horace Walpole wrote to Sir Horace Mann in July 1774 upon James Bruce's return from Abyssinia. In January 1799 Mungo Park's *Travels in the Interior Districts of Africa* was a best-seller.[1] Its 1,500 copies sold out within a few months, and three other editions were issued before the end of the year. Translated into French and German and published in an American edition as well, the book testified to the appetite for consuming Africa, including its representations, its raw goods, and its human commodity, slaves. As Robin Hallett has written, "By 1750 no countryhouse library could be reckoned complete without one of those great multi-volumed *Collections of Travels*,"[2] and Africa, the unknown continent, nearly always figured prominently in these collections (Plate 12.1). European ignorance about West Africa persisted until increased trade prompted penetration beyond the coast, and Mungo Park's narrative especially sparked the imagination of layperson and merchant, scientist and missionary. Joseph Banks, himself a voyager and the treasurer of the African Association, wrote that Park had opened a road "for every nation to enter and extend its commerce and discovery from the west to the eastern side of that immense continent."[3] And the preface to a book which was part of Joseph Banks's library, *A New*

Voyage to Guinea (1744), acknowledges that it aims to satisfy the public's appetite for the foreign: "The present Curiosity of the Publick for whatever may contribute to the rendring the Produce of distant Countries and the Manners of Foreign Nations, fully and certainly known, was what encourag'd the Publication of this Work. . . . There is no part of the World with which we are less acquainted than the interior Part of *Africa*."[4] Willem Bosman anticipated these ideas in his voyage to New Guinea written earlier in the century: "But 'twas an ancient Saying among the Romans, that *Africa* always produces something *New*; and to this day the Saying is very just."[5] Africa and its products, material and human, sold well in the expanding market, and it was regarded as a welcome producer of the new and the novel.

These travel accounts encouraged commerce deep into the unmapped interior, and European manufactures were sent to West Africa in exchange for African slave labor in the Americas. As was characteristic of the larger print world in the eighteenth century, explorers' accounts were seldom dependent on patronage for publication and more exactly aimed at writing for an anonymous market.[6] As "Africa" was invented and consumed, its description in the printed word gained a commodity status. Africa was increasingly included in the extraordinarily popular collections of travels in spite of the fact that the same accounts were often simply reprinted or slightly altered before Park's monumental voyages are undertaken at the end of the century. Compelling information or fantasy, recycled as new, produced the desire for more such travel narratives and novels, even though very little new information emerged after the travels of Labat in 1725 and Moore in 1738, apparently because the urge to exploit Africa's wealth was not sufficient to overcome the obstacles to penetration.[7] Though the struggle for power over West Africa (colonized by the Portuguese, French, English, and Dutch) was intense in the eighteenth century, Africa's interior remained largely unmapped by Europeans. In short, the commercial market, especially in the mid- and late eighteenth century, gave evidence of a passion to consume the unknown and uncharted, the "new" blank space of Africa.

When the human object of obtaining something "new" from Africa speaks, however, in the case of Ignatius Sancho, an African living in England, it is with incredulity, anger, and contempt for the misuse of his land and people. Sancho writes in his letters (1782):

> The grand object of English navigators – is money – money – money – for which I do not pretend to blame them – Commerce attended with strict honesty – and with Religion for its companion – would be a blessing to every shore it touched at. – [but] In Africa, the poor wretched natives – blessed with the most fertile and luxuriant soil – are rendered so much the more miserable for what Providence meant as a blessing: – The Christians' abominable traffic for slaves – and the horrid cruelty and treachery of the petty Kings – encouraged by their Christian customers. . . . But enough – it is a subject that sours my blood.[8]

The European pleasure in consuming Africa exacted a high cost, and its apparent "blankness" to the European eye veiled massive human suffering.

Here I want to consider one aspect of those power relations between nations, specifically the consumption of the Other. I mean to define this Other woman both geographically and sexually – that is, the African woman who is the " 'other' of the 'other,' "[9] doubly colonized, *and* the other woman of polygamy, women at home and abroad who make others of each other in competition for the male prize. Focusing on women and polygamy as central terms in the eighteenth century provides an alternative way to analyze the connections between England and its empire.

Polygamy is constituted by a multiplicity of practices that may set women against each other or, contradictorily, may bond them together in collective pleasure or to their mutual benefit. In the eighteenth century polygamy was defined variously as a husband's taking more than one wife, as his marrying after the death of his first wife, and even as his seducing a woman while married to another and therefore being held responsible for her ruin. Johnson's *Dictionary* (1755) explains polygamy as "a plurality of wives," but polygamy may also mean simply having sexual commerce with more than one woman on an ongoing basis. As Caleb Fleming writes in *Oeconomy of the Sexes . . . the Plurality of Wives* (1751), "I shall use the term, *polygamy*, for a man's having more than one wife at one and the same time; without any regard to the term bigamy or digamy [a second legal marriage after the death of the first spouse]: because monogamy be transgressed, for the same reason that a man has two wives, he might have twenty."[10] Here I will explore some of the profound historical contradictions that emerge when polygamy, a crux of desire and domination, is invoked in British travel narratives of West Africa, the polygamy tracts of eighteenth-century England, and Samuel Richardson's *Pamela* II. England's national imperative to manipulate control of women's sexuality in the later eighteenth century derives in part from the increasing demands of colonization, and polygamy serves as a crux to negotiate the erotic and the exotic.

In spite of the century's passion to create taxonomies of the species and maps of colonial territories, the Other can never be fully "known" except in reference to the self. If imperialism uses the Other to consolidate the imperialist self, the Other also consolidates the European woman. The domestic monogamous Englishwoman who personifies chaste maternal womanhood frequently contrasts to the wanton polygamous Other. "Colonial power produces the colonized as a fixed reality which is at once an 'other' and yet entirely knowable and visible," Homi Bhabha argues.[11] The European woman is in large part represented by travel narratives rather than a speaking subject herself. But the African woman is even less likely than the Englishwoman to speak for herself. Africa is frequently, of course, visually figured as a naked woman, a scorched mother under the heat of the sun, flanked by devil and lion, carrying gifts to Europe, a pharoah's head and pyramids in the background, and tropical trees behind.[12] Certainly "Africa" was invented for European consumption in the eighteenth century, but what has been less recognized is the way in which the African *woman* (and other women of empire) were invented as well as made coherent and consistent, yet represented as inscrutable and sexually polymorphous in relation to the European domestic woman. "Woman," like other colonial territories, is treated as something to be defined, charted, probed, exploited, and overcome. Metaphors of seduction, penetration, and conquest permeate the language of colonialism to tame the wild exotic and the imagined unbridled sexuality of the Other.

Discussions of polygamy in England were nearly as common as discussions of divorce because of its religious and political implications, and notables such as William

Cowper, Lord Chancellor of England, defended polygamy in order to vindicate his own *ménage à trois*. Bishop Burnet, Bernardino Ochino, Lord Bolingbroke, Patrick Delany, and the deists also took up the pressing questions surrounding the timely issue.[13] In *Reflections upon Polygamy* (1737) the pseudonymous P. Dubliniensis writes, "Polygamy is a doctrine daily defended in conversation, and often in print, by a great variety of *plausible* arguments.[14] One popular pamphlet compares polygamous practices in England to participating in a seraglio: "Polygamy, according to the *spirit* of the law, is still punishable; but the *dead letter* lets it every day escape with impunity. There was a time when a man, who openly kept one mistress, though a bachelor, was considered as a very bad man; but a man of fashion now should be ashamed of not keeping three or four mistresses, even under the nose of his wife."[15] In England the issues focused on establishing scriptural authority for or against polygamy, as well as determining whether seduced women would significantly benefit from it.

Polygamy is often treated in remarkably benign ways in the African travel accounts written before missionary zeal began to preach monogamy as a tenet of civilization. John Millar's treatise draws distinctions between polygamy in "opulent and luxurious nations" and in "barbarous countries." In the former women are reduced to slavery by polygamous practices. Further, children are so numerous that paternal affection is severely diminished, wives demonstrate great jealousy amongst each other, and they are strictly regulated by the father/husband. On the contrary "in barbarous countries, where it is introduced to a great measure from motives of conveniency, and where it is accompanied with little or no jealousy, it cannot have the same consequences."[16] According to Millar, when combined with luxury polygamy is clearly destructive to women but the terms of evaluating it differ in "barbarous" countries.

The popular African narratives nearly always mention polygamy or, in a few instances, its remarkable absence. Most notable is Olaudah Equiano who reports of his native Ibo tribe that "The men . . . do not preserve the same constancy to their wives, which they expect from them; for they indulge in a plurality, though seldom in more than two."[17] Jerom Merolla da Sorrento comments about the Congo that "Every one of these Negroes takes to wife as many women, be they slaves or free, it is no matter, as he can possibly get: these women, by his consent, make it their business to charm men to their embraces." Moore and Stibbs remark that every man may take as many wives as he wishes, even up to a hundred, in the Gambia, and Barbot says that "as many wives as he can keep" enhances a Guinean man's reputation. Grazilhier comments that every man in Guinea "may have as many Wives as he pleases." William Smith reports that men may take as many wives as they want in Barbary, as many as they can maintain in Cape Monte, that there is much polygamy in Dahomy, and that wives are a measure of status ranging from the ordinary man's 40–50 to the king's 4,000–5,000. He believes, following Alexander and Millar, that such practices are vestiges of an earlier time.[18] Sometimes distinctions between wives and concubines are reported, though not always. In some instances, polygamy is presented as commercially sound, and the wives are treated as inheritable property. The women work excessively hard in the field and in the bed, and all the wives except the rich man's foremost two, may prostitute themselves to other men. In other cases, a wife's infidelity is grounds for selling her to the Europeans.

William Smith's *Voyage to Guinea* follows the popular assumption that African women are excessively sexual, the climate rendering the African coast and interior a torrid zone:

> As for all the rest, they may be accounted little better than his Slaves, never-theless they live in Peace together without envying each other's Happiness, and he in their Turns, renders to them all, if able, due Benevolence: But if that be not sufficient for those hot constitution'd Ladies, they very well know how to supply such Defects elsewhere, without fearing any check from the Husband, who generally makes himself easy in those Cases, provided he duly receives such Profits.
>
> (Smith, *A New Voyage to Guinea*, p. 146)

According to Paul Lovejoy's recent findings, women slaves for export apparently cost up to one third more than men in spite of the greater supply of women. Lovejoy's explanation for this disparity is that women are in greater demand as sexual objects: "The extraction of surplus labour is certainly a factor in explaining why the price of female slaves was greater than that for males. . . . Women worked hard at most tasks, and sometimes they could be made to work harder than males. But women's 'work' also included sexual services."[19]

William Smith also comments that polygamy helped propagate sufficient numbers for slavery and allowed explorers to take sexual advantage of the indigenous population – "a man sometimes in one Day [may] . . . have Half a Dozen Children born to him" (p. 202) because polygamous men do not cohabit with pregnant or menstruous wives. Francis Moore writes of his witnessing the apparent willingness of Gambian women: "The Girls would have People think they are very modest, especially when they are in Company; but take them by themselves, and they are very obliging . . . if any White Man has a Fancy to any of them, and is able to maintain them, they will make no Scruple of living with him in the Nature of a Wife, without the Ceremony of Matrimony" (p. 121). Smith adds, "Most of the Women are publick Whores to the *Europeans*, and private ones to the *Negroes*" (p. 213). The women "miss no Opportunity [for sex, he writes], and are continually contriving stratagems how to gain a Lover. If they meet with a Man they immediately strip his lower Parts, and throw themselves upon him, protesting that if he will not gratify their Desires, they will accuse him to their Husbands" (p. 221). Claiming this kind of seduction, Smith of course takes an African woman for his own. Polygamy, Smith suggests, varies not so greatly from European practices under the guise of courtship: "We often spend several Years therin [*sic*; in courtship]; in which we at one Time, address this young Woman, write to that, and keep criminal Conversation with a Third" (p. 260). Smith elides the differences among sexual practices, and his point is to show the superiority of Europeans while allowing for the strange excellence of "savage" ways. Smith concludes his account with a description of a paradisial liaison: "At Midnight we went to Bed, and in that Situation I soon forgot the Complexion of my Bedfellow, and obey'd the Dictates of all-powerful Nature. Greater Pleasure I never found" (p. 254). Portraying African women, especially the wives of other men, as unabashedly seductive and unclaimed for mono-gamy provided a legitimating rationale for European travelers who were impregnating African women and fathering illegitimate children of mixed race.

The sexual traffic between European men and African women is much remarked upon in the British travel voyages, as is the troubling question of color. For John Barbot too the women of Guinea are also proud and lascivious, seeking to attract Europeans even at a small profit: "such manner as might prove sufficiently tempting to many lewd *Europeans*; who not regarding complexions, say, *all cats are grey in the dark*" (p. 239). (Barbot also notes that most Europeans keep three or four women "as if they were marry'd to them" [36].) This trope of the European male congratulating himself for ignoring the color of his female bedmate in the dark is common in these accounts. Color is very much on the minds of the travelers who give fantastic reports of spotted or mottled women, children who are half black and half white, twins in which one is black and the other white, and children born white who turn tawny or black in a matter of time, all presented as accurate history. Male sexual desire erases the color of the bedfellow, and men's sexual oppression of women is justified by their assertion of the absence of racism. Similarly the issue of polygamy becomes grimly relevant when we remember that white slaveowners participated in unacknowledged polygamy and used the slave woman's womb for increasing slave population. Harriet Jacobs's *Incidents in the Life of a Slave Girl*, though written in the nineteenth century, gives voice to a slave woman's perspective: "Southern [white] women often marry a [white] man knowing that he is the father of many little slaves. They do not trouble themselves about it. They regard such children as property, as marketable as the pigs on the plantation."[20] In short, one threat of public polygamy is that it makes legal and visible that which has occurred all along – serial monogamy and especially adultery by white men who claim African women as their sexual property and who wish to bring to market their progeny in such unions. Polygamy is further justified as a practical solution to slavery's disruption of family life in *Some Historical Account of Guinea, Its Situation, Produce, and the General Disposition of its Inhabitants with an Inquiry into the Rise and Progress of the Slave Trade* (1788) when male slaves are wrenched from their wives and children and taken to another state.

In Henry Neville's popular erotic novella *The Isle of Pines*, the political rule of the polygamous protagonist is also a sexual monopoly.[21] First published in 1668, reissued thirty times during the eighteenth century and translated into six languages, the novella recounts the prince's tale of shipwreck and his being left with four women. His polygamous relationship with all of them repopulates the island. Polygamy here is figured as male magnanimity in spreading the sexual wealth to his sex-starved female companions. He writes:

> Idleness and Fulness of every thing begot in me a desire of enjoying the women, beginning now to grow more familiar, I had perswaded two Maids to let me lie with them, which I did at first in private, but after, custome taking away shame (there being none but us) we did it more openly, as our Lusts gave us liberty; afterwards my Masters Daughter was content also to do as we did; the truth is they were all handsome Women when they had Cloathes, and well shaped, feeding well. For we wanted no Food, and living idly, and seeing us at Liberty to do our wills, without hope of ever returning home made us thus bold.

(Neville, *The Isle of Pines*, p. 12)

Racial difference becomes something to reckon with, though class seems less significant:

> One of the first of my Consorts with whom I first accompanied (the tallest and
> handsomest) proved presently with child, the second was my Masters
> Daughter, and the other also not long after fell into the same condition: none
> now remaining but my *Negro* who seeing what we did, longed also for her
> share; one Night, I being asleep, my *Negro*, (with the consent of the others) got
> close to me. . . . I [he continues] willing to try to difference, satisfied my self
> with her.
>
>   (Ibid.)

The shipwrecked group enacts the ultimate male fantasy as the women become the
breeders and the protagonist a stud: "So that in the year of our being here, all my
women were with child by me, and they all coming at different seasons, were a great
help to one another" (p. 12). The women produce the community of workers he needs
to populate the island. Race and class, subordinate to fulfilling the fantasy of male
sexual desire and voyeurism, are erased as the sexually available women become
interchangeable in the hero's mind. These and other discourses of polygamy locate the
libidinal energy needed to colonize the Other in the body of the woman.

Polygamy in these travel narratives works both as a male fantasy and as an economic
rationale for dealing efficiently with excess women. Eroticizing having more than one
wife tends to obscure polygamy's economic uses. If one considers these matters within
the context of nascent empire, rather than simply the English domestic scene, Martin
Madan's massive 1780 vindication of polygamy, ostensibly written to protect seduced
women, becomes nuanced in surprising ways.[22] Those who argue in defense of polygamy, and those who argue against it, often claim to have the women's interests at
heart. Madan, William Cowper's cousin, incited a controversy of over two dozen
responses. Madan's ill-received book espouses the views published a decade before by
his great-uncle, Lord Chancellor Cowper. In spite of his having been an enormously
popular preacher, Madan was forced to resign as the chaplain of the Lock Hospital
because of the resulting controversy.

Madan's *Thelyphthora* proposes polygamy as a serious solution to an epidemic of
seduction or female ruin. Polygamy in England would be a means to deal with excess
females and to dispose of their living carcasses that simply become wastage after sexual
consumption. In the explorers' accounts as well as in the English pamphlets a kind of
litany arises concerning the loss of control over female sexuality, and it is particularly
troublesome in its *public* manifestations. Prostitutes are visible everywhere: "our streets
abound with prostitutes and our stews with harlots at present" and the crimes of
adultery and *seduction* are grown to an enormous height."[23] Richard Hill believed that
Madan's proposal would actually *increase* the number of prostitutes. "Prostitutes swarm
in the streets of this metropolis to such a degree," wrote Saunders Welch, "and bawdy-
houses are kept in such an open and public manner, to the great scandal of our civil
polity, that a stranger would think that such practices, instead of being prohibited had
the sanction of the legislature, and that the whole town was one general stew."[24]
Polygamy resolves "the woman problem," and is a way to deal with the public
embarrassment of unmarried and ruined women who show themselves in the street.

Yet *Thelyphthora* was paradoxically crucial in fixing the monogamous family and in claiming private property. Madan proposes to control women's superfluity of desire in the purported cause of alleviating women's oppression, while those who opposed him also cited emergent feminist sentiments in defense of women's investment in monogamy.

Another important justification for polygamy is to relieve the sexual deprivation of men, especially when eighteenth-century middle-class Englishwomen are being urged to suckle their own children for long periods of time. As is well known, the practice of women's nursing their children, rather than giving them over to a wetnurse, was firmly reinstituted during the eighteenth century. Sexual intercourse was discouraged during nursing as spoiling the milk, men's sexual deprivation became the object of concern, and sexuality was separated from maternity. (Not surprisingly, the question of women's sexual deprivation during this time seldom arose.) These matters became subject to comment when British voyagers represented foreign practices as exemplary or instructive to Englishwomen. John Matthews, for example, in his *A Voyage to the River Sierra-Leone* (1788) commends the domesticity and attentive maternity of the African women: "They never wean their children till they are able to walk . . . for, during the time a child is at the breast, the woman is not permitted to cohabit with her husband, as they suppose it would be prejudicial to her milk."[25]

David Hume's essay on the subject, while it finally argues against polygamy, also treats polygamy as potentially releasing men from their extreme passions for women by allowing them to indulge them to the fullest.[26] Hume openly acknowledges the political nature of sexual mores. Dividing and conquering the women who quarrel for his favors, the polygamist resembles a sovereign who politically manipulates one group against another in order to maintain his power. By analogy then, the best ruler is the monogamist who maintains authority over his wife because he need not confront the difficulties of conflicts between wives or of one faction against another. Similarly Mungo Park in his *Travels in the Interior Districts of Africa* sets up a paradigm of benevolent colonialism through the metaphor of polygamy. Park observes that husbands hold complete command, but the wives do not resent it, and in fact remain cheerful and compliant. The husband is not cruel, but the community supports his right to mete out punishment. Polygamy encourages women to quarrel, and the husband rules, judges, and punishes. "When the [African] wives quarrel among themselves, a circumstance which, from the nature of their situation, must frequently happen, the husband decides between them; and sometimes finds it necessary to administer a little corporal chastisement," he writes. In these public hearings, the wife's complaint is seldom taken seriously, and if she protests "the magic rod of *Mumbo Jumbo* soon puts an end to the business."[27]

The British travelers in Africa and elsewhere had considerable investment in reporting that polygamy was completely acceptable to the women involved. As I will show, women's resistance within polygmamy is possible; it may have encouraged female companionship and allowed an excess population of women to be protected through marriage, but it seems especially tied to patriarchal practices in most of its manifestations. England's toying with and ultimate rejection of polygamy near the end of the eighteenth century is part of the nation's defining itself both as distinct from and as morally superior to the polygamous Other. Monogamy is instituted as part of England's national definition, and whatever practices its explorers might find to tempt them in other worlds, England asserts its public stance that marriage means one man, one wife, at least in law. As David Hume writes, "The exclusion of polygamy and divorces sufficiently recommends our present European practice with regard to marriage" (p. 195). Yet polygamy of one sort or another is common practice in eighteenth-century England.

II

I want to turn now to Richardson's *Pamela* II (1741) as a local instance of the tensions between women set in play to sustain monogamy's public face before turning finally to three Englishwomen's views of the Other woman. In Richardson's hastily composed sequel to the popular *Pamela*, *Pamela* II, a penchant for polygamy is one of Mr. B's tendencies. By "polygamy" Mr. B seems to mean an adulterous affair – sexual relations with more than one woman – and the tantalizing possibility of keeping both available to him. *Pamela* II is a response to the commodification of *Pamela* I and the need to purchase another when the first has been consumed. According to Richardson's biographers Eaves and Kimpel, "By January 1741 the whole town had read *Pamela* I and by the summer Richardson had determined to write a sequel to counter a spurious continuation."[28] The first version, like the first wife, is somehow not sufficient to the desire – though of course Pamela proves her virtue and sufficiency at the cost of the sauciness that enlivened and complicated Part I. The Pamela of the sequel, an Other woman to Mr. B's countess, works out the difficulties of the other woman on the domestic terrain but the polygamous woman abroad is remarkable for her absence from the novel and its sequel. Pamela II is as unchanging in her maternal virtue as the Pamela of the first part is volatile, maddening, and uncertain in her sexuality. Part II, as Terry Castle has shown, offers "a paradoxical kind of textual doubling" to its predecessor.[29] Part II revises and refutes Part I's empowering of Pamela and places her within a more familiar sexual traffic in which women are a form of exchange between men. Pamela II, a polygamous second wife to Mr. B, is a realization of the driving fantasy of providing different women for different functions. In *Pamela* I this was already displayed in Mr. B's liaison with Sally Godfrey and manifested in the embodiment of his illegitimate daughter. In *Pamela* II Mr. B meets Pamela's demand for breast-feeding with his own threat of "that vile word *polygamy*."[30] This debate centers on Pamela's belief that it is her natural duty, and thus a divine duty, to nurse her child, but "if the husband is set upon it [wetnursing] it is a wife's duty to obey" (III. 48). Appealing to scriptural, legal, medical, natural, and parental authority, she musters considerable argument to insist on her duty to the child. To do otherwise, she believes, would be to indulge in "the sin of committing that task to others, which is so right to be performed by one's self" (III. 50). But Mr. B defines the question as one of hierarchy and priority – is the husband's will to be honored as superior to divine or natural law? How much authority over his wife does a husband have? Pamela wonders to her friend Miss Darnford, "Could you ever have thought, my dear, that husbands, have dispensing power over their wives, which kings are not allowed over the laws?" (III.5). Male sexual desire is encoded as male sexual prerogative boldly intertwined with the political. Mr. B's sovereignty rests on his authority over Pamela.

In the sequel Pamela (Mrs. B) becomes the ideal wife who limits the demands of maternity in order to remain sexually available to her husband. The wetnurse assumes those aspects of the maternal which threaten Mr. B's sexual prerogative, and she keeps the two functions of the breast distinct. Pamela is tormented everywhere she turns by other women who are under Mr. B's control: he flirts with Pamela's nemesis, the countess, with whom he travels, dallies, and converses in Italian. Pamela daily confronts a reminder of Mr. B's sexual liaison with Sally Godfrey in the presence of their child Miss Goodwin; and Pamela herself is confined within Mr. B's increasingly intense strictures to submit her will to him. No longer the feisty Pamela of the first book who can withstand male prerogative, she decorously withdraws into the tempering of her "self."

For Mr. B the issue of breast-feeding involves both class privilege and male prerogative.[31] He wishes to prevent Pamela's descending to her origins. He fears that she will become "an insipid, prattling nurse . . . a fool and a baby herself" (III.56) absorbed in the nursery instead of learning French and Latin. Calling on patriarchal authorities, Mr. B teases Pamela with the threat of polygamy but then retreats: "The laws of one's own country are a sufficient objection to me against polygamy: at least, I will not think of any more wives till you convince me, by your adherence to the example given you by the patriarch wives, that I ought to follow those of the patriarch husbands" (III.53).[32] When Pamela intones, "*Polygamy* and *prerogative*! Two very bad words! I do not love them," Mr. B demands that she ought to be angelic about the matter rather than a "mere woman" who despises competition from other women.

Until Pamela becomes pregnant in *Pamela* II, there is little to say about the virtuous domestic married woman, no story to be told. Polygamy seems to be inextricably linked to pregnancy as an assertion of male prerogative when men find themselves faced with the female authority that women's pregnancy releases: "For ladies in your way," Mr. B argues, "are often like encroaching subjects: They are apt to extend what they call their privileges, on the indulgence showed them; and the husband never again recovers the ascendant he had before" (III.63). Pregnancy paradoxically enables her to invade his "province." Mr. B's patriarchal retort here and elsewhere is a physical reminder of his authority: a tap on her neck as he says, "Let me beat my beloved saucebox." Later Mr. B commands, "Speak it at once, or I'll be angry with you; and tapped my cheek" (III.153). The community of readers, just as in the case of Mungo Park's Africa, supports the husband's right to mete out physical punishment and to regulate the women who quarrel over him.

For Pamela, the question concerns a woman's authority over her own body, her child, and her will, and she perseveres though Mr. B finds her saucy and perverse: "Upon my word, he sometimes, for argument's sake, makes a body think a wife should not have the least will of her own. He sets up a dispensing power, in short, although he knows that the doctrine once cost a prince his crown" (III.53). Her parents do not hear her plea: "But do you take it *indeed*, that a husband has such a vast prerogative?" (III.56). Pamela succumbs, and the two are reconciled. But Mr. B has been duplicitous throughout the sequel in becoming involved with the countess who is dressed as a bold Italian nun at the masquerade even though the reader is encouraged to believe that they indulged only in a harmless platonic flirtation. Mr. B expresses the longing upon which monogamous marriage in the eighteenth century is based, the longing that *love* will mask the power relations that guarantee male prerogative.

Mr. B's alleged affair with the countess occurs near the time of Pamela's first lying-in. The rest of the novel is, after all, about polygamy, the production of a redundance of female desire directed towards Mr. B, and the regulation of that desire. Mr. B is able to take plural "wives" in the sense of one sexual Pamela and one maternal Pamela, but also more literally a former chambermaid and a countess. The sympathetic Lady Davers reports to Pamela, "What vexes me is, that when the noble uncle of this vile lady [the countess]. . . . expostulated with her on the scandals she brought upon her character and family, she pretended to argue, foolish creature! for polygamy; and said, "She had rather be a certain gentleman's second wife, than the first to the greatest man in England" (III.171). The wily Pamela who had survived the wicked Mrs. Jewkes now finds herself a meek domestic cowering at the prospect of meeting her nemesis, the countess. Again as in the first volume, the reader remains uncertain if Pamela is overreacting. If *Pamela* I has links with pornography, *Pamela* II roots out the connection between debauchery and male tyranny to foster benevolent monogamy.

Mr. B literally plays the two women off against each other in arranging for them to meet. The countess excels at the harpsichord when each plays, and her equestrian skills are also reported to be superior to those of the class-bound Pamela. Seldom is a comparison between women so blatant except in misogynous satire. Mr. B reports the countess's questioning concerning the superiority of face, hair, forehead, brows, complexion, eyes, cheek, nose, lips, smiles, teeth, chin, ears, but when he threatens to move lower, the lady calls a halt. No need, however, since the facial features may easily be read as codes for sexual parts.[33] In the second telling of this twice-told tale of the encounter between Pamela and the countess, the beauty contest between the "incomparable" ladies is made very particular:

> For black eyes in my girl, and blue in your ladyship, they are both the loveliest I ever beheld. – And, Pamela, I was wicked enough to say, that it would be the sweetest travelling in the world, to have you both placed at fifty miles distance from each other, and to pass the prime of one's life from black to blue, and from blue to black; and it would be impossible to know which to prefer, but the present.

> (III.229)

The countess cuffs him in response, and he "kissed her in revenge." Pamela cries out in disgust: "Fine doings between two Platonics!" which leads Mr. B again to exercise his physical authority and tap her neck. The former chambermaid and the countess, reduced to body parts as they compete for the polygamous male, are interchangeable women in spite of social class differences. Mr. B, like the weak sovereign of David Hume's essay "Of Polygamy," "must play one faction against another, and become absolute by the mutual jealousy of the females. *To divide and govern*, is an universal maxim" (p. 185). Hume says polygamy means male prerogative, male governance, and male authority. This enables us then to see the way masculine privilege is integrally connected to the territorial prerogative of empire. Pamela is Mr. B's territorial domain to conquer as the power relations of *Pamela* I are reversed, and she fully submits her will to his. Pamela wins out over the nobility through the display of her superior beauty and virtue, but we can imagine Mr. B's continuing to produce polygamous rivals throughout their marriage only to be once again chastened by the moral order of monogamy.

The progress of *Pamela* II reveals Mr. B's apparent libertinism yet supposed fidelity. In the unsatisfying resolution of the plot, Pamela rather than Mr. B is put on trial. The countess, it turns out, was quoted out of context, and the entire epistolary affair may now be reread and reinterpreted to free Mr. B from imputation. He unequivocally rejects polygamy as outside the bounds of his country. He claims that it was advanced only "in the levity of speech, and the wantonness of argument" (III. 223). In sum, *Pamela* II re-establishes an order in the world made topsy-turvy in *Pamela* I. It replaces the first Pamela with Pamela II, a maternal Pamela who strains at sexuality. One nursing breast is equal to another, one sexual organ substitutes for another. But Mr. B recognizes that polygamy is un-English. It is an exotic tease more suitable for masquerades than real life, and *Pamela* II becomes finally a triumphant assertion of monogamy at Mr. B's expense. Richardson, like Hume, seems to argue that the best ruler, in the home as well as the state, is the monogamist who does not need to pit factions against each other in order to maintain authority. He rules by the willing submission of woman's will which relies on her sexual competition with other women – her signaling her new class status by relinquishing nursing to the working-class woman, the Other.

Polygamy operates on two fronts at once – the domestic and the colonial. At home its imagined possibility maintains a husband's sovereignty over his wife's body and its parts by threatening to replace it with another female body. Yet to legalize its practice, even for the benevolent purpose of providing husbands for ruined women and taking up a surplus of useless women (as Martin Madan's *Thelyphthora* proposed), proves too disturbing for England's sense of itself as moral, Christian, western. On the colonial front, polygamy involves men's control of women as property. The colonizers penetrate and possess the African continent; they may also take pleasure in penetrating another man's property. The sovereign male, the counterpart to the woman who realizes her civic duty in mothering, freshly expresses his patriotism and his Englishness in public monogamy at home at the historical moment when private property and the monogamous family form are linked.[34] Mr. B's threats of philandering in order to prevent Pamela from breast-feeding their child play out on the domestic front the issues of maternity, sexuality, and male monogamy purchased through the profoundly tedious declaration that Pamela (and even quite literally her body) is his private possession. These apparently domestic issues have larger political implications in an emerging empire and help to define the differences between the European and its polygamous others – the African, the Indian, the Turk, and the Pacific Islanders. The use of the exotic for Mr. B, as in the passage from Montesquieu that Samuel Johnson cites in the epigraph to this chapter, is to make the strange practice of polygamy familiar. Thus Mr. B justifies polygamy to a credulous wife who, in ultimately refusing to accept Mr. B's Other woman and rejecting a foreign pollutant to her marriage, remains the firm moral center of the domestic English novel.

III

For the Englishwoman, the stance is even more intensely fraught with contradiction. In this context I want to turn briefly to three Englishwomen's responses to polygamy abroad: Anna Falconbridge, Lady Mary Wortley Montagu, and Mary Wollstonecraft. In tension with the cult of domesticity represented in *Pamela* is an increasingly strong female voice, readership, and authorship – a tension between empowerment and domestication. The profound historical contradiction revealed is that Africa and other countries of the emergent empire provided the justification for exotic practices, but also presented a threat that the Other may have been too similar for comfort to the European if the practice is justified and shared. The polygamous, sensualized, yet supposedly ugly African woman is produced as a contrast to the monogamous, domestic, and lovely Englishwoman. One effect is to de-politicize the bourgeois woman and to insist that the domestic sphere remains confined to its local region.

Falconbridge, Montagu, and Wollstonecraft, all women with feminist sentiments, voice both admiring and antagonistic reactions to women of empire. In this context we might well ask what use pitting women against each other in class, race, and national conflicts might serve at a time of emergent feminism, of newly rigidified differences between the sexes, and of the formation of empire. Both Falconbridge and Montagu focus on the female body of the Other in their accounts of polygamy, while Mary Wollstonecraft concerns herself instead with its social implications. In these three accounts the Other is the self displaced in a veiled and even skewed recognition of its own colonization under domestic patriarchy.

Anna Falconbridge, writing a narrative of her voyages to Sierra Leone where in 1791–3 she traveled with her Abolitionist husband, comments on how ususual it is for an Englishwoman to visit Africa.[35] In conversation with a Portuguese woman who envies Englishwomen, Falconbridge acknowledges her similarity to the European lady, their sameness and their mutual oppression: "I thanked her in behalf of my country women, for her good opinion, but assured her they had their share of thorns and thistles, as well as those of other countries" (p. 122). But her initial reaction to African women she finds there is to remark on her distance from them: "Seeing so many of my own sex, though of different complexions from myself, attired in their native garbs, was a scene equally new to me, and my delicacy, I confess, was not a little hurt at times" (p. 21). She champions "My own sex" yet considers their "different complexions"; she positions herself as the delicate and squeamish one, for they are not yet mapped in terms of gender because of the difference in color.

Falconbridge, like other travelers, locates racial difference in the fetishized breasts of the Other, the exposed breasts of the polygamous king's many wives. These breasts place the women in a conjunction of the sexual and maternal which is difficult, if not impossible, to reconcile in the Englishwoman, and the way she reconciles them in the African woman is by judging them to be aesthetically repellent. Breasts, like pudenda, mark racial differences between European and African women. Their breasts – large, long, stretched by nursing, "disgusting to Europeans," are reminiscent of the near constant invocation of the legendary Hottentot breasts which women supposedly threw over their shoulders for the comfort of the nursing child on their backs. Most of the women, Falconbridge believes, are attached as mistresses to the various English gentlemen, and their appearance of occupying "superior rank" stymies the conventional response of assuming their inferiority to her. Polygamy, she notes, "is considered honorable, and creates consequence" (p. 77).

When faced with these naked African women, Anna Falconbridge also records her frustration in attempting to convince Queen Clara, the first of the king's wives, to dress in the European manner. Instead she finds her "impetuous, litigious, and implacable" as Queen Clara tears the clothes off her back: "Finding no credit could be gained by trying to new fashion this *Ethiopian Princess*, I got rid of her as soon as possible" (p. 62). Falconbridge, attempting to wash the Ethiop white, resists the recognition that her body resembles the body for which she has contempt; the bond of the female body which transcends race is instead made the unmistakable marker of conflictual difference. The European woman's Other cannot logically possess a female body so Falconbridge wishes to rid herself of its sight and clothe it in the spoils of empire.

Lady Mary Wortley Montagu's Other is exotic and various in the Turkish Embassy letters of 1716–18 extracted in part from her journal and published after her death.[36] The preface by Mary Astell angrily dismisses men's travel narratives as inaccurate and "stuft with the same Trifles."[37] Unlike men's travel narratives, Montagu's remarkable letters probe the private women's quarters in Turkey and offer "a new path." Women travelers were contemptuous of exact descriptions from male travelers since men were unlikely to have been eye-witnesses to the private women's quarters. In Billie Melman's recent history of women travelers to the Middle East she writes. "The Third Court with its women's quarters and the quarters of black eunuchs were the most impenetrable territory in the Ottoman Empire and, before the nineteenth century, were hermetically sealed to adult males other than the Sultan himself, his sons and the black eunuchs."[38] European women travelers, disempowered by their gendered identification with the women confined, were empowered in their ability to describe a part of the world which could be conquered only by a woman's eye, and the seraglio invited the description of women by women as did few other sites.

In Montagu's vision of the Other, a romantic vision of 200 women of the Turkish baths, she admires their nude splendor and the nudity of the slaves who tend them, and they provoke her aesthetic and erotic pleasure, "their skins shineingly white" (I.314). She commends the ladies' "finest skins and most delicate shapes," and she wishes Mr. Gervase [Charles Jervas the portrait painter] could share her voyeur's attitude "to see so many fine Women naked in different postures, some in conversation, some working, others drinking Coffee." In bold contrast to usual notions of the female tea-party and other private domestic sites, Wortley Montagu conjures up a vision of female community. She remarks on their resistance to mutual disdain and backbiting: "In short, tis the Women's coffée house, where all the news of the Town is told, Scandal invented, etc." In spite of polygamy, she believes the Turkish women to be the "only free people in the Empire." The veil allows them freedom to move invisibly, flitting from one scene to the next without detection: "This perpetual Masquerade gives them entire Liberty of following their Inclinations without Danger of discovery" (I.328). She goodhumoredly portrays herself as the one imprisoned, caught as she is in the "machine" the Turkish women assume her husband has locked her in, her stays. Yet there is also sameness: "Thus you see, dear Sister, the manners of Mankind doe not differ so widely as our voyage Writers would make us beleive" [*sic*]. Polygamy is synonymous here with female collectivity, female beauty, and sexuality, and in a magnificent reversal *her body* is imprisoned rather than theirs. The Other – not racially different, but different in kind – is free, and polygamy (because the women under its aegis are able to move surreptitiously within it) represents liberty rather than restraint to Montagu.

In sharp contrast, when she regards "the Companies of the country people" in North Africa "eating, singing, and danceing [*sic*] to their wild music" (I.425), class and race surface as more significant than gender. The creatures appear to her to be animal-like instead of human, and their ugliness and exotic tattooed ornamentation safely distinguish them from European women:

> They are not quite black, but all mullattos, and the most frightfull Creatures that can appear in a Human figure. They are allmost naked, only wearing a piece of coarse serge wrap'd about them, but the women have their Arms to their very shoulders and their Necks and faces adorn'd with Flowers, Stars, and various sorts of figures impress'd by Gun-powder; a considerable addition to their natural Deformity.
>
> (I.425)[39]

Later:

> many of the women flock'd in to see me, and we were equally entertain'd with veiwing [*sic*] one another. Their posture in siting [*sic*], the colour of their skin, their lank black Hair falling on each side their faces, the features and the shape of their Limbs, differ so little from their own country people, the Baboons, tis hard to fancy them a distinct race, and I could not help thinking there had been some ancient alliances between them.
>
> (I.427)

These North African women, like Queen Clara of Falconbridge's account, refuse to wear the clothing of empire or to commodify themselves according to its ideal of femininity and virtue. Here the European woman narrator, Lady Mary Wortley Montagu, wishes to claim as female the exquisite naked beauty of the Turkish harem while rejecting any gender, class, or racial connection to the near-naked mulatto women. Their nakedness in her eyes is bestial rather than evoking the homoerotic sensuality of the harem. Wortley Montagu is not unlike the male traveler she scorns in pitting the "shineingly white" Turkish women against the tattooed African women.

Mary Wollstonecraft, adamant in her opposition to polygamy, established the feminist position that was to prevail. "Polygamy," writes Mary Wollstonecraft in *A Vindication of the Rights of Woman* (1792) "is [another] physical degradation [of women by men]; and a plausible argument for a custom, that blasts every domestic virtue. . . . If polygamy be necessary, women must be inferior to man, and made for him."[40] She cites *Observations Made During a Voyage Round the World* (1778) by John Forster who claims that in Africa, polygamy enervates men while women "are of a hotter constitution, not only on account of their more irritable nerves, more sensible organization, and more lively fancy; but likewise because they are deprived in their matrimony of that share of physical love which, in a monogamous condition, would all be theirs."[41] Forster claims that this sexual deprivation for women leads to a hotter constitution, and the sex of the hotter constitution prevails in the population, women outnumbering the men. In other words, in his representation Africa is a torrid zone of sexuality where large numbers of passionately sexualized women roam unsatisfied. Wollstonecraft does not explicitly contrast the cold and less desirous European woman to her lascivious polygamous African counterpart but the implication is there. It is rhetorically unclear whether Wollstonecraft believes that polygamy protects seduced women in countries where more women are born than men and is therefore justified. Recognizing polygamy's social use in the cause of women's common feminist interests and arguing against those who find polygamy arises to respond to some natural law rather than within a particular social formation, Wollstonecraft nevertheless demonstrates little interest in the situation of African women as she argues forcefully in behalf of European women.

The relation of feminism to polygamy and the Other woman is indeed a vexed one that is charged with unresolved contradictions. Arguments in behalf of polygamy on the domestic front encourage providing economic support for seduced women, but both feminism and domestic femininity are united in their antagonism to polygamy. At the same time that Enlightenment feminism emerges in the west claiming liberty and equality, differences among women make feminism's progress exclusionary. Western women attempt to supervise the Other woman abroad. The Other is undressed and dissociated, admired yet held fast in the voyeuristic and aestheticizing gaze, freed within confinement, a princess yet a slave, a noble female savage, superior yet inferior, various yet the same, erotic, repulsive, excessive. The Englishwoman abroad finds in the Other something that aids her in granting herself an identity and thus contributes to the now suspect liberal feminism, so closely bound up with monogamous marriage and motherhood, of the latter part of the century. Englishwomen are pitted against African women and other women at the emergence of empire, as colonizing men lay claim to the female body and to imperial territory. Monogamy, with the support of feminism, is established as a national imperative; the Englishwoman is contained within the boundaries of marriage and nation, and her superiority is confirmed by her difference from the sexuality of empire's polygamous women. The exemplar of the domestic feminine woman, Pamela musters her moral power to make a convincing, if tedious, case for monogamy at home.

European-American feminism may find in its eighteenth-century manifestations, a harbinger of its current urgent need to produce alternative trajectories when confronted with the problems that African-American and Third World feminist theorists in the USA and elsewhere aptly reveal. In postcolonial feminism, polygamy also maintains a potential subversive power and threatens to become radically uncontained. Feminist theorist Trinh T. Minh-ha suggests that "difference" need not be opposed to "sameness, nor synonymous with separateness." She cautions against using difference as an attempt to locate racial essence: "When women decide to lift the veil one can say that they do so in defiance of their men's oppressive right to their bodies. But when they decide to keep or put on the veil they once took off they might do so to reappropriate their space or to claim a new difference in defiance of . . . standardization."[42] The Other woman of polygamy turns out to be, not surprisingly, both self and Other. What may be more surprising, less predictable, at home and abroad, is the way the Other woman's differences may instead be the occasion for unsettling "essences," sabotaging conflicts that arise because of those supposed essences, and preserving the enigma of speaking at once as the domestic woman, the Other woman at home, and the Other woman abroad. In the metaphor of *Pamela* II and the women's narratives of the Other, such a feminist position, a position of collective illusion, emanates from a hybrid subjectivity as it simultaneously regards itself and the world from one black eye and one blue eye, speaks from the mouth of Queen Clara, and is embodied in the tattooed skin of the North African countrywomen. Such a woman, embodied between the permeable boundaries of the real and the virtual worlds, between collective illusion and lived experience, may well refuse to be anyone's other woman.

Notes

1   *Horace Walpole's Correspondence with Sir Horace Mann*, ed. W. S. Lewis, Warren Hunting Smith, and George L. Lam (New Haven, CT: Yale University Press, 1967), Vol. XXIV, p.21. Mungo Park's *Travels in the Interior Districts of Africa: Performed under the Direction and Patronage of the African Association, in the Years 1795, 1796, and 1797* (London: 1799). For a publication history, see Kenneth Lupton, *Mungo Park the African Traveler* (Oxford: Oxford University Press, 1979), esp. p.109.

2   *Records of the African Association 1788–1831*, ed. and intro. Robin Hallet for the Royal Geographical Society (London: Thomas Nelson, 1964), p. 10. The African Association, a group of wealthy aristocratic men, grew to 109 members by 1791.

3   *Records of the African Association*, p. 31.

4   William Smith, *A New Voyage to Guinea: Describing the Customs. . . . Appointed by the Royal African Company to survey their settlements, etc.* (London: 1744), p. iii. The preface to this volume is apparently not written by Smith.

5   Willem Bosman, *A New and Accurate Description of the Coast of Guinea, Divided into the Gold, the Slave, and the Ivory Coasts*, trans. from the Dutch (London: 1705), Preface.

6   Captain Philip Beaver, *African Memoranda: Relative to an Attempt to Establish a British Settlement . . . on the Western Coast of Africa, in the Year 1792* (London: 1805) writes that "slaves are the money, the circulating medium, with which great African commerce is carried on; they have no other" (p. 395). For a discussion of the parallel commodification of the novel, see Terry Lovell, *Consuming Fiction* (London: Verso, 1987).

7   Jean Baptiste Labat, *Voyages and Travels along the West Coast of Africa, from Cape Blanco to Sierra Leone* (1731), Vol. II in *A New General Collection of Voyages and Travels; Consisting of the most Esteemed Relations, which have been hitherto published in any Language: comprehending every thing remarkable in its Kind in Europe, Asia, Africa, and America* . . . [compiled by John Green?], 4 vols. (London: 1745–7); and Francis Moore and Captain B. Stibbs, *Travels into the Inland Parts of Africa: Containing a Description of the Several Nations* . . . (London: 1738). See also *Records of the African Association*, p. 25.

8   Ignatius Sancho, *Letters of the Late Ignatius Sancho, an African to which are prefixed Memoirs of his Life*, 2 vols. (London: 1782), Vol. II, pp. 4–5.

9   Michele Wallace uses this term in reference to all black women in *Invisiblity Blues: From Pop to Theory* (London and New York: Verso, 1990).

10 Caleb Fleming, *Oeconomy of the Sexes, or the Doctrine of Divorce, the Plurality of Wives, and the Vow of Celibacy Freely Examined* (London: 1751), p. 32.

11 Homi K. Bhabha, "The other question: difference, discrimination and the discourse of colonialism," in *Literature, Politics and Theory: Papers from the Essex Conference 1976–84*, ed. Francis Barker *et al.* (London and New York: Methuen, 1986), pp. 148–72 (p. 156). For the concept of "consolidating the imperialist self," see especially Gayatri Spivak, "Three women's texts and a critique of imperialism," *Race, Writing and Difference*, ed. Henry Louis Gates, Jr. (Chicago: University of Chicago Press, 1986), pp. 262–80, and Aihwa Ong,

"Colonialism and modernity: feminist representations of women in non-western societies," *Inscriptions* 3/4 (1988): 79–93.

12   For representations of Africa in the period, see V. Y. Mudimbe, *The Invention of Africa: Gnosis, Philosophy, and the Order of Knowledge* (Bloomington, IN: Indiana University Press, 1988).

13   A. Owen Aldridge's articles, "Polygamy and deism," *Journal of English and Germanic Philology* [*JEGP*] 48 (1949): 343–60, and "Polygamy in early fiction: Henry Neville and Denis Veiras," *JEGP* 65 (1950) 464–72, remain the definitive studies. Defoe opposes polygamy in *Conjugal Lewdness: A Treatise Concerning the Use and Abuse of the Marriage Bed* (London: 1727) stating that if it had been destined, God would have made Adam's rib into six wives (p. 23).

14   P. Dubliniensis, *Reflections upon Polygamy, and the Encouragement given to that Practice in the Scriptures of the Old Testament* (London: 1737), p. 1. This treatise also argues that in polygamous relationships women are deprived of their natural right, sufficient sexual gratification. This defense of women's sexuality as a natural right appears in several of Madan's antagonists including T. Hawkes, *A Scriptural Refutation of the Argument for Polygamy Advanced in a Treatise entitled Thelyphthora* (London [1781]), p. 101. Bigamy was apparently common practice. According to Lawrence Stone, *The Road to Divorce: England 1530–1987* (Oxford: Oxford University Press, 1990), p. 191, "The most common reason in the late seventeenth and early eighteenth centuries for declaring a marriage intrinsically void was bigamy arising from a previous marriage. . . . The Act followed custom in exempting persons whose spouses had been overseas or absent without news for seven years or more." Famous cases include *Tipping* v. *Roberts*, 1704–1733, Teresa Constantia Phillips's many bigamous marriages described in Lawrence Stone, *Uncertain Unions: Marriage in England 1660–1753* (Oxford: Oxford University Press, 1992), pp. 232–74; and the duchess of Kingston who was accused of bigamy while in Rome in 1776. Legal cases of multiple marriage, often involving a wife from another country or a different religion, debated the status of such marriages under English law. *Warrender* v. *Warrender* (1835) rules that "Marriage is one and the same thing substantially all the Christian world over. Our whole law of marriage assumes this: and it is important to observe that we regard it as a wholly different thing . . . from Turkish or other marriages among infidel nations, because clearly we never should recognize the plurality of wives, and consequent validity of second marriages . . . which . . . the laws of those countries authorise and validate"; J. H. C. Morris, *The Recognition of Polygamous Marriages in English Law* (Tübingen: J. C. B. Mohr, 1952), p. 291.

15   [Sophia Watson] *Memoirs of the Seraglio of the Bashaw of Merryland* (London: 1768), p. 2.

16   John Millar, *The Origins of the Distinctions of Ranks: or, an Inquiry into the Circumstances which give rise to the Influence and Authority in the Different Members of Society*, 3rd edn. (London: 1781), p. 124.

17   Olaudah Equiano, *The Interesting Narrative of the Life of Olaudah Equiano or Gustavus Vassa, the African*, in *The Classic Slave Narratives*, ed. Henry Louis Gates, Jr. (New York: New American Library, 1987), p. 13.

18   For these references to polygamy, see Jerom Merolla da Sorrento, *A Voyage to the Congo and Several other Countries* (1682) in *A General Collection of the Best and Most Interesting Voyages and Travels in all Parts of the World*, ed. John Pinkerton, 17 vols. (London: 1814) Vol. XVI, p. 231; Moore and Stibbs, *Travels into the Inland Ports of Africa*, p. 133; John Barbot, *A Description of the Coasts of North and South Guinea, and of Ethiopia Inferior, Vulgarly Angola* (1732) in Awnsham and John Churchill, *A Collection of Voyages*, 6 vols. (London: 1732), Vol. V, p. 240; J. Grazilhier, *Voyages and Travels to Guinea and Benin* (1699) in *New General Collection*, comp. John Green (London: Frank Cass, 1968), Vol. III, p. 113; and Smith, *New Voyage*, pp. 26, 102.

19   Paul Lovejoy, "Concubinage in the Sohoto Caliphate 1804–1903," *Slavery and Abolition* 11, 2 (1990): 158–89 (180). He adds, "Concubinage is virtually ignored in the literature on slavery, yet it was the central mechanism for the sexual exploitation of women in Islamic societies" (159). Alexander Falconbridge, *An Account of the Slave Trade on the Coast of Africa* (London: 1788), for example, maintains that women slaves seldom exceeded a third of those transported (p. 12). Claire Robertson, "The perils of autonomy," *Gender and History* 3, 1 (Spring 1991): 91–6, convincingly suggests that transporting more males than females was

due to African "desire to retain women slaves, *not* to European's preference for male labor. Women slaves were kept primarily because of their agricultural labor value and secondarily due to their reproductive capabilities that were useful for expanding African lineages" (95).

20   Harriet Jacobs's *Incidents in the Life of a Slave Girl: Mrs. Harriet Brent Jacobs, Written by Herself* (1861) (New York: AMS Press, 1973), p. 57. The narrative by "Linda Brent" was edited and framed by white women.

21   Henry Neville, *The Isle of Pines, or A Late Discovery of a fourth Island near Terra Australis, Incognita by Henry Cornelius Van Sloetten* (London: 1668).

22   Martin Madan, *Thelyphthora; or, a Treatise on Female Ruin in its causes, effects, consequences, prevention, and remedy; considered on the basis of the Divine Law*, 2 vols. (London: 1780). One of Madan's most unusual arguments is that polygamy is justified because Christ was born of a polygamous relationship. See John Towers, *Polygamy Unscriptural; or Two Dialogues Between Philalethes and Monogamus* (London: 1780), p. 8.

23   Richard Hill, *The Blessings of Polygamy Displayed, in an Affectionate Address to the Rev. Martin Madan occasioned by his late Work, entitled Thelyphthora, or A Treatise of Female Ruin* (London: 1781), p. 39; and Martin Madan, Letter 4 to Rev. Mr. G (April 14, 1781), *Letters on Thelyphthora: with an Occasional Prologue and Epilogue by the Author* (London: 1782).

24   Saunders Welch, *A Proposal to Render Effectual a Plan to Remove the Nuisance of Common Prostitutes from the Streets of the Metropolis* (London: 1758), p. 7.

25   John Matthews, *A Voyage to the River Sierra–Leone, on the Coast of Africa* (1788), p. 99.

26   David Hume, "Of polygamy and divorces" (1742), reprinted in *Essays Moral, Political and Literary* (Oxford: Oxford University Press, 1963), pp. 185–95. Hume believed that blacks were "naturally inferior to the Whites. There scarcely ever was a civilised nation of that complexion. . . . Such a uniform and constant difference could not happen, in so many countries and ages, if nature had not made an original distinction between these breeds of men"; "Of national characters," p. 213, n. 1. Hume, in charge of the British Colonial Office from 1766, added this note to the 1753–4 edition, and it was later used as a basis for scientific racism. See Richard H. Popkin, *The High Road to Pyrrhonism* (San Diego, CA: Austin Hill Press, 1980), pp. 251–66.

27   Mungo Park, *Travels*, p. 268. According to Frances Moore and Captain Stibbs, Mumbo Jumbo is a cant language spoken exclusively by men (p. 40). Mumbo Jumbo, as a folkloric invention dressed in a long coat and a tuft of straw on top, kept women in awe of masculine authority. Women flee when Mumbo Jumbo arrives.

28   T. C. Duncan Eaves and Ben D. Kimpel, *Samuel Richardson: A Biography* (Oxford: Clarendon Press, 1971), p. 135.

29   Terry Castle, *Masquerade and Civilization: The Carnivalesque in Eighteenth-Century English Culture and Fiction* (Stanford, CA: Stanford University Press, 1986), p. 132. Though she does not mention polygamy, Castle richly describes the way the sequel to *Pamela* must "be different, but also *exactly the same.*"

30   *Pamela; or, Virtue Rewarded* in *The Works of Samuel Richardson*, ed. Leslie Stephen (London: Henry Southeran, 1893), Vol. III, p. 53; text citations hereafter give volume no. and page no. (III. 53). For a subtle analysis of Pamela's double jeopardy as wife and mother, see Ruth Perry, "Colonizing the breast: sexuality and maternity in eighteenth-century England," *Journal of the History of Sexuality* 2, 2 (October 1991): 204–34.

31   It seems possible that breast disfigurement was associated with the milky lower class. See Gail Paster, *The Body Embarrassed: Drama and the Disciplines of Shame in Early Modern England* (Ithaca, NY: Cornell University Press, 1993), pp. 163–280.

32   Mr. B's sentiments resemble Lovelace's in *Clarissa*: "Polygamy is a doctrine that I am very far from countenancing; but yet, in an argumentative way, I do say, that the law of nature, and the first command (increase and multiply) more than allow of it; and the law of God no where forbids it. Throughout the Old Testament we find it constantly practiced" (June 24, 1752).

33   Fatna A. Sabbah, *Woman in the Muslim Unconscious*, trans. Mary Jo Lakeland (New York: Pergamon Press, 1984), p. 25, discusses the way that Muslim women's visible physical attributes are openly interpreted as indicators of veiled sexual organs.

34 The classic statement of this view is, of course, Friedrich Engels, *The Origin of the Family, Private Property and the State* (New York: Penguin, 1985).

35 A[nna] M. Falconbridge, *Narrative of Two Voyages to the River Sierra Leone during the Years 1791–2–3*, 2nd. edn. (London: 1802). Falconbridge despised colonial policies but equivocated about abolishing the slave trade.

36 These revised and elaborated letters were published later as *Letters of the Right Honourable Lady M—y W—y M—e: Written during her TRAVELS in Europe, Asia, and Africa*, 2 vols. (London: 1763). I have cited the modern edition, *The Complete Letters of Lady Mary Wortley Montagu*, ed. Robert Halsband, 2 vols. (Oxford: Clarendon Press, 1965); (I. 314). See also Joseph W. Lew, "Lady Mary's portable seraglio," *Eighteenth-Century Studies* 24, 4 (Summer 1991): 432–50. Lew believes that Lady Mary "subverts both Orientalist discourse and eighteenth-century patriarchy itself."

37 Leslie P. Peirce, *The Imperial Harem: Women and Sovereignty in the Ottoman Empire* (New York and Oxford: Oxford University Press, 1993) believes that "in the absence of indigenous descriptions of the workings of the harem institution, we must turn to accounts written by European observers of the Ottomans, our only contemporary sources" (p. 114).

38 Billie Melman, *Women's Orients: English Women and the Middle East, 1718–1918: Sexuality, Religion and Work* (Ann Arbor, MI: University of Michigan Press, 1992), p. 72.

39 On tattoos, see Harriet Guest, "Curiously masked: tattoing, masculinity, and nationality in late eighteenth-century British perceptions of the South Pacific," in John Barrell (ed.) *Painting and the Politics of Culture* (Oxford: Oxford University Press, 1992).

40 Mary Wollstonecraft, *A Vindication of the Rights of Woman*, ed. Miriam Kramnick (Harmondsworth, Mx: Penguin, 1975), Ch. IV. Wollstonecraft compares the weakest and most frivolous Englishwomen to women in a seraglio (p. 76). Mahometanism is defined as woman's brutish enemy.

41 John Reinold Forster, *Observations Made During a Voyage Round the World on Physical Geography, Natural History and Ethic Philosophy* (London: 1788), pp. 425–6.

42 Trinh T. Minh-ha, "Not you / like you: post-colonial women and the interlocking question of identity and difference," *Inscriptions* 3/4 (1988): 71–7 (73). For a discussion of the use of the veil in protest against the Shah of Iran, see Nayereh Tohidi, "Gender and Islamic fundamentalism," in *Third World Women and the Politics of Feminism*, ed. Chandra Talpade Mohanty, Ann Russo, and Lourdes Torres (Bloomington, IN: Indiana University Press, 1991), pp. 251–67.

13

The good, the bad, and the impotent

Imperialism and the politics of identity in Georgian England

Kathleen Wilson

> Britain will never want a Race of Men, who prefer the publick Good before any
> narrow or selfish Views – who choose Dangers in defence of Their Country
> before an inglorious safety, an honourable Death before the unmanly pleasures
> of a useless and effeminate life . . . it is now the Birthright of Englishmen, to
> carry, not only Good Manners, but the purest Light of the Gospel, where
> Barbarism and Ignorance totally prevailed.
>
> (Richard Brewster, *A Sermon preach'd . . . on the*
> *Thanksgiving Day* [Newcastle: 1759])

The cultural construction of state power is a topic that has been curiously neglected by scholars of eighteenth-century Britain. Historical narratives of politics, empire, and culture have typically gone their separate ways, leaving it to literary critics and art historians to draw some impressionistic, though fruitful, connections. This has led to two separate, though intimately related, interpretive problems. First, the latest distinguished efforts to analyze the growth and nature of the state have left largely unexplored questions about the ideological significance of eighteenth-century state- and empire-building, and the impact of both on domestic cultural production.[1] And second, cultural studies of imperialism and difference have tended to elide politics as a constitutive arena of culture that both constructed and disseminated competing images of the state and nation, Englishness and otherness, citizenship and exclusion.[2] This chapter will attempt to bring together two disparate interpretive strands by examining the cultural representations of empire in the period of the Seven Years and American wars.

Such a task is a formidable one in light of historians' uneven treatment of this crucial period in British imperialism. Although the expansion of Britain in the Hanoverian decades was a central subject of historical inquiry for generations of scholars, their accounts invariably eschewed large-scale political, ideological, or cultural forces in favor of great events, of battles won and lost and military and naval strategies that in the long run succeeded in wrenching some colonies from France and Spain. From this perspective, "empire" consisted of a series of wars between Britain and her European rivals for domination in the Americas and East Indies; and, once that domination was achieved, of a series of policies (some just, some badly calculated) designed to consolidate and build upon a hard-won imperial ascendancy.[3] Such an approach, however useful in understanding the international and diplomatic contexts of war and peace, colonial acquisition and loss in the eighteenth century, is of limited usefulness to those who wish to know the meaning and significance of empire at home. How was empire retailed and understood in Britain, by those for whom it existed more in ideology and imagination than in policy? The rich and resourceful work that has appeared in the past decade on popular politics, class relations, and protest unfortunately has equally elided the significance of empire in public and national conscious-ness.[4] This omission is all the more remarkable in light of the broad social basis within Britain of investment in the imperial project, from the financing of ships, investment in cargoes, and colonial land speculation to the distribution, consumption, and population patterns which spread colonial and British goods across regions, oceans, and nations.[5] Even the most recent distinguished assessment of eighteenth-century nationalism has obscured rather than illumined the multifaceted impact of empire on the public politi-cal imagination, for it positions overseas expansion as an overarching and invariably unifying force that produced uncontested and latently loyalist "British" identities among those at home.[6] It is, then, the historical complexities of eighteenth-century imperialist sensibilities that need to be recovered: the various ways in which the empire was imagined, the forums through which it was represented, debated, and discussed, and, above all, the frequently contested meanings which empire held for the various groups involved in or engaged by the mesmerizing spectacle of Britain's global expansion.

Empire – its existence, aggrandizement, and concerns – permeated Georgian culture at a number of levels: literature (both adult and children's), theater, music, painting, leisure pursuits, gardening, philanthropy, fashion, religion, politics, and graphic and literary propaganda.[7] This chapter will examine just a few of the ways in which a popular (in the sense of socially inclusive) vision of imperial greatness was embedded in domestic culture and politics. I have argued elsewhere that the cultural, political, and ideological significance of empire was both greater and less straightforward than much current scholarship has led us to believe. Empire was intimately linked with opposition patriotism and libertarian politics throughout the century, and was central to contem-porary arguments about the nature of consent, liberty, and authority in the British political system, the limitations of state power, and the effectiveness and legitimacy of its counsels.[8] What I will sketch in below are some of the ways in which a mercantilist, libertarian view of empire was disseminated in three important discursive structures within Georgian culture – the press, theater, and politics – with a view to uncovering the ideological significance which empire had for the wider and predominantly urban, middle-class public of this period. Specifically, I will argue that the competitive and militaristic contexts of imperial acquisition and loss worked to establish and naturalize exclusive, gendered definitions of citizenship and political subjectivity that valorized an aggressive masculinity as a touchstone of Englishness, while devaluing and marginaliz-ing "effeminate" others both within and without the polity.[9] In this way, the discourses of imperialism embedded normative definitions of class, gender, and nation in English culture that shaped men and women's perception of Britain's place within the world and their own place within the polity.

I

Belief in the desirability of empire in the eighteenth century rested upon a bedrock of nationalistic, mercantilist, and libertarian beliefs that lay behind commercial thinking of the period generally, all of which were galvanized in this period by Britain's obsessive rivalry and protracted wars with the continental Catholic powers. Put simply, the British Empire was imagined to consist of flourishing and commercially viable colonies, populated with free British subjects, that served as bulwarks of trade, prosperity, naval strength, and political virtue for the parent state.[10] As one commentator put it, colonies were the "sinews of our naval strength, on which avowedly the very being of this kingdom depends"; while another extravagantly claimed that all British wealth and grandeur were attributable to her colonies – "She draws from thence . . . all that is *good* and *valuable*."[11] The imperial project existed to maximize trade and national power, in other words, and colonies were considered crucial to the "empire of the sea" that contemporaries believed Britain had, or should have, dominion over.

Behind this view of empire lay the tenets of an adulterated mercantilism, popularized through a plethora of pamphlets, essays, newspaper articles, and parliamentary speeches that had debated commercial issues since the early years of the century. These principles could be summarized as follows: the world was possessed of finite amounts of wealth and resources; national power and prosperity depended upon capturing the greatest proportion of these riches relative to other nations; attaining national self-sufficiency and a "favorable balance of trade" (that is, more exports than imports) were means to this end, which depended in turn upon procuring a monopoly of international trade and colonial markets, and pursuing policies geared to increasing population and industry at home; and if trade was the best means of civilizing the world (and most agreed that it was), then colonies were the most useful way of maximizing its benefits for the mother country. Within this framework, the navy was considered to be the prime instrument of national power and the guarantor of commercial wealth; colonial interests were to be subordinated to those of the mother country; and the state was to support and pursue these goals, not only through the encouragement of the production of people and goods at home, but also through a foreign policy that concentrated on maintaining England's naval power and colonial supremacy – "The Acquisition of Tracts of Land and Territories to Enlarge Dominion and Power," as one writer put it – which by 1730 represented the most recent incarnation of the "blue-water policy" advocated since Anne's reign.[12]

If contemporaries were to give this amalgam of beliefs a slogan, it would perhaps have been "Production at Home, Acquisition Abroad" – a motto which may not have rivalled "Wilkes and Liberty" in evocative pithiness but which certainly states the priorities of the imperial vision. It was also one which highlighted the orientation of mercantilist thinking towards counting, measuring, and assessing national wealth numerically against that of other nations. The eighteenth-century press brilliantly reflected and encouraged such sentiments, for, among other things, it provided the information necessary to make endless calculations about incoming and outgoing wealth, goods and profits, production and consumption. From mid-century, the very structure and content of newspapers in London and the provinces mirrored a world-view in which trade and the accumulation of wealth appear to be of the highest national and individual good. The progress of wars in Europe, America, Africa, and the East Indies, and the prizes taken in battle; the comings and goings of merchant ships, often with lengthy lists of the products of their laden bottoms; prices, stocks, and bullion values; and advertisements for luxury goods from international and colonial markets – tea, coffee, chocolate, and tobacco; calicoes and silks; wines, rum, and spirits; fruits and seeds; furs, exotic birds and plants, and ivory: together they could account for one third of the contents of individual issues of eighteenth-century newspapers from the capital and outports, and an even higher proportion in wartime.[13] As one scholar has noted for the imaginative literature of the period, both the enumeration of goods and their seemingly endless variety encapsulated on a small scale the contemporary fascination with the moveable products of imperialist accumulation.[14] They also evinced a widespread interest in the processes of colonial acquisition and possession. By the 1740s and 1750s, several provincial papers and most magazines had sections on "American affairs" or "British Plantations" that included not only current news on politics and trade, but also the histories and settlement patterns of individual colonies, the competing claims of European powers to them, and the "etiquette" of colonization.[15]

In conjunction with other items in the papers,[16] the format and content of newspapers mirrored contemporary conceptualizations of power and market relations, at home and abroad, and expressed the interests and priorities of those who read them, from landed elites and overseas merchants to humble middling tradesmen, shopkeepers, and artisans – all individuals who had an interest, material or ideological, in commerce and colonies. Newspapers were thus central instruments in the social production of information: both representing and verifying local experience, they functioned like imaginative literature in reproducing and refracting world events into socially meaningful categories and hierarchies of importance; and the processes of imperial acquisition were clearly significant here. In this way, newspapers produced an "imagined community" of producers, distributors, and consumers on both sides of the Atlantic, who shared an avid interest in the fate of the "empire of goods" that linked them together in prosperity or adversity.[17] They also, significantly, familiarized their readers with a discourse that diagnosed the structure, location, or distribution of power in the state as the source of many imperial, political, and social discontents and grievances.

Naturally, these patterns were not limited to newspapers: pamphlets, novels, travel books and histories, and the periodical press were similarly caught up in the mechanics and fruits of imperial acquisition. John Oldmixon's two-volume *British Empire in America*, for example, provided a history of each colony which included the most salient points about its history, settlement, current state and products, and the unassailable claims of the British to it, as well as beautifully produced maps with towns, plantations, and settlements clearly marked. His histories of the northern mainland colonies included detailed recountings of their settlement and constitutional evolutions, while his

1.1 Willem Kalf, *Still Life with Nautilus Cup, c.* 1664. Reproduced by courtesy of the Fundación Colección Thyssen-Bornemisza, Madrid.

1.2 Antoine Watteau, *L'Enseigne de Gersaint*, 1721. Reproduced with the kind permission of Berlin, Verwaltung der Staatlichen Schlösser und Gärten, Schloss Charlottenburg.

3.1 Joshua Reynolds, *Theophila Palmer Reading "Clarissa Harlowe,"* 1771. Private Collection: photograph by courtesy of the Paul Mellon Centre for Studies in British Art.

3.2 Pierre-Antoine Baudouin, *Le Midi*, engraved by E. de Ghendt, *c.* 1770. From Edward Fuchs, *L'Element érotique dans la caricature* (Vienna: Harz, 1906), fig. 92.

3.3 Joshua Reynolds, *Emilia, Duchess of Leinster*, 1753. Private Collection: photograph reproduced by courtesy of the Courtauld Institute of Art. **3.4** Cesare Ripa, "Meditation," from his *Iconologia* (London: Motte, 1709). Special Collections Department, Northwestern University Library, Evanston, IL.

5.1 John Singleton Copley, *Watson and the Shark*, 1778. National Gallery of Art, Washington, DC; Ferdinand Lammot Belin Fund.

5.2 John Singleton Copley, *Charles I Requesting from Parliament the Five Impeached Members*, oil on canvas, 71¾ × 90½ ins., 1782-95. Reproduced by courtesy of the Trustees of the Public Library of the City of Boston.

5.3 James Gillray, *Shakespeare Sacrificed, or, The Offering to Avarice*, 1789. Reproduced by courtesy of the Trustees of the British Museum.

5.4 Joseph Wright of Derby, *The Corinthian Maid, c.* 1783-4. National Gallery of Art, Washington, DC; Paul Mellon Collection.

5.5 Joseph Wright of Derby, *Penelope Unravelling Her Web*, 1785. Collection of the J. Paul Getty Museum, Malibu, California.

5.6 Benjamin West, *Etruria, or British Manufactory*, 1789-91. The Cleveland Museum of Art, Gift of the John Huntington Art and Polytechnic Trust, 19.1018.

6.1 François-André Vincent, *Belisarius Begging Alms*, 1776. Musée Fabre, Montpellier.

6.2 François-André Vincent, *Socrates Admonishing Alcibiades*, 1776. Musée Fabre, Montpellier.

6.3 Jean-François-Pierre Peyron, *Belisarius Receiving Hospitality from Peasants Who Had Served Under Him*, 1779. Musée des Augustins, Toulouse. Photograph by courtesy of the Atelier Municipale de Photographie, Mairie de Toulouse.

6.4 Jacques-Louis David, *Belisarius Begging Alms*, 1781. Musée des Beaux-Arts, Lille. Photograph by courtesy of Photographie Bulloz.

6.5 Jean-Germain Drouais, *The Return of the Prodigal Son*, 1782. Church of Saint Roch, Paris. © Ville de Paris, S.O.A.E.

6.6 Jean-Germain Drouais, *Christ and the Canaanite Woman*, 1784. Musée du Louvre, Paris. © PHOTO R.M.N.

6.7 Jacques-Louis David, *Oath of the Horatii Between the Hands of Their Father*, 1784. Musée du Louvre, Paris. © PHOTO R.M.N.

6.8 Jean-Germain Drouais, *Marius at Minturnae*, 1786. Musée du Louvre, Paris.
© PHOTO R.M.N.

6.9 Jean-Germain Drouais, study for *Marius at Minturnae*, *c.* 1786. Musée des Beaux-Arts, Lille.

6.10 Jean-Germain Drouais, study for *Marius at Minturnae*, *c.* 1786. Musée des Beaux-Arts, Lille.

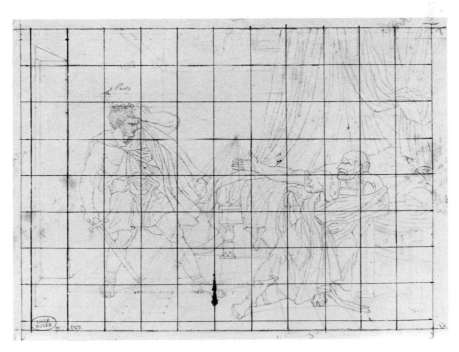

6.11 Jean-Germain Drouais, study for *Marius at Minturnae*, *c.* 1786. Musée des Beaux-Arts, Lille.

6.12 Jean-Germain Drouais, *Philoctetes on Lemnos*, 1788. Musée des Beaux-Arts, Chartres.

7.1 Flemish school, *A Collector's Cabinet*, 1620. Reproduced by courtesy of the Board of Trustees of the National Gallery, London.

7.2 Albrecht Dürer, *Pond in the Woods, c.* 1497-8. Reproduced by courtesy of the Trustees of the British Museum.

7.3 Giorgione, *Tempesta*, *c.* 1505. Reproduced by courtesy of the Galleria dell'Accademia, Venice. © Reale Fotografia Giacomelli.

8.1 Angelica Kauffmann, *Miss Cornelia Knight*, 1793. © The City of Manchester Art Gallery.

8.2 Angelica Kauffmann, *Hector Taking Leave of Andromache*, 1768. Saltram House, Plymouth. Reproduced by courtesy of the National Trust Photo Library, London.

8.3 Gavin Hamilton, *Andromache Bewailing the Death of Hector, c.* 1761-4. Photograph reproduced by kind permission of the Courtauld Institute of Art.

8.4 Thomas Burke after Angelica Kauffmann, *Andromache Weeping Over the Ashes of Hector*, 1772. Reproduced by courtesy of John Freeman & Co., London.

8.5 Maria Cosway, *The Progress of Female Virtue*, plate IV (London, *c.* 1800). Reproduced by permission of The Huntington Library, San Marino, California.

8.6 Maria Cosway, *The Progress of Female Dissipation*, plate IV (London, *c.* 1800). Reproduced by permission of The Huntington Library, San Marino, California.

8.7 Mary Moser, *Flower Painting, c.* 1770. Reproduced by courtesy of the Board of Trustees of the Victoria and Albert Museum.

12.1 Frontispiece by F. Child to *A New General Collection of Voyages and Travels*, vol. II (London, 1745), 4 vols [compiled by John Green?] (London,1745-7). Reproduced by permission of the British Library.

14.1 Ramsden's Dividing Engine of 1777. Reproduced by courtesy of the National Museum of American History, Smithsonian Institution.

14.2 Ramsden's Dividing Engine of 1777; detailed view from above. Reproduced by courtesy of the National Museum of American History, Smithsonian Institution.

15.1 Marie-Pierre Nicolas Ponce-Camus, *L'Abbé de L'Epée*, 1802. Reproduced by courtesy of the Collection Institut National des Jeunes Sourds de Paris.

15.2 Jerome-Martin Langlois, *Sicard Instructing the Deaf-Mutes*, 1806. Reproduced by courtesy of the Collection Institut National des Jeunes Sourds de Paris.

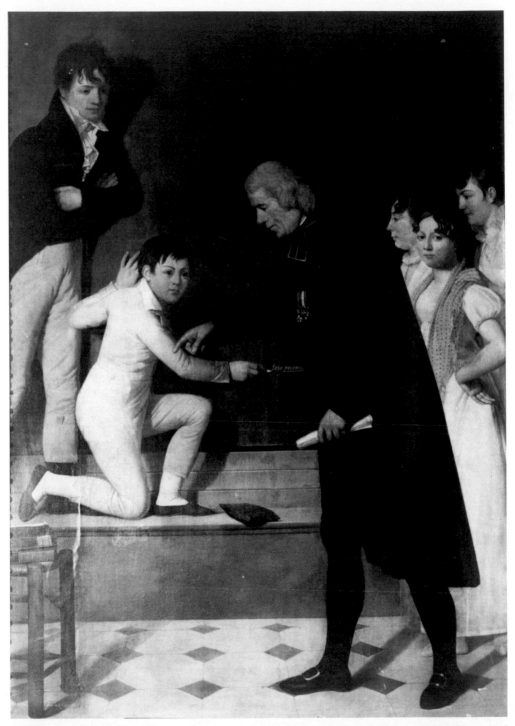

15.3 Jerome-Martin Langlois, *Sicard Instructing the Deaf-Mutes*, 1814. Reproduced by courtesy of the Collection Institut des Jeunes Sourds de Paris.

16.1 F. Lemot, *Henri IV*, 1818. Pont Neuf, Paris. Photograph: Anne Wagner.

16.2 Helman after Monnet, *Fountain of Regeneration*, 1793, reproducing an element in the Festival of Unity, August 10, 1793. From David L. Dowd, *Pageant Master of the Republic* (University of Nebraska Studies, no. 5, June 1948).

16.3 Anonymous, *Monument erected on the Place des Victoires in Honor of General Desaix*, 1810. Document B.H.V.P.

16.4 Anonymous, *Caricature of Vivant Denon, c.* 1815. Paris, Cabinet des Estampes, Bibliothèque Nationale.

A FRENCH ELEPHANT.

16.5 Anonymous, *Louis XVIII: A French Elephant, c.* 1814. Paris, Cabinet des Estampes, Bibliothèque Nationale.

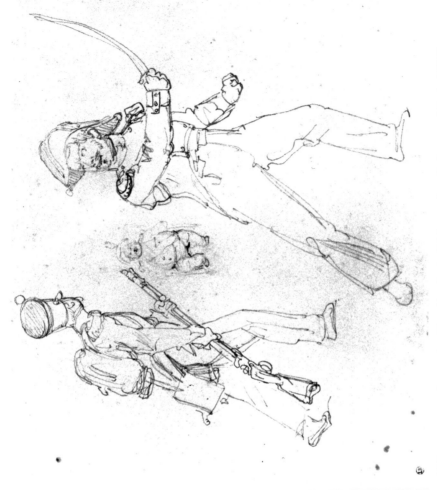

16.7 Théodore Géricault, *Two Napoleonic Soldiers and a Caricature of Louis XVIII*, *c*. 1815. Reproduced by courtesy of the Musée Bonnat, Bayonne.

16.6 Anonymous, *Louis XVIII*, *c*. 1815–24. Reproduced from A. Dayot, *La Restauration*, p. 94, by courtesy of the Doe Library, University of California at Berkeley.

16.8 Merlet, *Anthousiasme des français pour Henri IV, lors de la translation de sa Statue au Pont Neuf*, 1818. Paris, Cabinet des Estampes, Bibliothèque Nationale.

16.9 Anonymous, *Louis de notre amour, amant de Gabrielle*, 1818. Paris, Cabinet des Estampes, Bibliothèque Nationale.

16.10 Prieur, *Busts of Necker and the duc d'Orléans Carried to the Place Louis XV*, 1789. Paris, Cabinet des Estampes, Bibliothèque Nationale.

16.11 Vêve and Girardet, *Gathering on the Pont Neuf, September 16, 1788*, 1788. Paris, Cabinet des Estampes, Bibliothèque Nationale.

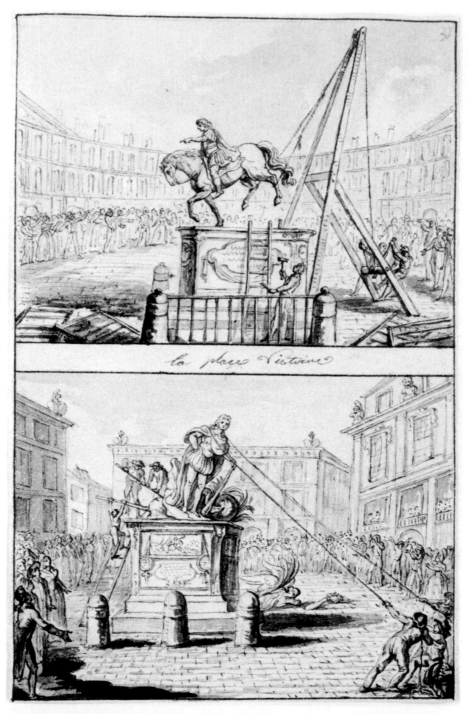

la place Victoire

16.12 Anonymous, *Destruction of the Statues of Louis XIV, Place Vendôme and Place des Victoires*, 1792. Musée du Louvre, Département des Arts Graphiques, Collection Edmond de Rothschild. © PHOTO R.M.N.

La place Royale

16.13 Anonymous, *Destruction of the Statues of Henri IV, Pont Neuf and Louis XIII, Place Royale*, 1792. Musée du Louvre, Département des Arts Graphiques, Collection Edmond de Rothschild. © PHOTO R.M.N.

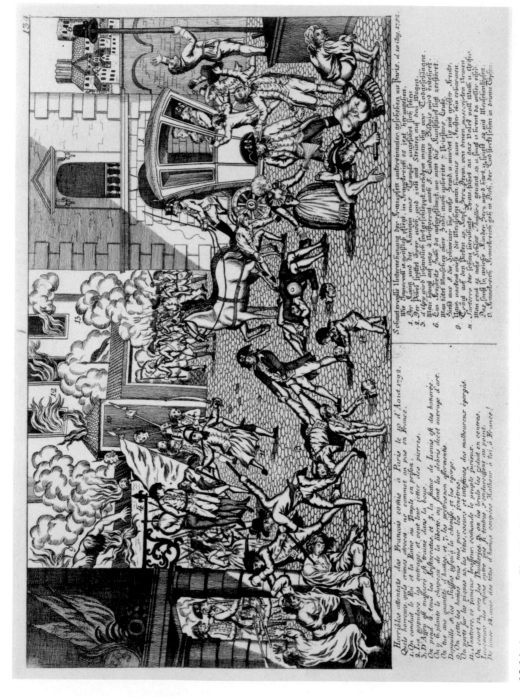

16.14 Anonymous, *Horrible Crimes Committed in Paris, August 10, 1792*, 1792. Paris, Cabinet des Estampes, Bibliothèque Nationale.

16.15 N. Lesueur, *Equestrian Figure of Louis XIV*, after 1699.

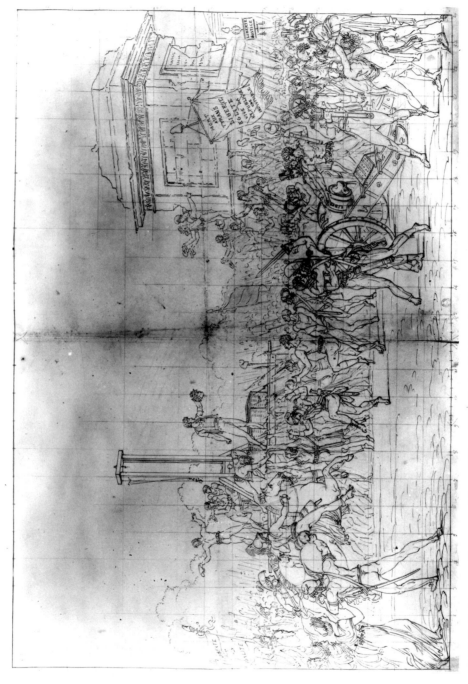

16.16 P. E. Lesueur, *Execution of Louis XVI*, *c.* 1793. Paris, Cabinet des Estampes, Bibliothèque Nationale.

16.17 Anonymous, *Death of Louis XVI*, 1793. Musée du Louvre, Département des Arts Graphiques, Collection Edmond de. Rothschild. © PHOTO R.M.N.

16.18 G. Opiz, *Descente de la Statue de Napoléon de la Collonne [sic] triomphale sur la Place Vendôme*, 1814. Paris, Cabinet des Estampes, Bibliothèque Nationale.

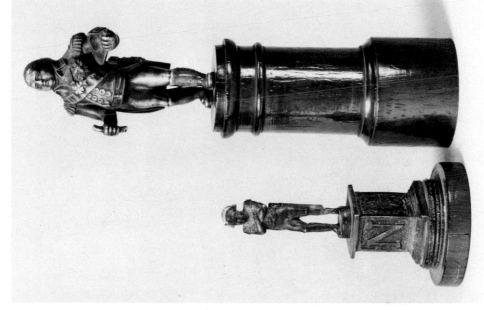

16.19 F. Lemot, *Henri IV* (detail), 1818. Paris, Pont Neuf. Photograph: Anne Wagner.

16.20 Anonymous, *Cane with Handle Representing Louis XVIII, Concealing an Image of Napoleon, c.* 1815–24. Musée Historique Lorrain, Nancy. © Gilbert Mangin.

19.1 Johannes Kip after J. Badslade, *The Pantiles at Tunbridge Wells*, engraving, from John Harris, *The History of Kent*, 1719. Reproduced by courtesy of the William Clark Memorial Library, UCLA.

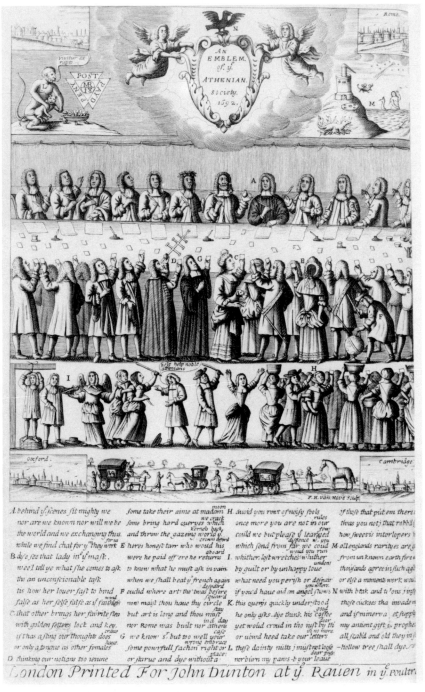

19.2   F. H. van Hove, frontispiece to John Dunton's *The Young Students Library* (London, 1692). Reproduced by courtesy of the William Clark Memorial Library, UCLA.

19.3 Anonymous, frontispiece and title page to J. Hill's *The Young Secretary's Guide*, eighth edition (London, 1697). Reproduced by permission of the Huntington Library, San Marino, California.

19.4 Anonymous, frontispiece and title page to *The Mysteries of Love and Eloquence*, third edition (London, 1685). Reproduced by permission of the Huntington Library, San Marino, California.

20.1 William Hogarth, *A Harlot's Progress*, Plate 1, First State, 1732. Reproduced by courtesy of the Trustees of the British Museum.

20.2 William Hogarth, *A Harlot's Progress* Plate 2, First State, 1732. Reproduced by courtesy of the Trustees of the British Museum.

20.3 William Hogarth, *A Harlot's Progress*, Plate 3, First State, 1732. Reproduced by courtesy of the Trustees of the British Museum.

20.4 William Hogarth, *A Harlot's Progress*, Plate 4, First State, 1732. Reproduced by courtesy of the Trustees of the British Museum.

20.5 William Hogarth, *Boys Peeping at Nature*, Second State, 1730/1. Royal Library, Windsor Castle. © Her Majesty Queen Elizabeth II.

20.6 William Hogarth, *A Rake's Progress*, Plate 1, Third State, 1735. Reproduced by courtesy of the Trustees of the British Museum.

20.7 William Hogarth, *A Rake's Progress*, Plate 2, Third State, 1735. Reproduced by courtesy of the Trustees of the British Museum.

20.8 William Hogarth, *A Rake's Progress*, Plate 3, Third State, 1735. Reproduced by courtesy of the Trustees of the British Museum.

20.9 William Hogarth, *Marriage à la Mode*, Plate 1, Fifth State, 1745. Reproduced by courtesy of the Trustees of the British Museum.

20.10 William Hogarth, *Marriage à la Mode*, Plate 4, Second State, 1745. Reproduced by courtesy of the Trustees of the British Museum.

20.11 William Hogarth, *The Distrest Poet*, Third State, 1741. Reproduced courtesy of the Trustees of the British Museum.

21.1 Hubert Robert, French, 1733-1808, *Four Decorative Paintings from the Chateau of Méréville: The Obelisk*, oil on canvas, 1787/8, 256 × 222 cm, Gift of Clarence Buckingham, 1900.383. © 1991, The Art Institute of Chicago. All Rights Reserved.

21.2 Hubert Robert, French, 1733-1808, *Four Decorative Paintings from the Chateau of Méréville: The Old Temple*, oil on canvas, 1787/8, 256 × 223 cm, Gift of Adolphus C. Bartlett, 1900.382. © 1991, The Art Institute of Chicago. All Rights Reserved.

21.3 Hubert Robert, French, 1733-1808, *Four Decorative Paintings from the Chateau of Méréville: The Fountains*, oil on canvas, 1787/8, 254.5 × 223.5 cm, Gift of William C. Hibbard, 1900.38. © 1991, The Art Institute of Chicago. All Rights Reserved.

21.4 Hubert Robert, French, 1733-1808, *Four Decorative Paintings from the Chateau of Méréville. The Landing Place*, oil on canvas, 1788, 256 × 223 cm, Gift of Richard T. Crane, 1900.34. © 1991, The Art Institute of Chicago. All Rights Reserved.

24.1 Elisabeth Vigée-Lebrun, *Peace Bringing Back Abundance*, Salon of 1783. Musée du Louvre, Paris. © PHOTO R.M.N.

24.2 Elisabeth Vigée-Lebrun, *Self-Portrait*, Salon of 1783. Reproduced by courtesy of the Board of Trustees of the National Gallery, London.

24.3 Peter Paul Rubens, *Le Chapeau de Paille*, 1630-24. Reproduced by courtesy of the Board of Trustees of the National Gallery, London.

24.4 Elisabeth Vigée-Lebrun, *Portrait of Marie-Antoinette "en chemise,"* Salon of 1783. Darmstadt, Schlossmuseum.

24.5 Elisabeth Vigée-Lebrun, *Portrait of the duchesse de Polignac*, 1783. Reproduced by courtesy of the National Trust Waddesdon Manor and the Courtauld Institute of Art. © National Trust Waddesdon Manor and Courtauld Institute of Art.

24.6 Elisabeth Vigée-Lebrun, *Portrait of the duchesse de Polignac*, 1787. Private Collection.

24.7 Gustave Lundberg, *Portrait of François Boucher*, 1752. Paris, Musée du Louvre. © PHOTO R.M.N.

24.8 Antoine Vestier, *Portrait of Nicolas-Guy Brenet*, 1786. Versailles, Musée national du château.
© PHOTO R.M.N.

24.9 Anton Raphael Mengs, *Self-Portrait*, 1774. Reproduced by courtesy of the Galleria degli Uffizi, Florence.

24.10 Louis Tocqué, *Portrait of Galloche*, 1734. Musée du Louvre, Paris. © PHOTO R.M.N.

24.11 Nicholas Largillière, *Portrait of Coustou*, 1710. Reproduced by courtesy of the Staatliche Museen Preussischer Kulturbesitz, Berlin.

24.12 Jacques-Louis David, *Self-Portrait*, 1794. Musée du Louvre, Paris. © PHOTO R.M.N.

24.13 Jean-Baptiste Greuze, *The Broken Jug*, 1773. Musée du Louvre, Paris. © PHOTO R.M.N.

25.1 Nikolas Willem von Heideloff, *Gallery of Fashion*, vol. II, April 1795. Fig. 87, "New Dresses in the Roman Style". Reproduced by courtesy of the Yale Center for British Art, Paul Mellon Collection.

25.2 Nikolas Willem von Heideloff, *Gallery of Fashion*, vol. V, October 1798. Fig. 120, "Afternoon Dress." Reproduced by courtesy of the Yale Center for British Art, Paul Mellon Collection.

25.3 George Romney, *Caroline, Viscountess Clifden and Lady Elizabeth Spencer*, 1791. Reproduced by courtesy of The Huntington Library, San Marino, California.

25.4 Edward Francis Burney, *A Fashionable Academy for Young Ladies*, c. 1800. Reproduced courtesy of the Board of Trustees of the Victoria and Albert Museum.

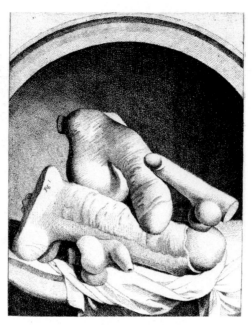

25.5 Wax Ex-Voti from Isernia, from Richard Payne Knight's *Discourse on the Worship of Priapus* (London, 1786). By permission of the Huntington Library, San Marino, California.

25.6 Frederick Rehberg, *Three Attitudes of Emma Hamilton*, 1794. Reproduced courtesy of the Department of Printing and Graphic Arts, The Houghton Library, Harvard University.

25.7 Johan Zoffany, *Charles Towneley and Friends in the Park Street Gallery, Westminster*, 1781-3. Reproduced courtesy of Towneley Hall Art Gallery & Museums, Burnley Borough Council.

25.8 Johan Zoffany, *The Tribuna of the Uffizi*, 1772–8. Royal Collection, St. James's Palace. © Her Majesty Queen Elizabeth II.

26.1 Robert Dighton, *Fashion Plate for February*, *c.* 1780. Reproduced courtesy of the Minneapolis Institute of Arts.

26.2 Johan Zoffany, *The Armstrong Sisters, Mary and Priscilla*, late 1760s. Reproduced by courtesy of the Leger Galleries Ltd, London.

26.3 Henry Pickering, attr., *Family Gathered Around a Harpsichord*, c. 1760s. Reproduced by courtesy of the Leger Galleries Ltd, London.

26.4 Joseph Francis Nollekens, *Conversation Piece*, 1740. Reproduced by courtesy of the Yale Center for British Art, Paul Mellon Collection.

26.5 Lady Dorothy Savile, Countess of Burlington, *Woman at Harpsichord, with a Dog and a Cat*. Devonshire Collection, Chatsworth. Reproduced by permission of the Chatsworth Settlement Trustees. Photograph: Courtauld Institute of Art.

26.6 Paul Sandby, *Two Women at Music Seated Under a Tree*. Windsor Castle, Royal Library. © 1991, Her Majesty Queen Elizabeth II.

26.7 John Hoppner, *Quartet*. Whereabouts unknown.

26.8 Gavin Hamilton, *Family Scene*. Whereabouts unknown.

26.9 Samuel Collins, *Musical Party*. Whereabouts unknown.

26.10 Nathaniel Dance-Holland, *Musical Party*. Sabin Galleries, London.

26.11 Johan Zoffany, *Musical Party*. Reproduced by courtesy of the Ashmolean Museum, Oxford.

histories of the islands also dwelt on their character as exotics, with origins, customs and culture different from the metropole's. The projection of absolute identities or differences onto colonial cultures, of course, was a salient feature of European imperialist mentalities as a whole in this period.[18] But Oldmixon's enthusiasm for "foreign" cultures, like that of many other writers on empire, was clearly attributable to their status as potential or actual contributors to Britain's favorable balance of trade.[19]

The periodical literature of the day was similarly marked by broad and sustained interest in the imperial project and its contribution to Britain's national stature and strength. At least a third of periodicals such as *Gentleman's Magazine*, *London Magazine*, and *Newcastle General Magazine* were taken up in foreign and imperial affairs in the mid-century, and articles, essays, songs, and poems which concerned themselves, either directly or indirectly, with the state and health of the empire. The *Gentleman's Magazine*, for example, which prided itself on its judgment in selecting and condensing news and cultural items and representing a balance of different views for its broad and hetero-geneous audience, was a prodigious chronicler of imperial affairs, particularly in the 1750s. The volume for 1756, for example, included full accounts of the loss of Minorca, public reaction to it across England, and the first months of the trial of Admiral Byng, which stretched out across several issues (and continued well into the next year). There were also pointed reminiscences about Britain's historical escapades as an intrepid and robust imperial power, from the swashbuckling performances of Raleigh and Drake to Vernon's much more recent, and vividly remembered, siege of Porto Bello in 1739. At the same time, the "Journal of American Affairs," which had been a regular feature of each monthly issue since the magazine began, providing snippets of information on colonial curiosities, cultivation, politics and trade, was expanded to include more extended accounts of individual colonies which sought to establish the clear right of possession by the British. They also included histories of French, Spanish, and Indian aggression against the brave, stalwart, and virtuous English settlers, who managed to survive and triumph despite the odds against them. The columns of the *Gentleman's Magazine*, and of rival publications like it, thus exuded not only contemporary fasci-nation with the processes of colonization, but also the importance of their recounting to germinating conceptions of the national and patriotic character.[20]

Graphically expressive of imperial aspirations were the scores of maps produced from the 1730s onwards that demarcated British possessions, past, present, and future. Indeed, maps of the colonies seem to have predated the proliferation of English gazetteers and trade directories that took off in the 1750s and 1760s. In the 1730s and 1740s it was, naturally, the West Indies that riveted cartographers' attention, while from the early 1750s on it was maps of America and Canada that competed for prominence.[21] The periodical press, again, was prolific in this respect. Like the *London Magazine*, the *Gentleman's Magazine* in 1756–60 printed dozens of maps which ranged from the theaters of war in Europe, Africa, America, and India, to Caribbean islands, the possession of which was or could be contested, all appropriately scaled in "English miles" and longitude from London.[22] It is within the context of extensive cartographic mania over the colonies, providing emblematic evidence of British global aspirations and claims, that the production of trademen's directories must be seen. Publications like *The general shopbook: or, the tradesman's universal directory. Being . . . a . . . compendium . . . comprehending and explaining the domestic and foreign trade of Great Britain and the plantations . . . by companies or private persons . . . [with] commodities and manufactures exported and imported*, published in 1753, must be read against a tradition of colonial "directories," which first refined the technique of making the empire palatable and comprehensible for domestic consumption.

A wide range of printed materials, made available through commercial printing, were instrumental in supporting and extending consciousness of and attitudes about the empire in the wider public, though they are beyond our scope here. What is suggested by the brief overview above is the degree to which the newspaper and periodical press, even in its most apolitical manifestations, supported an accumulationist and mercantile view of empire – that is, that empire was at heart about trade, commerce, accumulation, and consumption, and as such augmented national, as well as individual, standing, wealth, and power. Such accounts, in conjunction with histories and topographies of the colonies, also produced forms of ethnocentric knowledge about the colonies that supported British superiority and power, fed the growing enthusiasm for the exotic and primitive, and legitimated British domination in terms comprehensible to the empire's domestic consumers.[23] They were thus instrumental in disseminating a particularly self-serving version of the significance of Britain's imperial project among an avid public at home.

II

Theater was deeply implicated in the imperial project as well as in the struggles for national definition that eighteenth-century imperialism entailed, providing a focus and a forum for debates about the empire and its relationship to Britain's international stature and prosperity.[24] Theaters, both licensed and unlicensed, flourished not only in the capital but also in the localities, such as Newcastle, Liverpool, Bristol, Hull, Norwich, and Manchester, where audiences were comprised of the same urban classes who made up the wider political nation, from local gentry and government officials to merchants, tradesmen, and artisans. They thus represented a lively and frequently volatile cross-section of social classes, a feature that did not change until the late eighteenth and early nineteenth centuries.[25]

The connections of eighteenth-century theater with the imperial project were both implicit and explicit, and empire provided both a context for understanding the significance of theater as a cultural arena and a text for specific plays. In the first instance, theater was certainly a forum in which national stereotypes were constructed and perpetuated with a vengeance. French fops, adventuring Irishmen, ridiculous Italians and bullying Spaniards – as well as rowdy, robust, but essentially honorable Englishmen – were all stock characters in farce, sentimental comedy, and tragedy in this period. But the nationalist and imperialist sensibilities embedded in much English theater were more subtle and complex than the presentation of "others" as grotesques. For theater both drew upon and exaggerated national cultural identities, and socialized audiences into the mores of differentiation on the basis of sex and nationality in ways that directly affected domestic conceptions of the imperial project.

For example, the legitimacy and morality of the English stage were frequently defended against its critics by protestations of its importance to national manners and character in a way that endowed theater with particular patriotic significance. In the context of Britain's obsessive competition with France – particularly of fears that the British nation had declined into "effeminacy" and effeteness, largely through French influence and contagion, that were fanned by a host of cultural, political, and social commentators in the 1740s and 1750s[26] – theater proponents marshalled the images and rhetoric of patriotism to make their case that English theater was a crucial bulwark of national manners, language, morality, virtue, and spirit – both an offensive weapon and a defensive battlement against "foreign" and especially French contagion, that could also contribute to British expansion abroad.

Not only was theater instrumental, indirectly, in spreading English culture throughout the world – the high proportion of ship-captains and seafaring men in the audience "thereby carry abroad a Taste of Politeness and Generosity, and give the World a Better Idea of *English* Manners," as one advocate argued in the 1730s – but a flourishing theater was also a sign of flourishing liberty, honor, and national vigor, as the support given to Shakespeare by good Queen Bess had shown.[27] That the Whig government should attempt to curtail *English* theater while permitting foreign acting troupes to perform and, it seemed, flourish, was seen as a doubly insidious form of betrayal, both of national honor and of countrymen. Not surprisingly, attacks on both licensing acts and imported actors and genres could take the form of strident xenophobic diatribes against perceived foreign contagion. As one particularly vitriolic defender of English theater put it, "Barbarous Thought! . . . A Freeman of *London*, a Native of England . . . shall be denied the Liberty that is allowed *French* Dancers and [Italian] Harlequins, – to Effeminate Eunuchs, and Sod [omitica]l *Italians*; yet such shall be encouraged, and *Englishmen* despised!" Is it any wonder, he went on, that England is "so debauch'd with Effeminacy and *Italian* airs . . . [that] we daily see our Male Children . . . dwindle almost into Women? Is the antient *British* Fire, Spirit and Bravery, to be supported by such as these?" Clearly, only indigenous British theater could inculcate the appropriately manly, civilized patriotic virtues and manners in its audience. Such nationalistic attitudes, which defined the "other" as barbarous, ignorant, effeminate, or obscene (and hence defined Englishness as their opposites: civilized, cosmopolitan, manly, and virtuous), were deeply entrenched in the entire imperial effort, from the competition with other European countries for empire to the confrontation with the "primitive" and exotic indigenous cultures of the lands being colonized.[28]

Nationalistic and protectionist defences of the stage were not confined to extremist reviewers or high-placed cultural arbiters, however; they were also shared by a wider public. Theater riots (for which the century was notorious) were frequently precipitated by the use of "foreign" entertainers on London and provincial stages, such as those against French and Italian comedians at the Haymarket in 1738 and 1749, and against French dancers at Drury Lane in 1755. These disturbances, where the rioters cried "Remember the poor English players in Gaol!" and "No French Strollers" can quite plausibly be seen as crude attempts to enforce the tenets of balance of trade through the institutional imperatives of theater, protecting its territory and labor force from foreign domination. They were certainly interpreted by their participants as supremely patriotic activities. At the 1755 Drury Lane riots, occurring at a time when war with France was imminent, the leader of the disturbances was alleged to have faced the gallery and exclaimed, "O Britons! O my countrymen! You will certainly not suffer these foreigner dogs to amuse us. Our destruction is at hand. These sixty dancers are come over with one desire, to undermine our Constitution!" Significantly, the rioters included many members of the francophobic Anti-Gallican Society, an association of merchants, tradesmen, and craftsmen dedicated to promoting English manufactures and art in order to eliminate French imports.[29]

Indeed, the riots of 1755 were defended in print by no less a theatrical luminary than Theophilus Cibber, actor, playwright, and son of the poet laureate, in a way which clarified what some observers saw as an evident link between the fate of theater in Britain and the fate of Britain in the world. Cibber began his *Second Dissertation on the Theatre* with a prefatory address to the "Anti-Gallicans, and the Trading Part of the Nation," lauding them for their superior and patriotic actions in removing the French dancers from the stage. The appearance of the French troupe "at so critical a Juncture, when the Minds of Men were naturally inflam'd, against an insidious Enemy, who premeditated a daring Invasion of our Country," was bound to provoke a disturbance, Cibber declared. The audience's actions proved to the world that

> the Natives of this Sea-Girt Island will not readily forget our Navy's our best Bulwark, that our Traffic is the best Support of that Navy: that not only Riches, but Power, and Glory, are added to this Nation, by its extended Commerce. With that, our Arts and Sciences Increase. In you, then, Gentlemen, we trust for an Amendment of our Taste, by a sensible Correction of our Public Diversions.[30]

Although Cibber had no little degree of self-interest in adopting these patriotic arguments – he wanted to diminish the popularity of his rival, David Garrick, who had hired the French troupe to perform in the Drury Lane production of *The Chinese Festival* – the francophobia and identification with the imperial project would strike resounding chords in the public, and indicate how deeply theater was involved in the social and political debates of the day.

Cibber's arguments also underscore the close and deliberate identification of contemporary theater with the attitudes and personnel that supported the imperial project. In the outports, for example, such as Bristol, Liverpool, and Newcastle, it is clear that the commercial middle classes made up a major portion of the theater audience, and merchants were prodigious contributors to new theater buildings.[31] Theatrical prologues and epilogues of the period reflected this social milieu in their employment of the language and metaphors of trade and commerce to explain the significance of particular plays or the English stage generally, purposefully catering to audience sensibilities.[32] Clearly, the precarious existence of theater, both as a closely supervised political medium dependent upon magisterial tolerance, and as a commercialized cultural arena requiring the sympathy and support of its audience, necessitated the adoption of the "patriotic," commercial idiom, which vindicated the stage simultaneously as a nursery of loyalty to the state and as bolsterer of an appropriately aggressive and imperial national identity and spirit. In this regard, too, theatrical benefits held in London and the provinces for patriotic, imperial causes – such as the Anti-Gallican Society, the Marine Society, which apprenticed young paupers to seamen, or various institutionalized charities, such as foundling hospitals, which preserved the nation's youth for useful and productive employment – no doubt served to underline the stage's advanced sense of civic responsibility and its stature as a prop of patriotic sentiment.[33]

The role of eighteenth-century theater in promoting and supporting pro-imperial sensibilities extended beyond its location in a nexus of cultural and ideological issues to the content of the plays themselves. Such a topic is too vast to do justice to in a short space, so two examples must suffice. George Farquhar's comedy *The Recruiting Officer*, first performed in 1706, and George Lillo's *The London Merchant*, first performed in 1731, had many successful runs at London, provincial, and colonial theaters throughout the eighteenth century. Both provided, in different ways, images, rhetoric, and attitudes through which the imperial project could be comprehended by those at home.[34] Farquhar's comedy is a highly topical and amusing account of the dubious recruiting practices during the War of the Spanish Succession (when Farquhar himself served as a recruiting officer in Lichfield and Shrewsbury). Its continued popularity, particularly in wartime, when it became standard fare at provincial theaters during recruitment drives, was based not only on its witty dialogue, multiple plot lines (involving love, masquerade, and social and gender inversion, as well as recruiting), and splendid spectacle, but also upon public familiarity with the chicanery and bribery that were so essential a part of the processes of recruiting soldiers and seamen from the civilian population. Equally important for our purposes, it uses Britain's military and imperial efforts abroad as the standard for illustrating relations between the sexes at home, thus pointing up the ideals of manliness and masculinity for both. Indeed, the dominant trope of the play is conquest – sexual, military, imperial, and recruiting; the language and images of sexual – and national – potency that suffuse the play are one and the same. The army officers, though lampooned for their vices and conceits, are nevertheless local agents of wider international processes, and are worldly, experienced, and above all inexhaustibly virile. Captain's Plume's expression of surprise at the shortage of bastards in the town for impressment is just one of the many lines which play on the supposed libertinism and virility of England's fighting service:

> What! No bastards! And so many recruiting officers in town. I thought 'twas a maxim among them to leave as many recruits in the country as they carried out.
>
> (I.i.218–20)

The use of the language of balance of trade neatly links sexual and national commerce with the military effort, giving an old theme of English comic drama – the equation of sex and commerce – a topicality that forcefully played on eighteenth-century sensibilities and experience.

The conceited Captain Brazen – whose slogan with regard to women is "*veni, vidi, vici*" – equally illustrates the connections between domestic and foreign, military and sexual conquest; in one scene, he brags of his amorous intrigues abroad to Melinda, whom he hopes to make his current prize:

> you must know, madam, that I have served in Flanders against the French, in Hungary against the Turks, and in Tangier against the Moors. . . . I have always had the good luck to prove agreeable . . . I might have married a German princess worth fifty thousand crowns a year. . . . The daughter of a

Turkish bashaw fell in love with me too, when I was prisoner among the infidels. She offered to rob her father of this treasure and make her escape with me, but I don't know how, my time was not come.

(III.ii.47–65)

As Brazen's self-parodic speech implies, women were a highly prized part of the booty of warfare, at home and abroad. The female characters in the play are well aware of the double significance of sexual conquest:

Melinda: Flanders lace is as constant a present from officers to their women as something else is from their women to them. They every year bring over a cargo of lace to cheat the Queen of her duty and her subjects of their honesty.
Lucy: They only barter one sort of prohibited goods for another, madam.

(III.ii.7–12)

And of course it is the army officers' role as the defenders of British liberties and properties (including property in women) against foreign aggression that ultimately valorizes and excuses their libertinism. As Justice Balance points out, echoing stock arguments of the period in support of the army,

They expose their lives to so many dangers for us abroad that we may give them some grains of allowance at home . . . were it not for the bravery of these officers we should have French dragoons among us that would leave us neither liberty, property, wife, nor daughter.

(V.i.3–5, 9–12)

The interchangeability of the language and images used to describe recruiting, foreign conquest, love, marriage, and sex – and even relations between the localities and the state – thus both plays on and coaxes awareness of the links between Britain's glory, liberty and property, successful sexual relations, and the military-imperial effort: conquest and defence were the ends, and manliness and virility the means. Indeed, *The Recruiting Officer*'s comedic representation of martial virility and potency was undoubtedly reassuring at a time when fears of creeping "effeminacy" were impinging on public perceptions of Britain's military performance. In the hands of Farquhar's amorous officers, British sexual and military power (and British masculinity) were safe from "illegitimate" appropriations, whether from women or rival nations.[35]

An equally successful play with a different but related agenda was the "excellent moral tragedy" *The London Merchant*, written by the former merchant George Lillo. A tale of the ruin of a young merchant apprentice, George Barnwell, by a scheming vixen who has declared war on the opposite sex, it satisfied contemporary requirements for moral drama by giving vice its just deserts (Barnwell dies in the end, a broken and betrayed young man, the knowing victim of lust and greed). But the whole play was a cautionary tale about the links between national prosperity, commerce, empire, and virtue that spoke to current sensibilities and concerns. Set in Queen Elizabeth's reign, it skillfully played on the growing anti-Spanish sentiment in London and the outports in the 1730s that arose from continued *guarda costa* attacks on English merchant ships and Spanish encroachments on English colonies. Hence the anachronistic setting in the England which had repelled the Armada evoked what Lillo obviously saw as a more intrepid age, when the English were successful in thwarting Spanish pretensions; it was also an effort to rewrite the history of that era to give the starring role to English merchants themselves. Deliberately didactic, *The London Merchant* differs from earlier, Elizabethan attempts to write tragedies based on middle-class life, not merely by being written in prose, but also by being exceptionally militant in its pride in the middle classes, especially merchants.[36]

The hero of the piece is Barnwell's master, Merchant Thorowgood. He is prosperous, upright, principled, stern, kindly, and fond of repeating mercantilist platitudes, which are worth examining for what they reveal about the marketing of empire at home. Mercantile capitalism is a "science," Thorowgood asserts, "[which] promote[s] humanity . . . keeps up an intercourse between nations . . . and . . . promote[s] arts, industry, peace and plenty" (III.i.5–9). "It is the industrious merchant's business to collect the various blessings of each soil and climate, and, with the product of the whole, to enrich his native country," he instructs his eager apprentice Truegood (III.i.30–3). Truegood agrees, reflecting that trade diffuses "mutual love," allowing English merchants "to tame the fierce and polish the most savage; to teach them the advantages of honest traffic by taking from them, with their own consent, their useless superfluities, and giving them in return what, from their ignorance, in manual arts, their situation, or some other accident, they stand in need of" (III.i.11–19). As these excerpts illustrate, the languages of science, mutuality, consent, love, and duty are employed to emphasize the paternalistic, romantic, and fair-minded nature of British commercial imperialism. This, in turn, is contrasted to the imperialism of the "haughty and revengeful Spaniard[s]" (I.i.5–7) who, in their colonies in the New World, "plundered the natives of all the wealth they had and then condemned the wretches to the mines for life to work for more" (I.iii.25–7).[37] It is, then, English merchants who stand as a buffer between their "happy island" and the world, keeping both out of the hands of the "revengeful Spaniards." Needless to say, Thorowgood is the fulfillment of mercantile ideals: honest and prompt in his accounts with aristocrats and tradesmen alike, virtuous and upright in his personal life, generous in hospitality and charity, he succeeds in teaching Truegood "how honest merchants may sometimes contribute to the safety of their country, as they do at all times to its happiness" (II.i.16–18).

Barnwell, on the other hand, is ruined by not attending to the advice and example set by his master, thus becoming victim to the wicked seductress Millwood. Significantly, Millwood herself provides the domestic counterpart to the meanness and immorality of "foreign" imperialism; she is the domestic "fierce savage," the woman who refuses to be tamed, and she expresses this role in her pledge to dominate the enslaving sex of men, to treat them as the Spanish treat the conquered and plundered natives of the New World (I.iii.24–7). She accordingly promises love to Barnwell and delivers instead ruin, betrayal, defeat, and death. Such is the punishment for weakness and corruption, in private as in public, in individual as in national life. The upright apprentice Truegood, on the other hand, stands to gain all of Thorowgood's wealth through marriage to his beautiful daughter: hence the principles of virtuous acquisitiveness prove victorious, at home as well as abroad. The play is clearly the ultimate mercantilist fantasy and morality tale, in which commerce, empire, and their agents, the merchants, are admired and supported as the founts of national wealth and the conduits of civilization, while the colonies serve to display English paternalism to the world by aggrandizing both the nation and individual Britons at home. As such, it remained popular in the theaters and fairs of the outports throughout the middle decades of the century.

Other plays of the period are equally revealing when read against the imperial effort and sensibilities of the day, such as Southerne and Hawkesworth's version of *Oronooko* (1759), Colman's *English Merchant* (1763), Cumberland's *West Indian* (1771), Colman Jr.'s *Inkle and Yarico* (1787), Foote's francophobic *Englishman in Paris* (1753), or his pillorying of empire as a source of domestic corruption in *The Nabob* (1772). Clearly, theater contributed to public discourse on empire in a number of ways, converging with other branches of the contemporary "media" to promote language, images, and ideologies through which the empire could be comprehended and signified at home. At the same time, the imperial effort provided the context which gave theater a particular cultural and nationalistic significance.

III

Political culture was perhaps most crucial in coaxing, focusing, and disseminating beliefs about and support for empire in public consciousness. Here empire was linked not only to material interests but also to opposition and libertarian ideologies, to strategies of extra-parliamentary organization and resistance, and to the form and content of popular political consciousness. This can be seen at several important junctures, but I will limit my discussion here to two: the Minorca crisis in 1756, and the opening years of the American war.

The mercantilist vision of the empire as the sole means to national greatness was first aggressively retailed to a wider public during the 1730s and early 1740s, when it became a central part of the "patriotic" campaign against the stultifying corruption of the Walpolean state.[38] The imperial project of the period was represented as the ultimate patriotic one: it diffused wealth among the entire population, protected domestic freedoms (including freedom of trade and navigation in the world) from the threats of both foreign powers and rapacious ministries, coaxed "public-spiritedness" from British subjects, and extended Britons' birthrights to the colonies. Simultaneously libertarian and mercantilist, this conceptualization of empire celebrated an aggressive imperial presence and flourishing colonies as bulwarks of trade, power, liberty, and virtue, for Britons at home and abroad. Similar patterns emerged at the inauguration of Britain's greatest imperial effort in the century, the Seven Years War. In this period it was French power and the colonies in North America that were the focus of public attention, and popular imperialism became attached to anti-aristocratic critiques of the state and polity.

By the early 1750s, imperial anxieties and widespread francophobia had become mutually reinforcing, producing much oral and printed obsessing over the security and viability of Britain's American colonies and the dangers posed to them by the strong French presence in Acadia and the upper Ohio country. A large number of histories, pamphlets, and maps of British holdings in America were published, for example, arguing for the need for better management of the colonial defence, particularly after the French defeated American and British troops in confrontations along the Ohio in

1754–5.[39] These demands were bolstered by a chorus of voices both in and out of Parliament that stressed the "High Importance of the *British* Possessions and Rights in America to the Trade and Well-being of these Kingdoms" and called for colonial conquest – particularly of Canada – as the most effective means of defence.[40] The clamor for a strong and aggressive policy in America, along with the sheer wealth of detailed information provided in the daily and periodical press about the French naval and military build-up in the first half of the decade, made the fall of Minorca in May 1756 appear doubly damaging to the Newcastle administration, and doubly catastrophic to the political nation, for it seemed to augur both the beginning of French imperial supremacy and the hopelessly ineffectual and effete nature of the British aristocratic state.

Minorca, situated on the main trade route to Italy and the Levant, was deemed of vital strategic importance for the protection of English commercial interests, and its fall, in conjunction with other territorial losses in America and India and the threat of French invasion, precipitated a sense of crisis that reverberated at all social levels. The unlucky commander of the British squadron sent to defend Minorca, Admiral Byng, was burned in effigy by outraged crowds across the country soon after news of the island's conquest, and a barrage of addresses and constituency instructions demanded a national inquiry into the disaster, as well as a change in ministry, greater accountability from the government, the establishment of a militia, and even parliamentary reform.[41]

The significance of the Minorca crisis and of the ultimate success of Britain in the Seven Years War must be seen, however, against a broader political and cultural context. The early 1750s were marked by a deepening sense of national malaise, stimulated by xenophobia and tinged by sharpening anti-aristocratic sensibilities. Gerald Newman has documented the cultural protest against foreign and especially French "influence" that was so marked an aspect of much literature and propaganda in the 1750s, whereby the aristocracy (and the sycophantic *nouveaux riches* who aped them) were seen as the agents of "alien cultural influence and the associated moral disease."[42] These fears and grievances were further aggravated by the perception that the cultural contagion from above had infiltrated political channels. A virulent strand of anti-aristocratic sentiment had entered political discourse by the mid-1750s, instilled by hostility at government neglect in America, the subsidizing of troops on the continent and the use of foreign mercenaries at home, and such self-regarding pieces of legislation as the game laws, which were presented by their critics as the ultimate in class legislation, mean-spirited and self-serving in orientation and reflecting the genuine priorities of the nation's aristocratic leadership. The letter addressed "To the Nobility and Gentry, Associated for the Preservation of the Game" and printed in a number of newspapers and periodicals, aptly indicated the prevailing mood when it praised the society for its "most useful, most excellent, and most laudable purpose" before reminding them of another issue, "however trifling it may appear to you, and how much soever hitherto neglected . . . the preservation of our country."[43]

Equally damaging, the aristocracy's feckless pursuit of self-interest was also held responsible for the chilling spectacle of the British nation's inexorable, and, some feared, irreversible slide into "effeminacy." According to this theory – the most recent variant of a perspective forged by both anti-Catholic and English civic humanist discourse that condemned the iniquitous effects of luxury and wealth in society – the effeteness and selfishness of Britain's ruling classes had seeped down and corroded the polity, sapping patriotic fervor and leaving weakness, ineffectuality, and supiness in its place. "Effeminacy" denoted a degenerate moral, political, and social state that opposed and subverted the vaunted "manly" characteristics – courage, aggression, martial valor, strength – that constituted patriotic virtue. In the current circumstances, "effeminacy" was chiefly objectionable because it had produced a weak and enervated fighting force that was undermining Britain's position in the world by relinquishing to France her "Empire of the Sea."

The Rev. John Brown of Newcastle, in his *Estimate of the Manners and Principles of the Time*, perhaps most forcefully propounded the theory of "effeminacy" as the cause of Britain's distress, which he pointedly identified as the "ruling character" of the age and the chief characteristic of the ruling classes, both having underwritten the nation's recent disgraces abroad.[44] But Brown was merely systematizing ideas that were percolating through the heated political and cultural debates of the mid-1750s (and, indeed, of the previous two decades). A variety of observers, from almanac writers and political journalists to village shopkeepers, decried the nation's corrupted and "effeminate" spirit that had resulted in displays of national "impotency" abroad and ignominious imperial decline as that evinced in 1755–7.[45] The instructions that poured into Parliament on the heels of the Minorca crisis expressed similar beliefs and fears, while placing responsibility squarely on the nation's leadership.[46] And anti-Byng demonstrators in the localities were no more reticent in identifying the Minorca disaster with ineffectual aristocratic counsels; the fact that Byng was himself the son of a peer added further credibility to the connection.[47]

Hence the aristocratic state was identified with "French influence" and corruption at home, and timidity, effeminacy, and ignominy abroad, and because of this it looked as if France would triumph. The demands for an inquiry into Minorca were, therefore, also demands for an uncorrupted and accountable government that actively protected and pursued the national – that is to say, the *imperial* – interest. As the *Monitor* reminded the Newcastle ministry, after reviewing the crisis in public and imperial affairs, "Remember that government is not given you for venal ends, nor power delegated for your convenience and pleasures . . . forget not that you are accountable servants of the public, and that a learned and inquisitive people are to be judges of your actions."[48]

Equally important, in the context of the public outcry against Minorca and Britain's poor initial performance in the war, empire represented not only the antidote to aristocratic "cultural treason" and effeteness, but also the bulwark and proving-ground of the *true* national character – potent, fearless, virtuous, and *middle-class*. As a number of writers noted, it was among the middle ranks alone that a "spirit of liberty" and national defence still thrived, as was proved in the martial valor of colonial militias.[49] Prints of the period gave visual form to these perceptions, such as *The English Lion Dismember'd; Or, the Voice of the Public for an Enquiry into the Loss of Minorca*, which associated imperial decline and national disgrace with courtiers, game laws, and foreign troops; the way out is shown through stout-hearted and patriotic middling Englishmen, willing to defend their country's interests.[50] Significantly, the creation of extra-institutional supports for a formalized anti-gallicanism was achieved in this period largely through the associative activities of private middle-class citizens, who sought to make England less permeable to French influence and commodification, and more formidable as a counter to French power. The Marine Society, the Anti-Gallican Society, and the Society for the Encouragement of Arts, Manufactures and Commerce, all nurtured a strident nationalism and a good dose of middling anxieties about national impotency, as revealed in both their rationales and memberships. Jonas Hanway, founder of the Marine Society, chose a common trope when he asserted that "They [the French] ever behold with envious eyes the bounties which heaven bestows on this nation, and are watchful of opportunities to *Ravish* them from us," for the imagery of rape was central to the current cultural representations of Britain as a voluptuous maiden poised to be violated by France's lustful aggression.[51]

In the context of these nationalistic anxieties and concerns, the anguish at the loss of Minorca, and indeed the ecstasy and euphoria over the victories of 1758–60, which removed the French from the North American colonies, take on their full significance. The Seven Years War was the fulfillment and ultimate expression of mercantilist imperial aspirations: it bolstered the Atlantic economy, especially the colonial trade in sugar, slaves, tobacco, and rum; produced profits for speculators and privateers alike; and catapulted Britain to the status of a world power, correspondingly (so it was thought) plummeting France to a new low of despair and defeat.[52] And through the fears about French influence and cultural contagion, the war also allowed British global expansion to be portrayed as an ultimately benevolent and patriotic act.[53] The imperialist vision was, in other words, one of expansive wealth and liberty for British citizens on both sides of the Atlantic, mystifying, through nationalistic competition, the exploitative relations upon which the empire was based.

The war and its leaders, particularly the mercurial William Pitt, brilliantly played on and orchestrated the libertarian and pro-imperial sentiment in the nation, producing the unlikely convergence, for the eighteenth century, of a popular war and a popular ministry.[54] The victories at Louisburg, Quebec, Guadeloupe, Niagara, Ticonderoga, Goree, and Montreal demonstrated and valorized the national character – courageous, aggressive, conquering, manly – in a way that surpassed even those spectacular historic conquests which had passed into national mythology. If the loss of Minorca constituted the symbolic emasculation of the British nation, in other words, then the war and its representation at home reconstituted national masculinity, potency, and power. The recovery of British patriotism and manliness through the imperial cause was epitomized, perhaps, for those at home by the death of General James Wolfe at the Battle of Quebec, as the expressions of national pride and grief on the occasion indicated. In a significant anticipation of Benjamin West's famous painting, *The Death of General Wolfe*, a tableau of this historic moment, which ended a performance at the Manchester Theatre in 1763, depicted

> the *General* expiring in the Arms of *Minerva*, while she crowns him with a Laurel; the Figure of *Hope* with a broken Anchor, weeping over him, an Emblem of past Recovery. *Britannia*, the Genius of *England*, seated in *Commerce*, with an *Indian Prince* kneeling at her Feet, resigning up *America*: And *Fame*, triumphing over *Death*, with this Motto: *He never can be lost, Who Saves His Country*.[55]

The war had demonstrated, then, that "Britain will never want a Race of Men . . . who choose Dangers in defence of Their Country before an inglorious safety, an honourable Death before the unmanly pleasures of a useless and effeminate life" as the Rev. Brewster proclaimed on the Thanksgiving day in 1759. Britain's spectacular successes clearly constituted a forceful repudiation of the anxieties of three years before, while reifying the imperial effort into both a national duty and an international blessing.

The imperialism supported and confirmed by the Seven Years War was, however, short-lived, fractured by differing perceptions of the significance and purpose of Britain's expanded empire. To many members of the public, the end of the war promised to inaugurate a new era of British imperial ascendancy and American expansion that would diffuse civilization throughout the globe.[56] To the government, newly acquired territories meant burdensome and expensive imperial responsibilities, necessitating revenue-raising schemes and restrictions on colonial settlement west of the Ohio.[57] And to patriots at home, Pitt's resignation and the Peace of Paris indicated that the old disjunction between the virtuous and imperialistic public and corrupted and self-serving "court" government had returned. Further, within a decade, conflicts with the American colonies and apprehensions about the socially and morally corrosive force of empire raised doubts about the viability of the libertarian, imperial dream. The war for America thus revealed the limitations of the libertarian-imperial nexus that had suffused popular and anti-government politics for most of the century, and underlined its central contradictions.

Certainly once hostilities had commenced, coercive actions in America were easily interpreted as but the latest instance of the simultaneous assault on empire and liberties by a corrupt and tyrannical government. The London and provincial radical press propagated such views with great fervor, identifying the outbreak of "civil war" across the Atlantic with government despotism at home. In prints, pamphlets, newspapers, broadsides, and periodicals, both the ministry and its apologists in Britain were indicted in the "Butean" conspiracy to overthrow legal authority, crush colonial and domestic liberties, and introduce popery and slavery throughout the empire.[58] It was these perceptions that the war emanated from the corrupt, occluded institutions of the aristocratic state which prompted the organization of anti-war petitions and addresses in London and dozens of provincial towns, and which ultimately galvanized new demands for measures of democratic political reform.[59]

But even from the early stages, many English observers were aware that the issues stemming from the war were ones connected not only with political liberty and authority, but with the mercantilist vision of empire itself. In this context, some of the most forceful anti-war arguments were those which emphasized the commercial and imperial, as well as libertarian, reasons for opposing the war. The City of London's "Letter to the Electors of Great Britain," printed in most provincial newspapers, castigated the folly of loyalist writers who argued that government actions would preserve the British empire and colonial commerce: "Desolated fields, and depopulated provinces, are little likely to contribute to our necessities," the address stated: "To secure our commerce, therefore, can neither be the aim, nor the issue of this war."[60] Other writers attacked government aggression for its sheer impracticality and the mercantilist system itself for its shortsightedness. "It is a war of absurdity and madness," one opponent of the war declared; "We shall sooner pluck the moon from her sphere, than conquer such a country"; while another contended that it was folly to believe Britain could forever "tie the hands of the inhabitants of a great continent abounding with raw materials . . . restrain them from using the gifts of nature, and . . . force them to take the products of your own labour."[61] Although virtually all those who opposed the war did so in the hopes of preserving the British Empire in North America, the anti-war arguments, simultaneously commercial and libertarian, clearly contradicted certain tenets of the mercantilist imperial vision that had been articulated in previous decades. Yet they drew a substantial, and, after 1779, an increasing number of citizens of all ranks into the anti-war camp, even from among the middling groups for whom empire and colonial acquisition had always had an appeal, and who were, in the present crisis, hardest hit by the economic dislocation of credit and currency caused by the war.

At the same time, the American crisis undermined long-held beliefs in the morality and virtue of the imperial project. British commentators had long insisted that Britain's greatness as an imperial nation lay in not seeking conquest, but having conquest thrust upon her: colonial acquisition in the Severn Years War was thus continually justified, in and out of Parliament, as a *defence* against French aggression.[62] Further, traditional libertarian doctrine on colonies insisted that force could have no place in their government: as "Cato" stressed, "liberty and encouragement" alone would allow colonies to flourish, which is why "arbitrary countries have not been equally successful in planting colonies, with free ones."[63] But government policies in America clearly contradicted these notions. The Quebec Act, which provided for the continuation of French civil law, government without representative bodies, and the "free exercise" of Roman Catholicism, was justified as a requirement of empire by North and his supporters, and vehemently denounced by his opponents for contradicting what were believed to be established principles of imperial government.[64] Hence, the establishment of "despotic" government in certain colonies, as well as the inefficacy and immorality of forcing submission upon an unwilling population, threatened the loss of a virtuous empire, once "as much renowned for the virtues of justice and humanity as for the splendour of its arms," as the Middlesex electors lamented in their address for reconciliation with America in 1775.[65]

As such, the colonial crisis created an opportunity and an audience for the arguments of the anti-imperialists (always an articulate minority) that empire itself was the primary source of national luxury and corruption.[66] Even those sympathetic to the American cause could perceive that the empire could be a corrupting and enervating force. Foote's scathing indictment of the moral corrosiveness of empire in India in *The Nabob* was paralleled by other condemnation of the Asian empire's polluting impact, which was increasingly seen as a conduit of "luxury, effeminacy, profligacy and debility" to those at home.[67] The West Indian planters or "Creoles" were equally seen as potent sources of parliamentary corruption and mismanagement, who, "being bred the tyrants of their slavish blacks, may endeavor to reduce the whites to the same condition by an aristocracy." The Beckfords of London were similarly lampooned in political ballads.[68] Further, the wave of anti-Americanism that broke out after the fighting had commenced made some observers despair of the mindlessly authoritarian attitudes that empire had produced among English subjects, who clearly saw their cousins across the Atlantic as possessions.[69] And both the war and the reaction to it at home led some observers to attack the acquisitive, machismo model of patriotism and the national character which the imperial project had crystallized. A lecturer at a philosophical society in Newcastle thus claimed that "in every point of view, the laws of war, and the laws of thieving, are exactly alike," both valorizing conquest, self-interest and force, while a local writer suggested that the safety and glory of the state may best be found in its adoption of "feminine" values, as the alleged "weakness of women hath not ushered in such a flood of calamities, as these fatal virtues of men."[70] Clearly, empire benefited some English citizens more than others, and could warp as well as nourish libertarian and public-spirited sensibilities.

Hence, the American crisis had forced a recognition that the empire of virtue, founded in consent and nurtured in liberty and trade, had been irrevocably altered. For British radicals in particular, the colonial conflict exposed the internal contradictions of the libertarian, mercantilist imperialism that had played so large a part in dissident political agitations since the 1730s. An anonymous writer in the *Norfolk Chronicle* in 1778 unwittingly illustrated this predicament when he decried colonial loss as the relinquishing of Britain's "glorious dependencies," for that very notion was an oxymoron in the patriotic, oppositionist ideology that exalted independency as the highest political, moral, and national good. The view articulated by Trenchard and Gordon in the 1720s that colonies, like slavery, were an abrogation of the laws of nature accordingly gained currency along with Smith's exposé of mercantilism and balance of trade theory in 1776.[71] Anti-war activists in the late 1770s were forced to face the essential incompatibility of mercantilist imperialism with the increasingly expansive and participatory views of Englishmen's birthrights, and with the new notions of the just relationship between the individual and the state that were articulated in the radical politics of the day. Other members of the British public, of course, would transfer their imperial confidence and aspirations eastward, to India, as the foundation of a grander, more glorious – and more authoritarian – empire. But for all, imperial identities would have to be reformulated on less tarnished bases than those of a discredited mercantilism and a tenacious, if embattled, libertarianism.

IV

It remains to consider in more concerted fashion the ways empire constructed and embedded normative definitions of class, gender and nation in English culture. "Imperialism" in eighteenth-century Britain was clearly an amalgam of mercantilist, libertarian, and nationalistic beliefs, given form and substance by the contexts in which they were invoked. For most of the period, the imperial project – the "empire of the sea" consisting of colonies and markets – was clearly believed by contemporaries to maximize trade, liberty, prosperity, and national power, and thus appealed to a heterogeneous range of interests, grievances, and aspirations at any given moment. Nevertheless, empire, although never straightforwardly repudiated by the government, was linked in extra-parliamentary political culture with oppositionist ideologies and a popularized mercantilism that castigated the state for not pursuing a more expansionist or nurturing imperial policy. At such junctures as the Vernon agitation, the Minorca crisis, and the beginning of the American war, imperial aspirations were enmeshed with the patriotic critique of corruption and a populist, libertarian vision of the polity, in which accountable government, a public-spirited citizenry, and imperial ascendancy all went hand in hand. The discourses of patriotism, in other words, were complicit with those of imperialism. Linked in this way with the development of extra-parliamentary political culture, empire entered popular political consciousness as a birthright, as much a part of the national identity as the liberties and constitutional traditions for which Britain was celebrated the world over. This outlook, embedded in a range of cultural artifacts and pursuits, justified British imperial ascendancy as a salvation to the world, and erased, or mystified, the exploitation and bloodshed at home and abroad through which imperial dominance was achieved and perpetuated.

Even within their own terms, however, the discourses of empire produced as many contradictions as unities, championing both libertarianism and chauvinism, and celebrating the birthrights of white English (and largely propertied) men while denying those rights to Britons. But because empire was not represented as an end in itself in the eighteenth century, but as the means through which national power and ascendancy could be proved and demonstrated, it could serve as a potent symbol of the innate superiority of the national character in which all social classes could share. This was particularly the case in wartime, when the effort to define and vindicate the nation in opposition to other nations, whether it was Britain against Spain, Holland, or France, or Britons against the native "others" – Indians, Africans, "savages" – coaxed the expression of strident nationalistic sentiments that glossed over domestic differences and divisions. Through Britain's rivalry with France, anti-gallicanism and imperialism became mutually reinforcing: both were reified in this period into patriotic duties, a connection which endured through the years of the American war and beyond. It is in the context of these nationalistic struggles that eighteenth-century imperialism justified both the rights of Britons to trade freely with the world, and their domination of it: they were fairer than the French, less barbarous than the Spanish, more civilized than the savages.

But the Others generated by the imperial project were never limited to those outside the national boundaries. Empire mediated notions of class that were articulated in and through conceptualizations of the dangerous and hostile forces lurking in the domestic polity. Aristocratic "effeminacy" and corruption, for example, presented a distinctive threat to a virtuous polity, for they seeped into the body politic from above, through social and cultural patronage and political power, corroding both national manners and martial might. Aristocratic effeteness was proven, above all, in the inability or disinclination of the "court" to pursue the national, imperial interest. Empire – its acquisition, settlement, and protection – was represented in graphic and literary propaganda as a middle-class paradise, promoting wealth, strength, independence, and virtue, for both individuals and the nation. The antidote to court and aristocratic corruption, empire was, in contemporary conceptualization, the means to becoming more independent and self-contained as a nation, rejecting "foreign" influences, circumscribing degeneracy, and introducing English virtue wherever the latter dared to tread.[72]

Above all, the misogynistic rhetoric and images of eighteenth-century imperialism point to the most threatening Other lurking within. Despite the persistence of an iconography which symbolized the British imperial presence as the female figure of Britannia,[73] colonial conquest was described and glorified as a *manly* occupation, the proving ground for national, as well as individual, potency, strength, and effectiveness, and the vehicle of paternalistic largesse and duty. The basic categories through which the imperial project was valorized (or, later in the century, denigrated) thus both reinforced and exaggerated dominant cultural categories of sexual difference. Empire cultivated and bolstered "manly" characteristics – strength, fortitude, courage, aggression – or it fostered an insidious and "effeminate" moral luxuriousness and corruption. In either case, the "feminine" was contained and devalued in its constructions of patriotism and the national character. Women's place may not have been in the home in the Georgian decades, but "feminine" qualities had no place in the political imaginary of the nation-state in this crucial moment of its development. As Brown had charged, "What strength of thought or conscious Merit can there be in *effeminate* Minds, sufficient to elevate them to . . . Public Spirit?" An "effeminate nation" is "a *Nation which resembles Women*," characterized by cowardice, "irrational pity," and a "dread of suffering," and thus clearly destined for international ignomy and derision.[74] As the antidote to national effeminacy, the imperial project was described and valorized in the images of an aggressive masculinity. It was thus the male conquerors who appeared as the heroes of the imperial saga, and empire became a crucial instrument in constructing exclusive definitions of the British nation and the requirements for citizenship – as nineteenth-century experience would prove.

Notes

This chapter is a reworked version of an essay originally presented at the Shelby Cullom Davis Center at Princeton University. I would like to thank the discussants there as well as at the Clark Library for their lively commentary. For helpful suggestions and advice on this chapter I would like to thank John Brewer, Ann Bermingham, Larry Klein, Jay Tribby, and especially Nicholas Mirzoeff. Portions of the research were funded by a grant from the National Endowment for the Humanities.

1   The best work on the eighteenth-century state is John Brewer, *The Sinews of Power: War, Money and the English State, 1688–1783* (London: Hutchinson, 1988).
2   See the otherwise excellent collection of essays in Felicity Nussbaum (ed.) "The Politics of Difference", special issue of *Eighteenth–Century Studies* 23 (1990).
3   See, for example, H. H. Dodwell, *The Cambridge History of India*, Vol. 5 (Cambridge: Cambridge University Press, 1929); Richard Pares, *War and Trade in the West Indies* (Oxford: Oxford University Press, 1936); Frank W. Pitman, *The Development of the British West Indies* (New Haven, CT: Yale University Press, 1917); Kenneth Andrews, *Trade, Plunder and Settlement: Maritime Enterprise and the Genesis of the British Empire, 1480–1630* (Cambridge: Cambridge University Press, 1984); and, most recently, Paul Langford, *A Polite and Commercial People: England, 1727–1783* (Oxford: Oxford University Press, 1989). More balanced are Richard Koebner, *Empire* (Cambridge: Cambridge University Press, 1961), and the fine studies of Peter Marshall on ruling-class attitudes to the colonies: see "Empire and authority in later eighteenth-century Britain," *Journal of Imperial and Commonwealth Studies* 15 (1987): 105–22, and " 'A free though conquering people': Britain and Asia in the eighteenth century," inaugural lecture, Rhodes Chair of Imperial History, Kings College, London, March 5, 1981. I would like to thank Professor Marshall for making this lecture available to me. Ironically, some of the most distinguished work on the ideological ramifications of the imperial project has focused on *anti-imperial* sentiment and theory in Georgian England: see J. G. A. Pocock, *The Machiavellian Moment: Florentine Political Thought and the*

Atlantic Republican Tradition (Princeton, NJ: Princeton University Press, 1975), and *Virtue, Commerce and History* (Cambridge: Cambridge University Press, 1985).

4 See, for example, Douglas Hay *et al.*, *Albion's Fatal Tree* (New York: Pantheon, 1975); Linda Colley, "Eighteenth-century radicalism before Wilkes," *Transactions of the Royal Historical Society*, 5th series, 31 (1982): 1–19; Linda Colley, "The apotheosis of George III: loyalty, royalty and the British nation, 1760–1820," *Past and Present* 102 (1984): 94–129, and Linda Colley, "Whose nation? Class and national consciousness," *Past and Present* 113 (1986): 97–117; Paul Monod, *Jacobitism and the English People* (Cambridge: Cambridge University Press, 1989); John Stevenson, *Popular Disturbances in England, 1700–1870* (London: Longman, 1979), and Gerald Newman, *The Rise of English Nationalism* (New York: St. Martin's Press, 1987). Nicholas Roger's recent work has taken the imperialist dimensions of popular politics into account: see *Whigs and Cities* (Oxford: Oxford University Press, 1989). Raphael Samuel (ed.) *Patriotism: the Making and Unmaking of British National Identity*, 3 vols. (London: Routledge, 1989), also makes an important contribution but focuses largely on the post-1789 period.

5 Bernard Bailyn, *The Peopling of British North America: An Introduction* (New York: Knopf, 1986), pp. 20–85; T. H. Breen, "Baubles of Britain: the American and consumer revolutions of the eighteenth century," *Past and Present* 119 (1988): 73–104, and T. H. Breen "An empire of goods: the Anglicization of colonial America, 1690–1776," *Journal of British Studies* 25 (1986): 467–99; John Brewer, "English radicalism in the age of George III," in J. G. A. Pocock (ed.) *Three British Revolutions* (Princeton, NJ: Princeton University Press, 1980), pp. 322–67, and John Brewer, *The Sinews of Power*; Ralph Davies, *The Rise of the Atlantic Economies* (Ithaca, NY: Cornell University Press, 1973); Kenneth Morgan, "Shipping patterns and the Atlantic trade of Bristol, 1749–70," *William and Mary Quarterly*, 3rd series, 46 (1989): 506–38; Jacob Price, "The excise affair revisited: the administrative and colonial dimensions of a parliamentary crisis," in Stephen B. Baxter (ed.) *England's Rise to Greatness* (Berkeley and Los Angeles: University of California Press, 1983), pp. 257–321; S. P. Ville, "Patterns of shipping investment in the port of Newcastle-upon-Tyne, 1750–1850," *Northern History* 25 (1989): 135–52; and Kathleen Wilson, "Empire, trade and popular politics in mid-Hanoverian Britain: the case of Admiral Vernon," *Past and Present* 121 (1988): 74–109.

6 Linda Colley, *Britons: Forging the Nation 1701–1837* (New Haven, CT and London: Yale University Press, 1992). Colley argues that "Britishness was superimposed over an array of internal differences in response to contact with the Other, and above all in response to conflict with the Other" (p. 6), and identifies the predominant "Other" as France. But national identities are not unitary entities to be discovered or superimposed but dense ideological constructions that are fissured, contested, and exclusionary of those *within* as well as, or more than, those *without*. The "Other" that is battled with is, as Edward Said has noted, "a surrogate and even underground self": *Orientalism* (London: Routledge, 1978), p. 3.

7 As scholars have just begun to point out: see, for example, G. S. Rousseau and Roy Porter (eds.) *Exoticism in the Englightenment* (London: Routledge, 1989); Felicity Nussbaum and Laura Brown (eds.) *The New Eighteenth Century* (London: Methuen, 1987); and Terry Castle, *Masquerade and Civilization* (Stanford, CA: Stanford University Press, 1986).

8 See Wilson, "Empire, trade and popular politics in mid-Hanoverian Britain", and Kathleen Wilson, *The Sense of the People: Politics, Culture and Imperialism in England, 1715–85* (New York: Cambridge University Press, 1995), *passim*.

9 My conceptualization of the problem has been influenced by Gayatri Chakravorty Spivak, "Three women's texts and a critique of imperialism," *Critical Inquiry* 12 (1985): 243–56; and Homi Bhabha, "The other question: difference, discrimination and the discourse of colonialism," in F. Barker *et al.* (eds.) *Literature, Politics and Theory* (London: Methuen, 1986).

10 See the discussions in Koebner, *Empire*, pp. 85–90, and Marshall, "Empire and authority," p. 106.

11 *London Magazine* 24 (1755): 403–5; *Craftsman*, December 28, 1728.

12 Wilson, "Empire, trade and popular politics," p. 97.

13   These observations are based on extensive examination of London and provincial news-papers, including *London Chronicle, London Evening Post, Public Advertiser, Farley's Bristol Journal, Bristol Gazette and Public Advertiser, Cumberland Pacquet, Newcastle Journal, Newcastle Courant, Norwich Gazette, Norwich Mercury, Liverpool General Advertiser, Manchester Mercury,* and *Worcester Journal*; I would also like to thank J. Jefferson Looney for important information on Yorkshire newspapers. For rare birds and plants, see J. H. Plumb, "The acceptance of Modernity," in Neil McKendrick, John Brewer, and J. H. Plumb (eds.) *The Birth of a Consumer Society: The Commercialization of Eighteenth-Century England* (London: Hutchinson, (1982), pp. 321–2; for ivory, *Liverpool General Advertiser*, July 6, 1770. Kenneth Morgan has also noted the propensity of newspapers from the outports to track the movement of vessels and provide lists of ships' names, masters, and destinations: Morgan, "Shipping patterns," p. 537.

14   Laura Brown, "The romance of empire: *Oroonoko* and the trade in slaves," in Nussbaum and Brown, *New Eighteenth Century*, pp. 51–2.

15   See, for example, *Newcastle Journal*, January 27, June 9, 1750; *Newcastle Magazine* 8(1755): 7–15, 241–4, 405–9; *Liverpool General Advertiser*, November 17, November 24, December 8 December 15, 1769; June 15, July 6, July 27, August 3, 1770; *Lancashire Magazine*, 1 (1763): 11–12; *London Magazine* 24 (1755): 307–12 and issues for July, August, September, *passim*.

16   Such as the marriages of local gentry and wealthy bourgeoisie, national politics, local philanthropic and economic initiatives, land and properties for sale or rent, and notices of the meetings of clubs and societies.

17   For the discussion of the role of "print capitalism" in producing the "imagined community" of the nation, see Benedict Anderson, *Imagined Communities: Reflections on the Origins and Spread of Nationalism* (London: Verso, 1983), pp. 50–79. By the 1740s the economic balance of power in literary and newspaper production had shifted from individual printers to associ-ations of bookseller-publishers and the reading public. See Michael Harris, "The structure, ownership and control of the press, 1620–1780," in George Boyce, James Curran, and Pauline Wingate (eds.) *Newspaper History: From the 17th Century to the Present Day* (London: Constable, 1978), pp. 94–6.

18   John Oldmixon, *The British Empire in America*, 2 vols. (London: 1708), 2nd. edn. (1741); Brown, "The romance of empire," in Nussbaum and Brown, *New Eighteenth Century*, pp. 48–50; V. G. Kiernan, "Noble and ignoble savages," in Rousseau and Porter, *Exoticism*, pp. 86–116; P. J. Marshall, "Taming the exotic: the British and India in the seventeenth and eighteenth centuries," in Ibid., pp. 46–65; and Roy Porter, "The exotic as erotic: Captain Cook at Tahiti," in Ibid., pp. 117–44. See also William Robertson, *History of America* (London: 1777); Admiral Anson, *Voyage Round the World* (London: 1748); and Daniel Defoe, *A Tour Through the Whole Island of Great Britain* (London: 1726), who is eager to note the wider imperial connections of individual towns.

19   See Carole Fabricant, "The literature of domestic tourism and the public consumption of foreign property," in Nussbaum and Brown, *New Eighteenth Century*, pp. 256–7.

20   *Gentleman's Magazine* 26 (1756): *passim*. See also: *Lancashire Magazine* 1–2 (1763–4); *London Magazine* 24–9 (1755–60); and *Newcastle General Magazine* 8–9 (1755–6) *passim*.

21   *Caribbeana* (London: 1740); [Nathaniel Crouch], *The English Empire in America* (London: 1739); Thomas Jeffreys, *The West Indies, exhibiting the English, French, Spanish, Dutch and Danish Settlements* [London: 1752]; Emanuel Bowen, *A Map of the British American plantations extending from Boston in New England to Georgia; including all the back settlements in their respective provinces, as far as the Mississippi* ([London]: 1754); John Bowles, *A new of North America wherein the British dominions in the continent of North America, and on the islands of the West Indies, are carefully laid down from all the surveys . . . and the most accurate accounts and maps lately publish'd. Also the French encroachments on the English provinces particularly described* (London: 1754).

22   See, for example, *Gentleman's Magazine* 26–9 (1756–9): *passim*. *London Magazine* 24–7 (1755–8) includes separate maps of North America, the French settlements in North America, Virginia, Senegal, and Quebec, and the table of contents for 1758 refers the reader to twenty-seven different maps published in earlier issues.

23 Said, *Orientalism*, pp. 2–11; Kiernan, "Noble and ignoble savages," and Porter, "The exotic as erotic," in Rousseau and Porter, *Exoticism*, pp. 86–116, 117–44.

24 Of course, eighteenth-century drama was retailed not only as performance but also as literature. As such, plays should be considered equally a part of the culture of print, read by an even wider audience than that which viewed them.

25 This paragraph and most of what follows is based upon archival research that is part of my work-in-progress on provincial theater. For additional information on theatrical audiences in this period see also Harry William Pedicord, *The Theatrical Public in the Time of Garrick* (New York: King's Crown Press, 1954), pp. 19–43; Sybil Rosenfeld, *Strolling Players and Drama in the Provinces* (Cambridge: Cambridge University Press, 1939), pp. 32–5; and J. Jefferson Looney, "Cultural life in the provinces: Leeds and York, 1720–1820," in A. L. Beier, D. Cannadine, and J. Rosenheim (eds.) *The First Modern Society: Essays in Honor of Lawrence Stone* (Cambridge: Cambridge University Press, 1989), pp. 483–510.

26 See, for example, John Brown, *An Estimate of the Manners and Principles of the Times* (London: 1757–8); Newman, *Rise of English Nationalism, passim*; and section III below.

27 *To the H--nble Sir J-- B--* [London: 1734], reprinted in Theophilus Cibber, *Two Dissertations on the Theatres* (London: 1756), Appendix, pp. 74–5; Cibber, *Two Dissertations*, p. 83. I am grateful to Michael Dobson for drawing my attention to this reference.

28 *To Sir J-- B--*, pp. 74, 76, 73; for the role of nationalistic identities in the imperial effort, see Oldmixon, *British Empire in America, passim*, and Hans Sloane, *A Voyage to the Islands of Madera, Barbadoes, Nieves, S. Christophers and Jamaica*, 2 vols. (London: 1707), which detail the cultural, botanical, and topographical marvels of these lands admiringly, yet in a way which managed to uphold the superiority of English difference; and the essays by Kiernan, Marshall, and Porter in Rousseau and Porter, *Exoticism*.

29 *London Evening Post*, October 10/12, 1738; George Winchester Stone, *The London Stage: A Critical Introduction 1747–76* (Carbondale, IL: Southern Illinois University Press, 1968), pp. lx–lxi, clxxxvi–vii; quote from Ibid., p. clxxxvi.

30 Cibber, *Two Dissertations*, p. 11.

31 G. T. Watt, *Theatrical Bristol* (Bristol: 1915), p. 69; Liverpool County and Reference Library/Record Office, Holt–Gregson Papers, vol. 12, ff. 12–15; Newcastle Central Library, List of Subscribers to the Theatre Royal [1789].

32 See, for example, George Colman, *The English Merchant*, 2nd. edn. (London: 1768), pp. i–iii; Garrick's opening prologue for the Theatre Royal in Bristol, in Avon County Library, Calcott MS 22477, pp. 25–8; and Liverpool County and Reference Library/Record Office Holt–Gregson Papers, vol. 12, ff. 15–18, for a similar prologue written by Colman for the opening of the Liverpool Theatre in 1772.

33 To take one example, the Manchester theater had benefits for the local Infirmary, the Marine Society, bounties on volunteer seamen, and freemasons: see Manchester Central Library, Playbills, Marsden Street Theatre and Theatre Royal: November 27, 1753; October 30, 1757; December 11, 1759; November 26, 1760. For foundling hospitals, see Stone, *London Stage*, cvii–cviii.

34 George Farquhar, *The Recruiting Officer*, ed. Michael Shugruc (Lincoln, NB: University of Nebraska Press, 1965); George Lillo, *The London Merchant*, ed. William H. McBurney (Lincoln, NB: University of Nebraska Press, 1965); all citations from these editions. *The Recruiting Officer* had eighteen runs at the Drury Lane theater and eighteen at the Covent Garden between 1747 and 1776, with the best runs coming in 1750–1 and 1754–5; Lillo's play had nine runs at Covent Garden and twenty-four at Drury Lane in the same period, with the best coming in 1749–50 and 1767–8: Pedicord, *Theatrical Public*, Appendix C. Both were also performed regularly in provincial theaters, such as those at Bristol, Canterbury, Liverpool, Manchester, Newcastle, Norwich, and Richmond: Harvard Theater Collection, Provincial Playbills, 1760 ff.; Bristol Central Library, MS 11204, Jacob Wells Theatre Account Book [1741–8]; Playbills, 1672–1841, MS 1976–80, vols. 1–2; Liverpool County and Reference Library/Record Office, Holt–Gregson papers, MS 942 HOL/12, and Playbills, 1767 ff.; Manchester Central Library, Playbills, 1750 ff.; Rosenfeld, *Strolling Players*, pp. 58, 207, 224, 286, 301. They were also popular in New York and Philadelphia: J. N. Ireland, *Records of the*

New York Stage, 1750–1860, 2 vols. (New York: 1866–7; repr. 1968), Vol. 1, pp. 22–5, 37, 58–60; T. C. Pollack, *The Philadelphia Theatre in the Eighteenth Century* (Philadelphia, PA: University of Pennsylvania Press, 1933), pp. 74–5, 123.

35   Contemporaries were obviously well aware of the significance of these connections in the play: *The Recruiting Officer* was a perennial object of attack in Reformation of Manners campaigns to close down the stage, for its bawdiness and representations of army officers as whoremongers and libertines were alleged by dour observers to undermine respect for authority. "The Debauching of the Country Wenches is represented as a main Part of the Service," the Rev. Arthur Bedford rightly charged in *The Evil and Danger of Stage Plays* (Bristol: 1706; repr. 1730), p. 152; and these objections to the play were repeated by George Pryce in *The Consequences of a New Theatre to the City of Bristol Considered* (Bristol: 1765), pp. 29–30.

36   G. Nettleton, A. Case, and G. W. Stone (eds.) *British Dramatists from Dryden to Sheridan* (Carbondale, IL: Southern Illinois University Press, 1969), pp. 595–6.

37   Cf. the remarks of Brown in *Estimate of the Manners and Principles of the Times*, Vol. II, p. 143: "The Spaniards, in Course of Time, will have converted one-half the vast Southern Continent [to popery], and murdered the other." Favorable comparisons of (virtuous) British with (evil) continental imperialism were well established in economic and political literature by the eighteenth century.

38   See Wilson, "Empire, trade and popular politics in mid-Hanoverian Britain," for a detailed discussion of the way in which empire was inserted into patriotic ideology, and its appeal to a wide range of interests in the extra-parliamentary political nation in the 1730s and 1740s.

39   *Newcastle General Magazine* 8 (1755): 10–15, 241–4, 405–9; *French Policy Defeated. Being An Account of all the hostile Proceedings of the French, Against the Inhabitants of the British Colonies in North America, For the Last Seven Years* (London: 1755); *A Miscellaneous Essay Concerning the Courses pursued by Great Britain in the Affairs of her COLONIES: with some Observations of the Great Importance of our Settlements in America, and the Trade thereof* (London: 1755); *The State of the British and French Colonies in North America, With Respect to Number of People, Forces, Forts, Indians, Trade and other Advantages; in which are considered, I. The defenseless condition of our Plantations . . . II. The Pernicious Tendency of the FRENCH Encroachments and the fittest Methods of Frustrating them . . . With a Proper Expedient proposed for preventing future Disputes* (London: 1755). See also, Dan E. Clark, "News and opinion concerning America in English newspapers, 1754–63," *Pacific Historical Review* 10 (1941): 75–82.

40   *Proceedings and Debates of the British Parliaments Respecting North America, 1754–83* (ed.) R. C. Simmons and P. D. G. Thomas, 5 vols. (Milwood, NY: Kraus International Publications, 1982), Vol. I, p. 81. See also, Ibid., pp. 11–16, 65–7, 94–106, 195–6, 299–301; *Newcastle General Magazine* 8 (1755): 15–16; *A Letter from a Merchant of the City of London*, 2nd edn. (London: 1757), p. 26; John Shebbeare, *A Letter to the People of England, on the Present Situation and Conduct of National Affairs*, 4th edn. (London: 1756).

41   For demonstrations, see *Newcastle Journal*, July 24, July 31, 1756; *Salisbury Journal*, August 2, August 16, 1756; *Worcester Journal*, August 5, September 2, 1756; *York Courant*, September 14, 1756; for addresses and instructions, see *The Voice of the People: A Collection of Addresses to His Majesty and Instructions to Members of Parliament by their Constituents* (London: 1756); most of these are also reprinted in the London and provincial newspapers for August–November 1756. The Newcastle administration was only too aware of the extent and seriousness of the opposition that had broken out across the country, and took steps to contain it, though with little effect: see Add. MSS 32, 866–35, 964, British Library. The ministry was also eager to place the blame for the disaster on Admiral Byng, even though there was ample evidence that Byng was only executing bad and belated orders from the government: see Wilson, *Sense of the People*, Ch. 3.

42   Newman, *Rise of English Nationalism*, pp. 68–84.

43   *Gentleman's Magazine* 26 (1756): 384; *Newcastle General Magazine* 9 (1756): 434–6.

44   Brown, *Estimate*, Vol. I, pp. 66–7.

45   Bernard Capp, *English Almanacs* (Ithaca, NY: Cornell University Press, 1979), pp. 253–4, 260–1; Shebbeare, *Letters to the People of England, passim*, esp. the *First Letter, Fourth Letter,* and

Fifth Letter (London: 1755–7); *Newcastle General Magazine* 9 (1756): 484–94; David Vaisey (ed.) *The Diary of Thomas Turner, 1754–1765* (Oxford; Oxford University Press, 1984), pp. 124–5.

46 *The Voice of the People*, pp. 19, 53–4.

47 See the description of the anti-Byng demonstration in Darlington, in *Newcastle Courant*, September 11, 1756: the effigy of Byng wore a sign with the following message: "A curse on French gold, and great men's promises / I have never done well since I took the one, / And depended on the other: but / take heed my countrymen, *I am not alone*." Byng was the son of Viscount Torrington.

48 *Monitor*, October 30, 1756.

49 Brown, *Estimate*, Vol. II, p. 30; *The Monitor*, December 13 and December, 19, 1755, March 13 and September 11, 1756, January 8, 1757; *Gentleman's Magazine* 27 (1757): 509–12; Shebbeare, *A Letter to the People of England*, pp. 46–8.

50 Lewis Walpole Library, Yale University (British Museum catalogue #3547). Shebbeare and Brown reinforced these themes, insisting that virtue, principle, and manliness remained only among the middling ranks: Shebbeare, *First Letter*, pp. 6–7, 47–8, 50–6; Brown, *Estimate*, Vol. II, pp. 25 6.

51 Isaac Hunt, *Some Account of the Laudable Institution of the Society of Antigallicans* (London: 1781); *Rules and Orders of the Society, Established at London For the Encouragement of Arts, Manufactures and Commerce* (London: 1758); Jonas Hanway, *A Letter from a Member of the Marine Society, Shewing the Piety, Generosity and Utility of their Design* (London: 1757), p. 4. Branches of these societies existed in a number of provincial towns, such as Newcastle, Norwich, Liverpool, Manchester, Bristol, Portsmouth, and Edinburgh; see Wilson, *Sense of the People*, Ch. 1.

52 Pares, *War and Trade*, pp. 85–125; R. Davis, "English foreign trade, 1700–74," *Economic History Review*, 2nd. series, 15 (1962): 285–303; Marie Peters, *Pitt and Popularity* (Oxford: Oxford University Press, 1980), pp. 150–1.

53 See, for example, *London Magazine* 27 (1758): frontispiece, which gives mythological form to this construction.

54 Pitt's genius consisted in playing to the bellicose, patriotic imperialism of the mercantile and middling classes, pursuing an aggressive and expansionist policy in the New World (where the monopoly companies had little sway), and emphasizing the primacy of colonial over continental campaigns: see Add. MSS 32,885 ff. 523–6; *Proceedings and Debates of the British Parliaments*, pp. 265–7.

55 *The Death of the late General Wolfe at the Siege of Quebec*, Manchester Central Library, Playbills, Marsden Street Theatre, August 17, 1763.

56 See the Address of the Protestant Dissenting Ministers of London and Westminster to the King, printed in *Gentleman's Magazine* 33 (1763): 291.

57 Klaus Knorr, *British Colonial Theories, 1570–1850* (Toronto: University of Toronto Press, 1944), pp. 108–10.

58 The evidence on this point is vast, and is documented in Chs. 5, 7, and 8 of Wilson, *Sense of the People*, as well as in several already published monographs.

59 See, for example, James Bradley, *Popular Politics and the American Revolution in England* (Athens, GA: Mercer University Press, 1987); Brewer, "English radicalism"; Kathleen Wilson, "Inventing revolution: 1688 and eighteenth-century popular politics," *Journal of British Studies* 28 (1989) 349–86.

60 *London Evening Post*, October 3/5, 1775; *Norfolk Chronicle*, October 7, 1775.

61 *Peace with America, or RUIN to England*, printed in *Norfolk Chronicle*, March 7, 1778; *Newcastle Journal*, December 16, 1776.

62 *Proceedings and Debates*, pp. 104–9, 265–7; Jonas Hanway, *Thoughts on the Duty of a good citizen* (London: 1759), p. 10.

63 *Cato's Letters. Essays on Liberty, Civil and Religious, and Other Important Subjects*, 4 vols. (London: 1755), pp. 7–8.

64 J. Wright (ed.) *Debates of the House of Commons in the Year 1774, on the Bill for Making More Effectual Provision for the Government of Quebec* (London: 1839; repr. 1966), pp. 89, iii–iv, 15–24. For demonstrations against the Act see *London Evening Post*, June 11–14, 1774, *Newcastle*

Journal, July 9, July 30, 1774; and Jonathan Paul Thomas, "The British Empire and the press, 1763–74" (DPhil. thesis, University of Oxford, 1982), pp. 329–68.

65   Petition of the Freeholders of the Country of Middlesex to the King, PRO HO 55/13/2, reprinted in Bradley, *Popular Politics*, pp. 230–1.

66   See, for example, Josiah Tucker, *Four Tracts and Two Sermons on Political and Commercial Subjects* (Gloucester: 1774); *A Letter to Edmund Burke, Esq.* (Gloucester: 1775); and *An humble Address and earnest Appeal to those Respectable Personages in Great Britain and Ireland* (London: 1776) repr. in *Gentleman's Magazine* 46 (1776): 78–9. See also, Pocock, *Virtue, Commerce and History*, pp. 37–50, 157–92.

67   *Public Advertiser*, March 14, 1774; Samuel Foote, *The Nabob* (London: 1772). Foote's protagonist, Sir Matthew Mite, was a moral grotesque, ruthlessly exploitative of the Indians and equally so of the English at home, whom he strove to rob of their ancestral and native rights. For other expressions of distaste for the Asian empire's enervating and corrupting effects, see *Public Advertiser*, July 10, 1769, March 26, 1771; *Lancashire Magazine* 1 (1763): 60–2; 2 (1764): 515–16; Marshall, " 'A free though conquering people" ', pp. 7–10, and Thomas, "British Empire and the press," pp. 232–328.

68   *Daily Gazetteer*, November 2, 1767; Seymour Drescher, *Capitalism and Antislavery* (New York: Oxford University Press, 1987), pp. 178–9.

69   These attitudes were displayed in anti-American demonstrations in which colonial patriots were burned in effigy, in sermons, pamphlets, and addresses to the Crown, and in prints, ballads, and drinking songs: see Wilson, *Sense of the People*, Ch. 5.

70   "On the folly of war, and love of our country," *Newcastle Weekly Magazine* (Newcastle: 1776), pp. 4–5, and "On the equality between the sexes," in Ibid., pp. 201–4.

71   *Norfolk Chronicle*, January 17, 1778; Cato's Letter no. 106, *London Journal*, December 8, 1722; Adam Smith, *Wealth of Nations* (London: 1776), Book 4. For a discussion of the impact of Smith's work on contemporary thinking about the colonial conflict, see Pulteney MSS, Box 15, WA to Air WP, May 18, 1778. The social contours of support for the war, and particularly the extent of merchant hostility to the colonists' claims, also forced radicals to recognize that there was no necessary connection between merchants, empire, and liberty: "Merchants and genuine patriots are *not* synonymous terms," one observer fumed on surveying the loyalist merchant addresses to the throne. *London Evening Post*, September 8–10, 1778 (I owe this reference to Nick Rogers).

72   In this respect, the contagion of effeminacy was also apprehended to seep up through the polity from below, that is, through the degenerate and disorderly lower classes whose potential for "manly patriotism" was eternally suspect. Not surprisingly, these groups were as much the target of the didactic, middle-class patriotic charities of the 1750s as national ascendancy was the goal. See Wilson, *Sense of the People*, Chs. 1 and 4.

73   See Madge Dresser, "Britannia," in Samuel, *Patriotism*, Vol. III, pp. 25–49; Herbert Atherton, *Political Prints in the Age of Hogarth* (Oxford: Clarendon Press, 1974), pp. 90–6.

74   Brown, *Estimate*, Vol. I, p. 62; Vol. II, p. 40.

14
The state's demand for accurate astronomical and navigational instruments in eighteenth-century Britain

Richard Sorrenson

In 1772, as the Admiralty planned Captain Cook's second voyage to the extreme southern regions of the world (in what was to become the exemplar of all scientific voyages), the first Lord of the Admiralty, the earl of Sandwich, ordered that each of the "watch machines" on board ship be secured with three locks, the key to the first to "be kept by the commander . . . the [second] by the 1st lieutenant . . . [and] the third by one of the [astronomers]" (Cook 1961: 723). Thus, as in the launch of a nuclear missile, no single person was entrusted with the use of these new and accurate machines; when one was to be wound and its dial to be read, all three men had to gather around the box that contained the watch, unlock its three separate locks, check each other's readings of the time that the watch displayed, and make sure that the watch was wound correctly. Other crucial instruments were treated with similar care. When a sextant, which enabled the observer to measure the angle between the horizon and a particular star, was stolen by a Tahitian on another of Cook's voyages, Cook wrote in his journal: "I punished him with greater severity than I had ever done any one before." Another officer noted in more detail: "Cook . . . [made] a publick and severe example of him, in consequence of which . . . he was deprived of his ears and turned on shore" (Cook 1967: 236).

Why was such extraordinary care taken in the use of these instruments and such uncharacteristically grim punishment meted out for their theft? First, as is well known, both clocks and sextants were crucial to accurate navigation; their loss or misuse might have seriously imperiled Cook's voyages. Secondly, they had been made in response to the British state's demand for accurate and robust instruments, and it was the duty of the state's servants (Admiralty naval officers and Board of Longitude astronomers) to use them, test them, and protect them. Finally, they were of great symbolic importance, since, by reflecting the apparent circularity of the observed heavens and the actual circularity of the spinning earth, they accurately mirrored the workings of the clockwork universe. Though timekeepers and angle measurers do not have to be circular or have components that move in circles in order to function, they invariably did so in the eighteenth century, in part because their circularity reified as well as measured the spinning of the globe.[1]

The British state took the study of the clockwork universe very seriously in the eighteenth century and adopted several strategies to give its armies and navies a firmer grip on the globe. In the previous century it had founded the Royal Greenwich Observatory in 1672 to observe the more minute motions of the stars and planets for the use of navigators, and in the eighteenth century it created the Board of Longitude in 1714 to solve the central navigational problem of the century (namely, how to find one's way east or west), and commissioned the Board of Ordnance in 1783 to begin an accurate survey of Great Britain. While the Royal Greenwich Observatory and the Board of Ordnance commissioned instruments for direct purchase, the Board of Longitude, somewhat similarly to the patent system, gave rewards to inventors on the condition that they made their inventions public. As the principal consumers of the most accurate and robust instruments available in Britain and Europe, all three institutions became crucially dependent on instrument makers who could both mimic and measure the precise regularity of the clockwork universe.

The London trade in instruments throughout the eighteenth century was the largest in Europe (Bennett 1985: 13). The forces driving this trade were many, and it would not be easy to rank them in order of importance. On the supply side were a domestic brass and glass industry supplying products that were at least as good and cheap as any in Europe (Hamilton 1926; Macleod 1987); a flexible and well-capitalized system of subcontracting; a loosely controlled apprenticeship system that did not restrict workshop size; a vigorous and innovative retailing trade supplying the huge London market (McKendrick, Brewer, and Plumb 1982); an easy availability of popularized natural philosophy, which instrument makers understood and made use of; a mechanically skilled and ambitious provincial labor pool; and a craft tradition in mathematical instrument making and watchmaking stretching back to the late sixteenth century. On the demand side were domestic, colonial, and European consumers purchasing marine, surveying, and household instruments; natural philosophers in Britain and abroad ordering experimental and observational instruments; popular lecturers and schoolteachers buying a whole range of demonstration instruments to explicate the new natural philosophy; and finally, as this chapter will show, the British state itself, buying gauging instruments for the customs and excise, marine instruments for the navy, astronomical instruments for the Royal Greenwich Observatory, and surveying instruments for the Board of Ordnance, as well as offering prizes for navigational instruments through the Board of Longitude.[2]

The market for scientific instruments in the eighteenth century was a complex one and I have analyzed it by breaking it up into four classes listed in Table 14.1. Although the same maker often supplied more than one class, there were important differences in the creation and supply of consumer demand in the different types of market. The class II market (Natural Philosophical) came into existence in the seventeenth century, and it contained newly invented instruments (pendulum clocks, telescopes, air pumps, and microscopes) as well as older mathematical instruments used in the new context of natural philosophy (quadrants, magnetic compasses). Classes III (Natural Philosophical Lecturing) and IV (Household) were entirely new markets created in the late seventeenth and early eighteenth centuries, as natural philosophy moved out of the courts and academies of princes and into the newly burgeoning commercial market-place of consumers. Only the class I market (Marine, Astronomical, Surveying, Weights and Measures) existed before the scientific revolution, though with far fewer instruments than it contained by the eighteenth century. The "pre-scientific-revolution" instruments included magnetic compasses, quadrants, globes, levels, drawing instruments, gauges, and balances, while pendulum clocks, telescopes, microscopes, barometers and thermometers were added in the seventeenth century. The most important newcomers in the eighteenth century were chronometers, dividing engines, large theodolites, and achromatic lenses, all of which became commonly available only after they had first been developed in response to the demands of the British state.

For the remainder of this chapter I will examine the important nexus of circular instruments from class I – timekeepers (watches or clocks) and angle measurers (sextants, quadrants, and theodolites) – that the British state continuously developed as its navies and armies began to encircle the globe. To do this I will focus on the three most important instrument makers – John Harrison (chronometer), George Graham (quadrant), and Jesse Ramsden (dividing engine and theodolite) – who responded to the demands of the state, and in particular the demands of the Board of Longitude, the Royal Greenwich Observatory, and the Board of Ordnance, to produce masterpieces of accuracy.

I   John Harrison and the Board of Longitude

The Board of Longitude's mission was defined in terms of accuracy. Under an Act of Parliament of 1714, £20,000 was offered by the board for the invention of a method that would be practicable and useful for finding the longitude at sea, such that on a voyage to the West Indies the error of longitude would be less than 30' of longitude or 2 minutes of time over the whole voyage (Taylor 1956: 253). Thus if a watch could be made that varied by less than 2 minutes of time over a typical voyage of eighty days, no matter how rough the passage or how variable the temperature and humidity, it would win the prize. A watch that would do this would almost exactly mimic the perfect motions of the Newtonian clockwork universe. Just as the earth turned on its axis back to exactly the same point in a day (by definition), so too would the dial of the watch return to almost exactly the same place after one day. The success of the watch would mirror the mathematical success of Newtonian natural philosophy.

The board, by offering such a huge prize accompanied by occasional smaller grants to encourage promising methods, stood in a rather unusual patronage role. It could not commission pieces of work, since the technology it was encouraging was not yet certain. On the other hand, those inventors trying to satisfy the board had no certainty of immediate success in satisfying this single consumer.

The eventual winner, John "Longitude" Harrison, a carpenter by training who devoted his entire adult life to winning the prize, was alternately encouraged and discouraged by the board. Up to 1765 the board had given him piecemeal grants for the three watches he made, and in 1765 they gave him half the prize for his fourth watch, which was even more accurate than the board required. They refused, however, to give him the other half of the prize until he had revealed his methods of chronometer

Table 14.1 Markets for scientific instruments in the eighteenth century

---

Class I: Marine/Astronomical/Surveying/Weights and Measures

General Market

Mathematical
chronometers, compasses, globes, sextants, quadrants, theodolites, levels, drawing instruments, gauges, balances, hygrometers, weights, rules

Optical
telescopes

Philosophical
barometers, thermometers

Special Market

Mathematical
chronometers and dividing engines for the Board of Longitude; pendulum clocks, quadrants and sectors for the Royal Greenwich Observatory; theodolites for the Ordnance Survey; standard yard for the Royal Society

Optical
telescopes and achromatic refracting lenses for the Royal Greenwich Observatory

Class II: Natural Philosophical

Mathematical
pendulum clocks, globes, sectors, quadrants, micrometers, pyrometers

Optical
telescopes, microscopes, optics for mathematical instruments, burning lenses

Philosophical
air pumps, pneumatic and chemical apparatuses, magnets, compasses, electrical machines

Class III: Natural Philosophical Lecturing

Mathematical
orreries, globes

Optical
burning lenses, prisms

Philosophical
air pumps, pneumatic and chemical apparatuses, magnets, electrical machines, apparatuses to demonstrate principles of mechanics, models of machines, "toys"

Class IV: Household

Mathematical
clocks, orreries, globes

Optical
spectacles, telescopes, microscopes, prisms, magic lanterns, opera glasses, camera obscura

Philosophical
thermometers, barometers, air pumps, electrical machines, "toys"

---

making to the board and instructed several watchmakers in the art of constructing his "watch machines." Despite the intervention of the king in his favor (George III even tested one of Harrison's watches himself), Harrison was forced to train several watchmakers in his methods to gain the other half of the reward (Quill 1963: 151–7). One of these copies was placed on Cook's ship for further testing. Since potentially large sums of money were at stake the word of one officer (even if a gentleman) was not enough; three different men had to keep their eyes on each other, and all three were given separate keys.

Harrison's chronometer of 1765 was the culmination of nearly a century of effort to develop a timekeeper that kept accurate time aboard ship so that a navigator could find his way east or west. Such an accurate shipboard timekeeper – initially a pendulum clock, but eventually a spring-regulated watch – was called a chronometer. Christian Huygens was the first to devote a major effort to making such a timekeeper in the 1650s, but while he failed to invent a watch that worked at sea, the mathematics that he developed to describe the motion of the timekeeper's regulator (either a spring or a pendulum) became the exemplar of the best sort of mathematics to apply to physical problems (Mahoney 1980: 236–7). Out of the study of the motion of springs and pendulums came a style of mathematics that survived into the late twentieth century. Thus not only did the clock serve as the dominant machine for creating metaphors of the universe, but the mathematics it engendered led to what Stephen Kellert has called the clockwork hegemony in the mathematics of science – a hegemony that lasted until very recently (Kellert 1993: 145).

Even after Harrison was awarded the second half of the longitude prize, the Board of Longitude continued to offer premiums for improvements in chronometers until 1828. At that time the board was dissolved, since the longitude problem was judged to have been sufficiently solved such that the normal marketplace could supply enough accurate chronometers without the encouragement of the government.

II George Graham and the Royal Greenwich Observatory

The Royal Observatory at Greenwich was founded by the Crown in the seventeenth century to improve astronomy for the benefit of navigation and more specifically of the English navy, whose elegant officers' college the Observatory still overlooks. Greenwich was the first successful military-scientific complex in Europe, and the knowledge created there was both of the most arcane and the most useful kind imaginable.[3]

When, in 1725, it was found that the Observatory could no longer operate properly, since the previous Astronomer Royal's widow had taken many of the instruments upon her husband's death, a number of new instruments were ordered. The principal instrument needed was a quadrant that would be fixed to a wall facing north and measure the angle above the horizon at which stars passed the meridian. Operating in quite a different manner from the Board of Longitude, the Observatory commissioned George Graham, a mathematical instrument maker and a Fellow of the Royal Society, to make the quadrant for a fixed price. The Observatory did not specify the accuracy of the quadrant; they simply expected it to be the most perfect possible because it was being made by Graham, who already had a reputation for extraordinary ability.[4]

Graham did not manufacture the whole quadrant himself – Jonathon Sisson undertook the construction of the brass arc and the iron frame – but he did "direct the whole design . . . [and] was pleased to perform the divisions of the arch and all the nicer parts of the work with his own hands" (Smith 1738: 332). The method of division rested on a sound understanding of the geometry of the circle and a delicate and precise touch; the angles were marked off by compasses and rulers, and the process of division took several months.

The Observatory did indeed get the best possible quadrant it could have had at the time, and the praise for this instrument was consistent from the beginning. In 1738, Robert Smith, the Master of Mechanics to His Majesty, asserted that its "particular accuracy . . . excels all others . . . owing to the extraordinary skill and contrivance of Mr. *George Graham!*" (Smith 1738: 332). Nearly fifty years later, the Cambridge don William Ludlam thought that Graham had "carried the art of constructing and graduating [this] instrument . . . to such perfection, that from this time we may date a new era in Astronomy" (Ludlam 1786: iii). This new era in astronomy worked not only to the advantage of the Observatory (and hence of the navy), whose astronomical observations were made greatly more accurate by this instrument, but also of other English instrument makers who copied Graham's quadrant. On the strength of Graham's reputation they exported their versions throughout Europe, so that Graham's quadrant became the model for virtually all large observatory quadrants for the next fifty years (Chapman 1990: 71).

III   Jesse Ramsden and the Boards of Longitude and Ordnance

Though both John Harrison and George Graham had produced masterpieces of accuracy, the Board of Longitude also wished to encourage the production of a great number of accurate instruments for the use of naval and civilian mariners; to this purpose it turned to the most distinguished optical and mathematical instrument maker of the day, Jesse Ramsden, who was beginning to apply industrial techniques to instrument making. He had already made an instrument to make instruments – in other words a machine tool – and they wished to encourage him to make its construction public knowledge. The main object of his machine tool, called a dividing engine, was to mechanize the process of marking off angles on quadrants and sextants. In principle, with a machine like Ramsden's, unskilled workers could make accurate instruments; in practice, however, this became true only for smaller instruments that could be mounted on the dividing engine. Large instruments, which could not be fitted on his dividing engine, remained individual masterpieces.

In 1775 the Board of Longitude paid Ramsden £615 to write an account of his dividing engine, instruct other instrument makers in its use and construction, and divide other makers' octants and sextants at a fixed rate. In his "Description of an engine for dividing [circular] mathematical instruments," which appeared in 1777, Ramsden boasted that his machines could divide an instrument "without an error of the 1/4000th part of an inch," going on to note that "as this can be done by any indifferent person, and so very expeditiously, its uses for dividing all sorts of navigation scales, sectors, etc. must be obvious."

Ramsden's first dividing engine is shown in Plates 14.1 and 14.2. The large bell-metal wheel, mounted on a mahogany stand, is 45 inches in diameter, and its edges have been cut into 2,160 teeth on which an endless screw acts (the screw is shown from above in Plate 14.2). Six turns of the screw move the wheel one degree, and the brass circle to be divided is fixed to the wheel. The divider (Plate 14.2), which slides along the rectangular frame, is fixed when it is over the circle to be divided. The endless screw is rotated a small amount, corresponding to the fraction of a degree wanted for the instrument being divided, and the divider is pressed down to make a mark on the instrument. Thus the dividing arm of the engine creeps minutely and precisely around the circular instrument, inscribing the circularity that the instrument will then reveal when it is used to measure angles from the earth to the sky.

Ramsden was ordered to charge three shillings for dividing octants and six shillings for dividing sextants on this machine. The Board of Longitude printed 500 copies of the pamphlet describing its operation and construction (Ramsden 1777: Maskelyne's preface). The Royal Society also expressed its gratitude for this machine, "by which an accuracy unheard of before except in the most expensive instruments had been transferred to the cheap sextants used by our Merchant Sailors," and gave Ramsden (who was also a Fellow of the Society) the Copley Medal in part for its construction (Banks 1795).

While the Board of Longitude could command Ramsden (once he had made his machine tools) to get workmen in his shop to make a great number of sextants and quadrants, no one could force him to finish his large masterpieces on time. He was an artist whose work could not be copied by others; to the President of the Royal Society, Sir Joseph Banks, Ramsden was "Promethean" (Banks 1795), while to the head of the Paris Observatory, the comte de Cassini, he was a "genius" (Wolf 1902: 288). Ramsden kept everyone waiting. He is even supposed to have kept the king waiting – the *Dictionary of National Biography* relates that on one occasion he attended Buckingham House exactly a year later than invited, though he was punctual as to the day and hour – and he certainly kept lesser mortals waiting several years for delivery of his telescopes, mural quadrants, zenith sectors, and theodolites. The record length of time to fill an order was probably the twenty-three years that the Dublin Observatory had to wait for delivery of an altitude and azimuth circle (King 1955: 169). Yet buyers throughout Britain and Europe, rather than acquire some other maker's lesser instrument sooner, chose to get an excellent Ramsden instrument later. These clients did eventually have their orders filled, so that, as Banks noted in 1795, five years before Ramsden's death:

> Few Observatories were without something that bore his name and no expence was spared by those persons who were able to induce him to undertake the construction of capital instruments, for indeed, there was scarcely one instrument made use of in the whole circle of Astronomical Observations, that had not received eminent improvement from his masterly touch.
>
> (Banks 1795: November 30)

With Ramsden's theodolite, the Ordnance Survey of Great Britain, begun in 1784, saw the levels of accuracy that had been recently applied to astronomy and navigation applied to surveying. The French Astronomer Royal, Cassini, had proposed a survey to fix the relative longitudes of Paris and Greenwich in 1783, and the Royal Society quickly took him up on it. This project was soon expanded by the Board of Ordnance into a survey of all of Great Britain; the main force behind the effort was Major-General William Roy, who had first seen the usefulness of accurate maps when he had surveyed the Scottish highlands in order to provide roads for the subduing British army after 1745. Ramsden took over three years to complete the new theodolite, much to the displeasure of General Roy. Joseph Banks, the President of the Royal Society, in his speech awarding Ramsden the Society's Copley Medal, diplomatically stated that

> before so large a number of capital improvements could be brought to perfection a considerable portion of time was consumed; during the lapse of which, both General Roy's character as a man of patience and Mr. Ramsden's as a man of punctuality, underwent some severe trials.
>
> (Banks 1795: November 30)

Despite Roy's impatience, however, he had no alternative but to wait for Ramsden to finish, and when Ramsden did so the massiveness, intricacy, and accuracy of the theodolite left it beyond criticism.

With Ramsden's theodolite, as with Graham's quadrant and Harrison's chronometer, the British navy and army demanded and were provided with instruments that mapped with the greatest available perfection the land, the heavens, and the sea. Thus the state created and defined a small but important type of market for British instrument makers, who in turn gained a reputation that allowed them to dominate the European market for such complicated, expensive, and accurate instruments. At the same time, however, the state, primarily through the Board of Longitude, also helped finance the construction of cheaper, but still reasonably accurate, instruments (especially chronometers and sextants) that could be made in far greater numbers than the large observatory instruments. Thus, by encouraging both the construction of unique large instruments and the mass production of smaller instruments, the state, through such organs as the Royal Greenwich Observatory, the Board of Longitude, and the Ordnance Survey, ensured that instruments of near perfection became readily available both to its servants and its subjects.

Notes

1   The modern digital watch and atomic clock do not rely on circularity of components or dials to function; nor did the sixteenth-century cross-staff, which measured angles.

2   Brewer (1988) makes a convincing case for the size and strength of the British state's excise service and navy, both of which made extensive use of mathematical instruments. Brewer also notes that wartime embargoes of French goods between 1688 and 1714 allowed "the British glass, paper, silk, cutlery, watch and toy industries . . . to improve the quality of their work . . . [and] also to capture a sizable portion of the domestic luxury goods market" (1988: 196). These remarks apply equally well to scientific instrument making. Howse (1975) gives extensive evidence of the Observatory's patronage of instrument makers. There are no histories of the Board of Longitude of which I am aware. Turner (1987) gives an excellent account of scientific toys which were used to demonstrate principles of mechanics.

3   While the Royal Observatory in Paris was commissioned two years earlier, the French navy never made much use of its work (Gillispie 1980: 100–1).

4   For the sources of, and reasons for, Graham's reputation see Sorrenson (1993: Ch. 5).

Bibliography

Banks, J. (1795) "Copley Medal address," Royal Society Journal Book, November 30.

Bennett, J. (1985) "Instrument makers and the 'decline of science in England': the effect of institutional change on the elite makers of the early nineteenth century," in P. R. de Clerq (ed.) Nineteenth-Century Scientific Instruments and their Makers, Amsterdam: Rodopi.

Brewer, J. (1988) The Sinews of Power: War, Money and the English State, 1688–1783, New York: Knopf.

Chapman, A. (1990) Dividing the Circle: The Development of Critical Angular Measurement in Astronomy, 1500–1850, New York: Ellis Horwood.

Cook, J. (1961) The Journals of Captain James Cook, Vol. II, The Voyage of the "Resolution" and "Adventure" 1772–1775, ed. J. C. Beaglehole, Cambridge: Hakluyt Society.

—— (1967) The Journals of Captain James Cook, Vol. III, The Voyage of the "Resolution" and "Discovery" 1776–1780, ed. J. C. Beaglehole, Cambridge: Hakluyt Society.

Gillispie, C. C. (1980) Science and Polity in France at the End of the Old Regime, Princeton, NJ: Princeton University Press.

Hamilton, H. (1926) The English Brass and Copper Industries to 1800, London: Longman, Green.

Howse, D. (1975) Greenwich Observatory, Vol. 3, The Buildings and Instruments, London: Taylor & Francis.

Kellert, S. (1993) In the Wake of Chaos, Chicago: Chicago University Press.

King, H. (1955) The History of the Telescope, London: Charles Griffin.

Ludlam, W. (1786) "An introduction and notes on Mr. Bird's method of dividing astronomical instruments," London.

McKendrick, N., Brewer, J. and Plumb, J. H. (eds.) (1982) The Birth of a Consumer Society: The Commercialization of Eighteenth-Century England, Bloomington, IN: Indiana University Press.

Macleod, C. (1987) "Accident or design? George Ravenscroft's patent and the invention of lead-glass," Technology & Culture 28: 776–803.

Mahoney, M. S. (1980) "Christiaan Huygens: the measurement of time and longitude at sea," in Studies on Christiaan Huygens, ed. H. J. M. Bos et al., Lisse: Swets & Zeitlinger.

Quill, H. (1963) "John Harrison, Copley medallist, and the £20,000 Longitude Prize," Notes and Records of the Royal Society 18: 146–60.

Ramsden, J. (1777) "Description of an engine for dividing mathematical instruments," London.

Smith, R. (1738) A Compleat System of Optics, Cambridge.

Sorrenson, R. (1993) "Scientific instrument makers at the Royal Society of London, 1720–1780," PhD dissertation, Princeton, NJ: Princeton University.

Taylor, E. G. R. (1956) The Haven Finding Art: a History of Navigation from Odysseus to Captain Cook, London: Hollis & Carter.

Turner, G. L'E. (1987) "Scientific toys," British Journal for the History of Science 20: 377–98.

Wolf, C. (1902) Histoire de l'Observatoire de Paris, Paris: Gauthier-Villars.

15
Signs and citizens
Sign language and visual sign in the French Revolution

Nicholas Mirzoeff

If we had neither voice nor language, and we wished to show things to one another, would we not try, as in effect mutes do, to indicate them with our hands, head and the rest of our body?

(Plato, *Cratylus*, XXXIV, 422d–423b)

The forms of men must have attitudes appropriate to the activities that they engage in, so that when you see them, you will understand what they think or say. This can be done by copying the motions of the dumb, who speak with movements of their hands and eyes and eyebrows and their whole person, in their desire to express that which is in their minds. Do not laugh at me because I propose a teacher without speech to you . . . for he will teach you better through facts than will all the other masters through words.

(Leonardo da Vinci, *Treatise on Painting* [1956: 105])

I understood, moreover, that in every Nation speech and writing only signify something by a purely arbitrary agreement amongst the people of that country, and that everywhere there must have been signs which would have given to both speech and writing – and as perfectly by writing as through speech – the virtue of recalling to the spirit the ideas of things whose names one had pronounced or written, whilst showing them by some sign of the hand or the eyes.

(Abbé Charles-Michel de l'Epée, 1984 [1784]: 110)

Reading signs

The hearing have always been aware of the signs made by the deaf to communicate with each other.[1] But, until very recently, they have not fully understood what those signs have meant. Nonetheless sign language has often been referred to by artists, critics, and philosophers as a source for (mis)understanding the meaning and origin of language and of depicting the body's gestures. This chapter is concerned with the transition between two moments of that (mis)reading in the Enlightenment and the French Revolution. In order to approach this task, I highlight the interaction between two visual signifying systems, sign language and painting. The sign was read very differently in 1810 than it had been in 1775 and it is part of my concern to show that this process was not a logical unfolding of semiotic thought but a radical disruption of that Reason.

In so doing, I will offer a "semiotic turn" to the emphasis on consumption which has been prominent in recent cultural studies. In such work, the traditional Marxist concept of the mode of production has come to be replaced by the study of an almost autonomous consumer, validating him or herself through consumption (Krauss 1991). But it is precisely the resonance of poststructuralism that there are no fixed and immutable structures of signification by which we can interpret culture. As Bal and Bryson have observed: "Once launched into the world, the work of art is subject to all the vicissitudes of reception; as a work involving the sign, it encounters from the beginning the ineradicable fact of semiotic play" (Bal and Bryson 1991: 179). Thus, the reception or reading of the sign is a vital precondition for its consumption and is in no way a "given" that does not require analysis. A cultural sign must be understood, even if the sense gained is not that intended by its originator, if it is to be received or consumed. As Roger Chartier has recently emphasized: "The diffusion of ideas cannot be held to be a simple imposition. Reception always involves appropriation, which transforms, reformulates, and exceeds what it receives" (Chartier 1991: 19). That is to say, consumption takes place only after the sign has been transformed into a culturally acceptable format which may radically differ from its original form. The means by which this transformation occurs, and the changes in such techniques, are the focus of this chapter. The switch in cultural studies from, broadly speaking, production to consumption requires a further recognition that the itinerary of the sign cannot be known or predicted either in the eighteenth century or the present. Here the gestural sign and the artwork are considered not as exclusive categories but as semiotic processes that should be seen as analogous.

The signs of the deaf were of particular importance to Enlightenment philosophers who believed that they could find in them the key to the much-desired universal language which would obviate the need for such an interpretive process. It was the semiotic concept of the sign proposed by Condillac, Locke, and Rousseau as a means of understanding language that both enabled and necessitated an interaction with the gestures of the deaf which could now be "read" as signs. This interaction is indeed justified, for a handshape in sign language is a signifier that indicates a signified. If sign language were universal, as such writers hoped and believed, the gestural sign might, as it were, belong to that which it signified in a relationship that could not be divided or shown to be possible in another form. But we now know this to be wrong, both empirically and theoretically. It is a fact that the sign languages of different nations are mutually unintelligible – British Sign Language is different from American Sign Language, for example – and, furthermore, sign has been shown to use precisely the same conventions and grammatical constructions as spoken languages (Stokoe 1982).

Gestural signs are no more universal than spoken or written signs and must be treated as such.

The interaction between the semiotic and the gestural is one of the key fields of investigation in this work. It is not enough, however, simply to equate the gestural sign and the semiotic sign as premissed by Saussure and others. Rather, it should be emphasized that, like all semiotic systems, sign language is constituted by difference. For if the gestural sign does not have a transparent, natural relationship to the referent, it cannot be self-evident what the sign means. Instead it operates as Saussure's sign does, with signifier and signified combined into the arbitrary unit of the sign: "*In language there are only differences*. What's more: a difference in general presupposes positive terms between which it is established; but in language there are only differences *without positive terms*" (Saussure 1964: 166). The inescapability of such difference is clear when considering the gestural sign for, in this instance, "sign" refers both to the verb, to sign, and the noun, sign. "Sign" is thus both a practice and a register of gestural sign language, whilst also referring to the semioticians' abstract notion of the sign. The sign cannot be neatly defined and separated, so that at one moment it is a linguistic construct and at another a particular handshape: it is always both of these at once.

Sign language draws our attention to the notion that signs are not simply different from one another but are constituted by their difference both from other signs and from the three components – signifier, signified, referent – of the individual sign. Any attempt to classify and order the sign can never fully encompass this system of difference and will produce anomalies and inconsistencies that belie the overall veridic power of the system. In moments of reformulation, the network of signification will attempt to exclude such aporia in order to retain and revive its power to produce knowledge. The "third term" of difference does not simply disrupt the sign-in-itself but involves it in a wider intersection with a variety of discursive practices. Perhaps precisely because of the uncertainty over its status and meaning, debates over sign language were a point of intersection for discourses of anthropology, gender, language, medicine, race, and vision. Difference has been widely shown to be constructed in its various instances, most noticeably those of gender and race. However, it may now be appropriate, without denying the validity of such specialized studies, to concentrate on such moments of interaction between divergent discourses of difference. This chapter, then, seeks to examine how the sign, specifically the sign language of the deaf, was transformed in conception, reception, and institutional practice in the moment around the French Revolution without seeking to privilege as causal one or other of the series of interactions upon the sign.

In the beginning, there was the sign

Sign was accepted, if little understood by the hearing, in Renaissance and early modern Europe.[2] It was assumed that signs were pantomime icons, imitating objects or needs, making the meaning of signs transparent. Leonardo's *Treatise on Painting* (quoted above) marked the first written advice to artists that such gestures might well represent an important source. Consistent with the belief in the artistic imperative of copying nature, Leonardo saw sign language as a "[f]act," a product of nature rather than culture. But true sign language is not pantomime. It has a grammar, vocabulary, and syntax of its own, giving it the full range of a spoken language as well as its own particular strengths. In the early modern period, it had numerous regional, as well as national, variations. The painter seeking to draw the gestures of the deaf would have needed to learn it from deaf friends or relatives. Certainly, deafness was far more common as an acquired condition in early modern society, for it was a side-effect of such diseases as scarlet fever, smallpox, mumps, and even the common cold.

The imitation of sign language was first prescribed for artists in France by du Fresnoy in his Latin poem "On the art of painting" (1668), which was soon translated into French by Roger de Piles: "Mutes have no other way of speaking (or expressing their thoughts) but only by their gesture and their actions; 'tis certain that they do it in a manner more expressive than those who have the use of speech, for which reason the Picture, which is mute, ought to imitate them, so as to make itself understood" (Dryden 1695: 129).[3] For the moderns in the Academy, the cliché of Academic theory that painting was *la poésie muette* had some literal, as well as metaphorical, sense.[4] For the first forty years of the eighteenth century, the Academy of Painting was controlled by the Coypel family, who were friends of de Piles, and who often repeated his advice on sign language to students and members of the Academy. Charles-Antoine Coypel was also a playwright and drew upon the popular tradition of deaf characters in French theater. At least as early as the sixteenth century, deaf characters appeared in comedies, most often involving a hearing romantic hero pretending to be deaf in order to gain access to his love. Sign language was used as a piece of "business" to attract the attention of the often unruly crowd.[5]

Throughout this period, however, the gestural sign was simply taken to be a pantomime imitation of speech with no importance of its own. But in the eighteenth century, the search for both the origin of language, and hence a universal language, became widespread. One critic noted that: "The great advantage of a universal language would consist in rendering the communication of *lumières* easier, surer, more prompt and more general" (*Décade Philosophique* an IX: 24). Gesture was held to have been one of the first stages of language and might hence hold clues for the establishment of an advanced, philosophical universal language. Diderot's interaction of theater, art, language, and deafness in his "Lettre sur les Sourds et sur les Muets" [Letter on the deaf and dumb] (1755) was entirely consistent with this tradition. He transformed the status of gesture from popular entertainment into a philosophical and linguistic sign. It took the peculiar genius of the abbé de l'Épée for sign to again be of importance to artists. Diderot conversed with a prelingually deaf person to test his theories of the origins of language. He believed that gestural sign was a natural language that preceded the evolution of the artificial, spoken languages. Diderot found a quality in the sign language of the deaf that could not be matched by the orators:

> One could almost substitute the gestures with their equivalents in words; I say almost, because there are sublime gestures which all the eloquence of oratory will never capture.

> (Diderot 1978: 142–3)[6]

He found this language so convincingly natural that he decided that, when looking at paintings, he would pretend to be a deaf man watching other deaf people conversing about a subject known to them. If the scene was convincing, looked at in this manner, he judged it to be successful.[7] In this respect, Diderot had simply taken the earlier recommendations of the Academy's teachers and used them as a guide for his criticism. In turn, his ideas on the sublimity of gesture quickly found their way into Academic theory. In his Academic textbook, Dandré-Bardon, who taught David at the Academy, observed: "One gesture alone . . . can be sublime. Such is the gesture which Poussin gave to Eudamidas' doctor in that painting where this Philosopher left his testament" (Dandré-Bardon 1972: 60)

Supplementing the sign

Just as art critics and theoreticians suggested that painters learn from the deaf, so too did the abbé de l'Epée use art as a means of theorizing the instruction of the deaf. In the early 1760s, Charles-Michel de l'Epée, an obscure Jansenist priest, encountered two deaf sisters in a poor district of Paris. Epée observed the women signing and realized that they were in fact conversing, providing him with an unsuspected opportunity to save their souls for the Church.[8] Working with the sisters, he taught himself the rudiments of their language and proceeded to attempt to teach them written French. He believed that he had found a primitive universal language in deaf sign. Once refined out of its crude, natural state by his hearing intervention, Epée believed it "could become a meeting place for all men" (Epée 1776: 136). He saw himself as applying the linguistic logic of Condillac who had held that the first form of language was the gesture, accompanied by a cry. Soon the sound became regularized and, in due course, came to replace the gesture altogether. Sounds were then combined to form phrases and sentences. It was thus impossible for a gestural language to have grammar, as it preceded the grammatical stage in the evolution of language. I have argued elsewhere that this form of linguistic practice needs to be understood in terms of Derrida's analysis of the supplement (Mirzoeff 1992). The supplement completes something, but in so doing it reveals that it was not previously whole. In Derrida's view, the logic of the supplement thus cuts both ways:

> The supplement supplements. It adds only to replace. It intervenes or insinuates itself *in-the-place-of*; if it fills, it is as if one fills a void. If it represents and makes an image, it is by the anterior default of a presence. Compensatory and vicarious, the supplement is an adjunct, a subaltern instance which *takes-(the)-place*.

> (Derrida 1976: 145)

Thus a supplement, which is exterior to the sign, reveals the lack of plenitude in the sign by the necessity of its addition. If the sign is truly complete, it would not have any need of the supplement. Christopher Norris has made a useful comparison of this idea with the *Oxford English Dictionary* and its regular supplements. The dictionary, which one presumes complete when issued, is in fact completed by the publication of the supplements. These volumes then call into question not only the status of the original dictionary but their own importance as additions. This complicated relationship between what is proper to a thing and what is not is, Derrida suggests, ultimately irresolvable; it may be very widely understood, but never completely. I have argued that both sign language and painting in the eighteenth century were systems of signification that operated by the combination of fragmentary signs into a whole by the supplementary addition of an exterior logic, whether that be grammar in the case of sign language or beauty in the case of art. For Epée the parallel between the two visual languages was clear: "Like painting, the art of methodical signs is a silent language which speaks only to the eyes" (Epée 1776: 181–2).

An empire of signs

Such arguments were well understood by the administrators of the National Assembly. In July 1791 the Jacobin Prieur de la Marne proposed to the National Assembly that Epée's school for the deaf should now be administered by the government. Prieur indicated that he believed the government should make use of "[t]he utility which one can extract from these men deprived of their two most precious organs."[9] For once the school was established, he believed that "[t]he pupils themselves will be able to provide free places by means of their labour; and, consequently, the establishment can maintain itself."[10] As a result, numerous workshops were created at the school for printing, painting, drawing, sculpture, and engraving. In a speech which neatly encapsulated the results of over a hundred years of thought on the sign, Prieur declared:

> What is more, the deaf have a language of signs which can be considered as one of the most fortunate discoveries of the human spirit. It perfectly replaces, and with the greatest rapidity, the organ of speech. . . . It does not consist solely of cold signs and those of pure convention; it paints the most secret affections of the soul. . . . If one were ever to realize the much desired project of a universal language, this would perhaps be that which would merit preference.
>
> (Prieur 1791: 202)

Prieur appreciated that gestural sign was, as Condillac had said, the first language, but that, as Epée maintained, its natural signs had required the addition, or supplement, of conventional ones to make it a fully operative language. He recognized that its uniquely visual quality made it a variety of painting, which provided it with the possibility of becoming a universal language. Art became an important subject of study in the newly open National Institute for the Deaf, and as well as François-André Vincent's painting class, Pajou offered sculpture, Bervick taught engraving and Madame Labille-Guiard directed the women in embroidery and tapestry (Prieur 1791: 203). The neo-classical artists who taught there appreciated the possibilities of this seemingly universal language for artists attempting to communicate with the mass, revolutionary public. But, like Prieur, their notion of both the visual and gestural sign was still that of the Enlightenment. State involvement had not brought with it any significant transformation in the reception of the sign.

It was during the Consulate and the Empire that a radical and unprecedented shift in the understanding of the deaf and their sign language by the hearing took place. Its consequences echoed down the nineteenth century and have only very recently been challenged. In 1799, precisely the moment when historians have traditionally declared the French Revolution over, attitudes to deafness were revolutionized. This change was part of a wider and longer evolution described by Georges Canguilhem as "normaliz-ation": "Between 1759, the date of the first appearance of the word *normal*, and 1834, the date of the first appearance of the word *normalized*, a normative class conquered the power to identify the function of social norms with its own uses and its own determi-nation of content" (Canguilhem 1991: 246). In this one example of that process, by which hearing was categorized as normal and deafness as pathological, we can date matters more precisely to the Consulate and Empire.

In making this distinction, it should not be assumed that the Enlightenment's view of the deaf was indeed enlightened, only to fall to a less sympathetic imperial order. In fact, it operated a hierarchical notion of the citizen which, whilst at first appearing emancipatory, later came to reinforce and institutionalize difference. For Epée believed that the deaf were irredeemably stuck at a lower, more primitive level of humanity. Roch-Ambroise Sicard (1742–1822), the successor to Epée at the deaf school, drew his own more radical conclusions from this assumption, seeing the deaf as

> [a] sort of walking machine, whose organization is inferior to that of animals. . . . What kind of sentences could a man write in a foreign language who knew only the meaning of each word without knowing its syntax, above all if he had as a native language only the language of nature, the language of the peoples of Africa, the language of the deaf and dumb. We know the sentences of the Negroes; we can judge those of the deaf and dumb, who are even closer to nature.
>
> (Lane 1984a: 423)

Sicard's view of nature was very much in tune with Enlightenment tropes of the natural. The natural was not a simple given but a hierarchical construct, operating between the parameters of *la belle nature* and *la nature empirique*.[11] Nature as it existed was found insufficient and in need of correction by reason. Thus the natural state of deafness was amongst the accidents of nature and not to be considered part of the potentially ideal nature which the Enlightenment was striving to describe and create. In applying Condillac's theory of supplementarity, it had been possible for the deaf, as it were, to climb the linguistic ladder away from the state of nature and attain a degree of parity with the hearing. The Revolution attempted in its early years to institutiona-lize that change in its search for the "whole" citizen who could play a full part in the revitalized social body. The belief in the Rights of Man led to an empirical effort to render all citizens worthy of participation in the civic process.

However, after Thermidor, this effort was redirected. Now the hierarchy of nature, which had previously been seen as a malleable field, became the very state of nature. Under the influence of the *idéologues*, the new discourses of social reform had the effect of removing mobility from those classified as pre-civilized. The deaf were one early instance of what Allan Sekula has called "[t]hat privileged figure of social reform discourse: the figure of the child rescued by a paternalistic medico-social science" (Sekula 1986: 14). The infantilized status of the deaf was reinforced and given new meaning by the application of anthropological and racial theory.[12] As Sicard's remarks quoted above indicate, race, "disability," and class were inextricably interlinked in this period. The transformation is not so much in the racial dimension of *idéologue* thought, as its use of them in a disciplinary and normative framework. The insertion of such disciplinary theories into the hierarchical framework of supplementarity legislated difference as natural and irrevocable. For Destutt de Tracy, "to think is to sense and nothing but to sense," leaving no possibility of compensating for deficiencies in perception (Kennedy 1989: 66). Inequality was inevitable and one should organize both education and society in recognition of that fact. Thus the *classe savante* was naturally worthy of education whereas the *classe laborieuse* would not benefit from it at all.

This moment of transformation can be observed in the proceedings of the Société des Observateurs de l'Homme, founded in 1799 to advise the colonialist expeditions of Nicolas Baudin to Australia and Levaillant to Africa (Rabinow 1989: 18–24). The membership was a cross-section of those intellectuals who benefited from 18 Brumaire, that *coup d'état* of the Institut. Destutt de Tracy and the other leading *idéologues* were members along with physicians such as Philippe Pinel and Jean-Marc-Gaspard Itard; colonial explorers; scientists like George Cuvier; and the head of the Institute for the Deaf, the abbé Sicard and his pupil Massieu. As such, their broad range of interests, united in the observation of Man and the description of the natural and the savage, serve as an indication of the polysemicity of difference at the outset of the modern period, subsumed within the disciplinary apparatus of the panopticon. For the society, the fascination of studying the "savage" lay not in itself but in the clues such study would bring to the understanding of civilized man. As Joseph-Marie de Gérando, a rising star of the Institut, and a future director of the Institute for the Deaf, put it: "Here we can find the necessary materials to compose an exact scale of the different degrees of civilization and to assign to each one the properties which characterize it" (Copans and Jamin 1978: 131).[13] For de Gérando, the hierarchy of nature described by the *idéologues* could be empirically researched in the New World. The colonized Other was thus, as so often, a means for the colonizing self to validate itself through comparison and contrast. Baudin's expedition was itself an anthropological failure, although his ship was infiltrated by a group of British convicts whom he abandoned on a remote island (Hughes 1987: 121–2, 210); Baudin himself died on the return voyage.[14]

The society was scathing about the efforts of previous expeditions which had failed to communicate with the people they encountered. Jauffret, the secretary of the society, declared that language was at the heart of their investigations, since "[s]peech is, after reason, the most beautiful prerogative of man ... it is above all [speech] which distinguishes man from the crowd of animals which surrounds him." This emphasis on speech was no longer simply a question of its utility but was couched in heavily moralistic terms. Jauffret emphasized that "[t]he observation of physical man is intimately linked to that of moral man and it is virtually impossible to study either the body or the spirit in isolation. . . . Each illness is almost always the product of a vice" (Copans and Jamin 1978: 73–85).[15] Humans were distinguished from the animals by reason of their speech, as had often been argued. Jauffret's addition of a moralizing dimension to such distinctions made it reprehensible not to be able to speak. For him, the deaf were "[t]hese disgraced beings of nature" whose silence clearly indicated a moral fault. In this sense, one might see Jauffret as fulfilling Kant's categorical imperative which, as Gayatri Spivak has argued, "[c]an justify the imperialist project by producing the following formula: *make* the heathen into a human so that he can be treated as an end in himself" (Spivak 1985: 267). For Jauffret, this notion of the human as an end in itself refuted Condillac's assertion of the arbitrary nature of the sign. Rather, there was simply an ignorance of the means by which words had come into existence that might be rectified by the study of primitive deaf sign (Copans and Jamin 1978: 73–85).

De Gérando reversed this formula and advised colonialists to learn sign language in order to be able to communicate with the native peoples they encountered: "For travellers, to whom these reflections are directed, one cannot recommend too highly the detailed study of the methodical signs which citizen Sicard has used with such success to establish his first communications with the deaf-mute. For the deaf-mute is also a savage, and nature is the only interpreter which can translate for him the first lessons of his masters" (Copans and Jamin 1978: 140). In the view of these early anthropologists, civilized man was everywhere surrounded by savages and animals, an important resource for his narcissistic study of himself. This racial terminology applied as equally to the morally deficient classes in France as to the colonized territories. Jauffret carefully noted that the savage to date revealed by exploration was not the noble savage, or man of nature. Whereas for Diderot and Condillac the deaf had presented a philosophical conundrum – how was it possible to know the world with only four senses? – they were now seen as one class amongst the ranks of the "primitive," subject to disciplinary control and observation. The deaf provided no important clues to understanding the cognition of the "civilized," ending a philosophical tradition which stretched back to Plato. Philosophy no longer distinguished itself from speech, for it conceived of itself as a voice, as de Gérando noted in seeking to move beyond the "egoism" of the preceding period: "True philosophy, always in accord with morality, offers us another language. . . . But what is the best means of studying Man? Here the history of philosophy, the voice of the *monde savante*, answers us. The time for systems is past. Far from agitating itself for centuries in vain theorizing, the genius of knowledge is finally set on the route of observation." The voice of philosophy no longer theorized, it simply spoke of its observations. In an attempt to circumvent the logic of supplementarity, speech became philosophical, disconnected from the material language of gesture. Destutt de Tracy argued that "[s]ounds have the two properties of being the most natural and most commodious of all signs." He considered the alphabet as a direct representation of sounds and thus not a sign system but an authentic transmission of thought (Tracy 1817: I, 370).[16] The moralized and philosophical voice had connection with gesture, being of an altogether different and higher order. The new social body of France was constituted only by those "whole" citizens, whose eligibility for membership depended upon fulfilling the corporal and disciplinary norm.

The society was clear that a new political moment had dawned and brought with it the need for a new knowledge: "The Society, in searching to raise human dignity, that beautiful prerogative which was so cruelly ignored, so insolently outraged, during the awful regime which recently ruled France, will have the advantage of completing, by the sole influence of its observations, the extinction of a crowd of abuses to which this odious regime gave birth, and which the existing government has not yet succeeded in destroying" (Copans and Jamin 1978: 140). In the wake of Bonaparte's expedition to

Egypt, power was colonial and disciplinary, relying on its all-seeing observations, both at home and abroad. The scale of supplementarity that had made a sign language epistemologically intelligible was now subsumed within what Foucault has described as "[t]he *medical bipolarity of the normal and the pathological*. Consciousness lives because it can be altered, maimed, diverted from its course, paralyzed; societies live because there are sick, declining societies and healthy, expanding ones; the race is a living being that one can see degenerating; and civilizations, whose deaths have so often been remarked on, are also, therefore, living beings" (Nye 1984: 47). Thus the success of the colonizing race depends on its health at home as well as its dominance abroad. In the agenda drawn up by the *idéologues* to ensure such health, the deaf found themselves newly categorized as savage and immoral. Foucault has highlighted "[t]hat moment when the sciences of man become possible . . . the moment when a new technology of power and a new political economy of the body were implemented" (Foucault 1977: 193). Out of the revolutionary crisis had emerged both a new science of man and an accompanying political economy of the body. For the deaf, this new power of the Norm was deployed through the power of the Word (*parole*) to which they were to be forced to submit.

Theater of the deaf

This marked change can be observed within a series of paintings by and about the deaf, initiated by David's students. These works mark a cultural moment in the Consulate and Empire in which the cultural metaphoricity of deafness acquired a new urgency. Marie-Pierre Nicolas Ponce-Camus (1778–1839) was amongst those of David's 500 students who have been forgotten by art history, yet David rated him as one of his best (Hautecoeur 1954: 225). He joined the studio in 1791 but then enlisted in the Revolutionary armies and so did not exhibit in the Salon until 1801. He later won medals of honor at the Salons of 1804 and 1812 and painted a series of military portraits of Napoleon, later hung at Versailles (Michaud 1845: 387–8). He remained loyal to David throughout his career and signed the letter written in 1816 by a group of former pupils, requesting the Minister of the Interior to allow David to return from exile (Wildenstein 1973: 260). In 1819, one of his works was refused for the Salon as demonstrating unacceptable revolutionary sympathies and he spent the remainder of his career as a successful portrait painter.

At the Salon of 1802, Ponce-Camus exhibited a *Tableau représentant une anecdote de la vie du célèbre Abbé de l'Epée, prise dans les causes célèbres* (Plate 15.1) (Lane 1984a: 44).[17] Two figures dominate the scene, edged in by the frame and, because of the proximity of the wall behind, they seem close to the space of the viewer. The elderly priest is the abbé de l'Epée, seen returning one of his abandoned deaf pupils to his rightful home and inheritance. The Salon catalogue provided a lengthy description of the scene, which presents the abbé de l'Epée's actions as an *exemplum virtutis* for the moral edification of the viewer. What is unusual is that Ponce-Camus has used the methodical signs for the deaf to give visual meaning to the upward gesture of the abbé. His hand correctly forms the sign for Heaven (Epée 1984: 86), and is the counterpoint to the natural gesture of the child in taking Epée's hand to his heart in gratitude. The thanks, Epée signs, are due to God. Ponce-Camus has used gesture exactly as formerly prescribed by the

Academy, in imitation of deaf sign language. In comparing this version of the scene with others in popular prints, it is immediately noticeable that the abbé's sign is the innovation of the painting.[18] Ponce-Camus, on the other hand, was able to incorporate his knowledge of sign language as a resource in history painting, acknowledged by contemporaries as the most complex genre of painting.[19] As the lengthy Salon catalogue entry showed, this one gesture removed the image from potential silence (*la poésie muette*) and rendered it extremely discursive. This painting in fact combines and deploys numerous strategies of representation that require close attention. Like Epée's signs for the deaf, Ponce-Camus' painting sought to bring the silent artwork within the realm of utterance. Furthermore, the stillness of the artwork allows for one gestural sign to be isolated and emphasized in a way that was impossible in deaf conversation.[20] It is truly silent poetry. For if poetry can be defined as a language that resists intentional dissolution into other forms, the visual sign is certainly poetic (B. Johnson 1989: 6–7).

Ponce-Camus' painting depicted a scene from Jean-Nicolas Bouilly's play *The Abbé de l'Epée*, based on the scandalous history of the comte de Solar. In June 1775, the abbé de l'Epée used sign language to discover that one of his impoverished pupils was the abandoned heir of a noble family. A chance visitor to one of Epée's demonstrations of sign language identified the child as the comte de Solar. Investigation seemed to prove that the child was indeed Joseph, the deaf eldest son of the now-deceased comte de Solar. In Toulouse, where the family lived, it was discovered that Joseph had last been seen traveling with his tutor, a young law student named Cazeaux. Cazeaux had reported that the child had died from smallpox on the journey, and no more was thought of him – he had been something of an embarrassment to his family.

It now seemed clear that Cazeaux had in fact abandoned the child in order to facilitate his affair with Joseph's widowed mother. Cazeaux was arrested, taken to Paris and thrown into an oubliette. The identity of Joseph seemed secure, for he had an extra tooth in his upper jaw, an unusual feature matching one which the comte had been known to have. Yet Cazeaux protested his innocence and, before his trial, the famous lawyer Eli de Beaumont produced a sensational defence. Cazeaux was known to have left Toulouse on September 4, 1773 on which date "Joseph" had already been committed to Bîcetre, having been discovered in Picardy a month before that! Cazeaux's lawyers bitterly protested that his arrest was based on no evidence other than Epée's interpretation of sign language: "It is thus, in all history, that deception and fanaticism, aided by certain singular circumstances, have caused the multitude to adopt the reveries of the imagination, and the fictions of illusion" (Annales 1825: 217).

The judges ordered Cazeaux released and an investigation was set up in Toulouse with Joseph present. This, in fact, was Joseph's only return to Toulouse, as depicted by Ponce-Camus, but Epée did not accompany him. Initial evidence proved inconclusive so the judges ordered that the tomb of the boy Cazeaux had buried be opened. Inside was the skeleton of an 8- to 10-year-old child and, sensationally, the child's skull showed an extra tooth in the same place as that of the comte. The judges arrived at an extraordinary verdict. Cazeaux was innocent of abandoning the comte and the young deaf man was indeed the comte de Solar. The defence lawyer's claims that Cazeaux was the victim of aristocratic privilege, allied with popular sentiment, seem amply confirmed in this verdict. For if the child in Paris was Solar, Cazeaux had committed an offence in fraudulently registering the corpse in Charlas as that of the comte.

Alternatively, if he was fully innocent, then "Joseph" had no connection with the family whatsoever (Lane 1984a: 43–66). But Cazeaux was not satisfied and nor was Caroline, Joseph's sister, who lost half her inheritance to her "brother." In 1791, they appealed the decision together and not only won the case but were restored to the family property, with compensation. It seems that once the patronage network of the *ancien régime* had crumbled, so too did Joseph's defence.

Ponce-Camus thus appears to have painted an event that not only did not happen but was actually part of a criminal conspiracy. Rather than a depiction of actual events, as prescribed by history painting, the work can only be understood as a depiction of a scene from Bouilly's play, *The Abbé de l'Epée*, which opened in December 1799 at the Comédie Française. The play was an enormous success, second only to the *Marriage of Figaro* in the period. Jean-Nicolas Bouilly was a lawyer and writer who successfully reactivated the earlier theatrical tradition of using deaf characters but he was now able to use Epée's methodical signs to give them exact meaning. The character of "Theodore," as the young count was called by Bouilly, was played by Mme. Talma, who went to study sign with Massieu in preparation for her role. It is noticeable that the character of the signing deaf boy was considered an appropriate role for a woman.

Both the play and the painting were remarkable popular successes, leading to distinctly unfavorable reviews in the literary journals and newspapers. Ponce-Camus' painting was dismissed as a "bizarrerie of composition" which placed emphasis on achieving "marvelous" effects over the true responsibilities of history painting: "In the end, it is nothing but the stamp of ignorance" (*Journal des Débats* an X: 227). The exhibition as a whole was so badly received that the Academy was forced to bring out some old favorites from previous years by Girodet and Gérard. At the same time *The Abbé de l'Epée* was having a rerun at the Comédie Française, which encountered renewed hostility. The critics noted that "chamberwomen and servants" (*Journal des Débats* an X)" – that is, the audience of the parterre, the popular theater audience – enjoyed the marvelous and the adventures in the story. But they denounced the play as being historically inaccurate – which it was – and for being the ally of superstition and *séméiomancie* (*Mercure de France* Messidor an X: 130–1) – which it was not. Bouilly's response was to dismiss all such debate: "I know that power, intrigue and, above all, the hate which the archbishop of Paris bore towards the abbé de l'Epée, had prevented this latter from obtaining all the rewards of his long and precious researches. . . . No matter! It was no less true that the great man whom I celebrate was able to make an interesting man out of this young deaf mute" (Bouilly an VIII: ix-x). His defence was enough to cloud the issue, although it seems to have had little substance in fact. His work remained "[t]he play of the people, always the friend of marvels and adventures" (*Mercure de France* Messidor an X: 130–1).

This dismissive, elitist tone is identical to that pursued by the Directory in its attempt to shape a national culture out of the confused heritage of monarchical and Republican France. For example, one government commissioner in the Basses-Pyrénées reported: "There fanaticism had erected its stage; there the most ridiculous farces were played out. In the end all the phantasmagoric tricks had so disturbed the minds of the spectators that many poor unfortunates thought they had witnessed miracles" (Ozouf 1988: 223). The passage could easily have been a review of Bouilly's play from one of the literary magazines. As Mona Ozouf has emphasized: "One could not be content simply to allow public opinion to emerge: it had to be formed" (Ozouf 1976: 220). But the Directory were unable to impose their rational, ordered schemes on the population at large which stubbornly remained attached to their patois, their superstitions and their religion.[21] Why, one critic complained, did a revival of *Brutus* close immediately whereas the *Abbé de l'Epée* played to packed houses (*Décade Philosophique* an IX: 285–94)? The Directory's control over discourse, given concrete form as the Institut, did not always entail political control in the widest sense, particularly in the cultural sphere. Since Thermidor, the popular forces had been separated from political power and continued to adhere to their own sense of sentiment, the marvelous, and the power of signs, which contradicted official thought. It was part of the genius of Bonaparte that he was able to harness and control that popular sentiment which gave him the authority the other post-Thermidorean governments had lacked.

Bouilly's play was a striking early example of that process. It was a production of the inner circle of Josephine's salon, where Bouilly was a regular and David was often in attendance with various pupils (Spengler: IV, 1905). It was first read at the salon, after which both she and Bonaparte came to the second night, leading to some prearranged theatricals in the audience (Bouilly 1835: 183–90).[22] At a particularly poignant moment of the play, the writer Collin d'Harleville, another regular at the salon, made a resounding appeal for Sicard's liberty. Sicard had been sentenced to deportation by the Directory in 1797 for his pro-royalist journalism. The First Consul noted the lively, and no doubt pre-arranged, support for d'Harleville's appeal and granted it shortly afterwards. Bonaparte's gesture symbolized his fusion of a renascent private, salon politics with tightly controlled public display. Sicard's liberty was no threat to the Consular regime whose ideological politics aimed less at individual participation in Republican culture than at a generalized subservience to discipline. Foucault has well described the Napoleonic aura:

> At the moment of its full blossoming, the disciplinary society still assumes with the Emperor the old aspect of the power of spectacle. As a monarch who is at one and the same time a usurper of the ancient throne and the organiser of a new state, he combined into a single, symbolic, ultimate figure the whole of the long process by which the pomp of sovereignty, the necessarily spectacular manifestations of power, were extinguished one by one in the daily exercise of surveillance.
>
> (Foucault 1977: 217)

Thus, although Ponce-Camus' picture showed a scene that referred only to a contemporary play, it was still possible to think of it as a history painting. The surveillance exemplified by the Emperor extended its gaze into the symbolic panoply of the time, in which history painting played a full and important role. As Michael Fried has commented: "The ubiquitous gaze at play in Napoleonic painting is ultimately that of the Emperor himself, or rather of the Imperial regime of systematic surveillance" (Fried 1990: 22). Visual signs took on new meanings and were read in altogether different ways as a result of this important shift, which would have immediate repercussions for the Institute of the Deaf and its teaching of sign language.

In Ponce-Camus' painting, the fusion of traditional spectacle with new discipline can be strikingly observed. The virtue it exemplified was twofold: on the one hand, it recalls the general virtue of the abbé de l'Epée as a teacher of the deaf, as set out in the Salon catalogue, but it also recalls the specific action of Bonaparte in showing clemency. More specifically still, Epée's gestural sign recalls Bonaparte's gesture of civic virtue in healing political divides for the common good, in anticipation of Gros' famous depiction of *Napoleon in the Plague House at Jaffa* (Paris: Musée du Louvre, 1804). The theatrical values of neo-classicism had now been deployed within an explicitly dramatic setting.[23] This strategy of representing representation – combining sign language, theater and politics – offered interesting new possibilities for history painting. This interaction between sign language and history painting can be appreciated by comparing an exactly contemporary painting from England, involving deaf sign. James Northcote, a former pupil of Joshua Reynolds, painted a half-portrait of *Miss St Clare performing the deaf alphabet* (1801), in which the young Miss St Clare forms the letter D in a manual alphabet. Although Northcote was at this time attempting to become a history painter, he saw no wider possibilities in the subject. The deaf alphabet is presented as a feminine accomplishment, rather like drawing or embroidery.[24] It was only in the French Revolutionary context that deaf sign had a broader signification.

Founding fathers

Ponce-Camus' work further highlights the irreducibility of difference in the period. We have already seen that discourses of discipline, race, and imperialism provide the ground through which his work could signify. But the interaction of philanthropy and governmental authority evoked by Ponce-Camus has a further dimension that might be described as paternalism, for both the figure of the Father and ideas of fatherhood are central to his work.[25] Epée's age contrasts strikingly with that of the child but is not a problem because of the institutionalized relationship between them. In this sense, Ponce-Camus continued David's strategy for rescuing the "fallen fathers," to use Carol Duncan's phrase, found in Greuze's painting (Duncan 1981). David had painted Socrates and Belisarius with much younger dependants or disciples but their relationship was paternalist, mediated by moral authority and thus not felt to be problematic. Ponce-Camus echoed David's use of gesture in the *Socrates*, the father of the Horatii, and especially *Bonaparte Crossing the Alps* in his depiction of Epée.[26] Behind these risen fathers was a new moral and legal authority, comparable in power with that of Michelangelo's Moses. This sense of paternal authority runs through the various different levels of interpretation that the use of gestural sign gave Ponce-Camus' work. The picture shows the "comte de Solar" finding his paternal home once more and being recognized as part of the family by the dog at the gates. Bouilly's play, from which the scene is taken, had as its central dramatic device the transformation of an evil father into a natural father. As a result, the elderly Darlemont finds peace for himself and avoids prosecution, whilst restoring Solar's rightful property and thereby permitting his own son to marry. It is through the paternal authority of Epée, often referred to in Bouilly's play as "the father of the deaf," that Solar gained access to sign language without which none of this could have happened. Epée's semantic sign contrasts with the natural gesture made by the boy, demonstrating that it was only through Epée's paternal intercession that the child has escaped the state of nature. Finally, the painting invoked the joint power of God, who inspired Epée, and the state, which ordered police searches on his behalf and funded his school. Paternalism thus held sway in the state, society, and the family, as the nineteenth century recast power around the model of the bourgeois family. It provided an overarching metaphor for Ponce-Camus, keeping his polysemic representation from degenerating into meaninglessness.[27]

Deafness, display and the word

This newly problematic status of the deaf can be seen in two paintings from the Napoleonic period, representing the deaf and their education. Jerôme-Martin Langlois (1779–1838) was a hearing student of David who also painted the deaf. He assisted David on his *Bonaparte Crossing the Alps* and was placed second in the *Grand Prix de Rome* of 1805; he won the prize outright in 1809 with his *Priam at the feet of Achilles*, a composition that owed much to David's *Belisarius* (Grunchec 1989: II, 40–1). In his later career, Langlois had a triumph at the Salon of 1819 with his *Diana and Endymion*, was awarded the Légion d'Honneur and became a member of the Institut in 1838 (Soubies 1909: 185–6). He painted two canvases of Sicard educating the deaf, the first in 1806 (Plate 15.2) and the second in 1814 (Plate 15.3). In contrast to Ponce-Camus' use of visual sign, Langlois resorted to writing in order to explain his painting. On the left stands Jean Massieu, the gifted deaf teacher who was the prodigy of the school, a writer and a member of many learned societies. The blackboard on which the figure of Massieu has written is both the screen of our vision and the field of writing. The words hang in a typically gloomy neo-classical background, as if at an understated Belshazzar's Feast. Massieu gestures towards the text which he has written with the chalk in his left hand: "Means of making sounds articulated by the feeling of pressure." But he, a signing deaf person, is not connected to the words, which are taken from Sicard's *Course of Instruction* for the deaf, and his gesture is reduced to a mere pantomime of indication. Sicard is engaged in demonstrating the ability of a deaf woman to speak. She is accompanied by two other young deaf women and a woman teacher. The gloves worn by the taller woman indicate that she is Mme. Laurine Duler, a speaking *répétitrice* at the school who wore gloves in order to make her signs more intelligible (Berthier 1873: 63). But it is Sicard alone who possesses the gift of speech, conveyed by his hand that reaches across this divide, not in sign, but in the attempt to instruct the woman to speak. She tries to form particular sounds which she has been taught in reponse to Sicard's cue of pressure on her arm. She attempts to measure her own voice by feeling the vibrations of her throat, for her endeavor is based upon imitating the vibrations of sound which she has learned from Sicard. Such methods, known as *phonomimie* (phonomimicry) were, and remain, successful only with those who became deaf after acquiring language, or who are only partially deaf. The composition partially obscures Massieu from our view and reinforces the hierarchical concepts of language discussed above. In the foreground, and in the light, are those who speak or are trying to speak. In the background, in the shadows of deafness, is Massieu. Above them all, in an uncertain but powerful position, hangs the writing. Writing has been the means by which the deaf have become educated but is also, in the philosophy of the time, a debased form of speech. It was writing that seduced the deaf away from the effort of learning to speak and therefore writing was suspect. Derrida has described how the eighteenth century "[c]onsiders writing as a dangerous means, a menacing aid, the critical response to a situation of distress. When Nature, as self-proximity, comes to be forbidden or interrupted, when speech fails to protect presence, writing becomes necessary. It must *be added* to the word urgently" (Derrida 1976: 144).[28] It was thus to writing that the hearing artist had to turn in order to make his image comprehensible, having abandoned the gestural language of sign.

Recent restoration has indicated that the text has in fact been changed to its present state from an earlier version which read. "*La reconnaissance est la mémoire du coeur*" (Recognition is the memory of the heart), a famous aphorism of Jean Massieu. It was his answer to the question "What is memory?," a staple of the signing demonstrations organized by Sicard. For the deaf, not having the use of speech, were thus incapable of memory, according to Enlightenment philosophy. Massieu's response was widely known as a riposte to that charge. It seems that, as so often, Sicard has obliterated the words of the deaf to emphasize his own importance and let his own stand in their place.[29] If Massieu's words had remained, Langlois' image would have presented both sign and speech as means of deaf education, whilst still giving first place to speech. Nonetheless, the writing would have acted as a means of communication between the deaf as represented and the hearing viewer, rather than as a caption and means of classifying the action. In the 1814 version, Langlois again emphasized the importance of communication between the deaf and the hearing not in sign but via writing. The scene represents Sicard testing the ability of his student to understand his action. He gestures towards the book lying on the chair and the boy interprets this to mean that he will soon fetch the book and hence writes "[s]era prenant" on the board. In contrast to the dominating words of Sicard in the first picture, the deaf boy's writing is small and hard to see. The composition appears disjointed and was widely criticized (Soubies 1909: 186). Only Sicard's pointing hand and the boy's writing hand can be seen, as if to preclude even the possibility of a gestural sign. One boy has his arms folded and one palm can be seen but the signing hands remain inactive.

The impact of Langlois' painting can be seen in a striking work by the deaf artist Augustin Massé, *Une Séance Publique des Sourds-Muets* (1814). Langlois' image hangs on the wall beyond the blackboard, a visual representation of the events actually taking place on the stage. It is directed towards the hearing audience and is almost invisible to the waiting deaf in the wings, indicating the lack of signification it held for the signing deaf. The figure of Massieu stands center stage and this time his saying on memory remains inscribed on the blackboard. The room is crowded with the Parisian bourgeoisie, fashionably dressed as if for the theater. Many of the spectators have turned their heads in conversation with their neighbors, rather than attending to the demonstration, for this is the audience of the *loges* and not that of the parterre. But the image is most remarkable for its depiction of the scene as a deaf student might have seen it. The space is rendered from the margins, both of the demonstration theater and of the society which fills its seats. As a result, instead of the narrow perspectival box traditionally prescribed, there is a sense of width and space that is almost alarming. The viewpoint feels distanced from the scene because of the very awareness of the artificial construction of pictorial space. Similarly, the lighting is not, as was traditional, from the side but from the window confronting the spectator. Thus, for the hearing audience depicted, the scene was "correctly" lit, as it would have been for Langlois, but for the deaf participant a different light is seen. The luminosity of the window suggests a point of escape from the confines of being an object on display. Massé's work conveys the anxiety of being seen, caught in the full glare of the light so as to be best observed, with only the writing of Massieu as a means of response to an inattentive audience. Massieu stands as the man in the middle, caught between hearing society and writing which is increasingly seen as inextricably linked to speech. Similarly, he is isolated between Langlois' history painting and the spectators in front. The anxiety of this painting came from the knowledge that the possible space between such binary poles was closing.

   One casualty of that exclusion was to be sign language. In 1813, Paillot de Montabert, the author of a vast theory of painting, dismissed the former tradition of drawing gesture from the deaf. Rather than finding an enhanced means of communication "by this means you will paint nothing other than the deaf who could never be the man of nature" (de Montabert 1829: V, 445). Deafness had lost its philosophical dimension and become just another disease. The gestural sign language of the deaf, far from being the privileged resource for artists that it had been since Leonardo, now represented nothing more than a pathological symptom. The Empire sought ever more transparent means of communicating with the mass of the people but rejected the Enlightenment hope of a universal gestural language. The gestural sign failed to achieve a place in the new sciences and no longer had anything to offer the hearing artist. In the nineteenth century, culture was to be consumed verbally at all costs.

But this seemingly neat and clear resolution is misleading. Gesture, sign, and supplement could not be so neatly elided, and returned in different guises. In fact, this is the beginning of another story, that of a deaf cultural politics, which presented sign language not as Other but as "mimicry." The mimicry referred to was not of speech but of the ideas which precede speech, presenting sign as almost the same as spoken language – but not quite (Bhabha 1987). Thus the deaf sought to evade the disciplinary norm by camouflaging themselves as the *semblables* (fellows or likenesses) of the hearing, rather than by active resistance in the form of counter-discourse or political activity that has traditionally attracted historical attention. In this more nuanced cultural politics, art was a key weapon. The nineteenth century saw the emergence of a school of deaf painters – over ninety exhibiting artists in France alone – who used the inevitably silent media of the visual arts to demonstrate to an increasingly hostile hearing majority that deafness was no hindrance to the intelligent perception and representation of exterior reality. Further, by using the "official" style of the Academy, deaf artists were able to assert their "normality," in the eyes of the majority, as well as their capacity to formulate and comprehend abstract ideas. Such an artistic style might, then, be thought of as a mimicry of the mimesis of the Salon style, raising interesting questions about both modes of representation. It was precisely this kind of ambiguity that oralism sought to eliminate in concert with the modernist aesthetic which increasingly came to distrust representation as a reliable grid for the knowledge of things. The seeming ambiguity of sign language as a system of visual representation made it intolerable. It is no coincidence that oralist educationalists described themselves as the "modern school" of deaf education. Modernism's problematizing of representation meant that, as Richard Terdiman has noted: "The sign comes to figure something like an elemental *machine for domination*" (Terdiman 1985: 33). Mimicry had proposed that sign language and speech were essentially two versions of the same kind of representation. The visual arts were the privileged ground in which that equivalence became exact. Modernism was not content to accept this ambiguous balance. In contemplating binary oppositions, it valorized the pathological over the normal, speech over gesture, and abstraction over representation. Enormous achievements resulted from this moment of elimination but it may now be time, in this postmodern era, to count the costs: one of them was the culture of mimicry. That culture had its roots in the Institute for the Deaf and was both made possible by, and made in opposition to, the normative institution created by the French Revolution.

Notes

This paper is the first version of what became Chapter Two in my book *Silent Poetry: Deafness, Sign, and Visual Culture in Modern France* (Princeton: Princeton University Press, 1995). I would like to thank the Center for Seventeenth- and Eighteenth-Century Studies at UCLA and its director John Brewer in concert with Clark Professor Ann Bermingham, for providing me with a fellowship in 1990–1 when this chapter was first researched and drafted. My thanks are also due to my Center colleagues Lawrence Klein and Jay Tribby; also to Alexis Karacostas, Gwynne Lewis, Richard Shiff, and especially Kathleen Wilson.

1   Lane (1984a) is the most comprehensive and authoritative history of the deaf, with an extensive bibliography.
2   See "Une histoire à découvrir" in Karacostas (1989) for the medieval period and Mirzoeff (1992) for the *ancien régime*.
3   Dryden's translation of de Piles. Until the late eighteenth century the deaf were assumed to be naturally dumb and thus de Piles's reference would have been clear to his readers.
4   For a discussion of *la poésie muette*, see W. J. T. Mitchell (1986) "Eye and ear: Edmund Burke and the politics of sensibility".
5   See Mirzoeff (1992) for details.
6   Diderot, "Lettre sur les Sourds et sur les Muets à l'usage de ceux qui entendent et qui parlent" (1755).
7   Ibid., p. 146.
8   See Lane (1984a) p. 55 f. for details of this encounter.
9   Quoted in *Journal des Débats et des Decrets* 792 (July, 22 1791).
10 Prieur's comments seem to contradict Professor Dora Weiner's assertion that "[t]he nation was obligated by its new mandate of fraternity and equality to aid those citizens whom nature had shortchanged at birth" (Weiner 1974: 67). Rather than a prototype health care system, Prieur offered a short-term investment capital to the Institute. Although the government continued to fund the school once it became clear that the initial project would not succeed, it was not administered by the Education Ministry but by the Interior Ministry.
11 As Ehrard (1963: I, 252) puts it: "In order to liberate man from the misfortunes which weighed upon him, the eighteenth century was forced to substitute for empirical nature a nature reconstructed according to the exigencies of reason."
12 One might compare Derrida's critique of Lévi-Strauss's intervention into the culture of the Nambikwara people. Lévi-Strauss believed that he had sullied a natural society by his introduction of writing which Derrida shows to have already been present as "archi-écriture." Likewise, Sicard and Epée felt they were bringing such enlightenment as was possible into the deaf's natural ignorance when they already had a functioning language and social system. This reading is caution against endowing the deaf, or other marginalized

groups, with a kind of "authenticity" that the mainstream might somehow wish to recover (Derrida 1976: 101–40).

13 J.-M. de Gérando, "Considérations sur les méthodes à suivre dans l'observation des peuples sauvages."

14 See the introduction by F. C. T. Moore to de Gérando (1969) for a detailed account of Baudin's rather disastrous expedition. Refused medical supplies at Mauritius for fear that they might seek to enforce the French decree abolishing slavery, many of the scientists jumped ship. Once in Australia, little contact was made with the Aborigines and revictualling voyages to Timor led to the death of many of those on board. Baudin died unmourned, according to his junior officer, on account of his severity.

15 L. F. Jauffret, "Introduction aux Mémoires de la Société des Observateurs de l'Homme."

16 Tracy accepted that deaf sign was a language but he argued that a gestural language could never become as habitual or flexible as a spoken language, and further could not be translated into other languages. Gesture was a part of the original "language of action" along with cries and touches, but was not a separate stage, as Condillac and Rousseau had argued (Tracy 1817: I, 302–88).

17 See catalogue of the 1802 Salon in H. W. Janson (1977). Several other of Epée's pupils were artists, including the sculptor Deseine, the painter Grégoire, and the engraver Boutelou (Notice 1896: 91–4).

18 For example, the frontispiece to Kotzebue (1805) or the print reproduced by Karacostas (1989: 49). Cruikshank also engraved this scene, again without reference to sign language.

19 Chaussard commented on Ponce-Camus' painting *Rollon et Poppa* at the Salon of 1806: "Si les faits sont beaux, honorables, portant un grand caractère de vertu, de morale, de philosophie, le peintre d'histoire aura rempli son but" (Chaussard 1806: 381).

20 Barthes has commented: "Painting . . . has frequently reproduced a gesture apprehended at the point in its course where the normal eye cannot arrest it" (Barthes 1982: 32). Painting thus makes use of a pathological vision with capabilities beyond that of the normal eye.

21 See Ozouf (1976) on the failure to control religion and de Certeau (1975) on the survival of patois and the attempts to control it.

22 See Gilbert Spengler 1905, Tome IV, "Les Ecrivains et les Comédiens," for details of Josephine's salon. Bouilly (1835: 168) notes David, Gérard, and Girodet as amongst regular habitués, which casts a sidelight on Delécluze's notion that David became a "monarchist" at this time.

23 On the theatricality of David – in a very different tenor to that of Michael Fried – see Thévoz (1989).

24 My thanks to Susan Alon, archivist at the Washington University School of Medicine, MI, for drawing my attention to the Northcote.

25 I distinguish such paternalism, which I see as a constituent part of the disciplinary system of power that had just emerged, from patriarchy which I take to be a trans-historical domination of the female by the male. In other words, I do not feel that the disciplinary power described by Foucault is first and foremost registered in gender, without, of course, denying that gender plays a significant role. It is part of my thesis that the interacting discursive practices which constitute the sign in this period do not have either Althusser's "relative autonomy" or Gramsci's "hegemony" but were always and already in a state of *différance* which it would be reductive to ascribe to any one factor.

26 See, D. Johnson (1989) for a discussion of David's use of gesture, especially in the *Horatii*.

27 Jacques Lacan has emphasized the importance of what he termed "[t]he paternal metaphor" in the construction of language: "the attribution of procreation to the father can only be the effect of a pure signifier, of a recognition, not of a real father but of what religion has taught us to refer to as the Name-of-the-Father" (Lacan 1977: 199).

28 See ". . . that dangerous supplement . . ." (Derrida 1976: 141–64) for a full discussion of this important point, which informs my discussion of Langlois.

29 For example, after Sicard's arrest in 1792, Massieu organized a delegation to the National Assembly which, in carefully crafted Republican terms, appealed for his release as "he has

never hurt anyone, he has always helped who he can and has taught us to love the Revolution and the sacred principles of liberty and equality" (Karacostas 1989: 63). Sicard, whose virulent monarchical principles were rather contrary to this account, published Massieu's comments as follows: "He loves us as if he were our father. It is he who taught us what we know. Without him, we would be like animals" (Barrière 1858: 67–102).

Bibliography

Annales (1825) *Annales du Barreau Français, ou choix des plaidoyers et mémoires les plus remarquables*, Tome VI, Paris: B. Warée.

Bal, Mieke and Bryson, Norman (1991) "Semiotics and art history," *Art Bulletin* LXXIII, 2 (June): 174–208.

Barrie, Lita (1989) "New York, new art," *Art and Design* 5, 7/8.

Barrière, F. (ed.) (1858) *Mémoires sur les Journées de Septembre 1792*, Paris.

Barthes, Roland (1982) *Camera Lucida*, trans. Richard Howard, New York: Noonday Press.

Berthier, Ferdinand (1873) *L'Abbé Sicard*, Paris: Charles Douniol.

Bhabha, Homi (1987) "Of mimicry and man: the ambivalence of colonial discourse," in *October: The First Decade*, ed. Annette Michelson *et al.*, Cambridge, MA and London: MIT Press, pp. 317–25.

Blum, Carol (1986) *Rousseau and the Republic of Virtue: The Language of Politics in the French Revolution*, Ithaca, NY and London: Cornell University Press.

Bouilly, Jean-Nicolas (an VIII) *L'Abbé de l'Epée: comédie historique*, Paris: P. André.

—— (1835) *Recapitulations*, Paris: L. Janet.

Canguilhem, Georges (1991 [1966]) *The Normal and the Pathological*, intro. Michel Foucault, trans. Carolyn R. Fawcett, New York: Zone.

Certeau, Michel de, Julia, D., and Revel, J. (1975) *Une Politique de la Langue. La Révolution française et les patois. L'enquête de Grégoire*, Paris: Gaillard.

Chartier, Roger (1991) *The Cultural Origins of the French Revolution*, trans. Lydia G. Cochrane, Durham, NC and London: Duke University Press.

Chaussard, Paul (1806) *Le Pausanias Français*, Paris.

Condillac, Etienne Bonnot de (1973) *Essai sur les origines des connaissances humaines*, précédé par *L'Archéologie du Frivole* par Jacques Derrida, Paris: Galilée.

Copans, Jean and Jamin, Jean (eds.) (1978) *Aux Origines de l'Anthropologie Française: Les Mémoires de la Société des Observateurs de l'Homme en l'an VIII*, Paris: Sycomore.

Cornié, Adrien (1903) *Sur l'Institution Nationale des Sourdes-Muettes de Bordeaux 1796–1903*, Bordeaux: F. Pech.

Dandré-Bardon (1972 [1765]) *Traité de Peinture*, repr. Geneva: Mlnkoff.

Da Vinci, *see* Leonardo.

Décade Philosophique (an IX), "L'Abbé de l'Epée."

De Gérando, Joseph-Marie (1969 [orig. an. VIII]) *The Observation of Savage Peoples*, trans. F. C. T. Moore, Berkeley and Los Angeles, CA: University of California Press.

De Montabert, Paillot (1829) *Traité Complet de la Peinture*, Paris; originally published as *Traité de geste* (1813).

Derrida, Jacques (1976) *Of Grammatology*, trans. Gayatri Chakravorty Spivak, Baltimore, MD: Johns Hopkins University Press.

Diderot, Denis (1978 [1755]) "Lettre sur les Sourds et Muets à l'usage de ceux qui entendent et qui parlent," repr. in *Oeuvres Complètes*, Tome IV, Paris: Hermann pp. 135–91.

Duncan, Carol (1981) "Fallen fathers: images of authority in pre-Revolutionary French art," *Art History* 4, 2 (June): 186–202.

Dryden, John (1695) *De Arte Graphica: The Art of Painting by C.A. du Fresnoy*, London: J. Hepinstall.

Ehrard, Jean (1963) *L'idée de la Nature en France dans la première moitié du XVIIIe siècle*, 2 tomes, Paris: S.E.V.P.E.N.

Fort, Bernadette (1989) "Voice of the public: the carnivalisation of salon art in pre-Revolutionary pamphlets," *Eighteenth-Century Studies* 22, 3 (Spring): 368–97.

Foucault, Michel (1977) *Discipline and Punish: The Birth of the Prison*, trans. Alan Sheridan, Harmondsworth, Mx: Penguin.

Fried, Michael (1990) *Courbet's Realism*, Chicago and London: University of Chicago Press.

Grunchec, Philippe (1989) *Les Concours des Prix de Rome 1797–1863*, 2 tomes, Paris: Ecole Nationale Supérieure des Beaux-Arts.

Hautecœur, Louis (1954) *Louis David*, Paris: La Table Ronde.

Holcroft, Thomas (1801) *The Deaf and Dumb or the Orphan Protected*, 4th edn., London: J. D. Dewick.

Hughes, Robert (1987) *The Fatal Shore*, New York: Alfred A. Knopf.

Janson, H. W. (1977) *Catalogues of the Paris Salon 1673–1881*, 60 vols., New York and London: Garland.

Johnson, Barbara (1989) *A World of Difference*, Baltimore, MD: Johns Hopkins University Press.

Johnson, Dorothy (1989) "Corporality and communication: the gestural revolution of Diderot, David and 'The Oath of the Horatii'," *Art Bulletin* LXXI (March): 92–114.

Journal des Débats (octobre an X) "Salon de l'An X."

Karacostas, Alexis (ed.) (1989) *Le Pouvoir des Signes: Sourds et Citoyens*, Paris: Institut de Jeunes Sourds de Paris.

Kennedy, Emmet (1989) *A Cultural History of the French Revolution*, New Haven, CT and London: Yale University Press.

Kotzebue, Augustus von (1805) *Deaf and Dumb; or the Orphan*, trans. Benjamin Thompson, London: Vernor & Hood.

Krauss, Rosalind (1991) " 'Nostalgie de la boue'," *October* 56 (Spring): 111–20.

Lacan, Jacques (1977) *Ecrits: a Selection*, trans. Alan Sheridan, London: Tavistock.

Lane, Harlan (1984a) *When the Mind Hears: A History of the Deaf*, New York: Random House.

—— (1984b) *The Deaf Experience*, trans. Franklin Philip, Cambridge MA: Harvard University Press.

Leonardo da Vinci (1956) *Treatise on Painting*, trans. Philip McMahon, Vol. 1, Princeton, NJ: Princeton University Press.

L'Epée, Abbé Charles-Michel de (1776) *Institution des Sourds et Muets*, Paris.

—— (1984 [1784]) *La Véritable Manière d'Instruire les Sourds et Muets*, repr. Paris: Fayard.

[Lesuire, R. M.] (1781) *La Muette qui parle au Salon de 1781*, Amsterdam & Coll. Deloynes, no. 257.

Mercure de France (Messidor an. X) "Abbé de l'Epée."

Michaud, J. F. (1845) *Biographie Universelle, ancienne et moderne*, Tome 77, Paris: Michaud.

Miller, Nancy K. (1986) "Rereading as a woman: the body in practice," in Susan R. Suleiman (ed.) *The Female Body in Western Culture*, Cambridge, MA and London: Harvard University Press, pp. 354–62.

Mirzoeff, Nicholas (1992) "Body talk – deafness, sign and visual language in the *ancien régime*," *Eighteenth-Century Studies* 25, 4 (Summer): 561–86.

Mitchell, W. J. T. (1986) *Iconology: Image, Text, Ideology*, Chicago: Chicago University Press.

Notice (1896) *Notice sur l'Institution Nationale des Sourds-Muets de Paris depuis son origine jusqu'à nos jours (1760–1896)*, Paris: Typographie de l'Institution Nationale.

Nye, Robert (1984) *Crime, Madness and Politics in Modern France: The Medical Concept of National Decline*, Princeton, NJ: Princeton University Press.

Ozouf, Mona (1976) *La fête révolutionnaire 1789–99*, Paris: Gallimard.

Prieur de la Marne, Nicolas (1791) *Réimpression de l'ancien Moniteur* (1854), Tome XIII, no. 205, Paris.

Rabinow, Paul (1989) *French Modern: Norms and Forms of the Social Environment*, Cambridge, MA and London: MIT Press.

Rousseau, Jean-Jacques (1966) *On the Origin of Language*, trans. John H. Moran and Alexander Gode, Chicago: Chicago University Press.

Saussure, Ferdinand de (1964) *Cours de Linguistique Générale*, ed. Charles Bally and Albert Sechehaye, Paris: Payot.

Seigel, Jules Paul (1969) "The Enlightenment and the evolution of a language of signs in France and England," *Journal of the History of Ideas* XXX, i (January–March): 96–116.

Sekula, Allan (1986) "The body and the archive," *October* 39: 3–65.

Soubies, Albert (1909) *Les Membres de l'Académie des Beaux-Arts depuis la fondation de l'Institut,* deuxième série, 1816–1852, Paris, E. Flammarion.

Spivak, Gayatri Chakravorty (1985) "Three women's texts and a critique of imperialism," in Henry Louis Gates (ed.) *"Race", Writing and Difference,* Chicago: University of Chicago Press, pp. 243–61.

Spengler, Gilbert (1905) *La Société Française Pendant le Consulat,* 8 vols., Paris: Perrin.

Stokoe, William (1982) "The study and use of sign language," in W. Stokoe (ed.) *Sign and Culture: a Reader for Students of American Sign Language,* Silver Spring, MD: Linstok Press, pp. 10–52.

Terdiman, Richard (1985) *Discourse/Counter-Discourse: The Theory and Practice of Symbolic Resistance in Nineteenth-Century France,* Ithaca, NY and London: Cornell University Press.

Thévoz, Michel (1989) *Le Théâtre du Crime: Essai sur la peinture de David,* Paris: Minuit.

Tracy, Destutt de (1817) *Elémens d'Idéologie,* 3rd edn., Paris.

Weiner, Dora (1974) "The Blind man and the French Revolution," *Bulletin of the History of Medicine* 48, 1 (Spring): 60–89.

Wildenstein, Daniel and Wildenstein, Guy (1973) *Documents complémentaires au Catalogue de l'oeuvre de Louis David,* Paris: Fondation Wildenstein.

16
Outrages
Sculpture and kingship in France after 1789

Anne M. Wagner

> In books history speaks only to individuals; often it is heard only by the
> inquisitive idler or the unmindful philosopher; in public monuments it speaks
> to everyone at once; it cries out and makes itself heard in every corner of the
> world.
>
> *(Sur le projet d'un monument à ériger à la mémoire de Louis XVI, 1814[1])*

August 1991: it did not take long after the hardliners' coup failed and Gorbachev
resurfaced from Crimean detainment – a mere matter of days – for the statues to
topple. The massive effigies of Lenin and Stalin, Khrushchev and Dzerzhinsky soon lay
in still-massive ruins which citizens inspected and the press services photographed.
Their prints were wired westward without delay, so that we, at our breakfast tables,
could have an imagery of revolution appropriate to the momentous political news. We
needed pictures both of men manhandling statues and the resultant rubble to give the
circumstances their proper historical form. And if we could not remember or never
knew that such events *have* proper forms – that is, that they have happened before –
on-the-spot interviews gave us the facts, and more: "The bemedaled grandfather . . .
turned thoughtful. 'No, I can't say this is good,' he said. . . . 'We trashed the old
statues, now we've trashed these, then we'll be trashing the next ones. There's got to be
a better way' " (Schmemann 1991: A7).

If it seems as though this thoughtful patriarch was supplied by Central Casting, this
is doubtless because of both his medals and his pessimism (it helps to read that while
he chatted with the interviewer his little grandson was clambering over the fallen
idols). But despite the stereotypes, it is nonetheless important, to my mind, that this
stock character also *remembers*, and performs that function textually; he makes it clear
that the memory of the iconoclasm of the first revolution survives in the destructions of
the second one; he assumes, moreover, that new statues will be raised and recognizes
that each succeeding set of images invites a similar fate. Revolutions inevitably dispose
of the old symbolic order only to invent it anew, he declares – thus explicitly disavow-

ing the process as any real agency of change. Destruction, to him, is simply more of the same.

September's newspapers gave plenty of hints that despite their symbolic necessity falling statues do not necessarily signal a complete reordering of cultural priorities and public belief. Consider the odd phenomenon that while images of Lenin were being destroyed, the line of people waiting to see his embalmed remains – to inspect an object which, despite the embalmers' repeated attentions, still passes for his body and not an image of his body – grew steadily longer; until, on September 9, it meandered through Red Square for almost a mile. Evidently the ruler, if he had lost his effigies, had not yet lost his charisma, at least in the minds of some. Does it not seem fair to assume that the two orders of belief – regard for the agents of power and confidence in its symbols – are not necessarily one and the same?

What struck me in September 1991, and continues to seem relevant, is the extent to which the Russian events reconfigure and illuminate the questions which occupy me here. The general province of this chapter is the complex and sometimes contradictory weave of the fates of power and its images, as those fates are legible in the histories of the ruler's body and its surrogates; I wish particularly to attend to the roles of use and belief and memory in animating and reinventing those forms over time. I hope, that is to say, to provide a means of interpreting public sculpture which will attend to issues other than aesthetic ones – though I do not intend to leave aesthetic questions un-addressed. On the contrary, one main focus of the chapter is the demonstration of the claim that formal considerations are of the essence when sculptural sites of memory – or *lieux de mémoire*, to borrow Pierre Nora's useful phrase – are being created. And though I find myself wishing to agree with Nora that such sites, though apparently the province of history, are actually the places "where memory crystallizes and secretes itself," I nonetheless cannot assume, as he does, that memory is some active, authentic, and disembodied agent – the opposite number to a history which is relentlessly critical, relative, and lethal: "Memory is a perpetually actual phenomenon, a bond tying us to the eternal present; history is a representation of the past. History is perpetually suspicious of memory, and its true mission is to suppress and destroy it" (Nora 1989: 8–9). Does history really exist less in the present than does memory? I doubt it. Such polarities make for good rhetoric because they fix and simplify, policing boundaries, denying shared terrain, and removing from consideration both agents and intentions, to say nothing of controversy, resistance, and sheer confusion. In what follows I hope to be able to restore such considerations to a cultural moment to which they were essential.

The time which specifically concerns me is the crucial, final phase in the tradition (as opposed to the actuality) of French kingship – a phase punctuated by two linked sets of significant public acts. When with the return of Louis XVIII to France and the throne, the statues of kings were likewise returned to their pedestals, those events were meant to close a chapter opened a generation before, in August 1792. In less than a week, the bronze and marble monarchs in Paris squares had been cast down by determined citizens, and their disappearance (necessarily) broadcast by a spate of engravings. With the execution of the current Louis then only five months in the future – he was guillotined on January 21, 1793 – perhaps it is to be expected that the images of his more immediate ancestors, Louis XIII, Louis XIV and Louis XV, were the first to fall. The *bon et vaillant* Henri IV was the last to be unseated – reluctantly toppled, it was said, amidst observers with tears in their eyes, singing "Vive Henri IV" under their breaths.[2] These popular loyalties were not soon forgotten, not when they offered the most palatable means for the restitution of a royalist imagery: thus Henri IV was the first of the lot to be returned to its former position, when in 1818 his image was reerected on the Pont Neuf.

There can be no doubt that the new bronze *Henri* (Plate 16.1) remade by the sculptor Frédéric Lemot with an exacting fidelity to its destroyed seventeenth-century proto-type, was meant to stand for both the past and the present, with its ability to do so predicated on the special, if elusive, mix the sculptor was asked to make of the imagery of those two moments – or, in the terminology of the time, of imitation and genius.[3] Thus it was decided that the new statue would recall the old as much as possible, "without the artist being constrained to a too-servile imitation, a constraint which could be harmful to the execution of the work." Its willed archaism was meant to be marvelous, in other words, the resemblance intended from the outset to be strong enough to "create the sweet illusion," according to the prospectus making the provisions of the commission public, that "virtuous hands had hidden it from view during the days of trouble, only to make it appear with new brilliance in times of peace and happiness" (Lafolie 1819: 277).[4] And if this were not enough, the statue was meant to link past and present in slightly different terms as well: it was intended to serve as the artistic emblem of the connectedness of the present monarch to the most palatable and populist of French rulers, beloved above all others for his beneficence, courage, and manly prowess in bed. Hence the choice of Louis's name day, August 25, St. Louis' Day, for the inauguration – though the range of connections went far beyond this, as we shall see. Finally it proclaimed the return to the public realm of a royal representation cast in a purely and recognizably French idiom, as opposed to the hybridized exoti-cisms, even downright barbarism, of the Revolutionary and Napoleonic symbolic languages (Plates 16.2, 16.3): no more Egyptianizing goddesses, like the one used for a Fountain of Regeneration in 1793, her breasts spouting improbably great jets of water meant to succor the new citizen. No more obelisks with their unintelligible markings and no more giant bronze generals sent naked into the middle of the square: both heroic nudity and hieroglyphs must have looked odd plunked down in the Place des Victoires; when juxtaposed by the sculptor Claude Dejoux to form a single monument to the dead Desaix, they seemed positively outlandish. (Little wonder that the monu-ment was dismantled in 1817, only seven years after its inauguration, and the bronze melted down to make up Lemot's work.) Taking its distance from such imported babel, Henri's statue speaks the native dialect with a comfortably oldfashioned inflection – at just the moment, mind you, when Napoleon's former cultural administrators, men like the Baron Vivant Denon, were being satirized for their exotic tastes and misplaced political allegiances (Plate 16.4). Meantime Napoleon's artistic trophies, the naked Apollos and the rest, were being packed off eastward, back to Italy where, their former owners insisted, they rightfully belonged.

Above all the restored bronze *Henri* doubled, doublet and all, in a useful, indeed necessary way, for the body of the present king, Louis XVIII. That body, though monumental in its proportions, was hardly heroic (Plates 16.5, 16.6): portraitists soft-pedalled in vain; cartoonists made it their butt; in fact it was at the heart of the matter, so to speak, where the sincerity of Louis' address to his subjects was concerned: "Je vous porte tous," he declares, "dans mon coeur." The songsters likewise could not let his size alone: Louis, they sang, was "un gros homme, imposé par l'Europe ennemie" (Barbier and Vernillat 1958: 21); or he was "un gros roi nommé Cotillon: Boire, manger, manger et boire, / Voilà le plaisir de Bourbon" (Barbier and Vernillat 1958: 17–18). The problem, to take a slightly different tack, was not that Louis astride cut a less-than-impressive figure, but that he apparently could not mount a horse at all; he could not even get up from his chair without assistance. His body resisted representation – or at least that kind of representation meant to do work of a positive, public kind. His physical envelope was anti-heroic, a matter for caricature, not the admiration and emulation public sculpture should inspire. Théodore Géricault put the matter in a nutshell in a drawing of about 1815 (Plate 16.7): sandwiched between two Napoleonic soldiers whose physical vigor exemplifies the current masculine ideal sits the unfortunate monarch, comedically squat and stool-bound, all jowls and thighs and belly. This is a body with plenty of weight, yes, but almost none of it the ceremonial kind.

So when in 1818 the regenerated bronze *Henri* (some said *resurrected*) was paraded through the Paris streets with all the splendor that could be laid on for the occasion, the ceremonial did double duty: first, it stood in for a monarch whose body could not be publicly manipulated to such advantage; and at the same time the display addressed and corrected the memories of other public paradings of the monarch through Paris streets – the indifference and downright hostility to the entry of Louis XVIII in 1814 certainly among them.[5] (Hence the initial plan, spoiled by delays in the casting, to inaugurate the *Henri IV* on May 4, 1818, the anniversary of Louis' return. The date of August 25 was a second choice.)[6] Perhaps no memory was so relevant as the ignominious forced return of Louis XVI in June 1791, after his botched flight and arrest at Varennes. On that occasion the people stood silently watching his entry under guard; in 1818, we are told, the event was an altogether more joyful and participatory affair, so much so that when the oxen broke down under the sheer weight of their burden, the young men – the teenaged Victor Hugo among them – took up the yokes and dragged the statue the rest of the way (Plates 16.8, 16.9).

The event of course inspired lithographs – such a demonstration of "popular sentiment" could not go unrepresented – and it likewise moved Hugo to pen an ode to the occasion, "Le Rétablissement de la statue de Henri IV," a poem whose twelve stanzas versify the official gloss on the implications of the day's events, and repeat the litany of popular participation and affection: "Par mille bras trainé le lourd colosse roule. / Ah! volons, joignons-nous à ces efforts pieux. / Qu'importe si mon bras est perdu dans la foule! / Henri me voit du haut des cieux" (Hugo 1964: 311). This is not now among Hugo's most appreciated poetic moments – though it was well esteemed at the time – and the current critical neglect of his royalist verse is entirely consonant with the critical fate of the works and circumstances which inspired it (Spitzer 1987: 130).[7] We are long since accustomed, that is to say, to ignoring or dismissing works like Lemot's *Henri IV*. We lack both the terms and the inclination to discuss it; we are not entirely clear on what story it has to tell: one about quality, perhaps – another version of the same sad tale of nineteenth-century state patronage, and its too frequently malign and stultifying effects on sculpture (certainly this is still the dominant art-historical assumption; it has not yet been sufficiently contested). Or perhaps its lesson is moral: perhaps it illustrates another chapter in the annals of artistic coat-turning, given that in 1796 its then 24-year-old author had hotly and successfully competed, at the Convention's behest, to make a colossal statue of *le peuple français*, and in 1808 worked as dutifully and well to show Minerva crowning Napoleon, as he eventually would to remake Henri, or, a few years later, to remodel Louis XIV for Lyons (Lami 1914–21: 306–10; Moulin 1975). Or perhaps a third explanation best fits the case – is it that the art-historical machinery just seizes up, frozen in the face of such a late manifestation of a genre, equestrian statuary, so clearly at the end of its rope?

My argument takes its distance from these various approaches. I want to claim, by contrast, that the monument's archaism is its interest, not its failure, and moreover that the intimate connectedness of its maker to the events of the revolution and empire is altogether typical, and more revealing than morally charged. What the work typifies are the ways, in both theory and practice, that the *Henri IV* could not and cannot be severed from those circumstances which made its re-erection a necessity. Nor should the apparent obviousness of the decision to restore this monarch to his pedestal before all the other kings were returned to their places obscure the complexity of the representational work being done by the statue in question. The assertion of complexity takes some proving, I realize, given its archaizing form; the proof lies above all in the irrevocable entanglement of this statue's history with the fates of other monuments and other monarchs; both were present at its unveiling, lodged in the form of the statue itself, in the minds of observers, and in the patrons' explicit purposes. In such a situation only archaism would do.

Moreover all these intertwined events – the waves of Revolutionary iconoclasm and the restoration of simulacra of those same destroyed icons, the execution of the king and the restoration of his simulacrum, in the (problematic) shape of his brother – are specific sites and decisive events in what Michael Walzer calls the long and difficult process of the destruction of kingship (Walzer 1974: 88). That destruction may be most definitively symbolized in the display of the king's severed head – the physical head of the man who was in turn the symbolic head of the French body politic – but it was tested, quite literally prefigured, in the increasingly outraged and outrageous treatments which his surrogates, the royal statues in the city, received at the hands of the populace in the months and years after 1789.[8] And the restoration likewise is part and parcel of the destruction of kingship, even though its belonging to that process may at first seem counterintuitive. Its contribution to the process lay in the fragility and extremism – ultimately the patent impossibility – of the claim central to restoration: the assertion of a royal body once again made whole and unimpaired. Lemot's statue of Henri IV, I shall claim, images exactly that impossibility, in no uncertain terms.

This chapter is also meant, then, as a contribution to the as yet incomplete study of the erosion of the ideology of royalism. Moreover it proposes public sculpture as a particularly revealing site at which to measure such erosion: revealing because it is placed in public space, thus literally marking a point of intersection between power and its audiences. In so doing, it simultaneously embodies assertions and invites responses, as if quite overtly elected – not only at this moment in particular but repeatedly thereafter – to play a specially visible, sometimes self-sacrificial social role. Wherever there is a notion of a public, sculpture is attributed the ability to speak, if not always to be heard. Hence, among other things, the exuberant confidence of my epigraph, which insists that sculpture, not books, is the real historical textbook, at least when the audience is the people. Such assumptions have deep roots and historical justification: remember, for example, that in the very first moments of the Revolution, on July 12, 1789, when news of the dismissal of the minister Necker spread through the streets, his bust and that of the duc d'Orléans were paraded forth in order to admonish the crowd and incite it to action (Plate 16.10). Carlyle discerned just how fraught, and how necessary, their display was:

> And now to Curtius' Image-shop there; to the Boulevards; to the four winds, and rest not till France be on fire! France, so long shaken and wind-parched, is probably at the right inflammable point. – As for poor Curtius, who, one grieves to think, might be but imperfectly paid, – he cannot make two words about his Images. The Wax-bust of Necker, the Wax-bust of D'Orleans, helpers of France: these, covered with crape, as in funeral procession, or after the manner of suppliants appealing to heaven, to Earth, and Tartarus itself, a mixed multitude bears off. For a Sign! As indeed man, with his singular imaginative faculties, can do little or nothing without signs: thus Turks look to their Prophet's Banner; also Osier *Mannikins* have been burnt, and Necker's Portrait has erewhile figured, aloft on its perch.[9]

(Carlyle 1894: 138)

"For a Sign! [Man] . . . can do little or nothing without signs." So Carlyle claims, and looking at the range of visual documents from both revolution and restoration – whether it is the imagery of the Jacobin clubs, with their requisite bust of Marat as resident quasi-ancestral deity, or selections from the stream of Bourbon propaganda, which time and again present Henri IV *en buste*, in his ancestral guise – we can only agree with him.[10] And if such signs are essential presences, they are also at this moment in history actively manipulated, animated, and invoked in ways which give a clear-cut measure of their real utility. For instance: already in 1787, two years before the parade of busts, the statue of Henri IV had become the negative surrogate of Louis XVI: on the ruling monarch's *jour de fête*, the wreaths and flowers were ostentatiously piled up at the foot of the bronze king. Then in September 1788 while the Parlement sat in historic session, passers-by were forced to salute the statue (Plate 16.11); in the words of a nineteenth-century historian, "it became impossible not to see a sort of insult to the living king in the ironic homage paid to the dead one" (Fournier 1862: 442).[11] And then in the days following the fall of the Bastille, the Pont Neuf and its statue once again became the focus of popular sentiment: someone put a tricolor cockade behind Henri's ear; a painted decor was raised up round the pedestal so that horse and rider seemed to move atop an impressive rocky outcrop; and medallions of La Fayette and mayor Bailly were stuck in place on either side. With this the stage was set: according to a 1791 guidebook, "dances, concerts, songs and purest joy completed these civic celebrations; on them *le bon Henri* seemed to smile" (Dulaure 1791: 298).[12]

We are still a long way off, it is clear, from the destructions of August 1792. The distance of course is more than simply temporal; such calculated and affectionate appropriations of the imagery of kings had no place in Paris as the summer came to its bloody end. Yet even so it is not entirely easy to give those events a fixed historical character, though the difficulty does not simply arise from lack of information. The problem is that the accounts on hand make such uneasy bedfellows. On the one hand, there is the absolute matter-of-factness of many versions. Most visual representations, like the prints in *Les Revolutions de Paris* executed after the drawings reproduced here (Plates 16.12, 16.13), give pride of place to block and tackle rather than furious hordes, and their prose is matched by the workaday way in which the engraver J.-G. Wille recorded their breakup in his journal; they had fallen, end of story. Even when on August 12 it was finally the turn of Henri IV – an event which Wille saw from his own window – he remarked only that "it raised a cloud of dust as considerable as the smoke from a cannon shot" (Duplessis 1857: 356).[13] Any symbolism here was, I am convinced, entirely unintentional; to this observer, at least, who had been in the Place Vendôme in June on the night an immense quantity of *titres de noblesse* were put to the torch, the latest destructions were merely what had to happen when and if events were to run their course. The Assemblée Nationale was forced to come to just such a conclusion when news of the fall of the statues came to its ears. The first reaction was less sanguine than Wille's:

> *M. Sers:* At this very moment the people are busy tearing down all the statues in the various public squares. Trusting such operations to unskilled hands may bring about the gravest possible misfortunes. I ask that the *commissaires* of each section be charged with sending engineers and architects to preside over the work.
> [*Another voice*] I insist that we move on to the business of the day, given that the Assemblée did not authorize the destruction of these monuments.
> *M. Fauchet:* I oppose the business of the day. The Assemblée must regulate the movements of the people if it wishes to prevent real trouble.
> *M. Thuriot:* Since it's impossible to prevent the overthrow of these statues, I think it's all the more important to get some trustworthy men to take charge of the work. . . . In these circumstances the Assemblée should show real character, and not shirk from authorizing the suppression of all these monuments to pride and despotism.[14]

Not, perhaps, the Assemblée's finest hour. Nonetheless it does appear that a certain measure of order did rule the day, though whether or not it was the result of the Assemblée's actions is very much open to question. The sheer labor involved in demolishing monumental statuary – to say nothing of the potential danger – demanded deliberate action. Thus workmen were selected from among the men of the sections, and their names recorded – one Paillot was put in charge – along with any relevant debate about the matter; the duly appointed *commissaires* likewise did their duty, ensuring that the bronze debris was salvaged for cannons and coins and more statues. When a commemorative capsule was found inside the first *Henri IV* it was promptly collected and dispatched to the new Archives Nationales.[15] All this seems a far cry from other versions of the events in question: from Carlyle's trenchant association of the fallen statues with the "constitution burst into pieces" (1894: 122–4); from Fournier's cynical and suggestive characterization, borrowed from Dio Chrysostome, of Parisians as *"enfants terribles de la moderne Athènes"* to whom statues are given like playthings, in full knowledge that sooner or later they will be broken (1862: 482); and farthest of all, perhaps, from the *petit bonhomme* squatting gleefully in the corner of one engraving of the August days, putting paid to centuries of misrule with one long, triumphant, vengeful shit deposited atop the wreckage of a royal statue (Plate 16.14).

All these texts speak from a hostile position, of course – though none more so than the engraving. With text in German as well as French, its version of events is elliptical to say the least, though pointed; it is meant not so much to inform as to provoke with its news of "Horrible acts committed in Paris on the tenth of August": among them, iconoclasm. Thus the caption "La statue de Louis est deshonoré. On y plante le chapeau de liberté où sont les debris de cet ouvrage d'art." And looking at those artistic remains, we are meant to take in their macabre analogy to the all-too-human fragments with which the children play. At the same time the grinning mistreatment of these generic ruins of a ruler points to the charge of affect even a fragmentary royal body – or its image – could still contain.[16] Hence the sack of the royal tombs at St. Denis, and the despoiling and dispersal of their still-numinous contents; little wonder too at the marvelous report that the visage of Henri IV alone had withstood the ravages of time – though not for long: the grenadiers in attendance promptly pulled out tufts of mustache, even teeth, for souvenirs. If they took such trophies to dispel the royal numen, their act nonetheless maintains a belief in a bodily magic which can still work even when the body itself is destroyed. And acting from similar reasons, the members of the Section de la Place Vendôme collected, not some conspicuous body part, but just the forefinger of the right hand of the statue of Louis XIV, a work by François Girardon of 1699, which had dominated their home turf till they put matters right (Plate 16.15). They sent it as a token to another section, the Marseillais, in thanks for their crucial contribution to the events of August 10, because in just that small fragment was embodied enough of the essence of its model to recall his "atrocities" and to keep their revolutionary indignation at a fever pitch. One finger alone was a powerful enough talisman to keep alive their shared hope that, in the words of Arthur, president of the Vendôme section, "the downfall of the kings would follow close on the heels of the ruin of the idols that a blind people once erected to their glory" (Arthur 1792: 5).

Of course it was impossible not to read auguries of the real king's fate in that of his surrogates – although it is not now entirely clear that in August 1792 the proximity and character of that fate were as yet entirely apparent. The fallen statues certainly were either ominous or encouraging, depending on one's point of view; in either case they carried real predictive weight. But exactly *whose* fate was being predicted, to say nothing of whether it would involve death or merely deposition, was still open to some small measure of doubt. For all the plain speaking of the Section de la Place Vendôme – they brand Louis XVI a traitor months before the courts do, and their judgment has a prescience to which we will return – they hold back from naming him outright when the future is predicted; the "*chute des rois*" of which they write in August is decidedly plural, and generalized as a result. And according to another writer, an anonymous contributor to the *Moniteur universel*, whose letter to the editor is dated August 17, if the destructions can be assigned a more specific meaning, their message is nonetheless still cast in the future tense:

> Yesterday while crossing the Pont Neuf I saw a man stopped in front of the
> square where the statue of Henri IV used to be; he seemed plunged into deep

reflection. I stood beside him for some time without speaking. Two or three minutes later I said to him, "Monsieur, do you think it's the statue of the bold and good Henri IV which was demolished here?" "Yes, monsieur," my man answered, "don't you see it?" "No," I answered, "it's not Henri at all I see on the ground, it's Louis XVII" [*sic*]. Surprised, the man seemed to look at me with a brighter air, and I went on my way.[17]

The events of December 1792 and January 1793, when the king was tried, and then executed a few yards away from the empty pedestal where his ancestor's effigy had but lately stood, forestalled any further discussion of the exact meaning of the August vandalism; its significance was now incontrovertible, and the wastage of those bronze figures a clear prefiguration of the decisive and declarative breakup of the royal body and institution. The terms seemed final at the time and were meant to: the royal head was necessarily displayed to the body politic and the grisly ostentation duly imaged and broadcast. The king's remains were then carefully consigned, the head neatly tucked between the legs, to a thick bed of lime lest any fleshly talisman or charm survive (Anchel 1924: 190–200).[18] All this, it now was clear, had been tested out, had been seen to be effective, in the businesslike assaults on the king's surrogates five months before. Hence the insistence, when the king's demise was drawn and engraved (Plates 16.16, 16.17), on coupling the scene at the guillotine with a bare ruined pedestal which sometimes even sported the ruin's requisite tufts of grasses – what better way to declare the monarchy resolutely part of the past?

The king's ultimate fate likewise brings into final focus the three years of public debate concerning the future of royal statuary. I want to keep those discussions to some degree separate here from what I have termed the public *uses* of the monuments – that is, their treatments and mistreatments, the ways they were addressed in actions, not in words. The debates, by contrast, were carried out in print and on the Assemblée floor; they repeatedly imagined and reimagined a variety of futures for public sculpture in terms which kept pace with – perhaps even anticipated – the parallel debate concerning kingship. The medium of those imaginings is pamphlets and speeches and the occasional drawing, but that fact lessens neither their immediacy nor their contingency; on the contrary we should think of their shared purpose as providing a means to negotiate the terms under which kingship might be made viable within the Revolution.

Should the monuments stay or go? The questions had begun to be sounded by the summer of 1790, when it was first proposed, then enacted, that the four slaves which ornamented the base of Desjardin's image of Louis XIV in the Place des Victoires be removed; the insult that they offered to the suppressed peoples they represented, the four French provinces brought into the realm by Louis' conquests, had by then become intolerable (Boislisle 1888: 87–8). But this move already seemed too much of a half-measure to some members of the public, among them one Simonne, a self-styled "*simple citoyen qui aime la patrie*," former under-engineer in the Public Works Department of Burgundy, member of the Club Patriotique de Dijon (Simonne 1790). To his mind, the slaves were not the problem. It was Louis XIV who should go, making way for the statue of Liberty which would fill his place. And as for the slaves, their chains removed, they could be quickly rebaptized as Abuse, Prejudice, Feudalism, and Arbitrary Power, a new inscription added, "To Liberty. On the ruins of despotism," and, hey presto, a statue for the moment, with a minimum of fuss.

Simonne's was one solution to the problem; destruction of the slaves another. It is no small measure of the flux and indecision of the moment that still other proposals should have been mooted; enquiries were launched into the real meaning of those four benighted captives. Did they represent modern peoples after all? Were their attributes not those of Parthians or Armenians subjugated in some distant past by a Roman ruler, not a French one?[19] And if so, could they not be left alone? If removal was necessary, did destruction have to follow? This last question was the concern of a group of artists, Jacques-Louis David at their head, who tried to stave off the final indignity for a work of art they could not help but admire, regardless of its politics.[20] Remove the slaves by all means, they urged, but rather than destroy them, turn them into a monument in their own right; group them on a pedestal without their chains and blighted attributes, explain their presence with an appropriate inscription, and they will become exemplary rather than oppressive.

In the end neither the slaves nor the king were spared removal. But what is striking about this early debate is the way hostility to the oppressor is here displaced on to the figures of the oppressed; only in this guise, apparently, was hostility admissible, when it did not take aim too directly or too violently at the king or his institution. Even Simonne, who while able to imagine the Place des Victoires without Louis XIV, makes it clear that he contemplates dispensing with the monarch at that site only because his image exists elsewhere in the city. To his mind, that single figure would not only be sufficient, but also necessary; Simonne is not yet ready to do without a royal imagery altogether. In fact, to some ways of thinking, at least in 1790, what the capital needs is *more* signs of the sovereign, not less. What better way to symbolize the Revolution than by a monument to the enlightened monarch under whom despotism has been destroyed, and law and liberty recognized? So argued the Chevalier de Mopinot, a former military man, in his *Proposition d'un monument à élever dans la capitale de la France, pour transmettre aux races futures l'époque de l'heureuse révolution qui l'a revivifiée sous la règne de Louis XVI* (1790). He did not stipulate how his monument should look, although he allowed as how it could very properly serve to replace the imprudent militarism of the ensemble in the Place des Victoires; better to have a competition among sculptors to fix on a final "magnificent and expressive" terminology, drawing their conceptions from the "ideas and inspirations of the academies and citizens." Given the tone of his proposal, I doubt that Mopinot would have objected to some of the other projects that were forthcoming in the early 1790s; to the well-timed idea, due to MM. Varenne and Janinet and recorded in an engraving of 1790, that Louis XVI should be monumentalized and memorialized in the company of Henri IV, for example (Hargrove 1989: 32). And then in March 1792 the painters Adelaide Labille-Guiard and Jacques-Louis David were each asked to supply an equally timely portrait of the king, in this instance showing a copy of the constitution to the young dauphin (Bordes 1983: 78–80, 166–73). Such designs, like the debates, instance and are keyed to the ebb and flow of the king's public reputation. Their context and their source are the various efforts made first to temporize and revitalize the monarchy, then to qualify its powers by vesting them in the constitution of 1791, rather than the now inadmissible principle of divine right.

Thus when in August 1792 the Section Henri IV bore witness before the Assemblée

Nationale to their particular motivations in unseating their eponymous master from his horse and his pedestal, their testimony could not help but hinge on the *immediate* climate in which kingship was to be understood. Their orator declared, "The virtues of Henri, we will confess to you, made the citizens hesitate for a moment, but then they remembered that he was by no means a constitutional king; they no longer saw anything but the despot, and all of a sudden he was down" (Letronne 1843: 46–7). Surely we cannot help but notice that Henri is here being judged by an anachronistic standard; constitutions had yet to be mooted in his day; his efforts went as much to solidify absolutism, as to temper it. Clearly the measure in use here has been designed for Louis XVI, not his ancestor; it was not found to fit him any better than it does Henri.

Or to cite one further example, when the Section de la Place Vendôme set down an account of the destruction of its neighborhood monarch, it made even more explicit the connectedness of the action with the betrayals of the king. It is worth quoting the argument at some length:

> Once again Louis XVI has been seen to be guilty of treason towards his country, but even more criminal is the fact that at the moment of his flight of June 21 – since he has just carried out something that before he only contemplated doing – he consummated his crime in spilling the blood of the people. Now his actions leave no more room for glamor or illusion or prejudice in favor of a tyrant whose hypocrisy has so astutely kept the revolution at bay, and who only pretended to accept the constitution so as to undermine its basic principles. Now every person of understanding gathers around the same goal, opinion makes itself heard loud and clear.
>
> (Arthur 1792)

Does it not seem, given the intransigent hostility of these few lines, that what must follow is the call for the death of the king? This is partly an effect of the vehement Vendôme house style: no surprise to learn that one of the section's chief orators was Robespierre himself and that he was deeply involved in the group iconoclasm; on August 14 it was he who set before the Assemblée a proposal to replace the fallen effigy with a new monument to liberty and the martyrs in its cause. But as it happened, the writer in this instance was Arthur, the section's president, though his fervor reaches a Robespierrist pitch; in recounting the fall of the Vendôme statue he is already able to produce the argument which will be used to cause the ruler's death a few months hence. Louis XVI will be formally charged in the dock with treason, the betrayal of his people – his execution followed almost as a matter of course. But in this earlier context the argument takes a different, and oddly abrupt turn: the destruction which is actually urged, which is here most relevant, is that of the king's surrogates, the statues. And so the passage continues apace: "These are no longer only names and simple effigies which are to be veiled from the gaze of a free people which opposes royalty; down with them; the statues must disappear." The shift from ruling monarch to his symbols is abrupt, yes, but it leaves us in no doubt about why their destruction was mandated; the monarch's conduct, his treason, brings it on. And it also works a transformation on the monuments themselves. If they are not, or, better stated, *no longer* "simple effigies," then what are they? The text is quite clear on this point, and once again the elision between sculptural form and the contemporary gloss on royal conduct and prerogatives is spelled out. Take the Vendôme statue itself, the mounted Louis XIV produced by Girardon; this, for the Vendôme section, is the salient example. In its form are read "presumptuous bearing" and a "proud attitude"; such verdicts are perhaps not surprising. But in the same forms they also see an "insolent despot" who has abused his power, a "crowned brigand" who has committed atrocities: in fact so apparent are these malign qualities that they can be remarked anywhere, even in the smallest part of the odious whole. And thus the index finger of the statue's right hand was preserved by its destroyers and packed off to the Marseillais section; in it, the whole history of monarchy was contained – and predicted.

It is sometimes said of Louis XVIII that he learned nothing, and forgot nothing (Walzer 1974: 84). An exacting judgment, certainly, but a fair one, quite properly measuring the decade of his reign by its outcome: when Louis died in 1824, royalists and liberals were more deeply polarized than ever before, and the way had been cleared for his brother and successor Charles X to stage an all-out intensification of the counter-revolution and an ill-fated comeback for royal absolutism. The final ouster of the Bourbons followed on apace. But the utility of the phrase is not only as a verdict on Louis' place in history. Even more to the point, it sums up the issues confronting the restoration with clinical exactitude. A regime unable either to profit from or to forget the past was doomed, and at the outset of his reign, at least, Louis seemed to recognize that fact full well. Hence the motto chosen for his reign, *Union et Oubli*, with its call to heal old rifts and to adopt a restorative amnesia. A fine idea, perhaps; certainly a necessary one, but nonetheless an idea belied on all sides: by the intolerances of state censorship, for example, which though hardly new in France – every previous regime had had its own censorship machinery, with that of Napoleon reaching an unprecedented level of efficiency – certainly managed to impose limitations on republican speech (Goldstein 1990: 92–118); in the legislature, with its violent struggles between left and right; and not least, by the urgent revivalism of Louis's cultural policies and practices. In fact the whole force of royalist representation was directed not at forgetting, but at remembering: restoring, repairing, reenacting, re-creating, returning to the past. The new royal festivals picked up where the *ancien régime* left off, calling on the Church, its calendar and rituals, again to become active collaborators in the ceremonial life of the country, or opening barrels of wine in the public squares to summon up the memory of an indulgent royal bounty (Wacquet 1981). The royal lineage was repeated like a litany; kings cropped up at every juncture, in medallions and prints and festival decors. Their tombs were repaired, and a chapel to the memory of the last king and his queen erected (Darnis 1981). A special enquiry was conducted to see if any shreds of the body of the late dauphin – Louis XVII, as he had come to be known – could be discovered. A demanding schedule of expiatory masses for guillotined royals was put into operation. And so on: this was the meaning of restoration; it was explicitly conceived as an antidote to revolution, with monuments meant to play a leading role as, in the words of *La Quotidienne*, "*une barrière éternelle qui nous sépare de la République*" ("Ch." 1818). And if such monuments seemed backward-looking, this was the result, another commentator wrote worriedly, of a fatally misguided "mania to replace everything that is so as to reestablish what was" (Etienne 1818: 352).[21] So urgently, so extremely, were these policies pursued that the language had to expand to accommodate them: hence the verb "to bourbonize."[22] But bourbonization was objectionable, even risky, some critics recognized, above all for the official policy of *Union et Oubli*. For some the threat was to public order; restored monuments increased the risk of revolútion. Read Chateaubriand on this topic: "In the present time, it is to be feared that a monument erected with the aim of instilling fear of popular excesses can produce the desire to imitate them; evil is more tempting than good; in wishing to perpetuate the memory of pain, one often perpetuates its cause."[23] This is the voice of prudent royalism, but passionate liberalism also spoke out on the issue. "When a state has two parties" – wrote the young editors of the liberal periodical *La Minerve française* in an editorial titled, tellingly, "Union et oubli":

> two parties each with its own customs and even its own language, which oppose principle with principle, memory with memory, it can be said that civil war exists in that state, not openly, it is true, but secretly, as if shut away in its veins and entrails. An excellent way to make that war interminable is with monuments and commemorations – everything which speaks to the eyes, which, dare I say it, embodies the injury, which brings the past into the future, in order to rob from time its most beautiful quality, that of consolation.[24]

These two opinions, make no mistake about it, are the two sides of a single coin; they share many of the same doubts about statuary. They agree, for example, that if monuments of expiation or restoration present a threat, it is because they act differently on different audiences; what is at issue is how those audiences could best be characterized. To Chateaubriand the risk involved emanates from a single source, from the excesses – "*les excès populaires*" – of a people easily tempted into evil. There is no question here of his seeing his opponents as equal or worthy; they evidently belong – as *le peuple* traditionally does – to a lower order of folk (Chartier 1991: 230). Not so, according to *La Minerve française*: there the image is steeped in another view of restoration politics, indeed of modern politics in general; they see equal opponents, each deaf and blind to the other, facing off across a formidable barrier built of principles and memories.

I want to claim that both attitudes animate – are present in – the campaign to restore the imagery of kingship. They are there in different measures and at different sites, to be sure, with Chateaubriand's opinion getting rather more play, for obvious reasons, but nonetheless each is legible in the terms in which the campaign was cast by its instigators, and received by its audiences. Perhaps this is not surprising, given that the specter of the destructions *was* necessarily raised as the inevitable by-product of reconstruction, as both my specimen texts insist. In fact it is difficult to overestimate how present that phantom was in the minds of all and sundry. Its traces are various and omnipresent. They are visible, for example, in the very first pamphlets printed after Napoleon's defeat, which cannot frame their calls for expiation without reference to the crimes which made it necessary; and in the Crown's own programmatic publications of its restorative purposes; and of course, in its own selected sculptural disestablishments (Plate 16.18). These were addressed not so much at any tenacious vestiges of the Revolutionary decor, but at the extraordinarily vigorous Napoleonic appropriation of an imagery of state power best embodied in the form of the ruler himself. But as

Chaudet's statue of the former emperor was laboriously lowered to the ground from its perch atop the Vendôme column – it was soon to be melted down and recycled to make up Lemot's bronze *Henri* – or as portraits of Napoleon were recarved, improbably, to resemble the new monarch, the recollection of the first wave of iconoclasm, that of August 1792, surely rankled as much as did the presence of the imperial iconography which had so efficiently and successfully filled the void.

Certainly it was very much present when the time came to restore Henri's image to the Pont Neuf. That time came early, as we know, and even before the figure had been given permanent form in bronze, a plaster version was mocked up and put in place by royalists and opportunists eager to come – or to come back – into their own. Much more careful thought was given to how the statue's second, permanent restoration was to be characterized and accomplished. There was no doubt that if Henri was the most popular king, he was also the most useful; a guise for a revitalized kingship could certainly be found in the precedent that his rule – he was, after all, the first royal Bourbon – could be taken to provide. Henri and Louis must be thought of as kith and kin, that was the first, essential point, though as we will see, their relationship – *la ressemblance*, as it was termed – would be claimed to entail more than just shared blood-lines. The more difficult issue – the one that required more subtle negotiation – was the business of this talismanic king's relationship to the very people who had so recently and decisively caused his destruction. That same people must now be seen themselves to have elected and effected his return, while their violent destructive act had to be displaced and relocated as the work of some other agency, some external force.

These purposes are explicit in virtually every aspect of the statue's history, from the financial administration of the project to the finer grain of contemporary writing about the work. It is for this reason, for example, that the commission was handled from beginning to end as a public subscription, rather than being financed out of royal or administrative coffers; when princes sought to contribute, their donations were ceremoniously refused (Lafolie 1819: 102). Lists of subscribers were regularly published in the government newspaper, and much play given to the widow's mite and orphan's penny. And when in 1816 it was found that, widows and orphans being rather slow to cough up, the fund was short 120,000 francs, a letter was sent to every departmental prefect urging him to dun his region harder. Its terms are worth savoring: "This enterprise is eminently national, and spontaneous. The name of the head of the august house who reigns over us has animated French people of every class. We cannot have recourse to the government without robbing the enterprise of the inestimable advantage of being the result of the simple love of the French for their Princes."[25] Reading this letter to a governmental appointee, sifting through documents housed in governmental archives, copying out reports of governmental inspectors as to the progress of the statue, looking at the plans of governmental architects for the pedestal and grille and pavement round the work: it is hard to do all this and not fall prey to some small measure of skepticism as to the public – that is to say, private – nature of the enterprise. Hitting upon a copy of a letter sent to the sovereign himself to solicit a formal royal blessing only increases that doubt still further.[26] One has the sense of definitions being stretched to the breaking-point, and beyond, simply because this particular claim was so essential. It could not be surrendered; in it was lodged one crux of the rhetorical value of the work.

But if the public had restored the statue, then it could by no means be held accountable for its destruction in 1792. Of course not. So ways had to be found to attribute such an unfortunate fact to other causes. Perhaps the richest fund of figures for "popular excess" is the dozens of poems written to celebrate Henri's reappearance on the Pont Neuf: there are Hugo's verses, of course, and Valant's "Henri-Quatre renaissant de sa gloire," and Baour-Lormian's "Vers à l'occasion de le Fête de Saint Louis et du Rétablissement de la Statue de Henri IV," and a whole crop of other odes by a variety of authors. Collectively they yield a rich harvest of circumlocutions; synecdoche and personification are the order of the day. Vandalism did it, or Anarchy, or an impious horde, or Discord, or Vengeance, or Barbarism, or Hate, or Fury, or Daunting Tempests, or simply, an Ax.[27] And the people? The injunction rings out: "N'accuse point le peuple! Ils les abhorra tous."[28]

It must be said of this truly dire poetic corpus that even some contemporary readers approached it with a certain skepticism, to put it mildly. Not least the critics of *La Minerve française*; only the efforts of the academician Baour-Lormian win their approval. "The other verses which have been printed are excessively mediocre" – this is their verdict – "union is depicted there even while fresh seeds of discord are being sown; moreover their ideas are vague and their expressions colorless; they have neither verve, nor warmth; this is poetry made to the minister's orders."[29] No doubt the minister did smile on these efforts, even if he did not solicit them; they toe the official line too closely to have been anything other than welcome.

But there is a text about Lemot's statue that was made to the minister's orders; not a poem but a history, it was the work of one Charles Lafolie. An inspector in the restoration Ministry of Fine Arts, Lafolie was a former Napoleonic functionary who tactfully used a pseudonym to publish his memories of the French administration in Italy, in which he had played a part. When Lafolie was appointed to produce the official account – the work he would title *Mémoires historiques relatifs à la fonte et à l'élévation de la statue équestre de Henri IV sur le terre-plein du Pont Neuf à Paris* – Lemot proclaimed himself delighted.[30] Understandably so: Lafolie was a man of parts, entirely able to meet the challenge such a task presented. It was not merely a matter of getting the facts straight, though Lafolie, as the liaison between the subscription committee and the Fine Arts office, was in a position to do just that. And virtually no fact seemed too trivial for inclusion there: we learn the colors of the trappings of the beasts who bore the statue to its destination, and the name of the foundry worker who died a few days after the ceremonial dedication; we are given the titles of the books and the subjects of the medallions sealed inside the bronze; we discover the identities of all the subscribers, by department, Ain to Yonne, from M. Ailland, private collecting agent in Nantua, to M. Viart, *curé* of Auxerre. The list alone demands 100 pages.

But Lafolie's real skills lay elsewhere. He understood with uncommon penetration that he wrote, in quite special circumstances, for three different audiences: for history, of course; for the book's subscribers, since the publication was presold rather than consigned to the vagaries of the open market; and not least for the king, its dedicatee. Hence the particularly charged and ambitious nature of the message. Not only was circumstantial detail provided in abundance for readers scattered throughout France. Long chapters on casting – its history from ancient times and the peculiar material problems encountered and solved in this instance – documented technological venturesomeness in knowing emulation of the eighteenth-century treatises which were the explicit prototypes of this account. And a path was threaded with real dexterity through the minefield of the meanings and memories attributable to public sculpture: "Too often," writes Lafolie in his lead sentence, "flattery or fear have erected monuments to sitting monarchs while giving to such homages the appearance of issuing from the general will; but posterity, ever just, despoils these simulations of supposed gratitude of their fawning inscriptions, and the citizen, in the midst of so many statues offered to his gaze, stops to interest himself only in those of men who have contributed to the happiness and glory of the land" (1819: Prospectus).[31] Here is a remarkable way of speaking of the past, one which takes its distance from the poets' clichéd figures and circumlocutions. It is not the destruction of monuments that is here repudiated; but the suspect conditions under which they were first erected. Enter the citizen, the representative of a just posterity able to discriminate; he can admire only those rulers who have actively contributed to their nation's happiness and prosperity.

Lest it seem too remarkable to read such sentiments in an official history, rather than, for example, in a liberal paper like *Le Constitutionnel* or *La Minerve française*, let me hasten to say that Lafolie is here echoing, among other things, Louis' own taboo against a public monument to his own august person. And of course he does not fail to locate Louis, as well as Henri, in that specially admirable group of men who might worthily attract a citizen's interest. Addressing the king directly, he repeats the key equation between the two rulers like a brief checklist of the modern monarch's duties: "Your majesty, you who in placing wisdom and goodness on the throne and ruling according to law, each day heal the wounds of the state, reopen the wellsprings of prosperity, you know as Henri did how to extinguish dissension, calm resentments, and conciliate all factions" (1819: Prospectus).[32] The obligatory invocations of monarchical virtue should not deceive us. Lafolie's equation of the first and last Bourbons, with its quite special emphasis on law and conciliation, offers its own, decidedly presentist view of the monarchical institution, and the role Louis was being asked to play within it.

And so we come to understand, even from this unlikely source, the ways in which Lemot's *Henri IV*, for all its conscious archaism – or better, *because* of that very archaism – could be taken to enunciate a reinvention, rather than a simple repetition, of the ideology of kingship. The statue is here seen, no longer as the embodiment of despotism that it so lately had seemed to be, but as the very figure of legality and tradition – those principles most essential to the constitutional monarchy that France had by then become. Same location, same horse, same rider, same gait and trappings and stance: the only direct departure from the past which Lemot was allowed involved working from the death mask cast when Henri's tomb was opened at St. Denis – a "departure," needless to say, aimed at shoring up authenticity, rather than undermining it. And the other qualities of the work – above all the meticulous, even fussy attention to the surface detail of the ruler's armor, the horse's trappings, and the like, the places in which Lemot's "genius" might legitimately most make itself felt – have the same authenticating effect. But if Lemot's work thus both re-creates and reinvents its prototype, it also does so by a still more subtle exercise of "genius": the final form of the work decisively undercuts any seventeenth-century Italianate elegance the original may once have had, instead casting both horse and rider into a particularly clipped, contained version of themselves. The body's parts are crisp and distinct, their outlines clearly accented, maybe even a bit guttural – remember that Henri spoke French with a

Gascon burr – and their surfaces are laboriously articulated. There are no smooth transitions here, but rather the repeated visible marks of the chisel used to describe the curls of a beard, the swathe of a sash, the cut of a doublet, and in so doing, summoning past traditions of guild labor and the *objet de vertu* (Plate 16.19). All this, I think, lends Henri a kind of presence which is less transcendent than literal. That literalness *is* its illusion, perhaps even what its supporters may have meant by a "sweet illusion"; the strength of the image, that is to say, lies in the impression it can create of a familiar actuality, the less threatening by virtue of its familiarity, and its Frenchness.

It is tempting to associate to this reading of the *Henri IV* the terms which Chateaubriand used in 1814 to explain to Frenchmen what a king is:

> The king stands simultaneously for the idea of legitimate authority, order, peace, and legal and monarchical liberty. Memories of *vieille France*, religion, time-honored customs, the family's ways of doing things, the pastimes of our childhood, the cradle, the tomb, all this is linked with the sacred name of the king; he frightens no one; on the contrary, he reassures. King, magistrate, father: a Frenchman makes no distinction among these ideas. . . . [A] king is a leader whose paternal power is regulated by institutions, tempered by custom, sweetened and made outstanding by time, just like a full-bodied wine born from native soil and ripened by the sun of France.
>
> (1814: 45)

All this, of course, in contradistinction to Bonaparte, who needless to say has nothing French about him, either in his habits or his character: "even the features of his face betray his origin. The language which he learned in his cradle is not ours, and his accent, like his name, reveals his nationality" (1814: 52–3). It is ironic, of course, that the *Henri IV* might likewise have been accused of betraying a tell-tale accent, had anyone been prepared to invoke its foreign origins in Italy two hundred years before. That no one did, I suspect, was not just because the work was genuinely familiar, but because familiarity had become the main value of the piece.

What is new, then, is political context, so much so that an artistic form whose motivating principle was revivalism could nonetheless here be seen to innovate, to instance a conception of monarchy still not yet deeply rooted in France. Moreover this very revivalism, to underline the contradiction still further, is essential to that significa-tion. To reimagine Henri, rather than simply reimaging him, would have been to risk eroding the royalist claim that the French monarchy had always been constitutional; constitutionality, like kingship, thus meant continuity with the monarchical tradition, rather than the revolutionary one. And it would further have jeopardized the possibility of provoking and tapping any widespread confidence in a populist kingship claimed to bear Henri's stamp. It is exactly the statue's archaism which left it open to either interpretation. To defend either the king or the Charter – and not necessarily both – or even to be among those who pulled Henri's statue to its final destination: all these were ways of proclaiming some kind of adherence to the new doctrine of constitutional royalism. Though exactly what kind of constitutionalism was, like Henri's statue, itself open to interpretation: "each thought of it in his own terms according to his leanings" (Roberts 1990: 78). So spoke the comte de Vitrolles, the royalist who negotiated the Bourbon return with the allies in 1814. Does the king grant the constitution, or is it imposed on him? Does he rule by right, or at the people's pleasure? Does the very fact of the Charter, with its guarantees of the personal liberties first framed by the constitution of 1791, mean that the Revolution lives on in restoration? Or does its entitlement of only a minuscule electorate of wealthy and propertied men signal a blow struck for counter-revolution? The urgent undecidedness of those questions in France from 1816 to 1820 – by far the most liberal moment of the fifteen years of restoration – helped decide the tone and range of responses to Lemot's image of *le bon Henri*.

But what of the audiences the statue could never hope to address? Were not some barriers too wide, some principles too strong, some memories too fresh ever to be bridged by any royalist image, no matter how conciliatory? Were there no counter-proposals to the imagery of monarchy? The answer to all these questions is certainly yes. To locate them, one need only remember that conciliatory speech is not the same as free speech; to put the matter crudely, one could shout "Vive Henri IV!" in public, but never "Vive l'Empéreur!" You could purchase a print of the ancestral Bourbon with no trouble at all, but images of Bonaparte were kept off the market – at least, that is to say, off the *legal* market. The proscriptions meant that the black market for such imagery flourished; its stock in trade was the industrialized image, sometimes printed, often sculpted – the tiny figurine, or the snuffbox, or the portrait which reproduced the familiar dangerous features to the delight of the devoted. In any case their size was never monumental; the whole point was their personal, portable scale. Their messages were often couched in a secret language legible only to the initiated: there are the engravings of pansies (and even of irises!) which conceal the familiar Napoleonic profile among the blossoms, in a special political version of the rabbit/duck effect – the meaning all depends on how you look at it. There are poems with secret tidings, and canes with special handles.[33] One type consists of an apparently innocuous carving which casts a shadow of Napoleon's features when held to the light. Another has a figure of Louis XVIII which a flick of the wrist unscrews to display a little Napoleon within (Plate 16.20). The work of art here enters the age of mechanical reproduction, with a vengeance and for a cause. Its market was large, it was clandestine, and it moved like lightning: one merchant, when apprehended by the police in 1819, claimed to have sold 8,000 small busts of Napoleon's son in the brief space of four days.[34] Policing such a thriving and resilient commerce was no easy business; constant vigilance was the watchword and increasingly minor infractions could mean arrest: in 1827, one fellow was picked up for selling, not canes, but simple pieces of cut cardboard which would cast the shadow of the beloved profile. Add to these disciplinary duties the thankless task of prosecuting every threatening utterance aimed at the king. There were plenty of them, and they grew more frequent – or were more assiduously policed – as the monarchy became increasingly less liberal. There was the surgeon Guyomard, who when confronted with the celebration of the king's birthday in his local *auberge*, spoke up: "I say Vive le Roi, or Vive la Merde! – it's all the same to me!" Or the prostitute Dubarry, who while in a butcher shop at St. Cloud declared, "I'll stick a dagger in Louis's heart, and give my life for his death"; or the day laborer in his *auberge* at Massoté, who pronounced the king a "*gros cochon*" and asked nothing more than the royal tongue and heart, dished up with vinaigrette, for dinner.[35]

Now add to these affronts to order and conciliation the not infrequent attacks on Louis' bodily surrogates – the busts which represented him in churches and barracks and *mairies* across the land.[36] Smashed or disfigured, or merely decorated with a cockade, they received treatment which *Henri* was apparently spared. But only apparently; remember that this is a state with a "civil war shut away in its veins and entrails." Many things might be meant by that phrase – the ultimate irreconcilability of liberal and royalist, for example, or the pulse of popular clandestine resistance. How uncanny to discover that the civil war, so to speak, is actually shut away inside the statue of Henri itself! Let me explain: it seems that one of the team of founders who cast the statue, a certain Mesnel, decided to insert his own choice of mementoes inside the great bronze before it left his hands. His motivations are open to speculation – not least, I reckon, was his chagrin at having failed to prevent the melting down of Chaudet's huge Napoleon from the Vendôme Column for reuse in Lemot's *Henri*; he had worked on the earlier figure, and seen it put in place; such was his fondness for the piece that he even went so far as to offer to pay for the equivalent weight of bronze from his own pocket in order to see it spared. All to no avail, however: so before the resurrected *Henri* left his hands he literally filled it with Napoleonica – all potentially contraband and seditious. He deposited a statuette of Napoleon in the ruler's right arm (he says it was a cast after the model by Taunay) and a description of his own action in the head, and in the horse's belly what he calls "several boxes filled with various papers, like songs, inscriptions, diatribes – monuments to the flavor of the times which I wanted to conserve for history."[37] Do these objects sit cheek by jowl with the official mementoes, one wonders, next to the lives of Henri and the medals commemorating Louis' return, and the copy of the Charter and so on? (True to the political complexities of this conciliatory moment there was even a copy of Voltaire's once-taboo *Henriade*.) Or did Mesnel's act involve a strategic substitution, a clandestine removal as well as a secret contribution? His description (which he prudently waited until 1831 to set down) does not say. He adds only that he fashioned the seams of the statue in such a way as to retrieve his special collection in only half a day.

Short of retrieval we shall not know exactly what outrages sit at the heart of Henri's statue: surely Béranger's verses – perhaps the bitterly ironizing "Cocarde blanche" or "La Sainte-Alliance Barbaresque" – figured among the songs and diatribes. And I hope, given his fight to save Chaudet's *Napoleon*, that Mesnel included the words to Dubraux's "La Colonne," the seditious hymn to the "*gigantesque monument*" which was the hit of the workers' *goguettes* that year. And what about that apposite little ditty, "La Ressemblance," which concludes: "Ravaillac assassine Henri / Un autre tuera celui-ci [Louis XVII] / Voilà la ressemblance / On pleura pour le grand Henri / Nous rirons pour le gros Louis / Voilà la différence" (Barbier and Vernillat 1958: 61)? But I suppose it does no good to let one's imagination run amok; though I will confess that when I picture Mesnel making his deposit in my mind's eye he has some of the glee of the grinning *bonhomme* of August 1792. He is no longer a *sans-culotte*, of course; he makes statues, rather than breaks them, but the impulse to leave his mark, however outrageous, is entirely unchanged. How satisfying, the terms in which Mesnel names his mark-making: he leaves a statuette, at once the symbol of his trade and his politics (as so often, the two go hand in hand), and a collection of texts – together, he writes, these are "monuments to the flavor of the times which I wanted to conserve for history." They are, by Mesnel's lights, as much "monuments" as the huge bronze object in which he conceals them, and insofar as they may be thought to be representative of the political allegiances and utterances of a class which is to play a decisive role in the revitalization of the Revolution, he is right. Mesnel seems quite confident, moreover, that history will receive and learn from his offering, confident, that is, that its contents will one day be revealed to instruct the future. And again he was right, though not exactly in the way he would have predicted. His various documents unread, Mesnel's lesson is a general one, though with its own special uncanny allure. It concerns the fate of the very institution represented by the statue in which it was housed. The restoration itself, in its necessary, even strategic insistence on replicating rather than reinventing the iconography of kingship, seems tacitly to admit to the dis-animation of the tradition it represented and meant to foster. The sheer artistic caution, the frozen lifelessness, of its reedition of the king's body bears witness to the difficulty of reviving the mystic ethos of royalism, once it is hedged round with the qualifications necessitated by constitutionality and political compromise. How bizarre – how representative of ideological crisis – that it is *Mesnel* who believes most in the talismanic quality of the royal body; so much so that at its core he secretes his own dangerously numinous devices – devices which represent the explicit taboos of the royalist regime. Unreadable, unseeable, nonetheless they need simply be lodged in the king's vitals to work their special predictive magic. There they embody the revolutionary Other, giving it form in the figure of Napoleon, and voice as seditious speech.

Notes

1 This anonymous pamphlet was published in Paris in 1814; Bibliothèque Nationale LB 41 469, p. 17: "Dans les livres l'histoire ne parle qu'aux individus; souvent elle n'est entendue que du curieux oisif, de l'indifférent philosophe; dans les monuments publics elle parle à tous à la fois; elle crie et se fait entendre jusqu'aux bouts du monde."

2 This is according to an eye-witness, Jean Louis Soulavie, a priest and art collector who after the revolution took the clergy's oath of loyalty to the civil constitution, married, and joined the Club des Jacobins. Present in the Place Dauphine as the statue fell, he noted his observations on the back of a drawing of the scene which was part of his collection. See Musée du Louvre 1989: 55, no. 54.

3 The official dossier of the statue in Paris, Archives Nationales, F 21 582, no longer contains a copy of Lemot's contract with the state. But references to it in the course of documentation which *is* included there – for example, at the moment that Lemot's model is inspected by the committee appointed to weigh its quality and suitability – as well as the tone adopted by Charles Lafolie in his commemorative text (Lafolie 1819) implies that the artist was held to such a standard. Hence the supervising *comité*'s decision that "la nouvelle statue rappelleroit, autant que possible, celle qui avoit été détruite, sans que néanmoins l'artiste fut astreint à une imitation trop servile, dont la gêne pourroit nuire à l'exécution de son ouvrage" (Lafolie 1819: 96).

4 "Rétablissement de la Statue de Henri IV. Aux Français . . . il est à désirer que [la statue] soit assez ressemblante à celle qu'on y a vue si long-temps, pour qu'une douce illusion fasse demander si des mains vertueuses ne l'auroient pas soustraite à tous les regards dans des jours de malheurs, pour la faire reparoître avec un nouvel éclat dans des jours de paix et de bonheur."

5 Chateaubriand gives that hostile reception an unforgettable guise in his description of the Napoleonic troops lining the monarch's route from the Pont Neuf to Notre Dame: "Je ne croix pas que figures humaines aient jamais exprimé quelque chose d'aussi menaçant et d'aussi terrible. Ces grenadiers couverts de blessures, vainqueurs de l'Europe, qui avaient vu

tant de miliers de boulets passer sur leurs têtes, qui sentaient le feu et le poudre, ces mêmes hommes, privés de leur capitaine, étaient forcés de saluer un vieux roi, invalide du temps, non de la guerre, surveillés qu'ils étaient par une armée de Russes, d'Autrichiens, et de Prussiens, dans la capitale envahie de Napoléon. Les uns, agitant la peau de leur front, faisaient descendre leur large bonnet à poil sur les deux coins de leur bouche dans le mépris de la rage, les autres, à travers leurs moustaches, laissaient voir leur dents comme des tigres. Quand ils présentaient armes, c'était avec un mouvement de fureur, et le bruit de ces armes faisait trembler. Jamais, il faut en convenir, hommes n'ont mis a une pareille épreuve et n'ont souffert un tel supplice. Si dans ce moment ils eussent été appelés à la vengeance, il aurait fallu exterminer jusqu'au dernier, ou ils auraient mangé la terre." *Mémoires d'Outre Tombe*, Vol. II (Paris: Edition du Centénaire, 1948), pp. 531–2, cited by Wacquet (1981: 140).

6   This detail is evident from the document recording the financial terms under which Lemot undertook to supervise the execution in bronze of the statue, a measure he seems to have decided on in order to have both a free hand and final say over its appearance, as well as to avoid the problems which beset the casting of the Desaix. See "Marché pour l'entière exécution en bronze de la statue equestre de henry IV, qui doit être érigée sur le pont neuf à Paris, présenté à Messieurs les Membres composant le Comité formé pour le rétablissement de ce monument, par M. Lemot, statuaire, membre de l'Institut et Professeur aux Ecoles Royales des beaux-arts de Paris," AN F 21 582. In it Lemot contracts to deliver the finished statue by March 1, 1818, "afin que le transport et l'exécution puissent avoir lieu dans le courant du dit mois, et l'inauguration le 4 mai suivant, jour anniversaire de l'Entrée de Louis XVIII dans la capitale."

7   Hugo's ode was the recipient of a golden lily in a special competition sponsored in 1819 by the *Jeux floraux de Toulouse*, and the poet himself published it in the May 1820 *livraison* of *Le Conservateur Littéraire* (Marsan 1935: 5–10).

8   Historians of the monarchy and the Revolution nowadays agree that the trial and execution of the king were merely the terminus of a process begun long before, though exactly how long before is open to interpretation. Did the process begin in the 1750s, with the representative event signalling its start being Damiens' attack on the king? Or had it already begun more than a century before, when in 1610 the new king Louis XIII disrupted the traditional usages governing the display of the king's mysterious body? See Chartier (1991: 111–35); Merrick (1990); Ozouf (1989: 105); Furet (1989: 243).

9   The Curtius in question was the Swiss-born Philippe Guillaume Curtius (1714–94; sometimes John Christopher), uncle and teacher of Mme. Tussaud, and founder of the first wax museum, the Caverne des Grands Voleurs; his shop and exhibition were on the Boulevard du Temple. His own uncannily realistic wax self-portrait is now at the Musée Carnavalet, Paris.

10   As an example of such sculptural imagery, let me cite the bust of Marat, painted plaster, Musée Carnavalet, S533; a monochrome version is at the Musée du Château Gontier and during the Revolution was displayed in the local Temple de la Raison.

11   "Il devenait impossible de ne pas voir une sort d'insulte au roi vivant dans l'ironique hommage rendu au roi mort."

12   "Le lendemain du jour de la fédération, les soirs du 15, 16, et 17 juillet 1790, on célébra devant cette statue des fêtes magnifiques. Une décoration très bien peinte, placée au-devant du piédestal, représentait un vaste rocher sur lequel la statue d'Henri IV semblait placé; aux deux côtés étaient des medaillons de MM. de la Fayette et Bailly. Des concerts, des danses, des chants et la joie la plus pure complèterent ces fêtes civiques, auxquels la figure du bon Henri semblait sourire."

13   "Je vis de mes fenêtres la chute de la statue à cheval de Henry IV. Il s'éleva une poussière aussi considérable que la fumée d'un coup de canon."

14   *Gazette Nationale, ou le Moniteur Universel* 13, 226 (Paris: 1853), Monday, August 13, 1792.

15   Concerning the first statue of Henri IV, the work of Giovanni Bologna and Pierre Tacca, and the dedicatory capsule found within it, see Lafolie (1819: 82–6). Letronne (1843: 46–7) cites the case of the first *Henri IV*, and the 1614 *procès-verbal* secreted within the statue, as an

immediate parallel to a lead inscription found within a Greek kouros acquired by the Louvre in 1834, and in the course of his discussion quotes from the *Registre des délibérations de la Section de Henry IV, du 13 août (l'an iv de la liberté)*, the report that the Section Henri IV addressed to the Assemblée Nationale concerning its actions towards the statue; the report was duly published in the *Gazette nationale, ou Moniteur Universel*, August 16, 1792. It is given here in its entirety: "Législateurs, vous avez ordonné la destruction de tous les monuments du despotisme qui, après trois années de liberté, fatiguoient encore les yeux des hommes libres et donnoient dans nos places publiques le démenti le plus formel et le plus authentique à la révolution. A votre voix les citoyens de la section de Henry IV se sont empressés de renverser la statue du roi dont cette section porte le nom. Les vertus de Henry, nous vous l'avouerons, les ont fait hésiter un instant, mais ils se sont souvenus qu'il n'était point roi constitutionnel, ils n'ont plus vu que le despote, et soudain il est tombé. Toutes les marques, toutes les noms qui peuvent rappeler le despotisme doivent avoir le même sort. Les signes de la liberté et de l'égalité doivent les remplacer, et les citoyens qui nous ont députés vers vous, nous ont chargés de vous prier de faire élever à la place de cette statue deux tables sur lesquels seront gravés les droits de l'homme. Leur oubli a seul produit le despotisme, et chaque citoyen les liroit en passant sur le Pont-Neuf.

Ils nous ont chargés de remettre sur le bureau l'acte de fondation de cette statue qui a été trouvé dans les *flancs du cheval* [*sic*] et de vous déclarer qu'ils ont changé le nom de la section de Henry IV en celui de la section du Pont-Neuf."

16 Perhaps it should be noted that another event of "*vandalisme excrémental*" is recorded by Louis Réau as having followed on the heels of the removal of the Galerie des Rois from Notre Dame; the debris was piled behind the cathedral, according to Sebastien Mercier in *Le Nouveau Paris* (2nd. edn., Geneva, 1795), Réau's source, where it served as an open-air latrine (Réau 1959: 230).

17 *Gazette Nationale, ou le Moniteur Universel* XIII (Paris: 1853): 422, August 17, 1792: "Au redacteur. Hier, Monsieur, j'ai vu en passant sur le pont neuf un homme arrêté vis à vis la place où était la statue de Henri IV; il paraissait plongé dans des profondes réflexions. Je me suis tenu quelque temps à côté de lui sans lui parler. Deux ou trois minutes après, je lui ai dit: 'Croyez-vous, Monsieur, que ce soit la statue du brave et bon Henri qu'on ait renversée?' 'Oui, Monsieur,' m'a répondu mon homme, 'est-ce que vous ne le voyez pas?' 'Eh bien, non,' lui ai-je répliqué, 'ce n'est point Henri IV que je vois là par la terre, c'est Louis XVII.' Cet homme étonné m'a regardé d'un air qui m'a paru moins triste, et moi, j'ai passé mon chemin."

18 Anchel's conclusion casts doubt on the likelihood of any authentic remains having been found in 1814, when an effort at exhumation was made, and bones collected for reburial in the *Chapelle expiatoire*.

19 This was the argument of the sculptor Jean-Jacques Caffieri, as outlined in a letter of June 27, 1790, to Bailly, mayor of Paris, and published in the *Journal Général de France*, July 5, 1790 (Guiffrey 1877: 406–11, 456–8).

20 David was joined in this proposal by Restout, Jullien, Robin, Echard, Massard, Beauvallet, Bouillard, Henriquez, Wille *fils*, Monnot, Giroust, Huet, and Pasquier (Guiffrey 1877: 454–5).

21 "Rien du reste ne me semble plus mal imaginé, j'oserai même dire plus funeste, que cette manie de démolir tout ce qui est pour rétablir tout ce qui était."

22 The term did not, however, have a necessarily negative cast, as is clear from its usage in the title of a pamphlet by one Auguste Hus, *La colonne de la Place Vendôme Bourbonisé, suivi de quelques pensées sur l'éloquent ouvrage de M. de Chateaubriand, contenant la noble et héroique vie de l'immortel Duc de Berry, et quelques mélanges en prose et en verses* (Paris: 1822).

23 *Mémoires d'Outre-Tombe*, Vol. II, pp. 544–5, cited in Wacquet (1981: 131). "Par le temps actuel, il serait à craindre qu'un monument élévé dans le but d'imprimer l'effroi des excès populaires donnât le désir de les imiter: le mal tente plus que le bien; en voulant perpétuer la douleur, on en fait souvent perpétuer l'exemple."

24 "Union et Oubli," *La Minerve française* 1 (1818): 190: "Lorsqu'il existe dans un état deux partis, chacun avec ses moeurs et même son langage, qui opposent principes à principes,

souvenirs à souvenirs, on peut dire que la guerre civile existe dans cet état, non point manifestement, à la vérité, mais sourdement, et comme renfermée dans ses veines et dans ses entrailles. Un excellent moyen de la rendre interminable, ce sont les monuments et les commémorations, tout ce qui parle aux yeux, tout ce qui donne, si j'ose le dire, un corps à l'injure, tout ce qui ramène le passé dans l'avenir, afin de ravir au temps sa plus belle qualité, celle de consolateur."

25 Dijon, Archives de la Côte d'Or, 7M140, Rétablissement à Paris de la Statue de Henri IV, letter of July 9, 1816, to the prefect of the Côte d'Or: "Cette entreprise est éminemment nationale; elle a été spontanée. Le nom du chef de la maison auguste qui règne sur nous a animé les français de toutes les classes. Nous ne pouvions avoir recours au gouvernement sans ôter à l'entreprise l'avantage inestimable d'être le résultat du seul amour des français pour leurs Princes."

26 This is a brief digest of the types of documents contained in the official records of the work, Paris, AN F 21 582.

27 This brief vocabulary list is culled from the following poems, in addition to those mentioned above (note 4 and below (note 35): J. H. Vallant, "Henri-Quatre renaissant de sa gloire, Poême" (Paris: 1818); Félix Vidal, "Ode sur le rétablissement de la statue de Henri IV" (Paris: Firmin Didot, 1818); C. L. Mallevant, "La Restauration de la Statue de Henri IV" (Paris: 1818); Comte de Coëtlogon, "Ode sur le rétablissement de la statue équestre d'Henri IV, le 25 août, 1818" (Paris: Delaunay, 1818); J. Brisset, "Statue de Henri IV" (Paris: 1818); P. Baour-Lormian, "Vers à l'occasion de la fête de St.-Louis et du rétablissement de la statue de Henri IV," *Moniteur universel*, August 25, 1818: 1021.

28 F. J. Depuntis, "Ode sur le rétablissement de la statue de Henri IV" (Montauban: 1818).

29 E. [Etienne], "Lettre de Paris," *La Minerve française* (August 1818: 182–3: "les autres vers qu'on a imprimé sont d'une médiocrité excessive; on y parle d'union en jetant de nouvelles sémences de discorde; les pensées en sont d'ailleurs vagues et l'expression décolorée, il n'a ni verve, ni chaleur; c'est de la poésie tout-à-fait ministérielle."

30 Paris, Archives Nationales, F 21 582, Henri IV; Dossiers Divers: Mémoires Historiques; Lemot to Lafolie, November 19, 1817.

31 "Trop souvent la flatterie ou la crainte ont élevé des monuments aux souverains pendant leur vie, en donnant à ces hommages l'apparence du voeu général; mais la postérité, toujours juste, dépouille de leurs inscriptions adulatrices ces simulacres d'une reconnoissance [sic] supposé, et le citoyen, au milieu de tant de statues offertes à ses regards, ne s'arrête avec intérêt que devant celles des hommes qui ont contribués au bonheur et à la gloire de la patrie." Bound with the *Mémoires*, the prospectus also preceded them; it was the means by which subscriptions to the complete publication were meant to be secured.

32 "Votre majesté qui, plaçant la sagesse et la bonté sur le trône, et regnant par les lois, cicatrise chaque jour les plaies de l'état, rouvre les sources de la prospérité, sait, comme Henri, éteindre les dissensions, calmer les ressentiments, concilier tous les intérêts."

33 The collections of Napoleonica in the Musée historique lorrain, Nancy, and the Musée national des Châteaux de Malmaison et Bois-Préau, Malmaison, are rich in this kind of material. I am grateful to Claire Aptel and Jérémie Benoit, curators at these two institutions respectively, for their responses to my inquiries. The following verses, which were circulating in Paris in December 1827, are an example of the poetic trickery I mean: they can be read as two separate royalist poems, or a single Bonapartist one:

Vive vive à jamais	L'Empéreur des français
La Famille royale	est indigne de vivre.
Oublions desormais	La branche des capets
La race impériale	A Jamais doit survivre.
Soyons donc le soutien	du Fier Napoléon
du grand duc de Bourbon	que l'âme soit maudite
C'est à lui que revient	cette punition
l'honneur de la nation	à son juste mérite.

(Paris, AN F7/6706. Ecrits et objets séditieux)

34   These references are culled from a variety of dossiers in the series BB 18 and F 7 in the Archives Nationales, Paris: BB 18 974, 980, 981, 982, 983, 993, 994, 1113, 1114, 1115; F 7 6706; this final reference is the source for the detail of the sale of 8,000 little busts.

35   AN BB 18 1113, 1114.

36   AN BB 18 980, 991, 993, 1026, 1113, 1114.

37   "La Colonne de la Grande Armée," *Le Cabinet de Lecture*, August 10, 1839, 121–2: "Permettez-moi d'ajouter quelques détails sur la statue d'Henri IV. On trouvera dans le bras droit de cette statue, un petit Napoléon d'après le modèle de Tonnet [*sic*] La tête contient le procès verbal du dépôt que j'ai fait moi-même dans le bras droit d'Henri IV. Dans le ventre du cheval se trouvaient plusieurs boîtes renfermant divers papiers tels que chansons, inscriptions, diatribes, monuments de l'esprit du temps que j'ai voulu conserver à l'histoire. En une demi-journée, je pourrais retirer de ce dépôt tous ces objets sans endommager en aucune façon la statue." There can be no doubt that Mesnel was an actual historical personage, since his name figures in the documents concerning the erection of the Henri IV; it was he, for example, who did the job of breaking up the bronze Desaix for recycling in the later work. See AN F 21 582; Dossiers Divers. The letter in which he reveals his deed may have been first published in July 9, 1833 in *L'Estafette* (I am grateful to Jacques de Caso for this reference), and continued to circulate in various forms well into the twentieth century. It was the kind of story, for example, about which readers would write in to *L'Intermédiaire des Chercheurs et Curieux* (1058, November 20, 1904, 736–7) for confirmation or denial by other readers, both of which were provided. Here it was alleged, for example, that the statue is full of gold, and in another account that it is filled to the brim with statuettes of Napoleon all cast by the founders from the bronze of Chaudet's massive statue. The Mesnel letter was also referred to by Fournier (1862: 604–5), by Reinhard (1935: 146), who claims, against all odds, that the secretly Bonapartist Lemot was the instigator of the deed, and by Herbert (1974).

Bibliography

Anchel, R. (1924) "La Commémoration des rois de France à Paris pendant la Restauration," *Mémoires de la Société de l'histoire de Paris et de l'Ile-de-France* 47: 173–208.

Arthur (1792) *Les Citoyens de la Section de la Place Vendôme aux Marseillois*, Paris: Imprimerie de la Section de la Place Vendôme.

Barbier, P. and Vernillat, F. (1958) *Histoire de France par les chansons*, Paris: Gallimard.

Boislisle, A. de (1888) "Notices historiques sur la Place des Victoires et la Place Vendôme," *Mémoires de la Société de l'histoire de Paris et de l'Ile-de-France*, 15: 1–272.

Bordes, P. (1983) *Le Serment du Jeu de Paume de Jacques-Louis David*, Paris: Editions de la Réunion des musées nationaux.

Carlyle, T. (1894) *The French Revolution, A History*, London: Chapman & Hall.

"Ch." (1818) "Des Suites du 21 janvier et des causes qui devaient s'opposer à la durée de la république et du règne du Bonaparte," *La Quotidienne*, March 4.

Chartier, R. (1991) *The Cultural Origins of the French Revolution*, trans. L. G. Cochrane, Durham, NC and London: Duke University Press.

Chateaubriand, F.-R. (1814) *De Buonaparte, des Bourbons et de la nécessité de se rallier à nos princes légitimes pour le bonheur de la France et celui de l'Europe*, Paris: Mame frères.

Darnis, J. M. (1981) *Les monuments expiatoires du supplice de Louis XVI et de Marie Antoinette sous l'empire et la Restauration, 1812–1830*, Paris: published by the author.

Dulaure, J. A. (1791) *Nouvelle Description des curiosités de Paris*, 3rd edn., Paris: Lejay.

Duplessis, G. (ed.) (1857) *Mémoires et Journal de J. G. Willi, Graveur du Roi*, Paris: Renouard.

Etienne (1818) "Lettres sur Paris," *La Minerve française* 3.

Fournier, E. (1862) *Histoire du Pont Neuf*, Paris: Dentu.

Furet, F. (1989) "Louis XIV," in F. Furet and M. Ozouf (eds.) *A Critical Dictionary of the French Revolution*, trans. A. Goldhammer, Cambridge, MA and London: Harvard University Press, pp. 234–43.

Goldstein, R. J. (1990) *Censorship of Political Caricature in Nineteenth-Century France*, Kent, OH and London: Kent State University Press.

Guiffrey, J. (1877) *Les Caffieri, sculpteurs et fondeurs ciseleurs*, Paris: De Morgand et C. Fatout.

Hargrove, J. (1989) *The Statues of Paris: an open-air Pantheon*, Antwerp: Mercantorfonds.

Herbert, R. (1974) "Baron Gros's Napoleon and Voltaire's Henri IV," in F. Haskell (ed.) *The Artist and the Writer in France, Essays in Honour of Jean Seznec*, Oxford: Oxford University Press, pp. 52–71.

Hugo, V. (1964 [1819]) "Le Rétablissement de la statue de Henri IV," in *Oeuvres Poétiques*, Vol. II, Paris: Bibliothèque la Pléiade.

Lafolie, C. (1819) *Mémoires historiques relatifs à la fonte et à l'élévation de la statue équestre de Henri IV sur le terre-plein du Pont-Neuf à Paris, avec des gravures à l'eau-forte représentant l'ancienne et la nouvelle statue; Dediés au Roi*, Paris: LeNormant.

Lami, S. (1914–21 [1919]) "Lemot," in *Dictionnaire des sculpteurs de l'école française au dix-neuvième siècle*, Vol. III, Paris: E. Champion, pp. 306–10.

Letronne, A. J. (1843) *Explication d'une inscription grecque trouvée dans l'intérieur d'une statue antique de bronze, avec des observations sur quelques points de l'histoire de l'art chez les anciens*, Paris: Imprimerie royale.

Marsan, J. (ed.) (1935) *Le Conservateur Littéraire 1819–1821*, Vol. II, Paris: Libraire E. Droz.

Merrick, J. W. (1990) *The Desacralization of the French Monarchy in the Eighteenth Century*, Baton Rouge, LA and London: Louisiana State University Press.

Moulin, M. (1975) "Le Thème de la statue équestre dans l'oeuvre de François-Frédéric Lemot (1771-1827)," *Bulletin de la Société de l'Histoire de l'Art Français*: 227–36.

Musée du Louvre (1989) *Un collectioneur pendant la Révolution, Jean Louis Soulavie (1752–1813)*, Paris: Edition de la Réunion des musées nationaux.

Nora, P. (1989) "Between memory and history: *Les Lieux de Mémoire*," *Representations* 26: 7–25.

Ozouf, M. (1989) "King's trial," in F. Furet and M. Ozouf (eds.) *A Critical Dictionary of the French Revolution*, trans. A. Goldhammer, Cambridge, MA and London: Harvard University Press, pp. 95–106.

Réau, L. (1959) *Histoire du Vandalisme, Les Monuments Détruits de l'art français*, Vol. II, Paris: Hachette.

Reinhard, M. (1935) *La Légende de Henri IV*, Paris: Librairie Hachette.

Roberts, J. (1990) *The Counter-Revolution in France, 1781–1830*, London: Macmillan Education.

Schmemann, S. (1991) "Moscow memo: the old order, like its idols, is toppled, but the victors find words of bereavement," *New York Times*, September 4.

Simonne (1790) *Lettre d'un citoyen à M. le Président de l'Assemblée Nationale sur l'enlèvement des statues de la Place des Victoires*, Paris: Imprimerie de Calixte Vollard.

Spitzer, A. (1987) *The French Generation of 1820*, Princeton, NJ: Princeton University Press.

Wacquet, F. (1981) *Les fêtes royales sous la Restauration, ou l'ancien régime retrouvé*, Paris: Libraire Droz et Arts et Métiers Graphiques.

Walzer, M. (1974) *Regicide and Revolution: Speeches at the Trial of Louis XVI*, London: Cambridge University Press.

17

Dante's Restaurant
The cultural work of experiment in early modern Tuscany

Jay Tribby

Civility requires you to be polite, but it does not expect you to be homicidal towards yourself.

(Antoine de Courtin, *The New Treatise of Civility* [1672])

Anyone who has been to Florence knows that the city promotes its Renaissance past to visitors with the full knowledge that, during their stay, they are going to comport themselves as consumers of that past. This Florence does not promote nostalgia trips, it promotes shopping trips. This Renaissance is not an object of intellectual reverie, it is an object of mass consumption. In the center of town, for example, not far from Dante and Beatrice's Restaurant, marble tablets inscribed with passages from the *Divine Comedy* point out sites mentioned in the *Inferno*, the *Purgatorio*, and the *Paradiso*. Just a few blocks down the street, the index finger of Galileo greets visitors during their tour of the Museum of the History of Science. Among the items for sale in the museum (which, to be honest, tries very hard not to be a single-themed memorial to Tuscany's most famous astronomer) are sturdy cardboard replicas of the telescope used by Galileo to observe the moons of Jupiter. And everywhere, it seems, postcards and T-shirts with neon writing screaming "Ouao!" (the Italian transliteration of the English "Wow!") offer reproductions of the anatomical highlights of Michelangelo's David for them to purchase and take home with them.

Whose Renaissance is this, anyway? Or rather, just what traces of just whose Renaissance do we have here?

The first grand-scale packaging of a touchable, collectable, and visitable Renaissance past may be traced to the middle decades of the sixteenth century, when the recently installed court of Cosimo de' Medici more or less created it to promote a new social identity for the two groups of political subjects who were to be the Medici's staunchest allies in the decades following the family's definitive return to power in 1537: members of the established Florentine patriciate, on the one hand, who could render useful services to the court once their suspicions about the Medici had been overcome, and, on the other, members of the new court bureaucracy, many of whom were not yet notables, but who aspired to that status.[1] A new ideology celebrating the "Tuscanness," or *toscanità* of the court and these two groups shaped the contours of their new social identity, ignoring the categories through which political culture in Florence had been organized for centuries (categories arising from long-standing family alliances and rivalries) and putting in their place categories based upon individual and group capacities to make a style of life of an obsession with a trio of poets from the thirteenth and fourteenth centuries who, under the Medici, would be transformed into ornaments of unprecedented social prestige. This Renaissance was dangled before the members of these groups as the key to their social success within the new culture of the court. In court circles the period became known as the "Good Century," with Dante, Petrarch, and Boccaccio its "Good Authors." These poets meant different things to different people, of course, and therein lay their appeal: to the members of the Florentine patriciate they were, among other things, reminders of a kinder and gentler past when political life had been organized around them; to the new court bureaucrats they were the symbolic capital of the members of the dominant culture, a culture whose ranks they now had the chance of joining.

The Medici "Good Century" bore about as much relation to a thirteenth- and fourteenth-century Florentine moment as the Disney Imagineers' "France" or "Morocco" at Epcot Center in Orlando, Florida, bears to . . . Well, suffice it to say that the Good Century was very much the product of the later culture that gave it a name and of the wide range of texts, institutions, commodities, and social practices that gave it a social profile. Although one could certainly say a great deal about the ways in which good centuries, renaissances, and golden ages have been invoked in recent years in the rhetoric of the American right, and although one could say even more about the ways in which they have been used by dominant cultures in many different historical periods to fashion social identities and foster social antagonisms, my immediate point here is that this particular thirteenth- and fourteenth-century Renaissance is a product of the sixteenth and seventeenth centuries, and that the first sustained use of it as a shaper of social identity was one with the emergence of absolutism in Tuscany. For the sixteenth-century Medici, as for many late twentieth-century scholars, the Good Century was a floating signifier emptied of historical content, a period on to which the court could project its own fantasies. An imagined epoch out of which tumbled an entire political imaginary, the Good Century and its Good Authors quickly became code words in the service of fledgling social hierarchies. At issue for the new court, as for its most privileged new subjects, were questions such as the following. To whom does the Florentine Renaissance belong? To whom, for that matter, does Florence or the past in general belong? How can the identity of a group of individuals be shaped so that they come to regard themselves as having a privileged relationship to historical time, intellectual property, and the human social fabric?

In this chapter I want to consider the emergence of Medici interest in natural experiment between the later 1650s and the 1680s as part of the history of the means by which the court established the terms of social privilege in the grand duchy of Tuscany. Experiments provided the Medici and the members of their court with the delicate rose-waters they used in their baths, the fine extracts of orange with which they scented their living quarters, the cool ices with which they refreshed their palates between courses, and the watermelon salts with which they regularly cleansed their intestines. Through experiment, distance from bodily discomfort became an analogue to the court's distance from the law. The production of other distances was also at issue in experiment. Since many experiments were staged by the court as explicit checks on the statements once made by ancient natural philosophers, experiments made it possible for the court to assert what it saw as its privileged relationship to historical time. Similarly, experiments transformed imported objects into fodder for the stories that the court would tell itself about the grand duchy's superiority to the foreign cultures which were its contemporaries.

Much of the analysis to follow is driven by an assumption that may be stated in roughly the following terms: experiments based in or sponsored by courts during much of the seventeenth century proceeded according to a local logic of practice, a social or cultural logic that derived in large part from the pretensions and aspirations of the specific courts that sponsored them and the individuals who performed them. As I shall suggest throughout this chapter, a focus in Medici-sponsored experiments on keeping palates, intestines, languages, and reputations as clean as a whistle reflects these local realities. This kind of approach to the study of court-sponsored natural experiment requires a sensitivity to the general dynamics of court culture, something about which we know a good deal thanks to the past decade of poststructuralist criticism by scholars of early modern Europe, and to the ways in which specific courts used experiment to reproduce or supplement their power in a given space and time, about which we still have much to learn. Although my analysis engages the wide range of experiments performed in and around the Medici court between the later 1650s and the 1680s, my comments in this chapter will focus on one particular aspect of the Tuscan art of experimenting: the work of experiment in the production of what, following the insights of Benedict Anderson, we might call the imagined community of the grand duchy of Tuscany. Experiments and accounts of experiments telegraphed significant, but fragmented, messages about political power, social identity, and cultural character to those who commanded that they be carried out, those who performed and witnessed them, and those who read about them, to say nothing of those whose bodies were at times the objects of direct experimental intervention, violation, and observation. In this chapter I shall be arguing that natural experiment was one means, if only one means among many, by which the Medici court "imagined" "Tuscany" to itself, to its subjects, to other courts, and to posterity.

In the section that follows I want to consider some of the many cultural sites in which this Tuscany came into being, beginning with an account of Medici-sponsored attempts in the sixteenth and seventeenth centuries to define the social category, "Tuscans," through existing forms of social organization in Florence, and in particular through its academies. I shall also point to a few examples from early modern Florentine material culture in which this Tuscany was represented. The court's understanding of the ways in which academy-based interactions and the products of material culture shaped social identity is important to our own understanding of the cultural work of experiment in the grand duchy, since it would turn to similar forms of social organization and similar uses of material culture in its experiments of the mid-seventeenth century.

The academies of sixteenth- and seventeenth-century Florence were the high-tech laboratories for the new state of mind called "Tuscany."[2] The Medici's first use of an academy to promote a repertoire of social comportments that looked resolutely court-ward, towards a Tuscany of a collective political imaginary that could be shared by the court and its most privileged subjects, came only a few years after Cosimo's election as duke of Tuscany in 1537. The Good Century's entrance into the academy setting bears specific mention here, since it established the terms of the court's involvement with and interest in a number of other academies over the course of the sixteenth and seventeenth centuries, including the Accademia Fiorentina and the Accademia della Crusca (Medici academies of language reform), the Accademia del Disegno (the Medici academy of the visual arts), the Accademia degli Apatisti (whose members prided themselves on their parodies of the discourses delivered at meetings of the Fiorentina and the Crusca), and the Accademia del Cimento (the Medici academy of natural experiment).[3]

Between December 1540 and February 1541, the recently installed court of Cosimo I transformed Florence's youngest literary academy, the Umidi, into an office of linguistic censure for all works printed in the territories under Medici rule.[4] Censure in this context turned less on questions of publication or non-publication than on questions of language and style, on the appropriateness of word choices, and the like, precisely the kinds of questions that occupied increasingly large portions of the court day in the sixteenth and seventeenth centuries. In January 1541, the Medici enlarged the academy's numbers with important members of the court. By the end of January the academy, guided by these new academicians, had revised its statutes to suit the court's new plans for the group: it was to focus its "lessons" on what we would now call the Tuscan canon – Dante, Petrarch, and Boccaccio – a canon which was in many significant ways to be the invention of this new Medici court. In February the academy changed its name to the Accademia Fiorentina. Soon thereafter Cosimo transferred to the academy's *consolo*, the highest officer of the group, the political power once wielded by the rector of Florence's university, thereby placing under court control the rector's authority over printers and booksellers. Under a succession of *consoli* and *arciconsoli*, and through the highly stylized staging of censure in the give and take between academicians during academy meetings, Dante, Petrarch, and Boccaccio were transformed into the shared icons of the group.

Dante, Petrarch, and Boccaccio would oversee other groups as well. If the process by which the Accademia Fiorentina was founded gives us a good sense of the cultural pretensions of the early years of Cosimo I's reign, the independent founding in the 1580s of the Accademia della Crusca, another academy of language reform and one whose members showed great skill at using the Good Authors to raise their status in the eyes of the court, marked the realization of the court's hopes for the social realignment of power in the region. The Crusca brought together, voluntarily, the two groups of individuals whose fortunes were becoming increasingly linked with those of the Medici, the members of the old Florentine patriciate and the members of the new court bureaucracy. The early activities of the Crusca were similar to those of other academies in early modern Europe, consisting primarily of elections, the delivery of prepared discourses, and preparations for elaborate banquets, known as *stravizzi*, which the academy held twice a year. In 1589, a few years after the founding of the Crusca, the members of the academy revised their constitution, and with it an already elaborate code of in-house conduct, in hopes of raising their corporate status within the realm. Now their principal activities would revolve around the compilation of a massive lexicon of "authoritative" examples of "approved" Tuscan usage, primarily passages taken from works written during the Good Century.[5] Just as speaking knowledgeably about a bottle of expensive wine from the region might bring one the approval of a certain privileged segment of Florentine society in this period, speaking knowledgeably about a passage from a manuscript copy of thirteenth-century Florentine or Aretine poetry and then submitting it for inclusion in the Crusca's lexicon would now serve as a means through which to purchase one's "Tuscanness." The first edition of the Crusca's *Vocabolario* appeared in 1612, with subsequent seventeenth-century editions appearing in 1623 and 1691. By 1640 the project of the lexicon had proved itself so congenial to the interests of the Medici that the academy was placed under the protection of Grand Duke Ferdinando II's brother, Prince Leopoldo de' Medici.

The academicians' sense of themselves as the keepers of Tuscan culture, and of the Crusca as the repository of that culture, was rehearsed in a number of ways; among them, through the academy's many custom-made "machines," or *macchine*, and pieces of furniture, all of which had flour, flour mills, and flour storage as a running theme – a play on the academy's name, which in English means the Academy of Bran. The comportment of academy members was themed accordingly. For example, members had to place in a wooden hopper, known to the group as the *tramoggia*, the written works which they wished to submit for the approval of the group's censors. If the works met with the censors' approval, they were then moved to a wooden container resembling a sack of flour, which held the academy's most important papers, including its statutes and all the works which had been approved during that particular academy year. Like the Medici, who during this period were commissioning a series of family histories to trace the origins of their political power back to the Good Century, the members of the Crusca came to see the group as the sum of all the linguistic artifacts they could collect, a perception which was meant to be reinforced every time they placed a sonnet or a discourse into the *tramoggia*. In this way, the language that had been a vehicle of political critique in Renaissance Florence was made a vehicle of political consolidation for those who, two centuries later, considered themselves above politics altogether.

Over the course of the sixteenth century in Tuscany, inside as well as outside the academies of Florence, the period we now call the Renaissance was recast as something worthy of the attentions of all who wished to serve the Medici. The pretensions and aspirations to which the Good Century was made to appeal found their complement in an eclectic range of texts, institutions, commodities, and social practices which had the Good Century as a recurring motif. No other epoch was so important to the thematic self-representation of social privilege under the Medici, and none was so conspicuously consumed in their home city of Florence. For example, not just anyone ate or drank at the well-known Florentine tavern called the Inferno. It was the tavern of Medici favorites. Not far from the Inferno, around the shops that dotted the neighborhood near the Piazza del Granduca (now known, as it was in Renaissance Florence, as the Piazza della Signoria), these same individuals would have purchased busts of Dante, Petrarch, and Boccaccio to display at home in their libraries and museums. A contemporary board game, based on Dante's own inner journey in the *Divine Comedy*, even tested their ability to recall short passages of his poetry to the applause of their peers.[6]

By imagining the Good Century as a period in which style reigned – and politics, at least in the Florentine republican sense of the term, was nonexistent – the court came to represent itself as an entity that existed outside of historical time. Cosimo I's celebration of the pre-Roman "Etruria," and the Etruscomania that subsequently swept the court during the sixteenth century, configured the grand duchy's relationship to time in similar ways. Existing outside of or at one remove from previously existing social categories was another concern in this milieu. Hopes of serving the court thus came to depend upon one's ability to reproduce gestures of social and temporal distance in every aspect of one's life. Even the distancing mechanisms that court-based experimenters employed so as to place themselves at one remove from the knowledge they produced is likely the product of this court-based *sprezzatura*, a studied disinterestedness and nonchalance that writers from Castiglione on regarded as an essential attribute of successful courtiership. The ostensibly "unique" "geniuses" and "timeless" "masterpieces" through which Florence and many scholars of Florence promote its Renaissance past today began to acquire much of their "uniqueness" and "timelessness" during this period of Medici imagineering. Through them the thirteenth- and fourteenth-century Florentine past was put in the service of this new dominant culture as it was being constituted.

Over the course of the seventeenth century, a second epoch – the first hundred years of Medici rule – came to play an increasingly visible role in the court's representations of Tuscany and Tuscanness. Like the Good Century, this epoch came with its own heroes. Michelangelo, Galileo, and Torricelli, among others, joined Dante, Petrarch, and Boccaccio as icons of Tuscan culture, and like them they attained that status through the interaction of a wide range of texts, institutions, commodities, and social practices. From 1620 on, for example, just a half-century after Michelangelo's death, many of the same individuals who ate at the Inferno and collected busts of Dante, Petrarch, and Boccaccio for their domestic museums were paying the Buonarroti family a small fee to tour the artist's house on the via Ghibellina. Of the rooms opened by the artist's descendants the most famous by far contained no pictures, drawings, or sculptures by Michelangelo at all, but rather an elaborate visual program by a contemporary painter, Domenico Cresti, celebrating Michelangelo's most lucrative commissions, including those from the Medici family. After the tour these individuals might have returned home to an evening meal in which they dined from plates decorated with scenes taken from Ariosto's *Orlando furioso*. Later, they might have spent some time searching the works of Ariosto or Galileo for potential vocabulary entries for the third edition of the Crusca's lexicon, which would appear in 1691. And if they were very fortunate (in this particular instance, it would have helped if they were foreign royalty), they might have spent part of the evening gazing at the stars through one of the many "Galilean" telescopes made for the Medici Grand Dukes Cosimo II and Ferdinando II to distribute as gifts following the astronomer's discovery of the moons of Jupiter, which Galileo had presented to Cosimo as Medici property.

Natural experiment played an important role in the process by which the first century of Medici rule came to join the Good Century as a privileged thematic source for the court's self-representations, as, for example, when the experiments of Galileo and Torricelli were restaged for the benefit of foreign visitors, or when observations they had once made were tested for their accuracy through court-sponsored experiments. More generally, however, the natural experiments undertaken by the court between the later 1650s and 1680s established some of the terms of social privilege in the grand duchy, standards by which all other groups, inside and outside Tuscany, ancient and contemporary, would come to be measured. In the next section I want to consider the court as a culture in which these terms were constantly being negotiated, and to examine some of the ways in which the experiments performed at the command of Grand Duke Ferdinando II and his brother, Prince Leopoldo, made it possible for the court to regard itself as a kind of laboratory for the production of what, in light of Pierre Bourdieu's work in *Outline of a Theory of Practice* and *Distinction: A Social Critique of the Judgement of Taste*, we have come to know by the term "distinction."

Although the court of the Medici Grand Duke Ferdinando II has never occupied a prominent place in political histories of early modern Europe, it has always been important to histories of modern science, for it was during Ferdinando's reign that a number of court-based groups of experimenters in Europe – including a Medici-backed group known as the Accademia del Cimento – were constituted as academies or societies under the protection of a king, a prominent cabinet minister, or, in the case of the grand duchy of Tuscany, the grand duke's brother, Prince Leopoldo.[7] Until recently, historians tended to look at the practices of two of these groups, the Royal Society of London and the Parisian Royal Academy of Sciences, and extrapolate from them a narrative about the origins of much of modern science, with its state-sponsored research projects, its sizeable numbers of individuals brought together in common cause, and its emphasis on the production of "useful" knowledge. These days, however, and especially for historians with interests in sociological and anthropological approaches to the history of knowledge production, the groups active in London, Paris, Florence, Rome, Munich, and elsewhere during this period may seem as striking for their dissimilarity as for their similarity. From these perspectives, the Cimento that is familiar to most historians of science and historians of early modern Tuscany looks like the projection of a collective fantasy from another era in western culture and academia whose attractions are no longer as compelling as they once were. In this sense, much of the scholarship on the Accademia del Cimento now has its own stories to tell: about the discourse of modernism, about the links between narrative politics and disciplinary politics in academia, about the transformation of programs in the history and philosophy of science into programs of science studies. Like the Medici "Good Century," this "Cimento" could benefit from being placed within a different constellation of historical narratives.

By comparison with the groups in London and Paris, for example, Leopoldo's academy of experiment was never awarded a letter of patent, its numbers were never great, and its members were not much interested in producing the kind of knowledge that monarchs or academicians in London and Paris would have recognized as "useful." We need to keep these differences in mind, not in the interests of rating the "usefulness" of one group's experiments over another's (in the secondary literature, the Cimento is inevitably compared with the groups in London and Paris and, just as inevitably, found wanting), but in the interests of foregrounding the local logic and meaning of experimental practice in this period. The members of Leopoldo's group certainly did not regard their work, nor should they have regarded it, as anything less than useful. The kinds of activities which engaged one group of experimenters in the middle decades of the seventeenth century, and the meaning those activities were given, differed from one group to the next. In fact, as recent studies by Simon Schaffer, Steven Shapin, Mario Biagioli, and David Lux have made clear, many of the disagreements between academies, and between academicians of the same academy, arose because each was producing knowledge that was in some ways specific to a culture, a social group, or a profession.

Among the factors which most distinguished those who served the Medici through experiment from those who served other courts through experiment during this period is the extent to which those in the grand duchy of Tuscany could exploit their experiments to praise the prince and increase the status of the court, and, in so doing, increase their own status. The difference in the opportunities offered from one court to the next derived from, among other things, the difference in the size of each court (the Medici court was a small one by comparison with, say, the French courts of Louis XIII and Louis XIV), the kinds of interaction experimenters could expect with members of the ruling family (they seem to have been possible, and frequent, in Tuscany), and the local, regional, and extraterritorial pretensions of each court. When natural experiment caught the eye of the Medici during the middle decades of the seventeenth century, it did so, I want to argue, as one means among many by which to preserve and enhance the collectively imagined state of social privilege that went by the name of "Tuscany."

Better Tuscan living through experiment. My reading of experiment under Ferdinando II is less concerned with the place of the Cimento within the history of science than with the place of the *cimento*, the wide range of tests through which individuals displayed their social capacities and purchased their social status, within the culture of the court. Life under the Medici was full of these tests. As we know from the work of Jacques Revel, Sergio Bertelli, Norbert Elias, Stephen Greenblatt, and Frank Whigham, among others, early modern European courts gained much of their power through psychological games which kept the social status of their most privileged political subjects always at issue and nearly always in doubt. The uncertainties which these games produced were reproduced and multiplied through similar games which those subjects played on each other and on individuals of lower social status. Truthfulness, civility, disinterestedness, and fidelity were a few of the many virtues that were rendered visible to the court through these tests. Under the Medici the absence of these virtues placed one's Tuscanness in doubt.

If Tuscany was a state of mind, then, it was the product of a state of anxiety. To mention only a few of the tests that filled the courtier's day, there was the *cimento della tavola*, or the inner court's after-dinner test of wits; the *cimento regio dell'oro*, or royal test of gold; and the *censura*, which was practiced in academies such as the Crusca and gauged one's ability to judge the ostensible Tuscanness of a word or phrase employed in another's speech and writing. Many of these tests, including those we commonly think of as experiments, were carried out during the two periods of the day that Florentine men of high social status devoted to the formal, group-oriented exercise of their judgment-making faculties: mid- to late morning and late evening. These were the hours set aside for what were known in this milieu as Florence's "markets of virtue," for academy meetings, post-dinner conversations, court entertainments, and other activities that brought members of the dominant culture together for conversation-based exchanges of opinions, or *opinioni*, on various subjects deemed worthy of the group (Garuffi 1688: n.p.). Through these conversation-based exchanges, as Emanuele Tesauro noted in his *Filosofia morale* of 1670, they purchased their "mutual conservation" as a collectivity (Tesauro 1765: 75). "Virtue," the diary accounts of the Crusca's meetings repeatedly note, was "tested" (*esperimentata*) here.

Although some of these tests of individual and group virtue appear in venues and practices (such as pharmacies and the creation of vacuums in sealed containers) which have always figured in accounts of the history of science, a good many others appear in venues and practices which have not (such as dining-rooms, bathing-rooms, and the drinking of iced beverages). For this reason, it may be helpful if I describe a few here. The *cimento della tavola*, for example, began with a question or observation directed by the grand duke to one of his family members at the conclusion of the inner court's evening meal. The strawberries served for dessert could function as the catalyst for a *cimento*, as could a bottle of chianti served with the meal.[8] After the family had engaged in a bit of very public, and often very well lubricated, give and take on a topic, the grand duke might direct that the question be turned over to one or more of the courtiers in the room for further investigation. To produce an opinion on the matter the courtier would scour the writings of ancient and modern authors, speak with others, undertake a series of experiments, or do whatever else he considered appropriate. Later, his opinion on the question would be conveyed back to the grand duke. These tests made it possible for the courtier to respond to the grand duke with the degree of assurance and apparent disinterestedness that a ducal command demanded of him. The bodily pleasure of the grand duke and his family was often the focus of these experiments because it was often the focus of their after-dinner conversation, at least as far as one can tell from the manuscript accounts of the court's diarist. Given the relatively public forum in which these conversations took place, their pleasures became the concern of the court as a whole: while the family interacted on a slightly raised platform in the dining room, the assembled company of dinner guests listened and watched from their tables some distance away, with the court diarist recording the proceedings.

Outside the meal setting, experiments could be just as motivated by this court-centered preoccupation with the production of opinion. Upon receiving a gift from a foreign ambassador, for example, the grand duke might command that it be examined by a courtier or group of courtiers to see if there was anything "notable", or *notabile*, about it (which is to say, worthy of the time of someone who was himself the first among notables in the grand duchy). He might do the same after bagging an animal during a hunting expedition, or when he was unwell and wished to be entertained.[9] Here, too, the experiment that might follow was not an end in itself, but a means of producing an opinion for the grand duke. The grand duke's brother, Prince Leopoldo, might make a similar demand of a courtier, sometimes in conjunction with an evening meal, but most often after having read or heard an opinion that, to his mind, was potentially notable enough to warrant the court's attentions.[10] Judging from the content of Leopoldo's letters to those who served him in the Cimento, he directed many of his questions concerning the opinions he encountered between 1657 and 1662 (the years the Cimento was most active) to the members of his private academy of experiment. These commands left a lasting impression on those to whom they were addressed. Courtiers collected them with the same diligence that the court collected opinions, because commands, like opinions, fueled the projects of promotion which were a central feature of court life. In their letters and conversations courtiers displayed these commands like trophies and brandished them like swords. The commands elevated courtiers in the estimation of their peers, they promoted jealousies and rivalries, and they increased, however slightly and momentarily, a courtier's status within the court. These tests were concerned, then, with the production of multiple insiders and outsiders, and they derived much of their power from their ubiquity.

The objects and topics which were the focus of experimental investigation in this milieu reflected the objects and topics which were the focus of the court's conversations: the grand duke's health; a remark once made by Galileo; food and drink; the unpleasantness of the summer heat in Florence; the gullibility of the ancients; and the rustic ways of those who were not fortunate enough to be born Tuscan.[11] The published accounts of court-sponsored experiment that appeared in this period, including the Cimento's one published work, the *Saggi di naturali esperienze fatte nell' Accademia del Cimento* (Reports of Natural Experiments Undertaken in the Accademia del Cimento) of 1677, all turn on these topics and themes. Lorenzo Bellini's *Gustus organum* (The Organ of Taste) of 1665, which is dedicated to Prince Leopoldo, is an illustrated anatomical treatise on the tongue which includes experiment-based opinions on the ostensibly refined Tuscan sense of taste, while texts such as Pietro Paolo di Sangallo's *Esperienze intorno alla generazione delle zanzare* (Experiments on the Generation of Mosquitoes) of 1679 and Giovanni Cosimo Bonomo's *Osservazioni intorno a' pellicelli del corpo umano* (Observations on the Little Worms that Cause Itching in the Human Body) of 1687 display to the reader the process by which experiment-based opinion itself is produced in the grand duchy. Sangallo's account, for example, takes place between a group of Tuscan interlocutors as they stroll near Florence's cathedral on a hot summer evening.

These texts are compendia of the opinions produced by Tuscany's most privileged social group. They are also much more. They are treasuries of the symbolic capital of Tuscany, containing dozens of what Lorenzo Magalotti calls, in his proem to the *Saggi*, the individual "jewels" of the Medici court under Ferdinando II (Magalotti 1667: n.p.). As a treasury of Tuscan culture, the *Saggi* contains a relatively restricted number of experiment-based opinions about a relatively restricted number of topics of interest to the court. There are opinions on statements once made by Torricelli and Galileo, the two individuals who, with Michelangelo, had brought the Medici their greatest fame in the first century of their reign as the dukes and grand dukes of Tuscany. Others are produced by testing the assertions of ancient and modern non-Tuscans, such as Plato and Plutarch, Boyle, Kepler, and Gassendi. Others, involving summertime experiments with the court's prized ice-makers or experiments on precious and semi-precious stones, exotic purgative salts, and distilled waters, speak to the kinds of activities by which any court and its courtiers attempted to distinguish themselves from other courts and courtiers in the seventeenth century. The experiments that produced these jewels were repeated off and on for years, in the court's pharmacy, in private homes, and elsewhere, before their outcomes were judged by the members to be certain enough to be conveyed, like exquisitely cut and polished gems, back to the court.[12]

The Medici's interest in the opinions that could be produced through experiment came at a time when they were filling the spaces of the Pitti Palace and the hours of the court day with increasing numbers of people, objects, and activities. Indeed, by the mid-seventeenth century the Pitti had become a site of conspicuous consumption the likes of which Florence had not seen in decades.[13] The manuscript diaries of the court's experiments tell us a lot about what the court and those who served it expected of experiment, including why it was important to keep records of these activities at all. Filled with references to everything from the time of day in which a particular experiment was undertaken to the precise quantity of materials it consumed, a diary was not so much a record of nature's ways as it was a record of the ways of the court. As an artifact of court culture, it documents individual and group hopes of pleasing the prince by keeping careful track of his property, and of making a graphic impression of service to him on the diary page. Experiments assessed the opinion-generating value of all this property, in much the same way that the discussions and private correspondence between members of the Accademia della Crusca assessed the value of Tuscany's linguistic wealth. *Il più bel fior ne coglie* was the Crusca's motto, and it was reproduced on everything the academy published. Translated into English with late twentieth-century mass-marketing sensibilities in mind, it might read, "We use only the best flower."

Nancy Armstrong and Leonard Tennenhouse write in their introduction to *The Violence of Representation: Literature and the History of Violence* that "a class of people cannot produce themselves as a ruling class without setting themselves off against certain Others. Their hegemony entails possession of the key cultural terms determining what are the right and wrong ways to be a human being" (Armstrong and Tennenhouse 1989: 24). Those who served the sovereign courts of early modern Europe were introduced to these terms and, perhaps more importantly, the means of generating them, at a very young age. In the Jesuit classroom, for example, where the social identity of many aspiring courtiers was first fashioned, adolescent boys were taught to see themselves as individual showcases of centuries of social privilege. There they learned that every aspect of their self-presentation, from their speech to their gestures, was a vehicle of social meaning and, moreover, an active force in the production of social distinction.[14]

We know from the work of Pierre Bourdieu that claims of social distinction are not made in a vacuum. Rather, they are made by means of a dynamic in which individuals or groups of individuals imagine themselves as separate from other individuals or groups. They are made at the expense of others, often at the expense of many at the same time. This dynamic was set into motion in any number of the activities intended for the acculturation of Jesuit pupils. One was the practice of recording in pocket-sized notebooks examples of words, deeds, and social scenarios, drawn from books and the comments of others, which the pupil intended to make part of his social capital. In these notebooks court dwarves, Moors, the mentally handicapped, and donkeys, to name only a few, frequently appear as the objects of endless jokes played upon them by their princes and masters. These anecdotes – to say nothing of the conceptual categories that made these individuals humorous, and collectable as stock characters, within this milieu – are artifacts of early modern European male identity formation. They were not clothes that one sheds during a rite of passage, nor were they toys to which one clings but which one eventually leaves behind. They were cultural baggage, and they accompanied the adolescent male through his rites of institution into an adulthood of social privilege.

If these notebooks were miniature museums of social antagonisms, the court itself was their Smithsonian, a living theater of the presiding terms and strategies of social distinction. This is clear in a poem which Francesco Redi, the Medici family's head physician for much of the second half of the seventeenth century, composed as a youth and placed in his personal notebook of "witty phrases, enigmas, games, and other jokes," the same notebook from which came the sampling of stock characters in the list above.[15] In the poem, entitled "On the court," Redi writes of a place filled with "drunken traitors, homicidal vices," "vain men, and false idols," where social division reigns supreme.[16] It is difficult to regard the young Francesco, whose father was himself a Medici physician, as a naive observer of this scene. Rather, it seems more plausible that the act of giving a name, through the process of composition, to the cynicism he sees at the court is part of a much longer process of acculturation through which he will come to acquire the terms of cultural dominance, and the capacities for generating endless variations based upon those terms, that are the concern of Armstrong and Tennenhouse in their introduction.

In accounts of Medici-sponsored experiment, everything and everyone lacking or potentially lacking *toscanità* – from hardshell crabs and ancient Roman philosophers to imported cocoa beans and local peasant farmers – is the focus of intense scrutiny and, often, ridicule. Issues of social identity, difference, and distinction figure in the earliest correspondence between Prince Leopoldo and those who would serve him in the Accademia del Cimento, and they continue to inform court-based experimental practices long after the Cimento ceases its activity. In a 1657 letter to Leopoldo, for example, Paolo del Buono writes that the work of the group will make it possible for Florence to surpass the glory of ancient Athens.[17] One of the less-than-glorious moments in the history of ancient Rome is the focus of another text, Francesco Redi's *Osservazioni intorno alle vipere* (Observations on Vipers) of 1664, which records the experiments undertaken by a group of court pharmacists and physicians in response to Grand Duke Ferdinando's command that they solve the centuries-old riddle of the suicide of Cleopatra. In Redi's text the "truthfulness" of the opinions about the suicide which have been generated by dozens of ancient writers, such as Galen and Dio Cassius, is assessed through the live, experiment-based reenactment of the scenarios proposed by each writer, a task which involves dozens of recently imported Neapolitan vipers. A few years later, Redi's *Esperienze intorno a diverse cose naturali, e particolarmente a quelle che ci son portate dall'Indie* (Experiments on Diverse Natural Things, and Particularly on Those which Have Been Brought to Us from the Indies) of 1671 shifts the focus of a peculiarly Tuscan form of conspicuous consumption from the intellectual property of ancient cultures to the natural resources of other contemporary cultures.

"Never a stable body," Leonard Tennenhouse has noted, "the aristocratic body was constantly changing" (Tennenhouse 1989: 79). The same may be said of the aristocratic body politic in a city such as Florence. The Medici went to great lengths to bring about a Tuscany that would prove attractive to a select group of individuals, and they did so through multiple public performances of that Tuscany. The work of Norman Bryson, Michel Foucault, Martin Jay, and Louis Marin has explored the ways in which dominant cultures in early modern Europe multiplied the signs of their power, whether on the bodies of courtiers and condemned criminals, through modes of address, in the designs of palaces, or through mass-produced images of the sovereign. Florence under the Medici was full of these signs, and they separated those for whom an investment in good centuries and good authors would be socially profitable from those for whom it would not. The sounds of lions, bulls, and other large animals fighting in the grand ducal menagerie near the church of San Marco, for example, was said to remind the occupants of the neighboring prison of the kind of power that the court held over their lives. The precisely timed ringing of bells from the tower of the Palazzo Vecchio performed a somewhat less ominous, but nonetheless similar, function in the lives of court bureaucrats, signaling the beginning and end of a work day that was carefully orchestrated (indeed, legislated) by the court.[18]

Tuscanness came with its own set of specular privileges in Florence. At the menagerie, for example, high social status gave one access to a private room with a view on to the animal-on-animal violence there. The gallows that dotted the city from the Porta al Prato to the Piazza del Granduca provided privileged physical, aural, and visual access to the hanging and subsequent evisceration of the convicted thieves of the city. The same was true of experiment. Here is a diary entry which narrates one of the experiments performed during the meeting of the Accademia del Cimento on August 19, 1662. It is fairly typical of those found in the diaries of the group's activities.

> A hardshell crab and a frog were placed in the vacuum together. As for the crab, it was seen to move about with little alteration in its body right up to the end of its life, although it did seem to slow down a bit [as the air was removed from the glass]. The frog, on the other hand, was noticeably affected [by the removal of the air]. It puffed its cheeks out wide, to the point that they nearly obscured its snout, and in all parts of its body one could see it become bloated, vomiting lots of slobber through its mouth, which now remained wide open and prevented from closing by its own tongue, and the other vescicles and membranes in its body, monstrously swollen, remained stuck in that swollen position. When air was returned to the container, it deflated completely, and all at once, and it remained in this flattened state for two more extended periods as the air was removed. When the frog was removed [from the glass container] it was dead. There was little interest among the group at the time to look for other novelties by cutting it up.[19]

In this entry and others like it the scene of experiment in the Pitti Palace becomes a staging in miniature of the scene at the menagerie near San Marco. In it the court records its own fascination with the technologies of spectatorship, technologies that enable it to monitor and control the movements, the bodily integrity, and even the lives of animate beings, often without ever having any direct physical contact with them at all. The order in which experiments are recorded in these diaries even suggests that the Cimento's meetings were endowed with a dramatic structure not unlike that of a baroque entertainment, in which the most spectacular visual effects of the court's power and wealth were saved for last, as the final entry on any given day often tells of controlled explosions of glass containers filled with live moths, spontaneously ignited fires, the slow drowning of small animals, and the mysterious steaming of iced beverages in silver-plated goblets.

The diary of a series of experiments undertaken at the court between May and December of 1660 is another case in point. The experiments are set in motion when Grand Duke Ferdinando II commands that his court physicians develop a gentler laxative than those then in use by the Medici, one, he says, that can "satisfy" his own needs as well as those of the many "delicate persons" who visit and have commerce with the court.[20] Thus begins an eight-month search for a laxative that can function within the same social register as the poetry of Dante, Petrarch, and Boccaccio, a laxative that can be regarded by others as one more mark of Tuscany's ostensibly special place in history and culture. Between May and December at least fifty individuals, possessing little social capital, and who are identified in the diary through the use of stock categories similar to those found in the commonplace books of Jesuit schoolboys – through terms such as "a mercenary," "a vagrant," and "a lackey," or through diminutives such as the "Little Moor" and the "Little Dwarf Girl" – were administered various quantities of laxative "salts," or *sali*. These salts were made by roasting to their ash or powder form great quantities of delicate-tasting fruits, vegetables, flower petals, and spices, such as water melon, laurel, cucumber, and rose. Many of those who became the subjects of these experiments were brought in from the streets around the Pitti Palace in Florence or the Medici palace at Poggio a Caiano, provided with something to eat, given the laxative, and then locked in a room, where their physical reaction to the laxative could be carefully monitored by a court servant. Their bowel movements, which each subject was to deposit into color-coded chamberpots, would be weighed carefully by a physician's assistant, inspected by a court physician, and then described, often in great detail, in a diary entry, which might include comments such as the following (this is one of the least detailed and graphic of the entries): "His urine was of a good color until 11:00 that night, at which time it began to be tinged with red, and he was not much troubled at all, except for needing to pass a bit of wind and some agitation in his stomach. He slept well that night and in the morning he had a good bowel movement. Another came an hour and a half later."[21]

In these experiments and others like them, the eventual bodily pleasure of the grand duke and the court was produced through the bodily and psychological distress of political subjects who possessed none of the social capital of those who could have considered themselves "Tuscans" in the court's sense of the term. The isolated instances in these accounts in which the voices of these non-Tuscans were even recorded only emphasize the complexity of the work that all experiments perform in culture and on culture. They remind us that there is nothing natural about natural experiment. The diary record of the court's search for a proper Tuscan laxative includes only one instance in which a subject of experiment speaks, and that instance appears early in the first day of tests. In it, each member of that first group of experimental subjects shouts, "I'm too young to die," as he prepares to drink the mysterious beverage handed to him by a physician's assistant. Here as elsewhere – in the act of shouting and in the act of recording that shouting – is the mark of a Tuscan politics of contact with time, the body, the material world, and the social fabric. Here as elsewhere natural experiment is one means by which the court of Grand Duke Ferdinando II rehearses and refines that politics.

Notes

Much of the preliminary research for this chapter was done while I was an NEH Fellow at the UCLA Center for Seventeenth- and Eighteenth-Century Studies. I would like to acknowledge the intellectual support of John Brewer, Ann Bermingham, Nicholas Mirzoeff, Lawrence Klein, and Mario Biagioli during my year at UCLA. This chapter was written and revised while I was a Fellow at the Cornell University Society for the Humanities. I would like to thank Jonathan Culler, the director of the Society, for creating such a stimulating environment for thinking and writing. My special thanks to Julia Emberley, Eric Garberson, and Nicholas Mirzoeff for their comments on an earlier draft of this chapter, and to Michael Aaron Dennis for inviting me to present that draft to members of Cornell's Program in the History and Philosophy of Science and Technology.

1 According to Norbert Elias, these kinds of social alignments are typical of early modern European courts. See *The History of Manners* (Elias, 1978). On the Medici court's promotion of a concept of Florentine "nobility" that gradually won the allegiance of these two groups to the court see C. Donati, *L'Idea di nobilità in Italia. Secoli XIV–XVIII* (1988: 214–27), and F. Diaz, *Il granducato di Toscana – I Medici* (1987: 424–7).

2 On academies and academy-based interactions in the grand duchy of Tuscany during this period see Eric Cochrane's classic study, *Tradition and Enlightenment in the Tuscan Academies* (1961).

3 Indeed, according to Michel Plaisance, it provided a template for the cultural politics practiced by the court throughout the region. See his "Une première affirmation de la politique culturelle de Côme I: La transformation de l'Académie des 'Humidi' en Académie Florentine (1540–1542)" (1975: 361–438). See also S. Bertelli, "Egemonia linguistica come egemonia culturale e politica nella Firenze cosimiana," *Bibliothèque d'Humanisme et Renaissance* (1976: 249–83); and Diaz (1987: 199–206). Joel Reed examines similar motivations in the language projects of the early Royal Society in "Restoration and repression: the language projects of the Royal Society" (1989: 399–412).

4 *Annali dell'Accademia degli Umidi poi Fiorentina*, MS Bandini B.III.52.

5 See "Le leggi dell'Accademia della Crusca riformate l'anno 1589," MS Λ.46.

6 On Florence in the seventeenth century see G. Imbert, *La vita fiorentina nei Seicento secondo memorie sincrone 1644–1670* (1906); F. L. del Migliore, *Firenze città nobilissima illustrata* (1684); and T. Rinuccini, "Considerazioni sopra l'usanze mutate nel passato secolo del 1600" (1840: 270–89).

7 On the Cimento and experimental practice under Ferdinando II see W. E. K. Middleton, *The Experimenters: A Study of the Accademia del Cimento* (1971); P. Galluzzi, "L'Accademia del Cimento: 'Gusti' del principe, filosofia e ideologia dell'esperimento" (1981: 788–844); among other works by M. Biagioli, "Scientific revolution, social bricolage, and absolutism" (forthcoming); and among other works by P. Findlen, *Possessing Nature: Museums, Collecting and Scientific Culture in Early Modern Italy* (forthcoming), and "Rhetoric, court patronage and the experimental method of Francesco Redi (1626–1697)" (1994). The classic study of experiment in this period is Giovanni Targioni Tozzetti's three-volume *Notizie degli aggrandimenti delle scienze fisiche accaduti in Toscana nel corso di anni LX. del secolo XVII* (1780).

8 See, for example, the "Diari di Etichetta" 5 (covering the period 1657–9) of the Guardaroba Medicea, Archivio di Stato, Florence, f. 54. Ottaviano Falconieri's letter of June 13, 1665, to Prince Leopoldo refers to this kind of test as "the usual after dinner discussion" of the court. MS Galileiana 313, Biblioteca Nazionale Centrale, Florence, ff. 839r-v. On dining practices in the Medici court see a number of essays in S. Bertelli and G. Crifò (eds.), *Rituale cerimoniale etichetta* (1985).

9 See, for example, Lorenzo Magalotti's letters to Ottavio Falconieri, in which he writes of some of the objects given to Leopoldo's academy by Ferdinando, and of Ferdinando's interactions with the group, in L. Magalotti, *Lettere scientifiche et erudite* (1721: 58–63), and *Lettere familiari* (1769: 93–4).

10   This particular investigative procedure is outlined for Leopoldo, at his request, by Carlo
     Rinaldini in a number of letters written during the period immediately preceding the first
     experiments of the group we know as the Cimento. See, for example, Rinaldini's letter of
     November 6, 1656. MS Galileiana 275, Biblioteca Nazionale Centrale, Florence, ff. 44r–46v.
     That this continues to be the mode of investigation favored by Leopoldo may be seen in later
     correspondence as well. See, for example, Lorenzo Magalotti's letter of January 15, 1666, to
     Alessandro Segni, in F. Massai, "Sette lettere inedite di Lorenzo Magalotti al Cav.
     Alessandro Segni (1665–1666)," (1917: 137–8), and his letter to Leopoldo, "Sopra la mara-
     vigliosa stravaganza d'un flore," in Magalotti (1721: 21–4).
11   On court-based experiment as a means of staging what was known in court circles as a "civil
     conversation" between courtiers and ancient natural philosophers see J. Tribby, "Cooking
     (with) Clio and Cleo: eloquence and experiment in seventeenth-century Florence" (1991:
     417–39).
12   See, for example, the July 31, 1662, entry in the manuscript diary of the Accademia del
     Cimento, which states that the group met in Lorenzo Magalotti's home that day to "repeat a
     few experiments" which, once they became easier to do, "had to be done again in the
     presence of His Most Serene Highness." MS Gallieiana 262, Biblioteca Nazionale Centrale,
     Florence, ff. 132r–v.
13   On material culture and its social functions in this period see P. Burke, "Conspicuous
     consumption in seventeenth-century Italy" (1987: 132–49), and N. McKendrick, J. Brewer,
     and J. H. Plumb, *The Birth of a Consumer Society* (1982).
14   On the body and the domestic museum of the early modern European courtier as showcases
     of social capacity see J. Tribby, "Body/building: living the museum life in early modern
     Europe" (1992: 43–67).
15   F. Redi, "Motti, enigmi, giuochi, et altri bagattel" (n. d.: f. 121r).
16   Ibid., f. 111r.
17   P. del Buono, letter of October 6, 1657, to Prince Leopoldo, MS Gallieiana 275, Biblioteca
     Nazionale Centrale, Florence, f. 78v.
18   On the menagerie see del Migliore, (1684: 242–8), and M. M. Simari, "Serragli a Firenze al
     tempo del Medici" (1985: 23–6). On the regulation of the court bureaucracy see S. Berner,
     "Florentine society in the late sixteenth and early seventeenth centuries" (1971: 242–5). On
     the gallows of the city and policing practices under the Medici see Imbert (1906: 189–211).
     On the state control of violence in early modern Europe and its ties to the construction of
     aristocratic identity see N. Elias, *Power and Civility* (1982), and a number of essays in N.
     Armstrong and L. Tennenhouse (eds.) *The Violence of Representation: Literature and the History of
     Violence* (1989), including S. Jed, "The scene of tyranny: violence and the humanistic
     tradition," and L. Tennenhouse, "Violence done to women on the Renaissance stage."
19   MS Gallieiana 262, Biblioteca Nazionale Centrale, Florence, f. 143r.
20   See the "Memorie nella fabbrica de sali fattizi, e loro operazioni" and the "Memorie de sali
     che si sono prima provati in poco quantita, e poi dati con dose proporzionata comincato alla
     Villa imperiale di comandi di SAS" (1660: ff. 2r–15r and 77r–92v, respectively).
21   "Memorie de sali che si sono prima provati in poca quantita . . ." (1660: f. 77v).

Bibliography

Altieri Biagi, M. L. and Basile, B. (eds.) (1980) *Scienziati del Seicento*, Milan: Ricciardi.
Anderson, B. (1983) *Imagined Communities: Reflections on the Origin and Spread of Nationalism*, New
     York: Verso.
Annali dell'Accademia degli Umidi pol Fiorentina, MS Bandini B. III. 52, Biblioteca Marucelliana,
     Florence.
Armstrong, N. and Tennenhouse, L. (1989) *The Violence of Representation: Literature and the History of
     Violence*, New York: Routledge.
Barzman, K. (1989) "Liberal academicians and the new social elite in grand ducal Florence," in

I. Lavin (ed.) *World Art. Themes of Unity in Diversity: Acts of the XXVIth International Congress of the History of Art*, University Park, PA: University of Pennsylvania Press, pp. 459–63.

Basile, B. (1987) *L'invenzione del vero. Studi sulla letteratura scientifica da Galilei ad Algarotti*, Rome: Salerno.

Berner, S. (1971) "Florentine society in the late sixteenth and early seventeenth centuries," *Studies in the Renaissance* 18: 203–46.

Bertelli, S. (1976) "Egemonia linguistica come egemonia culturale e politica nella Firenze cosimiana," *Bibliothèque d'Humanisme et Renaissance* 37: 249–83.

—— (1990) *Il corpo del re: Sacralità del potere nell' Europa medievale e moderna*, Florence: Ponte alle Grazie.

—— and Crifò, G. (eds.) (1985) *Rituale cerimoniale etichetta*, Milan: Bompiani.

Bhabha, H. (ed.) (1990) *Nation and Narration*, New York: Routledge.

Biagioli, M. (1990) "Galileo the emblem maker," *Isis* 81: 230–58.

—— (forthcoming) *Galileo Courtier*, Chicago: Chicago University Press.

—— (forthcoming) "Scientific revolution, social bricolage, and absolutism," in R. Porter and M. Telch (eds.) *The Scientific Revolution in National Context*, Cambridge: Cambridge University Press.

Bourdieu, P. (1977) *Outline of a Theory of Practice*, trans. Richard Nice, Cambridge: Cambridge University Press.

—— (1984) *Distinction: A Social Critique of the Judgement of Taste*, trans. Richard Nice, Cambridge, MA: Harvard University Press.

—— (1991) *Language and Symbolic Power*, Cambridge, MA: Harvard University Press.

Bryson, N. (1990) *Looking at the Overlooked: Four Essays on Still Life Painting*, Cambridge, MA: Harvard University Press.

Burke, P. (1987) "Conspicuous consumption in seventeenth-century Italy," in *The Historical Anthropology of Early Modern Italy*, Cambridge: Cambridge University Press, pp. 132–49.

Cochrane, E. (1961) *Tradition and Enlightenment in the Tuscan Academies*, Chicago: University of Chicago Press.

Cohen, S. (1986) *Historical Culture: On the Recoding of an Academic Discipline*, Berkeley, CA: University of California Press.

Collezione Galileiana, MSS 262, 275, 313, Biblioteca Nazionale Centrale, Florence.

"Diari di Etichetta," Guardaroba Medicea, Archivio di Stato, Florence.

Diaz, F. (1987) *Il granducato di Toscana – I Medici*, Turin: UTET.

Donati, C. (1988) *L'idea di nobilità in Italia, Secoli XIV–XVIII*, Bari: Laterza.

Elias, N. (1978) *The History of Manners*, New York: Pantheon Books.

—— (1982) *Power and Civility*, New York: Pantheon Books.

Findlen, P. (1994) *Possessing Nature: Museums, Collecting and Scientific Culture in Early Modern Italy*, Berkeley, CA: University of California Press.

—— (forthcoming) "Rhetoric, court patronage and the experimental method of Francesco Redi (1626–1697)," in J. V. Field and F. A. J. L. James (eds.) *Renaissance and Revolution: Humanists, Scholars, Craftsmen and Natural Philosophers in Early Modern Europe*, Cambridge: Cambridge University Press.

Foucault, M. (1979) *Discipline and Punish: The Birth of the Prison*, trans. Alan Sheridan, New York: Vintage Books.

Galluzzi, P. (1981) "L'Accademia del Cimento: 'Gusti' del principe, filosofia e ideologia dell'esperimento," *Quaderni storici* 16: 788–844.

Garuffi, G. M. (1688) *L'Italia accademica*, Rimini: Gio. Felici Dandi.

Goldberg, J. (1990) *Writing Matter: From the Hands of the English Renaissance*, Stanford, CA: Stanford University Press.

Greenblatt, S. (1980) *Renaissance Self-Fashioning*, Chicago: University of Chicago Press.

Halpern, R. (1991) *The Poetics of Primitive Accumulation: English Renaissance Culture and the Genealogy of Capital*, Ithaca, NY: Cornell University Press.

Hobsbawm, E. and Ranger, T. (eds.) (1983) *The Invention of Tradition*, Cambridge: Cambridge University Press.

Imbert, G. (1906) *La vita fiorentina nel Seicento secondo memorie sincrone 1644–1670*, Florence: Bemporad & Figlio.

Jay, M. (1988) "Scopic regimes of modernity," in H. Foster (ed.) *Vision and Visuality*, Dia Art Foundation, Discussions in Contemporary Culture 2, Seattle, WA: Bay Press, pp. 2–23.

Jed, S. (1989) "The scene of tyranny: violence and the humanistic tradition," in N. Armstrong and L. Tennenhouse (eds.) *The Violence of Representation: Literature and the History of Violence*, New York: Routledge, pp. 29–44.

Kellner, H. (1989) "Boundaries of the text: history as passage," in *Language and Historical Representation: Getting the Story Crooked*, Madison, WI: University of Wisconsin Press, pp. 3–25.

LaCapra, D. (1989) "History and psychoanalysis," in *Soundings in Critical Theory*, Ithaca, NY: Cornell University Press, pp. 30–66.

"Le leggi dell'Accademia della Crusca riformate l'anno 1589," MS A.46, Accademia della Crusca, Florence.

Lux, D. (1989) *Patronage and Royal Science in Seventeenth-Century France: The Académie de Physique de Caen*, Ithaca, NY: Cornell University Press.

McKendrick, N., Brewer, J., and Plumb, J. H. (1982) *The Birth of a Consumer Society: The Commercialization of Eighteenth-Century England*, London: Europa.

Magalotti, L. (1667) *Saggi di naturali esperienze fatte nell'Accademia del Cimento*, Florence: La Stella.

—— (1721) *Lettere scientifiche et erudite*, Florence: Tartini & Franchi.

—— (1769) *Lettere familiari*, Florence: Gaetano Cambiagi.

Marin, L. (1988) *Portrait of the King*, Minneapolis, MN: University of Minnesota Press.

Massai, F. (1917) "Sette lettere inedite di Lorenzo Magalotti al Cav. Alessandro Segni," *Rivista delle biblioteche e degli archivi* 28: 137–8.

Middleton, W. E. K. (1971) *The Experimenters: A Study of the Accademia del Cimento*, Baltimore, MD: Johns Hopkins University Press.

Migliore, F. L. del (1684) *Firenze città nobilissima illustrata*, Florence: La Stella.

Plaisance, M. (1975) "Une première affirmation de la politique culturelle de Côme I: La transformation de l'Académie des 'Humidi' en Académie Florentine (1540–1542)," In A. Rochon (ed.) *Les écrivains et le pouvoir en Italie à l'époque de la Renaissance*, première série, Paris: Université de la Sorbonne Nouvelle, pp. 361–438.

Poggi Salani, T. (1961) "L'atteggiamento linguistico di Lorenzo Magalotti e il lessico del *Saggi di naturali esperienze*," *Acme* 14: 7–69.

Redi, F. (n.d.) "Motti, enigmi, giuochi, et altri bagattei," MS Rediana 45, Biblioteca Medicea–Laurenziana, Florence.

—— (1660) "Memorie nella fabbrica de sali fattizi, e loro operazioni" and "Memoria de sali che si sono prima provati in poco quantità . . ." MS Rediana 199, Biblioteca Medicea–Laurenziana, Florence.

Reed, J. (1989) "Restoration and repression: the language projects of the Royal Society," *Studies in Eighteenth-Century Culture* 19: 399–412.

Revel, J. (1985) "Les usages de la civilité," in R. Chartier (ed.) *Histoire de la vie privée*, Vol. 3, Paris: Éditions du Seull, pp. 169–209.

Rinuccini, T. (1840) "Considerazioni sopra l'usanze mutate nel passato secolo del 1600," in *Ricordi storici di Filippo di Cino Rinuccini*, Florence: Piatti.

Shapin, S. and Schaffer, S. (1985) *Leviathan and the Air-Pump: Hobbes, Boyle, and the Experimental Life*, Princeton, NJ: Princeton University Press.

Simari, M. M. (1985) "Serragli a Firenze al tempo dei Medici," in M. Mosco (ed.) *Natura viva in casa Medici*, Florence: Centro Di, pp. 23–6.

Targioni Tozzetti, G. (1780) *Notizie degli aggrandimenti delle scienze fisiche accaduti in Toscana nel corso di anni LX. del secolo XVII*, Florence: Bouchard.

Tennenhouse, L. (1989) "Violence done to women on the Renaissance stage," in N. Armstrong and L. Tennenhouse (eds.) *The Violence of Representation: Literature and the History of Violence*, New York: Routledge, pp. 77–97.

Tesauro, E. (1765) *La filosofia morale*, Macerata: Giuseppe Piccini.

Tribby, J. (1991) "Cooking (with) Clio and Cleo: eloquence and experiment in seventeenth-century Florence," *Journal of the History of Ideas* 52: 417–39.

—— (1992) "Body building: living the museum life in early modern Europe," *Rhetorica* 10: 43–67.

Whigham, F. (1984) *Ambition and Privilege: The Social Tropes of Elizabethan Courtesy Theory*, Berkeley, CA: University of California Press.

White, H. (1987) "The politics of historical interpretation: discipline and de-sublimation," in *The Content of the Form: Narrative Discourse and Historical Representation*, Baltimore, MD: Johns Hopkins University Press, pp. 1–25.

Part IV

The social order:
culture high and low

18

"The most polite age and the most vicious"
Attitudes towards culture as a commodity, 1660–1800

John Brewer

This chapter investigates a paradox about eighteenth-century England epitomized in Richard Steele's remark in *Spectator* 6 of March 7, 1711 that "the most polite Age is in danger of being the most vicious" (Addison and Steele 1965: I, 30). Its aim is to explore this tension or potential contradiction in three ways: to examine the emergence of an overtly commercial "high" or "polite" culture in what Jürgen Habermas has called the "public sphere" (Habermas 1989; La Volpa 1992: 79–116); to explore the ambiguities inherent in the eighteenth-century debate about the nature of taste and the aesthetic; and to investigate the debate about culture and gender, one which revolved about issues of the feminine and effeminacy. Overall, my focus is upon the tension between the efforts to create a culture that was polite, moderate, reasonable, morally instructive, decorous, and restrained (the culture of Shaftesbury in the eighteenth century and Habermas in the twentieth), and the palpable intrusion of impulses – notably sexual passion and pecuniary greed – which were Rabelaisian and commercial and which undercut the claim that culture could and should be impartial, disinterested, dispassionate, and virtuous. In order to create a story in which art, virtue, and politeness could plausibly be united, there was much that had to be masked or suppressed.

What do I mean by culture? I am not using the term in the inclusive, all-embracing way deployed by anthropologists. Rather what I am discussing is what came to be defined in the eighteenth century as what Edmund Burke called "works of imagination and the elegant arts" (Burke 1958: 13). I am aware, of course, of the historically specific and highly problematic nature of this definition; indeed, questions about what is meant by and contained within this category – about its historical emergence and contentious character – are the subject of my chapter.

I

Let me begin my account of the emergence of a public sphere by pointing to the conjunction of two historical circumstances which I believe to have been distinctive to eighteenth-century England. The first is the remarkable weakness of court culture. The civil war, Commonwealth, and Protectorate effectively destroyed a court culture in which the monarch stood at the centre of a complex system of cultural signs and artistic practice intended to represent his or her monopoly of power. Never again was there to be a royal cult analogous to that which surrounded Elizabeth as the Virgin Queen (a sort of English, secular madonna); no British monarch was ever to match Charles I either as a patron of the arts or as the fabricator of an astonishingly rich and complex "illusion of power" (Orgel 1975). Though we can exaggerate royal control and the univocal message of the early seventeenth-century court, it was far more important as a site of cultural activity and display than it was ever to become again.

Charles II and his brother James aspired, of course, to re-create the monarchy of old and even to emulate the lavish embodiment of royal authority epitomized by Louis XIV's Versailles. Both, however, failed. This is not to say that the Restoration court was not an important social and cultural site. But the Restoration court suffered from two overwhelming difficulties – public penury and private misconduct. Palaces remained incomplete and the royal musicians unpaid because of the parlous state of royal finances. The court failed to represent itself as a seat of heroic power. Private pleasure, not public duty, appeared to be its end; the aspirations of Dryden were undercut by the antics of Rochester (Bucholz 1987: 12; Harley 1968: 66; Paulson 1989: 101).

Subsequent monarchs and their courts were less licentious but also less successful in becoming centers of cultural power. Neither the Whig supporters of the Hanoverian regime nor its Tory and Jacobite opponents wanted a cult of monarchy focused on the new dynasty and its court. Between the late seventeenth century and the accession of George III the court shriveled in size and shrank in stature (Beattie 1967). The monarch certainly patronized musicians, painters, the theater, opera, and, less frequently, men of letters, but the Crown was only one of many sources of patronage and certainly did not offer the most lucrative rewards. At the end of the eighteenth century Haydn could earn more at a single public benefit concert (£350) than at an entire series of private royal concerts (Geiringer 1964: 116). The greatest value of royal patronage lay in its use as currency in the larger market for cultural goods, as social cachet that could be parlayed into rich commissions. In short, the monarch acted as a private patron; there was no sustained attempt to use the arts as an adjunct of kingship, nor did the court, as an institution or site, manage to establish the sort of cultural eminence that it achieved under the early Stuarts and promised under Charles II and James II.

If court culture was the victim of politics, church culture fell foul of religion. Since the Henrician Reformation of the 1530s, royal cupidity and Protestant suspicion of images as idolatrous had combined to ensure the destruction or removal of relics, images, and ornaments from the English church, notably in the two great waves of iconoclasm of the mid-sixteenth and mid-seventeenth centuries. The effect of the English Reformation on the arts was twofold. Despite the efforts of Laudians and high

Anglicans in the early and late seventeenth century, it left churches bereft of what Archbishop Laud had called "the beauty of holiness"; and it created a profound suspicion of images in general, and of religious images in particular (Paulson 1989: 15–17). The strength of this fear is difficult to underestimate. It explains the remarkable absence of religious painting, especially of non-biblical subjects, until the late eighteenth century when attitudes towards ecclesiastical art seem to have softened. It is epitomized in the public outcry when a painted altarpiece was erected in a church in Whitechapel in 1714 (Pears 1988: 44–5). And its durability can be seen in episcopal opposition to the Royal Academy's proposals for the decoration of St. Paul's.

Apart from a few great cathedrals, churches were not important sites for music. In Salisbury, at the Three Choirs Festival held at Hereford, Gloucester, and Worcester, and in such cathedral cities as Chichester and Canterbury, annual concerts were held in grand ecclesiastical buildings. But in the great majority of English parishes there was no organ and in many there was no choir. Any singing, before the reforms of the Evangelical revival encouraged large congregational choirs, often consisted of a weak dirge (Temperley 1979: I, 105–8, 117–18, 123, 141, 158, 202, 230).

In short, in the early eighteenth century culture was without a clearly determined site. Or, to shift the metaphor, there was a cultural vacuum. Culture failed to thrive as an artifact of state power, court intrigue, or religious instruction and understanding. No doubt I have overstated the case for the weakness of royal, courtly, and ecclesiastical influence. But, when compared with France, Spain, Russia, Sweden, Prussia, and the small states of German princelings, royal and court power was extraordinarily attenuated. And the church, though its individual officers were a force in music and literature (Barry 1985: 39; Gregory 1991: 82–109), lacked the institutional presence enjoyed by Catholicism through much of Europe and by Lutheranism in Sweden and Prussia.

This cultural void in England has not gone unnoticed and it is often argued that it was filled by the formation of a culture in the public sphere, by the creation of a culture that was the expression of social and economic power in society at large. Habermas defines the "public sphere" as "a forum in which private people come together to form a public, readied themselves to compel public authority to legitimate itself before public opinion" (Habermas 1989: 25). He sees this phenomenon as having a specific site (the term "forum" is significant here), one which is urban rather than courtly, and which is embodied in a number of institutions, most notably the clubs, salons, coffee-house coteries and tavern societies that flourished in such abundance first in the English metropolis and later in the British provinces (Habermas 1989: 30–6).

These institutions, Habermas argues, had several distinctive features. First, in contradistinction to the hierarchical polity of which they were a part, they observed within their institutions an ethos of equality which self-consciously disregarded or ostensibly elided differences of social status among their members (Habermas 1989: 36). Secondly, though these institutions were not equivalent to or coterminous with the public, they nevertheless claimed to speak for the public and to define who its members were. They saw the public as potentially or in principle inclusive, capable of embracing all members of civil society, though in practice this inclusive view of the public was elided into one that confined membership to the male owners of property. Thirdly, they took their brief to be the discussion of the arts and of those matters of policy which had formerly been defined as the "mysteries" of church and state. Fourth, if their brief was culture and politics, their judge was "reason," the exercise of human deliberation free from either domination or coercion. And, finally, their court and schoolhouse was the press, notably the periodical press, exemplified in the English case by the greatest of what Habermas erroneously calls "the moral weeklies," the *Spectator* of Addison and Steele. Such publications, Habermas argues, enabled the public to hold "a mirror to itself; it did not yet come to a self-understanding through the detour of a reflection on works of philosophy and literature, art and science, but through entering itself into 'literature as an object' " (Habermas 1989: 43).

Habermas's analysis is consonant with a considerable body of recent historical literature which has sought to map the formation of a public and a public sphere in eighteenth-century England (Langford 1989; Borsay 1989; Brewer 1976; McKendrick, Brewer, and Plumb 1983; Money 1977). The eighteenth-century European phenomenon that Habermas discusses is usually understood in the English case as an attempt by politically moderate (but usually Whig) aristocrats and gentlemen, liberal and latitudinarian clergy, and prosperous Dissenting/Nonconformist interests to create a polite culture (Klein 1984–5: 186–214). This culture was characterized by its proponents as moderate and reasonable. Usually Christian (though it eschewed clerical controversy and theological dispute as the divisive dogmas of the academy and priesthood), it invariably rejected the court as the focus of culture, even though, in some of its manifestations, it was committed to aristocratic leadership. Its object, as Habermas stresses, was to constitute and instruct a public – a body of arbiters of taste, morality, and policy – and the means by which this goal was to be achieved was through the art of politeness. Politeness was construed both as a technique and an end. Its aim was to shape and unify a disinterested, reasonable, and discriminating public, without which there could be neither good taste nor moral virtue (Klein 1984–5: 186–214; 1989: 583–605). Anthony Ashley Cooper, third earl of Shaftesbury, the exemplar of aristocratic politeness, was sure that "where absolute power is there is no PUBLICK" (because, to use Habermas's terms, domination and coercion prevented free and disinterested deliberation). He was also sure that

> without a public voice, knowingly guided and directed, there is nothing which can raise a true ambition in the artist; nothing which can exalt the genius of the workman, or make him emulous of fame, and of the approbation of his country, and of posterity. . . . When the free spirit of a nation turns itself this way, judgments are formed; critics arise; the public eye and ear improve; a right taste prevails, and in a manner forces its way.
>
> (Shaftesbury 1914: 22–3)

The creation of a public entailed, as Habermas recognizes, the simultaneous representation, to an unprecedented degree, of the private, domestic world. For, if the formation of the public sphere depends upon the fabrication of a certain civic personality through the shaping of attitudes and manners, then it also legitimates the representation of the private world of conversation as a means of moral instruction. The public sphere is Janus-faced: it seeks to intrude upon matters of state but it also threatens to colonize the domestic sphere. And, just as its claims against the state provoked an attempt to define more clearly those areas which the state believed it ought to control, so the notion of what is truly private was more sharply focused. The scope, forms, and detailed content of private life were given unparalleled public exposure. Indeed, we might say that a clearly defined sense of the private, or what Habermas calls "the intimate," sphere depends symbiotically upon a developed notion of what constitutes the public.

Now this version of the public sphere, offered by Habermas and endorsed by Shaftesbury, is an extremely orderly and tidy one. It presupposes, in Habermas's case, a public of rationally and critically thinking bourgeois intellectuals – a sort of eighteenth-century equivalent of the Frankfurt school – while in the case of Shaftesbury it assumes a public of enlightened, moral, and aesthetically sensitive landed proprietors. Both cases assume a public which, by virtue of either its intellectual powers or its propertied independence, is capable of acting in a manner that is reasonable, disinterested, and impartial; a public which is capable, in other words, of transcending partial interests and passions in order to represent and embody a universal public good.

But these are only two possible versions of how the public was constituted. They had and have to compete with different ideas about who made up and was entitled to contribute to what Shaftesbury called "the public voice." And they also have to deal with the untidy and disorderly world of eighteenth-century social practice: to recognize that those who vociferously claimed a public voice were, as Bernard Mandeville tartly pointed out, not reasonable, moderate, and disinterested but rather driven by powerful, egoistic passions (Mandeville 1924).

I do not wish here to embark upon a general discussion of the history of the problem of the passions and the interests, nor of its different resolutions, of which the most important was undoubtedly the science of political economy. But I do want to emphasize the degree to which it was recognized that the formation of a public cultural sphere – the emergence of reading, theatrical and musical publics – was heavily compromised by but dependent upon two forces that undercut its impartiality, namely pecuniary gain – acquisitiveness – and sexual passion. This tension between disinterestedness, on the one hand, and the interests and the passions, on the other, was a source of profound unease, and it also goes far to explain the difficulties that eighteenth-century commentators had in determining the scope and character of the cultural public. To understand these contradictions we need first to turn to the workings of the eighteenth-century cultural sphere.

II

In the eighteenth-century culture became, to an unprecedented degree, a commodity. Let me cite one anecdote by way of example. It comes from the world of the visual arts rather than from the culture of print which was normally taken by contemporaries as the most obvious example of trafficking in culture. In 1714 Joseph Highmore visited a fellow artist, Vanderstraeten, in a garret in Drury Lane:

> He hired a long garret . . . where he painted cloths many feet in length . . . and painted the whole at once, continuing the sky . . . from one end to the other, and then several grounds etc., til the whole was one long landscape. This he cut up and sold by parcels as demanded . . . and those who dealt in this way

would go to his house and buy three or four, or any number of feet of landscapes.

(Whitley, 1928: I, 23)

This is no isolated anecdote. In every field of cultural endeavor culture was for sale: paintings, books, and prints passed through the auction houses and into the hands of specialized dealers. In the decade of the 1680s alone there were more than 400 painting and print auctions in London (Pears 1988: 58). The property of authors and engravers in their work was established (though not properly protected) through government legislation of 1709 and 1736. In the half-century after 1716 there were over 200 sales of book copyrights, chiefly at auction. It was possible to buy shares in a copyright. Thus two thirds of the copyright of the works of William Shakespeare was sold for £1,200 in 1767 (Belanger 1982: 18).

The marketing of culture became a trade separate from its production: theatrical and opera impresarios, picture-, print- and booksellers, became the new capitalists of cultural enterprise, peddling culture in almost every medium and art. The publisher John Dunton was one of the first booksellers to recognize the importance of women as cultural consumers. J. J. Heidegger, the opera impresario who partnered Handel, orchestrated the Hanoverian monarchy's public ceremonies, and introduced the masquerade into the English theater. John Rich, theatrical manager and patentee, changed the format of the London stage, introducing pantomime, comic dancing, complex machinery, and extravagant scenery. Jonathan Tyers, the proprietor of Vauxhall Pleasure Gardens, patronized the painters Hogarth and Hayman and the musicians Handel and Thomas Arne. Andrew Hay, having failed as a portraitist, became the first professional art dealer. James Lackington, humble apprentice, pioneered the mass secondhand book trade. John Boydell, printseller, developed the English export trade and established the Shakespeare Gallery as a shrine to British culture (Rogers 1985: 11–17, 28; Pears 1988: 77–87; Edelstein 1983; B. Allen 1987: 16, 32, 62; Bruntjen 1985; Shevelow 1989: 3–5, 39–40, 58–92; Lackington 1790).

These impresarios were responsible for the dissemination of new literary and aesthetic forms that emerged in the eighteenth century: the novel, the periodical essay, the conversation piece, the ballad opera, comic history painting and a variety of pastiche. They were agnostic when it came to the question of culture as a means of moral improvement. Though they were happy to support tragedy, epic poetry, and history painting, especially when these forms seemed particularly profitable, they did not hesitate to promote forms of entertainment which were neither morally elevated nor instructive. Their aim was to appeal to the appetite, to cater to changing taste, and to satisfy an audience eager to enjoy novelty and variety. As far as they were concerned, culture, as a commodity, was an end not a means. Its pleasures lay in its pursuit – in participation and possession. Moral purpose was secondary. This did not of course preclude them from being extremely sanctimonious about culture when it suited them; and there were many occasions on which fashion, the desire for respectability, or a combination of the two, induced entrepreneurs to promote morally elevated cultural forms and practices. But at bottom their concern was to titillate their customers.

The mix of commerce and hedonism promoted by cultural middlemen was embodied in the chief cultural sites of eighteenth-century London. The city's theaters – Covent

Garden, Drury Lane, Goodman's Fields, Lincoln's Inn Fields, the Haymarket – were run as sophisticated and profitable businesses. They were capable of staging an astonishing number of productions designed to cater to a wide variety of taste; they were also houses of pleasure whose delights were not confined to the plays, music, pantomime, and dancing performed on the stage. Above all, theaters were places of sexual assignation: the Green Boxes at Covent Garden, described by Bonnell Thornton in the *Connoisseur* as "the flesh Market," were dominated by prostitutes and their potential clients (Pedicord 1954: 50); more than one dramatic elopement – one thinks of Susan Fox–Strangways' flight and furtive union with the impossibly handsome actor, William O'Brien – was planned in a theatrical box. And not only the lobby but the auditorium of the theater was a place of social display in which the performance of the audience was a significant part of the spectacle. Mr. Lovel, the beau in Burney's *Evelina*, who declares that he "has no time to mind the stage" and affectedly asks his theatrical companions "pray – what was the play tonight" (Burney 1970: 80), was clearly not exceptional. As the *Theatrical Monitor* of 1768 complained, "During the time of the representation of a play, the quality in the boxes are totally employed in finding out, and beckoning to their acquaintances, male and female; they criticize on fashions, whisper cross the benches, make significant nods, and give hints of this and that, and t'other body" (R. D. Hume 1980: 43). On occasion the line between performer and audience was totally eroded, as in the masquerades that were held at the Haymarket, as well as at such London pleasure gardens as Vauxhall and Ranelagh (Castle 1986).

If the theater was the great centre of cultural entertainment in the winter, the pleasure garden was its home in summer. The most famous garden – Jonathan Tyers's Vauxhall – offered its customers a variety of entertainments and spectacles. The first public rehearsal of Handel's Fireworks Music was heard there by an audience of more than 12,000. The outdoor orchestra offered exciting and eclectic programs of songs, small-scale operas, overtures, and concertos. Thomas Arne, the composer of "Rule Britannia," was retained as the house musician. The buildings in the grounds included some of the finest rococo architecture in Britain, as well as a display of over fifty works of art. Visitors could dine in booths decorated with designs by Hogarth and Francis Hayman, visit the Rotunda whose entranceway was hung with history paintings and scenes from Richardson's *Pamela*, admire the statues of Handel and Milton, witness a number of *tromp-l'oeil* effects, which changed from season to season and year to year, or walk in the alleyways that crossed the grounds. Like the theater, Vauxhall, as Evelina was to discover to her cost, was also a place of sexual assignation: a spot which, according to the many Vauxhall songsheets that were published, encouraged young nymphs and shepherds to innocent sport and dalliance, but which was better known, as Casanova discovered, to be "a rural Brothel" (Casanova 1958–60: V, 218–19, 316–17; Edelstein 1983: 11–12, 14; B. Allen 1987: 62–70; Burney 1970; Anon. 1752; Anon. 1762).

Vauxhall was the most famous and enduring of the pleasure gardens, a model to which others aspired. It was also one garden among many: in Islington, Spa Fields, Sadlers and Banigge Wells, Marylebone, Bermondsey, Chelsea and Lambeth, at Ranelagh and at Cuper's Gardens, and even in Wapping proprietors offered orchestras and vocalists, picture galleries, illuminated transparencies and fireworks, sculpture and jugglers, dancing and equestrian performances (Wroth 1896).

Several features of this commercialized culture stand out. The first is the extraordinary variety of entertainments on offer and the apparent absence of discrimination between cultural forms that we would consider "low," popular or simply "entertainment" and those that we would view as edifying, improving, or highbrow. Juggling, music, dancing, opera, pantomime, entr'act, tragedy, and comedy were all lumped together on the London stage. Similarly, the eighteenth-century periodical brought together within its pages not only literature, music, painting, and theatrical performance but town gossip, political news, epistolary advice, remarks on exotic places as well as on current medical and scientific topics. The pleasure gardens offered some of London's finest music and some of its cheapest effects. On the stage, in the periodical, and at the pleasure garden, different genres and forms, both high and low, were jumbled in together. The classical, courtly, and didactic types remained, but now constituted a patrician elite that was increasingly outnumbered, jostled, and challenged by their much more culturally heterogeneous companions.

A second feature was the comparatively easy access which "the public" had to this culture: it was available to almost anyone who could pay. Coffee-house newspapers and periodicals could be read for the price of a beverage; printsellers' shops and auction houses were entered gratis by those able to muster the appearance of respectability; until 1792 access to Vauxhall Gardens cost one shilling; entrance to other pleasure gardens was free. Some entertainments and cultural artifacts were, of course, beyond the purse of all but the most affluent: a portrait by Reynolds or a box at the opera excluded all but the very richest members of society. And most entertainments were not available to the laboring poor, except on the rarest of occasions or when they participated at one remove as servants wearing livery. But for an exceptionally large social stratum culture was available as never before. When the London haberdasher, Robert Fotherby, died in 1709, he had no fewer than forty-four pictures hanging in his dining-room. A mercer who died four years earlier left his heirs almost a thousand books (Earle 1989: 295–6). The cultural audience was clearly not confined to the aristocracy and the leisured classes.

Thirdly, this culture was characterized by an emphasis upon social display: cultural sites were places of self-presentation in which audiences made publicly visible their wealth, status, social and sexual charms. The ostensible reason for an individual's presence at a cultural site – seeing the play, attending an auction, visiting an artist's studio, listening to a concert – was often subordinate to a more powerful set of social imperatives. An audience did not passively attend a performance separate from the social world. It incorporated culture as part of its social performance. And, from the individual's point of view, access to culture and self-presentation in the cultural arena was a vital means of maintaining or attaining social status and of establishing social distinctions.

Fourth, this was a culture steeped in hedonism and sexual intrigue. With the exception of reading (an activity whose representation was also often eroticized; see de Bolla 1989: 236–7; Barker–Benfield 1992: 327–9; Pawlowicz, this volume), culture was bound up with the giddy round of social pleasures that its critics found so morally offensive. It provided the public space for gustatory and bibulous excess, the venue for courtship, seduction, and the pleasures of the flesh.

Seen from the entrepreneurs' perspective the public was defined as those who possess and consume. What validated cultural artifacts and practices was their exchange-value; what enhanced their exchange-value were the pleasures that they and their surroundings offered. This made entrepreneurs both extremely sensitive to the wishes of the public and remarkably untroubled about the role of the public in determining good taste. From their point of view, the audience was the uncontested arbiter of taste. The point was well made by John Boydell, when he was accused by Joseph Wright of Derby of categorizing artists into different classes by offering them different fees and rewards. "I never presumed to class the Painters," he wrote, "I leave that to the public, to whose opinions and judgement I bow with great reverence and respect" (Bruntjen 1985: 79).

In short, the cultural entrepreneur created a culture that was driven by luxury, social emulation, human appetite and desire. Here we are in the realm of the senses. Taste is active, energetic, almost carnal; a matter of immediate sensation, whether culinary or sexual. Dash, in a remark to Blotpage in Henry Fielding's *Author's Farce*, captures this feeling perfectly: "A titlepage is to a book what a fine neck is to a woman, [and] therefore ought to be the most regarded as it is the part which is viewed before the purchase" (Fielding 1966: 28). His comment epitomizes the view, on which I will elaborate later, that culture, like the female harlot, is envisaged and consumed as the male object of desire.

To all appearances this cultural realm did not accord easily with the notion of an impartial cultural sphere free from concupiscence and commercial greed. For all their differences, the many commentators who attacked or defended this culture were largely agreed that it was blatantly commercial and that, in its pursuit of profit, it frequently sacrificed moral instruction for entertainment and cheap sensation. Clerics, conservative commentators, and social reformers censured the theater, pleasure garden, and printshop as venues of social and sexual license, populated by "the giddy, lewd and vain," and condemned the abandonment of instructive and morally elevated cultural forms for crude entertainment. The expansion of the public audience was reprobated as the greedy seduction of the vulgar and the ignorant into the belief that they, like their social superiors, could be men and women of taste. It was feared for the way it undermined social distinctions by creating a heterogeneous public. And it was loathed for the possibilities that it afforded for social dissembling and disguise (Sekora 1977: 77–109; Langford 1989: 607–13; Castle 1986: 2–7.).

Even Bernard Mandeville, who was often accused by contemporaries of supporting a culture characterized by "Lust and vanity" and the pursuit of "Objects of Mutability" (Mandeville 1924: I, 18, 25), concurred with critics who ascribed the excesses of the age to the passions and the interests. His point was not that the critics' analysis of the motives that animated a commercial culture was at fault, but that their complaints about its wickedness were misplaced. What they regarded as reprehensible he saw as inevitable. Passions governed men "whether they will it or no"; to pretend otherwise was rank hypocrisy. Modern "vast, potent and polite societies" could flourish only thanks to the depravity of man. Modern vices made the pleasures of polite society possible; private vice was inextricably a part of public virtue (Mandeville 1924: I, 6–8, 10, 12–13).

Mandeville clearly derived much pleasure in exposing what he saw as the sanctimoniousness of critics who wished to pretend that all men were not irredeemably creatures of passion. Similarly he had contempt for those who failed to see that the most remarkable feature of modern culture was its ability to harness the energies fueled by lust, greed, and ambition. Yet, in his triumphant demonstration of the costs of modernity and in his occasional hankering for a pre-lapsarian state, Mandeville is closer to his critics than might at first appear. For both he and his opponents conveyed with astonishing power the seductiveness and energy of a commercially vibrant, protean, and fertile culture suffused with lust and greed. The most astringent critics were also the most revealing. In the writings of Pope and Swift, in the sermons and tracts of William Law and John Brown, and the stoical republican disquisitions of James Burgh, we can detect a disgust that is close to desire. I want to explore this theme of ambivalence by pursuing not the well-worn path that leads to the debate about luxury, but a rather less familar track that leads to discussions of taste.

III

Even as the range of cultural goods and pleasures on offer grew to unprecedented proportions, there was a parallel – in some ways contradictory, in others complementary – tendency to define culture in a new way. What Edmund Burke called "works of imagination and the elegant arts" were distinguished from other products of human endeavor as objects of taste, whose purpose was to stimulate, in the famous phrase of Joseph Addison, "the pleasures of the imagination." The notion that there was a new cultural category of "the fine arts," sometimes called "elegant arts" or "arts of taste," which could be distinguished from the "necessary," "mechanical," or "useful arts" on the one hand, and from those intellectual matters that were the object of human understanding on the other, was well established by the mid-eighteenth century (Kristeller 1965: II, 193–210). Indeed, it had become a cliché of the British periodical press (Spector 1966: 245–6; Hooker 1934; B. S. Allen 1937: I, 110; II, 235).

There was a certain amount of disagreement, however, about what cultural activities fell into this new category. Poetry, painting, and music – what Archibald Alison in his *Essays on Taste* (1790) specified as "the landscapes of Claude Lorraine, the music of Handel and the poetry of Milton" (Alison 1790: 3) – were invariably included. Architecture, dance, gardening, sculpture, and, with declining frequency, oratory and eloquence were also identified as "fine or elegant arts" (Gerard 1759: 22; Harris 1744: 53; Britannica 1771: 887–8; Chambers 1788–91: Vol. I, "Arts"; Vol. IV, "Taste"). All were, at one time or another, recognized as proper objects of taste. Burke put it succinctly in his *Philosophical Inquiry into the Origin of our Ideas of the Sublime and Beautiful*: taste, he says, is "that faculty, or those faculties of the mind which are affected with, or which form a judgment of the works of imagination and the elegant arts" (Burke 1958: 13). In short, there was now presumed to be an entity that we might call "high" or "polite" culture whose defining characteristic was that it was the object of taste.

One (albeit rather naive) way of reading the eighteenth-century literature on taste is to interpret it as a positive response to, or at least as consonant with, changes in cultural practice. Certainly one of the most conspicuous features of almost all works on this subject, whether they are philosophical discussions about the nature of taste or self-consciously didactic works intended to shape particular sorts of taste, is that their key figure is a member of the public, a person – usually a man – of taste. The perspective is that of the spectator or consumer of culture, of those members of the expanding public who presumably need both guidance and instruction.

At times, it appears as if this body is potentially limitless. Appreciation of the arts and imaginative literature was viewed as not restricted by the understanding because it was a matter of sense rather than reason. Views on this subject seemed beguilingly democratic. The principles of taste, wrote one commentator, "are common to our whole species, and arise from that internal sense of beauty which every man, in some degree at least, evidently possesses" (Bate 1946: 52). The sentiment is echoed by Archibald Alison: "In so far as the beauties of art and nature affect the external senses, their effect is the same upon every man who is in possession of those senses" (Alison 1790: 5). And Francis Hutcheson in his influential *Inquiry into the Original of our Ideas of Beauty and Virtue* (1725) was emphatic that our appreciation of beauty was not enhanced by or dependent upon knowledge:

> The Pleasure does not arise from any Knowledge of Principles, Proportions, Causes, or of the Usefulness of the Object; but strikes us at first with the Idea of Beauty: nor does the most accurate Knowledge increase this Pleasure of Beauty, however it may super-add a distinct, rational Pleasure from prospects of Advantage, or from Increase of Knowledge.
>
> (Hutcheson 1725:10)

Because the arts were deemed to work on the senses, unconstrained by reason or knowledge, they were seen as capable of extraordinary effects. In *Spectator* 421 Addison remarks "how great a Power . . . may we suppose lodged in him, who knows all the ways of affecting the Imagination, who can infuse what Ideas he pleases, and fill those Ideas with Terrour and Delight to what Degree he thinks fit" (Addison and Steele 1711–14: III, 580). Dr. Johnson took a similar view in his "Life of Dryden": "Works of imagination excel by their allurements and delight; by their power of attracting and detaining the attention" (Johnson 1905: I, 454).

Allurements, delight, attraction: all of these terms speak to the exceptional sensuality and seductiveness of culture. They remind us of the cultural impresario's view of the public as a body whose pleasure is derived from cultural pursuit and possession, and they are redolent of Fielding's image of the title-page as the neck of a fine woman, something or someone that is viewed before acquisition. We are back in the realm of the senses, back in the Mandevillian world of cupidity and concupiscence.

Yet this was precisely what most commentators on taste desperately wished to avoid. They did not want "works of the imagination and the elegant arts" to be seen as commodities or products – comparable with things whose functions were practical or of use and which could be deployed for gain or profit – nor did they wish to equate the pleasures of the imagination with the pleasures of the flesh. The way in which they sought to distinguish the realm of culture – to purge it of these associations – is extremely revealing.

One of the most conspicuous absences in almost all eighteenth-century discussions of aesthetic appreciation is that of a social milieu: the man of taste exists in individual isolation. He is not part of a larger public or audience, except in the most abstract sense as a person who appreciates culture; he is certainly not placed in a public gallery, theater, or pleasure garden. Indeed, there is an increased emphasis in discussions of taste on the importance of avoiding any impediment to the direct enjoyment of the cultural object or experience. As David Hume put it: "A perfect serenity of mind, a recollection of thought, a due attention to the object; if any of these circumstances are wanting, our experiment will be fallacious, and we shall be unable to judge of the catholic and universal beauty" (D. Hume 1788: I, 208). Increasingly, isolation, a retreat from the hubbub of social and city life, is seen as necessary to the full appreci-ation of the pleasures of the imagination. Alison's man of taste is someone "who, from the noise and tumult of vulgar joy, often hasten[s] to retire to solitude and silence, where they may yield with security to . . . illusions of Imagination" (Alison 1790: 117). (We can almost see Alison's man of taste fleeing the theater audience and the crowd at the pleasure garden.) And, if physical retreat is not possible, then the imagination offers the pleasures of mental escape. Speaking of Claude, Handel, and Milton, Alison remarks: "we feel the sublimity or beauty of their productions, when our imaginations are kindled by their power, when we lose ourselves amid the number of images that pass before our minds, and when we waken at last from this play of fancy, as from the charm of a romantic dream" (Alison 1790: 3).

As these remarks of Alison make clear, the spectator, the man of taste, is represented not as the active consumer, the pursuer or acquirer of culture, but rather as passive, as someone on whom the pleasures of the imagination work. The man of taste does not taste, he has taste. Indeed the two most important writers on taste in the mid-eighteenth century, Alexander Gerard and Edmund Burke, concurred in the view (which seems, in turn, to have been derived from the aesthetics of Shaftesbury) that disinterestedness rather than self-interest or passion was essential to the appreciation of art and nature. Gerard explicitly cites "gratification of appetite" and "pursuit of gain" as the two conditions that distort or occlude taste, while Burke distinguished aesthetic appreciation "from desire or lust; which is an energy of mind, that hurries us on to the possession of certain objects" (Stolnitz 1961–2; 134–5; Burke 1958: 91).

We seem to be perilously close here to pleasure without sensation (or is it sensation without pleasure?), just as in the *Spectator* essays on the imagination we come close to possession without ownership. In *Spectator* 411 Addison remarks:

> A Man of Polite Imagination is let into a great many Pleasures that the Vulgar are not capable of receiving. [The passivity of the word "receiving" is typical.] He can converse with a picture, and find an agreeable companion in a Statue. He meets with a secret Refreshment in a Description, and often feels a greater Satisfaction in the Prospect of Fields and Meadows, than another does in the Possession. It gives him, indeed, a kind of Property in every thing he sees, and makes the most rude uncultivated parts of nature administer to his Pleasures: So that he looks upon the World, as it were, in another Light, and discovers in it a Multitude of Charms, that conceal themselves from the generality of Mankind.
>
> (Addison and Steele 1711–14: III, 538)

The pleasure is both perspicuous and covert, recognized and denied.

These ambiguities reveal the exceptionally unstable status of both the character of taste and the nature of the imagination. Most writers on taste wanted, on the one hand, to make clear that it entailed feelings that made it a matter of sense rather than understanding; on the other, they wished to make clear that sense was not sensual, a matter of the passions, but rather innate and natural. As an inherent attribute of man – like the innate capacity to understand truth and virtue – it existed prior to the passions and the interests, whose function was not to grasp or understand the aesthetic but to distort our ability to appreciate it (Caygill 1989: 47, 57, 59, 62).

In order to sustain this position, Hutcheson and others drew a distinction between "interior" and "exterior" sense. For Hutcheson our external senses arise from desire: they are active, "sensual," "voluptuous"; in this context taste is what Kant called "the taste of the tongue, the palate and the throat"; the appreciation or understanding of beauty, on the other hand, is associated with "internal sense," which is seen as passive, lacking appetite (Hutcheson 1725: 7–8, 88–92; Stolnitz 1961–2; 140). Alexander Gerard provided an excellent summary of this position, with all its attendant confusions, on the first page of his *An Essay on Taste* (1759):

> A fine Taste is neither wholly the gift of *nature*, nor wholly the effect of *art*. It derives its origin from certain powers natural to the mind; but these powers cannot attain their full perfection, unless they are assisted by proper culture [i.e. cultivation]. Taste consists chiefly in the improvement of these principles, which are commonly called the *powers of the imagination*, and are considered by modern philosophers as *internal* or *reflex senses*, supplying us with finer and more delicate perceptions, than any which can be properly referred to our external organs.
>
> (Gerard 1759: 1)

Gerard's account (as well as many others) does not deny that man has an innate capacity for taste, but, in order to introduce an element of discrimination (an inevitable move in a highly stratified social order and one which is also necessary if taste is to be something more than sensual gratification), he immediately qualifies his account by requiring "proper culture," the cultivation of proper judgment. Taste then becomes a notion which touches both sense and reason but which is not reducible to either; it is a floating middle term whose status is indeterminate and difficult to define.

As Kant pointed out, the issue of how to define taste was fudged by the likes of Hutcheson, Gerard, and Kames (Caygill 1989: 69). Its indeterminacy, which so exercised David Hume but which he typically refused to deny, was also grudgingly acknowledged by Burke. The difficulty that confronted commentators on the debate about taste was analogous to that faced by the critics of a commercialized cultural sphere. They recognized – and no one recognized this more forcefully than Burke – that in the fruit of taste lay the seeds of desire; yet it was this knowledge that they were so eager to suppress or deny.

There was one presence which, above all others, served as a constant challenge to this act of denial. Whether as cultural producers, impresarios, critics, or merely as the audience, women were a persistent reminder of the libidinal energies which the culture could unleash and which were so difficult to control. It is to this preoccupation with women and culture that I turn in my closing remarks.

IV

At its simplest level this concern might be explained by the shifting sociology of culture, by the emergence of women as cultural producers and consumers and, less frequently, as cultural entrepreneurs. Thanks to recent scholarship, we now know a great deal more about the cultural contribution of such playwrights and novelists as Aphra Behn, Eliza Haywood, Delarivier Manley, Sarah Fielding, Frances Brooke, Elizabeth Griffith, Frances Sheridan, Fanny Burney, Elizabeth Inchbald, Perdita Robinson, and Mary Wollstonecraft (*inter alia*, Spencer 1986; Todd 1984). The female actors who became increasingly important to the post-Restoration theatre (and from whose ranks such playwrights and novelists as Haywood, Griffith, and Robinson were recruited) have been equally well studied. But we know far less about women singers and artists. (Perhaps this is explained by reference works like Ellis Waterhouse's *Dictionary of British 18th-Century Painters*: the entries on the numerous women portraitists and exhibitors at the Society of Artists and Royal Academy are invariably disparaging and perfunctory. He writes, for example, of Angelica Kauffman, one of the founder members of the Royal Academy, as "one of the odder artistic phenomena of her time, as she was admired far beyond her artistic deserts and seems to have charmed, at different times, Winckelmann, Reynolds, Goethe and Canova" (Waterhouse 1981; 200; but see Roworth 1992 for a revisionist view).

For more than two hundred years female cultural producers have excited such enmity and disparagement. It is easy to see why. By presenting their works (with varying degrees of directness) to the public, by acting commercially in the public cultural sphere, such women violated the precept that, in the words of Hannah More, a woman's "talents are only a means to a still higher attainment . . . she is not to rest in them as an end . . . merely to exercise them as an instrument for the acquisition of fame and the promoting of pleasure, is subversive of her delicacy as a woman" (More 1799: II, 12). Husbands, fathers, and other members of the family, especially sons, were the proper objects of female attainment, not a wider public.

The woman who was a cultural producer, who appealed to or appeared before the public, compromised her virtue because such conduct was construed by many critics as inherently immodest. It laid women open to the charge of being tantamount to the only other independent woman in the cultural public sphere, the punk or prostitute.

This association was one that women could glory in, deny, avoid, or subvert – the tactics available to the highly visible actress were different from those of the partially concealed author – but the link was unlikely to be dispelled as long as women claimed the right not only to create their own representations and narratives but to speak publicly of matters, notably those of sex and love, of which they should either be innocent or about which they should display a proper, female modesty.

Yet there were compelling reasons why women were likely to play an important role in the cultural sphere, not only as creators and performers but as spectators and critics. For, as we have seen, imaginative literature and the elegant arts were defined by their ability to provoke the pleasures of the imagination. The emphasis on imagination, on the non-rational quality of the appreciation of beauty, on the importance of feeling, is consonant with contemporary perceptions of female personality. The same psychology that saw women as singularly benevolent and sympathetic also recognized their capacity for aesthetic and cultural appreciation (Todd 1986: 19–21; Barker-Benfield 1992: 218).

But this susceptibility, the sense that women's state of mind and sensibility made them open to cultural pleasures, was also seen as exceedingly dangerous. For the culture that was, in practice, available for women to enjoy in eighteenth-century London was, as we have seen, far from chaste. Its context – the opera and theater box, the painter's studio, the dark alley of the pleasure garden, the street crowd outside the printshop – provided other temptations: to sexual intrigue, prodigal living, and social emulation. And to these, as well, women were believed to be peculiarly prone. Hence James Burgh's tirade to women in his admonitary tract, *Britain's Remembrancer*, in the aftermath of the 1745 rebellion:

> Can you say you ever come away from the tumultuous scenes of Pleasure, which ingross the bulk of your Time, without having your Minds disturbed and thrown into a ferment of irregular and exorbitant desires, which, if you loved a life of sobriety, peace and retirement, would never have stirred in your breasts? Can you pretend that the sight of gorgeous dresses, of gawdy paintings, and all the various magnificence, which exquisite art supported by unbounded extravagance can put together; that the hearing of the most melting strains of music, and of the most rapturous and passionate flights of poetry; can you pretend, I say, that these have any other effect upon you than to fill your fancies with a thousand romantic wishes and desires altogether inconsistent with your station and above your rank in life, and to make your homes dull and tiresome to you?
>
> (Burgh 1746: 43)

Women, then, were viewed as susceptible not only to the acceptable and respectable aspects of culture (a topic on which Burgh is much less eloquent), but to its associated temptation to indulge the passions indiscriminately.

Many critics of culture argued that the sites that we have discussed – the theater, pleasure garden, opera house, and printshop – exacerbated female lubriciousness for they inflamed women's desire, agitated their imagination, and provided them with the opportunity for pursuing their passions by creating an environment – best exemplified in the masquerade – which removed conventional restraints. The author of *The Devil on Crutches* (1755) complained that women in the theater, "though they resent the least loose Discourse in private company, they are fond of the most fulsome Obscenity upon the Stage, and will not suffer a Blush to take Possession of their Cheeks, while they are attending to scenes that would disgrace the Stews" (Anon. 1755: 33), while another commentator bemoaned the "indecent attitudes, obscene labels, and similar decorations of the figures" in printshops, claiming that "girls often go in parties to visit the windows of printshops, that they may amuse themselves with the view of prints which impart the most impure ideas" (Corry 1804: 156–7). Such remarks were palpably infused with male anxiety about uncontrolled female freedom and pleasure.

Much of the public sphere, then, was seen as potentially compromising for women, a zone whose very attractions were its dangers and which could only be entered with proper caution and restraint. Fanny Burney's novel *Evelina* (1778) is only the best known of a large number of fictional and non-fictional works that make this point.

Evelina is a guided tour of London's sites of temptation which leaves not even its heroine, protected by her innocence, unaffected. In this genre, the journey through London's sites of pleasure becomes a peregrination in which young women travel from beguiling (and usually bucolic) innocence to a responsible and knowing maturity acquired through acquaintance with but not the enjoyment of the pleasures of the town (Kubek in Chapter 23 in this volume).

The astringent Hannah More in her *Strictures on Female Education* was sure that places of public resort as sites of female display were a formula for marital infelicity:

> If a man select a picture for himself from among all its exhibited competitors, and bring it to his own house, the picture being passive, he is able to *fix* it there: while the wife, picked up at a public place, and accustomed to incessant display, will not, it is probable, when brought home stick so quietly to the spot where he fixes her; but will escape to the exhibition room again, and continue to be displayed at every subsequent exhibition, just as if she were not become private property, and had never been definitively disposed of.
>
> (More 1799: II, 166)

In this example More, with characteristic acuity, identifies deeply felt anxieties about the control of women and culture. Both women and paintings are properly deemed the object and property of men. Though women are distinguished from pictures by their disturbing agency and mobility, More's explicit link between the two putative forms of male property, both acquired in a public space, reveals a larger apprehension about the exhibition room and its contents, pictorial and human, as an erotically charged site of male voyeurism. (This, incidentally, is a favourite theme of the drawings of Thomas Rowlandson [Paulson 1972: 80–92].) But More displaces this anxiety, representing it not as a male desire to see and to consume but as a female desire to be seen, "to be displayed," and to be consumed. Women's participation in the cultural sphere, even in the role of consumer, is thus rendered problematic; they are translated from consumers to the object of consumption.

Yet, as is well known, women would not be gainsaid; they would not suffer exclusion from the cultural marketplace. As the *Athenian Mercury*, a periodical that catered predominantly for women, put it, women are "a Strong Party in the World" (Shevelow 1989: 34). They were the readers of periodicals and novels; the devotees of the circulating library; a major part of the audience at the theater, opera, and pleasure garden; enthusiastic participants in the masquerade; the collectors of prints and the purchasers of paintings; the organizers of amateur dramatics and theatricals; in households the members who presided over most forms of decoration and furnishing. In short, they were women of fashion.

The power of women as cultural consumers is reflected in almost every cultural medium and at almost every site. There were women's periodicals like the *Athenian Mercury*, the *Ladies Mercury*, *The Visitor*, and the *Town and Country Magazine*; sentimental comedy and "she tragedy" in the theater, conversation pieces and domestic portraits in painting, even the funereal sculpture of Roubiliac: all were seen as especially catering to female taste (Paulson 1989: 231, 244).

To many critics and commentators this implied not simply a cultural market and production aimed at and devoured by women but, more insidiously, the feminization of a culture they believed should embody masculine values. Complaints about feminiz-ation were commonplace: Swift's remark to Stella that he'd "not meddle with the Spectator – let him fair-sex it to the world's end" (Shevelow 1989: 1); Joseph Wharton's dismissal of a tragic theater dominated by love "which, by totally engrossing the theatre, hath contributed to degrade that noble school of virtue into an academy of effeminacy" (*Adventurer* 1753–4: II, 253), and "Estimate" Brown's blanket condemna-tion of "unmanly dissipation" (Brown 1757: 118).

As these examples make clear, this cultural criticism contains a strong element of anxiety about masculinity. Brown makes the point explicit, complaining that "the one sex [have] . . . advanced in boldness, as the other have sunk into effeminacy" (Brown 1757: 51). For, if men were catering to the tastes of women, they were surrendering control over taste; equally, if they adopted or embraced feminine taste, their manliness was undermined, unless, of course, it were possible to construct a new notion of masculinity. This is not so much an anxiety about women as scholarly critics – despite the works of Charlotte Lennox, Elizabeth Montagu, and Elizabeth Griffith on Shakespeare, or Clara Reve on the history of the novel – rather, it is about the female arbiter who is able to escape masculine authority and to dictate taste. This is Daphne in Edward Young's fifth satire on women in his popular *Love of Fame, the Universal Passion* (Young 1728: 91–2):

> O'er the belle-lettre lovely Daphne reigns;
> Again the god Apollo wears her chains:
> With legs toss'd high, on her sophee she sits
> Vouchsafing audience to contending wits:
> Of each performance she's the final test:
> One act read o'er, she prophesies the rest;
> And then, pronouncing with decisive air,
> Fully convinces all the town – she's fair.

Young's Daphne is a far cry from the nymph of classical legend. She is neither passive nor a symbol of chastity. The classical Daphne is saved from Apollo's unwanted attentions by being transformed by her father into a laurel tree. (It sounds like a horticultural version of an eighteenth-century novel plot.) Her fate is usually taken to symbolize the triumph of chastity over love. But Young's Daphne is the authority figure, the arbiter of taste. Apollo (the god of poetry and music; the embodiment of masculine beauty and of man's rational nature) is her captive (he wears her chains), while she is free to be at once critic – "Of each performance she's the final test" – and author – "One act read o'er, she prophesies the rest."

But such assertion is, once again, compromising. The modern Daphne ought to be chaste and passive, captured within a classical narrative; her proper role is as the object and inspiration for the poet's art, providing him with the opportunity to celebrate the moral determination and moral superiority of women. But Daphne, on the contrary, asserts her powers as a critic and author by misusing her beauty, by exerting sexual power. She is not the passive object of male disquisition on the subject of female virtue, but an active, immodest ("with legs toss'd high"), and beautiful seductress. And that, the text makes clear, makes her a fair woman of the town, i.e. a whore. Young's text epitomizes a common eighteenth-century view: that, because women do not have the

358   John Brewer

requisite abilities to create and to judge, they can appear to do so only by deluding men with their charms, by acting seductively, and, therefore, by forfeiting their virtue.

In this respect the seductive woman is analogous to the culture of which she is a part. Culture itself comes to be seen not only as feminine but as a particular sort of woman. She (I use the pronoun advisedly) is a prostitute, a gaudy painted commodity put up for sale by the pimps of modern culture, the middlemen and cultural impresarios, whose task, like the bookseller's efforts to equate a title-page with the neck of a beautiful woman, is to titillate and entice the audience to possess and to buy. The harlot is a commodity that can be purchased and a person that can be pursued; she is exploited and in a position of vulnerability and weakness. But she is also seen to have powers, the ability, once modesty has been abandoned, to enjoy a sort of liberty not available to other women, and to turn her charms to pecuniary and social advantage. (This double message of advantage and exploitation was reinforced by the wide range of circumstance – from royal mistress to immiserated street-walker – covered by the term harlot.)

As Hogarth well knew, it is in the image of the prostitute that all the greatest anxieties about eighteenth-century culture – its debasement into a trade or business, its association with sexual license, its ambiguous status as a realm of sensuality, sense, or reason, and its potential to privilege women – are to be found. The harlot, neither male nor polite, neither above commerce nor able to deny the carnal senses, was "the other," the figure that exemplified the immoderate passions, desires, and pleasures that were integral to the most polite age but whose suppression could acquit it of the charge of being the most vicious.

Bibliography

Addison, J. and Steele, R. (1965 [1711–14]) *The Spectator*, ed. with notes and intro. Donald F. Bond, 5 vols., Oxford: Clarendon Press.

Adventurer (1753–4) *The Adventurer*, 2 vols., London: J. Payne.

Alison, Archibald (1790) *Essays on the Nature and Principles of Taste*, London: J. J. G. Robinson & G. Robinson; Edinburgh: Bell & Bradfute.

Allen, Brian (1987) *Francis Hayman*, London and New Haven, CT: Yale University Press.

Allen, B. Sprague (1937) *Tides in English Taste (1619–1800): A Background for the Study of Literature*, 2 vols., Cambridge, MA: Harvard University Press.

Anon. (1752) *A Sketch of the Spring Gardens, Vauxhall. In a Letter to a Noble Lord*, London: G. Woodfall.

Anon. (1755) *The Devil on Crutches in England, or Night Scenes in London. A Satirical Work. Written upon a plan of the celebrated Diable Boiteux by M. Le Sage by a Gentleman of Oxford*, London.

Anon. (1762) *A Description of Vauxhall Gardens. Being a proper companion and guide for all who visit that place. Illustrated with copper plates*, London: S. Hooper.

Barker-Benfield, G. J. (1992) *The Culture of Sensibility. Sex and Society in Eighteenth-Century Britain*, Chicago and London: Chicago University Press.

Barry, Jonathan (1985) "Religion in the Georgian town," in *Life in the Georgian Town*, Bath, Som.: Georgian Group Annual Symposium.

Bate, Walter Jackson (1946) *From Classic to Romantic. Premises of Taste in Eighteenth-Century England*, Cambridge, MA: Harvard University Press.

Beattie, J. M. (1967) *The English Court in the Reign of George I*, London: Cambridge University Press.

Belanger, Terry (1982) "Publishers and writers in eighteenth-century England," in Isabel Rivers (ed.) *Books and their Readers in 18th-Century England*, Leicester: Leicester University Press; New York: St. Martin's, pp. 5–25.

Borsay, Peter (1989) *The English Urban Renaissance. Culture and Society in the Provincial Town, 1660–1760*, Oxford: Clarendon Press.

Brewer, John (1976) *Party Ideology and Popular Politics at the Accession of George III*, Cambridge: Cambridge University Press.

Britannica (1771) *Encyclopedia Britannica: or a Dictionary of Arts and Sciences, compiled upon a new Plan*, 3 vols., Edinburgh: A. Bell & C. Macfarquar.

Brown, John (1757) *An Estimate of the Manners and Principles of the Times*, 2nd edn., London: L. Davis & C. Reymers.

Bruntjen, Sven H. A. (1985) *John Boydell: a Study of Art Patronage and Publishing in Georgian London*, New York: Garland.

Bucholz, R. O. (1987) "The court in the reign of Queen Anne," DPhil. dissertation, University of Oxford.

[Burgh, James] (1746) *Britain's Remembrancer: or, the danger not over*, London: M. Cooper.

Burke, Edmund (1958) *A Philosophical Inquiry into the Origin of our Ideas of the Sublime and Beautiful*, ed. with intro. James T. Boulton, London: Routledge & Kegan Paul.

Burney, Frances (1970 [1778]) *Evelina: or the History of a Young Lady's Entrance into the World*, London: Oxford University Press.

Casanova, Jacques (1958–60) *The Memoirs of Jacques Casanova de Seingalt*, trans. Arthur Machen, 6 vols., New York: Putnam's; London: Elek.

Castle, Terry (1986) *Masquerade and Civilisation: the carnivalesque in eighteenth-century English culture and fiction*, Stanford, CA: Stanford University Press.

Caygill, Howard (1989) *Art of Judgement*, Oxford and Cambridge, MA: Blackwell.

Chambers, Ephraim (1788–91) *Cyclopedia, or an Universal Dictionary of Arts and Sciences*, 4 vols., London: J. F. & C Rivington.

Corry, John (1804) *Satirical View of London: or, a Descriptive Sketch of the English Metropolis with Strictures on Men and Manners*, 3rd edn., London: R. Ogle.

De Bolla, Peter (1989) *The Discourse of the Sublime. Readings in History, Aesthetics and the Subject*, Oxford and New York: Blackwell.

Earle, Peter (1989) *The Making of the English Middle Class: Business, society and life in London, 1660–1730*, London: Methuen.

Edelstein, T. J. (1983) *Vauxhall Gardens; with essays by T. J. Edelstein and Brian Allen*, New Haven, CT: Yale Center for British Art.

Fielding, Henry (1966 [1730]) *The Author's Farce (original version)*, ed. Charles B. Woods, Lincoln, NB: University of Nebraska.

Geiringer, Karl (1964) *Haydn, a Creative Life in Music*, London: Allen & Unwin.

Gerard, Alexander (1759) *An Essay on Taste*, London: A. Millar; Edinburgh: A. Kinkaid & J. Bell.

Gregory, Jeremy (1991) "Anglicanism and the arts: religion, culture and politics in the eighteenth century," in *Culture, Politics and Society in England*, ed. Jeremy Black and Jeremy Gregory, Manchester and New York: Manchester University Press.

Habermas, Jürgen (1989), *The Structural Transformation of the Public Sphere: An Inquiry into a Category of Bourgeois Society*, Cambridge, MA: MIT Press.

Harley, David (1968) *Music in Purcell's London: The Social Background*, London: Dennis Dobson.

Harris, James (1744) *Three Treatises. The first concerning Art. The second concerning Music, Painting and Poetry. The third concerning Happiness*, London.

Hooker, E. N. (1934) "The discussion of taste from 1750 to 1770," *Proceedings of the Modern Language Association* 49: 577–92.

Hume, David (1788) *Essays and Treatises on Several Subjects*, 2 vols., London: T. Cadel, C. Elliot, T. Kay; Edinburgh: C. Elliot.

Hume, Robert D. (ed.) (1980) *The London Theatre World, 1660–1800*. Carbondale, IL: Southern Illinois Press.

Hutcheson, Francis (1725) *Inquiry into the Original of our Ideas of Beauty and Virtue*, London: J. Darby.

Johnson, Samuel (1905) *The Lives of the Poets*, ed. E. B. Hill, 3 vols., Oxford: Clarendon Press.

Klein, Lawrence E. (1984–5) "Shaftesbury and the progress of politeness," *Eighteenth-Century Studies* 18, 2: 186–214.

—— (1989) "Liberty, manners and politeness in early 18th-century England," *Historical Journal* 32: 583–605.

Kristeller, Paul Oskar (1961, 1965) *Renaissance Thought*, 2 vols., New York, Evanston, IL and London: Harper & Row.

Lackington, James (1790?) *Memoirs written by himself*, London: [published by the author].

Langford, Paul (1989) *A Polite and Commercial People: England 1727–1783*, Oxford: Clarendon Press.

La Volpa, Anthony J. (1992) "Conceiving a public: ideas and society in eighteenth-century Europe," *Journal of Modern History* 64: 79–116.

McKendrick, N., Brewer, J. and Plumb, J. H. (1983) *The Birth of a Consumer Society: The Commercialization of Eighteenth-Century England*, London: Europa.

Mandeville, Bernard (1924) *The Fable of the Bees: or, Private Vices, publick benefits*, with a commentary, critical, historical and explanatory by F. B. Kaye, 2 vols., Oxford: Clarendon Press.

Money, John (1977) *Experience and Identity: Birmingham and the West Midlands 1760–1800*, Manchester: Manchester University Press.

More, Hannah (1799) *Strictures on the Modern System of Female Education*, 2nd edn., 2 vols., London: T. Cadell & W. Davies.

Orgel, Stephen (1975) *The Illusion of Power: political theater in the English Renaissance*, Berkeley, CA: University of California Press.

Paulson, Ronald (1972) *Rowlandson. An Interpretation*, New York: Oxford University Press.

—— (1989) *Breaking and Remaking. Aesthetic Practice in England 1700–1820*, New Brunswick, NJ: Rutgers University Press.

Pears, Iain (1988) *The Discovery of Painting: The Growth of Interest in the Arts in England 1680–1768*, New Haven, CT: Yale University Press.

Pedicord, Henry William (1954) *The Theatrical Public in the Time of Garrick*, New York: Columbia University Press.

The Polite Lady, or a course of female education; in a series of letters, from a mother to her daughter (1759) London.

Rogers, Pat (1985) *Literature and Popular Culture in Eighteenth-Century England*, Sussex: Harvester; Totowa, NJ: Barnes & Noble.

Roworth, W. Wassyng (ed.) (1992) *Angelica Kauffman. A Continental Artist in Georgian England*, London: Reaktion.

Sekora, John (1977) *Luxury: the concept in Western Thought, Eden to Smollett*, Baltimore, MD: Johns Hopkins University Press.

Shaftesbury, Anthony Ashley Cooper, 3rd. earl of (1914) *Second Characters, or, the Language of Forms*, ed. Benjamin Rand, Cambridge: Cambridge University Press.

Shevelow, Katharine (1989) *Women and Print Culture: the construction of femininity in the early periodical*, London and New York: Routledge.

Spector, Robert Donald (1966) *English Literary Periodicals and the Climate of Opinion during the Seven Years War*, The Hague: Mouton.

Spencer, Jane (1986) *The Rise of the Woman Novelist from Aphra Behn to Jane Austen*, Oxford: Blackwell.

Stolnitz, J. (1961–2) "On the origins of 'aesthetic disinterestednes,' " *Journal of Aesthetics and Art Criticism* 20: 131–43.

Temperley, Nicholas (1979) *The Music of the English Parish Church*, 2 vols. Cambridge: Cambridge University Press.

Todd, Janet (1984) *A Dictionary of British and American Women Writers, 1660–1800*, London: Methuen.

—— (1986) *Sensibility: An Introduction*, London and New York: Methuen.

Waterhouse, Ellis (1981) *Dictionary of British 18th-Century Painters in oils and crayons*, Woodbridge, Suffolk: Antique Collectors Club.

Whitley, William T. (1928) *Artists and their Friends in England 1700–1799*, 2 vols. London and Boston, MA: Medici Society.

Wroth, Warwick (1896) *The London Pleasure Gardens of the Eighteenth Century*, London and New York: Macmillan.

Young, Edward (1728) *Love of Fame the Universal Passion in Seven Characteristical Satires*, London: J. Tonson.

19
Politeness for plebes
Consumption and social identity in early eighteenth-century England

Lawrence E. Klein

The English eighteenth century was an age of politeness, at least to judge by those contemporaries who used the word "polite" to describe not only their era, but themselves, their civilization and some of its important elements. "Politeness" and a related vocabulary, including "good breeding," "refinement," "sociability," and "manners," ranged widely in social and cultural discussion, referring to social behaviour, linguistic and artistic expression and the largest generalities to be made about society and culture. Indeed, politeness can be seen to correspond to a range of distinctive social and cultural practices in eighteenth-century England.

The prestige of politeness is, in part, explained by developments within elite culture. The "polite" were the "better sort," the Quality, the gentlemen and ladies of England. Since "politeness" was often used as a rough equivalent of "gentlemanliness" or "gentility," it marked distinctions in the social order, signifying and congratulating an elite. Indeed, "politeness" came into prominence as part of the process by which the English elite reconstructed itself in the later seventeenth and early eighteenth centuries: it helped to formulate the hegemony of the landed classes and their supporters, as religion was definitively subordinated to social and political discipline, as the royal court shrank in cultural stature, and as metropolitan London took over in generating cultural values.[1] In this way, politeness constituted an oligarchical culture for a post-courtly and post-godly society with a growing metropolis.

The same process, it can be argued, served to heighten the exclusivity of the upper classes so that the rise of politeness seems to fit with the model of a progressive divorce of elite from popular culture during the early modern period (Muchembled 1978; Revel 1989: 167 ff.; Everitt 1969: 48 ff.; Burke 1978; Wrightson 1982; Thompson 1973–4; Reay 1985a; Fletcher and Stevenson 1985; Borsay 1989: 284–308). The model asserts that while, in earlier centuries, clear and unquestioned distinctions in social rank were not matched by clear and self-consciously elaborated distinctions in cultural forms, this pattern changed in the seventeenth and eighteenth centuries, with European elites seeking more vigorously to assert differences between themselves and other members of society. Since "politeness" was a term of distinction that foregrounded cultural achievements, it appears to exercise exactly the sort of "exclusivizing" function called for by the model.

I wish to confront this line of interpretation with the fact that politeness was marketed in books to an audience wider than the gentry and pseudo-gentry. Politeness was purveyed to non-elite individuals in an array of manuals and encyclopedic guides, which are the center of this investigation. In this chapter, I have generally restricted myself to publications between 1660 and 1730, the period during which "politeness" rose to prominence in English discourse.[2] This period contains the lives of Shaftesbury, Addison, and Steele, whose writings did so much to promote "politeness." It also corresponds almost precisely to the dates of Daniel Defoe, who figures among the manual writers considered here and whose life experience was like that of many manual readers. Finally, this period corresponds to the London portrayed in Peter Earle's synoptic *Making of the English Middle Class* (1989). It was among the middling Londoners, surveyed in that book, that we would find readers of the material I have been investigating.

Interpreting this phenomenon raises questions on two levels. First, plebeian interest in politeness necessitates asking just who was polite in the eighteenth century. The phenomenon of plebeian politeness raises the possibility that the gentlemanly associations of politeness are not an altogether reliable guide to its social interpretation.

In turn, these questions necessitate reflecting on the question of identity itself, of selfhood or self-conception, in a society of the sort that England was becoming by the early eighteenth century. This society was characterized by rising expectations of material comfort, social mobility, and the consumption of artifacts and images that mediated economic and sociological fluidity. In such a society, social identities, at least for certain segments of the population, were adaptive and dynamic. Interpretation therefore requires a model of identity that can take account of the self's pragmatic adaptations in fluid circumstances.

I will return to this level of reflection in the conclusion of this chapter. However, the answer I offer to the first question is adumbrated in the observation of Guy Miège, published in 1707, that the English were characterized by "a general Emulation, striving to live Well, and make a good Figure" (Miège 1707: II, 4). In his unembarrassed coordinating of economic well-being with social self-presentation, Miège suggests the close and interesting relations that obtained between two zones of human experience: utility and economic productivity, on one hand, and ornamentation and display, on the other.[3] My straw man is the tendency to distinguish these zones too neatly and to set them in opposition.

One instance of this tendency is the very supposition, mentioned above, that "politeness" was restrictively an attribute of the landed elite and its fellow-travelers. Another is the matching supposition that the middling sorts were wholly given over to utilitarian production. According to one standard view, commercial society demanded a personality capable of rational calculation and accumulation (Weber 1927: 352–69; Weber 1930; Bell 1976; Macpherson 1962). Thus, the commercial personality was said to be constructed from such materials as industry, frugality, discipline, prudence, inner resourcefulness, integrity, and, generally, an orientation towards productivity and utility. Commerce, it was said, required a possessive individualist, a worldly ascetic, a vocational man, and the masculine gender of this construct was underscored by its putative embodiment in the figure of Robinson Crusoe.

However, as attention among economic historians has shifted in recent years to consumption as a key feature of the eighteenth-century British economy (in the words of one historian, from a supply-side to a demand-side approach to economic history [Neil McKendrick in McKendrick, Brewer, and Plumb 1985: 5]), there has been an accompanying shift in the assessment of the social personality of members of a commercial society.[4] Commercial personality conceived under the sign of consumption rather than accumulation required such qualities as the desire for pleasure and comfort, a willingness to spend, playfulness, and ambitions to emulate and display. The latter were expressed in capacities and interests concerned with the "ornamental" aspects of life, such as taste, style, fashion, and politeness. These aspects of commercial culture seem better personified by Roxana than Robinson.

Thus, the identity of the "polite" cannot be confined to patricians. I have called this chapter "Politeness for plebes" precisely because the model of eighteenth-century English society as fractured between a patriciate and plebs is inadequate to describe both social and cultural relations in the period.[5] This was not a society in which social boundaries were being tended, or could be, with maximal tidiness, especially when we think of those segments of the population whose paths intersected in the urban and commercial zone. As contemporaries recognized and historians have reiterated, English society was a finely calibrated gradient of conditions, without crude and easily legible gaps (Porter 1982: 63 ff.). Moreover, prosperity, social and geographic mobility, and consumerism meant that it was common for people to experience changes of condition during their lives, often for the better. Hence, as Miège pointed out, people were in a position to redefine their own horizons and identities by looking farther along the social incline. Prosperity allowed the commercial community to engage in the pursuits of gentility.[6] At the same time, the landed classes were closely tied to the upper segment of the commercial classes, through commercial investment, through the migration of younger sons into the business world, and through intermarriage (Earle 1989: 6–7, 86–9). As both response and stimulus to these patterns, London grew, serving as a matrix for social and cultural interchange among the middling and upper sorts.

Problems of social identification and classification

It is not surprising that this context complicated the discourse of social identification and classification. An obvious instance is the term "gentleman," which sagged into semantic limpness during this period. While members of the armigerous landholding elite might claim an exclusive right to be called "gentleman," many others appropriated the label. As early as 1691, Miège commented that the word was applied to anyone with "a liberal, or genteel Education, that looks Gentleman-like (whether he be so, or not) and has wherewithall to live freely and handsomely" (Miège 1691: 226; also, *Tatler* no. 207; *Spectator* nos. 75, 202; *Guardian* nos. 34, 137; Chamberlayne 1723: 174–6; Earle 1976: 158–60; Earle 1989: 6–7; Porter 1982: 64–5). The term's promiscuity reached an interesting extreme in the mid-century when a commentator exclaimed: "We are a Nation of Gentry. We have no such thing as Common People among us;

between Vanity and Gin the whole Species is utterly destroyed" (a 1755 number of *The World* cited in Corfield 1987: 44).

The bagginess of "gentleman" was only one component of the problem of social identification and classification in this period. Penelope Corfield (1987) has recently pointed out that in the eighteenth century social change and particularly social mobility disrupted inherited categories of social classification, making for a distinct epoch of categorial proliferation between the earlier age of "ranks" and the later age of "classes." Corfield, like other social historians (Cressy 1976; Wrightson 1986), takes a narrow approach to the question of social classification, focusing on language explicating social hierarchy and economic functions. However, her general point is underscored by taking a broader view of classificatory language and schemes, particularly a view that includes the range of cultural distinctions, among which "politeness" figured prominently. If anything, the impression of energy and unease in the realm of social classification is amplified when one looks at cultural categories.

Contemporaries were aware of the fluidity of classificatory language. The age abounded in censors and censoriousness, and, as classically educated contemporaries realized, the job of the Roman censors was initially to sort the population into groups for assessment, an activity out of which evolved their concern with maintaining moral standards. Isaac Bickerstaffe, the Censor of *The Tatler*, made clear (in no. 162) that moral criticism and categorization were closely related operations. (See the classificatory arabesque in *Spectator* no. 442. Some characteristic statements about censoriousness are: T. P. Blount 1691: preface; *The Character of the Beaux* 1696: A3r; Defoe, The Review: I, 2. John Barrell (1983) has written a stimulating account of the search for social comprehension in the eighteenth century.) More generally, throughout the *Tatler*, the *Spectator*, and many other publications of the period, categories of people proliferated, foregrounding the difficulties of social comprehension under contemporary conditions.

An instance of the complexity of social language is provided by the semantics of "politeness" itself. "Refined yet sociable gentility" expressed the gist of "politeness." (For a survey of "politeness" and its meanings, see Klein 1984–5.) At least, many usages of "politeness" contained one or more of the three elements in that formula: (1) sociability, submitting behavior or expression to social discipline; (2) refinement, polishing and making outwardly kempt; and (3) gentility, marking affinities with the highest group in the social order.

However, while that formulation is useful, it is also helpful to examine the terms to which "politeness" was opposed. One obvious antonym of "politeness" was "vulgarity." Indeed, it might be expected that a chapter concerning "politeness" and social identity would revolve principally around this antagonism. However, "vulgarity" was only one of several terms to which "politeness" was juxtaposed. Moreover, the polarity of "politeness" and "vulgarity" was not the principal motif for "politeness" in the early eighteenth century. (That polarity, it seems to me, grew more dominant in the course of the eighteenth century and into the nineteenth.) Another term with which "politeness" was juxtaposed was "rusticity," which facilitated cultural discriminations on the metropolitan–provincial axis. Still another was "barbarity," which enabled distinctions between modernity and the past, between England and the Continent, and between the "western" and the non-"western."

However, it is another juxtaposition involving "politeness" that is of particular interest here, the juxtaposition between the "polite" and the "productive" or "useful." For instance, writers often set "polite learning" against "useful learning." While "useful learning" was solid and substantial, "polite learning" was ornamental.[7] More pertinently, "polite" people could be contrasted to "useful" people. The "useful part of mankind" were "industrious" or "busy" or "business" people (the middling sorts) or they were "laborious" or "laboring" or "mechanick" people (the lower sort or the common people). The "useful" were "productive." Meanwhile, the "polite" were those who turned leisure to account through a dedication to the ornamental, to fashion, style, and display.

This polarity between the "polite" and the "productive" differed from the polarities "polite"/"vulgar," "polite"/"rustic," and "polite"/"barbaric." The latter relations were clearly antonymous and exclusive ones. Such an outright antagonism did not necessarily apply in the case of the "polite" and the "useful," since the two terms in the relation could be mutually dependent.

To be specific, the "polite" was often seen as supplemental to the "productive." For instance, a commonplace of the literature of "politeness" was that "Merit will not do the Work, if it be not seconded by Agreeableness" (Boyer 1702: 104). As the ability to present oneself, "politeness" was a way of setting off one's capacities so that they could operate effectively. "Politeness" was ornamentation, to be sure, but a necessary and useful form of ornamentation. In the words of one polite source: "The *How* does much in all Things" (Gracian 1685: 11; a similar idea appears in *Tatler* no. 30 and *Guardian* no. 149). Similarly, it was often said that "politeness" was a way to set off useful knowledge so that it became more useful, an idea conveyed in a couplet by the earl of Roscommon: "None have been with *Admiration*, read, / But who (beside their *Learning*) were Well-Bred" (Dillon 1685: 5; also, Hughes 1697: I, 247–8; Molesworth 1694: 40; S. C. 1677: A3r–A4r; Gracian 1685: 84).

Thus, compared with the antinomy between the "polite" and the "vulgar," the relation between the "polite" and the "productive" was both more flexible and more complex. This has a bearing on the use of "politeness" as a social classification. For, in this period, "politeness" did not serve principally as a wall to segregate a small polite elite from the vulgar. Rather, "politeness" was used to help articulate a complex and evolving set of social and cultural relations involving the traditional landed elite, along with the non-landed pseudo-gentry, and a spectrum of elements within the "useful" part of the population, the variety of middling sorts. Serving as a map for the socially mobile or even an ideal trajectory of social ambition, "politeness" helped to coordinate diverse elements in the population.

Coordinating effects are the subject of the rest of this chapter. However, a particularly graphic instance is worth mentioning. Since the public promenade was an ideal setting for enacting refined yet sociable gentility, many were constructed in British towns during the eighteenth century. In *The English Urban Renaissance* (1989), Peter Borsay describes at least two instances (the Gravel Walks at Bath and the Pantiles at Tunbridge Wells[8]) in which public promenades were built on two levels for the use of different populations: the upper, for the "better sort"; the lower, for the "common sort." Borsay uses these instances as evidence of widening social polarization and heightened exclusivity of the upper classes (1989: 293). However, these instances seem more striking as evidence of a reconstructed coordination of different elements in society during the eighteenth century. On these promenades, different elements in society shared a common form of sociability and social display, even if separated by an altitude of several feet.

Very Useful Manuals

"Politeness" was purveyed to plebeians in an array of non-fictional books of secular improvement, books offering people what they needed to pursue a given occupation or to assume or reinforce a certain social personality. Some taught the widely applicable skills of writing and arithmetic. Some contained technical information geared to specific occupations (for merchants and tradesmen, for "secretaries," scriveners, and clerks, for attorneys and solicitors). Some digested learned and/or practical information (from epitomes of astronomy and geography to collections of recipes and domestic techniques). And some instructed in social skills. (See the Bibliography section on Very Useful Manuals.)

Their titles misleadingly suggest a set of discrete subgenres: "companions," "vade mecums," "helpes," "manuals," "academys," dictionaries, encyclopedias, "family-books," and so forth. (There were also those that promised to embody a "compleat" practice.) However, any individual specimen is hard to classify since these books were usually amalgamations of heterogeneous materials. (See Plates 19.3 and 19.4.) Many were literally pastiches, assembled from previously published materials. (These were publishers' gambits rather than authorial projects. While some of the Very Useful Manuals imputed authorship to an individual, more were anonymous. Alleged authorship was sometimes purely fictive: a book's content might evolve strikingly over a century of republication while the title and "author" stayed the same. Cf. the versions of *A Helpe to Discourse*, discussed below, or the seventeen (at least) editions of *A Thousand Notable Things* published between 1579 and 1815 and all ascribed to Thomas Lupton. This Lupton is to *A Thousand Notable Things* as Noah Webster is to my *Ninth New Collegiate Dictionary*.) Their total lack of integrity is part of their claim on our attention: the very qualities that have made them seem below historical interest were those that appealed to their original readers.

Since these books were produced under the sign of utility, I call them (in deference to the title of one) Very Useful Manuals (Mather 1681). Their frequent claim to be "useful and necessary" was based on the fact that they were indeed guides to practice ("pearles of practice") (Hill 1688: A3r; N. H. 1737: A3r; Hatton 1699: A4v; G. J. 1720: preface; N. H. 1684: [full title] A2r–v; *A New Academy of Complements* 1715: A3r; *A New Academy of Complements* 1748 [a different work from the preceding one of the same title]: 1). However, this claim was often reinforced by a recognition that the practices with respect to which these books guided people were themselves useful ones, concerning the business of society. England (the manuals repeated) was a trading nation (N. H. 1684: 2; J. P. 1684: A4v), and, as one of the "companions" put it, "For as to the Subject of the Book in General, I have this satisfaction, that (morally speaking) there's none more useful, because none more advantageous; for 'tis to TRAFFICK that the Riches, Strength and Grandure of all Nations is chiefly owing, and particularly that of this our

Island" (Hatton 1716: A3v-A4r). (The passage continues: "which no Country (tho' much superior in Acres) exceeds in Universal Commerce, nor any that makes a greater figure in the World" – a close echo of Miège's coordination of economic well-being and self-presentation, discussed above.) A book concerned with trade was bound to be useful.

The Very Useful Manuals were practical reading for common readers. The books signalled their intended readership in a variety of ways. Despite the fact that some of these books were directed at occupational specialties, they generally aimed for inclusiveness. They proclaimed their universal usefulness, being designed for "every Man's Occasions," "for every Man's Garden," or for "Persons of all Ranks and Conditions" (Cocker 1675: A3v; Curzon 1712: I, iv; G. J. 1720: preface). They often aimed at the young without relinquishing the goal of edifying all ages (Hill 1689: A3r-v). They indicated their intellectual inclusiveness by stating that they were suitable for the "meanest Capacity" or "easie to an indifferent Capacity" or "useful to any understanding" (Winstanley 1684: A2r-v; Hill 1688: 3; Cocker 1675: A3v). Finally, they often advertised the fact that they sought a female readership, aiming at "all degrees of people of either sex" or, in other cases, at women alone (Hill 1689: A3r-v; *The Universal Family Book* 1703: A1r; N. H. 1694; M. B. 1639; M. B. 1654; M. B. 1667; *The Ladies Cabinet* 1743; W. M. 1655; W. M. 1710).

Such direct pronouncements were supported by other statements. Some of the manuals pointed out that, since they were free of the learned languages, they were educationally inclusive (Cocker 1675: A3v; Curzon 1712: iii). Many made a virtue of their concision, on the assumption that ordinary readers desired instruction without the temporal and financial burdens of erudition (Curzon 1712: iii; Hill 1688: A3v; N. H. 1684: A2r). The books often called direct attention to their modest price, which put them within the range of a wider part of the population (*An Universal, Historical, Geographical, Chronological and Poetical Dictionary* 1703: A4r; *The Complete Family-Piece* 1737: x; Mather 1681: A2r-v). They accomplished the same thing indirectly by promising to save the reader money. The information in the book, they claimed, would allow the reader to do for himself or herself what might otherwise have to be paid for. In particular, a number of the books emphasized that they would allow the reader to evade the necessity of paying for professional help, especially for lawyers or commercial writers (Cocker 1675: A3v; Hill 1689: A3r-v; *Universal Family Book* 1703: preface; *Complete Family-Piece* 1737: v).

Very Useful Manuals were, in fact, reasonably priced for people of the middling sort. Like many other small books (octavo- and duodecimo-sized books, of 100 to 300 pages, simply printed, with no engravings or crude ones), they cost about one shilling though sometimes 1s 6d (*Mundus Foppensis* 1691: final sigs. – trade list for John Harris, at the Harrow, in the Poultry; Lupton 1706: I, 2, II, 2, III, 2 – trade lists for G. Conyers, at the Gold Ring, in Little Britain; L. B. *et al.* 1671: A1r [title-page]; *A New Academy of Complements* 1715: A1r [title-page]). This was more than the cost of a typical chapbook (of 24 or 48 pages), which went for no more than sixpence, or an almanac, which usually sold for three or four (Burke 1985: 49; Spufford 1981: 91–8; Capp 1979: 41, 397 n. 114). However, it was a good deal less than the cost of the finely printed volumes that inhabited the shelves of gentlemanly libraries. It should be remembered that those who bought Very Useful Manuals were probably not habitual book-buyers.

Recognizing this, some Very Useful Manuals vaunted their heterogeneity as a kind of comprehensiveness obviating the need for further book purchases.

The very existence of this genre implies an environment in which the range of human employments was diverse and expanding and in which skill and merit were acquired. Servicing the occupational and social identities of common readers, these books projected a setting in which individuals had latitude to fashion themselves. Indeed, some Very Useful Manuals presented themselves explicitly as handles on an environment in which ambition combined with endeavor promised worldly success (e.g. N. H. 1737; Lupton 1702?; *The Way to Promotion* 1682; Campbell 1757).

Commercial selves

The Very Useful Manuals offered many representations of and appeals to the commercial self as conventionally conceived. John Hill wrote *The Exact Dealer* (1688) "for the Benefit of Traders, and Artists of sundry kinds," or those generally who comprise "the Industrious part of Men." "My main aim and drift," wrote Hill, "is, to admonish and direct Men how to improve themselves, and rise by Industry in Trading and managing Affairs." The commercial self engaged in a practical but not particularly polite sort of self-fashioning. Before launching a survey of heterogeneous materials, Hill announced that two "most desirable" objects were "*Profit* and *Advantage*" and that specific qualities (understanding, prudence, diligence, caution, and industry) conduced to them (1688: 1). Similarly, *The Compleat Tradesman* by N. H. endorsed intelligence, industry, caution, and frugality (1684: 1–17 *passim*). Edward Hatton's *Merchant's Magazine*, before moving on to its pastiche of information, dissected the merchant's requisite natural parts (apprehension, judgment, physical constitution), morals (fortitude, prudence, justice), and acquired parts (various linguistic and arithmetic skills and subject areas) (1699: A2v-A3r). This sort of writing, which points towards Defoe's *Complete English Tradesman* of the mid-1720s, does evoke a world of Weberian commercial vocation.

The gentlemanlike

However, Very Useful Manuals also held out the promise of a kind of gentility – if not the "really" gentlemanly, at least the "gentleman-like," a term suggesting a possible arc of social aspiration. Curzon's *Universal Library* (1712) claimed to embellish knowledge so that "Youth may be thereby Endued with Learning and Gentleman-like Qualities for their Advancement or Conversation" (1712: II, A2r-v). *The Young Secretary's Guide* by John Hill was a treasury of verbal models to enhance "Learning and Civility" (1689: 15). Meanwhile, the preface to *Wit's Cabinet* (1700?) was more implicit in its assertion to introduce the reader to the gentlemanlike by promising that the book would compensate the indigent reader for his or her inability to afford a Grand Tour. If books in this bibliography sometimes ascribed to themselves gentlemanlike purposes, they labeled their contents in a similar way. Charles Blount's *Janua Scientiarum* (1684) was subtitled "a compendious introduction to . . . all genteel sorts of literature" (Air). E. S.'s *Wit and*

Eloquence offered models of letters that were "curious" and "elegant" and done with "nicity" (1697: 1), while other Very Useful Manuals presented their contents as specimens of modishness and fashionability (Hill 1689: 2; Philomusus 1650: A1r; *Wit's Cabinet* 1700?: preface; *A New Academy of Complements* 1748: A3r).

One way in which the gentlemanlike was disseminated in Very Useful Manuals was the insertion in humble textual surroundings of actual rules of politeness. Rules of politeness appeared in a number of books intended for readerships which were not gentle at all. (Some examples are: *The Way to Promotion* 1682; E. S. 1697; *Wit's Cabinet* 1700?; *The Compleat Academy of Complements* 1705; *A New Academy of Complements* 1748.)

A particularly interesting example is a book directed to the commonest of readers and book-buyers in many editions through the seventeenth and eighteenth centuries. First published in 1619, it was called, in the early seventeenth century, *A Helpe to Discourse* and, in the later seventeenth and early eighteenth centuries, *The New Helpe to Discourse*.[9] It was a collection of material from a variety of authors, much of it digested into dialogues, dialogues "being," according to the 1669 preface, "the most easiest to the meanest capacity." According to the editor, the work aimed at those who, in the absence of accessible and cheap edification, might not pursue it on account of its "tediousness and chargeableness." However, his work offered these people an alternative to simply sitting "dumb" in the presence of "knowing persons" (Winstanley 1669: A2r-v).

Almost half of the 1669 edition's 300 pages consisted of questions and answers on religious, ethical, natural philosophical, and historical topics. Then came, among other matter, "A Discourse of Wonders, Foreign and Domestical," a thumbnail history of the English kings, jests, poems, epigrams, riddles, acrostics, anagrams, and a section of specialized information for the sake of the countryman. This sort of motley comprised the content of *A Helpe* and *The New Helpe to Discourse* throughout their history from the early seventeenth century through the eighteenth. Nonetheless, there were many revealing changes over that period: less space devoted to religious topics and to the supernatural (magic declined!); less space concerning the countryman (an increasingly urban audience!); the elimination of unseemliness, such as jokes about the body, and of anti-Jewish and anti-Papist remarks (the rise of politeness confirmed!). The additions were also interesting: some contemporary "political arithmetick"; information pertaining to English industries and trades; more classical references. Thus, the editions of *A Helpe* and *The New Helpe* offer a panorama of cultural change and stasis at the level of the grossest printed popularization.

A most interesting change in the content of *The New Helpe* was the addition in 1684 of a section called "Rules of Civility and Decent Behaviour." These "Rules" continued to appear through the eighteenth-century editions. Aside from invoking some general principles ("Every Action . . . ought to be done with some sign of respect to those that are present"), the rules covered several standard zones of politeness: bodily control, consumption of food, apparel, intercourse in general, and conversation in particular (Winstanley 1684: 272–93).

Such rules were entirely conventional. Indeed, their appearance in *The New Helpe to Discourse* offers a paragon instance of downward cultural trickle. These "Rules" were lifted wholesale from a book called *Youths Behaviour*, translated by Francis Hawkins, which first appeared about 1640 and, by 1692, was in its eleventh edition. *Youths*

Behaviour, in turn, was a translation of *Bienséance de la conversation entre les hommes*, written (so it said) by students at the Jesuit academy of La Flèche and first printed in French in 1617. It comprised a list of instructions for youngsters on behaviour, but its inspiration has been shown to be Giovanni della Casa's *Galateo*, published in 1559 and an ur-source for courtesy literature north of the Alps for the next two centuries.[10] In 1684, there was a new matching of this courtesy material with the audience of *The New Helpe*.

On the basis of the Very Useful Manuals, then, it would appear that politeness was being purveyed to plebeian audiences and that there was a quite common readership for some sorts of polite material. How do we account for this phenomenon?

To begin with, there was a large, eligible readership in London itself (leaving aside provincial and rural readerships). At the beginning of the eighteenth century, metropolitan London had a population of about a half-million. At least a fifth of these belonged to middling households, supported by manufacturing, trade, finance, and the professions. Among such people, literacy was almost universal (Earle 1989: 10, 65, 80–1). However, since the middling sorts of London ranged from an *haute bourgeoisie* of great merchants and successful professionals down to self-employed artisans and educated white-collar workers on salaries, politeness would have come in handy to different segments of the London middling population in different ways.

Social metamorphosis

At the upper end of the middling sort of early eighteenth-century London was a greater bourgeoisie of merchants and professionals, whose interests might explain the marketing of politeness in plebeian publications. It might be argued that, when a useful and industrious member of the upper middling sort really made it, he became anxious to leap from the realm of utility and industry to that of politeness and gentility. He therefore bought an estate, setting himself up as a country gentleman. Thus, it might be suggested, the inclusion of "polite" material in manuals served these special cases of social mobility.

Occasionally, the Very Useful Manuals represented themselves as instructing those making the metamorphosis from "industrious" to "polite." For instance, *The Complete Family-Piece* identified hunting, angling, and gardening as distinctive of the country gentleman's life and then provided chapters on these activities "for the Benefit and Advantage therefore of such Gentlemen who retire from Business to live in the Country" (1737: vii).

However, there are a number of objections to this suggestion. First, it seems unlikely that the merchant-prince who had achieved this level of success would have turned to the crummy books that constitute my bibliography of Very Useful Manuals. There were lots of tonier guides which represented themselves as exclusively for gentlemen. With titles such as *The Gentleman's Companion* (1672, by William Ramesay), *The Compleat Gentleman* (1678, by Jean Gailhard) and *The Gentleman's Recreation* (1686, by Richard Blome), they invited a readership of provincial gentry and pseudo-gentry, and they seem apt purchases for would-be landed gentlemen, retiring from business.

But would someone who had achieved such success really need a book to help him or his household make the transition? In *Tatler* no. 46, Steele depicted a City plutocrat who regularly adjourned his money-making on the Exchange late in the afternoon to go to Will's coffee-house "where the Tast is refin'd, and a Relish giv'n to Men's Possessions, by a polite Skill in gratifying their Passions and Appetites." This vignette suggests that the plutocrat was already engaged in a form of life that "refined" him and was therefore not in need of books to facilitate the process. Indeed, this was the sort of City personality who showed up on the subscription lists for the *Spectator* or for Pope's works (Speck 1982). In other words, he was capable of making good on a quite extensive definition of "politeness."

The fact that, as the vignette suggests, it was possible to combine the life of commerce with that of politeness points to a final objection to the idea that City gentlemen needed manuals on politeness to make the transition to landed status. The fact is that it was the rare City man who sought this transition. Whatever may have happened at other moments in English history, London successes of the early eighteenth century were not turning themselves into classic landed gentlemen. They did often buy estates, but generally in the Home Counties in easy reach of London. Thus, they became gentlemanlike owners of suburban estates, with continued ties to the City (Lang 1974; Horwitz 1987; Rogers 1979; Earle 1989: 152–7; Stone and Stone 1984).

Commercial affability

Another explanation for the appearance of "polite" material in Very Useful Manuals is indicated in some of the manuals themselves, which suggest that forms of politeness were intrinsic to commercial experience. While trading was fueled by the pursuit of gain, the actual practice of trade was sufficiently social to demand a good deal of social form. This was particularly true when trade was considered from the standpoint of consumption, and tradespeople were conceived as retailers to customers. Since, by the later seventeenth century, most Londoners bought many items in shops, shopkeepers comprised one of the largest subgroups within the middling order (Earle 1989: 44–5).

In his *Merchant's Magazine* (1699), Edward Hatton listed affability among the ethical traits of the commercial person. Affability, he wrote, "makes him of an easie Access, gains him Love and Affection, and makes all that know him delight to deal with him" (A2v). Affability was an aspect of politeness, of course, since politeness was the art of pleasing and thereby of gaining the love and esteem of fellows. (A typical statement is presented in a definition of complaisance as "an Art to regulate our words and behaviour, in such a manner as we may engage the love and respect of those with whom we Converse" – S. C. 1677: 1.)

Defoe (1725–7) made a similar point thirty years later when he wrote that one key to successful business was social discipline, a necessity imposed by the vicissitudes of interaction. In the face of impoliteness, the tradesman had to be patient, capable of bearing provocation and impertinence with outward equanimity. The tradesman's spontaneous and often passionate response to customers had to be mediated since "the man that stands behind the counter must be all courtesy, civility and good manners." In a short narrative anecdote contained in this discussion, the model tradesman was praised as "the most obliging, most gentleman-like man, of a tradesman" (I, 105, 110–11).

Thus, contemporaries perceived that commercial life itself demanded a kind of politeness, a commercial affability. One interesting aspect of commercial affability is that it defies the widely accepted idea that the spread of manners was all downward trickle, from courts to aristocracies in general and from aristocracies in general to the middling sorts. The fact is that the rules for courtly success and for commercial success were similar in many ways. Politeness arose in both quarters.

However, commercial affability is not a sufficient explanation for the "politeness" phenomena in the Very Useful Manuals. The role of politeness in commercial societies was more complex than this, and politeness impinged on plebeians in more complicated ways, as Defoe's *Complete English Tradesman* also makes clear.

The cultural contradiction of commercial society

The Complete English Tradesman can be seen as a Very Useful Manual, expanding on the existential aspects and shrinking the technical aspects of earlier Very Useful Manuals. However, it was also an exploration of the cultural contradiction of commercial society, which Defoe sought to unmask and confront. (This formulation is borrowed from Bell 1976. According to Bell, the cohesion of bourgeois values and society achieved in the nineteenth century has broken down in the twentieth in a radical disjunction between society and culture, between "an economic principle defined in terms of efficiency and functional rationality" and a culture that is "prodigal" and "promiscuous," involving, "in its emphasis on display, a reckless squandering of resources" (21–2, 36–7). The thrust of this chapter is to foreground the tension between these principles from the very start of the capitalist age.)

To Defoe, the necessary traits of a tradesman were obvious: sobriety, frugality, caution, industry, diligence, care, and pain. However, "the temper of the times" made fulfilling these expectations difficult for the tradesman. The tradesman could not survive without credit, but getting credit required certain forms of display, which were expensive and therefore dangerous to commercial health (Defoe 1725–7: vii–viii). (On the centrality of credit in the economic activities of the middling sort, see Earle 1989: 26, 115–16. The ubiquity of credit is attested in Very Useful Manuals, which frequently have sections on handling credit or bringing in debts.) In this way, the commercial person, for all his or her habituation to the zone of utility and productivity, had to broach the zone of ornamentation and display.

In other ways too, Defoe's tradesperson was tempted away from the straight and narrow path of calculation towards the more pleasurable route of display. Defoe defined commercial virtues against such temptations. Thus, industry was defined against abandonment of one's shop to spend time in the coffee-house or any other milieu of sociability. Frugality was defined against expenditure for one's own (or household's) clothing and entertainment or for the ornamentation of one's shop. Moreover, since the commercial person often entered into commerce with those who were wealthier or politer, he or she was liable to imitate them (Defoe 1725–7: 47, 48, 56–7, 119–20, 124, 127, 128 ff., 133–52, 312–20, 370–6).

While Defoe was very anxious to draw neat distinctions between the busy trading part of the population and the leisured gentle part, reality withheld from him the joys of

374   Lawrence E. Klein

tidy distinction. His consequent disappointment comes across nowhere more clearly than in his assertion that "this is an age of gallantry and gaiety, and never was the city transpos'd to the court as it is now: the play-houses and balls are now filled with citizens and young tradesmen, instead of gentlemen and families of distinction; the shop-keepers wear a differing garb now and are seen with their long wigs and swords, rather than with aprons on, as was formerly the figure they made" (67). What matters here is not the sociological accuracy of Defoe's observation but its plausibility and the significance of Defoe's anxieties.

Social "transvestitism"

Defoe was here describing a sort of social "transvestitism," people wearing the "wrong" clothing for their social estate. Nor was he alone in his alarm since his complaint was common (*Tatler* nos. 155 and 270; Miège 1691: 39. See Staves 1982 for an illuminating discussion of the cultural significance of men's apparel in this period.) Such anxieties do not make sense unless "useful" persons were in fact interested not just in making money or in making a living but also in making a figure. This is not to suggest that flower sellers were parading around like Hungarian princesses, but that a range of middling sorts in London assumed modes of politeness within their reach.

There were indeed modes of politeness within their reach, and opportunities to engage in them increased over time.

For one thing, it was not hard for a male of the middling sort to dress like a gentleman. In fact, the suggestion in Defoe and others that the middling were not keeping to the dress code was a red herring. The basic three-piece suit, which had arrived on the scene in the 1660s and 1670s, was worn by middling men as well as the Quality. While the cost of the suit could encode social distinction through the nature of the fabric, the quality of the tailoring, and the degree of detail, the suit was the basic form of male apparel shared by people of a wide social and economic range. Access to this standard apparel was facilitated by the existence of a ready-made clothing industry which imitated what tailors produced on order. The minimum for a ready-made suit was £6 7s, which was within reach of most of the middling sort. Of course, purchasing power could be enhanced by buying in the secondhand market. Moreover, most London apprentices began their career with several suits of this sort (provided either by parents or patrons or masters), and male servants, if not attired in a livery, often wore just such a simple suit. In addition, servants had easy access to gentlemanly clothing through the common perk of receiving their employers' cast-off clothing (Ribeiro 1984: 25, 30; Ribeiro and Cumming 1989: 28–31; Buck 1979: 103–13; Ginsburg 1972; Ginsburg 1980; Earle 1989: 19–21, 46, 281–90). Thus, a wide range of middling men, augmented by servants, were in a position to appear, more or less, gentle. (One could make much the same argument for women by considering the popularity and accessibility of the mantua from the early Restoration on.)

Moreover, early eighteenth-century London offered many opportunities for middling people to act out gentility. A wide range of places of public resort catered to people's appetites for pleasure, for sociability, and for consumption. In inns, taverns, and cookhouses, in coffee-houses and chocolate-houses, in shops and markets, in theaters and assembly rooms, and in gardens, parks, and spas, the busy of the world satisfied their needs, carried out business, and cut a figure. They ate and drank, conversed with friends, acquaintances, and strangers, bought things, consumed culture, danced, and advanced their erotic careers; but they also displayed themselves and watched others displaying themselves.

These institutions were not democratic since they excluded the entirety of the laboring poor (except for servants). However, these institutions were not tightly exclusive either, since they were often cheap. Entry to coffee-houses was generally one penny; to the suburban spas, threepence. Exclusivity could easily be structured into urban recreations through price: for instance, the concerts at York Buildings, intended to be smarter affairs, cost five shillings (Earle 1989: 51–8, 240 ff.; P. Clark 1986; Fisher 1948; Plumb 1985; Margetson 1970). Nonetheless, many urban recreations were within reach of the middling sort.

Aside from gentlemanlike or ladylike apparel, participation required a certain amount of discretionary income. Peter Earle uses an income of £50 a year as the lower limit for maintaining a comfortable middling style of life. Such an income would have allowed temperate participation in urban recreations. Indeed, many middling households, supported by manufacturing or commerce or professional activity, were much wealthier.

However, one of the most interesting things to emerge in Earle's survey (1989) of the middle classes of London is the presence of a proto-white-collar population. These people might make £50 a year but frequently made a good deal less. They were the pen-pushers and pedagogues of London. They included specialists in writing (writing masters, schoolteachers, scriveners, clerks), the lower ends of the professions (attorneys, court clerks, apothecaries), and bureaucrats in the small but growing civil service. Earle refers to the "shabbily genteel rank of the rapidly expanding educated lower middle class, a stratum of society which included book-keepers, clerks, customs officials and similar types of occupation, a world of prototype Pooters striving valiantly to retain some dignity on incomes well below what could be earned by many skilled artisans" (14, 31, 60–9, 73). Despite and at the same time because of their marginal incomes, these people seem highly eligible as seekers after politeness.

In addition to decent clothing and spare change, participation in the polite spaces of London required an ability to act somewhat politely. Very Useful Manuals would have given some guidance in this regard. Of course, the ability to act the part in a public place is a social practice, and most people learn most practices not by reading books but by observing, asking questions, and being instructed orally. My contention is not that plebeians learned how to behave in polite places by reading these books (though the possibility that people sometimes learn things from books should not be dismissed entirely). Rather, the contention is that the reason that politeness was being purveyed in these books to plebeian readers was that participating in a polite social milieu was an opportunity offered to middling Londoners in this period. Thus, the rules of polite practice in behavior and conversation were a matter of concern and curiosity, which their appearance in books could address.[11]

Social voyeurism

However, it is not necessary to maintain that readers of these books universally or even generally participated in the urban institutions to which I have been referring. Many readers would not have been in a position to avail themselves of the attractions of London: some were country people or provincial townspeople to whose towns such institutions had not yet come; some were too poor to participate or of a culture to which such institutions did not belong. In other words, Very Useful Manuals may have been read not only by people making brief excursions into the polite world but also by people wishing only to make imaginary visits to the social worlds of others.

A suggestive analysis of the reading population of Very Useful Manuals was offered in Guillet de Saint-Georges's *The Gentleman's Dictionary* (1705), a translation of a French volume concerned with distinctively gentle activities for men, such as equestrianism and military science. Its design was "to serve not only those who are bred to the Sword but all that pretend to a Gentlemanlike Education; and at the same time to gratify the Curiosity of others, who will, doubtless, be fond of knowing the true Import of such Terms and Phrases, as are daily met with in Common discourse, and are usually tack'd to the Busiest Actions of Life" (A3r-v). A three-tiered readership was here proposed. There were, first, the "true" gentlemen, second, those with pretenses to gentility, the "gentlemanlike," and, third, none of the above – people who just wanted to be oriented in a discursive and cultural world in which encounters with gentility were quite common.

This explains why in Very Useful Manuals alleged guides to "practices" often take on a lexicographical character. Howlett's *School of Recreation* (1696) was a guide to such gentlemanly pursuits as hunting, riding, and fencing. Its author commended these pursuits "as they are *viz*. Suitable *Recreations* for the *Gentry* of *England*, and others, wherein to please and delight themselves." Of course, the project of teaching people to ride horses in a book has a ludicrous side. Indeed, this book seems aimed less at teaching practices than at propagating a kind of cultural literacy. The chapters were not organized as step-wise procedures for activities but rather as taxonomies of kinds of activity. The chapter on hunting, for instance, was mostly a taxonomy of the sorts of hunts, with a separate listing of dog diseases. The section "of military discipline" was a glossary of commands for bearers of pikes and of muskets. Thus, the book seems to have conduced less to the furthering of certain athletic abilities and more to the furthering of a certain social capacity, recognizing a social and cultural world which was precisely not the reader's own. To be socially adept involved being, to an extent, a social voyeur.

Conclusion

Publishers pushed "politeness" in plebeian texts because there was a readership for it, and there was a readership for it for two reasons. For one thing, such texts offered a kind of cultural literacy, tendering useful knowledge of the master culture. For another, such texts relieved anxiety about and perhaps even provided some guidance for negotiating social moments that called for some mode of politeness. Such moments were common in the lives of a significant range of Londoners: in the lives of servants; in the lives of shopkeepers and others who dealt with customers; and in the lives of any who participated in the sociable and cultural pleasures of London.

Were these middling sorts therefore "polite"? The answer depends, first, on the standard of politeness one applies and, second, on the concept of identity one assumes.

In regard to the first, little of what I have been discussing would have been recognizable as "politeness" to the third earl of Shaftesbury or to Alexander Pope. They were, of course, princes of politeness. However, precisely because they devoted their careers to formulating "deep" or "high" conceptions and practices of politeness, their perspectives should not be privileged. Clearly, politeness was also a demotic idiom of historical significance. From a historical standpoint, therefore, they were polite who acted, or tried to act, in accord with politeness in any of its modes.

At this point, it may be objected that plebeian politeness was merely "pretense" or "social aping," but this objection is poorly formulated for two reasons. For one thing, "pretension" is just an arbitrarily condescending way to characterize processes of fashioning and refashioning in which selves necessarily engage under conditions of social fluidity. Second, since "pretension" exists only in relation to authenticity, talk of "pretension" invokes a normative interpretation of identity (an interpretation implicit in "identity"'s Latin derivation): the self as a cohesive, continuous, "same," unified thing. The weakness of this interpretation is that it can only worry (in the manner of Defoe) when confronted with shopkeepers who refuse to keep their smocks on.

However, if identity is not an essence but rather a set of skills adapted to a range of environments, multiplicity and even inconsistency become the self's natural condition. In the case at hand, the gestures towards politeness on the part of middling people were not transgressions but actualizations of identity. As soon as pretensions become social practices, they take on a reality and authenticity of their own. Even daydreams have their significance, since they map the trajectory of aspirations. Since, in a mobile society, people's careers are built on their aspirations, their social dreams and fantasies seem an ineradicable element of their identity.

Notes

1 On the material and ideological foundations of elite hegemony: Plumb 1967, Cannon 1984: 148 ff., Clark 1985: 93 ff., Holmes 1981. Here and elsewhere, this chapter is reliant on John Brewer's Clark lecture (October 12, 1990), " 'The most polite age and the most vicious': attitudes towards culture as a commodity, 1660–1800" (Chapter 18 in this volume).

2 In the long run, the analysis provided here has to be integrated into a larger chronological perspective. For the same phenomenon in the latter end of the century, see Benedict 1990.

3 The symbol for this convergence of commerce and politeness is Mercury, who frequently figured in the frontispieces of the manuals and guides to be discussed below. See Plates 19.3 and 19.4. Since Mercury was the guardian of borders, it is appropriate that this chapter is concerned with the border between two territories of which Mercury was also the guardian: trade and eloquence. The fourth edition of the *Encyclopedia Britannica* (1810) reported that "according to the confession of the emperor Julian, Mercury was no hero, but rather one who inspired mankind with *wit, learning, and the ornamental arts of life*, more than with courage. The pious emperor, however, omits some of his attributes; for this god was not only the patron of *trade*, but also of theft and *fraud*."

4   The best example is Agnew 1986. An important bibliography of works on the history of theatricality by Jonas Barish (1981), Michael Fried (1980), and David Marshall (1986), among others, is relevant here.

5   The model is that of E. P. Thompson 1973–4. My approach to these social and cultural relations is sympathetic to Paulson 1979: ix–xiv, and Barry 1985.

6   The pursuit of gentility is one theme in Earle 1989. See, for instance, 5–9, 31, 69, 73, 76, 85, 218. See also Rogers 1979 and Susan Staves's discussion of "the new class of the polite" (1988).

7   The actual contents of these categories were fluid, so that, among other things, this juxtaposition could express the contrasts between poetry and philosophy, between rhetoric and philosophy, and between literature, history, and ethics, on one hand, and "science," on the other.

8   See Plate 19.1. A similar parallel coordination of the "better" and "common" sorts is evident in the frontispiece to Dunton 1692, which shows the twelve secular "apostles" of the fictitious Athenian Society answering questions from a range of social types. The frontispiece purports to represent the whole of society in a coordinated search for normative guidance. The two levels of inquirers parallel the Upper and Lower Walks at Tunbridge Wells. See Plate 19.2.

9   *A Helpe to Discourse* was attributed to W[illiam] B[asse]. The edition of 1638 called itself the eleventh and that of 1682 called itself the seventeenth. *The New Helpe to Discourse* was assigned to W[illiam] W[instanley]. It first appeared in 1669 and was in its ninth edition in 1733. If one counts only editions for which copies are extant, there were at least twenty-two editions between 1619 and 1799. If one accepts the numbering of editions on title pages, there were as many as twenty-six.

10 The reliance on *Youths Behavior* is evident when one compares the two: cf. Hawkins 1646. *Youths Behaviour* was a translation of *Bienséance* according to the British Museum Catalogue. The derivation of *Bienséance* from della Casa is asserted in Heltzel 1928.

11 The analysis in this and the following sections accords with the idea that the foundation for popular literacy in early modern England was broadly cultural: common people were motivated to master reading and writing because these skills really helped them function in a wide range of situations. See Laqueur 1976.

Bibliography

I   Very Useful Manuals and other seventeenth- and eighteenth-century printed material

Place of publication is London unless otherwise noted.

Ayres, John (1682) *The New A-la-mode Secretarie.*
—— (1698) *A Tutor to Penmanship or The Writing Master.*
B., L. *et al.* (1671) *The New Academy of Complements.*
—— (1698) *The New Academy of Complements.*
—— (1713) *The New Academy of Complements.*
B., M. (1639) *The Ladies Cabinet Opened: Wherein is found hidden severall experiments in preserving and conserving, physicke, and surgery, cookery and huswifery,* 1st edn.
—— (1654) *The Ladies Cabinet Opened: Wherein is found hidden severall experiments in preserving and conserving, physicke, and surgery, cookery and huswifery,* 2nd edn.
—— (1667) *The Ladies Cabinet Opened: Wherein is found hidden severall experiments in preserving and conserving, physicke, and surgery, cookery and huswifery,* 4th edn.
Basse, William (1621) *A Helpe to Discourse,* 4th edn.
—— (1627) *A Helpe to Discourse,* 6th edn.
Beaumont, John (1701) *The Present State of the Universe.*
Bird, G. (1729) *The Practising Scrivener.*
Blome, Richard (1686) *The Gentleman's Recreation,* 1st edn.

—— (1710) *The Gentleman's Recreation*, 2nd edn.

Blount, Charles (1684) *Janua Scientiarum.*

Blount, T. P. (1691) *Essays.*

Boyer, Abel (1702) *The English Theophrastus.*

C., S. (1677) *The Art of Complaisance.*

Campbell, Charles (1757) *The London Tradesman*, 3rd edn.

Care, Henry (1699) *The Tutor to True English*, 2nd edn.

Chamberlayne, John (1723) *Magnae Britanniae Notitia.*

The Character of the Beaux (1696).

Cocker, Edward (1675) *The Young Clerk's Tutor Enlarged*, 8th edn.

—— (1705) *The Young Clerk's Tutor Enlarged*, 15th edn.

—— (1717) *The Young Clerk's Tutor Enlarged*, 16th edn.

The Compleat Academy of Complements (1705).

The Compleat Clerk, and Scriveners Guide (1655), 1st edn.

The Compleat Clerk, and Scriveners Guide (1683), 5th edn.

The Compleat Sollicitor (1672), 4th edn.

The Complete Family-Piece (1737), 2nd edn.

The Complete Family-Piece (1741), 3rd edn.

Curzon, H. (1712) *The Universal Library: Or Complete Summary of Science.*

Defoe, Daniel (1704–13) *The Review.*

—— (1725–7) *The Complete English Tradesman.*

Dillon, Wentworth, earl of Roscommon (1685) *An Essay on Translated Verse*, 2nd edn.

Dodson, James (1747) *The Calculator.*

Dunton, John (1692) *Young Students Library.*

England's Golden Treasury: Or, the True Vade Mecum (1700), 5th edn.

Fidell, Thomas (1658) *A Perfect Guide for a Studious Young Lawyer.*

Fisher, George (1742) *The Instructor: Or, Young Man's Best Companion*, 6th edn.

Gailhard, Jean (1978) *The Compleat Gentleman.*

Gough, John (1685) *The Academy of Complements: Or, A New Way of Wooing.*

Gracian, Baltazar (1685) *The Courtiers Manual Oracle.*

Guardian, ed. John Calhoun Stephens, Lexington, KY: University Press of Kentucky, 1982.

Guillet de Saint-Georges, Georges (1705) *The Gentleman's Dictionary.*

H., N. (1684) *The Compleat Tradesman: Or the Exact Dealers Daily Companion*, 3rd edn.

—— (1694) *The Ladies Dictionary: Being a General Entertainment for the Fair-Sex.*

—— (1737) *The Pleasant Art of Money Catching*, 4th, edn.

Hatton, Edward (1699) *The Merchant's Magazine*, 3rd edn.

—— (1716) *Comes Commercii: Or The Trader's Companion*, 3rd edn.

—— (1727) *Comes Commercii: Or The Trader's Companion*, 5th edn.

Hawkins, Francis (1646) *Youths Behaviour*, 4th edn.

Hill, John (1688) *The Exact Dealer: Being an Useful Companion for All Traders.*

—— (1689) *The Young Secretary's Guide*, 3rd edn.

Howlett, Robert (1696) *The School of Recreation.*

Hughes, John (1697) "Of style," in *Poems on Several Occasions. With Some Select Essays in Prose* (1735).

J., G. (1720) *Great Britain's Vade Mecum.*

The Ladies Cabinet, Or A Companion for the Toilet: consisting of letters, essays, tales, elegies, odes, songs, epitaphs, epigrams, &c. (1743).

Lupton, Thomas (1579) *A Thousand Notable Things, of Sundry Sortes.*

—— (1612) *A Thousand Notable Things, of Sundry Sortes.*

—— (1628) *A Thousand Notable Things, of Sundry Sortes.*

—— (1675) *A Thousand Notable Things, of Sundry Sortes.*

—— (1686) *A Thousand Notable Things, of Sundry Sortes.*

—— (c. 1700) *A Thousand Notable Things, of Sundry Sortes.*

—— (1720) *A Thousand Notable Things, of Sundry Sortes.*

Lupton, Thomas (1702?) *The Way to Get Wealth*.
—— (1706) *The Way to Get Wealth*.
M., W. (1655) *The Queens Closet Opened*, 4th edn.
—— (1710) *The Queens Closet Opened*, 11th edn.
Malcolm, Alexander (1731) *A Treatise of Book-keeping*.
Mather, William (1681) *The Young Man's Companion*, 1st edn., as *A Very Useful Manual.*
—— (1685) *The Young Man's Companion*, 2nd edn.
—— (1710) *The Young Man's Companion*, 8th edn.
—— (1727) *The Young Man's Companion*, 13th edn.
Miège, Guy (1691) *The New State of England*.
—— (1707) *The New State of England*, 6th edn.
Molesworth, Robert (1694) *An Account of Denmark*.
Mundus Foppensis (1691).
A New Academy of Complements: Or The Lover's Secretary (1715), 4th edn.
A New Academy of Complements; Or the Compleat English Secretary (1748).
P., J. (1684) *The Merchant's Dayly Companion*.
Phillips, Edward (1650) *The Mysteries of Love and Eloquence: Or the Arts of Wooing and Complementing*, 1st edn.
—— (1685) *The Mysteries of Love and Eloquence: Or the Arts of Wooing and Complementing*, 3rd edn.
—— (1699) *The Mysteries of Love and Eloquence: Or the Arts of Wooing and Complementing*, as *The Beau's Academy*.
Philomusus (1640) *The Academy of Complements*.
—— (1650) *The Academy of Complements*.
—— (1655) *The Marrow of Complements*.
Ramesay, William (1672) *The Gentleman's Companion*.
S., E. (1697) *Wit and Eloquence or the Accomplish'd Secretary's Vade Mecum*.
Saxton, John (1737) *The Merchant's Companion*.
Spectator, ed. Donald F. Bond, Oxford: Clarendon Press, 1965.
Tatler, ed. Donald F. Bond, Oxford: Clarendon Press, 1987.
The Universal Family Book: Or, A Necessary and Profitable Companion for All Degrees of People of Either Sex (1703).
A Universal, Historical, Geographical, Chronological and Poetical Dictionary (1703).
A Very Useful Manual, see *The Young Man's Companion*.
The Way to Promotion. Or the Young Man's Guide to Preferment (1682).
Winstanley, William (1669) *The New Helpe to Discourse*, 1st edn.
—— (1680) *The New Helpe to Discourse*, 2nd edn.
—— (1684) *The New Helpe to Discourse*, 3rd edn.
—— (1696) *The New Helpe to Discourse*, 4th edn.
—— (1721) *The New Helpe to Discourse*, 8th edn.
Wit's Cabinet: A Companion for Gentlemen and Ladies (1700?).
Wit's Cabinet: A Companion for Gentlemen and Ladies (1737), 16th edn.
The Young Clerk's Companion (1672).
The Young Clerk's Vade Mecum: Or Clerkship Improv'd (1723).

II   Secondary works

Agnew, Jean–Christophe (1986) *Worlds Apart: The Market and the Theater In Anglo-American Thought. 1550–1750*, Cambridge: Cambridge University Press.
Barish, Jonas (1981) *The Antitheatrical Prejudice*, Berkeley, CA: University of California Press.
Barrell, John (1983) *English Literature in History 1730–80*, New York: St. Martin's Press.
Barry, Jonathan (1985) "Popular culture in seventeenth-century Bristol," in Reay 1985b: 59–90.
Bell, Daniel (1976) *The Cultural Contradictions of Capitalism*, New York: Basic Books.
Benedict, Barbara M. (1990) "Literary miscellanies: the cultural mediation of fragmented feeling," *ELH* 57: 407–30.

Borsay, Peter (1989) *The English Urban Renaissance: Culture and Society in the Provincial Town, 1660–1770*, Oxford: Clarendon Press.

Buck, Anne (1979) *Dress in Eighteenth-Century England*, London: B. T. Batsford.

Burke, Peter (1978) *Popular Culture in Early Modern Europe*, New York: Harper & Row.

—— (1985) "Popular culture in seventeenth-century London," in Reay 1985b: 31–58.

Cannon, John (1984) *Aristocratic Century*, Cambridge: Cambridge University Press.

Capp, Bernard (1979) *English Almanacs, 1500–1800: Astrology and the Popular Press*, Ithaca, NY: Cornell University Press.

Clark, J. C. D. (1985) *English Society, 1688–1832*, Cambridge: Cambridge University Press.

Clark, Peter (1986) *Sociability and Urbanity: Clubs and Societies in the Eighteenth-Century City*, Leicester: University of Leicester (Victorian Studies Centre).

Corfield, Penelope (1987) "Class by name and number in eighteenth-century Britain," *History* 72: 38–61.

Cressy, David (1976) "Describing the social order of Elizabethan and Stuart England," *Literature and History* 3: 29–44.

Earle, Peter (1976) *The World of Defoe*, London: Weidenfeld & Nicolson.

—— (1989) *The Making of the English Middle Class: Business, Society and Family Life in London, 1660–1730*, London: Methuen.

Everitt, Alan (1969) *Change in the Provinces: The Seventeenth Century*, Leicester: Leicester University Press.

Fisher, F. J. (1948) "The development of London as a centre of conspicuous consumption in the sixteenth and seventeenth centuries," *Transactions, Royal Historical Society*, 4th series, 30: 37–50.

Fletcher, A. J. and Stevenson, J. (1985) "Introduction," in *Order and Disorder in Early Modern England*, Cambridge: Cambridge University Press, pp. 1–40.

Fried, Michael (1980) *Absorption and Theatricality: Painting and Beholder in the Age of Diderot*, Berkeley, CA: University of California Press.

Ginsburg, Madeleine (1972) "The tailoring and dressmaking trades, 1700–1850," *Costume* 6: 64–9.

—— (1980) "Rags to riches: the second-hand clothes trade, 1700–1978," *Costume* 14: 121–35.

Heltzel, V. B. (1928) "*The Rules of Civility* (1671) and its French source," *Modern Language Notes* 43: 17–22.

Holmes, Geoffrey (1981) "The achievement of stability: the social context of politics from the 1680s to the age of Walpole," in John Cannon (ed.) *The Whig Ascendancy*, London: Edward Arnold.

Horwitz, Henry (1987) " 'The mess of the middle class' revisited: the case of the 'big bourgeoisie' of Augustan London," *Continuity and Change* 2: 263–96.

Klein, Lawrence E. (1984–5) "The third earl of Shaftesbury and the progress of politeness," *Eighteenth-Century Studies* 18: 186–214.

Lang, R. G. (1974) "Social origins and social aspirations of Jacobean London merchants," *Economic History Review*, 2nd series, 27: 28–47.

Laqueur, Thomas (1976) "The cultural origins of popular literacy in England 1500–1850," *Oxford Review of Education* 2: 255–75.

McKendrick, Neil, Brewer, John, and Plumb, J. H. (1985) *The Birth of a Consumer Society: The Commercialization of Eighteenth-Century England*, Bloomington, IN: Indiana University Press.

Macpherson, C. B. (1962) *The Political Theory of Possessive Individualism*, Oxford: Clarendon Press.

Margetson, Stella (1970) *Leisure and Pleasure in the Eighteenth Century*, London: Cassell.

Marshall, David (1986) *The Figure of Theater: Shaftesbury, Defoe, Adam Smith and George Eliot*, New York: Columbia University Press.

Muchembled, Robert (1978) *Culture populaire et culture des élites*, Paris: Flammarion.

Paulson, Ronald (1979) *Popular and Polite Art in the Age of Hogarth and Fielding*, Notre Dame, IN: University of Notre Dame Press.

Plumb, J. H. (1967) *The Growth of Political Stability in England, 1675–1725*, London: Macmillan.

—— (1985) "The commercialization of leisure in eighteenth-century England," in McKendrick, Brewer, and Plumb (1985): 265–85.

Porter, Roy (1982) *English Society in the Eighteenth Century*, Harmondsworth, Mx: Penguin.

Reay, Barry (1985a) "Introduction: Popular culture in early modern England," in Reay 1985b: 1–30.

—— (1985b) *Popular Culture in Seventeenth-Century England*, London: Croom Helm.

Revel, Jacques (1989) "The uses of civility," in Roger Chartier (ed.) *Passions of the Renaissance*, Vol. III, *A History of Private Life*, ed. Philippe Ariès and Georges Duby, Cambridge, MA: Harvard University Press.

Ribeiro, Aileen (1984) *Dress in Eighteenth-Century Europe*, London: B. T. Batsford.

—— and Cumming, Valerie (1989) *The Visual History of Costume*, London: B. T. Batsford.

Rogers, Nicholas (1979) "Money, land and lineage: the big bourgeoisie of Hanoverian London," *Social History* 4: 437–54.

Speck, W. A. (1982) "Politicians, peers, and publication by subscription 1700–1750," in Isobel Rivers (ed.) *Books and Their Readers in Eighteenth-Century England*, Leicester: Leicester University Press, pp. 47–68.

Spufford, Margaret (1981) *Small Books and Pleasant Histories: Popular Fiction and Its Readership in Seventeenth-Century England*, Cambridge: Cambridge University Press.

Staves, Susan (1982) "A few kind words for the fop," *Studies in English Literature 1500–1900* 22: 413–28.

—— (1988) "Pope's refinement," *The Eighteenth Century* 29: 145–63.

Stone, Lawrence and Stone, Jeanne C. Fawtier (1984) *An Open Elite?*, Oxford: Clarendon Press.

Thompson, E. P. (1973–4) "Patrician society, plebeian culture," *Journal of Social History* 7: 382–405.

Weber, Max (1927) *General Economic History*, trans. Frank H. Knight, London: Allen & Unwin.

—— (1930) *The Protestant Ethic and the Spirit of Capitalism*, trans. Talcott Parsons, New York and London: Allen & Unwin.

Wrightson, Keith (1982) *English Society 1580–1680*, London: Hutchinson.

—— (1986) "The social order of early modern England: three approaches," in Lloyd Bonfield *et al.* (eds.) *The World We Have Gained*, Oxford: Blackwell, pp. 177–202.

20

Emulative consumption and literacy
The Harlot, Moll Flanders, and Mrs. Slipslop

Ronald Paulson

John Brewer's formulation of the prostitute as the image in which "all the greatest anxieties about eighteenth-century cultures" are summed up is, I presume, drawn from the great paradigm of the prostitute in the 1730s, Hogarth's Harlot (Plate 20.1). In one aspect of the Harlot, feminine beauty is shown in the context of danger, disease, and retribution: surrounded, threatened, and destroyed by figures of social authority, recalling the Ecce Homo or Christ Mocked tradition in painting (as in Massys's painting in the Prado, or Bosch's in the National Gallery, London). In another aspect, the Harlot is a human being and at the same time a commodity. She can be bought and sold by consumers as well as cruelly punished by the law. She enjoys a liberty (financial and otherwise) and a power over men unknown to other women of the age, but she is also utterly vulnerable, exploitable, and expendable. It is easy to see how Bernard Mandeville's brutal insight about the value of prostitution to society – concerning the butcher who saves his meat from the flies by "very Judiciously cut [ting] off a fragment already blown, which serves to hang up for a cure; and thus, by sacrificing a Small Part, already Tainted, and not worth Keeping, he wisely secures the Safety of the Rest" – is reflected in Moll Hackabout, "a Small Part, already Tainted," by which Mandeville meant the women in brothels, i.e. the poor, sacrificed to preserve the virtue of rich, respectable women.[1] The fate of the bawd Mother Needham, who appears in Plate 1, was paradigmatic: she was pelted to death in the pillory by a crowd that included – according to newspaper reports – the very men who patronized her brothel, and this was perhaps the reason Hogarth retained her face despite the fact that she was dead by the time the prints appeared.

Hogarth's Harlot is going to be the centerpiece of my story but I want to look at a third aspect: her emulation of respectable society. In a newspaper of 1730 that appeared while Hogarth was planning *A Harlot's Progress*, there was an account of a whore named Mary Muffet, "a woman of great note in the hundreds of Drury, who about a fortnight ago was committed to hard labour in Tothill-fields Bridewell . . . she is now beating hemp in a gown very richly laced with silver . . . to her no small mortification . . . and bestows many hearty curses upon her lawyers, &c." The editorial comment, "*This Lady's* Gown very richly laced with silver *does not well agree with* her no small mortification *in performing the Pennance of* beating hemp" suggests the ironic contrast Hogarth introduces in his fourth plate, which shows the Harlot beating hemp in Bridewell in a fashionable gown salvaged from her wardrobe in Plate 2 (Plates 20.2, 20.4).[2] The gown she wears in Bridewell indicates the remnants of her aspiration to gentility. This is the desire (literally figured in the emblem of *Imitatio* in Plate 2) to "ape" one's betters: in not only the Harlot, but her Jewish keeper, the monkey, and even (though one knows he is costumed by the Jew) the slave boy. The Harlot imitates the behavior of fashionable "ladies" by dressing up and taking a lover behind her keeper's back. The Jewish keeper has cut off his beard, taken a young Christian woman as his mistress, but above all – the example on which Hogarth puts most emphasis – collects old master paintings (a practice which the Harlot emulates in her own way in Plate 3 [Plate 20.3]).

The noticeable omission in Plate 2 is of the other attribute of *Imitatio* besides the mask, mirror, and ape which apply to the Harlot and her Jewish keeper: nowhere in sight are the artist's paint brushes. The brushes – symbol of the artist's proper imitation – Hogarth reserves for his subscription ticket, *Boys Peeping at Nature* (Plate 20.5), where they appear metaphorically in the hand of the putto copying Nature and literally in Hogarth's personal seal, impressed in wax, which shows a palette and brushes. Hogarth has displaced the theme of the artist's imitation from the social scene of the *Harlot's Progress* – the Harlot's imitation of fashion – to the subscription ticket, which is about *artistic* imitation. He consciously excludes himself from the Harlot's aping and the action of the scene, distinguishing this artist from those others. In his paintings he has consistently associated himself with the irreverent dog who never feigns. In the subscription ticket this is the satyr who lifts Nature's skirt to peek at the "truth." But in Plate 2 it is the monkey and not the dog who makes the comment of nature. The monkey is an animal who can indicate both art *and* animal nature, joining the upper and lower parts of the room, the paintings above and the human desires below. Thus emulation in *A Harlot's Progress* takes many forms, from the Londoner's imitation of good and bad social models to the artist's imitation of nature or of art.

The *Harlot's Progress* introduces my subject, the connection between emulation and consumption in the first half of the eighteenth century. We begin with the notion of a new, extended group of consumers, a product, and the new consumers emulating the taste of the old (experienced) consumers (Plumb 1973; McKendrick, Brewer and Plumb 1982). My attention will be primarily on the product. Of course, this applies to everything from dresses to candlesticks. But one implication – the strongest for the artist – is that the work of art is now objectified as a commodity, which is consumable on an individual basis and not limited, as it traditionally had been, to a patron or collector, and therefore is the most obvious sign of class status. The new market of consumers is huge (potentially everyone between the landless peasants and the landed aristocracy, the London journeymen and the great merchants, the laboring poor and the patrician elite) and yet has as its only model the patron and collector – or, often, simply what was referred to as the French taste. Typically, the observation of the *London Magazine* in 1738 that "the ridiculous imitation of the French is now become the epidemical distemper of this Kingdom . . . and what seems, at first sight, only very silly, is in truth the great national peril," referred to both the English imitation of French apishness and the specific imitation of French fashions (*London Magazine* 1738: 552).

Or more precisely, the new consumer has as a model the knowledgeability of the old consumer, which means essentially access to his discourse of collecting, that is, a certain form of literacy (or what we would call these days "theory"), which defines a canon of taste. Even Hogarth's subscription ticket, while it alerted the buyer that this series was about a low subject, an example of the imitation of "Nature" only, nevertheless, with its learned (Latin) inscriptions and allusions, made it quite clear that his maximal audience was made up of educated buyers, knowledgeable about classical texts, allusions, and notions. While there are many synonyms for "emulation" in this period, among them "imitation," "copying," and "affectation," they all share a common denominator of literacy. The discourse of collecting has to be *read*, even though it pertains to visual objects; and Hogarth's own pictures, with their learned and popular emblems, their visual and verbal puns, address – though by no means exclusively – an educated audience.

The new consumer is therefore tempted to climb (or appear to climb) from one class to the next higher – or (much the same thing) to replace his true identity, an Englishman become "Frenchified." His plight opened up a new space for the enterprising artist, who produced copies – single or in the hundreds or thousands – of the original and privileged objects owned by the patron. An alternative space, at the same time, was opened by the even more enterprising artist like Hogarth who sought to develop a *new* product that corresponds to (that catches) the expanding audience on its own terms, especially those who wish to maintain their identity and *not* merely emulate their betters.

Particularly significant, the exactly repeatable graphic image of the engraving extended the definition of "property" far beyond the collector of elite objects such as paintings. The print was seen in coffee-houses and shop windows by many more than actually purchased and owned it; recalling Addison's example in *The Spectator* of the nobleman's landscape which one can stand on the edge of and enjoy without owning. The work of art was no longer limited to the simple status of personal possession; indeed it put in question the whole matter of property as it did of class.

For Hogarth the artist, emulation meant copying – making and selling bad copies of old master paintings and often passing them off as originals, and copying Hogarth's own prints. Most significant for him in the 1730s was piracy, the commercial sense of copying: as long as the artist's mass-market commodity could be *copied*, his property and profits were endangered.[3] The question for the artist was whether ownership is determined by mere purchase or use, or, in Locke's terms, by the labor of the creating. Hogarth thus became a *property*-owner when he sold his own prints from his own copperplates. Later he would have other sorts of property (houses, a coach, and so on), but the essential property, beginning with the *Harlot* in 1732, and consolidated with the *Rake* and the Engravers' Act in 1735, was the fruit of his "labor" in his prints.

The woman laboring to hang out her laundry on the balcony in Harlot 1 (Plate 20.1) is the only indication in the series of an alternative way of life in London. The Harlot *could* be outside, with some space and fresh air around her, washing clothes and airing chamberpots; but she prefers to imitate the rich, wear gentlewomanly dresses, keep a servant woman, avoid physical labor, and be a piece of property herself. But the physical labor of the woman hanging out laundry also figures, for Hogarth and other engravers who read the art treatises, the mechanic labor of their humble craft, which was many steps beneath that of the painter. For the art treatises offered the artists their own equivalent of social climbing by urging them to emulate the old masters and affect gentlemanly behavior, including the collecting of pictures. The project of the *Harlot*, in short, places Hogarth himself within the process he depicts: He invents ("*invenit*," the word that carries the prestige) an original, unique object *and* engraves it ("*sculpsit*"). As artist he stands as a living rebuke to emulation, both in the sense that he does not copy the old masters but produces something new, and that he paints as well as engraves his product.

Thus he transferred the sense of the contemptibleness of labor to the copying – pirating – by others of his own *original* engraving; giving, from his point of view, what had been traditionally regarded as the result of a mechanical reproductive process the status of an original in relation to piratical copies (copies by someone other than the originator). Significantly, Hogarth's Act (as the Engravers' Act was popularly known), while protecting the engraver who is also the inventor of the original composition (Hogarth himself), did not protect engravers who copied old master paintings or sculptures.

As he lobbied for the Act, Hogarth thematized copying in the print series he was working on at the time, *A Rake's Progress* (Plate 20.6–8), which is *about* genuine vs. imitation, original vs. copy, in the story of the merchant's son who emulates the aristocratic rake; and whose publication included the story of the copyists who came into Hogarth's shop, pretending to be customers, and memorially reconstructed the *Rake* plates for a consortium of piratical printsellers who published them before the Act took effect. As a businessman, however, Hogarth exploited the fact of emulation itself among the purchasers of his prints, absorbing both the private collector and the mass audience. Not only are the *Harlot* and the *Rake* about emulation, their successful subscriptions were necessarily *based on* emulation, as were the piracies that followed in order to meet the unsatisfied demand. The first was good emulation, the second bad. The passing of the Engravers' Act meant that Hogarth defeated the bad emulation, and by authorizing cheap copies himself (and then, after the subscription, opening sales of the originals to the general public) he exploited the emulative urges of the lower orders – in a series that bases its rhetoric on the emulation of moral virtue.

The Engravers' Act, as it happened, took place not only following the success of the *Harlot* and the project of the *Rake* but in the same year as the founding of an art academy in St. Martin's Lane, also largely the work of Hogarth. In the academic context copying was the imitation of canonical sculptures, old master paintings, and ultimately, from the late 1740s, the principles of the French Academy – the proposed model for a national English one, despised of course by the anti-Gallican Hogarth.

A corollary was the subject itself of choosing and owning the product (old or new), of creating the new product, and so of projecting a scene or scenario in which the new consumer and the old patron, the artist who originates and the artist who copies, join in a more or less antagonistic relationship *within* the new, Hogarthian product. The most schematic representation of the scene I am describing was Hogarth's *Battle of the Pictures*

(1745) in which the old master paintings, rank on rank of copies (labelled "Ditto"), attack his new product, a modern equivalent, which he called a "modern moral subject"; a Penitent Magdalen punches a hole in her modern equivalent, Hogarth's Harlot, a desert saint goes after his contemporary churchgoer in *Morning*, a Feast of the Gods is set against Hogarth's brothel scene in the *Rake's Progress*, and a Bacchanal against his *Midnight Modern Conversation*.

I want to suggest some genealogies for the various senses of *imitation* we have seen in the case of Hogarth in three overlapping contexts: religious, aesthetic, and literary.

Defoe's *Moll Flanders* (published 1722) is posited upon Moll's desire to be a gentle-woman and is punctuated by Moll's sartorial disguises and genteel circumlocutions. It is useful to see it as the secularization of a conversion narrative with its built-in dichotomy of *then* and *now*, the protagonist's old self and new self. The conversion is the moment of transition from old to new self, but (as Bunyan, for example, demonstrates in *Grace Abounding*, his own conversion narrative) even following the conversion the convert continues to try on provisional scriptural selves – good and bad, of Peter and Judas or Esau – frequently enough to suggest the theatrical metaphor of role-playing. From this it is only a step to Defoe's chapter in *The Complete English Tradesman* (1726) on the tradesmen who emulate gentility, describing "their eager, resolved pursuit of that empty and meanest kind of pride, called imitation, viz., to *look like* the gentry" (Defoe 1726: 118; emphasis added).[4] In *The Great Law of Subordination Consider'd* (1724) he shows each class trying to pass in dress and behavior for the class above it. Even Robinson Crusoe tells us that he always ships out "in the Habit of a Gentleman" rather than a common sailor, and this upward-dressing becomes a major theme in *Moll Flanders*.

Moll, born in the condemned hold in Newgate, is lodged by the parish with a woman who lived formerly in "a good fashion," and who brings her up "as mannerly as if [she] had been at the dancing school." From her first role model, the "gentlewoman" down the street who proves to be a prostitute, to her disastrous choice of a second husband, a "gentleman tradesman," an "amphibious creature," a "landwater thing," and on down to her career as a thief, she dresses up to a status she does not in fact possess. Her emulation takes two forms – first, of dressing in a costume or of assuming a theatrical role, that is, a *visual* evidence; and second, distinct from her appearance, a verbal dimension: Moll's style of speech, her constant use of euphemisms, circumlocutions, and genteelisms ("*that which they call* the last favor," "as it is called," "that is to say").

Such emulation of the manners of the next higher social group becomes an obsessive theme of Defoe's fiction. The protagonist is either born of good parents and spirited away (Captain Singleton) or thinks he is a gentleman (Colonel Jacque) or actually is of good parents but come down in the world (Roxana). The upshot is that these figures affect (or in fact possess) a genteel sense which sets them off from the other denizens of their underclass. But they are unsure of their status, let alone their moral assumptions, and by trying to live up to the standards of gentility they ruin themselves – or, alternatively, as in the case of Colonel Jacque, save themselves. For Jacque's childhood experiences hinge on the fact that his mother and father were gentlefolk and that he knows it; his guardian will not let him forget it. Thus he is Colonel Jacque (no last name), while his playfellows are Major and Captain Jacque, depending on their decreasing gentility. In this case it is his gentlemanliness that prevents Jacque from being a rogue, or, as he says, "wicked." This little boy is completely alone in a hostile London, but he has the conviction that he is a gentleman and therefore keeps from sinking into Moll's degradation by behaving according to gentlemanly standards.[5]

Part of Defoe's context was the fact that emulative spending, the indulgence in fashionable consumption, was coming to be regarded by many as advantageous to the British economy (McKendrick, Brewer, and Plumb 1982: 14–15). As early as the 1680s, John Houghton had written that "our High-Living so far from Prejudicing the Nation . . . enriches it"; and Defoe is expressing in *Moll Flanders*, among other things, the economically conservative position for which *Luxuria* was still an evil (Houghton 1681: 60). At the same time, however, the form of his novel – its first-person narration, involving retrospection and adherence to conventional, often heteroglossial discourses – shows Moll invoking and internalizing the religious and economic discourses that represent her society's conventional moral plot of crime, punishment, penance, and conversion, and thus accepting the guilt of her life as her own rather than that of the heartless and venal society that made her.[7] Defoe raises the question of whether Moll's aspirations, disguises, and diction merely designate her sense of status uncertainty – or whether they project an image of the conformity society requires of its lower orders, including society's fear of her potential upward mobility.

Hogarth's Harlot, Moll Hackabout, represents a cross-breeding of Moll Flanders and John Gay's Polly Peachum. Polly reads romances and acts as though she were a romance heroine: Gay's phenomenally successful play *The Beggar's Opera* (1728) was a satire on the "great" whose model imposed (or excused) similar behavior on the part of the criminal class. It conveyed much the same message as *Moll Flanders* but through literary parody and analogy. Gay's satire was a dramatic equivalent to the mock-heroic mode in which Flecknoe sees himself as an Augustus, Aeneas, and John the Baptist; Shadwell sees himself as a Tiberius, Ascanius, and Christ; and so Macheath sees himself as a gentleman, Peachum sees himself as a respectable merchant, and so on. *The Beggar's Opera* transforms the high–low diction of the mock epic into a comedy of manners in which whores imitate ladies, highwaymen imitate gentlemen, and fences imitate merchants. As the Beggar says at the end of his play:

> Through the whole Piece you may observe such a similitude of Manners in high and low Life, that it is difficult to determine whether (in the fashionable Vices) the fine Gentlemen imitate the Gentlemen of the Road, or the Gentlemen of the Road the fine gentlemen.

Except, he adds, that the "lower Sort of People" "are punish'd for them." If Gay leaves open the possibility that the gentlemen may be imitating the highwaymen, Hogarth closes it. By having his characters plainly emulate their respectable counterparts, he adopts a much clearer way than Defoe of making society out to be the villain in the emulative situation.

A Harlot's Progress follows directly from Hogarth's several paintings of *The Beggar's Opera* (between 1728 and 1730), while also evoking Bunyan's role-playing with Peter, Judas, or Esau. But the visual equivalent he employs is the paintings his characters collect of their role models. If we look at the second and third plates of *A Rake's Progress*

(Plates 20.7, 20.8) we can see, almost schematically, a pictorial version of the Puritan conception of identity: the fallen man should wipe away his mirror image – his own face – and replace it with Christ's (an *imitatio Christi*). But, if he is reprobate, he will replace it with some worse image such as Nero (and, in a later state, to add gluttony, the chef Pontac). But Hogarth turns every picture into a bad, an authoritarian model – his characters collect only Neros. And this authority takes the specific form of "art." Spatially beneath these paintings are the Harlot or the Rake, capable of choice but limited by the socially accepted, fashionable models painted and affixed above them to the wall, which he/she has chosen, collected, and internalized; and, in crucial scenes, beneath the Harlot or the Rake, there is an animal, a monkey, dog, or cat – or, as opposed to "art," there is "nature."

Hogarth's model of identity owes much to the Puritan spiritual autobiography, but its particular reference is secular – to the central economic situation of consumption, and behind this to the intellectual phenomenon influencing artistic consumption in eighteenth-century England, the rise of Shaftesburyian aesthetics. After 1700 the emphasis in the art treatises shifts from the poet or painter (the producer) and the making of a poem or painting to the judgment or taste of the connoisseur (consumer). Taste and connoisseurship focus on the quality and rarity of the object. This aesthetic discourse is firmly in place by the end of the 1720s when all the treatises of the third earl of Shaftesbury, Francis Hutcheson, and Jonathan Richardson were in print. It was at that point in time that Hogarth began to produce his "modern moral subjects" which are about the imitators of the Man or Woman of Taste, the collector of pictures and other objects of virtu.

A sublimation of Whig politics, Shaftesburyian aesthetics (in his *Characteristics*, 1711) posited a civic humanist Man of Taste, the enlightened, moral, and aesthetically sensitive landed proprietor – therefore reasonable, disinterested, and impartial. He is essentially the Hercules at the Crossroads of Shaftesbury's treatise on history painting, *A Notion of the Historical Draught or Tablature of the Judgment of Hercules* (1713), a work reflected in more than one of Hogarth's scenes; and he is also the man Jonathan Richardson proposed in his *Science of a Connoisseur* (1773a) who understands that the function of art in polite society is to be collected, hung on the wall, and emulated. Emulation was the reason Richardson gave for collecting paintings of great men and their deeds: with these constantly before your eyes, you emulated their virtues. In his secular version of Bunyan's conversion narrative, Richardson showed man defining himself in terms of the art objects he lives among, in effect turning from salvation to self-realization.[8]

Richardson in essence creates the Hogarthian room when he recalls the uncivilized brute "inhabiting between bare walls" (the walls, it is implied, of a cave) and projects the pleasure and instruction gained by hanging pictures on these walls: "Our walls, like the trees of Dodona's grove, speak to us, and teach us history, morality, divinity; excite in us joy, love, pity, devotion; if pictures have not this good effect, it is our own fault in not chusing them well, or not applying ourselves to make a right use of them" (Richardson 1773a: 268–9).[9] As Hogarth saw, Richardson opened the door to *bad* models. At the same time, the extension of the market through exactly repeatable objects opened the door to bad copies, forgeries, and various kinds of artistic or entrepreneurial deceit.

Hogarth's model of the self is based on Shaftesbury and Richardson's emulative syndrome but mediated by Bernard Mandeville's satiric response to it in *The Fable of the Bees* (1724 edn.). For he replaces Shaftesbury's polite Man of Taste with the Mandevillian egoist, driven by powerful, egoistic passions, which are expressed in his Richardsonian choice of paintings. Mandeville's "Enquiry into the Origin of Moral Virtue" (introducing *The Fable of the Bees*) provided Hogarth with the metaphor of "rising" and of high and low which he materializes in the relationship of paintings to their collector in his rooms: Mandeville ironically opposes the "lofty," "higher qualities" of the ruling class to the "grovelling" of the "abject, low-minded People" (Mandeville 1924: I, 43–57). The higher or "superior" class creates morality in order to govern the lower or "inferior" ("inferior Brutes"); and the lower tries to "emulate" the higher, both in the sense of subservience and in the sense of endeavoring ("rising") to re-create a simulacrum of that status: a paradigm materialized in Hogarth's rooms. Thus virtue and vice are arbitrary power designations, "the Contrivance of Politicians" rather than "the pure Effect of Religion," as the civic humanist (in effect, the ruling class) discourse of Shaftesbury claims: they are "art" rather than the nature (or truth) of the actual life and death of a prostitute.

Mandeville in effect points out that it is only the function of Christianity to excite men to "virtue" and thus make them subservient which sets it above other (for example, classical) religions.[10] Both Shaftesbury and Mandeville were widely recognized as deists: in their different ways both replaced the deity with art (or custom or belief or some other emulative form). The equivalent of God versus Nature in the discourse of religion is, of course, in aesthetic discourse *Art* versus Nature, and Hogarth privileges Nature in both discourses.

The Harlot hangs portraits of Captain Macheath and Dr. Henry Sacheverell on her wall, and thus steals her client's watch and hopes she will escape the law as easily as Macheath and Sacheverell did. The Jew collects Old Testament history paintings and so desires the Harlot because David desired Bathsheba and casts her into outer darkness because Jehovah and Jonah were unmerciful.[11] In the *Rake's Progress* Tom Rakewell, collecting a painting of *The Choice of Paris*, follows Paris in choosing Venus, and in the next plate, appropriately in a brothel, he breaks the mirror, destroys his own image, and replaces it with the portrait of Nero (and in a later state Pontac as well). In every case Shaftesburyian disinterestedness and impartiality are undermined by acquisitiveness, sexual passion, and above all the desire to rise in society. The brutal egoism of Rakewell firms up the model adumbrated in the gentler Harlot: Hogarth starts with the Protestant conversion model of the self and the pictorial (aesthetic) model of Richardson's connoisseur, critiqued by Mandeville; and to this he adds in the *Rake* the theatrical model adapted from *The Beggar's Opera*.

He never valorizes the paintings on the walls: there is no difference between the painting of Paris in *Rake* 2 and the painting of Rakewell's father in 1 (Plate 20.6), who merely recalls the "framed" portrait of the Harlot's model Colonel Charteris in the doorway of *Harlot* 1 (vs. the unframed, preoccupied clergyman, who should be her model, and the similarly unframed Sarah Young in *Rake* 1). Hogarth markedly omits the figure of the deity from these paintings, while presenting religious myths which (as Mandeville points out) determine the actions of the figures beneath. He could have shown a *good* model in one of the paintings, secular if not religious, but he never does.

Good actions appear only as a natural human (but more often animal) action unconnected with the works of art on the wall. We never see a Good Samaritan painting on the wall of one of Hogarth's rooms, but we do see an occasional human behaving as a "modern" Good Samaritan – notably Sarah Young in the *Rake's Progress*. Yet Sarah's Samaritan actions – in truth Mandevillian actions – are based on her love of Rakewell and nothing else. We are never shown her carrying out a disinterested act of charity.[12]

Marriage à la Mode (1745) is the climactic work in Hogarth's thematizing of emulation. It presents the emulation of classes, a merchant marrying his daughter to a nobleman (Plate 20.9). By Plate 4 (Plate 20.10) she is shown to have all the characteristics of the late earl, her father-in-law, collecting art and seeking sex outside matrimony. In the artistic dimension, the paintings on the walls of each room show the actions of heroes, martyrs, Pharaohs, or of Dutch boors and drunkards, emulated by the various people (from aristocrats to City merchants) who live in those rooms and collect them. Moreover, it is implied that these are merely *copies* of paintings by Titian, Domenichino – the latter, presumably copied for Lord Squander, who has had the Divinity excised (Plate 20.9). He buys the picture because it is fashionable art, and then internalizes it, becoming its victim, whose actions are determined by its presence: neither is an act of free will. But one could also suspect that (along the line of the role-playing in *The Beggar's Opera*) he chooses the picture as self-justification. Squander chooses portraits and history painting to elevate himself, support his self-importance, pander to his megalomania; but the very paintings that portray his godhead dictate the tyranny, murder, and destruction of his own blood-line that godhead carries with it in the tradition of western art (whether the religion is classical or Christian).

Indeed, having shown the lower orders emulating the aristocracy (as in the *Rake's Progress*), in *Marriage à la Mode* Hogarth shows that the aristocracy itself is no different from the lower orders: Earl Squander also defines himself by emulating and upward aspiration – upward towards the monarch and the deity.

So meaning (or understanding) replaces possession as a sign of ownership, and meaning in the Hogarthian room emerges from pictorial signs under the close perusal of a spectator. The emergence of significance is from objects specifically regarded as commodities, and so the print is about the figures within the room as consumers who are indissoluble from their consumption. And given the "readability" of these objects, the important realization we find in the consumption of art objects is that class is primarily distinguished not by possession of the objects but by the ability to read them correctly – not, for example, as the consumer reads them but as the morally aware ironic spectator reads them. This is a distinction based on education and intelligence – only partly and tangentially (perhaps even negatively) on birth.[13]

For education – literacy – is primarily what distinguishes the emulous in Hogarth's prints from those who can recognize the satire on emulation: literacy does not mean simply "able to read" (i.e. Hogarth's Latin mottoes, inscriptions, and visual and verbal puns) but to rise above the literal – what is simply seen – to the figurative; for example, to interpret the relationship between the Rake or Lord Squander and his paintings.

One other genealogy of emulation remains to be mentioned, from the literary satire of Pope's *Dunciad*, a work of the same year as Gay's *Beggar's Opera*. Critics complained that Pope's ridicule in *The Dunciad* fell upon the unsuccessful, therefore poor and needy poets, and so in the second, *Variorum Dunciad* of a year later, Pope justifies his satire on the poor poets. In a letter attributed to William Cleland he marshals several arguments, but the climactic one asserts that the poor, incompetent, and deformed become justifiable objects of satire when they try to pass for the fashionable, talented, and beautiful: "Deformity becomes an object of Ridicule when a man sets up for being handsome; and so must Dulness when he sets up for a wit. . . . Accordingly we find that in all ages, all vain pretenders, were they ever so poor or ever so dull, have been constantly the topics of the most candid satyrists, from the Codrus of Juvenal to the Damon of Boileau" (Pope 1953: 17). Behind the satirists Pope cites there is, of course, the figure of Aristotle, who postulated in his *Poetics* that the subject of comedy is the low – which can be interpreted as an inferior class, one aspect of which is its poverty.

What is established in *The Dunciad* – that the poor poet is risible if he emulates, that is, desires and attempts to assume, or presume to, the status of the real poet – is, in a general way, explored by Hogarth in *A Harlot's Progress*, but then followed by a literal illustration in *The Distrest Poet* (1737), where (in the engraved version) *The Dunciad* is in fact cited in the appended verses. (I reproduce the third state of 1741, which replaces the verses with the title *Distrest Poet*, Plate 20.11.) The question Hogarth raised in *A Harlot's Progress*, however, was whether the object of the satire was the poor emulator or what she emulates. Obviously the emulator is "comic" because of the incongruity between her reality and aspiration; as in *The Beggar's Opera* one laughs at Macheath's gentlemanly diction, at Peachum's pose of the merchant and Polly's of the romance heroine. But the "villain" in both works is not the poor emulator but the figures emulated – the "great men," the lawyers, magistrates, and statesmen who, unlike these poor imitators, prosperously die in their beds. The Charterises, the Jewish merchants, the place-hunting clergymen and sadistic magistrates, the greedy physicians, are society's examplars that not only mislead but destroy the Harlot.

In *The Distrest Poet* Hogarth turns his attention to the fraudulent artist – the copyist who is the equivalent of Richardson's Italianate artist who battens on the continental tradition of painting. But who *is* the Distrest Poet's model of emulation? In fact, the picture he keeps above his head is of Alexander Pope – in the painting, a print of "Pope Alexander."[14] Moreover, the Poet himself has been traditionally identified as a portrait of Lewis Theobald, Pope's chief Dunce in *The Dunciad*, and certainly the author of a poem called *The Cave of Poverty, A Poem. Written in Imitation of Shakespeare* (1714), which is recalled by the Poet's "Poverty a Poem." In short, the Poet like the Harlot errs in trying to be like the great, in this case the "Great Poet" Alexander Pope. It is well to remember also that there were an inordinate number of exemplary portraits of Pope in paintings and prints – many commissioned by Pope himself and quite a few the works of Jonathan Richardson (and none the work of Hogarth) (Wimsatt 1965). The portrait of Pope was almost a blazon for the subject of emulative iconology.

In some ways Hogarth's print series of the 1730s served as the model for Samuel Richardson and Henry Fielding, who developed the two traditions of the novel in the 1740s – a subject I deal with elsewhere (Paulson 1992: Ch. 8). From the imitative syndrome came the realization that the subject of "modern" fiction is the emulators of the great and not the great themselves. Fielding and Hogarth of course shared an admiration for *Don Quixote*, which taught them both that not romance but the reader of romance was their subject. And so in the preface to *Joseph Andrews* (1742) Fielding defines his mode as neither burlesque nor epic tragedy but a middle area, the "ridiculous": "The only Source of the true Ridiculous (as it appears to me) is Affectation," which means the low *affecting* the manners of the high.[15] In his first chapter he lays out his subject as the emulation by the foolish reader of Pamela (or of Colley Cibber or of Richardson himself), and by anyone of any "fictional" exemplar. In the first extended comic exchange, Joseph is seen emulating the chastity of the biblical Joseph and his sister Pamela, while Lady Booby (in Joseph's terms, Potiphar's wife) emulates the ranting heroine of She-Tragedies.

In his discussion of "affectation," Fielding specifically alludes to the chamber in Hogarth's *Distrest Poet*, but he elides the crucial fact that it is a poet's chamber: he defines the subject of comedy as ugliness, deformity, and poverty but focuses on poverty, thus arguing that affectation in the poor consists of their filling their cold grate with flowers and decorating their empty sideboard with china dishes. In the narrative of *Joseph Andrews* poverty is an important subject (Adams and Joseph are always short of money); however, affectation follows the example of Pope's dunces and Hogarth's poet: it invariably comes down to literacy – the fishwife trying to speak like and indeed read Dido, the exemplary Dido, when only genteel Didos are capable of reading, understanding, and reproducing the diction of Dido. Recalling his starting-point in Pope's *poor* poet, we see that in his theory the poor can become comic only when they are connected with literacy, or poverty with the *writing* of poetry.[16]

Fielding's emphasis, coming directly from his reaction to Samuel Richardson's *Pamela* (1740), is on the poor servant who emulates gentility in order to rise above her station, specifically by writing. Imitation also figures in the public response to *Pamela* the novel as a model, and Fielding's Joseph begins by mediating his actions through the letters of Pamela and the sermons of Parson Adams. Fortunately, as we discover a bit later, he is only paying lip-service to Pamela's letters when he explains to her (in another letter) how he resisted the advances of Lady Booby ("it is owing entirely to [Parson Adams's] excellent sermons and Advice, together with your Letters, that I have been able to resist a Temptation"): it was in fact his love of Fanny, whatever he may have said or thought, that prevented him from succumbing. Nevertheless, Fielding hedges in a way that Hogarth does not: he also implies that without the texts of Pamela and Adams *even* his love of Fanny might not have kept him out of Booby's arms.

"Affectation" in *Joseph Andrews*, while reaching from the poor Joseph himself in London to the well-off Beau Didapper, who "was an excellent mimic," embraces the parallel phenomena of the way readers imitate the Pamelas and Cibbers of literary texts and the way authors imitate other literary texts. Joseph's and Lady Booby's role-playing in the bedroom scene is parallel to Fielding's (the author's) attempt to fit these figures in this scene into the genres of tragedy, comedy, or satire. Throughout, Fielding attempts to discredit the principle of emulation that determines what an author must write because other authors of the tradition and genre have done so. But his suspicion is directed to the *written* – whatever requires reading and can be misread – as opposed to the apparently transparent visual models of Hogarth's *Good Samaritan* and *Rake's Progress*; or to the living examples of the friends he cites from Hogarth to Hoadly, Chesterfield to Lyttelton, and Dodington to Ralph Allen.

The threat, of course, is less in the written text than in the *reading* of it. If every reader of *Pamela* had been as experienced (or educated) as Fielding, there would have been no need for him to write *Shamela* (1741) and *Joseph Andrews*. One threat resides in such credulous readers as Parson Tickletext who read and accepted *Pamela* at face value. But the greater threat, according to Fielding, is the servants with access to "a little learning" and especially writing (many servants were taught only to read): in particular, Pamela, whose writings convert the credulous Mr. B. to marriage with her. And so Fielding creates a semi-literate Shamela, whose book *Pamela* is really written by her lover Parson Williams; who is always being urged on by her mother's letters and Parson Williams's example towards the ideal of profit through hypocrisy (the emulative strategy *par excellence*). But poor Shamela, the real woman, cannot keep up to their mark; her passions carry her away, and Squire Booby (Fielding's parodic equivalent of Richardson's Mr. B.) discovers her in bed with her true lover Parson Williams.

Judith Frank has argued that the emulation of literacy in *Joseph Andrews* is localized as a badge of class[17] (Frank 1993–4). The two centrally "comic" cases of affectation are Parson Adams and Mrs. Slipslop. Adams *talks* in terms of models and their emulation, running from the Apostles to his own sermons and God's treatment of Abraham and Abraham's of Isaac; but when he *acts* it is from motives as simple and unobstructed as Joseph's love. In his joy at the reunion of Joseph and Fanny he throws his *Aeschylus* into the fire. On the other hand, Slipslop uses her "hard words" to lay claim to a gentility she does not possess. The spectrum of Joseph, Fanny, and Slipslop – the servant who can read and write (but does not know Latin); the servant who can do neither; and the upper servant, the curate's daughter, who affects learning – is capped by Parson Adams, whose class (obscured by penury and his ragged cassock and inappropriate outer garments) is nevertheless established by his literacy, which means his knowledge not even of English (he has not read Pope's English "copy" of Homer) but of the *original* Greek. When Parson Adams asks Joseph "if he did not extremely regret the want of a liberal Education," Joseph's reply is clearly normative (he does not yet know he is Mr. Wilson's son): "he hoped he had profited somewhat better from the Books he had read, than to lament his Condition in this World" (pp. 24–5). But if the servant's affectation is the center of Fielding's "ridiculous," and servants are Fielding's surrogates for the poor, then, following from Pamela, they are *female* servants, and the problem of literacy is anchored in gender as much as class.[18]

Hogarth's grounds for disagreement with Fielding are evident in his distinction in the *Harlot* between the Jew, who has money and power, and the Harlot, who is poor and powerless: both are "affected," but the Jew could be comic (cuckolds were traditionally comic butts); the Harlot was not comic, not finally (in Fielding's sense) "ridiculous." Hogarth must, after the fact of *Joseph Andrews* and its preface, have realized this.

In any case, once Fielding argues in *Joseph Andrews* that affectation is the way to make the poor a subject of comedy, Hogarth responds in two ways: first by looking up to his betters and creating a comedy of the rich in *Marriage à la Mode*, and then by looking down to the poor but without affectation, vanity, or pretension (let alone hypocrisy) and basing the structure of *Industry and Idleness* (1747) on the contrast of those qualities, of Francis Goodchild and Tom Idle, who are opposites, not one emulating the other, and whose comedy – if it is comedy – is in the way they cancel each other out.

So he gives us Tom Idle, who is poor and wretched but not ridiculous, not risible – detached from affectation, isolated as poor, needy, and desperate. By placing him in conjunction with the successful rise in status of Goodchild, Hogarth is daringly testing Fielding's (or probably, more likely, as in *The Distrest Poet*, Pope's) aristocratic definition of comedy – demonstrating that the poor are not comic; that indeed it is Goodchild who imitates his master and is "comic." In Plate 1 he is shown emulating his master, the example of Dick Whittington, and the *'Prentice's Guide*; in Plate 2 he is in church with his master's daughter, whom he has married by Plate 6, and in Plate 4 he joins his master, literally "a step up," in the counting-house. Idle, the iconoclastic *contra*-emulator, destroys his *'Prentice's Guide* and (in Plate 5) throws away his indentures. His only model is the ballad of "Moll Flanders," which he has tacked to his weaver's frame (and presumably other idle types like himself, people on his own level). In fact, contrasted with the proof of *Marriage à la Mode* that not only merchants but aristocrats themselves affect the poses of the next higher rank, *Industry and Idleness* demonstrates that the one class that does not demonstrate affectation, that cannot aspire to rise, is the poor.

Fielding continued to write about the poor's dangerous emulation of their betters in his *Enquiry into the Cause of the late Increase of Robbers* (1751), though now without comedy, replacing the servant with the criminal. But the poor whom Hogarth depicts at exactly the same time in *Gin Lane* and *The Stages of Cruelty* do not emulate the next class higher but rather are simply exploited or ignored by that class, the order that should protect them. This was what in effect Hogarth showed happening to them from the *Harlot* onward, but now without the theme of imitative consumption, for these are people who can afford only a pennyworth of gin (Paulson 1978: 3–8). Paintings no longer appear in the poor rooms depicted – indeed the scenes tend to move outdoors, where property is less well defined. The signs are public – pawnbrokers' signs and church steeples – and indicate society's shirked responsibility for the poor. The poor consumer in simple juxtaposition with civil authority is the subject towards which Hogarth has always been moving, but he had first to clear away the cumulative consumer before he could represent something as elemental as Tom Nero, who steals from and kills more vulnerable creatures than himself before being killed and dissected by the next order above him, who had ignored his needs in the first place.[19]

What emulation amounted to for Hogarth from the beginning was a simple contrast between *them* and *us*, and the danger of allowing ourselves to imitate *them*. It is likely that the primary lesson Hogarth (like other contemporaries, notably Defoe) learned from the experience of the South Sea Bubble (1720–1) was the knowledge that far from governing and protecting us, the higher orders are preying on us, exploiting and cheating us; far from stabilizing and controlling society, in fact they were victimizing the lower orders. This lesson informed the *Harlot's Progress*'s pictures of the clergy, magistrates, and prison warders, but by the 1750s it had been stripped down to the major theme of Hogarth's social commentary.

For Hogarth the danger (as well as his interpretation of the South Sea Bubble) went back to his father, Richard Hogarth, scrabbling up the social ladder and falling into debtors' prison, the victim of booksellers and patrons; or to his mentor and father-in-law Sir James Thornhill, who gave up the making (the labor) of his art in order to emulate a country gentleman.

For Fielding, the aristocratic Etonian and vain Latinist who nevertheless wrote *Shamela* in a sponging house (and whose father, recalling the experience of Hogarth's father, spent his last months within the Rules of the Fleet Prison), emulation meant something else (Fielding 1983: 300). His precarious financial situation during the writing of *Shamela* and *Joseph Andrews* made him acutely aware of his vulnerability and therefore defensive about the poor who lacked his education and breeding, if not his blood, but were at that moment indistinguishable from him. The experience of unruly servants at the theater may have influenced his response to that wily servant Pamela and to the servants he represents in *Joseph Andrews*. There was the stable audience in the pit and boxes, the masters; and in the galleries their servants (footmen, apprentices, etc., who had free access if accompanying their masters). Noisy and inattentive at the best of times, in the 1730s they were often riotous, sometimes locked out and battering at the doors. This was the experience (besides the Licensing Act) that Fielding carried away from his last season of 1737, from both Drury Lane and the Little Theatre in the Haymarket, in particular from his disastrous reception on the opening night of *Eurydice*. These illiterates who were criticizing his plays had no business being at a play, and their rioting was also a contributing force to the passage of the Licensing Act itself. Even Joseph Andrews, when he arrives in London, becomes fashionable and, in particular, "a little too forward in Riots at the Play-Houses and Assemblies." For Fielding literacy – with Latin at the peak – remains the test for gentility.

The principle of consumption was, of course, basically different for these two artists: Hogarth's prints, like a theatrical performance, were seen as well as read and studied by many more than purchased or owned them – constituting a genuinely social occasion; whereas the novels of Fielding (as a reaction against the democracy of the theater, although he paid lip-service to the theatrical model in *Tom Jones*) had to be read in private, and each book enjoyed a much more limited circulation. Hogarth's prints could assume both a collective and an individual, a mass and an elite, audience in a way that was impossible for Fielding, whose "readers" could not by definition include the illiterate (though he spends a great deal of space instructing his readers in how to read his text). It is the peculiar quality of Hogarth's prints to play back and forth between the written and legible parts of an image – between the textual and the purely visual or graphic, of which (as Addison says) "it is but opening the Eye, and the Scene enters." But in the later 1740s, after the climactic "comic history paintings" of *Marriage à la Mode*, in *Industry and Idleness* and the prints that followed, Hogarth begins to privilege the purely visual, and this is just as he coincidentally turns his attention to the plight of the poor and so precisely the illiterate. He launches into prints that distinguish – or at least open up a space for – the illiterate, the plebeian spectators of the theater galleries who bring a totally different mode of understanding to his prints. For one thing, they are specifically the non-purchasers of the prints, the apprentices who look at the prints purchased by the master and hung on their walls for their edification, but into which they can read their own meaning. At this point understanding radically breaks with both property and status.

Hogarth produces a scenario that does not, of course, cancel the educated readers, but it now privileges the naive immediacy of the apprentice's or the poor gin-drinker's apprehension, suggesting that there is a strength in this unmediated reading which the elite readers should try to appreciate – as they would also be turned by the contemporary poems of William Collins and the collections of Thomas Percy from the mode of Pope ("Pope Alexander") to a reading that draws upon the superstitions of the Scottish

Highlands and other ostensibly pre-literate, unmediated sources. This is what Parson Adams expresses when he throws his text of Aeschylus into the fire in his joy at the reunion of Joseph and Fanny, but also when he prefers Homer's Homer to Pope's. The part of Hogarth's audience closest to himself would have been not the readers of Dryden, Pope, Swift, Gay, and Fielding, either those who were consumers of high art or those who were irresistibly drawn to emulative consumption (and shamed); but rather the consumer who appreciates his belatedness, cannot himself afford to buy original old master paintings, and so is on a wavelength with the artist who wishes to circumvent the influence and reputation of those paintings – who cannot, for a variety of reasons as stringent as those that limited poor Tom Idle, paint them any more than his audience could purchase them. This is the consumer for whom Hogarth has been attempting to clear a path, with each new print, since his first exploration of the subject of consumption in *A Harlot's Progress*.

Notes

1   *A Modest Defence of Publick Stews* (1724), pp. xi–xii; Mandeville, *The Fable of the Bees* (1924: I, 100). Some of the materials I first sketched out in this Clark lecture have since been reworked into biographical narrative in my *Hogarth: The "Modern Moral Subject," 1697–1732* (1991) and *Hogarth: High Art and Low, 1732–1750* (1992).

2   Cf. *Daily Journal*, November 28, 1730. For further information on the prints, see Paulson, *Hogarth's Graphic Works* (1989).

3   If the upper social margin of society was distinguished by not having to earn a living, the line between the middle and lower orders was drawn at the possession of property. See Harold Perkin, *The Origins of Modern English Society, 1780–1880* (1969: 23).

4   See Michael Shinagel, *Daniel Defoe and Middle-Class Gentility* (1968), which educes many interesting facts but applies them to Defoe himself rather than his work.

5   Once this brilliantly realized situation is exhausted, however, and Jacque goes to Virginia, Defoe slips back into familiar genres: the conduct-book discussions between Jacque and his master and his own servants and slaves. But then Jacque returns to England and marries a fortune-hunting woman who fleeces him; when he leaves her and refuses to pay her bills, her bully confronts him in his own house with the code of a gentleman: he must pay her bill or fight a duel with the bully, who taunts him with his plebeian cowardice, and subsequently has him treated as a gentleman would treat one who refused his challenge: slashed and mutilated by hired bravoes. This humiliation forces Jacque to prove his gentility to himself by becoming a soldier and going to war. His next wife then allows him to correct the situation of his first one: her unfaithfulness is an excuse to treat her lover in the same way as he was treated by the first wife's lover.

6   See also John Sekora, *Luxury: The Concept in Western Thought, Eden to Smollett* (1977). Fashion, said Nicholas Barbon, "occasions the Expence of Cloaths before the Old ones are worn out" (see Joyce Appleby 1976: 506).

7   On one occasion Moll steals a necklace from a little girl. In Moll's reference to the little girl as not *she* or *her* but "it," we recognize a discourse of commodification, which at crucial moments (of choice, hunger, or danger) she replaces with the religious discourse of providence, the devil, temptation, and penitence. But these two discourses were initially obscured by Moll's discourse of gentility which, given her actual class status (unambiguous in terms of placement and cash, ambiguous in terms of her beauty and ability to learn), is emulated.

8   See Jackson Lears, "From salvation to self-realization: advertising and the therapeutic roots of the consumer culture, 1880–1930" (1983: 3–38). Of course, to be fair to Richardson – and as Professor Klein shows in his paper – emulation could be regarded as a good when

not accompanied by pretense, i.e. wishing to be what one is not or cannot be; when it does not too radically alter the authenticity of the self.

9   On originals and copies, cf. Richardson, *An Essay on the Whole Art of Criticism* (1773b: 225).

10   Mandeville on emulation: "We look above our selves, and, as fast as we can, strive to imitate those, that some way or other are superior to us" (1924: 129); which Mandeville praises in that it "sets the Poor to Work, adds Spurs to Industry, and encourages the skilful Artificer to search after further Improvements" (p. 130). And in "A search into the nature of society," appended to the 1723 edition as an attack on Shaftesbury: "that our Liking or Disliking of things chiefly depends on Mode and Custom, and the Precept and example of our betters and such whom one way or other we think to be Superior to us" (p. 330). See also McKendrick, Brewer, and Plumb (1982: 15–20).

11   A pictorial typology is perhaps the most accurate way of describing the relationship Hogarth establishes between his figures and the pictures they hang on their walls: X does Y because Z did it before; Z was the type that predicted the antitype X who must now fulfill his/her destiny. Thus the strong element of compulsion in imitation, based in the case of typology on a figure based on (determined by) history. In short, the painter copies old master paintings because rich men buy old masters because gentlemen buy them – because theorists like Richardson told them to do so. But also because the gentlemen have been taught by Richardson to believe in typology and example and to act according to them.

12   In *The Analysis of Beauty* (1753) Hogarth illustrates the Shaftesburyian principle of disinterestedness (the elision of ambition, possession, and consumption) by abstracting the aspect of property or consumption from his formal analysis, but then refutes it in his illustrative plates by demonstrating that animal (sexual) hunger and consumption – of a product, of property – are the two elements that *are* (or must be) connected with Beauty in order to define it. The first plate is set in a statuary yard where lead copies of the great canonical sculptures – the Venus de Medici, the Apollo Belvedere, the Laocoön – are precisely commodities, waiting to be purchased and carted away to country houses. And in the center is the triangle of Apollo, Venus, and (standing in for Vulcan, of whom there was not a canonical sculpture) Hercules. Again in Plate 2 the "possession" of marriage is questioned by an interloping lover. In the practical world of his own product, his prints, disinterestedness or detachment is replaced by various kinds of involvement, including the act of consumption, that extend beauty to moral and social issues and questions of class, and point towards *praxis*. But even in the text of *The Analysis of Beauty* his examples – stays, candlesticks, smokejacks – imply utility and the low status of commodities.

13   Addison emphasized in *The Spectator* no. 411 that the sense of sight (for him, as for Locke, the primary sense) is both immediate and democratic ("It is but opening the Eye, and the Scene enters"), but at the same time the "Man of a Polite Imagination is let into a great many Pleasures that the Vulgar are not capable of receiving . . . he looks upon the World, as it were, in another Light, and discovers in it a Multitude of Charms, that conceal themselves from the generality of Mankind." And this reflects the two audiences, the general reader and the reader of greater penetration, Addison described in his formulation of allegory (or perhaps more accurately irony) in *Spectator* No. 315.

14   In the first state of the print, "Pope Alexander" has been replaced by a print of Pope thrashing Curll, the bookseller whom he swindled into publishing his letters so he could then (without appearing conceited) bring out a "correct" edition himself. See Paulson, *Hogarth: High Art and Low* (1992: 119–20).

15   He defines burlesque as "the Exhibition of what is monstrous and unnatural," but as arising "from the surprizing Absurdity, as in appropriating the Manners of the highest to the lowest, or *e converso*": But the *e converso* is pro forma; he means in fact "appropriating the Manners of the highest *by* the lowest."

16   Fielding, as early as his farce *Pasquin* (1736), was echoing the Beggar's speech at the end of *The Beggar's Opera*: preparing to set out for London, the mayor's wife is asked by her daughter:

"But must I go into keeping, mamma?"
"Child, you must do what's in fashion."
"But I have heard that's a naughty thing."
"That can't be, if your betters do it; people are punished for doing naughty things; but people of quality are never punished; therefore they never do naughty things."

Even Jonathan Wild is shown imitating an ideal of greatness constantly held in front of him – by himself but also by the ironic narrator. Although the narrator claims that part of Wild's greatness lies in his preordained death on the gallows, a trace of pathos remains in the memory that "people of quality are never punished" and the knowledge that Wild never quite measures up to the ideal of greatness proffered by them.

17   Cf. Michael McKeon's view that Fielding, "attracted . . . to the energy of the career open to talents," was "appalled by the vanity and pretension of those who enacted that career with any success or conviction" (1987: 35).
18   Cf., in particular, Fielding's remarks on learned women in *Amelia* (and the character of Mrs. Bennet), and Battestin's note in his edition of *Amelia* (1983: 255). It is possible, of course, to argue that servants represent a middle area in themselves.
19   In short, Hogarth cancels the subject of emulative consumption by turning his attention, first, more directly to the poor and, second, to the Beautiful – the first in *Industry and Idleness* and the second in *The Analysis of Beauty* of five years later.

Bibliography

Appleby, Joyce (1976) "Ideology and theory: the tension between political and economic liberalism in seventeenth-century England," *American Historical Review* 81, 3: 506 ff.
Daily Journal (1730) 28 November.
Defoe, Daniel (1724) *The Great Law of Subordination Consider'd*, London: S. Harding, W. Lewis, etc.
—— (1726) *Complete English Tradesman*, London: Rivington.
Fielding, Henry (1983) *Amelia*, ed. Martin C. Battestin, Middletown, CT: Wesleyan University Press.
Frank, Judith (1993–4) "The comic novel and the poor: Fielding's preface to *Joseph Andrews*," *Eighteenth-Century Studies* 27: 217–34.
Houghton, John (1681) *A Collection of Letters for the Improvement of Husbandry and Trade*, London: Randall Taylor *et al.*
Lears, T. J. Jackson (1983) "From salvation to self-realization: advertising and the therapeutic roots of the consumer culture, 1880–1930," in Richard W. Fox and T. J. Jackson Lear (eds.) *The Culture of Consumption: Critical Essays in American History, 1880–1980*, New York: Pantheon Books.
London Magazine vol. 7 (1738).
McKendrick, Neil, Brewer, John, and Plumb, J. H. (1982) *The Birth of a Consumer Society: The Commercialization of Eighteenth-Century England*, Bloomington, IN: Indiana University Press.
McKeon, Michael (1987) *The Origins of the Novel*, Baltimore, MD: Johns Hopkins University Press.
Mandeville, Bernard (1724) *A Modest Defence of Public Stews*, London: A. Moore.
—— (1924) *The Fable of the Bees*, ed. F. B. Kaye, Vol. 1, Oxford: Blackwell.
Paulson, Ronald (1978) *Popular and Polite Art in the Age of Hogarth and Fielding*, Notre Dame, IN: University of Notre Dame Press.
—— (1989) *Hogarth's Graphic Works*, 3rd. rev. edn., London: Print Room.
—— (1991) *Hogarth: "The Modern Moral Subject," 1697–1732*, New Brunswick, NJ, Rutgers University Press.
—— (1992) *Hogarth: High Art and Low, 1732–1750*, New Brunswick, NJ: Rutgers University Press.
Perkin, Harold James (1969) *The Origins of Modern English Society, 1780–1880*, London: Routledge & Kegan Paul.

Plumb, J. H. (1973) *The Commercialization of Leisure in Eighteenth-Century England*, Reading, Berks: University of Reading.

Pope, Alexander (1953) *The Dunciad*, ed. James Sutherland, London: Methuen; New Haven, CT: Yale University Press.

Richardson, Jonathan (1773a) *The Science of a Connoisseur*, in *The Works of Mr. Jonathan Richardson*, Hildeshcim: G. Olms.

—— (1773b) *An Essay on the Whole Art of Criticism*, in *The Works of Mr. Jonathan Richardson*, Hildesheim: G. Olms.

Sekora, John (1977) *Luxury: The Concept in Western Thought, Eden to Smollett*, Baltimore, MD: Johns Hopkins University Press.

Shinagel, Michael (1968) *Daniel Defoe and Middle-Class Gentility*, Cambridge, MA: Harvard University Press.

Wimsatt, W. K. (1965) *Pope Portraits*, New Haven, CT: Yale University Press.

21

"La chose publique"
Hubert Robert's decorations for the "petit salon" at Méréville

Paula Rea Radisich

How the Academy's exhibitions have haunted the imaginations of historians of eighteenth-century French art! The reason for this is clear enough: the Salon furnishes us with a rich textual record – precious words and numbers – about works of art. Was the piece shown in the Salon, we ask? What did reviewers have to say about it? Thomas E. Crow's analysis of the Salon in *Painters and Public Life* made it even more central to our understanding of art and society. He emphasized the nature of the exhibition as a public space of political contestation, where various individuals and groups engaged in "a struggle over representation, over language and symbols and who had the right to use them" (Crow 1985: 5).

The kind of salon I am concerned with is the domestic salon. Less public than the Salon of the Académie Royale, the domestic salon's status as a discursive and signifying space had become, by the last third of the century, ambiguous and increasingly suspect. The challenge that faced artists who were commissioned to decorate the domestic salon was how to conceptualize this private sphere so that it shared – or at least appeared to share – the same formal and iconographic legitimating discourses of "la chose publique" that had come to characterize the politics of the Enlightenment and the art of the public Salon. It is this struggle that I believe we find played out in Hubert Robert's paintings for the "petit salon" of Jean-Joseph de Laborde at Méréville.

Ornament, decoration, and the Enlightenment

Ornament was not a great object of theoretical speculation for rococo artists. Architects and decorators in France during the first half of the eighteenth century had unproblematically applied a relatively standardized vocabulary of interior and exterior decoration to their buildings, matching form, style, and motif to the purpose of an edifice and the rank of its proprietor. Usage was determined by the doctrines of *convenance* (the correct relation of parts to each other and to their purpose) and *bienséance* (appropriateness or the correct form of the building to purpose and the patron's social rank).[1]

In the age of the *Encyclopédie*, however, something had changed. Reformers of the 1760s cast their eyes upon French ornament and recoiled in disgust, denouncing the "corruption of taste" and "depravity of style" into which practice had fallen (*Encyclopédie* 1778–9: *Index*, V, 94). Nowhere is the new instability of definition and purpose more strikingly indicated than in the discussion of decoration and ornament presented in the *Encyclopédie* itself, where the entries "decoration" and "ornament" are authored by different writers rooted in disparate discourses – one an artist and practitioner of the craft, the other a *philosophe* and critic. As one might expect, the call for change, for reform, emanated from the voice of the encyclopedist critic.

Jacques-François Blondel (1705–74) composed the *Encyclopédie*'s entry on decoration (1778–9: X, 452–4). His "decoration" is a conservative commentary which can stand for the views current in the first half of the century. Blondel, a practicing architect and teacher, had published his first book on building in 1738, *De la distribution des maisons de plaisance*; his celebrated four-volume compendium on French architecture, *Architecture françoise*, appeared in 1752–6. He begins his analysis by reiterating the primacy of the laws of *convenance* and *bienséance* (X, 452) to the field of decoration. Beyond one brief and slightly disparaging reference to certain "frivolous ornaments" introduced by past sculptors into their ensembles, he is full of praise for the French school: "This element of architecture," Blondel writes with pride, ". . . does France the greatest credit." "No nation . . . understands decoration as well as we do." And what is the object of decoration? Magnificence, states Blondel flatly – a magnificence exemplified by masterpieces like the Hôtels de Toulouse (1713–19) and de Soubise (1705–9),[2] enchanted abodes created by opulence "pour le séjour des grâces & de la volupté."

Magnificence, though, turns out to be the subversive agent that complicates the subject of decoration for vanguard artists and thinkers of the second half of the century, freighting it with an altogether different set of connotations connected to the philosophical debate about luxury. As defined in the *Encyclopédie*, magnificence belongs to the domain of morals (1778–9: XX, 741). The author of the article "magnificence" is a *philosophe*, the same man who will compose the entry on ornament, the chevalier de Jaucourt. Whereas Blondel had specifically associated magnificence with the opulent decoration of private, domestic space, Jaucourt identifies magnificence with the appropriate expenditure of wealth on objects "qui font de grande utilité au public," thus placing a value on the public, not the private, good. Jaucourt's concept, an expression of Enlightenment ideals typical of the *Encyclopédie*, differs distinctly from the definition of earlier lexicographers. Pierre Richelet, for example, had defined magnificence in his dictionary (1759 [1680]: II, 563) as a "virtue that loves glamor & to spend money prodigiously."

Entries on pomp and ostentation (*faste*) in the *Encyclopédie* resonate with the same castigating tone as the "magnificence" article. Furetière's earlier dictionary (1727 [1690]: III, n.p.) had defined pomp as an appropriate display of magnificence, such as the appearance an ambassador must present in order to do honor to his nation. The display of the French court, Furetière explains, indicates the power of its king. "*Faste*" in Diderot's *Encyclopédie*, on the other hand, speaks of the "pretensions" of the great and the "affectation" of demonstrating, by external signs, the idea of merit, power, or grandeur (1778–9: XIII, 863). Questioning the very value of pomp in his enlightened century, the author of one of the entries suggests that well-populated provinces, disciplined armies, and finances in good order will impress foreign nations more than the "*vain luxe*" of a royal court. As for the ostentatious individual, a short paragraph by Voltaire chides: "On peut vivre avec luxe dans sa maison sans faste, c'est-à-dire, sans se parer en public d'une opulence révoltante" (1778–9: XIII, 863).

Lying at the core of these expostulations by Enlightenment reformers is their passionate interest in the classical doctrine of liberality or right spending of riches.[3] On this count, Blondel's magnificence, the innocent objective of decoration, was clearly a misplaced expenditure which disturbed, even incensed, the encyclopedists on ethical grounds. If decoration was to take a place in the arena of cultural symbols in a post-encyclopedist age, its conceptual supports would have to be reformulated. Part of the old notions of *convenance* could be retained – notably the expressive manipulation of form to evoke sensation (what Blondel had called *caractère*) keyed to the purpose of the space and the comfort of its inhabitants (Blondel called this *commodité*) but those old signs of *bienséance* communicating the rank and status of the proprietor would have to be suppressed.

Through the *Encyclopédie*'s system of cross-references, Jaucourt posits, or at least points to, just such an Enlightenment revision of the ideas of decoration. First, in his article "*ornement (Peinture)*," Jaucourt, unlike Blondel, strikes an extremely bellicose posture towards the French school of ornament.[4] He writes contemptuously of ceiling paintings and overdoors which appear to have no end or purpose. Motivated only by a mindless desire to cover empty wall surfaces, French painters of ornamental ensembles had produced equally mindless pictures – "l'horreur du vuide remplit les murs de peintures vuides de sens" (1778–9: XXIV, 51). But – and here is how the cross-referencing is worked in – for an understanding of "how ornaments *ought* [emphasis added] to be handled in different works of art" Jaucourt sends the reader to an article in the *Encyclopédie* entitled "*exécution*" written by the German aesthetician, Johann Sulzer.

What could this have to do with wall decorations? In "*exécution*" (XIII: 502–5) Sulzer urges poets as well as graphic artists to infuse their artworks with coherent, forceful, clearly focused expression in emulation of masters ranging from Homer to Poussin. It seems that French ornament, heretofore constrained by simple artisanal considerations like "covering" the wall, was now to take on the means and objectives of poetry and easel painting. And indeed, as the century drew to a close, the theory and practice of ornament did change along the lines envisioned by Jaucourt. More specifically, by the 1770s, *caractère* had begun to replace *convenance* and *bienséance* as the aim and purpose of fashionable "enlightened" ornament.

In Paris, during the 1770s and 1780s, architects like Claude-Nicolas Ledoux, Alexandre-Théodore Brongniart, François-Joseph Bélanger, and Charles de Wailly designed buildings with the new norms and values in view.[5] The result was an architecture of mood and expression keyed to usage. As Jean Starobinski writes, "This architecture . . . wished to be expressive [*parlante*], that is, to indicate by the shape and arrangement of architectural forms the purpose of the space" ("Cette architecture . . . veut encore être 'parlante' par la façon dont elle ordonne ces figures afin d'en rendre la fonction extérieurement *évidente*" [1979: 61]. Today, the critical term *architecture parlante* is used to refer to the ideals and practices of these architects; eighteenth-century architects would have used the category of *caractère* to describe how their work differed from the past (Szambien 1986: 174–99).

One aspect of *caractère* omitted by Starobinski in his formulation is the significance of the beholder's response to the building: architecture now aimed to move the spectator emotionally. In his remarkable tract *Le génie de l'architecture ou l'analogue de cet art avec nos sensations* of 1780, Nicolas Le Camus de Mézières, a partisan of architectural *caractère* or expressiveness, articulated its fundamental premisses.[6] As Blondel had done in his *De la distribution des maisons de plaisance* of 1738, Le Camus examines in rich and lengthy detail the appropriate decor for each room of an elegant domestic house. But unlike Blondel, Le Camus has a theory to test on his readers: how inanimate objects evoke an emotional reaction in the spectator. That the sight of a monument will stir different "sensations" in a viewer is taken as axiomatic, for proof lies in theatrical stage-sets and English garden design, both able, Le Camus argues, to engage "facultés de l'âme, & parviennent à élever l'esprit jusqu'aux plus sublimes contemplations" (1780: 14). How much more powerful is the potential of "le génie de l'architecture," when architecture, painting, and sculpture are combined *intentionally* into one unified and overwhelming impression.

> C'est de ce principe qu'il faut partir, lorsqu'on prétend dans l'Architecture produire des affections, lorsqu'on veut parler à l'esprit, émouvoir l'âme, & ne pas se contenter, en bâtissant, de placer pierres sur pierres, & d'imiter au hazard des dispositions, des ornemens convenus ou empruntés sans méditation. L'intention motivée dans l'ensemble, les proportions & l'accord des différentes parties produisent les effets & les sensations.
>
> (1780: 7)

It is *this* conception of ornamentation as a tool to construct evocative and pointed three-dimensional ensembles in the domestic private space (interestingly Le Camus ignores the decoration of public buildings) that frames my analysis of Hubert Robert's salon decorations.[7]

Born in 1733, Hubert Robert is an exact contemporary of the architects associated with these ideas and practices. Emil Kaufmann called them the "generation of 1760": Ledoux was born in 1735, de Wailly in 1730, Brongniart in 1739.[8] These men were friends, colleagues, and occasional collaborators: when Ledoux built an hôtel for J.-B. Hosten in 1792, Hubert Robert painted the salon (Vidler 1990: 364–70).

Werner Szambien argues that *caractère* as an aesthetic ideal bore its first fruit among the *pensionnaires* studying architecture at the French Academy in Rome around 1750 (1986: 174–99).[9] The designs of architects like Marie-Joseph Peyre (1730–85) exemplify what he calls a "radical current" that developed there in response to the graphic works of Giovanni Battista Piranesi. That Robert's pictorial idiom was formed in the same crucible need hardly be stated.[10] Robert notwithstanding, Piranesi's vocabulary of centered arches and diagonally recessed columns was ubiquitous among the coterie of *pensionnaires* engaged in the representation of Roman buildings at the time. Indeed, Georges Brunel claims that the "language" of Piranesi was only truly comprehensible *to* architects (*Piranèse et les Français* 1976: 23). What *caractère* as a subsequent aesthetic formulation seems to share with Piranesi's imagery is the precedence attributed to the evocative properties of space and mass.

With the exception of Ledoux, perhaps, no French artist of the period was more of an impresario of the constructed space than Hubert Robert. Although we think of him primarily as a painter, one of Robert's royal pensions derived from his post as "Dessinateur des jardins du roi."[11] His fame rested on such marvels as the *Bains d'Apollon*, an assemblage of appropriated statues by Girardon, Guérin, and Gaspard and Balthazard Marsy set into a new fabricated grotto at the park of Versailles. The Island of Poplars at Ermenonville, site of the tomb of Jean-Jacques Rousseau, was another celebrated masterpiece of *sensibilité* designed by Hubert Robert. The aim of such pieces, which today we would call "environmental art" or "installations," was to create a "theater of experience centered on the garden" (Adams 1979: 114). Out of all the painters prominent in Paris during the 1780s, none matches Robert's involvement with garden art. Robert's interests in this regard should not be confused with those of a genuine gardener like André Le Nôtre, Robert's predecessor as "First Gardener to the King." The botanical dimension to gardening did not engage Hubert Robert's attention. His objective in working the terrain lay in creating a consciously artificial effect for the viewer through a carefully mediated intrusion of "art" into "nature." Both in the garden fabrications and, as I shall argue, in the ornamental ensembles he painted for salons, Robert created mood pieces infused with an "intention motivée dans l'ensemble," as Le Camus put it.

The salon

In 1787, Hubert Robert received a commission to ornament a salon for the immensely rich ex-banker to the court of France, Jean-Joseph de Laborde, in his château at Méréville. A "salon," as Dena Goodman points out in her study of the Enlightenment philosophical salon, referred in the eighteenth century to nothing more specific than a room in a house (Goodman 1989: 330, n. 2). Robert's salon was located on the ground floor of the recently remodeled château, to the right of the vestibule.[12] It was thus a "public" domestic architectural space designed for social gatherings. Under the aegis of the new weight given to *caractère*, the decoration of such a salon presented a stimulating creative challenge for the artist/decorator. How might the artist play with the constraints of "le local . . . l'utilité et . . . l'usage,"[13] and tie them into those relating to *caractère*?

It is this problem that I now wish to analyze as a case study of issues involving domestic space and consumption. Jean-Joseph de Laborde is the same patron who had commissioned, seventeen years earlier, *La Mère Bien Aimée* (1769) from Jean-Baptiste Greuze. There, in one of the more memorable images of eighteenth-century *sensibilité*, he had been pleased to see himself represented as the leisured aristocrat returning from the hunt into the bosom of his family, joyously gathered around "the well-loved mother," Laborde's wife Rosalie-Claire de Nettine. The hunt motif also appeared in his dining-room at the time. As Horace Walpole realized when he dined with him in 1765, the *salle à manger* of Laborde's Paris hôtel on the rue Grange-Batelière contained the same decoration it had held when Laborde had purchased the building from the farmer-general Etienne-Michel Bouret in the early 1760s. The dining-room, adorned with depictions of hunting dogs by François Desportes (Boyer 1962: 140), prompted Walpole to write home sarcastically: "your eating-room must be hung with huge hunting-pieces, in frames of all coloured-golds, and at top of one of them, you may place a setting-dog, who having sprung a wooden partridge, it may be flying a yard off against the wainscot" (Walpole 1937–71: XXXI, 80). Although hunting did not wane as a favored pastime of the wealthy elite during the course of the eighteenth century, imagery drawn from the hunt, an imagery that blatantly announced the prerogatives of privilege (and thus magnificence and display), had already begun to appear unfashionable. Neither of the dining-rooms in the new château of Méréville, purchased by Laborde in 1784, seems to have included references to the hunt.

Although the salon that Robert was commissioned to ornament in 1787 was a public, rather than a private, space in the house, it was not Méréville's grand, ceremonial salon, the Salon d'Eté.[14] In the correspondence between Laborde and Hubert Robert, the salon which concerns us is referred to as "*le petit salon de Méréville*," a sobriquet suggesting a comparatively more diminutive architectural space. Such spaces evolved during the *ancien régime* in connection with various new social practices stressing intimacy and informality. One of these, for example, was the *petit souper*. The *petit souper* took its eighteenth-century form during the reign of Louis XV when the monarch began to host intimate dinners in the private apartments of the palace at Versailles. Court protocol was set aside in the newly remodeled *salles à manger* in the Cabinets du Roi (the first appeared in 1732) and guests of both genders were invited to sit in no particular order at the same table with the king (Solnon 1987: 492). Quickly spreading to Paris, the intimate late supper eventually became a social event of more consequence than the traditional afternoon dinner. Vigée-Lebrun, who became famous for her *petits soupers*, described them in her memoirs as intimate gatherings of twelve or fifteen persons who would come together around nine in the evening "pour y finir leur soirée" (I, 82). At ten o'clock, guests dined on simple, light fare, and at midnight everyone retired. Conversation was lively, polished, and artful: "L'aisance, la douce gaieté, qui régnaient à ces légers repas du soir, leur donnaient un charme que les dîners n'auront jamais plus" (1986: I, 82). It was at these *soupers*, Vigée concludes nostalgically, that Paris society showed itself superior to the rest of Europe.

Vigée banned the subject of politics from her evening gatherings, but others did not. In Paris on a visit in 1784, William Beckford noted that "nothing so vulgar as religion is ever alluded to at those select great dinners and 'petits soupers' where the new light of doubly refined philosophy is shedding its beams in profusion." He owned that he was tired of the "pedantic gabble in such vogue . . . in the highest circles about political wants and political miseries . . ." (Oliver 1932: 192–3). Jean-Joseph de Laborde had been one of Beckford's hosts for "suppering out" on the "cold and snowy night[s]" of the Parisian winter of 1784; the Englishman complained about Laborde's hôtel being "damp as a grotto" in spite of its "blazing fires and blazing company" (Oliver 1932: 162).

As Beckford's remark suggests, Jean-Joseph de Laborde, though officially retired as banker to the court of France at this time, remained prominent in Paris society and politics.[15] Laborde was a reformer of the Enlightenment variety, a man who supported economic progress, individual freedom, and social harmony, but envisioned these reforms as evolving within a stable, monarchical political system. He was accordingly both a friend of the *philosophes*, proud to call himself the banker of Voltaire, *and* intimate with Mercy-Argenteau, the Austrian ambassador to the court (Vermale 1937: 48–64). An exemplar of the liberal aristocracy in the 1770s and 1780s (he had received the title of marquis in 1784), Laborde prided himself a virtuous citizen. As he declared in his memoirs, "J'ai toujours conservé l'attachement le plus décidé pour le commerce, c'est l'état d'un vrai citoyen,"[16] a strange avowal for a stupendously successful banker engaged in various financial dealings for over forty years. Laborde's confession becomes more comprehensible in light of the deliberations of the Assembly of Notables in 1787, though, for they clearly indicate that finance was seen in the 1780s, even in relatively conservative quarters, as a non-productive economic activity. Unlike commerce, industry, and agriculture, finance was thought to undermine national prosperity because it produced wealth but not employment (Gruder 1978: 207–32). Right spending of riches – the state's, his own, or both – was apt to be a theme of consuming interest in the Laborde salon.

After its purchase at the end of 1784, Méréville, located about seventeen leagues from Paris at Etampes, welcomed the cream of Parisian society. "La maison de mon beau-père," recalled the duc des Cars, Laborde's son-in-law, "réunissait la plus grande compagnie de Paris, en gens importants tant Français qu'étrangers, hommes de lettres et artistes distingués. . . . Il reçevait également beaucoup de monde chez lui à la campagne" (des Cars 1890: I, 342). As one might expect, among Laborde's more habitual guests were men of finance. The financier Simon-Charles Boutin, "immensément riche" (Vigée-Lebrun 1986: II, 243–4), often visited the estate. Charles-Alexandre Calonne, appointed Minister of Finances to the French court in 1784, was a frequent caller. Calonne's mistress, later his second wife, née Anne-Josèphe de Nettine, was Madame d'Harvelay, the sister of Madame de Laborde (both were daughters of Mathias de Nettine, Belgian banker to the court of the Low Countries). Calonne's disgrace in 1787, followed by the ministry of Loménie de Brienne, who resigned roughly one year later, led to the announcement of August 8, 1788 that the Estates-General would meet the following May to resolve the nation's crisis. The prospect pleased the citizen-elites of the Laborde family; Laborde-Méréville, Jean-Joseph's eldest son, would sit with the Third Estate to represent the bailliage of Etampes when it convened (Vermale 1937: 54).[17]

Hubert Robert, hired by Laborde to design and to supervise the creation of an extraordinary English garden at Méréville, often acted as cicerone for Laborde's visitors.[18] In fact, it is worth noting that Robert's circle of convives overlapped with that of his patron. Noted for the charm of a personality "as lively as light,"[19] Hubert Robert, along with the financier Boutin, Jacques Delille, Charles-Claude Labillarderie, comte d'Angiviller, and his wife, was a regular guest at Vigée-Lebrun's parties. Hence, the garden architect *qua* artist was optimally positioned to ornament *le petit salon de Méréville* according to the new aesthetic dictates of expression and appropriateness.

The image(s)

The paintings that Robert produced in 1787–8 for Laborde's *petit salon de Méréville* are now in the Chicago Art Institute.[20] Today, they bear the descriptive titles of *The Obelisk* (Plate 21.1, signed and dated 1787), *The Old Temple* (Plate 21.2), *The Fountains* (Plate 21.3), and *The Landing Place* (Plate 21.4). The sites represented in the four canvases are all imaginary, though vestiges of actual Roman statues grace two of them. *The Fountains* (Plate 21.3) features a reversed version of the celebrated *Dioscuri* fixed along the steps of the Campidoglio in Rome, and *The Landing Place* (Plate 21.4), a view of an antique port, includes the *Alexander and Bucephalus* from the Piazza del Quirinale as well as a statue adapted from the *Cesi Juno* and the *Farnese Flora*, both in the Capitoline Museum. A fanciful combination of figures in togate and modern dress enlivens the different scenes. In *The Old Temple* (Plate 21.2) and *The Fountains* (Plate 21.3), female figures are shown drawing water from lion-spout fountains lodged within the remains of colossal vaulted structures. And in *The Obelisk* (Plate 21.1) and *The Old Temple* (Plate 21.2) an enormous dog is added to the groups of figures who sit, stroll, or converse idly around the stairs.

Robert's imagery of Greco-Roman columns, vaults, statues, and reliefs reproduces a repertoire of ornament connected to dining-room decor in the 1780s. In his section on dining-rooms in *Le génie de l'architecture ou l'analogue de cet art avec nos sensations*, Le Camus de Mézières had proposed to decorate the *salle à manger* with a row of columns set against the wall, enframing, at regular intervals, white highly polished statues of pagan deities like Hebe and Flora (1780: 178–9), a decorative program similar to the dining-rooms at Méréville.[21] What Robert seems to have provided for his patron in the "*petit salon*" was a *painted* version of this ornamentation, albeit assembled into striking scenic units that draw on conventions of the eighteenth-century theater.

As John D. Bandiera (1989: 21–37) has shown in a recent article, Robert's imaginative combinations of diagonally recessed stairs and arcades owe an obvious debt to seventeenth- and eighteenth-century set designs and backdrops for tragedies, ballets, and operas. Indeed, the idiom of porticoes, obelisks, and antique statues was absolutely typical of the vocabulary used for theatrical productions of the period.[22] Since Robert is known to have assisted in the fabrication of certain theater sets and curtains, the formal correspondence between the two is perhaps not surprising (Desormes 1822: 124). Displaced from the theater to the domestic salon, though, the imagery acquires a rather different set of meanings.

In his ornamental ensemble for *le petit salon de Méréville* the artist plays with both the traditions of the stage-set and *trompe-l'oeil*, specifically the convention of the *trompe-l'oeil* hermitage exemplified by Charles-Louis Clérisseau's ruin room created at the convent of S. Trinità dei Monti in Rome in 1764 (McCormick 1990: 103–12). The painted space of Robert's four panels similarly approximates a fictive enclosure. At least two to three walls are shown in each canvas and all include the floor of the box. Diagonal recession draws the eye in all of them through a series of contoured apertures towards the light, illusionistically opening up the space of the room.

But the *petit salon de Méréville* was no hermitage harboring a retiring scholar weary of commerce with the world. (Clérisseau's ruin room was painted for the use of two mathematicians at S. Trinità.) It was rather a site of sociable gatherings. How do the ruined temples of Robert's pictures, then, relate to the use of this chamber? A closer look reveals that the Méréville canvases do, in fact, depict a public and discursive space, one with even a civic dimension. The vaults and arcades in *The Landing Place* (Plate 21.4) and *The Obelisk* (Plate 21.1) appear to line a piazza or a public square, while *The Old Temple* (Plate 21.2) and *The Fountains* (Plate 21.3) both include women drawing water from a fountain. Public water, like the piazza and the port, signals the presence of a polis.

By endowing the *petit salon* with the character of a civic space, Hubert Robert acknowledges the primary function of the salon as a space of sociability, a polite space, in which to shape and construct political discussion. The ancients, for once, furnished the eighteenth century with a negative exemplum in this respect. In Athens and in Rome, the public square and the Forum served as the site of political discourse. But, as Jacques Delille described it, what a vile precinct it became (Delille 1812: 20)! A place of tumult and chaos, the ancient public square sheltered unscrupulous demagogues who excited the populace with violent orations – harangues that inexcusably would accompany the listeners back with them to their homes, creating a virtual battleground out of their living quarters:

> Les fauteurs et les partisans de ceux qui se disputaient l'autorité, conservant les impressions qu'ils avaient reçues ou données, faisaient du salon un champ de bataille; aucun n'était lui: chacun était ou Marius ou Sylla, ou Pompée ou César, Antoine ou Auguste, et combattait pour un intérêt dont le désir de plaire ou de réussir avait fait le sien.

(Delille 1812: 21)

In the poem from which these prefatory statements are extracted, "La Conversation," Delille aims to contrast the unrestrained and irresponsible institutions of public rhetoric in antiquity with the civility of the French eighteenth-century salon conversation. What a difference, he exclaims, between those turbulent gatherings "et ces sociétés aimables, où la France admettait avec plaisir les étrangers les plus distingués par leurs titres ou leurs lumières" (Delille 1812: 21).

Robert's imagery, then, figuratively brings the polis into the bosom of the domestic salon where its unruly excesses will be curbed by the civility of polite conversation. It is not the content of Robert's pictures, a content notably lacking in gaiety or good cheer, that points to the room's use – but the *form* of the Méréville panels. The formal structure of the paintings imitates the "structure" of polite conversation practiced at the time. Conversational expression in the eighteenth century was controlled by rules designed to encourage the free flow of ideas among an assembly gathered together to discuss, develop, and refine a given topic. "One examines, one discusses, one attacks, one defends; one sees enlightenment born from the shock of ideas and opinions," wrote the abbé Morellet (cited by Gordon 1989: 315). Process was very much at the heart of the conversational enterprise. Since "enlightenment" was generated by the collective efforts of the conversationalists over time, a free posture and open, non-authoritarian atmosphere were pivotal to the success of the venture (Gordon 1989: 322). All ranks, all circumstances, and all ages participated equally in this commerce; all had a responsibility to contribute to the group's common pleasure, all shouldered blame for its collective *ennui* (Delille 1812: 22).

As a compositional ensemble, Robert's Méréville panels invite a similar meandering, fragmented, and non-hierarchical pattern of visual attention. Moreover, these are images in which the conversational unit, so to speak, is a shape – the semicircle, for example, which is repeated, contradicted, paraphrased, and scrutinized from different angles in each of the different canvases. As in a polite conversation, limits and edges are left deliberately obscure. Because the imagery in all the pictures is cropped by the framing edge, we are able to grasp only the fragment of what we are able to see in the visual field. Our ability to fathom the whole is impaired, a condition similar to the imperfect understanding of the dialogists generating "knowledge" through conversation.

The perspective in Robert's four compositions is brilliantly decentered and fragmented, technically resistant to the visual control of an omnipotent spectator. A composition like *The Fountains* (Plate 21.3) seems to dismantle the frontal alignments of a painting like Raphael's *School of Athens*, which in fact it seems to parody, setting the planes askew to the picture surface. The classical structure of the *School of Athens* – an image in which the configured elements are unfurled in layers parallel to the plane and then arranged within the semicircular frame on an imaginary axis with the centered eye of a single, stationary beholder – has been shifted, so the perpendicularity of Raphael's vaults (now ruined!) stands at an angle of forty-five degrees to the plane. As a result, in absolute contrast to the Raphael, we cannot see clearly what the opening in *The Fountains* frames for us. If to frame is to select and consequently to control, the perspectival apparatus of Robert's Méréville compositions eludes control. As in a conversation, the center of authority is radically dispersed, shifting around the circle as different subjects speak.

Although transience is unquestionably a theme in the four-panel series, evoked, for example, by the juxtaposition of ruined vaults in *The Old Temple* (Plate 21.2) and *The Fountains* (Plate 21.3) with the intact structures of *The Obelisk* (Plate 21.1) and *The Landing Place* (Plate 21.4), its sharp edge is blunted considerably by Robert's handling. Time may wear the trappings of antiquity in these representations but its nature is more geological than historical. Change, accordingly, appears in a very reassuring light. This is an imagery of orderly departures (*The Landing Place*) and arrivals (saddled horses in *The Fountains*). Within the stabilizing frame of Robert's representations, the historical and political vicissitudes of mankind occur without violence and conflict. From a vantage point hovering above the baseline of the panels, the spectator is able to take in the scene(s) with a broad sweep – a critical stance – at liberty to vacillate or to shift position.

And in *The Fountains* (Plate 21.3) the artist presents an amusing ontological conundrum centered around the stone sculptures placed above each fountain. Arranged in diagonal opposition, an implausibly lifelike statue leads a horse towards the plane of the canvas in counter-movement to two "real" saddled horses which face into the picture space; on the vertical supports of the arch, a roundel depicts horse and rider galloping off. A dizzying sequence of motifs representing different states of motion – at rest, at walk, at gallop – and contrasting directions of motion – in, out, parallel to the plane, to the left, to the right – these horses and men exist in a world where divisions between art and human life are mysteriously obscured. It is as if "real" steeds and "real" men and women have been reduced and refracted into a realm of art infused with sentient life. In Robert's painted world, calcified statues eye figures or their mounts slyly and gesture to them meaningfully. Similarly, the archaicized letters Robert inscribes on the pedestal beneath the female statue in *The Landing Place* ("H. Robert in aedibus merevillae pro d. delaborde pinxit A.D. 1788"; Plate 21.4) lift the "real" Robert and Laborde out of the present moment and deposit them seamlessly into the fictive time and space of the picture. If the imagery in Hubert Robert's pictures is taken seriously as a pointed example of a particular form of interaction between humankind and its art, a cue for Laborde and his guests to mimic in *le petit salon de Méréville*, then the interaction between these works of art and their viewers is expected to be an active and empathetic one.[23]

Performing the role of citizen

Hubert Robert's pictures consequently structure and shape the space of Méréville's *petit salon* in ways that remind us that elite culture in France at the end of the *ancien régime* was a performance culture (Stanton 1980; Huizinga 1955). Horace Walpole grumbled about this in 1765, complaining that in Paris "everyone sings, reads their own works in public, or attempts any one thing without hesitation or capacity" (Walpole 1840: V, 81). To be sure, artful conversation was part of the performance demanded in the "petit salon," but Robert's panels, so similar to backdrops used in tragic opera or drama, promoted another type of posturing as well. His pictures created a setting in which the patron and his guests were invited to recast themselves in the roles of "citizen-tribunes" acting in the service of the state.[24] This is an imagery resonating with the stirring chords of *The Social Contract*'s "la chose publique." As the baron de Frénilly recalled the temper of the 1780s, that was the very locution he used:

> Tout Français prenait alors un vif intérêt à la chose publique: l'artisan comme le marchand, le bourgeois comme le grand seigneur, s'informaient, se souciaient des événements, des guerres, des alliances; mais ce n'était pas cette agitation égoïste qui s'occupe de la chose publique pour redescendre d'elle à la chose privée et consulter l'intérêt de l'Etat comme le thermomètre de l'intérêt de sa boutique: c'était un sentiment inverse qui allait de soi-même à la France.
> (Frénilly 1909: 40)

Robert's ornamentation of *le petit salon de Méréville* allowed Jean-Joseph de Laborde, a "grand seigneur" of the 1780s, surely, if there ever was one, to play with and against a representation of "the public thing" at Méréville. Indeed, there is an assumption about the nature of art as a potent tool of socialization imbedded in Robert's panels that is equally present in Ledoux's imaginary city of Chaux and later, in the great Revolutionary fêtes staged by the government to refine the construction of the Republican citizen. A fundamental difference, though, separates the Roberts from the last two: the art produced by Robert for *le petit salon* was designed to complement activities and behaviors existing within the domestic space of the private salon, a space in which "tous les rangs, tous les états, tous les âges" (Delille 1812: 22), and, he might have added, all genders, participated visibly and volubly in both the consumption and the creation of culture.

Notes

I would like to thank Mary D. Sheriff and Ann Bermingham for the comments and suggestions they made on this paper.

1   These classifications are ambiguous. See Vidler (1987) and Szambien (1986) for fine studies of eighteenth-century architectural theory. See Szambien, especially, on the meaning of *convenance* in the eighteenth century (1986: 92–7).

2   The buildings mentioned are all masterpieces of the rococo. The adjoining Hôtels Rohan (1705–8) and Soubise (1705–9) were designed by Pierre-Alexis Delamair. The famous oval salon in the Hôtel Soubise was added in 1736–9 by Germain Boffrand. Robert de Cotte designed the Hôtel de Toulouse (1713–19).

3   The article on *liberalité* in the *Encyclopédie* was also penned by the chevalier de Jaucourt (1778–9: XIX, 977–8).

4   Hubert Robert's Méréville pictures, commissioned to embellish a particular room, fall into the eighteenth-century category of ornament. "Il était de mode, et très-magnifique, de faire peindre son salon par Robert," exclaimed Elisabeth Vigée-Lebrun in her recollections about her old friend, Hubert Robert (Vigée-Lebrun 1986: II, 308). The distinction made between simply owning a painting by the artist and hiring him to "paint your salon" is central to this study, which concentrates solely upon the problem of the decorative ensemble for the private space.

5   On this subject, see Braham (1980: Chs. 7, 10, 11, 12 and 13); Kaufmann (1955: Ch. 13); Dennis (1986: 136–87).

6   For an architect like Le Camus, as Werner Szambien notes, *convenance* hardly mattered next to *caractère*; Szambien also observes that *caractère* was not exactly an aesthetic principle like *symétrie* or *bienséance* but formulated rather as an objective, related to pleasure, of all architectural creation. Le Camus de Mézière's most well-known building is the Halle au Blé in Paris, designed in 1762.

7   The site of the canvas, then, along with its relationship to others in the series and the form of its display, become agents of meaning. Thus Robert could, and did, recycle compositions, using them more than once. Transposing an old picture into a new setting altered the character of the image. For example, versions of *The Old Temple* (Plate 21.2) exist in various forms. One pen and ink drawing, signed and dated 1780, is illustrated in *Piranèse et les Français* (1976: Figure 181). See Mary Sheriff's incisive analysis of Fragonard's *The Progress of Love* panels at Louveciennes for a discussion of these forces at work in erotic imagery (Sheriff 1990: 58–94).

8   Etienne-Louis Boullée, born in 1728, is another figure associated with *architecture parlante*. Unlike Ledoux, Brongniart, and de Wailly, though, Boullée seems not to have traveled in the same social and artistic circles as Hubert Robert. Brongniart and Robert were the two artists who were Vigée's closest friends. De Wailly was also a personal friend of Robert's, serving with him on the Louvre museum commission. Vidler notes connections between Ledoux and Robert at several points in his book (1990). For the record, Robert owned Ledoux's *L'Architecture considérée sous le rapport de l'art* . . . (item 376 in the 1809 studio sale).

9   While I tend to emphasize social factors in this study, Szambien sees several forces, beyond the Piranesi connection, behind the new priority given to *caractère*: a new concept of nature, tension between architect-engineers and architect-artists, a reaction to the explosion of facts in general, the appearance of new types of buildings, and the development of physiology.

10 On this subject, see *Piranèse et les Français* (1976: 22, 304–26). Five years into an extended Italian sojourn (from 1754 to 1765), Hubert Robert officially assumed the position of *pensionnaire* at the Academy. Robert, as is well established, knew Piranesi personally, occasionally sketched with him, and copied his work.

11 Robert received this honor as well as the post of "garde des tableaux du roi" and a *logement* at the Louvre in 1778.

12 The château was remodeled for Laborde by François-Joseph Belanger and Lhuiller; Lhuiller

was responsible for decorating the *rez-de-chaussée*, according to Stern, in "le style antique" (Stern 1930: I, 158).

13   The words are Germain Soufflot's, extracted from a *mémoire* he read to the Academy of Architecture on November 20, 1775; cited by Szambien (1986: 170).

14   The Salon d'Eté was to be decorated by eight canvases by Joseph Vernet, commissioned several years earlier for Laborde's country estate at La Ferté-Vidame (Stern 1930: I, 159; Cayeux 1989: 153).

15   In 1783, to cite one example of his political activity, Laborde averted a potentially disastrous run on the Caisse d'Escompte managed by his brother-in-law, Joseph Micault d'Harvelay. Laborde sustained the fund's credit with his own enormous cash assets. Afterward, Laborde was instrumental in seeing Lefèvre d'Ormesson, the Controller-General responsible for the crisis, replaced with a man enjoying more confidence from the Laborde clan, Charles-Alexandre Calonne.

16   The citation comes from a *mémoire* in the family archive reprinted in Michaud (1856: XXII, 288). Laborde may have written his *Mémoires inédits* in the 1790s. He was executed on April 18, 1794 in a sweep of old regime bankers and tax-farmers.

17   Like Lafayette, Laborde-Méréville had fought in the American war and returned to France imbued with republican ideals. In the early years of Revolution, he belonged to the party of the Lameth brothers and other very liberal aristocrats. Vermale notes that when the Estates-General met in Versailles, the salon of Laborde's eldest daughter, the baroness des Cars (sometimes written d'Escars), was also identified with the "patriots." The three Lameth brothers, Louis, vicomte de Noailles (into whose family Nathalie, Laborde's youngest daughter, would marry in 1790) and Laborde-Méréville were inscribed as members of the Jacobin Club in December 1790 (Bourquin 1987: 75). As was often the case in the eighteenth century, the entire extended Laborde family lodged together under the same roof, both in the Paris hôtel and at the country estate. Jean-François de Pérousse, duc des Cars, who married Pauline de Laborde in 1783, was an arch-royalist in the service of the *maison* d'Artois. He recalls his concern in July 1789 about the political temper of "ma propre maison de Paris, dans laquelle mon beau-frère [Laborde-Méréville] se déclarait déjà hautement du parti opposé à la Cour et entraînait ma femme dans ses opinions" (des Cars 1890: II, 63).

18   Space prevents me from developing the relation of the garden to the problem of luxury and magnificence, but the English garden becomes in France a primary new vehicle of liberality – an appropriate expenditure of wealth in the private sphere, while lavish interior decoration was deemed, as Voltaire said, "revolting." I am developing this argument further in my book on Hubert Robert, currently in progress. On the guests invited to Méréville, see Choppin de Janvry (1969: 96).

19   The quote comes from a letter by Beckford reprinted in Oliver (1932: 170). In the Laborde correspondence, Robert mentions dining with his patron in July 1786; he also alludes to visits to the estate by his wife in the company of Vigée-Lebrun in 1789 and again with Madame Dubarry in 1790. A trip to Méréville with Boutin is also discussed in 1789. Copies of the letters written by Robert to Laborde are in the Dumbarton Oaks Library in Washington, DC. Boutin, for his part, staged a *petit souper* for Vigée and her friends every Thursday; the friends are specified as Brongniart, Robert and his wife, Lebrun the poet (Ponce Denis Ecouchard Lebrun, known as Lebrun-Pindare), l'abbé Delille, and the comte de Vaudreuil.

20   In 1787, Hubert Robert had agreed to provide six pictures measuring 9 feet by 7 feet – four for "le petit salon de Méréville," as he put it, and two for the billiard room, at a price of 6,000 *livres* each. According to the terms of the contract, Robert was given six months to complete the paintings. The details are discussed in the Laborde correspondence cited above. Also see Cayeux (1989: 162–3). All the pictures are oil on canvas; all measure 256 × 223 cm.

21   The vestibule and the formal dining-room were both decorated with Tuscan columns. Stucco, marble paving, and statues in niches proliferated in the suite of room to the left of

the entry. Stern observes that each of the four pictures by Robert for the "petit salon" represents a different order of architecture: Doric, Ionic, Corinthian, and Tuscan (Stern 1930: I, 159).

22 On this subject, see *Piranèse et les Français* (1976: 15–16 and 21) and the illustrations of backdrop curtains by P.-A. Pâris on p. 12, by Bélanger on p. 45, and by Bernard Poyet on p. 299. Poyet's backdrop looks remarkably similar to an intact version of Robert's *The Old Temple* (Figure 21.2). On the relationship between theater and architectural imagery, see the excellent essay by Daniel Rabreau (1978).

23 The horse has a long history in western art as a symbol of state. Indeed, just seven years later, in 1795, the entrance to the Champs-Elysées would be transformed into a monumental republican civic space not unlike those pictured by Robert when Coustou's famous Marly horses were installed there by Delannoy (see Jacques and Mouilleseaux 1988: 92–7). In discourse, too, we find the metaphor used. In February and March 1787, Calonne had revealed to the public the stupefying extent of the nation's debt – a deficit that could be figuratively described as a wild horse. One ironic Parisian quip about the honest but unimaginative Lefèvre d'Ormesson, named to replace Necker as Controller-General of finances in 1783, was: "J'ai un cheval fougueux; je cherche pour le dompter un palefrenier plein de probité" (Lacour-Gayet 1963: 56, no. 2). As a patron, Jean-Joseph de Laborde was unlikely to enjoy decoding obscure references in the pictures he commissioned, although he was impressed by others who could. Des Cars wrote: "Mon beau-père était en littérature et en histoire aussi ignorant qu'il était fort en calcul et en spéculation de finance . . . connaître Horace, citer Horace fut pour lui une espèce de prodige dans un homme de la Cour, et dans un militaire" (des Cars 1890: I, 345).

24 On the wide political appeal of this idea in the 1780s, see Schama (1990). As an aesthetic conception, what I have in mind is a model in which the spectators are construed as part of the composition, a component which "completes" the artwork. We find this notion pervading the aesthetics of *architecture parlante*; in the design of Ledoux's theater at Besançon (1777–84), for example, he envisioned the spectators producing the major decoration of the auditorium. "Thirty-six rows of spectators," he wrote, "placed one behind the other. The dress of the first bench is in graduated opposition with the last. What varieties, what richness of tones!" (cited in Vidler 1990: 179).

Bibliography

Adams, W. H. (1979) *The French Garden 1500–1800*, New York: Georges Braziller.
Bandiera, J. D. (1989) "Form and meaning in Hubert Robert's ruin caprices: four paintings of fictive ruins for the Château de Méréville," *Art Institute of Chicago Museum Studies* 15: 21–37.
Bernois, C. (1968 [1903]) *Histoire de Méréville (Seine-et-Oise) et de ses seigneurs*, Orleans: Marcel Marrou, 1903; rpt. Villeneuve-le-Roi.
Bourquin, M.-H. (1987) *Monsieur et Madame Tallien*, Paris: Perrin.
Boyer, F. (1962) "Les collections et les ventes de Jean-Joseph de Laborde," *Bulletin de la Société de l'Histoire de l'Art Français*, année 1961 (1962): 137–52.
Braham, A. (1980) *The Architecture of the French Enlightenment*, Berkeley and Los Angeles, CA: University of California Press.
Cayeux, J. de (1989) *Hubert Robert*, Paris: Editions Fayard.
Choppin de Janvry, O. (1969) "Méréville," *L'Oeil* 180: 30–41, 83, 96.
Crow, T. E. (1985) *Painters and Public Life in Eighteenth-Century Paris*, New Haven, CT and London: Yale University Press.
Delille, J. (1812) *La Conversation, poème*, Paris: Michaud Frères.
Dennis, M. (1986) *Court and Garden from the French Hôtel to the City of Modern Architecture*, Cambridge, MA and London: MIT Press.
Des Cars, J. F. (1890) *Mémoires du Duc des Cars publiés par son neveu le Duc des Cars*, Paris: Plon.
Desormes, F. (1822) *Epître à Hubert Robert*, Paris: Persan.

Encyclopédie (1778–9) *Encyclopédie, ou Dictionnaire raisonné des sciences, des arts et des métiers par une société de gens de lettres. Mis en ordre et publié par M. Diderot . . .*, nouvelle edn., Geneva: Pellet.

Frénilly, A. F. de (1909) *Souvenirs du Baron de Frénilly, pair de France (1768–1828)*, publié avec introduction et notes par Arthur Chuquet, Paris: Plon.

Furetière, A. (1727 [1690]) *Dictionnaire universel contenant généralement tous les mots françois*, nouvelle edn., La Haye: Pierre Husson, Thomas Johnson, Jean Swart.

Goodman, D. (1989) "Enlightenment salons: the convergence of female and philosophic ambitions," *Eighteenth-Century Studies* 22: 329–50.

Gordon, D. (1989) " 'Public opinion' and the civilizing process in France: the example of Morellet," *Eighteenth-Century Studies* 22: 302–28.

Gruder, V. (1978) "Class and politics in the pre-Revolution: the assembly of notables of 1787," in Ernst Hinrichs *et al.*, *Vom ancien Régime zur Franzosischen Revolution*, Gottingen: Vandenhoeck & Ruprecht, pp. 207–32.

Huizinga, J. (1955) *Homo Ludens: A Study of the Play-Element in Culture*, Boston, MA: Beacon Press.

Jacques, A. and Mouilleseaux, J.-P. (1988) *Les architectes de la liberté*, Paris: Gallimard.

Kaufmann, E. (1955) *Architecture in the Age of Reason*, New York: Dover Publications.

Lacour-Gayet, R. (1963) *Calonne*, Paris: Hachette.

Le Camus de Mézières, N. (1780) *Le Génie de l'architecture ou l'analogue de cet art avec nos sensations*, Paris: Auteur ou Benoit Morin.

McCormick, T. J. (1990) *Charles-Louis Clérisseau and the Genesis of Neo-Classicism*, New York: Architectural History Foundation; Cambridge, MA: MIT Press.

Michaud, J. F. (1856) *Michaud's Biographie Universelle, ancienne et moderne*, nouvelle edn., Paris: C. Desplaces.

Oliver, J. W. (1932) *The Life of William Beckford*, London: Oxford University Press.

Piranèse et les Français, 1740–1790 (1976) exhibition catalogue, ed. Georges Brunel, Rome: Edizioni dell'Elefante.

Rabreau, D. (1978) "De scènes figurées à la mise en scène du monument urbain, notes sur le dessin 'théatral' et la création architecturale en France après 1750," in *Piranèse et les Français*, colloque tenu à la Villa Médicis 12–14 mai 1976, Etudes réunies par Georges Brunel, Rome: Académie de France à Rome, pp. 443–74.

Richelet, P. (1759 [1680]) *Dictionnaire de la Langue Françoise ancienne et moderne*, nouvelle edn., Lyons: Pierre Bruyset-Ponthus.

Schama, S. (1990) *Citizens: A Chronicle of the French Revolution*, New York: Vintage Books.

Sheriff, M. D. (1990) *Fragonard: art and eroticism*, Chicago and London: University of Chicago Press.

Solnon, J.-F. (1987) *La Cour de France*, Paris: Fayard.

Stanton, D. C. (1980) *The Aristocrat as Art, A Study of the Honnête Homme and the Dandy in Seventeenth- and Nineteenth-Century French Literature*, New York: Columbia University Press.

Starobinski, J. (1979) *1789: Les Emblèmes de la Raison*, Paris: Flammarion.

Stern, J. (1930) *A l'ombre de Sophie Arnould, François-Joseph Belanger, Architecte des Menus Plaisirs*, Paris: Plon.

Szambien, W. (1986) *Symétrie Goût Caractère Théorie et Terminologie de l'Architecture à l'Age Classique 1550–1800*, Paris: Picard.

Vermale, F. (1937) "Barnave et les banquiers Laborde," *Annales historiques de la Révolution Française* 14: 48–64.

Vidler, A. (1987) *The Writing of the Walls Architectural Theory in the Late Enlightenment*, Princeton, NJ: Princeton Architectural Press.

—— (1990) *Claude-Nicolas Ledoux, Architecture and Social Reform at the end of the Ancien Régime*, Cambridge, MA: MIT Press.

Vigée-Lebrun, E. (1986 [1835]) *Souvenirs*, 2nd edn. Paris: Editions Des Femmes.

Walpole, H. (1840) *The Letters of Horace Walpole*, 6 vols., Vol. V, London: Richard Bentley.

—— (1937–71) *Walpole's Correspondence with Hannah More* in *The Yale Edition of Horace Walpole's Correspondence*, ed. W. S. Lewis, 48 vols., Vol. XXXI, New Haven, CT: Yale University Press.

Part V

What women want

22

"News from the New Exchange"
Commodity, erotic fantasy, and the female entrepreneur

James Grantham Turner

> The Manufacture of this Town is Love.
> (Catherine Trotter)

In this chapter I examine several groups of late seventeenth-century obscene pamphlets that present the economic activity of women as a kind of prostitution. Every *entrepreneuse* is assumed to be an *entremetteuse*. Female discursive and executive institutions form, not merely one theme of male sexual phantasm, but its motive and core, as the titles of seventeenth-century pornography make abundantly clear: *L'Escole des Filles, L'Académie des Dames, The Poor Whores' Petition, Venus in the Cloister, The Parliament of Women.* Libertine dialogues like Nicolas Chorier's *Satyra Sotadica* (translated as *L'Académie des Dames* and *The School of Women*) spoke exclusively through female personae, and even claimed to be female-authored – a claim actually swallowed by a number of male readers, who felt "outdone" by women in "both acting and describing lust" (Oldham n.d.: 91). These texts attempt to sexualize and thereby ridicule the very idea of autonomous social or political action by women. In England as well as Europe, libertinism created counter-images to block female participation in any of the higher institutions of religion, politics, education – or commerce.

Since this chapter began as a paper for a 1991 Clark Library workshop on the theme of women's role in "The Consumption of Culture," I have concentrated on depictions and travesties of the marketplace. But even from the small sample presented here – focused on the New Exchange, a luxury shopping mall in London's Strand, and Bartholomew Fair, the famous carnival and market in the East End – it should be clear that the sites of women's agency are interchangeable in the libertine imagination, that all of them can be translated, in a universal system of equivalence, into houses of pleasure. The growth of new institutions like London girls' schools or the New Exchange, largely reserved for small "female" businesses such as haberdashery and needlework, prompted a hostile and belittling response: independent female enterprises – schools, lodging-houses, catering services, and luxury shops – *must* be covers for prostitution, and the only "commodity" a woman can sell is herself. The bawdy *Common-Wealth of Ladies* of 1650, produced in the power-vacuum that followed the execution of Charles I, shows women clamoring for "their owne *freedoms*" now that men have won theirs, voting themselves "the *Supreme Authority* both at home and abroad," and forming "an *Academy*" that exactly mirrors libertine male conviviality – anticipating or rehearsing the Restoration rake's love of buggery, smoking, and obscene toasts to the genitals (1 and *passim*). This comic provocation bears the alternative title *Newes from the New Exchange*, since it ends with the ultimate equation of political autonomy and manufactured love: a list of ladies on sale there.

1   News from the New Exchange

Before exploring these clandestine texts, it might be useful to trace the representation of marketing and consumption in a well-known and popular drama. A pivotal scene in William Wycherley's *The Country-Wife* takes place in the New Exchange and, like the pamphlets, exploits its local associations of sexual trade and commodification, fashionable display and false advertising. It is here that Margery Pinchwife browses at the bookstall and gazes at the shop signs, much to her jealous husband's distress, while Horner in turn reads or decodes her, seduces her with a highly suggestive gift of fruit, and (as Pinchwife remarks) squeezes her like an orange.[1] (The fact that Margery wears boy's clothes only enhances the luxurious "exchange" of pleasures and gender-identities, as Horner, pretending to admire "little Sir *James*," showers him/her with kisses and rushes him off to "the house next to the Exchange.") The "country-wife"'s own reading of the Exchange – the sight she most wants to see in London, to impress her neighbors back home – is both rustic and sophisticated; despite her naive inability to grasp the sexual codes and signals of the place, she takes instinctively to the pleasures of the town and registers its erotic subtext. Wycherley can use her "natural" responses to convey the true essence of the market beneath its gloss and fashion. Her excitement over the "power of brave signs" in the shopping aisles ("the Bull's-head, the Rams-head, and the Stags-head") identifies the central role of the New Exchange as a horn factory, and the action of the play bears this out; by the final tableau of act V, thanks in part to Margery's own sexual availability and in part to the "power of signs," the husbands do indeed form a display of "Cuckolds all a-row."[2]

A similar amphibiousness is expressed in the country-wife's attempt to buy books. She asks for rustic "ballads," urban "Playes," and the anthology *Covent Garden Drollery*, a text itself poised (as its title suggests) between the modish and the low, the "bawdery and drollery" of the cruder whore-pamphlet and the raffish associations of Covent Garden, where Horner lives. We know, as a matter of historical fact, that pornographical works like the English translation of Chorier's *Satyra* could be bought in the New Exchange (Foxon 1965: Plate I), so Wycherley's name for the bookseller, Clasp, might hint that something more intimate than plays appears on his table. If Mrs. Pinchwife had succeeded in buying this *Drollery*, this book that Wycherley desires her to consume, how would it have influenced her sense of female agency? Probably edited by Aphra Behn, the anthology shows female productivity penetrating the marketplace, but most of the pieces in the collection assume a more passive role for women. Opening it at random, Margery might have found a song that expresses very much the attitude that Horner wishes to plant in her:

> Since we poor slavish Women know
>   Like men we cannot pick and choose,
> To him we like, why say we no?
>   And both our time and labour lose.[3]

Like the pseudo-didactic *L'Escole des Filles*, this song purports to be the voice of an older woman exhorting her young friend to grasp the sexual moment; but both are actually effects of ventriloquism by the male author, in this case Wycherley himself. The split-level title that attracts Margery also prefigures, by a dramatic irony, the difference between her and Horner's responses to sexual pleasure; she thinks she has found a new improved "Husband" and wants to make a real exchange of partners (V.iv.346, 348), whereas he dismisses her as a "Changeling" or country idiot, and regards the whole affair as a mere Covent Garden drollery. The play oscillates between new and old associations of "exchange," corresponding to two contradictory models of women's agency – freedom and abjection.

Like its equivalent in real life, the "Change" serves in *The Country-Wife* as the gathering-place for multiple plots. Even before Margery Pinchwife brings out its erotic "Sign" system, the male characters have alluded quite heavily to its sexual meaning. Harcourt (the most honorable young man in the play) remarks of Alithea (the most honorable woman, only to be won on strict matrimonial terms) that "all Women are like these of the *Exchange*," lying to "their fond Customers" in order to "enhance the price of their commodities" (III.ii.289). This coarse allusion exploits the ambiguity of the place in the same vein as pamphlets like *Newes from the New Exchange* or *The Character of an Exchange-Wench* (printed in the same year as *The Country-Wife*). The modish word "Commodity" also served as slang for the vagina, as Wycherley himself reminds us in his labored poem on the "Juicy, Salt Commodity" of the woman who sells oysters (1924: III, 170). Harcourt here breaks down not only the status-barrier between the highest and the lowest form of retail, but also the conceptual barrier between the virtuous Alithea and the prostitute. Though Harcourt turns away from this rakish misogyny, and wins Alithea, when he refuses to believe the evidence of her apparent whoredom (V.iv.347), here he remains loyal to the cynicism of the Wits, and foreshadows the more brutal maxim that Horner will draw from his encounter with Lady Fidget and her friends: "that great Ladies, like great Merchants, set but the higher prizes upon what they have" (V.iv.344).

Horner's (and Wycherley's) aggressive attempt to impose a market model upon female sexuality backfires, however. The man who reduces women to purveyors of their own "commodity" finds himself, by the logic of trading, just another product. When Horner disguises a sexual assignation as a visit to buy "China" – an area of luxury consumption where women evidently helped to form élite taste – the image rebounds against the phallic confidence it is supposed to enforce: Horner becomes the salesman of a sexual product, in constant danger of running out of stock (IV.iii). This assimilation of the man to the commodity went beyond the confines of drama. John Dennis recounts an anecdote, told to him by Wycherley himself, in which the countess of Drogheda visits a bookshop in Tunbridge Wells in search of a copy of *The Plain-Dealer*; though she has never set eyes on the playwright, she is drawn to his text not only by the power of wit but by "the great Things which she had heard reported of his manly Prowess" (Dennis 1943: 411–12). The author happens to be in the same bookshop: " 'Madam,' says the male friend who acts as the procurer, 'if you are for the *Plain Dealer*, there he is for you,' pushing Mr. *Wycherley* towards her." This textbook romance blossomed (after the death of the count) into a marriage of extraordinary virulence, inspiring Wycherley to equate *male* sexuality with institutional labor: "Constrain'd to Drudg'ry, each dull Husband beats / The Hemp of Wedlock in the Wedding Sheets" (1924: IV, 192).

Pinchwife's references to the swarm of upper-class seducers who gather in the New Exchange, and who will "leave their dear Seamstresses" to follow Margery, gives some indication of the economics of the place. The trades that could set up shop there were strictly limited to luxuries – china (of course), intimate apparel, jewelery, embroidered silks, books, hats.[4] The seamstress-saleswomen were regarded as fashion models who would stimulate consumption by flirtatious exchanges with their "fond Customers"; in this commercial theater they acquire some of the contradictory associations of the actress. In *The Man of Mode*, for example, Etherege constitutes the New Exchange as a place of labile identity and female initiative: it is there that (according to the Orange Woman) Harriet watches Dorimant "fooling" with a shop assistant and starts to mimic his mannerisms, a strategy that effectively paralyzes him later in the play (1982: 222, 274). Her mimicry strips away and recirculates, as a commodity, his supposedly natural and intrinsic gestures, as it were alienating him from himself. The Exchange is thus a natural site for a woman who wants to trade or "make free" with signs, and in Harriet's case this freedom is well exercised. On the other hand, Lady Woodvill complains that young men nowadays are "civil to none but Players and *Exchange* Women," implying (like the pamphleteers) that both are little better than prostitutes (259).

Despite the comic setting, we can deduce something from these plays about material conditions in the New Exchange. I find it significant that, in this upmarket setting, the seamstresses themselves were displaying and marketing their manufacture. Except for the male pressure to sexualize the exchange, their labor seems relatively unalienated; the producer enjoys some influence on the consumer, some capacity to shape the fashion and to create desire for the product. This seems diametrically different from the experience of the rank-and-file textile worker, whose life Henry Fielding equates with slavery. (In his adaptation of Molière's *L'Avare*, the over-genteel upper servant complains that "no journeywoman sempstress is half so much a slave as I am," in a satirical context suggesting that she is unwittingly revealing her proper sphere.)[5] The relatively benign conditions of the New Exchange, generically compatible with the comedy of fashionable life, contrast violently with the abject scene revealed in Congreve's *Way of the World*; in a rage that tears apart the curtains of decorum and the fabric of comedy, Lady Wishfort threatens to reduce her maid Foible to the state she found her in, the conditions of the female proletariat – selling broken beads in the street, "washing of old gauze and weaving of dead hair, with a bleak blue nose over a chafing-dish of starved embers, and dining behind a traverse rag, in a shop no bigger than a birdcage" (1956: 356–7). Lady Wishfort's subsequent sarcasm – "these were your commodities, you treacherous trull! this was the merchandise you dealt in" – suggests that "commodity" was a high or genteel word; it would thus be all the more jarring to hear it vulgarized.

The local associations exploited by Wycherley and Etherege run throughout the period. They can already be found in Richard Brome's *The New Academy, or the New Exchange* (posthumously published in 1658), where "one of the Blades," a penniless Cavalier, is said to "Barter commodity for commodity . . . with Tradesmens wives" (1873: 24). In the early eighteenth century Edward Ward's *London Spy* still attempts to write these comic associations into the social geography of London, promoting the idea of a sexual collectivity by mingling together every possible female institution. He introduces the New Exchange as a "*Seraglio* of Fair Ladies" and indulges in the usual *doubles entendres* about selling themselves, dealing, and commodities: "I could willingly have Dealt among the Charming Witches, for some of their Commodities; but . . . I could only Walk by, and lick my Lips at their handsome Faces." The "Spy" occupies an ambiguous position, secure in the masculine perspective that converts all women's institutions into sexual markets, but marginal, even canine, in his exclusion from the feast of high consumerism. As he leaves he further identifies the place as a "Jilts Academy," where 9-year-olds become precocious adults, and as a "Cloister of kind Damsels" (1709: 212–15). Ward had already treated the less fashionable Royal Exchange in the City as a scaled-down version of the New, differing only in social cachet: the milliners and seamstresses in the shops upstairs seem to have "as much mind to dispose of themselves, as the Commodities they dealt in," and the place is declared "the Merchants Seraglio. A Nursery of Young Wagtails, for the private *Consolation* of *Incontinent Citizens*" (73–4).

This semi-automatic association of the female institution, the New Exchange, and the brothel helps a nouveau-picaresque fiction like Richard Head's *English Rogue* to renegotiate the boundaries between high and low. After a series of vulgar tricks and low-life brothel adventures, the picaro decides to spend his wealth in a "new-fashion Bawdy-house," masquerading as a respectable lodging-house. At first he is awed by the display of high-cultural status – the porter at the door, the gravity of the matron, the gallery of portraits in the dining-room, the invitation to show his own gentlemanly education by an aesthetic critique of these pictures, and the "celestial" demeanor of the lady he selects. After half an hour of silence and social diffidence, however, "confidence had repossessed her ancient seat in me," and this regaining of the seigneurial position allows him to recuperate the dominant language: as he emerges from the house the following morning, he declares it "A new Exchange" run by "a female Council." Latroon puzzles over the fact that this brothel looks like a "house of state" even though the bawdy-house *ought* to be easily distinguishable from the respectable mansion "by the shew"; the New Exchange provides him with exactly the image he needs to place this equivocal façade. Head seems uncertain whether to deplore or celebrate this lifting of the pornosphere to the level of genteel consumption, which gives him a chance to display his own erotic connoisseurship and procurative skills as he describes the portrait of his favourite courtesan. This exchange is "new" because it transcends, or even reverses, the usual cash transaction between rogue and whore: here "Ladies sell their Ware / To none; they scorn thereon to set a price, / But leave it solely to the Chapmans choice." The man is required to deposit ten gold sovereigns for the night, but receives a pound refund for each time he spends. (He later boasts, Boswell fashion, that the entire night cost him only two pounds.) Far from concluding, however, that this "female Council" has created a higher form of sexuality run on hedonistic rather than mercenary principles, Head uses the episode to level all women's desire to the lower stratum, trotting out the libertine generalization that would later be upheld by Harcourt and Horner: "What house is not a *Brothel-house* I pray?"[6]

This leveling device is especially clear in a group of pamphlets exactly contemporary with *The Country-Wife* and the "sex-craze of the 1670s." The title of *The Ape-Gentle-Woman, or the Character of an Exchange-Wench* (1675) spells out the conservative, regulatory attack on social climbing, and suggests the anxieties triggered by the seamstresses' participation in a luxury trade that might blur the caste distinctions between consumer and producer. The same note is struck (as we have seen) in satires against the social demeanor of another kind of "ape-gentlewoman," the genteel upper servant; the implication is that that they *should* be working in the abject conditions of the sweatshop, the "slavery" and starvation threatened by Lady Wishfort. In satires against women's sexual transgression the libertine vocabulary of "slavery" and "labor," deployed in Wycherley's song to persuade a woman to transgress, becomes grimly literal.

The ideological assault in the *Character of an Exchange-Wench* proceeds on two potentially contradictory assumptions: that she is, and that she is not, a whore. Her claim to economic viability (and thus to social respect) must be hollowed out by relentless sexual farce; she must be attacked for her social pretension and virtuous appearance, precisely for *not* conforming to the only two models of the working girl acceptable to the satirist – the proletarian textile worker or the rampant Cockney strumpet. Representations of the prostitute frequently stress her social aspirations and repudiation of traditional ties. The inmates of Bridewell "Say they were never bred to *Spin*," and adopt a disdainful air which "Proves that they are soft, Court like, and highly born" (*Troia* 1674: 7). The "London Jilt" was corrupted by her parents' social climbing and overindulgence, sending her to school to learn refined accomplishments rather than useful skills, and thereby guaranteeing that she would be "brought up in some sort of Libertinism" (*London Jilt* 1683: 2). In another libertine song from a "drollery" anthology, the male persona rebukes a mistress who has asked for money, invoking the dichotomy of liberal versus mechanical art, noble sex "for love" versus corrupt sex for cash:

> I'le never hire the thing that's free . . .
> Since Loving was a Liberal Art,
>   How canst thou trade for gain?

This seems like a worthy rejection of quantification and calculation, but the ending of the song strips away the idealist and reveals the bully, revealing at the same time how pitifully narrow were the economic choices for women; if she does not give him "the thing that's free" she will be reduced, quite literally, to a mechanical art: "Let's both to kiss begin; / To kiss freely: if not, you may go spin."[7]

In the *Character of an Exchange-Wench*, this anti-*arriviste* satire receives a topical anti-Puritan twist: she had been "intended for a Gentlewoman" by her Parliamentarian father, but the Restoration stripped him of his "Bishops Lands" (3). Her career then develops as the inverse of what her parents intended. She is apprenticed to a female linen-draper with an upper-class clientele (linen-drapers were indeed among the trades permitted in the exclusive New Exchange), but rather than rising to own the means of production herself after her apprenticeship, she is forced down through the circles of a sexual inferno. The businesswoman is, inevitably, a bawd: the entrepreneurial mistress uses her retail network to auction off the girl's maidenhead, delivering her with an order of linen. She is then passed on as a sexual bundle from gentleman-customer to master-craftsman, from master to apprentice, from linen-shop to brothel, and then to the most wretched condition of a field whore. Diseased and "turned out of Doors," she "carries such a *Hogo* along with her, one may smell her from hence to *Kingsland*" (5). With this disgusting evocation of the venereal hospital the pamphlet breaks off, its work of abjection done.

Parallel works like *The Character of a Town Misse* (1675) exploit this effect still further. Here the career of the "Miss" is told entirely through objects of possession, production, and consumption, which mark out the double trajectory of social climbing and descent to the lower depths. Her sexual adventures begin simultaneously with the squire and the ploughman, "Joint Tenants to her *Coppy-hold*" (the most plebeian form of land-tenure), but once she is "dispatcht" to London by the wealthy landlord she sets up a simulacrum of upper-class life, displaying the signs of colonial-mercantile power and acquisitive patronage: her retinue includes "a *Blackmoor*," a "*She-Secretary*, that keeps the Box of her Teeth, her Hair, and her Painting," and "a *French Merchant* to supply her with *Dildo's*" (4, 7). Here and throughout libertine discourse, the lady's power to form high taste by artistic patronage is reduced to an expertise in sexual implements. To drag this pretension down still further, she is passed through a cycle of metaphors that equate her with the marketing and disposal of meat, and thus alienate her, evacuate her (in every sense) from the social world: "She is a very *Butcher*, that exposes her own Flesh to Sale by the *Stone* . . . a *Cook* that is Dressing her self all day with *poinant Sauces*" (7). (To enforce the social satire the Town Miss's corruption, like the Exchange Wench's "*Hogo*" or haut-gout, must be equated with the most fashionable cuisine.) Finally "she becomes a *Loathesome* thing, too unclean to enter into *Heaven*, too *Diseased* to continue long upon Earth, and too foul to be *toucht* with any thing but a *Pen* or a Pair of *Tongs*: And therefore tis time to *Leave* her; – For, *Foh how she stinks*" (8). In this punitive distancing of social aspiration by stripping it to the level of garbage and excrement, however, the act of writing becomes implicated in the filth: the pen becomes equivalent to the tongs.

The *Character of an Exchange-Wench* and related pamphlets attempt to pillory the idea of free female agency, not only in the economic sphere, but also in the realms of culture and language. The saleswoman is equated not merely with passive or meaningless objects, but with the objects that constituted high culture, such as fancy *pâtisserie* (a "piece of Puff-past, or a bit extraordinary for those queasie Stomachs which can't digest a Bawdy-House") or expensive tropical products subject to wild speculation in the futures market: "She's a critical thing to deal in, having more Rises and Falls than Pepper or Indico's; She's one Comodity at several Rates" (2). (Confectionery and perfume, we recall, were the only perishable goods permitted at the New Exchange.) In the same vein as Harcourt's complaint in *The Country-Wife*, the Exchange woman (so by implication "all Women") becomes, not merely an object for sale, but a "Commodity" enhanced by verbal manipulation, by image management and sales talk that bring fashion and social envy into play. Like the "London Jilt" she is assumed to be a cultural product, supposedly "educated at 11 or 12 in Hackney" (3) – a pun that links the respectable girls' school, the horse for hire, and the whore. But this education only makes her more susceptible to a seduction that stresses the charms of literature; her customer-purchaser plies her with "Wine, a Neats tongue, and a little good Language, raising her desires with a little ob-Scene description of the sweets of enjoyment" (4). (Discourse modulates back into physical consumption in the suggestive form of a "Neats tongue.") Like the "Town Miss" who keeps a "Secretary" only to keep track of her false body-parts, so the Exchange wench participates in the new genteel culture, "the Play-houses, *Spring-Garden*, and the Park," only as a criminal parasite on the apprentices who take her there. As she proceeds down the social scale, language again confronts her with a mocking parody of a respectable career: she asks the Bawds, once they have finished with her, for "Letters of commendation" (5).

Two refutations of these pamphlets (also from 1675) appear to undo the damage, either by reappropriating "female" control over language or by arguing for the economic respectability of the New Exchange. *The Town-Misses Declaration and Apology* (also called her *Manifesto*) turns a critical eye on the practices of the accusing world. Men have ceased to be "Romance Hero's," congruent with their noble fictions. Marriage is so tainted with commerce that it resembles buying a horse at Smithfield market. How can men complain about the price of sex when it exemplifies their own commercial values so perfectly – "as if any man could expect to have any *Comodity* that's rare without a price proportionable" (3–6)? This ostensible counter-attack confirms the fundamental conceit of these pamphlets by assuming that "Town-Misses" are indeed prostitutes, and by identifying the area of hottest controversy as the conjunction of "public" women and linguistic agency. Still, the whore-figure allows the author to imagine a genuinely public language for women, at the same time discounting it by declaring it an adjunct of their sexuality: "'Tis not the first time that we have ventur'd to make ourselves *Publick*; and if our Rhetorick should prove too weak to make good our Cause, we have other Charms that we know are Irresistible" (4). Sex and rhetoric appear to be differentiated here, but those "other Charms" themselves generate fresh texts and shows, new discursive provocations in the public eye. The London mistress is "the Delight of Society and the very Soul of *Conversation*," especially for the poet: "she brings him in his Humours, and smart Repartees, for garnishing his next Play . . . without us the Theatres would be empty; the New Exchange Bankrupted; the Spring Gardens Ruin'd" (7). This impersonation of the prostitute thus allows the male pamphleteer to toy with an even larger claim, that illicit sexuality drives the entire machine of polite society, fashionable assembly, luxury consumption, and cultural-discursive display. The active exchange of ideas between patroness and author, a significant part of theatrical production in the Restoration, is at once acknowledged and belittled by this association with the *demi-monde* – a theme that continues in the whore-biographies of the following century.[8]

Another response to the original slander, *An Answer to the Character of an Exchange-Wench, or a Vindication of an Exchange-Woman*, seems to take the opposite tack by delibidinizing the consumer market and taking the saleswoman seriously. It praises the Exchange as an "Academy" of good manners, and stresses the value of female economic independence: "An Exchange-Woman does as far exceed a meer Gentlewoman, as a Civil Tradesman does a common Shark, having a commendable Calling to vouch for her honesty." But this too turns out to be a facetious work, overstating its case to provoke amusement and reinforcing the idea that relations with Exchange-women must be sexual; its last words are "And since you're Sinners too, I only wish / That we may sin in better sheets than this" (1, 6). The "sheets" of the innocent pamphlet are thoroughly imbued with the sexual matter of prostitution.

The ironies of this pamphlet warfare deepen when we recognize that, for women in the material world, retail and illicit sexuality were in fact absolutely opposed. If "commendable Calling" vouched for female honesty, the reverse was also true. Both as consumers and as traders, women whose sexual "credit" was broken could not obtain financial credit or employment. In practical terms, as Alice Browne reminds us, to be classified as fallen "made it impossible to earn a living in any of the few ways open to middle-class women" (1987: 141). These pamphlets should be seen as textual versions of a gesture ritualized in the riotous behaviour of bachelor gangs, manifested throughout early modern Europe by male apprentices and *confrèries de jeunesse* (Rossiaud 1985: 84), but brought to fever pitch in the upper-class hooliganism of post-Puritan England. Window-breaking, defacing the façade both literally and metaphorically, and so rewriting the occupant as a whore to punish her for resisting: such gestures of stylized violence were intended to destroy the independent woman's credit in every sense. That this was a huge joke to the upper classes may be gathered from the comic dramatists, who ascribe these aggressive demarcatory impulses to their most positive characters.

Sir Frederick Frolick in Etherege's *The Comical Revenge*, for example, who evolves from a high-spirited buffoon into the hero of the comedy, indulges in just such a quasi-military "alarm" of a friend's mistress's "Quarters." Like the raids of the violent youth gangs, this assault has the effect of stigmatizing her in the community and destroying her economic viability: "You and your rude ranting Companions hoop'd and hollow'd like Mad-men, and roar'd out in the streets, *A whore, a whore, a whore*. . . . We had so much the good will of the Neighbours before, we had credit for what we wo'd; and but this morning the Chandler refus'd to score a quart of Scurvy-grass" (1982: 11–12). Court records show that sexual defamation did have serious economic consequences, particularly for women in employment or business: men could be acquitted for smashing the windows and furnishings of women's houses if neighbors could be found to assert the victim's reputation for prostitution.[9] In the case of the bachelor's "frolic" the attack itself, often motivated by the woman's *refusal* to yield, was meant to create such a reputation, to mark the house as a military officer would mark houses for free-quarter. Those who "won't be civil," those who have ideas above their station (such as resisting rape by drunken aristocrats, or making a career in consumer society) are thereby isolated from their civil neighbors and written into an exclusively sexual script. The chambermaid states the case quite plainly – "Unhand me; are you a man fit to be trusted with a womans reputation?" – yet the audience is invited to align, not with her complaint, but with Sir Frederick's immediate response; he claims "intimate acquaintance" and makes a sexual advance. Such moments conceal, by a process we might call "comedification," the truth they put into words: that male discourse and gesture actually did control reputation, and that reputation translated directly into financial life or death, credit or ruin.

Further research would, I suspect, show some correspondence between real-life case histories and those projected in the phantasmagoria of libertinism, however different their consequences. Shop assistants *were* regarded as fair game both by cruising male customers and by working bawds. Pepys recorded that a saleswoman in Cheapside ("the pretty woman that I always loved" and thus defined as a sexual object), had been snatched up by the procuress "Lady" Bennett, to whom Wycherley would later dedicate his *Plain-Dealer* (September 22, 1660).[10] But Pepys's past tense and lamenting tone ("poor soul") suggest that the victim had disappeared from her position, that Mrs. Bennett's success had obliterated her from her visible place. The two careers could not run concurrently. Again, Randolph Trumbach has found some evidence of seduced and abandoned women having been apprenticed to luxury trades like mantua-making and millinery (both allowed in the New Exchange), to show how aptly Cleland lodges Fanny Hill with Mrs. Cole the "milliner." Trumbach proves that Cleland portrays the circumstances of prostitution correctly, but leaves out the horror, destitution, and disease. It is unwise, however, to cite as evidence for non-phantasmic reality a text like *The London Tradesman*, which solemnly advised parents not to apprentice their daughters to millinery because "nine out of ten of the young creatures who are obliged to serve in these shops are ruined and undone" (Trumbach 1988: 79). Here the serious conduct book merges and colludes with the scandalous pamphlet, both forms of male discourse enforcing the sexual interpretation of luxury production and its "new exchange." Rather than assuming that a female-run fashion industry naturally shaded off into prostitution, we should try to assemble the contrary evidence. Bridget Hill reminds us that female apprenticeship – particularly in expanding luxury trades like dressmaking – still represented an important career opportunity, and sometimes meant working for independent mistresses. Moreover, millinery was the most lucrative and had the highest prestige, to judge by the large premiums paid for daughters' apprenticeships (1989: 95). It is surely no coincidence that libertine fictions and libertine practices – each following and confirming the other – should be directed against this particular bastion.

A case history from the eighteenth century may help to drive home the cruelty of the sexual comedy that links market freedom with prostitution. Laetitia Pilkington's *Memoirs* show that, after she was publicly repudiated by her husband, the aristocracy and their procuresses felt free to visit her lodgings at any time of the day or night, even taking the locks off her door (1928: 137–41). Sexual discourse played a crucial role in this licensing of intrusion: one of the gentlemen who burst into her bedroom, in the early days of the separation, justified his assault by claiming that she was "publicly known through all the coffee-houses in Dublin . . . I had a full history of you from the maid" (137). Pilkington's correspondence with Samuel Richardson, her main hope of relief once she had moved from Dublin to London, shows that to be "misrepresented" is to be refused even minimal charity by "those falsely styled virtuous." Her relationship with Richardson seems to have consisted entirely of an exchange of "sheets" – letters, writing-paper, poems, banknotes, linen for her destitute daughter (Richardson 1804: II, 114–39). She sent him poems (blasting the meanness of others and lauding his generosity); he entrusted her with a prepublication manuscript of *Clarissa*. But one kind of writing, apparently, she could not obtain: "I can get a most compleat beautiful shop, in the Strand, exactly opposite to Buckingham-street; but the gentleman who owns it wants some person of credit to give me a character." She applied to the novelist for a character, to avoid the fate described in *The Character of an Exchange-Wench*. Richardson's response has not survived (he refused to see her in person), but on the same day she wrote a similar letter to the bishop of London, the Lord Almoner, enclosing a piece of her embroidered "work" to prove her skill in luxury production. Text and textile together constituted her qualification for the genteel world of entrepreneurial retail, in the vicinity of the New Exchange itself. The bishop returned her writing "torn to pieces." Her poverty and damaged reputation also prevent her from creditable writing on behalf of others, like the beloved maid she is forced to dismiss (121); in this context the witticism about the Exchange-wench's "Letters of commendation" seems particularly vicious.

2   Taking liberties

The negative "Character" pamphlets of 1675 attempted, not merely to sexualize female participation in the cycle of luxury production–retail consumption, but to "unfashion" it, to declass or alienate it by association with the lowest stratum of economic life – with coarse, native, perishable goods sold in the open air, with scavenging and street vending. We should not talk of "the marketplace" but of many markets, stratified by class divisions as vast as those dividing the society as a whole. At the upper level we can locate the marriage market of the propertied classes, displaying itself as a glittering social recreation, but conducted behind the scenes in the brutal language of trade; Edward Wortley's courtship letters to Lady Mary Pierrepont talk quite openly of "the bargain" and the "high rate set upon you" (Montagu 1956: 48, 51). Satirists liked to deflate these pretensions by equating the prenuptial negotiations of the *beau monde* with the lowest form of horse-trading, and "a Smithfield bargain" became a common synonym for an arranged marriage. That other upper-level market, the Bourse or Stock Exchange, likewise found its sexual analogy. One Dutch satire is actually entitled *De Beurs der Vrouwen* ("the Stock Exchange of Women"), and the frequency of lucrative suits for "criminal conversation" led one Fielding character to remark that it was "a stock-jobbing age, every thing has its price; marriage is traffic throughout; as most of us bargain to be husbands, so some of us bargain to be cuckolds."[11] A fashionable shopping center like the New Exchange occupies an amphibious position, differentiating itself both from the City financial markets and from the vulgar food markets, taverns, and street fairs that provided London with a zone of carnivalesque misrule. In fact the New Exchange had more in common with the popular markets than it would care to admit, with its focus on retail, its rows of individual stalls, its Orange-Women and pornography-sellers, and its atmosphere of license and sociability.

Each kind of trading floor generated its own sexual analogy and its own commodified discourse, its own form of the "news-novel" mélange of reportage and fiction.[12] "News from the New Exchange" should therefore be considered as part of a system that includes the 1660 *Strange and True Newes from Jack-a-Newberries Six Windmills* – an exposé, or celebration, of a notorious London brothel – and the 1661 *Strange Newes from Bartholomew-Fair, or the Wandring-Whore Discovered*. The newsy pornography of this low-market stratum, like the "Characters" generated by the New Exchange, focuses obsessively on the conjunction of public sexuality and female discursive agency. Billingsgate fishmarket, for example, becomes not only a zone of women's "free" speech (meaning licensed scurrility), but a university for the training of prostitutes: in Ward's

Rambling Rakes, or London Libertines (1700) we learn that a whore's "Education is chiefly owing to her Mothers late Seminary, which was *Billingsgate*, and are both well vers'd in its *Lingua*" (4). Language, schooling, and fishwife obscenity merge into one vast *double entendre* that can mean only one thing. The title of a chapbook from the Pepys collection, *The Womans Brawl, or Billingsgate against Turn-Mill-Street* (1680), suggests that the market itself is speaking, and that market discourse is identical to the foul-mouthed London dialogue represented in the *Strange News* and *Wandring Whore* pamphlets: Doll, the complaining wife, turns out to have kept a bawdy-house next door to Damaris Page, a real-life brothel-keeper recorded both in the 1660s whore-dialogues and in Pepys's diary.[13] The language of this "woman's brawl" mingles the cries of the market-vendor with sexual invitation, turning "the Poulterers wives cryes, *No mony, no Cony*" into an obvious pun, and so producing the self-commodification, or self-butchering, that we saw elaborated in the "New Exchange" pamphlets.[14]

This fusion of sexual display and market vocalization is most blatant, predictably, in *Strange Newes from Bartholomew-Fair*, supposedly authored by "Peter Aretine" but narrated by the folkloric figure of the "wandering whore" herself. The title-character tells how she cries: " 'Lads, here's a can of the best liquor in the fair,' claping my hand on my market-place," and Peg of Pie-Corner adds: "I for my part cry, 'here boys, here's the best Pigs head in the Fair, a rare quarter of Lamb, pure Mutton, and the best buttock bief in England' " (3). In recounting her own "wandering" sexual adventures, she elaborates this imagery of gross consumption with allusions to the European picaresque, the low literary genre mingling with the "blackguard" labor of the pig-booth: "I spread my Colours, and receive the Spanish Rogue into my *French* quarters, where he turn'd the Pig so long till one of his best members was lost in the dripping-pan" (ibid.). The genitals, the "low" and "hot" zone of the politic body, become synonymous with the low topography of marketplace and roasting-tent – areas of license, vulgar theater, and unbridled plebeian commerce. In a related image from the *Wandring Whore* series, a prostitute who earns half a crown for "stroaking the marrow out of a mans Gristle" bears the name of the pig-woman from Jonson's *Bartholomew Fair*, Ursula.[15]

Pepys's diary (September 1, 1668) records one man's furtive response to the discursive and erotic provocations of the low market. He was obviously drawn to Bartholomew Fair as a libidinous zone, or more precisely an occasion for lowering his threshold of sexual fastidiousness. In 1668, the same year that he records ejaculating while reading the French pornographic *Escole des Filles*, he kissed "a mighty belle fille" at the fair and then went in search of the famous "Horse of knowledge" (the same side-show that Wordsworth recorded at Bartholomew Fair over a century later). For the Restoration philanderer, however, the "knowledge" produced at the carnival was exclusively carnal; when the horse was asked which man in the audience "most loved a pretty wench in a corner" it picked out Pepys, and received a shilling reward. Following the subterranean logic of the fairground pamphlets, Pepys then gave another shilling to a common prostitute for masturbating him in a coach – was this "Ursula"? – and then made straight for a bookshop in Duck Lane, where he tried to seduce the bookseller's wife. Perhaps he was again acting out a fantasy schooled by his bawdy reading; "Moll of Duck Street" is one of the dialogists in *Strange Newes from Bartholomew-Fair*.

Another by-product of the low market was the quasi-pornographic printed catalogue of women for sale, alluding perhaps to the actual use of fairs for the sale of wives (sometimes by the pound). As we saw, the 1650 *Newes from the New Exchange* ends with a list of the women on sale there, a genre that began with the Aretinesque *Tariffa delle Puttane di Vinegia* of 1535 and continues in entrepreneurial ventures like *An Auction of Whores, or the Bawds Bill of Sale for Bartholomew Fair*.[16] Since Narcissus Luttrell's copy of the *Auction*, now in Harvard, is dated on St. Bartholomew's Day, August 25, 1691, we can assume that such pseudo-commercial bawdy was produced by and for the fair itself, and treasured as a souvenir by the respectable visitor; buying the pamphlet may safely substitute for buying the sexual commodity itself. Most of the later elaborations of this genre, which apply the sale catalogue or lottery to marriage as well as to prostitution, maintain a similar double focus; they provide both a subversive comic commentary on mercenary marriage, and a conservative, regulatory insistence that the trading classes must be seen as mere products of their manual occupation. The tailor's daughter "knows exactly how many inches goes to the making of a yard," the "cutler's daughter in Cheapside, who is true metal to the back . . . will endure grinding to the end of the chapter," and so on to the end of the pamphlet.[17]

The preposterous imaginings of low-libertine literature serve to model the world of illicit sexuality as an institution, either to integrate the marginal and forbidden into official culture, or to rehearse changes in the larger world at a time of social and political upheaval. The text and the brothel are both forms of cultural action, centers or stages for the production of behaviors and discourses which themselves may influence future institutions. The power vacuum of early 1650 provokes the equation of the equivocal-respectable New Exchange with the "Commonwealth of Ladies," and the parliamentary legislation on marriage later that year generates the first of the English whore-pamphlets, in which Macquerella, Scolopendra, and Pimpinello lament the Adultery Act (*Dialogue* 1650). The English Rogue, advancing socially in the libertine 1660s when the king's promiscuity had thrown public morality into confusion, imagines the amphibious upper-class brothel as a "New Exchange" and as a "Council" of women. Comic phrases like "*Cunny-hall*" and "Ballock Hall" project the idea of an official guild of whores, gravely regulating the trade in sex (Phillips 1653: 14–15). In the "strange news" pamphlets studied in this section, which poured out after the Restoration but before the settlement of a civic, ecclesiastical, and economic order, we encounter a double institutionalization: the male author does not simply take non-sexual agency and render it sexual, but responds to what appear to be real events in the sexual underworld, the emergence of elaborate brothels actually run by female entrepreneurs. The prostitute's enterprise is invested with the grand negotiations of state politics.[18] Mrs. Fotheringham's posture-house-cum-tavern, the Six Windmills, is established as a parodic government, complete with policies, ministries, and ancient precedents, even before the new constitutional norms of Great Britain had been properly defined. "*Priss Fotheringhams* Chuck-office," the device that triggered the entire series of pamphlets, refers both to the pub-brothel itself, organized like a government office with its elaborate regulations, and to the orifice into which her clients fling their money rather than their seed: "*Priss.* stood upon her head with naked breech and belly whilst four Cully-rumpers chuck't in sixteen Half-crowns into her Comodity."[19] The institution and the body reduplicate the same tortured conceit – reenacting, in the hysterical theater of the "chuck-office," the national panic over the direction and control of trade, the getting and spending of estates. By the same token commerce is sexualized: the influx of coinage ("French Dollars, Spanish Pistols, English Half-crowns . . . plentifully pour'd in")[20] corresponds to the emerging heroic-erotic image of the Thames as the recipient of the world's trade, familiar from *Cooper's Hill* and *Annus Mirabilis*.

Furthermore, the parodic institution of the sexual marketplace pretends to regulate cultural consumption as well as physical and monetary behavior. Like a miniature court, the whore's "Offices" promote and control cultural production, appointing a poet laureate, setting up a panel of literary critics, and commissioning paintings; these include versions of "Aretino's postures," of course, but also a uniform series of portraits of "our principal beauties," such as Lely would later paint for the court of Charles II and Kneller for William III.[21] These erotic-Utopian fantasies go beyond satire to express the wish that the new anti-Puritan order might be more tolerant of sexual alternatives, that the court may even come to resemble the courts of whoredom. In the great brothel riots of 1668, when the apprentices direct their stones against the little bawdy-house and murmur that they should be pulling down the "great bawdy-house at White hall," they are actually endorsing an image rehearsed in the brothels of litera-ture. As the "English Rogue" discovered in the intervening years, even "palaces" may be "courts of bawdry."[22]

When parliamentary politics once again went into a deep crisis, in the early 1680s, the whole mass of monetary-erotic associations rose again to the surface. In the English *Whores Rhetorick* of 1683, as compared with the Italian original of 1642, not only have metaphors of commercial and mercantile enterprise been greatly expanded, but the courtesan's art has been as it were politicized and nationalized; as a public figure "her actions ought to seem publick-spirited, though Statesman-like she should contrive them all to meet in the centre of her own particular advantage." Her house is not only a center of cultural consumption, emulating the upper-class residence with its (suitably equivocal) pictures and furnishings, but "an amorous Republick." Her mirrors are now called her "privy Counsellours."[23] This high-level image of a political economy is explicitly contrasted to the low-market model that men seek to impose; the procuress-mentor recognizes that, in fashioning herself as a discreet courtesan rather than a vulgar whore, her protégée must resist the customer's desire to force her down to fairground level. In advising young prostitutes never to "rashly addict themselves to a scandalous liberty in drinking, lewd swearing, and open ribaldry," she evokes the lower stratum of London sexual discourse, the *Wandring Whore* pamphlets and the punitive-comical bawdy of the fairground, associating them not with "free" merriment but with the brutal policing of plebeian sexuality. Rather shrewdly, she explains that men "encourage all the vile excesses that the most profligate stripping Whore can act, yet at the same time they applaud, they must need entertain a secret hatred and scorn. . . . They are solicitous for this wild diversion, as they are for the sight of a *Bartholomew Shew* . . . but once a year, and then too the Farce grows nauseous before it is half ended."[24] As in the Town Miss's manifesto, however, the defence against this forced carnivalization itself takes the form of a sexual language, a "whore's rhetoric."

In another eroto-political fantasy of these years, the 1684 *Parliament of Women*, the rhetoric of institutional and economic liberty reaches its fullest expression since the

Common-Wealth satires of 1650. A riotous female assembly establishes Antinomianism as the official religion and a commonwealth as the form of government, sets up a national curriculum consisting of only three books (Aretino's *Postures, L'Escole des Filles*, and Chorier's *Académie des Dames*), and regulates market-trading by revising all weights and measures: a 3-foot yard is too sad a reminder of better days (29–32, 84–5, 137–8). This parodic "Female Pile of Man-modelling" (125) sometimes points unwittingly to a powerful truth, however. Since marriage is no more than a meat-market (husbands say "this Chump of Beef is mine because I have put a Scewer into it") the solution is for every woman to take men at board wages, and swap them with her neighbors according to "fair Exchange, as the Change goes" (126, 129). Since market values prevail, women must "beware how ye expose your selves; for women, like all sorts of Commodities, lose their intrinsick value by being too often exposed; we are not therefore to expose our selves, but to oppose our selves; we are to oppose our selves against the Crafts, wiles, Subtilties and Polices [*sic*] of those that have for so many hundred years enslav'd us" (8). It goes without saying that these masculine "Crafts" and "Polices" include the very pamphlet that gives voice to this call for freedom. Women's agency becomes one of the "liberties," a trivial zone of sex and carnival, unthinkable as a serious alternative.

3 Work in progress?

A fuller treatment of this *topos* would document the extent of male anxiety about "mercenary" relationships, about becoming a "property," about the "drudgery" and "slavery" of sexual intercourse even when it is supposedly "free." As we have seen, the market-imagery men impose on woman converts the phallus, too, into a "Commodity" to be bartered or metered by the pound, a Bartholomew piglet that melts away in the roasting pan. Is it possible that men felt "outdone" by women on the page, and in the shops, as well as in bed? Though the materials studied here are mostly facetious, serious discourses on marriage agreed with libertine satire that women's increasing economic power as consumers must be neutralized by equating it with sexual promiscuity. A. B.'s *Letter of Advice Concerning Marriage* (1676), for example, calls the new spenders "Female-sparks," "She-gallants," and "a sort of Legal Concubines" whose cry (made audible only in this letter) resembles that of a Bartholomew Fair whore: "no Penny, no *Pater noster*" (15, 16, 21). His solution is to impoverish women completely by abolishing jointures. At a stroke, all taint of mercenary consideration and economic thought will be banished from the noble institution of marriage: "What price, and consequently what life, it would give to the languishing Virtues of Women. . . . 'Tis the best bargain you will ever drive" (27, 28).

In these economically obsessed attacks on women's political, discursive, and economic agency, history reverses Marx's aphorism: world-changing ideas seem to appear first as farce, and only later in serious form. I would like to suggest, however, that such phantasms are in part hysterical responses to existing phenomena, reactions to the actual sites and practices where women forged their own economic, educational, and political history. I would like to be able to prove that the new genres of libertine discourse – the "School of Venus," the whores' petition, the "character of an Exchange-wench" – evolve in response to women's own activities and voices, whether in traditional zones of misrule like the gossips' feast, or in the new feminist polemic of the Revolution and Restoration. Women's petitions had played a dramatic role in the revolutionary events of the 1640s (e.g. *True Copie* 1641), and the bawdy mock-petition appears thereafter as a back-formation. With almost scientific inevitability, a significant contribution by women will throw up its bawdy pamphlet: John Brewer has reported, for example, that women played an increasing role in bookkeeping and gauging for the Excise; sure enough, in 1733 "Timothy Smoke" creates *The Commodity Excis'd, or the Women in an Uproar*, with all the usual jokes.

But if we are to characterize men's attitudes as reactive and defensive, we need to show what actions and discourses they react against. Literary historians should follow, and contribute to, the new historiography of women's work, and should help to develop a theory of agency that recognizes (without overstating or romanticizing) the concrete achievements of women as well as their exclusion and victimization. Such a history could explore those institutions marked as significant by hostile pornographers – schooling, luxury trade, political influence – but it could also look directly at the institutional production of sexuality. Though I treat male depictions of prostitution skeptically, I do not want to suggest that "sex work" did not exist or played no part in women's economic autonomy; Trumbach notes (1988: 80) that "many of these houses were certainly run by women," and that male-owned brothels were still the minority. (The English whore-biography *The Practical Part of Love* [1660] describes the life of the working prostitute as a kind of "slavery" worse than "*Argier* bondage" [42], but the exploiter is assumed to be the independent female "Mistress" rather than the male patron.) Outside the clandestine realm, we should be looking at the whole process whereby men were "formed" and fitted for society by the conversation of women. Though this theme is more familiar in France than in England, and more explicitly linked to sexual initiation there, the aspiration to civil society frequently involved the fabrication of gentlemen through an élite cult of Love administered by "the Ladies." Artisanal and social production are neatly combined in the prologue to Catherine Trotter's *Love at a Loss*:

> The Manufacture of this Town is Love;
> Love in great Minds bears undisputed sway,
> A Shapeless Anarchy when that's away.

> (1701: f. A4)

Sexual identity was in some sense fabricated or woven by women's hands and tongues; men were "worked" as well as waistcoats.

Obviously this revisionist history of production and consumption must include the economy of texts and representations. This requires a more extensive reading of women's own writings, their proposals for new institutions, their "Man-modelling" creation of "Romance heroes," their comments on language, libertinism, and the mercantile-erotic nexus. When Laetitia Pilkington confronts the destruction of her own credit, her recourse is to create a counter-text in the public medium of print, to regain some control over her own reception and transmission; indeed, she threatens to name more of her abusers and would-be seducers in subsequent editions of the *Memoirs*, unless they immediately take out a subscription (1928: 141). When Sarah Fyge confronts the obscene misogynist satire of Robert Gould, she defines in two pungent

phrases the entire project I have been studying in this chapter. She understands the
"low" representation of female sexuality as an assault, an attempt to train perception
and form identity, an attempt to rewrite woman as a pornographic text and to mock the
very institutions through which she advanced herself: such writers "would have all bred
up in *Venus*-School." And in sharpening this accusation she creates a counter-image to
the foul prostitute-saleswomen imagined by the pamphleteers:

> You would adult'rate all Womankind,
> Not only with your Pen.

Sexual discourse involves both adultery and adulteration, the rake's seduction and the
market-trader's cheat.[25]

We should beware, however, of treating economic and discursive agency as parallel
and equivalent. Without falling into the academic folly of ascribing absolute power to
discourse *per se*, we must recognize the peculiar dangers of language, especially in the
public forms of "rhetoric" or print; in this slippery medium dissent is expressed *and*
neutralized, ideology challenged *and* internalized. A professional writer like Aphra
Behn, for example, provokes endless debate over her possible collaborationism. When
she expropriates the cruel song from *Westminster Drollery*, inviting the woman to give
herself gratis or "go spin," she puts it in the mouth of the dashing Willmore; is she
criticizing her "rover" or adorning him?[26] When she adopts the persona of the prostitute, does she fashion a new model of female authorship, or does she confirm the
ideology that equates women with their sexuality? At times she rages against the
"mercenary" and scorns those allegedly virtuous women who "exchange desire" (1915:
VI, 359); at times she seems to accept the prevailing image of a free market in
sexuality. In "To Lysander . . . asking more for his Heart than 'twas worth," for
example, she adopts the economic metaphor completely, but plays up the contrast
between fair and foul practices. Trade must be free, love must be properly appraised;
man must "not take / Freedoms you'll not to me allow," must "give her so much
Freedom back / That she may Rove as well as you" (1915 VI,: 202–4). In returning the
monetary image upon him, Behn shifts its class-register, not downwards, as in the
"characters" of Exchange-women who end in the gutter, but upwards. At the start of
the poem, she adopts the role of the consumer advocate confronting a shopkeeper
caught trying to "inhaunce" the price of his own heart. By the end, however, economic-
amorous activity has been transformed into a speculative, aristocratic, and non-
consumerist transaction. Behn's dominant metaphor is now the fashionable vice of
gambling, a field where she can equal him, either in honest play or "trick for trick."

Notes

1   1979: 298–303 (act III, scene ii) and 310–11. Subsequent references to Wycherley's plays
    include act and scene number, followed by the page where appropriate.

2   III.ii.292. I accept Gerald Weales's ingenious conjecture that the "Dance of Cuckolds"
    specified at V.iv.352 might have been identified by the folk tune "Cuckolds all arow"
    (Wycherley 1967: 370–1).

3   The *Covent Garden* text is here reconstructed from Wycherley 1979: 171–2 (notes to *The*

Gentleman Dancing–Master, II.i); in the published text of the play, which appeared after Behn's anthology, the ambiguous "Like men" (which could suggest that men have as little choice as women) is changed to "Our men," and "labour" to "Lover."

4   For the regulations limiting the kinds of retail at the New Exchange (54–64 Strand), see *Survey* 1900–: 96. The full list is: haberdashers, stocking-sellers, girdlers; linen-drapers, silk-mercers; seamsters, tiremakers, milliners, hoodmakers; goldsmiths, jewelers, perfumers; confectioners; sellers of china ware, pictures, maps, and prints; stationers and booksellers. For neighboring houses, where Horner might have taken Margery, see pp. 59, 94, 98.

5   *The Miser* I.ii, cited in *OED*, "journeywoman."

6   1666: 3rd. pagination, 36–9 (ff. Ccc2v–4); for the genteel language of aesthetic consumerism, cf. "as you are a Gentleman, you may have some knowledge in that noble Art of Limning."

7   Reprinted from *Westminster Drollery* by Montague Summers (Behn 1915: VI, 173), on the grounds that Willmore quotes it in Behn's *Rover II*.

8   "Sally Salisbury," for example, was encouraged by her aristocratic keeper to improve a young dramatist's work ("Every Scene was brought to her, and was continued, altered or left out, as she approved or disliked it; and she always gave very good Reasons for the Objections she made"); inevitably, "she could not forbear intriguing with the young Poet" (Walker 1723: 15).

9   Ingram (1987: 308–11) records cases of economic damage following on loss of reputation; though he discounts this as a major consequence, it is clear that any woman in service would be thrown out if sexual misconduct could be proved. The case of the acquitted window-breaker appears in the Old Bailey records, brought to light in Doody (1989).

10   All references to Pepys's diary come from the Lathan–Matthews edn. (1970–83), but will be cited by entry date; for other references to "Lady" Bennett, see May 30, 1668 and Wycherley 1979: 365–72.

11   Cf. Schama 1988: 382–3; Staves 1982: 290, citing Fielding's *Modern Husband*.

12   An idea developed in Davis 1983.

13   Thompson 1977: 252; cf. Pepys, March 25, 1668, and "Spenser" 1660.

14   Thompson 1977: 251; cf. Garfield 1660a: 6.

15   Garfield 1660b: 12 (cf. 1660a: 15, for a listing of "Ursula" among the whores). The descriptions of grotesque and violent sexual routines, which fill these early Restoration whore-pamphlets, should be seen as the textual equivalent of the "Monsters" or raree-shows of Bartholomew Fair; in *Strange and True Newes* (1660), for example, women are ordered to "stand upon their heads . . . with all their cloathes and smock about their ears bare breeches to the cold wall (like Monsters) legs spread at large with the door of their Chuck office open"(2).

16   For the *Tariffa*, attributed to Antonio Cavallino, see Aretino 1975: 185; the genre later flourished in such publications as *Harris's List of Covent-Garden Ladies* (annually from 1760 onwards). For wife-sales, see Hair 1972: 139. As we saw in section 1, the "Exchange Wench" was auctioned off by her employer.

17   Tom Brown, *The Auction of Ladies* (1699), cited in Pinkus 1968: 45. Among many other examples, cf. *The Ladies Projection [or] Marriage Lottery*, in *Dirty Dogs* (1732).

18   In Garfield 1661: 4–5, for example, the elaborate list of legal *"Articles"* that Julietta draws up before marrying the rich dupe Francion resembles an international treaty (and anticipates the "proviso" scene in *Way of the World*).

19   Garfield 1660b: 8; "Spenser" 1660 *passim* (occasioned by Fotheringham's imprisonment in Newgate, presumably because of her scandalous performances); *Strange and True Newes* (n. 15 above). Roger Thompson suggests, ingeniously, that "Chuck Office" may be a pun on the Poultry Office (1979: 93).

20   Garfield 1660a: 6–7; for later instances of the physical insertion of cash into the vagina, cf. Walker 1723: 66–8 (aristocrats throw guineas into Sally Salisbury's "merry *Chuck–Hole*") and the Victorian *My Secret Life*, cited in Marcus (1966: 159–60) as the "logical conclusion" of a system in which sex and money have become the agents of masculine power, and in which sexual acts must maintain "the maximum distance" between partners.

21 "Spenser" 1660: 8 (appointment of an official poet "to make baudy drollery for the Sportive Wits among us"); *Strange and True Newes* 1660: 5 (order for the examination, adoption, and prohibition of certain books); Garfield 1660a: 5–6 (presenting an ancient precedent for the toleration of brothels) and 1660b: 13 (list of pictures "in our private rooms").

22 Pepys, March 25, 1668; Head 1666: 3rd. pagination, 39 (f. Ccc4).

23 For commercial images (many of them already in the Aretino passages plagiarized here), see e.g. 80–1, 88, 179 (she should emulate "industrious and thriving merchants"); for politics, 42, 57 (cf. 60), 217.

24 177–8; for reminders of severe policing cf. 37 (the expert whore "need not fear the Constables Staff, or the justices Warrant, a publick whipping, or a private one in *Bridewel*").

25 1687: 4, 7. Rather than praising Fyge for this act of resistance to slander, her father treated it as itself a sexual transgression, and bundled her off to the country (Lonsdale 1989: 26). Fyge's counterblast is discussed in Nussbaum 1984: 30–4.

26 Behn 1915: I, 195; VI, 364, 430–1 (and see n. 7 above). I assume that when Willmore exits from La Nuche "singing," he continues the song whose penultimate stanza appears in the text; the final "go spin" would sound from the wings as the slighted courtesan laments "where's all your Power, ye poor deluded Eyes?" For Behn's use of the prostitute-as-author figure, see Gallagher 1988.

Bibliography

Works of unknown authorship are listed by title. Publishers are not given for early modern books, whose place of publication is London unless otherwise indicated.

An Answer to the Character of an Exchange-Wench, or a Vindication of an Exchange-Woman (1675).

The Ape-Gentle-Woman, or the Character of an Exchange-Wench (1675).

Aretino, P. (1975) *Sei Giornate*, ed. G. D. Bonino, Turin: Einaudi.

An Auction of Whores, or the Bawds Bill of Sale for Bartholomew Fair (1691).

B., A. (1676) *A Letter of Advice Concerning Marriage*.

Behn, A. (1915) *Works*, ed. M. Summers, London: Heinemann.

Brome, R. (1873 [1658]) *The New Academy, or the New Exchange*, in *Dramatic Works*, Vol. 2, London: J. Pearson (paginated separately).

Browne, A. (1987) *The Eighteenth-Century Feminist Mind*, Brighton, Sussex: Harvester.

The Character of a Town Misse (1675).

Congreve, W. (1956) *Complete Plays*, ed. A. C. Ewald, New York: Hill & Wang.

Davis, L. (1983) *Factual Fictions*, New York: Columbia University Press.

Dennis, J. (1943) *Critical Works*, ed. E. N. Hooker, Vol. 2, Baltimore, MD: Johns Hopkins University Press.

A Dialogue between Mistris Macquerella, a Suburb Bawd, Mrs. Scolopendra, a noted Curtezan, and Mr. Pimpinello an Usher (1650).

Dirty Dogs for Dirty Puddings (1732).

Doody, M. A. (1989) "Women as witnesses and victims," paper delivered to the Midwest Conference on British Studies, University of Illinois at Chicago, October.

Etherege, Sir G. (1982) *Plays*, ed. M. Cordner, Cambridge: Cambridge University Press.

Foxon, D. (1965) *Libertine Literature in England 1660–1745*, New Hyde Park, NY: University Books.

Fyge (later Egerton), S. (1687) *The Female Advocate, or an Answer to a Late Satyr against the Pride, Lust and Inconstancy of Woman*.

Gallagher, C. (1988) "Who was that masked woman? The prostitute and the playwright in the comedies of Aphra Behn," *Women's Studies* 15: 23–42.

Garfield, J. (1660a) *The Wandring Whore: A Dialogue between Magdelena a Crafty Bawd, Julietta an Exquisite Whore, Francion a Lascivious Gallant, and Gusman a Pimping Hector*.

—— (1660b) *The Wandring Whore Continued, Number 2*.

—— (1661) *The Fifth and Last Part of the Wandring Whore . . . By Peter Aretine*.

Hair, P. E. H. (1972) *Before the Bawdy Court: Selections from Church Court and Other Records Relating to the Correction of Moral Offences in England, Scotland and New England, 1300–1800*, London: Elek.

Head, R. (1666) *The English Rogue Described in the Life of Meriton Latroon.*

Hill, B. (1989) *Women, Work, and Sexual Politics in Eighteenth-Century England*, Oxford: Blackwell.

Ingram, M. (1987) *Church Courts, Sex and Marriage in England, 1570–1640*, Cambridge: Cambridge University Press.

The London Jilt, or the Politick Whore . . . Interwoven with Several Pleasant Stories of the Misses Ingenious Performances (1683).

Lonsdale, R. (ed.) (1989) *Eighteenth-Century Women Poets: An Oxford Anthology*, Oxford: Oxford University Press.

Marcus, S. (1966) *The Other Victorians: A Study of Sexuality and Pornography in Mid-Nineteenth-Century England*, New York: Basic Books.

Montagu, Lady Mary Wortley (1956) *Complete Letters*, ed. R. Halsband, Vol. 1, Oxford: Clarendon Press.

Newes from the New Exchange, or the Common-Wealth of Ladies (1650).

Nussbaum, F. A. (1984) *The Brink of All We Hate: English Satires on Women, 1660–1750*, Lexington, KY: University Press of Kentucky.

Oldham, J. (n.d.) MS Rawl. Poet. 123, Bodleian Library, Oxford.

The Parliament of Women (1684). *Pace* Thompson (1979: 107) this cannot be the same as the 1640 *Parlament of Women.*

Pepys, S. (1970–83) *Diary*, ed. R. Latham and W. Matthews, Berkeley, CA: University of California Press.

Phillips, J. (1653) *Sportive Wit, the Muses Merriment: A New Spring of Lusty Drollery, Jovial Fancies, and Alamode Lampoons*, second part (*Lusty Drollery*).

Pilkington, L. (1928 [1748–52]) *Memoirs*, ed. I. Barry, London: Routledge.

Pinkus, P. (1968) *Grub Street Stripped Bare*, London: Constable.

The Practical Part of Love (1660).

Richardson, S. (1804) *Correspondence*, ed. Anna Laetitia Barbauld.

Rossiaud, J. (1985) "Prostitution, sex and society in French towns," in P. Ariès and A. Béjin (eds.) *Western Sexuality*, trans. A. Forster, Oxford: Blackwell.

Schama, S. (1988) *The Embarrassment of Riches: An Interpretation of Dutch Culture in the Golden Age*, Berkeley, CA: University of California Press.

"Smoke, Timothy" (1733) *The Commodity Excis'd, or the Women in an Uproar.*

"Spenser, Megg." (1660) *A Strange and True Conference between Two Notorious Bawds, Damarose Page and Pris. Fotheringham.* Since Spenser is listed among the bawds and whores, her pretended authorship is clearly a front.

Staves, S. (1982) "Money for honor: damages for criminal conversation," *Studies in 18th-Century Culture* 11: 279–97.

Strange and True Newes from Jack-a-Newberries Six Windmills (1660).

Strange Newes from Bartholomew-Fair, or the Wandring-Whore Discovered, Her Cabinet Unlockt, Her Secrets Laid Open, Unvailed, and Spread Abroad (1661).

Survey of London (1900–), vol. 18, London: London County Council and Survey Committee.

Thompson, R. (ed.) (1977) *Samuel Pepys' Penny Merriments*, New York: Columbia University Press.

—— (1979) *Unfit for Modest Ears*, London: Macmillan.

The Town–Misses Declaration and Apology (1675).

Troia Redeviva [sic], or The Glories of London Surveyed in an Heroick Poem (1674).

Trotter, C. (1701) *Love at a Loss, or Most Votes Carry It.*

A True Copie of the Petition of the Gentlewomen and Tradesmens–Wives, in and about the City of London, . . . with Their Severall Reasons Why Their Sex Ought Thus to Petition (1641).

Trumbach, R. (1988) "Modern prostitution and gender in *Fanny Hill*: libertine and domesticated fantasy," in G. S. Rousseau and R. Porter (eds.) *Sexual Underworlds of the Enlightenment*, Manchester: Manchester University Press.

Walker, C. (1723) *Authentick Memoirs [of] Sally Salisbury.*

Ward, E. (1700) *The Rambling Rakes, or London Libertines.*

—— (1709) *The London-Spy Compleat, in Eighteen Parts*, "4th edition."

The Whores Rhetorick, Calculated to the Meridian of London (1683). A loose adaptation of Ferrante
    Pallavicino, *La retorica delle puttane* (Venice: 1642).
Wycherley, W. (1924) *Complete Works*, ed. M. Summers, London: Nonesuch Press.
—— (1967) *Complete Plays*, ed. G. Weales, New York: Norton.
—— (1979) *Plays*, ed. A. Friedman, Oxford: Clarendon Press.

23
Women's participation in the urban culture of early modern London
Images from fiction

Elizabeth Bennett Kubek

> I was now about the Age of Fifteen, at which time my Mother thought fit to send me to *London*, to remain under the Government of my Aunt, my Lady *Martial*, under whose prudent Conduct, I might learn a little of the Town Politeness; its Civilities without its Vanities; its Diversions without its Vices, *&c*. This Journey was extreamly pleasing to me, which is usual to any young Country Creature. *London!* the Idol of all the World, might naturally create Longings in a young female Heart.
>
> (Barker 1713: 6–7)

Jane Austen's rejection in her novels of the urban setting is typically explained by critics as the result of a personal aversion to fashionable society, and perhaps of painful romantic associations (Poovey 1984: 209). But Austen's expressions of distaste for the city also participate in an anti-urban tradition that dominates British women's literature of the later eighteenth century. During the Restoration and the early eighteenth century, many women writers depicted London as potentially a fulfilling environment for women. The repudiation of urban experience typical of later works by women was a concession to social pressures that sought to limit the female role in urban culture to that of the passive object of sexual consumption and/or the restrained consumer of material goods and appropriate social events.

London played a leading role in the lives of early modern British writers. F. S. Schwarzbach points out that

> London dominated literature in much the same way as it did the economy; it was the largest, most compact market for printed matter . . . The slow but steady collapse of patronage and the growth of the literary market economy left authors more and more dependent upon the sale of copyrights for income. This drew them inevitably to London, for one needed to be on the spot to negotiate

with booksellers and editors, and to keep one's hand on the pulse of fickle readers' changing interests.

(Schwarzbach 1982: 101)

The playwright Catherine Trotter was to find in 1701 that absence from London at the wrong time could mean a poorly edited published edition of a successful play (Morgan 1981: 26). The philosopher Mary Astell moved to London to pursue her intellectual goals; "[i]ntellectual, single, poor, and urban, she could not have existed out of London" (Perry 1986: 119). Urbanity was also an important professional resource for women writers in the Restoration and early eighteenth century. Writers like Aphra Behn and Delarivier Manley repeatedly drew themes and plots from the latest political events or "town-talk." Later women writers used the London marriage market to expose their heroines to adventures. Yet, Perry notes, "for literary, 'scribling' women, life in the city meant notoriety, derision, and unwanted attention" (Perry 1986: 128). As I have argued in an earlier article, feminine virtue and urbanity were always already defined as binary opposites (Kubek 1990: 303–40).

The present chapter examines images of consumption in Restoration and eighteenth-century English texts to demonstrate that early modern women writers sought to explore and capitalize on the scandal of urban womanhood. But as a special image of professionalism evolved for the woman writer,[1] moral and market forces demanded that women's representation and appropriation of their own commodity status be limited. Consumption and its control, in the early modern period freely treated by writers of both sexes as sexual issues, came to be represented to/by/for women by choices of material and cultural objects.

The first section of this chapter examines texts by male writers that represent urban women and their "histories" as objects to be sexually, visually, or verbally consumed. From this literature of the early modern city emerge strategies for the visual or narrative classification of urban women, part of a social system within which women were expected to remain in order to fulfill emerging bourgeois expectations concerning self-development, chastity, and social education. Texts from this category manifest an obsession with strategies for controlling the bodies of urban women. Mary Russo, writing on the grotesque female body, claims that "women and their bodies, certain bodies, in certain public framings, in certain public spaces, are always already transgressive – dangerous, and in danger" (Russo 1986: 217). Restoration and eighteenth-century male writers conventionally represent the urban woman as grotesque, fragmented and overly eroticized, and tend to offer as an alibi for specularizing their female subjects an agenda of reform, in a manner Jacqueline Rose describes occurring in the nineteenth century (Rose 1986: 113). Active scopophilia, which necessitates the relegation of the object of desire to a passive state (Mulvey 1989: 16–18), is excused in these texts by insistence on the dangerous indeterminacy of the urban female subject, usually represented as a criminal or a prostitute.

Section II of this paper examines works by three early professional women writers, roughly contemporary with the male writers discussed in section I. Fictions by early modern women writers appropriate existing literary forms, and to some degree capitalize on the market for urban women's adventurous and erotic narratives, while at the same time using irony and satire to oppose or resist the tendency to represent women's bodies and narratives as commodities. These texts suggest that a positive and active female response to the city is possible.

Section III demonstrates that mid- to late eighteenth-century works by women tend to represent women's London experience as necessarily limited to certain forms of consumption. These works for the most part accept with distaste both the commodification of women represented by the marriage market, and the idea that women experience the city primarily as consumers of goods, services, and social events. This limited view of urban experience leads to a rejection of London values as mercenary and hedonistic. A trope emerges which depicts the virtuous woman as one who voluntarily limits her own consumption and commodification by avoiding urbanity.

I

Popular London literature of the Restoration and early eighteenth century tends to depict urban women crudely as mere sexual commodities. These fictions also commodify women by making them the objects of a narrative strategy which exposes not only their bodies, but their lives, to a normative masculine gaze. While claiming an intent to protect men (and sometimes "virtuous" women) from female wiles, these texts focus obsessively on the signs of female identity – clothing, residence, employment, and name, as well as sexual status – in the service of a desire to contain women as narrative/sexual commodities. The figure of the urban woman is revealed to be the site of both pleasure and anxiety in the male subject; her control through commodification emerges as an essential element of early modern urban culture.

In *The English Rogue*,[2] Meriton Latroon struggles to disguise himself as a woman:

> Nothing troubled me more, than how to dress myself, when my clothes were off. I durst not lay two things together, for fear I should mistake; there were so many baubles, I wished for a pen and ink, to write on them what places they properly belonged to. Viewing them on the table together, they represented to my thoughts bable [*sic*], or a great confusion, and nothing but a miracle could produce order out of them.
>
> (Head and Kirkman 1665: I, 132)

Latroon complains that he finds female dress emblematic of "bable" – semiotic and structural chaos – and wishes for a masculine implement to inscribe order on this "great confusion." Latroon's long, rambling tale "produces order" out of the threatening babble of female existence by providing a series of narratives locating the image of the urban female body in/as a readable (and marketable) text. His first mistress is a "cunning quean" who deceives her husband by her changes of name, clothing, and lodging: she "never went abroad but with her vizard mask, and in as many varieties of suits as there are months in the year, which though but thirteen, yet did she make them ring as many changes as Bow Bells" (Head and Kirkman 1665: I, 58). She is the first of many dangerously clever women Latroon encounters. *The English Rogue* and its many imitators control the image of the urban woman through overdetermination: the "cunning quean" becomes a sign, an exchangeable and knowable object, which represents all urban women.

True to the nature of such signs, the "cunning quean" myth proves capable of coopting historical as well as fictional images. *The Counterfeit Lady Unveil'd* represents Francis Kirkman's framing and continuation (1961 [1673]) of an autobiographical sketch written by the famous "German Princess," Mary Carleton. Carleton's first-person narrative, embedded in Kirkman's text, tells of her marriage to a man who thought she was a foreign heiress; after discovering that she was in fact neither foreign nor wealthy, her husband's family attempted to have Carleton convicted of bigamy (Kirkman 1961 [1673]: 21–37). Kirkman makes Carleton's autobiography conform to the urban rogue format by appending to it a series of conventional anecdotes alleged to represent Carleton's "infamous carriage . . . in and about this city of London" (Kirkman 1961: 12). By appropriating and "editing" Carleton's own narrative, Kirkman transforms her history into another signifier for the "truth" of the "cunning quean" myth; he also converts her attempt at self-representation into a commodity for his own profit.

The myth of the "cunning quean" provides adequate justification for its own commodification in the form of narrative by representing all urban women as prostitutes, and thus always already commodities. The "moral" purpose of these texts is to deprive these women of the ability to benefit from their own commodification, and to turn the moral and financial profits of their actions over to men, by conventionalizing their behavior and/or their histories. Thus prostitution is fantasized in such texts as both the "true" condition of all women and a structuring device amenable to masculine knowledge. The first volume of *The English Rogue* describes a high-priced "new fashion *Bawdy-house*" in which some of the women are "persons of no mean quality" gratifying their lusts by masquerading as prostitutes; this leads Latroon to speculate that all urban houses are in "truth" brothels (Head and Kirkman 1665: I, 381). Another such fantasy is provided by Latroon's mistress Mary, the graduate of a "private and reserved" brothel in which she is passed off as "a private Lady a Merchant's wife, and several other Titles and qualities" (Head and Kirkman 1665: II, 345–7). Here women are classed, salaried, and priced according to freshness. Having "act[ed] the part of a Virgin" and masqueraded as a lustful City wife, Mary escapes being made to "serve in common, for all Gentleman customers that came," by finding a keeper (Head and Kirkman 1665: II, 347–8). A similar "freshness dating" scheme was (perhaps ironically) proposed by Bernard Mandeville in his 1724 *Modest Defence of Publick Stews*, which sketches an ideal brothel containing four "classes" of women, spatially separated according to appearance and price (Mandeville 1724: 13). The fantasy of the "new fashion *Bawdy-house*" reassuringly reflects the simultaneous existence of social roles in the brothel and of the brothel in society: all women are whores, but even whores acknowledge patriarchal structures. The patriarchy imagines women's natural condition as semiotic chaos; as commodities they lack innate difference and their only value is that given them by men (Irigaray 1977: 175).[3]

Edward Ward's *London-Spy* follows this logic by describing London in terms of heterosexual and scopophilic male desires. The narrator describes Bedlam as "a *Showing-Room* for *Whores*, a *sure Market* for *Leachers*," where the spectator can be "entertained" by the display of "Mistresses . . . to be had of all Ranks, Qualities, Colours, Prices, and Sizes; from the *Velvet Scarf* to the *Scotch Plad Petticoat*," or by the "Whimsical Figaries" of the female inmates (Ward 1709: 67). The City woman, or "Belsa," to be seen in Gray's Inn Walks, is "[t]rain'd half in School, and t'other half in Shop" for marriage (Ward 1709: 391). The "Court Ladies," glimpsed in the Mall and St. James's Park, are "shews of Cœlestial Harmony, in that most Beautiful and Curious Creature, WOMAN" (Ward 1709: 177–80). The bourgeois male reader learns the proper level of consumption for each class of woman: while the women of the court are commodified on the purely scopic level of the "shew," working women in the New Exchange "sat in their pinfolds, begging of Custom, with such Amorous Looks, and after so Affable a manner, that I could not but fancy they had as much mind to dispose of themselves, as the Commodities they dealt in" (Ward 1709: 73). Restoration discomfort with women's active participation in the city's economic life contributes to the transformation of active female members of London society into commodified objects of a scopophilic gaze, an operation *The London-Spy* also performs on female mountebanks, "gossips," inn-keepers, fortune-tellers, and thieves.

In scopophilic texts women's resistance to commodification is represented as an excuse for sadistic disciplinary measures. In *The English Rogue* Meriton Latroon's pursuit of his former wife, a prostitute, through such red-light areas of London as "*Sodom*, and *Dog* and *Bitch-yard*," ends with a description of its pox-raddled object being whipped in Bridewell, to Latroon's delight (Head and Kirkman 1665: II, 362–3). In *The London-Spy*, a similar scene involves the display of a female criminal's "tempting Bubbies," while two "Punks" in a coach are pelted by the crowd for the pretension of donning masks (Ward 1709: 141–2, 294).[4] John Dunton's *The Night-Walker: Or. Evening Rambles in Search after Lewd Women, with the Conferences Held with Them, &c.*, "to be publish'd Monthly, 'till a Discovery be made of all the chief *Prostitutes* in *England*, from the *Pensionary Miss*, down to the *Common Strumpet*," under the guise of moral reform obsessively narrates the display and punishment of urban female sexuality. The visual and the sexual are represented as identical modes of consumption as the Night-walker warns

> our Citizens, to take heed how they expose their *fine wives in their Shops*; . . . who sit Trickt and Trim'd, and Rigg'd in their Shops as if they had more mind to expose themselves to Sale, than their Goods . . . and in truth no man can well put any other Construction upon it, when he sees a fine Woman exposed in a Shop.
>
> (Dunton 1696: II, 11–12)

The Night-walker uses threats of public exposure to elicit from "lewd women" such signs of remorse as swooning, weeping, and confessions. Repeatedly the female body must be coerced into verbal representation. One woman's offer of "the pleasures of – (Throwing herself on the bed, and pulling up her Clothes)," is rejected in favor of a repentant narrative of her former transgression (Dunton 1696: IV, 19–20). "[W]hen women are exchanged, woman's body must be treated as an *abstraction*" (Irigaray 1977: 175); through narrative, women's bodies are deprived of the ability to represent themselves. These anecdotes clearly display the psychological and economic tensions embedded in the scopophilic "mapping" text. As Laura Mulvey points out, the woman as object of the gaze is a source of both pleasure and anxiety for the male subject, for she brings with her the unpleasurable reminder of the threat of castration; she must therefore be either punished or transformed into a fetish lest the subject's sexual pleasure be interrupted by castration anxiety (Mulvey 1989: 21). The punishment of these female "transgressors" is meant to reassure the male reader that patriarchal society protects his sexual "investment" in a scopic economy.

Clearly, these popular tales about urban women fulfilled a variety of social needs. They presented the Londoner to himself as a clever survivor in a dangerous world; they were titillating and yet seemingly moralistic; they gave new life to such class stereotypes as the cuckolded Cit and the clever 'prentice; they described the city as a world of pleasures and intrigues, and told the reader where those pleasures were to be purchased or glimpsed; and they established a spatial system of specular classification which would allow the reader to derive pleasure from women as commodities on various socially appropriate levels. Women could be visually sorted for degree of virtue, and thus the male consumer could decide whether to bargain for a particular woman as a mistress, whore, or wife. These narratives reassured men of their power over women in an urban society where social "place" seemed unstable, and provided female readers with an image of their own sexuality that, while ostensibly erotic, reinforced conventional standards of virtue and domesticity.

Yet the London-centered texts also established how conventional, and therefore open to manipulation, the spatial and visual signs of morality could be. In *Masquerade and Civilization*, Terry Castle points out the subversive potential of the understanding that dress is not an immutable sign of the wearer's "true" nature (Castle 1986: 55–6). The "cunning quean" narratives embody deep anxiety about the urban woman's ability to misappropriate the signs of her rank and moral nature, and attempt to reassure male readers by providing a signifying network which asserts women's status as always already a commodity controlled by men. But when women's narratives acquired commodity value, women were given an economic motive to appropriate this value to themselves.

II

The section which follows examines works by three Restoration and eighteenth-century women writers who capitalized on contemporary interest in the image of the urban woman to further their careers. The texts discussed below play upon the reader's assumed desire to purchase narratives by and about urbanized women and to see such women represented as sexual commodities. However, these texts also reflect satirically upon the readers' desires, and deconstruct the image of woman-as-whore by depicting heroines who resist consumption and containment by male values, who attempt to act as sexual and economic consumers, or who themselves profit by their commodity status.

As Jane Spencer notes, Aphra Behn complained of the sexism of her peers but was not above using the novelty of her femininity to promote her career (Spencer 1986: 42–3). Behn's awareness of women's reputation and sexuality as commodities is expressed not only in her self-promotion, but in the content of her works. Two of her short "novels," *The Black Lady* (1915 [1684]) and *The Unfortunate Happy Lady* (1915 [1696]), exemplify Behn's use of this knowledge. In *The Black Lady*, "the fair Innocent (I must not say foolish)" Bellamora, pregnant by her betrothed Fondlove, flees to

London and falls in with "a good, discreet, ancient Gentlewoman, who was fallen to decay, and forc'd to let Lodgings" (Behn 1915 [1684]: 4) – a description which the Restoration reader was conditioned to read ironically as signifying a bawd. The story invokes the code of a "harlot's progress" narrative, a tale of female betrayal and degradation. But the landlady and her female tenant prove resourceful and loyal; they conspire to hide Bellamora from the parish officials until Fondlove arrives. The lovers are safely wedded and gone shopping at the Exchange by the time "the Vermin of the Parish (I mean, the Overseers of the Poor, who eat the Bread from 'em)" arrive in search of a pregnant "young Blackhair'd lady," and are mocked by being shown "a black Cat that had just kitten'd" (Behn 1915: [1684]: 10). This short tale invokes the pattern of urban female sexual victimization and punishment in order to satirize the voracious desires of the reader and of patriarchal law: the heroine ends up as a happy consumer rather than an object of consumption.

The second of Behn's short London novels, *The Unfortunate Happy Lady*, recasts the "cunning quean" narrative by showing a virtuous heroine enriched through urban adventures. Again the tale begins as a victimization narrative: the heiress Philadelphia is betrayed to a bawd by her avaricious brother Sir William Wilding. However, she resists her first purchaser, Gracelove, so strenuously that he rescues her from the brothel and asks her to marry him. When Gracelove is believed lost at sea, Philadelphia becomes the wife and then the wealthy widow of his elderly cousin Counsellor Fairlaw. Her wealth allows her anonymously to redeem her brother from prison and her returned lover from poverty. The story ends with a banquet at which Philadelphia, in the presence of her many powerful suitors, reclaims and enriches Gracelove, and arranges a match for her bankrupt brother with her own stepdaughter (Behn 1915 [1696]: 37–63). Philadelphia's fairy-tale narrative allows its heroine to realize a profit on the sale of her virginity and to make a public purchase of the two men who once treated her as a commodity.

Behn's sophisticated manipulation of convention in these tales reveals the extent to which Restoration writers could rely on readers' interest in the commodification of urban women's bodies and narratives. Both tales begin by using as bait the image of the sexual victimization of women; both end by representing women as consumers and marriage as a choice rather than an inevitable destination. Although she does not question sexual consumption as a social practice, Behn balances capitulation to market forces, which demand that women be depicted as commodities, with her desire to create heroines who exploit the potentials of urban life.

The Tory satirist Delarivier Manley wrote two fictionalized accounts of her scandalous life in order to capitalize on public fascination with the writer's adventures as the source of her knowledge of sexuality (Spencer 1986: 53–62). Manley also made the victimized-woman narrative the basis of a deep critique of social values. *Secret MEMOIRS and MANNERS Of Several Persons of Quality . . . from the New ATALANTIS* (1709) and *MEMOIRS of EUROPE, Towards the Close of the Eighth Century* (1710), thinly disguised satirical attacks on prominent Whigs, ridicule wealthy and powerful members of London society, and through them the psychological and economic attitudes which demanded the commodification of women.

Like the works of Ward and Dunton, the scandalous chronicles are voyeuristic texts whose narrators protest reforming motives. *Atalantis* begins with the resolve of the goddess Astrea, or Justice, to "go to the Courts, where *Justice*, is profess'd . . . to the *Courts* and *Cabinets* of Princes . . . to the *Assemblies* and *Alcoves* of the Young and Fair to discover their Disorders, and the height of their Temptations" (Manley 1709: I, 8–9). But by depicting her narrators as motivated by desire, Manley ironizes the scopophilic text and turns the force of her satire back on the reader. Manley satirizes Whig wealth and privilege by demonstrating that urban capitalism, as represented both by the inhabitants of London's political power-sites and by the sites themselves, is based in the sexual consumption of women by men. Many of her female characters are portrayed sympathetically as victims of this process; a few escape by secretly pursuing desires of their own.

One key section in *MEMOIRS of EUROPE* simultaneously constructs a scathing characterization of the voyeuristic narrator, describes a Whitehall mansion as it reflects the commodification of sex, and provides an ambiguous portrayal of female desire.[5] The aristocrat St. Gerrone breaks a vow of silence to describe a mansion in "Constantinople" (London) to his gossip-hungry peers:

> *Sergius*'s beautiful Palace, built upon the *Constantinopolitan* Shore, has the *Asian* Side in an unlimited Prospect. . . . Along the Margin of the Water is rais'd a beautiful Terrass, adorn'd with flourishing and perpetual Greens. . . . Here you shall find those who hope to be happy Lovers, extended on the Grass, their Limbs all careless and supine, resting their Head [*sic*] (while stretch'd with an Air of Delight, at the Feet of the consenting Fair) upon their Mistresses Knees. . . . Disolv'd in more substantial Joys, the more forward Lovers tread the conscious adjoining Groves, enlighten'd as their Charmers Eyes, with thousands of Lamps blazing an artificial Day . . . the perpetually falling Blossoms furnishing the fragrant Couch.
>
> (Manley 1710: I, 282–3)

The grounds of this London mansion seem designed to encourage voyeurism and to display and classify conventional couples according to the sexual willingness of women. This staging of sexual activity continues within the palace, where "twenty noble Appartments [with] chrystal Doors" display more varied groupings:

> Each Appartment was accessible, all yielding to the Sight by their chrystal Lights, and an exact *Decorum* observ'd, not to intrude upon one anothers Pleasures; but as I was a Stranger and not very solicitous of Fame, I made no Scruple to pry about, and even to lean my Ears and Eyes to the magnificent Glass-Doors, that bestow'd a clear and noble Prospect of that Happiness I was in search of, and cou'd not forbear to envy.
>
> (Manley 1710: I, 297–8)

The "grand-salle" becomes a microcosm of the pornotopic city, and the glass doors, as "Perspectives," or lenses, focus the narrative/readerly gaze on the various sexual performances being enacted. St. Gerrone, the voyeur-narrator, is represented as the envious, unscrupulous, and impotent tool of the mansion's equally immoral owner, who has asked him to violate the "decorum" of the palace by spying on the alcoves' users (Manley 1710: I, 308).

Several of the scenes within the alcoves are drawn from the conventional iconography of "perversion" and satirical comedy: men dress as women or court young girls, while women dominate men (Manley 1710: I, 298–308). Within one alcove, however, St. Gerrone witnesses the lesbian embrace of "Ariadne" and "Philomela":

> I cou'd wear away a Life upon her Lips, press me closer, thou enchanting Girl: Not all Mankind can give me such *poignant* Joys! Here follow'd a very new and out-of-the-way Scene, but of what I can only imagine; for dexterous *Lydia* flipp'd a twisted Cord of Silk, which in a Moment left all in the Dark, the numerous Lamps being at one instant not extinguish'd, but cover'd by Silver-Machines artificially contriv'd. I heard tender Sighs and broken Murmurs succeed the Light, 'till after a convenient Season of Darkness, *Adroit Lydia* pull'd the Cord, and all was Day again.
>
> (Manley 1710: I, 300–1)

This scene, laden with ambiguity, both entices and threatens the voyeur. Ariadne chooses Philomela over a male companion disguised as Bacchus, thus rewriting the patriarchal myth which transformed the resourceful daughter of Minos into an abandoned victim of male treachery. The dressmaker Lydia can represent both fashion (an acceptable mode of feminine consumption) and the uncontrollable "ba[b]ble" of female dress. Rather than displaying sexual behavior, Sergius's palace and its "Silver-Machines" here protect the viewer from the spectacle of lesbian desire; this exclusion from narrative representation can be seen as a denial of the threatening "lack" which the female genitals represent to the male viewer. But the non-representational language of "tender Sighs and broken Murmurs" that "succeed[s] the Light" reinscribes female pleasure in the uncommodifiable form of "ba[b]ble," while the blocking of the gaze temporarily frustrates (castrates?) the voyeuristic male narrator/reader. Not content with merely satirizing the voyeur, Manley creates an image of female desire that escapes commodification by rejecting a male sexual partner and eluding the male viewer. Adriadne is in fact one of a series of heroines in Manley's "scandalous chronicles" who escape commodification by pursuing transgressive sexual desires.

Sergius's palace demonstrates the principles of displacement and exchange which govern the urban economy. Lamps, fountains, beds, tables, groves, and alcoves are all fetishized as sexual instruments, while sexuality itself is represented as a displacement of economic desires: "Interest . . . is the true Foundation, the invisible Spring on *Julius Sergius*'s Side, that moves the Machine even in this soft, this delectable Retreat" (Manley 1710: I, 281–2). Sergius himself is finally envisioned as a machine; Manley's "scandalous chronicles" deny the voyeuristic narrative's tendency to represent itself as guided by a reforming intelligence, and instead attack visual commodification as totally alienated and alienating.

Where Manley repeatedly depicted women's escape into sexual transgression, the heroine envisioned by the later satirist Jane Barker is chaste and retired; she resists sexual commodification by choosing urban professionalism over the London marriage market. Galesia, the heroine of Barker's *A Patch-Work Screen for the Ladies*, craves a classical satirist's laurels. Her narrative makes clear the gap between "masculine" and "feminine" response to urban society. Galesia first follows Horatian satire in comparing "the busy Town" unfavorably to "Rural Pleasures" (Barker 1723: 5–6). She then re-states her complaint in conventional "feminine" terms:

> the Town to me was a Wilderness, where, methought, I lost my self and my Time; and what the World there calls Diversion, to me was Confusion. The Park, Plays, and Operas, were to me but as so much Time thrown away.
>
> (Barker 1723: 42–3)

Where a male writer might complain of the drawbacks of fame or of political vice, Galesia is annoyed by the "Impertinencies" of consumer society (Barker 1723: 55). Pursuing her second avocation, the practice of medicine, Galesia is further distracted by the tales a female patient and nurse relate of their "Undoing" by men. Yet she still attempts to pursue traditional poetic experience:

> At last I found out a Closet in my Landlady's Back–Garret which I crept into, as if it had been a Cave on the Top of *Parnassus*; the Habitation of some unfortunate Muse, that has inspir'd *Cowley*, *Butler*, *Otway*, or *Orinda*, with Notions different from the rest of Mankind; and for that Fault, were there made Prisoners [sic]. . . .
>
> Here I could behold the *Parliament–House*, *Westminster–Hall*, and the *Abbey*, and admir'd the Magnificence of their Structure, and still more the Greatness of Mind in those who had been their Founders. . . . But with what Amazement did I reflect, how Mankind had perverted the Use of those Places design'd for a general Benefit.
>
> (Barker 1723: 64, 67)

This social satire is interrupted as a distressed woman appears, fleeing across the rooftops to bring Galesia a third narrative of male perfidy. Galesia is deprived of her "Parnassus" by her mother, who forbids her to return to the roof, lest she have any more "pernicious" "Adventures"; literary impulses lead her too close to sexual observations (Spencer 1986: 67–8). Galesia's female interlocutor compares this maternal ban to Ovid's "banish[ment] from all his pleasures and Injoyments in the glorious City of *Rome*" (Barker 1723: 78). Galesia's attempt at urban professionalism is defeated by the constant intrusion of woman's commodity value, in the form of Galesia's marriageability or of other women's tales of victimization. Ultimately, Galesia must retreat from London to avoid this intrusion; and Barker herself apparently must succumb to market forces by allowing conventional feminine narratives of betrayal to infest the text and interrupt its heroine.

Behn, Manley, and Barker all managed to produce and to have published fictions which depict women attempting to escape commodification in urban space; in so doing, all three demonstrated familiarity with various levels of London society and urban literature. However, the awareness manifested by Barker's Galesia of conflicting "masculine" and "feminine" visions of the city signifies the growing influence on women writers of the more limited vision of London society deemed appropriate for female consumption.

III

By the mid-eighteenth century, English fiction tended to represent "virtuous" heroines in terms of their important economic roles as consumers and as vehicles for the transmission of wealth, especially capital (Poovey 1984: 10–11). Consumption emerges as the major "fact" of women's experience of London. The privileged heroines of literature visit the city in theory as consumers of goods and culture, and in practice to marry. London still operates as a structuring mechanism for sorting women on the basis of their desirability as commodities, but the focus of the narrative gaze has shifted; the fictional heroine's choices as a consumer, rather than, or as causes of, her physical situation and appearance, become the primary signs of her value. Mary Poovey points out that "[a]ll attacks on female 'appetite' were also, implicitly, defenses of female chastity" (Poovey 1984: 20), and in this later fiction women's consumer choices metonymically represent all their desires.

At the same time, thematic and structural elements in fictions by and for women operate to deny the commodification of the virtuous heroine, even as the narratives prove her value. Marriage is romanticized as a spiritual rather than an economic transaction (Poovey 1984: 237), while the sexually experienced woman is anathematized. "[T]he history of a woman of honour" is paradoxically represented as being without novelty and therefore without commodity value (Lennox 1986 [1752]: 365), so that the "proper" woman writer could no longer profit from her own experience. Significantly, visual consumption is renounced as morally the most dangerous manifestation of desire for women, both as subjects and objects. These conventions led to the development of literary images of the urban environment that required no authorial familiarity with the city.

The novels by women discussed in this section depict heroines who consume a narrow range of urban pastimes on their way to marriage. These texts exhibit the narrative attitude described by Mary Poovey as that of "the proper lady" (Poovey 1984: 3–47) and by Jane Spencer as "the terms of acceptance" (Spencer 1986: 75–103). Both feminist critics locate in eighteenth-century British novels by women various postures of acquiescence to patriarchal standards of the "feminine," especially in the later eighteenth century. Examination of three texts by women from this period demonstrates that, indeed, representations of commodification and consumption are restricted or absent, ostensibly for moral reasons.

Eliza Haywood began her career in the 1720s, during which period she produced several short novels depicting women's urban adventures; she also imitated Manley's "scandalous chronicles," with some success. But *The History of Miss Betsy Thoughtless* (1986 [1751]), an ambivalent work, depicts a frivolous heroine who enjoys a typical list of urban pastimes: "The court, the play, the ball, and opera, with giving and receiving visits, engrossed all the time that could be spared from the toilette" (Haywood 1751: 12). Mr. Trueworth, Betsy's suitor, deliberately tests Betsy's sentiments by describing "the true felicity" of rural love. Betsy rudely interrupts his rhapsody: "What, to be cooped up like a tame dove, only to coo, and bill, and breed? O it would be a delicious life indeed!" (Haywood 1751: 196). Betsy also refuses to observe caution as to her social companions. Mr. Trueworth marries Harriot Loveit, who rejects "those amusements, which you gentlemen call the pleasures of the town," describes court as dull and expensive, and denounces London-style masquerades as "my utter detestation" for their "prophaneness and indecency." She finds plays and operas "improving" but argues that, having seen them once, she can enjoy them at home "in theory" by reading the texts (Haywood 1751: 285–8). Trueworth's values are further clarified by his rejection of the sexually aggressive Flora Mellasin, whose meetings with Trueworth at his coffee-house, a bagnio, and a tavern (sites of consumption off-limits to "virtuous" women) mark her as an adventuress (Haywood 1751: 279, 280, 417). *Betsy Thoughtless* contains a code that classifies women by the decorum of their consumption behaviors.

When Haywood's Betsy accepts decorous standards, she is rewarded with the conveniently widowed Trueworth. Other over-consuming heroines are not so lucky. Sarah Fielding describes the fall of *The Countess of Dellwyn*:

> Public Morning Diversions were the last dissipating Habit she obtained; but when that was accomplished, her Time was squandered away, the Power of Reflection was lost, her Ideas were all centered in Dress, Drums, Routs, Operas, Masquerades, and every kind of public Diversion. Visionary Schemes of Pleasure were continually present to her Imagination, and her Brain was whirled about by such a Dizziness, that she might properly be said to labour under the Distemper called the Vertigo.
>
> (Fielding 1759: I, 39–40)

Until exposed to urban society, Fielding's Miss Lucum leads a decorous life and resists paternal pressure to marry the wealthy Lord Dellwyn, a transaction she sees as "Prostitution" (Fielding 1759: I, 31). But once addicted to the pleasures of consumption, she marries him for money, is seduced into an affair, and descends to a demi-rep. As Spencer points out, the countess's fate is attributed not to love or lust but to vanity (Spencer 1986: 120). Female sexual desire is conspicuously lacking in *The Countess of Dellwyn*, whose heroine derives pleasure from her own commodification as a desirable object. Fielding indeed "attacks . . . the society that makes women saleable commodities" (Spencer 1986: 122), but she does not imagine any positive role for women as consumers. Her heroine's unmotivated progress from consumption of clothing and diversions to total commodification is naturalized as that of an illness. This mythologization is abetted by the narrative's lack of any concrete representation of "public Diversion"; Fielding effaces her own experience of London life, represented in such detail in her brother's works. Although *The Countess of Dellwyn* ostensibly represents and satirizes consumption it allows the reader no scopophilic pleasure.

The moral force behind this rejection of scopophilia as a narrative strategy is reflected in the later eighteenth-century novel by the representation of visual consumption as highly dangerous for the virtuous heroine, whether as subject or object. In Frances Burney's *Evelina* (1970 [1778]), the naive heroine looks forward to seeing the famed sights of London: "Two Playhouses are open, – the Opera-House, – Ranelagh, – the Pantheon. – You see I have learned all their names" (Burney 1970: 24). This guidebook view of the city has been described as typically masculine: "Landmarks represent the manmade world of work and achievement and these, according to Gilligan, are the areas that men particularly focus on" (Sizemore 1989: 130). However, Evelina's attempts at socially sanctioned consumption are thwarted by her own attractions as a visually pleasing commodity of indeterminate parentage, and therefore of unknown value. Constantly molested and embarrassed in public, Evelina is always in danger of being sexually consumed either as spectacle or as body. In order to escape commodification, she must avoid being seen in public; and thus cannot consume freely. Visual consumption also endangers the emerging sensibility heroine from within; in Mary Brunton's *Self-Control* (1986 [1810–11]), Laura Montreville, while watching Mrs. Siddons in *The Gamester*, is "exhausted by the strength and rapidity of her emotions." She declares that attending the theater "[o]nce or twice in a year would be quite sufficient for me. It occupies my thoughts too much for a mere amusement." Laura spends the next two days obsessively sketching "more than twenty heads of Mrs. Siddons" (Brunton 1986: 109–10). The sight of Mrs. Siddons's acting causes an eruption of affect in the female viewing subject that is immediately recognized as dangerous.

Miss Lucum, Evelina, and Laura discover that consumption always brings with it the specter of desire, either in the female subject or towards the female as object. Visual consumption is especially dangerous, not only when it is directed at women by men but also when it allows women to create "Visionary Schemes" or drawings that by-pass the verbal to express indeterminate desires. Women's consumption of urban culture is increasingly represented as necessarily limited only to those scenes that would allow them to imitate the manners and fashions of the upper classes, to pursue the latest luxuries, and to display some knowledge of professional performances of music and drama. This narrative mapping of London allowed the transgressive spaces depicted in earlier London-centered texts to remain the sole property of the male gaze, while less restricted texts by writers like Behn, Haywood, and Manley were convicted of lewdness and vulgarity. By refusing to represent the sexual aspects of consumerism, male and female novelists alike served capitalist society's need to commodify sections of society which had been isolated along allegedly moral lines. Women writers' acceptance of a policy of non-representation contributed to the development of the modern city as a text in which woman could only be represented as an object, and in which her desires had no self-knowledge and no place.

Notes

1   See Mary Poovey, *The Proper Lady and the Woman Writer: Ideology as Style in the Works of Mary Wollstonecraft, Mary Shelley, and Jane Austen* (1984); and Jane Spencer, *The Rise of the Woman Novelist: From Aphra Behn to Jane Austen* (1986). Both critics describe this process in detail.
2   The first volume of *The English Rogue* was written by Richard Head, the second by Francis Kirkman, and those that followed were the product of a collaborative effort; for clarity I have used "Head and Kirkman" to refer to the whole work, which went through numerous editions.
3   I would like to thank Ann Bermingham for her suggestions on the point of the fantasy brothel as a reflection of masculine values.
4   The obsession with venereal disease which characterizes Latroon's description of his search for his wife, and the contention in *The London–Spy* that public flogging is a just punishment for women's "capital crimes," in this analysis represent the irruption of castration anxiety into the scopophilic text.
5   Despite its change of setting, *Memoirs of Europe* was apparently considered by Manley's contemporaries a continuation of *Atalantis*; the latter title often is used to refer to both works.

Bibliography

Barker, J. (1713) *Love Intrigues: Or, The History of the Amours of Bosvil and Galesia. As Related to Lucasia, in St. Germains Garden. A Novel*, London: E. Curll; Cambridge: C. Crownfield. Facsimile edn. (Foundations of the Novel series: Representative Early Eighteenth-Century Fiction), New York and London: Garland Publishing, 1973.

—— (1723) *A Patch-Work Screen for the Ladies: or, Love and Virtue Recommended; in a Collection of Instructive Novels. Related after a Manner intirely New, and interspersed with Rural Poems. describing the Innocence of a Country-Life*, London: E. Curll and T. Payne. Facsimile edn. (Foundations of the Novel series: Representative Early Eighteenth-Century Fiction), New York and London: Garland Publishing, 1973.

Behn, A. (1915 [1684]) *The Adventure of the Black Lady*, in *The Works of Aphra Behn*, ed. Montagu Summers, Vol. V, London: William Heinemann; Stratford on Avon: A. H. Bullen.

—— (1915 [1696]) *The Unfortunate Happy Lady*, in *The Works of Aphra Behn*, ed. Montagu Summers, Vol. V, London: William Heinemann; Stratford on Avon: A. H. Bullen.

Brunton, M. (1986 [1810–11]) *Self-Control*, London and New York: Pandora Press.

Burney, F. (1970 [1778]) *Evelina: or the History of a Young Lady's Entrance into the World*, London: Oxford University Press.

Castle, T. (1986) *Masquerade and Civilization: The Carnivalesque in Eighteenth-Century English Culture and Fiction*, Stanford, CA: Stanford University Press.

Dunton, J. (1696) *The Night–Walker: Or, Evening Rambles in Search after Lewd Women, with the Conferences Held with Them, & c.*, London: James Orme. Facsimile edn. (Marriage, Sex, and the Family in England 1600–1800, Vol. 19), New York and London: Garland Publishing, 1985.

Fielding, S. (1759) *The History of the Countess of Dellwyn, In Two Volumes, By the Author of David Simple*, London: A. Millar. Facsimile edn. (The Flowering of the Novel: Representative Mid-Eighteenth-Century Fiction, 1740–1775), New York and London: Garland Publishing, 1974.

Haywood, E. (1986 [1751]) *The History of Miss Betsy Thoughtless*, London and New York: Pandora Press, 1986.

Head, R. and Kirkman, F. (1665) *The English Rogue*, Vols. I–II, London: Kirkman.

Irigaray, L. (1977) *This Sex Which is Not One*, trans. Catherine Porter with Caroline Blake, Ithaca, NY: Cornell University Press.

Kirkman, F. (1961 [1673]) *The Counterfeit Lady Unveil'd*, in Spiro Peterson (ed.) *The Counterfeit Lady Unveiled and Other Criminal Fiction of Seventeenth-Century England*, New York: Doubleday Anchor Books.

Kubek, E. B. (1990) "London as text: eighteenth-century women writers and reading the city," *Women's Studies* 17, 3–4: 303–40.

Lennox, C. (1986 [1752]) *The Female Quixote: or, The Adventures of Arabella*, London: Pandora Press.

Mandeville, B. (1724) *A Modest Defence of Publick STEWS; or, An ESSAY upon WHORING. As it is now practis'd in these Kingdoms. Written by a LAYMAN*, London: A. Moore. Facsimile edn. (Augustan Reprint Society publication number 162), Los Angeles, CA: William Andrews Clark Memorial Library, 1973.

Manley, [M.] D. (1709) *Secret MEMOIRS and MANNERS Of several Persons of Quality, of Both SEXES. From the New ATALANTIS, an Island in the Mediteranean, Written Originally in ITALIAN*, London: John Morphew and J. Woodward. Facsimile edn., Patricia Koster (ed.) *The Novels of Mary Delarivier Manley*, Vol. I, Gainesville, FLA: Scholars' Facsimiles and Reprints, 1971.

—— (1710) *MEMOIRS of EUROPE, Towards the Close of the Eighth Century. Written by EGINARDUS, Secretary and Favorite to CHARLEMAGNE; and done into English by the Translator of the New ATALANTIS*, London: John Morphew. Facsimile edn., Patricia Koster (ed.) *The Novels of Mary Delarivier Manley*, Vol. II, Gainesville, FLA: Scholars' Facsimiles and Reprints, 1971.

Morgan, F. (1981) Introduction to *The Female Wits: Women Playwrights on the London Stage 1660–1720*, London: Virago.

Mulvey, L. (1989) *Visual and Other Pleasures*, Bloomington, IN: Indiana University Press.

Perry, R. (1986) *The Celebrated Mary Astell: An Early English Feminist* (Women in Culture and Society series), Chicago and London: University of Chicago Press.

Poovey, M. (1984) *The Proper Lady and the Woman Writer: Ideology as Style in the Works of Mary Wollstonecraft, Mary Shelley, and Jane Austen.* (Women in Culture and Society series), Chicago and London: University of Chicago Press.

Rose, J. (1986) *Sexuality in the Field of Vision*, London: Verso.

Russo, M. (1986) "Female grotesques: carnival and theory," in Teresa de Lauretis (ed.) *Feminist Studies, Critical Studies* (Theories of Contemporary Culture, Vol. 8), Bloomington, IN: Indiana University Press.

Schwarzbach, F. S. (1982) "London and literature in the eighteenth century," *Eighteenth-Century Life* 7, 3: 100–12.

Sizemore, C. (1989) *A Female Vision of the City: London in the Novels of Five British Women*, Knoxville, TN: University of Tennessee Press.

Spencer, J. (1986) *The Rise of the Woman Novelist: From Aphra Behn to Jane Austen*, Oxford and New York: Blackwell.

Ward, E. (1709) *The London-Spy Compleat in Eighteen Parts*, 4th edn., London: J. Howe. Facsimile edn. (Marriage, Sex, and the Family in England 1600–1800, Vol. 19), New York and London: Garland Publishing, 1985.

24

The im/modesty of her sex
Elisabeth Vigée-Lebrun and the Salon of 1783

Mary D. Sheriff

What did women want?

In 1783 a Greek maiden dead more than three thousand years appeared at the Salon in Paris. As you might imagine she caused quite a stir. Not that Parisians were unaccustomed to singular persons visiting their Salon; after all, Momus the jester and the Greek painter Apelles were also there. But still, the young maiden was an exceptional presence, a "nymph" dead more than thirty centuries, who was as "fresh as a blooming rose."[1] Appearing first in the sculpture court, she was antique in form and costume and expressed a "virginal and primitive nature." Clearly she was from another time and place. A learned *abbé* said it must be Dibutadis who invented painting by tracing the head of her lover on a wall, and her comments on art confirmed his opinion.

It was indeed Dibutadis, and giving her due honor, the Salon visitors addressed her as the inventor (*inventrice*) of painting. Being an appropriately *modest* woman, however, she underplayed her achievement: "If I am an inventor then it is of the silhouette portrait for I have just heard called by that name a profile in black made by tracing the shadow of a young person. It is exactly the same procedure that love inspired in me and for which you claim to admire me" (*La Morte* 1783: 6–7).[2]

The report of the Greek maiden's visit was published as a letter from one unnamed monsieur to another, and although the encounter with Dibutadis is narrated in detail, the correspondent admits that she materialized only in an intoxicating dream inspired by art (*La Morte* 1783: 23). – What then made Dibutadis decide to appear, if only in a dream, in 1783? But why suggest that she chose the timing, that the game was her own? Maybe some god, or better yet some Pygmalion, fashioned and animated her to voice his concerns about the Salon of 1783.[3]

Just about a century later a reader looking at the Academy's records notices something that might suggest to us what Dibutadis – or her Pygmalion – was up to. This reader, Anatole de Montaiglon, is perusing the manuscript registers of the proceedings of the Royal Academy of Painting and Sculpture, which he will edit and publish in

1889. His eyes are fixed on the entry for June 7, 1783. He reads: "in opening the meeting Madame Lebrun, received as academician [*Académicienne*] at the last assembly, took her place in this capacity" (Montaiglon 1889: IX, 158).[4] But in the manuscript this statement is interrupted by an alteration in the text, something has been crossed out, even "*surchargée de ratures*." The erasure comes from the middle of the line quoted above; the record had once stated "in opening the meeting Madame Lebrun, received as academician at the last assembly *and who has brought her works with which the company was satisfied*, took her place in this capacity" (Montaiglon 1889: IX, 158).[5] Why was some academic authority so distressed with those words, "and who has brought her works with which the company was satisfied," that the phrase was "*surchargée de ratures*" and the official history of the Academy changed? With what works did the ambitious Madame Lebrun try to satisfy the assembled academicians?

The altered Academy record and Dibutadis's commentary on the Salon of 1783 have, I believe, much to do with one another. As we shall see, the work that Madame Lebrun brought to the Academy in June of 1783 substituted for the reception piece that in ordinary circumstances both determined and represented an artist's position as an academician. The *morceau de réception* gained its authority to signify the artist's acceptance by and position within the Academy from the Academy itself. Not only did the choice to accept the *morceau de réception* lie with the academicians, but often they assigned the subject. On the basis of this work they decided on the category or rank in which painters would be placed.[6] But the work that Madame Lebrun brought to the Academy in May of 1783 was not the usual reception piece. It was a dangerous substitution for that sign of official approval, dangerous because like Madame Lebrun herself, it could not be recognized in the normal academic categories.[7]

The status of Madame Lebrun's painting(s) was and is problematic precisely because Madame Lebrun did not enter the Academy in the ordinary way. On the day of her reception May 31, 1783, she was not elected by the voice vote of the assembled, she presented no *morceau de réception* and she was not positioned in a genre or rank. Rather she was admitted into the Academy, as the record shows, by order of the king.[8] If accepting Madame Lebrun by order rather than vote was extraordinary, there was much more that was unusual about May 31, 1783, at least as far as academic history goes. On that day the Academy admitted not one, but two women painters. And if this double admission linked them, it was perhaps to emphasize the distance between the two for the acceptance of the second woman, Madame Guiard, was conducted and recorded according to ordinary practice. But not quite.

Usually an artist seeking admission to the Academy presented at different times two reception pieces. But there were exceptions, and when the Academy found an artist's works particularly worthy, it could confer associate and full membership on the same day.[9] Such was the case for Madame Guiard, and the records indicate she brought to the Academy meeting paintings from which the academicians selected two portraits as her two reception pieces and entered her in the rank of portrait painter.[10] And here is an important point. Unlike Madame Lebrun's works, these paintings were not dangerous substitutions for those most important of academic symbols, they were – if you will – the real thing.

In the case of Madame Guiard the deviations from normal practice suggest a certain manipulation on the part of the academicians who contrived to have both women admitted on the same day. The record of the Academy, however, constructs a sense of ordinariness around this admission. Like any other candidate Madame Guiard was presented to the company by an established academician (in her case, the portraitist Roslin) and elected by the "customary" voice vote. It is clear that she submitted to and was validated by academic authority.

Judging from the Academy's *Procès Verbaux* the admission of Madame Guiard seems to have followed directly the irregular proceedings that placed Madame Lebrun within that priviledged body but left her without an officially sanctioned rank. The controversy surrounding Madame Lebrun's admission was apparently well publicized; in the *Correspondance Littéraire* of 1783 Grimm reports how finally seeing her paintings at the Salon recalled all the bickering and all the petty persecutions that for a long time kept the Academy door closed to her (Tourneux 1880: XIII, 440).[11] Madame Lebrun refers to this squabbling in her account of the event, written many years later and included in her *Souvenirs* published in 1827:

> Shortly after my return from Flanders in 1783 . . . several . . . of my works prompted Joseph Vernet to propose me as a member of the Royal Academy of Painting. M. Pierre, then first painter to the king, strongly opposed my admission, as he did not wish women to be received; yet Madame Vallayer– Coster, who painted flowers perfectly, had already been received, and I believe even Madame Vien was also an academician. Be that as it may, M. Pierre – a very mediocre painter who thought of painting only in terms of execution – was clever, and moreover he was rich, and had the means of ostentatiously receiving artists, who at that time were less well-to-do than they are today. His opposition would have proved fatal to me if at the time true amateurs had not been associated with the Academy of Painting. They formed in my favor a cabal against that of M. Pierre, and it was then that one of them wrote this couplet:
>
> > To Madame Lebrun –
> > At the Salon your triumphant art;
> > Will put you in the limelight,
> > Lise, To keep from you this honor,
> > One must have a heart of stone [*de pierre*], of stone, of stone.
>
> Finally I was received. M. Pierre then spread rumors that it was by an order of the Court that I was received. I think that the king and queen had been good enough to wish to see me enter the Academy, but that's all. I gave for my reception piece *Peace Bringing Back Abundance*. This painting is today in the Ministry of the Interior.
>
> (Vigée-Lebrun 1986: I, 76–8)[12]

You will notice a discrepancy between this account and the official records of the Academy. Madame Lebrun denies that she was received by an order of the king, yet there is just such an order included in the Academy records. Some may wish to dismiss solely on this point her entire account including her claim that the dispute focused on women in the Academy. Yet as we know, official documents hide as well as reveal, construct "truth" even as they claim to tell it. And any set of documents comprises only one story, one point of view among contesting ones. The king surely did give an order, but was the order necessary, really? Was it a façade for an entire conglomerate of (hidden) interests? Of what worth are the words of an elderly woman, a society portraitist, against the official records of the Academy?

A second significant point about Madame Lebrun's admission is made near the end of her account where she writes: "I gave as my reception piece *Peace Bringing Back Abundance*" (Plate 24.1, 1783–4). Recall that the Academy's proceedings record no reception piece, no rank. Yet this painting was, in fact, widely known as her *morceau de réception*. It is listed in the Salon *livret* and discussed throughout the Salon literature as such. Was this work the dangerous substitute, the proffering and approval of which some academic official erased? Is this the painting that is covered over, *surchargée de ratures*? And if it is, what larger story does the effacing conceal? Here is what I imagine it to be:

Madame Lebrun is both gifted and ambitious. The daughter of a guild painter and a hairdresser, she has become not only the court artist to Marie Antoinette, but an intimate of the noble and the accomplished. Through talent, achievement, hard work, and personal assets (beauty, grace, a lively mind) she has enjoyed considerable social mobility and has developed great self-confidence. Anticipating that the Academy doors will be opened to her, she sets out to demonstrate that she is not a mere portraitist. She plans to enter herself as a history painter, as an artist of the highest rank, the rank closed to women. (And perhaps she also plots a little revenge on her detractors.) On May 31 she sits through the Academy meeting where an entire scenario has been staged. She notices – perhaps with satisfaction, perhaps with rancor – that her enemy Pierre has chosen to absent himself from the proceedings. The corporate body accepts her by order and in pointed contrast elects Madame Guiard and chooses her reception piece(s) from among the portraits she has brought. Madame Lebrun is asked to bring her work to the next meeting. She has expected the request and on June 3 she presents to the academicians the allegory "Peace Bringing Back Abundance." Allegory, she knows, falls into the category of history painting. Seeing the work some faces set into stony grimaces, for given the protection of the queen and the order of the king, and given that they have already admitted the painter, the academicians are in no position to refuse her work. The beautiful Madame Lebrun is laughing.

Now this, of course, may not be the way things happened. No matter. One can paint other stories and imagine other motives, but my point remains: the academic officials would not have ratified her history paintings, and they would not have chosen her *Peace Bringing Back Abundance* as a reception piece. In selecting this work Madame Lebrun appropriated two kinds of symbol-making power: the power of the Academy to name the *morceau de réception* and the power of the male artist to dominate that genre devoted to texts of moral or intellectual significance.

If the *Procès Verbaux* contradicts Madame Lebrun's claim that the king did not order her admission, it also supports her contention that the main issue was the terms for accepting women. During the wrangling over her admission the Academy received two orders. The first was issued to fulfill the desires of the queen and assured one woman a place in the Academy. The second satisfied the academic body by limiting to four the number of places allowed for women. More significant than the order itself, however, is d'Angiviller's justification of it: "this number is sufficient to honor their talent; women cannot be useful to the progress of the arts because the modesty of their sex forbids them from being able to study after nature and in the public school established and founded by your Majesty" (Montaiglon 1889: IX, 157).[13]

Why have there been no great women artists?

Linda Nochlin argued in her groundbreaking work that women were excluded from the highest achievements in painting because they could not receive the necessary training (Nochlin 1971). Her argument recapitulates an eighteenth-century feminist position: lack of education, not lack of natural faculties, explained why women had contributed little to cultural development. These arguments seem fully justified by d'Angiviller's comments: women cannot be "useful" to the progress of the arts because they cannot study "in the public school established and founded by your Majesty." Although women did take classes from male artists in their private studios at the Louvre, one significant lesson they could not learn there was that of life drawing. Feminists have long stressed this point in accounting for the lack of women practicing the highest genres of painting. D'Angiviller justifies this exclusion by appealing to the natural law of a woman's modesty; modesty dictated that women neither mingle in the same classroom with men, nor look at the nude male body, which is what study after nature means in this context. Drawing after the male model was the only life drawing sanctioned in the Academy schools, and it was basic to d'Angiviller's conception of history paintings as subjects depicting the male body in heroic action. It is because women could not paint elevating subjects of the sort that d'Angiviller believed would revitalize the highest genre, that they could not be "useful to the progress of the arts."[14]

"Women cannot be useful to the progress of the arts because the modesty of their sex forbids them." In d'Angiviller's comment modesty is an attribute of, belongs to, the woman's sex. The French *sexe* refers to the (biological) category of woman, but the term also signifies the vagina – the woman's sex. D'Angiviller limits a woman's cultural role by invoking the modesty of her *sexe*, thus denying all responsibility for her restriction. Used in this way modesty functions as a regulator of social relations between men and women, a regulator which, because it belongs to woman's *sexe*, presents itself as natural.

In the late eighteenth century, nature's gift of modesty was most effectively dispensed to women by the master rhetorician Jean-Jacques Rousseau. In *Emile* Rousseau posits that women in society have boundless passions but no instinctual curb. So God, he supposes, gives them modesty (Rousseau 1966: 466–7). Modesty supplements nature and takes the place of the natural restraint belonging to female animals and women in the state of nature (Derrida 1976: 179–81). But Rousseau also insists it is natural, God-given, and where women are given modesty, men receive a far more useful, powerful, and effective curb: reason. Thus nature – Mother Nature (?), God the father (?) – gives men the gift necessary for cultural production, and reserves for women the restraint that effectively bars them from it.

Rousseau had earlier expounded on the naturalness of modesty in his *Lettre à M. D'Alembert sur les spectacles*. There it is central to a discussion of the relation between the sexes, a discussion framed within a more specific consideration of the differences between male and female actors. In conceptualizing the actor, Rousseau begins by describing him in terms applicable to the prostitute: he counterfeits himself, he performs for money, he engages in a servile and base traffic in himself. And his profession emasculated him for the actor is fit for all sorts of roles except for the most noble one, that of man (Rousseau 1948: 106–7). Yet the actor is not fully corrupted by his professions: for Rousseau the dissoluteness of actresses (who must be more like prostitutes) "compels and carries with it that of actors" (Rousseau 1948: 108). Having thus charged the actress with corrupting her male counterpart, Rousseau interrupts his arguments to pursue a more general consideration of the relation between the sexes.

This larger discussion raises a theme that will return Rousseau to the problem of the actress – the immorality of women who appear in public. The actress is the prototype of the immodest woman for actresses choose an occupation "the unique object of which is to show themselves off in public, and what's worse, to show themselves for money" (Rousseau 1948: 120). Later in the same text the notion of public woman will be extended to women who host salons and women who go to the theater to enjoy the decadent pleasures of self-display. The society that encourages such public display encourages the vices of the *toilettes* of artifice, of makeup and worse. For the married women especially, public display suggests sexual immorality, for why, Rousseau asks, would she seek the looks of men other than her husband? Rousseau elides the difference between being looked at and being possessed sexually; it is not just that one leads to the other, they are nearly the same thing. The indecent woman goes to the theater to see and to be seen, and in the public context both looking and being looked at are transgressions of modesty (Rousseau 1948: 110–11).

Having proclaimed modesty as the only virtue of women, Rousseau sets out to prove its naturalness by relating it to the economy of the sex act. The union of the sexes depends on attack and defense: man is strong and active, woman weak and passive. Rousseau asks what would become of the human race if the positions were reversed, if women were on top? Such a reversal would be disastrous because the success of the sex act depends on male arousal. If women were the attakers they might choose times when victory would be impossible, or leave the assailed in peace when he "needs" to be vanquished, or pursue him when he is "too weak to succumb" (Rousseau 1948: 112). If women were the attakers (that is, those on whose *will* sex depends) the will and the power to have sex would be disjoint, which assumes that power is located in male sexuality, in the power of having an erection.

Rousseau denied women the power to control their own passions through reason *and* the power to control sexual activity through erection. After defining women as bereft of natural power, Rousseau strips them of will, and having stripped them of will he compensates them with modesty. Modesty is their willpower and armament in the war between the sexes. True modesty insured women could withhold when they needed to, and feigned modesty – and here Rousseau finds a moral use for the artifice of women, which he ordinarily condemns – could inflame male desire, or more appropriately, the desire of the husband (Rousseau 1948: 111–13).

In a fundamental way, Rousseau cast modesty as what nature gave women because they lacked the penis, guarantor of power in the sex act. Although Rousseau's context is not psychoanalytical, the resonance with Freud's essay "On feminity" is not surprising given that Freud's works can be read (as Irigaray and other feminists have suggested) as revalidating traditional western attitudes towards women even as they open new possibilities for thinking the construction of human sexuality (Irigaray 1985a). I intend here to set up an association between Rousseau and Freud in terms of how they viewed the relation between a woman's body and her cultural, social, and intellectual development. Both Rousseau and Freud adjusted their feminine ideal to the "interests of society," which, as Carole Pateman has shown, coincided with the interests of a society whose fundamental right was that of paternity, of man's sexual right over woman (Pateman 1988: 44–60; 96–115). In various forms Rousseauist thinking about feminity permeated late eighteenth-century French culture as thoroughly as Freudian ideas, or notions derived from Freud, have permeated our own. If exploring the Rousseauian perspective is essential to the historicizing aspects of my project, introducing the Freudian one will emerge as central to my feminist analysis.

For Freud, modesty, or shame, is again both conventional and natural: "shame, while is considered to be a feminine characteristic par excellence but is far more a matter of convention than might be supposed, has as its purpose . . . concealment of genital deficiency" (Freud 1965: 117). Modesty covers woman's lack, and in Freud's essay is tied up with penis envy, which accounts for the predominance of jealousy in women's lives. Because in the Freudian account women do not have the same castration anxieties as men, they do not develop the same superego, the mechanism that controls behavior. Where men develop a sense of justice and self-control, women develop envy: "the fact that women must be regarded as having little sense of justice is no doubt related to the predominance of [penis] envy in their mental life . . . We also regard women as weaker in their social interests and as having less capacity for sublimating their instincts than men" (Freud 1965: 119). Rousseau also saw jealousy as characteristic of women, but he had no framework for conceptualizing an idea like Freud's penis envy. Instead of envy he gave women something to compensate for their lack – and that was modesty. Modesty became Rousseau's hook; he took a concept useful for subjugating women and made it attractive. And where Freud addressed his thoughts about women (and his essay on feminity, in particular) to men, Rousseau addressed *Emile* to women for whom he described the pleasures and rewards of virtue, modesty, and motherhood. Some were literally seduced into virtue while others found in Rousseau's seductive writing grist for their mills, bending his ideals to their own, sometimes feminist, ends. The feminist-female historians who today explore how symbolic constructions of feminine passivity and lack in the late eighteenth century shaped the actual societal role of women are themselves living through and struggling against surprisingly similar constructions, constructions that Lacan's influential readings of Freud have both unveiled and reinforced (Irigaray 1985b: 86–105).

When d'Angiviller called on woman's modesty to explain why she was excluded from artistic training, he was repeating Rousseau's gesture of attributing to natural law what was entirely a social convention. He blamed the victim, so to speak, for her own exclusion. It is modesty that dictates that women not be seen in public; that they neither look nor be looked at. So as not to "offend" a woman's modesty, men must keep women from compromising situations and especially in public arenas. But in this argument not flawed logically? If modesty is a restraint, if it is what allows women to refuse, should it not be precisely what would allow them to enter morally precarious situations and emerge unscathed? Do women armed with modesty need to be segregated? Could modesty not to be construed as precisely that which licensed women to enter life-drawing classes? To control themselves when seeing the male body? Perhaps . . . but what if people talked? Rousseau, in fact, regulates women by public opinion; they are slaves to public opinion, and they must avoid at all costs even the appearance of impropriety (Rousseau 1966: 471). And modesty was double-edged, both a restraint and a spur. Although modesty curbed women's uncurbable desires, it could excite the desire of men, make them want what was denied them. For Rousseau it is the basis of all desire. By denying satisfaction to need, it creates desire (Rousseau 1948: 113 and Rousseau 1964: 134–6). If modesty spurred male desire, can one imagine modest women drawing after the male nude, even in a class entirely populated by women? What if their gazes excited the model? Imagine his embarassment. And could modesty really be relied on to harness women's unruly sexuality? At play here is the fear of women polluting the serious and chaste male environment. In the same way that actresses led to the dissoluteness of actors, female painters could bring down their male colleagues.[15]

Morals, in fact, might be endangered in any instance where women artists looked at male models, whether clothed or unclothed. A woman portrait painter depicting a male sitter was often suspected of seducing or of being seduced by him through the exchange of glances. Rumors about Madame Lebrun's affairs with clients – in particular, M. Calonne and the Comte de Vaudreuil – circulated widely. Perhaps rumors of this sort provoked her to address the general issue of male sitters in her *Souvenirs*. She tells how when she was a young, unmarried painter several male admirers came to sit for portraits in the hopes of attracting her. As soon as she discovered they wanted to gaze on her with "*les yeux tendres*" she painted them with their eyes averted. "And then, at the least movement that would cast their eyes in my direction, I would say to them: 'I am just at the eyes'; which would annoy them a little, as you can suppose" (Vigée-Lebrun 1986: I, 39).[16] As in Rousseau's discussion of the sex act, the issue at stake in Lebrun's ploy is one of control. The incident is amusing because it reverses the expected positions. Rather than allow the male sitter to position her as woman, object of the gaze, Lebrun controls the model by speaking from the masculine position as painter, subject of the gaze. Moreover, the context of the comment is particularly illuminating as the section focuses on four issues: the young artist's attractiveness, her dedication to art, her impeccable morals, and the machinations of male admirers who pose as sitters. Seeing through their pose, the artist satisfies them as art patrons, but rejects them as suitors. Lebrun obviously enjoys the game of thwarting their amorous advances while satisfying her painterly ambitions, and she even shares her delight with another woman – her mother – who acts not only as chaperone to the sitting, but also as amused accomplice to her daughter's ploy. Yet even as Lebrun is savoring her powers of attraction, her accomplishment as an artist, and her clever manipulating of admirers, she is also reminding her readers that she preserved her virtue amidst the dangers presented by the male model.

But what about women portraying women? First consider drawing after the female nude, which in all cases was conducted outside officially sanctioned academic training. Artists who worked from nude female models did so in a private studio situation, thus there was ample opportunity to make the scene of drawing a female nude an erotic one, either in fantasy or actuality (Clements 1992). For women, modeling was an immodest profession; like the actress and the prostitute, the model was considered sexually accessible. As far as I know there is no evidence from the eighteenth century of women hiring other women to pose, but it is possible that women used their servants or their friends as models. As likely – or perhaps more likely – is that they used themselves. This latter possibility is the most interesting here. Given the contemporary discourse on modesty, could the audience construe the woman painter playing the role of the nude model as anything but doubly immodest? The *possibility* that Madame Lebrun used her own body offered Salon critics the opportunity to titillate their readers. Looking at her *Venus Binding the Wings of Cupid* (whereabouts of painting unknown) one writer criticized the proportions of Venus as not those of the goddess of beauty, but those of the Flemish school. He added the comment, "Surely in painting the nude woman the artist has not taken herself for a model, the contours would have been more delicate" (*Messieurs* 1783: 22). Although it might be construed as flattering, the comment actually asks the audience to imagine how Madame Lebrun's body looks, and thus uses her painting to make her an immodest woman. Another critic sets up a dialogue between a marquise, a chevalier, and an *abbé* as they stand before her *Peace and Abundance*. The marquise asks from where Madame Lebrun has taken her models. The *abbé* answers, "Has she not a mirror?" This exchange leads to a suggestive repartee were the *abbé* contends that women should not paint other women, but leave that pleasure to men. If "the Graces have learned to paint themselves," he says, "farewell to our rights" (*Momus* 1783: 10). To paint women here is assumed as both male prerogative and male pleasure, which are jeopardized when women presume to paint and give pleasure to themselves, and one another.

Painting like a man

As far as modesty was concerned, women artists were on the safest ground when they depicted other clothed women. And here they might also be positioned to meet the demands of *convenance*. As a general principle *convenance* held that the formal language – including the touches and paint handling – used to depict a figure must be appropriate to the figure depicted. The artist chose the paint handling appropriate to the sex of the sitter, but paint handling itself was also believed to be naturally connected to the sex of the artist. The touch "natural" to women painters was at best soft (*moelleuse*) and at worst too soft, lacking in force, effeminate (*molle*);[17] that "natural" to men was bold (*hardie*), vigorous and virile (*mâle*). Although recognizing that the gendered touch did not always correspond with the sex of the artist, critics still expected a soft touch from women artists and were surprised when they found instead firmness and force. These assumptions structure the criticism of Lebrun and Guiard at the Salon of 1783. Where some critics praised Lebrun's touch as "*moelleuse et suave*" (Fréron 1783: 160), others saw too soft (*molle*) a touch as a peril she must avoid (*L'Impartialité au Sallon* 1783: 28). Madame Guiard, on the other hand, had a surprisingly virile touch, one firm as a man's. In comparison to Madame Lebrun, Grimm finds her handling has "*plus de fermeté*" and that her touch is "*forte et vigoureuse*" (Tourneux 1880: XIII, 442). Another finds her brush "*ferme et vigoreux*" (*Messieurs* 1783: 24), a third praises her touch as "*mâle et ferme*", and finds that she has "made herself a man" (*L'Impartialité* 1783: 30).[18]

Apelles visiting the Salon notices that she has "a firm and bold touch which seems out of the reach of her sex" (*Apelle* 1783: 23). That she outstrips her sex, that she is nearly a man, surprises the critics pleasantly; this indicates, unsurprisingly, that the masculine touch – all consideration of *convenance* aside – was more highly valued.

The opposition between the artificial (associated with the ornate and the decorative) and the truthful (associated with the natural and the beautiful) also structured the way critics viewed the art of Madame Lebrun and Madame Guiard. The truthful seems to have had no overt sex; I take this as an instance of the masculine presenting itself as the general, as the unsexed, universal category. The artificial was gendered as the "feminine," and Jacqueline Lichtenstein has shown how since antiquity the problematic of ornament has never been separated from that of femininity (Lichtenstein 1987: 77–86). Throughout the rhetorical tradition excessive ornament was conceptualized through metaphors of femininity, and we have seen how in the mid-eighteenth century Rousseau associated artifice with women and their self-display. Madame Lebrun's works at the Salon of 1783 were often cited for the softness of their touch; they were nearly always either hailed for their brilliant color or criticized for their conspicuous artifice. The commentator for the *Mercure de France* is typical in citing the artist's tendency to make colors too brilliant, to make too great an "*éclat*" (*Mercure de France* 1783: 131). More precise was the critic for the *Journal de Paris*. Madame Lebrun's colors are too "*éclatantes*," in fact they are untruthful, unnatural: "Nature is less brilliant and it is nature that one must try to render" (*Journal de Paris* 1783: 1098).[19] Grimm repeats this sentiment (which becomes nearly a cliché in describing her work) in writing about the *éclat* of her *Peace Bringing Back Abundance*: "nature is less brilliant than art, and art that seeks to surpass nature lacks naturalness" (Tourneux 1880: XIII, 440).[20] The most interesting comment on this aspect of her work is that spoken by Apelles as he evaluates her self-portrait; he directly invokes the vices of the *toilette* and the coquette in his discussion of the painting. In the self-portrait, he says, painting plays beauty's dressing maid; "she [painting] takes care to embellish her [beauty] with all the arts of the most seductive coquetry," but does not see that "the art is in hiding the coquetry" (*Apelle* 1783: 22–3).[21] Here the "excessive" artifice of the colorist painter is compared with the artifice of the dressing-room, and both are aligned with the feminine. In contrast, Madame Guiard is held to paint nature and truth. She makes perfect resemblances, faithful images. Her work is "*naturel sans prétention*" (*Réponse à toutes les critiques* 1783: 54). Compared with the portraits of Lebrun hers are less flattering, but have more vigor and truth and a just resemblance (*Le Véridique* 1783: 19). Fréron says in the *Année littéraire* that she takes nature as her guide (1783: 264). The remarks suggest that Madame Guiard puts a faithful representation of the object (truth) above display of her artifice (manner).

I do not mean to suggest that all commentary about these artists falls neatly into the general structure I have outlined, but the tendency to categorize them thus persisted throughout the Salon literature from 1783 to 1789.[22] The paintings of these two women, then, were gendered differently; Madame Lebrun's work was feminine in its soft touch and artifice; Madame Guiard's masculine in its firm touch and truthfulness. The point is interesting on several counts. It suggests that, at least in the matter of execution, the sex of the artist and the gender of her painting need not coincide; no critic seems to be upset that Madame Guiard paints like a man. Far from it, they use the observation as a way to praise her. Moreover, the record suggests that from the beginning critics, academicians, and perhaps even casual observers, understood the relation between the two painters as one of opposition (masculine vs. feminine) within similarity (women who made portraits). This understanding in itself is not surprising; throughout the art literature of the eighteenth century, artists who worked in similar genres were constructed as opposing rivals: for example, the pastel portrait painters Perronneau and La Tour, or the still life painters Chardin and Oudry, or the flower painters van Spaendonck and Vallayer–Coster. The latter "competition" between a male and female painter suggests that women painters were not ghettoized – only compared with one another – as some have suggested (Chadwick 1990: 152). In fact, throughout the commentaries on Lebrun and Guiard they are compared with and contrasted to one another favorably or unfavorably, and they are also compared with a variety of men and women artists: Roslin, Duplessis, Rubens, Carriera, Vincent, Menageot, Raphael, and so on. Yet the constructed opposition between two women painters did come to rest on gendered categories, which suggests how fundamental the category of gender was in the 1770s and 1780s, a time when many feared the blurring of gender distinctions throughout culture. But why if there was a general cultural anxiety about gender distinctions and a move to shore up the categories through scientific proof (as Schiebinger [1989: 214–30] and Laqueur [1990: 193–207] have argued) was it so easy and common to see one of these women as painting like a man? Or to pose the question differently, to what extent did the "masculine" touch and manner of Madame Guiard upset gender boundaries?

The distinctions between the two women that we have discussed were distinctions within one aspect of painting – execution. In French painting theory, execution had long been that which could be varied according to subject; taken off and put on for the occasion. Although execution, and especially brushwork, were more and more taken as belonging to the "essential self" of the artist, the idea of a variable style of execution allowed, even demanded, that the artist learn to work in different modes (Sheriff 1990: 117–49). The tradition of viewing execution and touch as learned skills perhaps made it acceptable for a woman to paint like a man. More important, however, was the status of execution.

Since the founding of the French Academy, theorists had reckoned that there were two parts to painting, *la main* or execution, and *la raissonnement* or reasoning (Sheriff 1990: 47). The terms refer to body and mind synecdochically, and set up within painting a mind/body hierarchy.[23] Moreover, the lesser genres – portraiture, still life, landscape – were alleged to require only the skills of execution because in making them the painter did not imagine the subject but merely imitated nature as it was. History painting was the only genre that in theory required both execution and reasoning, and it appealed to the senses and mind of the beholder. It was, moreover, the kind of painting closest to literature and language. Not only did the highest genre require a knowledge of texts, it also required painters to have imaginative powers equal to those of authors. And history paintings easily lent themselves to verbal reconstruction. History paintings spoke – and they could be understood. Works in the lesser genres merely appeared; they were pleasant to look at, but usually said nothing of importance. Because they displayed and required imagination and judgment – the two central components of reason – history paintings belonged on the side of the masculine. And in this case it was important that the sex of the practitioners be aligned with the genre's gender, for what was at stake was the right to produce important cultural products. How could women, whose only resource was their modesty, be trusted with such an important mission?

As long as women practiced the lesser genres, it was acceptable, perhaps even desirable, for them to paint like men. Painting like a man took on entirely other connotations, however, when it was a question of history painting. For in that case to paint like a man was to assume the man's position, to wear his pants. And that was exactly what Madame Lebrun, the feminine painter, tried to do.

We find now that the opposition between Lebrun and Guiard is really a chiasmus. Madame Lebrun paints in an appropriately feminine mode (soft, suave, but also unnatural, artificial, seductive) but makes herself an immodest woman by claiming to be a history painter and working in a male genre. Madame Guiard paints in a masculine mode but is a suitably modest woman, she never claims to be more than a portraitist and she submits to academic authority. It is Madame Lebrun who incites controversy and who most seriously threatens the status quo. Here are two pertinent comments drawn from the Salon of 1783. The first is somewhat equivocal; is the writer praising Madame Lebrun or mocking some of her male rivals? "Madame Lebrun . . . raises herself even to history painting. I rightly refrain from advising her to give it up as so many critics have because they say she has not the force for it. I know that ordinarily one does not see this force in her sex. However, I know a number of men who would be honored to have painted her *Peace and Abundance*" (*L'Impartialité* 1783: 28).[24] The operative term in this discussion, force, did not refer merely to physical strength. Force, as the force of the connection one made between ideas, aided the production of new concepts forged in the process of imagining (Derrida 1987: 71–7). A second quotation taken from the *Mémoires secrets* is more equivocal than the first, for the praise lavished on Madame Lebrun's reception piece is prefaced with the comment that despite the abundance of history paintings at the Salon

> the scepter of Apollo seems fallen to the distaff side, and it is a woman who carries off the palm of victory. Let me explain. I do not want to say that there is more genius in a painting of two or three three-quarter length figures, than in a vast composition of ten or twelve life-size characters; in a painting in which the idea is simple, than in one in which the complex scheme equals an entire poem. I mean only that the works of the modern Minerva attract the first glances of the spectator, that they [the works] draw them [the glances] back unceasingly, seize them, make themselves master over them, wresting from the spectator the exclamations of pleasure and admiration that artists so covet, and which are usually the confirmation of superior productions.
>
> (Bachaumont 1780–9: XXIV, 4)[25]

But let us back up for a moment. Leaving aside all questions of mental equipment, if history painting depended on drawing the male nude, how could women practice it at all? Part of the answer lies in the feminization of history painting that went on in the first half of the eighteenth century. At that time the female body (as well as the child's body, which women of course could see) was often featured in mythological subjects, light subjects of the type popularized by Boucher. Such subjects, it could not be denied, were history paintings – they were based on stories drawn from literature, mythology, the allegorical tradition, and so forth. They demanded the painter visualize an event not seen, idealize the figures, imagine their passions, and choose the artistic language best able to express the meaning of the story. It could be argued, and indeed was argued, that such unedifying subjects debased history painting, eschewing its moral, serious (masculine) side and cultivating its erotic, frivolous (feminine) side. Indeed, the reform of history painting undertaken by d'Angiviller was to rescue the highest genre from the depths into which it had fallen in the hands of rococo painters, like Boucher. These erotic history paintings that featured the female body, however, opened possibilities for women practitioners. Madame Lebrun clearly took advantage of these possibilities in two of her Salon entries, *Juno Borrowing the Belt of Venus* (whereabouts of painting unknown), cited in the *livret* as a subject from the *Iliad*, and *Venus Binding Cupid's Wings*.[26] Salon critics mentioned that these paintings reminded them of the genre as practiced by Boucher.

Other elements of history painting provided openings for women as well. Within the allegorical tradition the idealized female body was used to represent any number of abstract ideas, and often made to stand for virtues that in the "real world" were not ordinarily ascribed to women or gendered as feminine (Hunt 1984: 113). Allegorical painting, interestingly enough, was considered by some theorists to be the most erudite of all history painting because in making an allegory the artist became both author and illustrator.[27] Perhaps Madame Lebrun had this notion in mind when she chose *Peace Bringing Back Abundance* as her reception piece. And finally, women could include male figures in their history paintings because they *could* draw after some male bodies – by copying other works of art, especially antique sculpture. Angelica Kauffman's ceiling design for the central hall of the Royal Academy in London (1778) and Hubert Robert's many paintings of women drawing either in the Louvre or outdoors amidst ruins make exactly this point. This practice, of course, left women open to the charge that they did not really draw after nature but only copied art. Copying another work of art literally represented a less advanced stage of artistic training, for all young artists drew after plaster casts before progressing to live models. Madame Lebrun did not use male figures in her history paintings, but this still did not protect her from the charge that she merely copied.

Three processes of art making – copying art, imitating nature, and inventing (or imagining) a composition – stood in a hierarchical relation to one another because of their relation to the intellectual powers. At the lowest level was copying art; it was held as merely mechanical (an operation of the hand), for in copying a work of art one merely took over another's conceptualization of nature rather than actually engaging in the process of conceptualization. Nature could also be copied by transcribing mechanically what was before the eyes. At the highest level was inventing or imagining a composition, which meant to form an idea about a story one wanted to depict, to visualize the scene in the imagination. In theory it was a purely conceptual process requiring reason as imagination and judgment. Imitating nature fell between the purely mechanical and the purely conceptual; painters worked from a model seen directly, but rather than merely copying, they idealized or conceptualized what they saw. History painters always were charged to idealize nature within the compositions they invented.

Some critics implied that Madame Lebrun's history paintings were imperfect – scarcely history paintings at all – because they were lacking the higher artistic processes. Commonly cited was her failure to idealize properly the figures of her goddesses. Some suggested that she copied her figures from Flemish art, which explained the "*courtes et lourdes*" proportions of the goddesses (*Changez-moi cette tête* 1783: 24). Others accused her of copying rather than imitating or idealizing nature. In reference to *Juno Borrowing the Belt of Venus* several repeated the witticism: "Take away the belt and you have two pretty women in conversation."[28] Alluding to the charge, another excused her because she (as a woman?) could not be expected to understand the ancients: "It would be unjust to expect of the estimable artist of whom we speak those grand and sublime forms that one only acquires by a profound study of the masterpieces of antiquity. The heads in the paintings of Madame Lebrun are very pretty surely, but they are pretty French heads" (Fréron 1783: 261)[29] Idealizing nature required that one enter into the mind-set of the ancients, not merely to copy their works of art, but to invent new ones based on their principles. Madame Lebrun is here held incapable of becoming like the ancients in their creation of timeless beauty. Hers is an art of the pretty, an art of the here and now. No introjection of an antique attitude is necessary for her to understand "pretty French heads."[30] She is/has one. Her inability to enter or to absorb the ancient spirit is perhaps best articulated by the narrator of *Apelle au Sallon* who tells us what the Greek painter noticed in looking at her *Juno Borrowing the Belt of Venus* and *Venus Binding Cupid's Wings*: "The artist [Lebrun], he [Apelles] said, should have joined the color of the one to the elegance of the other to form a single whole; I assembled all the beautiful women of Greece, and I painted only my Venus coming out of the water" (*Apelle* 1783: 23).[31]

Perhaps even more serious was the criticism of her reception piece *Peace Bringing Back Abundance*. Some critics intimated she had not invented the composition, but merely copied it from another work of art. Such remarks provoked a proper defense:

> To diminish the glory of the artist, some critics say that Madame Lebrun, who is more able than others to consult excellent models, has here only copied them. They claim to recognize in her painting Guido Reni, Pietro da Cortona, Cignani, Santerre, etc., but all that proves she has copied none of them. If she has sought to imitate them, nothing is more permitted, it is even a precept of art.
>
> (*Loterie pittoresque* 1783: 23)[32]

This last quotation suggests that the works of Madame Lebrun, and especially her history paintings, were by no means universally condemned. In fact, they had drawn quite a bit of positive notice since her first exhibition in 1774. And this positive notice may in part have provoked the negative evaluations that appeared in 1783 and continued until she stopped exhibiting history paintings in 1789. Both the positive and negative commentaries, however, interact with general cultural stereotypes and long-standing academic prejudices.[33]

Pretty woman

At times Madame Lebrun's supporters appear as belittling to women as her denigrators. Consider Grimm's discussion of her self-portrait (Plate 24.2),[34] which begins by summarizing all the negative evaluations offered by other critics. Grimm thereby reinforces the very criticisms he answers as he addresses these comments to Lebrun's detractors:

> notice there are thousands of defects more, but nothing can destroy the charm of this delicious work. . . . I have seen even alongside of this work beauties of a superior order, but never have I seen any work that better breathes the *je ne sais quoi* which pleases, which attracts, and which calls all attention to itself unceasingly. . . . One senses that only a woman, and a pretty woman, could have conceived of this charming idea and could have rendered it with a grace so brilliant and so naive.
>
> (Tourneux 1880: XIII, 441)[35]

Particularly in using the term *je ne sais quoi*, Grimm places the self-portrait with those works that, despite all technical faults, can be regarded as displaying genius. The eroticized aesthetic discourse widely applied to all sorts of colorist paintings during the eighteenth century, here applies to the artist as well (only a delicious woman could have made this delicious painting). In this suggestion we can read the most belittling aspect of the commentary. What Grimm has written as an extravagant compliment to the artist's person, works to remove her "*vrai chef-d'oeuvre*" from the sphere of intellectual calculation. Madame Lebrun knows intuitively how to make this portrait pleasing because as a pretty woman she knows how to please. These comments are particularly pointed because they follow what can only be called a mixed review of Lebrun's history paintings. In Grimm's discussion of the portrait, moreover, there is also an unpleasant eliding of woman and (art) object, with both held under the scrutiny of the male viewer. In his erotic involvement with the painter, her portrayal, and the painted surface, Grimm seems unthreatened by Madame Lebrun's self-presentation. He displays none of the (castration/death) jitters that the (image of) woman is held in some psychoanalytical and feminist discourses to provoke. He responds as a particular ideal of masculinity is supposed to respond to a particular ideal of femininity. He also – and we should not lose sight of this point – responds to the portrait as a successful work of art by a talented artist, for the whole discussion resonates with the influential writings of Roger de Piles, who saw the highest merits in painting as those of attracting, seducing, and fooling the eye of the beholder (Sheriff 1990: 127–8).

Other contemporary observers, however, did not find this self-portrait quite so charming as they read it against a tradition of representing artistic genius. For example, consider the commentary of Louis de Carmontelle who, writing as "Coup de Patte," produces a dialogue between a painter, a poet, and a musician. The trio pauses before the self-portrait of Madame Lebrun. Seeing the image of a pretty woman holding a palette, the musician asks about the work: whom does it represent? The sitter must be a student of Duplessis, the poet speculates, perceiving in the portrait the hand of that established portraitist. The painter knows better; the work, he explains, is a self-portrait. "Indeed! this pretty person has painted herself!" exclaims the surprised poet.

He is perhaps surprised because the work is magnificent; the painter thinks it would be difficult to make a more successful portrait. Nevertheless, the painter is troubled because the figure's hair is a little *négligé*. The musician takes this as a sign that she has the "taste" of great artists not focused on mundane details.[36] Addressing himself to the painter, the musician asks, "Is she a history painter?" And the painter replies:

> No. The arms, the head, the heart of women lack the essential qualities to follow men into the lofty region of the fine arts. If nature could produce one of them capable of this great effort, it would be a monstrosity, the more shocking because there would be an inevitable opposition between her physical and mental/moral [*morale*] existence. A woman who has all the passions of a man is really an impossible man. So the vast field of history, which is filled only with vigorously impassioned objects, is closed to those who would not know how to bring to it all the expressions of vigor.
>
> (*Le Triumvirat des Arts* 1783: 27)[37]

The dialogue is structured around two misrecognitions – the poet takes a woman portrait painter for a man portrait painter, and the musician takes a woman for a history painter. The first mistake produces only pleasant surprise; the second elicits a more outraged response. In the case of history painting there must be a fit between the sex of the painter and the gender of the genre, as is evident in the comment that only men can paint vigorous passions because they are naturally vigorous. Madame Lebrun can only be a history painter *manqué*. Yet she tries to become (and many say she succeeds in becoming) a history painter, and it is as a history painter that she presents herself at the Academy and at the Salon. Seen in this light her self-portrait as read by the musician shocks; it shows trouble lurking underneath her slipping chemise, beneath her reassuring feminity. And the painter raises the specter, shows the musician the monster, the woman with "force," the intellectual woman, the woman with a penis. Like Medusa, the monster has to be slain. The painter does it easily by denying that Madame Lebrun's history paintings are history paintings; the scenes she paints do not show vigorous, heroic male subjects. He (re)defines the categories, restores the balance of nature, and reinstates her feminity.

But has the painter really put the issue to rest? *Peace Bringing Back Abundance* may not represent vigorously impassioned male objects, but it is still a political allegory recognized by its contemporary audience as a commentary on France's international position during the reign of Louis XVI. Can it be, then, a history painting that is not a history painting? Despite the painter's vigorous denial the musician's question still lingers, "Is she a history painter?" Madame Lebrun's works raised the possibility that a woman could have the force – the strength (arms), reason (head), and passion (heart) – to produce significant works of art. Calling the manly woman he imagines "impossible," the painter holds that such a woman would not be a woman. Nor would she be a man. She might have the attributes of a man – his strength, reason, passion; she might even have some similar body parts – arms, head, heart; but she would lack the one part that organized and gave meaning to the others. Both impossible woman and impossible man, the creature he imagines is disjoint, forever divided by the irreconcilability of her "mental/moral" and "physical" existence. In this particular case the painter offers two options for the pretty woman holding a palette: either Madame Lebrun's history paintings arc not history paintings or Madame Lebrun is not a woman. Which does she prefer? To be a coherent subject, he believes there must be no split between her biological sex and gender identity. Without such coherence she simply cannot be. But such impossible subjects did exist, and more than a century later one sought help from the Freudian analyst Joan Rivière.

Rivière's analysis of that *femme-homme* published in her 1929 essay "Womanliness as masquerade," has recently received much attention in feminist writing. In posing the problem of the intellectual (masculine) woman – the problem that concerns us here as it relates to Elisabeth Lebrun – Rivière's work opens several avenues of investigation and illuminates from a psychoanalytical perspective both Carmontelle's commentary and Lebrun's dilemma. My aim here is not to validate or to apply Rivière's conclusions, nor is it to relate them to the complexities of the psychoanalytical debate over female sexuality, a debate that erupted among Freudian analysts in the 1920s and 1930s and was taken up by Lacan in the 1950s.[38] Rather, I want to use her conceptualization of the problem in an unauthorized and un-Lacanian fashion to elucidate various attitudes towards Lebrun's work by staging interactions between Rivière and Coup de Patte, between Rivière and Lebrun, and ultimately between Rivière and feminist interpreters of Lebrun.

Rivière has two goals: to categorize psychologically a particular type of woman and to chart more precisely the course of female sexual development. As in the Freudian account, femininity seems both constructed, something the little girl must achieve, and biologically determined, rooted in her lack of a penis. Positioning her essay in the context of the psychoanalytical debate over female sexuality, Rivière refers specifically to Ernest Jones's division of women into heterosexual and homosexual types. In his 1929 essay, "The early development of female sexuality," Jones postulated a number of "intermediate types," and it is with one of those intermediate types that Rivière is concerned:

> In daily life types of men and women are constantly met with who, while mainly heterosexual in their development, plainly display strong features of the other sex. This has been judged to be an expression of the bisexually [*sic*] inherent in us all. . . . The difference between homosexual and heterosexual development results from differences in the degree of anxiety, with the corresponding effect this has on development. . . . I shall attempt to show that women who wish for masculinity may put on a mask of womanliness to avert anxiety and the retribution feared from men.
>
> (Rivière 1986: 35)

Rivière is particularly interested in the intellectual or professional woman who nevertheless seems "to fulfil [*sic*] every criterion of complete feminine development" (36). In Rivière's criteria we find a mix of feminine social roles (they are "capable housewives"; they "maintain social life and assist culture"; they have "no lack of feminine interests, e.g., in their personal appearance") and heterosexual identity ("sexual relations with [the] husband included . . . full and frequent sexual enjoyment") (36). This mix opens on to the functions Rivière gives the feminine masquerade: warding off the (real and fantasied) threat of male retribution and warding off the woman's anxiety about her unconscious masculinity. In a fundamental way the masquerade covers over the wish for masculinity present in all women (recall Rivière's earlier invoking of the bisexuality inherent in us all) and so coincides with "normal" femininity or womanliness:

> The reader may now ask how I define womanliness or where I draw the line between genuine womanliness and the "masquerade". My suggestion is not, however, that there is any difference; whether radical or superficial they are the same thing. The capacity for womanliness was there in this woman [her patient] – one might even say it exists in the most completely homosexual woman – but owing to her conflicts it did not represent her main development and was used far more as a device for avoiding anxiety than as a primary mode of sexual enjoyment.
>
> (Rivière 1986: 38)

Rivière derived some of her conclusions from analyzing a patient who used the masquerade "more as a device for avoiding anxiety than as a primary mode of sexual enjoyment." She mentions that during the course of analysis, when the mask was being peeled away, her patient lost the desire for intercourse with her husband and had a love-affair with a woman. "It is striking that she had had no homosexual experiences (since before puberty with a younger sister); but it appeared during analysis that this lack was compensated for by frequent homosexual dreams with intense orgasm" (39). In this case the masquerade covers a wish for masculinity – which includes the patient's desire for other women. She guards, from men and from herself, not only her desire to have a penis, but also her lesbian desires. Rivière's essay thus presents at least two possibilities for the intellectual woman who is overtly heterosexual. (1) Her primary sexual gratification is heterosexual and her reaction-formations gave rise to "masculine" traits. (2) Her primary sexual gratification is not heterosexual and her reaction-formations gave rise to "masculine" traits. In the first case the woman has achieved heterosexuality by successfully repressing or masking half of her primary bisexuality. Her masculine traits (intellect, achievement) she hides through the masquerade of womanliness (conforming to the expected stereotypes of "feminine" behavior, acting the part of the thing men desire). In the second case the masquerade hides both her unrepressed "masculine" desires (that is, desires for women) and her masculine traits.

At first reading, Rivière's analysis of female sexuality, based as it is in infantile fantasies and debates within Freudian psychology, may seem to have little to do with an eighteenth-century Salon commentary or with a painting made in 1780. Yet, as Rivière and others have noted, there is a long tradition for thinking of womanliness as a mask behind which man suspects some hidden danger. To throw a little light on the question "What does woman want?" is for Rivière to analyze that hidden or masked danger (1986: 43). What Rivière suggests the feminine masquerade conceals is precisely what Coup de Patte so fervently denies and fears in women – masculinity as intellect, force, and desire. Her essay is compelling for the clarity with which she articulates how the intellectual or professional woman must perform in an ideological framework that conflates biological sex with societal role and constructs woman as modest and self-abasing (Heath 1986: 54–6). Such was the ideological framework (re)constructed for women in late eighteenth-century France by Rousseauist thinkers (Le Doeuff 1987: 184

and 190–3). Male anxiety over women's intellectual capacities, however, explains only one part of the masquerade. For Rivière the masquerade can also shield, from both the woman herself and the men around her, sexual desire directed towards other women.

Lebrun painted and Coup de Patte wrote at a time when the charge of lesbianism was increasingly leveled at prominent and/or intellectual women. I believe this charge is latent in the characterizing of a woman who has "all the passions of a man" as an "impossible man".[39] Coup de Patte's social text normalizes the "fit" between biological sex, gender role, and sexuality identity. Madame Lebrun subverted this fit in her Salon entries and in her self-portrait, which together suggested that she was both a desirable, feminine woman and a history painter. And her Salon entries might have also suggested – at least to some – that beneath the façade of the beautiful woman desirable to men, was a woman who also desired other women. We have already seen how Lebrun's practice of representing women's bodies in her history paintings was viewed erotically in a text where women are exhorted to leave for men the "pleasure" of painting women. By 1783 Madame Lebrun was also closely associated with the woman anonymous pamphleteers constructed as the most notorious tribade in France – Marie-Antoinette. Libels against the queen started as early as 1774 and suggested that unbridled female sexuality, once relegated to the margins of power (to the king's mistresses), had now moved to the center (Maza 1991: 68–9). One of the favorite charges accused the queen of sexual involvement with women, naming the Princesse de Lamballe and later the Duchesse de Polignac as her favorite lovers (Hunt 1991: 118–19).

In the 1770s and 1780s, Madame Lebrun was busy becoming the intimate of Marie-Antoinette whose influence finally opened the way for her to enter the Academy and Salon in 1783. The connection between the two women was suggested at the Salon where Lebrun showed a portrait of Marie-Antoinette "*en chemise*" (Plate 24.4). This fashionable style imported from England came to be associated with the queen, and was sometimes called the "*chemise à la reine*" or the "*robe en gaule.*" It was a simple gown of sheer cotton tied at the waist with a ribbon or sash, and, worn for informal occasions, it resembled what today we might call intimate apparel. That Madame Lebrun showed the queen in such dress indicates not only its fashionability, but also the painter's intimacy with her royal model.[40] Madame Lebrun, in fact, reserved this dress primarily (but not exclusively) for a small circle of women including the queen's favorite, the Duchesse de Polignac (Plate 24.5). And several times she portrayed herself "*en chemise*," constructing her own identity through her idealization of and association with this circle of powerful women.[41] The self-portrait shown at the Salon of 1783 (Plate 24.2) invokes that fashion – at least obliquely – with its sash at the waist, bow at the front, scalloped collar, and simple fabric. The plumed straw hat she wears was a favorite accessory, and one also sported by Marie-Antoinette in Lebrun's portrait.[42] Lebrun repeated the composition and costume of her self-portrait shown at the Salon of 1783 for another portrait of the queen's favorite, the Duchesse de Polignac (Plate 24.6). Since the time of the *Précieuses*, powerful and influential women were often labeled (rightly or wrongly) as tribades. And although the charge was never made against Lebrun overtly, could she entirely escape the talk surrounding the queen and her circle?[43]

A *Verse to Madame Le Brun* published as a Salon pamphlet highlighted in a positive way the association between artist and queen. It, too, can be read as suggesting more than friendship, although such a reading would not have been the one intended by the author – or at least I do not believe it was. Here is the stanza on the queen's portrait addressed to Lebrun:

> If the embellished throne offers you a worthy model,
> What enchanting features are soon recognized!
> The pride of Alexander called for an Apelles,
> It is Lebrun whom Venus needs.
> (Miramond 1783: 3)[44]

Madame Lebrun plays Apelles to Marie-Antoinette's Alexander, and through the two women the myth of the ruler honoring the artist is rewritten.[45]

But there is a further suggestion in rewriting the story of Alexander and Apelles for Lebrun and Marie-Antoinette. In the story of Alexander and Apelles the homosocial bond between men is cemented through the exchange of a woman, Campaspe. In the rewriting of this text (in the poet's verse, in Madame Lebrun's portraits, and later in her *Souvenirs*) women, traditionally the objects of exchange, circulate among themselves. The goods, as Irigaray says, get together (Irigaray 1985b: 192–7). Thus replacing Alexander and Apelles with Marie-Antoinette and Elisabeth Lebrun suggests a gyno-social and also an erotic bond between the two women.

We circle back again to Rivière's concept of masquerade and the fear that masculinity – even lesbianism – lurks behind the beautiful woman's façade. In exploring one function of the feminine masquerade – that of averting male reprisal – Rivière explicates the position of women in a particular patriarchal culture even as she validates many of the naturalist assumptions that straitjacketed them. She "throws some light on" Coup de Patte's response precisely because both are caught up in systems of thought (Rousseau's and Freud's) that base cultural difference on biological difference, ultimately tying the first to having or not having a penis. But if Rivière illuminates male anxieties about intellectual women, does she also throw some light on what women want? Or, to ask the question more specifically, does her concept of masquerade illuminate what Lebrun wanted in making her self-portrait, or what a feminist viewer wants in analyzing it?

I raise these questions because the only feminist reading of the work has understood it as a masquerade wherein the woman shows herself as precisely the object that male desires compel her to be. In this reading proposed by Rosizka Parker and Griselda Pollock in their pathbreaking survey *Old Mistresses*, the artist presents exactly the unproblematic fit of biological sex, sexual identity, and social role that Coup de Patte wanted to see. The analysis is framed by Lebrun's testimony that her self-portrait is based on Rubens's portrait of Susanna Forment, believed in the eighteenth century to represent his wife (*Le Chapeau de Paille*, Plate 24.3). Here is how Parker and Pollock describe Lebrun's appropriation of Ruben's work: "The coquetry and sensual feeling of that painting is hardly an appropriate model for an artist to use as a basis for a self-portrait, but it is a typical representation of woman, not just a woman, but Woman, sexual, physical, the spectacle of beauty" (Parker and Pollock 1981: 96). Their interpretation suggests that by choosing to represent herself within the codes for signifying "Woman," Lebrun constructed herself as not an artist. It is a claim founded not on an opposition between woman and history painter, but on a broader opposition between woman and artist. In setting the appearance of femininity at odds with professional or intellectual performance, their reading has a particular resonance with Rivière's analysis of the *femme-homme*.

Rivière observed that her patient reverted to stereotypical "feminine" behavior after a particularly compelling intellectual performance (for example, she openly flirted with "father figures" after giving an impressive lecture) (1986: 36–7). This appearing as Woman, Rivière concluded, worked to assuage the various anxieties and fears her performance raised. Can Parker and Pollock be understood as suggesting that Lebrun's masquerade is a similar tactical representation of herself as Woman? Such an under-standing would be appropriate given that these feminist viewers are sensitive to the complex historical and psychological position of women artists. Yet if we put Rivière's analysis beside this feminist reading, the results are unexpected.

From the start, viewing Lebrun's self-image as analogous to the display of feminine behaviour acted out by Rivière's patient is problematized by the move from per-formance to painted representation.[46] To see Lebrun's portrait as representing the masquerade is to concentrate on the artist masquerading as "the woman" to forestall anxiety, when we see simultaneously "the woman" unmasked as the artist and in fact producing it. In the case of a self-portrait, the painting (the physical object) is the professional performance – or at least its record – and the representation of that performance is inseparable from the representation of the woman. And because this particular self-portrait was part of a carefully orchestrated suite of Salon entries planned to present the woman not just as an artist, but as a history painter, it becomes difficult to see how in that public context the work could allay anyone's fears. It does not say, "I am merely a castrated woman," as much as it says, "I am a beautiful desirable woman artist who makes history paintings," or even to a certain audience, "I am a contradiction in terms."

A closer examination of Parker and Pollock's interpretation, moreover, reveals that the problem of simultaneity only emerges when their analysis is read intertextually with that of Rivière. Standing before Lebrun's work, Parker and Pollock allow the spectacle of Woman to eclipse any possibility of seeing or imagining an artist:

> Her self-portrait . . . carefully depicts the rich stuffs of her dress, the neat pleats of trimming, the textures of her soft hair and feathers. She holds the brush and palette with an elegant and unworkmanly gesture, the paint colors neatly arranged to echo the decorative arrangement of flowers on her hat. She offers herself as a beautiful object to be looked at, enjoyed and admired, but conveys nothing of the activity, the work, the mindfulness of the art she purports to pursue. As an image of an eighteenth-century artist it is wholly unconvincing.
>
> (Parker and Pollock 1981: 86)

Written more than ten years ago and published in a survey text, the judgment of "wholly unconvincing" needs rethinking both in light of more recent strategies of feminist interpretation (strategies that Parker and Pollock themselves have helped to produce) and in view of more current considerations of eighteenth-century French art.

Madame Lebrun's portrait was not "unconvincing" to its contemporary audience. Like the critic Grimm, commentators saw the artist as well as the woman. Even Coup de Patte, in denying that women could be history painters, suggests that Lebrun represents herself as one. Another critic describes the work as her "masterpiece" because it shows her "genius" vanquishing the difficulties of art (Fréron 1783: 262). Still another says she is represented in "an attitude of painting," that she holds in her hands "the instruments of the art that she practices with so much glory" (*Loterie pittoresque* 1783: 23). The neatness, elegance, and decorative arrangement of the work, moreover, typify a mode of painting common in the eighteenth century and widely discernible in many different kinds of subjects, including self-portraits and portraits of other artists.[47]

The notion of *convenance* would, however, constrict the types and modes of painting available to Lebrun in making her self-portrait. It would have been unconvincing for Lebrun to show herself as *not* a beautiful woman. But the display of physical beauty would not necessarily have produced an unconvincing image of an eighteenth-century artist. Such a (self-)presentation would have been advantageous to any artist – male or female – as La Tour's self-portrait (1751; Amiens, Musée Picardie), Lundberg's portrait of Boucher (Plate 24.7), or Madame Guiard's self-portrait (1785; New York, Metropolitan Museum of Art) show. These artists' portraits also suggest a much more important point: for the eighteenth-century painters and their audience there was never only one way to represent an artist or even "the Artist," the mythic genius.

To enhance their social position, artists showed themselves affluent, well dressed, or carrying themselves aristocratically. Although these types are more frequently associated with the earlier part of the century, they were not unknown in the later. Roslin's *Self-Portrait* of 1790 (Florence: Galleria degli Uffizi), Vestier's 1786 portrait of *Nicolas-Guy Brenet* (Plate 24.8) and Louis-Michel van Loo's 1763 *Self-Portrait with his Sister* (Versailles: Musée national du château) are all good examples here. These are particularly interesting because in each the artist, dressed as a gentleman, is posed before his easel or with his palette and brushes. Sometimes artists showed themselves in more informal garb, and they appear (at least to us) more workmanly. Chardin creates such effects in his pastel *Self-Portrait with Visor* of 1776 (Chicago: Art Institute of Chicago). More often artists appeared as intellectuals engaged in rational discourse, and this type spans the century, ranging from Antoine Coypel's *Self-Portrait c.* 1707 (Florence: Galleria degli Uffizi) to Mengs's *Self-Portrait* of 1774 (Plate 24.9). Indeed, it is to this tradition that the gesture made by Lebrun in her self-portrait refers – it is not merely an elegant gesture, it is a gesture drawn from rhetoric manuals and refers to the artist's reasoning.[48] With lips parted, she also can be construed as about to speak, perhaps to make a theoretical point. This presentation of the speaking, gesturing artist was often combined with the tradition of the artist distracted (i.e. concentrating on some mental conception; staring ahead or to the side; or looking through or past the viewer) and garbed in studio *déshabillé*. Tocqué's portrait of Galloche (Plate 24.10) and Largillière's portrait of Coustou (Plate 24.11) come readily to mind. Other eighteenth-century conventions for showing the distracted artist or the artist as "genius" include the secularized inspired gospel writer, and the artist who stares directly out of the painting. There is much of the latter in Lebrun's self-portrait: we can see in the work clear parallels with David's self-portrait (Plate 24.12) not only in the disheveled hair and clothes, but also in the full face frontal view and distracted gaze. My points are as follows. (1) "The artist" is not a stable, monolithic category; new ideologies never simply obliterated older types. (2) A single portrait could and indeed often did combine various codes for representing the artist. Sometimes codes that we might find conflict-ing were conjoined unproblematically (for instance, the elegantly attired working artist; the distracted speaking artist; the beautiful woman history painter). There were and are many "convincing" representations of the artist.

Returning to Lebrun's use of Rubens's portrait we might say that she rewrites it to suggest an artist inventing, speaking, reasoning. In comparing her portrait with its model, notice that Lebrun significantly diminished its more overt sexuality. She changes the position of the arms that in Rubens's portrait emphasize the protruding bosom. In her left hand she holds the attributes of her art, with her right she makes a rhetorical gesture. This configuration was common in portraits of artists (e.g. Van Loo's *Self-Portrait with Sister*; or Geuslain's portrait of Largillière, 1723; Versailles, Musée national du château) and pointed to the twofold nature of painting – practice or the hand indicated by the tools of the trade; mind or reasoning indicated by the rhetorical gestures.[49] But for the post-Freudian viewer the gesture made by Lebrun is particularly interesting. Given the placement of the hand near her pubic area could it not also be read as a dangerous substitute for the member she lacks?[50] Having that member entitled the bearer to the gift of reason, rather than the gift (?) of modesty. Lebrun here is no modest Venus turning her hand knuckle side up to cover her pubic area; in making her gesture of reasoning her hand figuratively takes the place of the penis, which guaranteed power, will, and reason to the male sex. Yet the gesture is hardly firm and virile; it is a gesture of reason appropriate to (in the sense of *convenance*) the beautiful woman who makes it.

Lebrun also significantly changed the gaze of Rubens's sitter in making her self-portrait. In the *Chapeau de Paille* the figure casts her eyes down coyly, perhaps showing us false modesty at work in exciting the viewer's desire. The viewer has free license to explore the image, for with eyes averted Forment cannot be imagined as confronting, challenging, or even acknowledging any viewer's gaze. Moreover, Rubens has pushed the figure so close to the picture plane that she seems in close intimate contact with those who look at her. Madame Lebrun, on the other hand, sets herself at more of a distance from the viewer and shows herself looking directly out of the painting. There is nothing coy about the presentation which, as we have already seen, invokes specific conventions for representing the artist. Some eighteenth-century critics, however, lam-basted the "expression" of the work. One said it reminded him of the *Broken Jug* (Plate 24.13) by Greuze in its immobile attitude and stupefied and vague expression (*Messieurs* 1783: 23). The choice of comparison is not, it seems, innocent. The young girl in Greuze's painting is not receiving inspiration; the *Broken Jug* is a loss-of-virginity theme. In comparing the two, the critic perhaps suggests that the lack of modesty, the lack of traditional feminine morality, can also be taken to characterize Madame Lebrun and her self portrait. His reading demonstrates again how codes overlapped, gaped, and opened possibilities for multiple interpretations.

Thus far we have concentrated only on Madame Lebrun's appropriation of a figure represented by Rubens. Her work also implies a comparison with the artist who made the representation – with Rubens. Competing with an established master was a stan-dard exercise for would-be academicians who could use such competition to claim alliance with their ideal. In making a self-portrait an artist could use the work of another to forge particular associations between them. Reynolds did this cleverly by presenting himself as Rembrandt contemplating the bust of his (Reynold's) ideal, Michelangelo (Paulson 1975: 82). The work establishes Reynolds's attachment to two painters: Rembrandt (his real model) and Michelangelo (his unattainable ideal). Lebrun's self-portrait, however, brings together the real and ideal, and emphasizes her connection to one artist, Rubens.

The work collapses other oppositions as well. In using the *Chapeau de Paille* as her model Lebrun becomes both the subject Rubens – the one who loves – and the object, Rubens's wife – the one who is loved.[51] Based in love, the portrait recalls the myth of painting's origin in which love inspires Dibutadis to trace the profile of her amour. Lebrun, however, does not declare her love for Rubens by literally painting *his* profile in the way Rubens drew his wife or in the way Reynolds showed the bust of Michelangelo. Rather Lebrun shows herself as the one whom Rubens loves and demonstrates her love (for him) by mirroring his artistic identity, by taking him as her ideal. Which brings us back to the notion of imitation. In absorbing another artist as an ideal, the imitator does not merely copy, but makes a work of art as if she were the other. Here Lebrun becomes Rubens not just by using his portrait as her model, but by using the same procedures as Rubens in making her composition and arranging her colors. Most important here is that Lebrun has taken up in her painting the singular light effect that characterizes Rubens's portrait. She describes that effect in her *Souvenirs*: "Its great effect lies in the two different lights that represent the simple daylight and the glimmering of the sun, so the lights [*clairs*] are in the sun; and that which it is necessary to call the shade, because there is no other word, is the daylight [*jour*]" (Vigée-Lebrun 1986: I, 75).[52] And these are the effects that Lebrun achieves in her self-portrait where her face, shaded by her hat, seems to be clearly lit even though it is actually bathed in shadow, as the line falling across her cheek and neck indicates.

But there is more. Notice, for example, how Rubens uses framing devices in the *Chapeau de Paille*. In the lower part of the painting Forment's bosom is framed by several irregular rectangles: the white inner drape, the black velvet of her dress, her crossed arms. Lebrun absorbs the notion of framing and transforms the rectangular format into an oval one whose major virtual line moves from the fingers of her gesturing hand to the tip of the feather on her hat down to her bent elbow. On her left side the oval is pulled open and its visual complexity increased by the intersecting and rhyming shape of the palette and the deliberate angle formed by the clasped brushes.[53]

Although not all of Madame Lebrun's audience could be expected to know the "source" of her self-portrait, the association with Rubens would have been otherwise available, as well. For example, her color tonalities were thought comparable with (but not equal to) those of the Flemish master: "I do not think that any woman [other than Madame Lebrun] has yet carried to as exalted a degree the seductive and true color tonality that would not displease the immortal *Rubens*" (Fréron 1783: 259–60).[54] Another wrote that her *Peace Bringing Back Abundance* was painted with all the force and brilliance of the Flemish (*Les Peintres volants* 1783: 12) and in the *Mémoires secrets* her figure of Abundance was called a superb woman *à la Rubens* (Bachaumont 1780: XXIV, 6). Other critics repeatedly cited her adherence to the principle of the Flemish school, either to praise or to damn her.

Having explored various meanings present in Lebrun's self-portrait, we find that the portrait seems to assume no one style or posture, to posit no stable or essential identity, and to present no contradictions between or among identities. In her self-portrait Madame Lebrun is all at the same time an intimate of the queen, the painter Rubens, his wife Helena Forment, a painted figure made by Rubens, a history painter, an inspired artist, an intellectual making a reasoned point, a speaking subject, a beautiful woman, an objectified commodity, an immodest woman/artist pleasuring in self-display. This is not to say, however, that the self-presentation puts the artist back in the place of woman as inchoate, formless mass, or indecipherable Sphinx. Nor is it to say that she is a product of poststructuralist thinking, although the contemporary notion of the decentered subject is perhaps more congenial to what we see in Lebrun's self-portrait than the fantasy of a "totalized self-contained subject present-to-itself" (Stanton 1987: 15). In a very fundamental way Lebrun constructs herself through her references and relatedness to others. Thus we could transfer Domna Stanton's conclusion about women's autobiography to Lebrun's self-portrait: "Because of woman's different status in the symbolic order, autogynography, I concluded, dramatized the fundamental alterity and non-presence of the subject, even as it asserts itself discursively and strives toward an always impossible self-possession" (Stanton 1987: 15). Yet this not totalized, incoherent subject was, as Felicity Nussbaum has argued, typical of both men and women's self-writing in the eighteenth century, especially before Rousseau's *Confessions* became the standard model for a new "modern" autobiography (Nussbaum 1989: 15–23).

Indeed, we might consider Madame Lebrun's self-portrait a kind of eighteenth-century self-writing. Felicity Nussbaum has characterized such self-writing as setting out the subject in fragments and discontinuities (Nussbaum 1989: 15). Eighteenth-century self-writing, she argues, presents multiple and serial subject positions that do not add up to a unified self (Nussbaum 1989: 21). Through such self-writing the (disunified) subject can assume agency in his or her contradictory positonings; identity is thus produced *by* the subject within a culture that is simultaneously urging an identity *on* the subject. Nussbaum argues that in eighteenth-century autobiographical writings men and women "experiment with interdiscourses and the corresponding subject positions to broach the uncertainties of identity," that they "envisage new possibilities in the interstices between discourses" and "weave them together in new hybrid forms" (Nussbaum 1989: 37). This conception of self-writing seems appropriate to what we see in Madame Lebrun's self-portrayal, where she is distracted, about to speak, and making a reasoned point, all at the same time. Thus she seems conceptually disunified, composed of discontinuous gestures or expressions. She is also disunified through time – presenting herself as various seventeenth- and eighteenth-century figures (Rubens, Rubens's wife, Madame Vigée-Lebrun, Marie-Antoinette's intimate) – through position (subject, object), and through sex and gender identity. These visual fragments and associations are framed together in a coherent pictorial structure, which perhaps encourages many viewers to imagine them in conformity with the dominant notion of a unified self, even though the image actually resists this reading. Moreover, each gesture and expression, each coded fragment, potentially has many meanings within the visual language, so that not only the identity of the figure represented, but also the references in the painting remain multiple and mobile.

If the illegibility of Madame Lebrun's identity might have proved problematic for some – and here I am thinking once more of Rousseau who longed to see the "essential self" through all appearances – her identity as a woman history painter produced a special anxiety for the art establishment in 1783. To return to the place where I opened this chapter – to Dibutadis at the Salon – let me use that commentary as one final example of the anxiety. The first Salon paintings discussed in the commentary are those of the women artists, and this discussion is separated from the rest of the pamphlet. After listing Madame Lebrun's works Dibutadis asks, "The sex which commands, has it anything more perfect to oppose to these exquisite pieces?" (*La Morte* 1783: 8). The rhetorical question is left hanging as the pamphlet goes on to consider the works by the other two women. Having cited and praised all the work by women, Dibutadis continues her visit to the Salon, moving to the paintings of Vien with these words, "But let me consider the history paintings. This genre, belonging only to the creative genuis; this genre, for which the artist must be filled by the heavenly fire stolen by Prometheus, this great genre comes to life again in the works of your artists" (*La Morte* 1783: 8).[55] That the genre came alive in the works of Madame Lebrun was, in 1783, a most debatable point. All would have agreed, however, that this immodest woman made ambitious claims.

I have tried in this chapter to reanimate Lebrun's claims by exploring the conditions under which she made them. A particular mode of painting, a particular set of influential friends, a particular theory of art, all cleared the way for this woman to make history paintings. Lebrun saw her opportunity and seized the advantage. At the same time another mode of painting, another set of allies, another theory of art, all resisted her claims and worked to close the space that the artificed rococo mode with its female patrons, effeminate practitioners, and pleasure-seeking viewers had opened. If my language here is loaded, it is because this conceptualization of the rococo dominates the (art-)historical narrative nearly as completely as a particular psychoanalytical and social construction of Woman regulates women's opportunities, behaviors, and desires. Although these two propositions may seem unconnected, in the eighteenth century there were significant points of contact between them, as cultural history is making increasingly clear.

In relating the problem of the intellectual woman – the female subject – to Elisabeth Lebrun, I wanted to throw a little light on some of those contact points. I also wanted more. I wanted to open the possibility of writing a narrative about eighteenth-century art that would interrupt the mythic oedipal story in which a male hero-subject (call him David) achieves his destiny and meaning by overcoming an obstacle gendered as feminine (call it the rococo, the aristocracy, Pompadour, or Boucher). In writing such a historical narrative one would take up Teresa de Lauretis's challenge "to enact the contradiction of female desire, and of women as social subjects" (Lauretis 1984: 156). This narrative is what I want, what I immodestly desire.

Notes

This work has been much improved by the insightful questions, comments, and suggestions of Ann Bermingham, Jane Burns, Whitney Davis, Bernadette Fort, Lynn Hunt, Felicity Nussbaum, Paula Radisich, Erica Rand, and, especially, Keith Luria. I also benefited greatly from discussions following the presentation of this material at the Clark Library, Folger Library, Emory

University, and Northwestern University. I am particularly indebted to my assistants, Helen Langa and Fiona Ragheb, for their intelligent and prompt handling of the tedious, as well as the challenging, research assignments. This essay was completed in 1991 and so represents the beginning of the work that resulted in my forthcoming book on Vigée-Lebrun.

1 The Greek maiden was one of many fictive Salon visitors invented by critics in the 1770s and 1780s. She appears in a pamphlet entitled *La Morte de trois milles ans au salon de 1783* (1783, Collection Deloynes, No. 286). For an excellent discussion of these "carnivalized" Salon pamphlets, see Fort (1989).

2 "Si je suis inventrice, répondit-elle, c'est donc des portraits à la *Silhouette*: car je viens d'entendre nommer ainsi un *profil noir*, tracé d'après l'ombre d'une jeune personne. C'est positivement le même procédé que l'amour m'avoit jadis inspiré, & pour lequel vous affectez de m'admirer" (*La Morte* 1783: 6–7).

3 Although I use this pamphlet here only to suggest some of my major themes, *La Morte* is an interesting text that reflects on both the credibility and origin of its story/dream. On the one hand, the correspondent suggests he is merely the medium or the body for a dream originating elsewhere, and on the other hand, he deems himself the mind that fabricated the fiction. The entire pamphlet, moreover, resonates with the myths of both Dibutadis and Pygmalion. The character Dibutadis is described nearly as if she were a piece of sculpture (*grande figure à la Grecque*) brought to life, she first appears in the sculpture court, and the *abbé* identifies her from likenesses seen on a medal and in an antique head. The two myths of the arts were often paired during the eighteenth century, as in Jean–Baptiste Regnault's overdoors in the Salon des Nobles at Versailles, painted for Marie-Antoinette in 1785.

4 "En ouvrant la séance Madame *Le Brun*, reçu Académicienne à la dernière assemblée, a pris séance en cette qualité" (Montaiglon 1889: IX, 158). I have chosen to call the artist Madame Lebrun throughout this chapter because in 1783 she used Lebrun (as opposed to Vigée-Lebrun, which she adopted sometime later). "Madame Lebrun" also highlights her status as a married woman, which is critical to several points of my argument.

5 As Montaiglon notes, "Il y avait d'abord cette phrase: 'Et qui a fait aporter des ses ouvrages dont la Compagnie a été satisfaite,' mais elle a été effacée et surchargée de ratures" (Montaiglon 1889: IX, 158).

6 This did not always mean that they placed the painter in the rank suggested by the subject of the painting. The obvious exception is in the case of Greuze, who presented his *Septimus Severus Rebuking Caracalla* (Paris, Musée du Louvre) for admission into the Academy in 1769. The academicians accepted Greuze, but ranked him as a genre painter based on his previous work. They found his *Septimus* an inadequate history painting.

7 I am here simplifying the issue by discussing what the Academy said and did as if that body were not composed of individuals in cooperation and conflict with one another. Like any academic group, it was rife with politics, gossip, intrigue, and jealousy. Among the members of the Academy there were many who supported Madame Lebrun. In referring to the Academy's decisions I have meant the "official" policies recorded in documents and represented by Pierre, the first painter, and d'Angiviller, the director. Evidence suggests, moreover, that while she had a hostile personal relationship with Pierre, she perhaps enjoyed a cordial one with d'Angiviller. Although this discussion of Madame Lebrun will highlight gender politics, arguments for and against her derived from multiple and complex motivations for she was positioned within several intersecting sociopolitical networks, which included the Academy, the court, and the salons.

8 The order was "necessary" because the Academy believed her admission would violate their statute that forbade members from engaging in the commerce of artworks. Lebrun was married to an art dealer, and "because in France a woman has no other status than that of her husband," Madame Lebrun was inadmissible to the Academy. The king, at the urging of Marie-Antoinette, made an exception to the rule for Madame Lebrun (Montaiglon 1889: IX, 152–7). I analyzed these documents more completely in the longer version of this chapter prepared as a paper for the Clark symposium.

9 Such an exception was made, for example, in the case of Chardin.

10   Actually, the record shows that they chose on that day as her *morceau de réception* her portrait of Pajou sculpting the bust of Lemoyne (Paris, Musée du Louvre). They left to d'Angiviller the choice of the first reception piece – that is, the *morceau d'agrément*. The record indicates that d'Angiviller was asked to select that portrait from among those Madame Guiard presented to the academicians on the day of her admission (Montaiglon 1889: IX, 154).

11   Her activities were widely known because long before 1783 Lebrun was a public figure who had managed her career skillfully. At 19 a member of the Académie de Saint–Luc de Paris (her father Louis Vigée had also belonged to this guild), she showed her art at its exhibition in 1774 and received very favorable notices in the press. She presented portraits of Fleury and La Bruyère to the Académie française in 1775, and the flattering letter of thanks she received from d'Alembert was published both in the *Mercure de France* and in the *Mémoires secrets*. In 1779, 1781, 1782, and 1783 she entered works in the Salon de la Correspondance, an enterprise founded by Pahin de la Blancherie to provide a Parisian meeting-place for the citizens of the Republic of Arts and Letters. By 1780 Madame Lebrun's talents, beauty, and wit had won her influential supporters, and she was the intimate of the comte de Vaudreuil, the comtesse de Polignac, the finance minister Calonne, and other members of the court circle whom she often entertained at suppers. She was, most importantly, the favorite painter of Marie-Antoinette.

12   "Peu de temps après mon retour de Flandre, en 1783 . . . plusieurs . . . de mes ouvrages décidèrent Joseph Vernet à me proposer comme membre de l'Académie royale de peinture. M. Pierre, alors premier peintre du Roi, s'y opposait fortement, ne voulant pas, disait-il, que l'on reçût des femmes, et pourtant madame Vallayer-Coster, qui peignait parfaitement les fleurs, était déjà reçue; je crois même que madame Vien l'était aussi. Quoi qu'il en soit, M. Pierre, peintre fort médiocre, car il ne voyait dans la peinture que le maniement de la brosse, avait de l'esprit; de plus, il était riche, ce qui lui donnait les moyens de recevoir avec faste les artistes, qui dans ce temps étaient moins fortunés qu'ils ne le sont aujourd'hui. Son opposition aurait donc pu me devenir fatale, si dans ce temps-là tous les vrais amateurs n'avaient pas été associés à l'Académie de peinture, et s'ils n'avaient formé, en ma faveur, une cabale contre celle de M. Pierre. C'est alors qu'on fit ce couplet: A MADAME LEBRUN . . . Au salon ton art vainqueur / Devrait être en lumière / Pour te ravir cet honneur, / Lise, il faut avoir le coeur / De Pierre, de Pierre, de Pierre. Enfin je fus reçue. M. Pierre alors fit courir le bruit que c'était par ordre de la cour qu'on me recevait. Je pense bien en effet que le Roi et la Reine avaient été assez bons pour désirer me voir entrer à l'Académie; mais voilà tout. Je donnai pour tableau de réception la *Paix qui ramène l'Abondance*. Ce tableau est aujourd'hui au ministère de l'Intérieur" (Vigée-LeBrun 1986: I, 76–8).

13   "Ce nombre est suffisant pour honorer le talent, les femmes ne pouvant jamais être utiles au progrès des Arts, la décence de leur sexe les empêchant de pouvoir étudier d'après nature et dans l'Ecole publique établie et fondée par Votre Majesté" (Montaiglon 1889: IX, 157).

14   For a discussion of d'Angiviller's participation in the revival of history painting, see Crow (1985: 178–209).

15   That d'Angiviller advocated the separation of male and female artists is evident from a letter he wrote to the king in November of 1785 concerning Madame Guiard's request for lodgings in the Louvre. There he points out that "the woman Guiard has a school for young students of her sex." He goes on to say that "all the artists have their lodging in the Louvre, and as one only gets to all these lodgings through vast corridors that are often dark, this mixing of young artists of different sexes would be very inconvenient for morals and for the decency of your Majesty's palace" (Passez 1971: 301). The argument recalls Rousseau's contention that the mixing of actors and actresses leads to corruption: "after what I have just said, I believe I need not explain further how the dissoluteness of the actresses leads to that of the actors; especially in a profession which forces them to live in the greatest familiarity with each other" (Rousseau 1948: 122).

16   "Alors, au moindre mouvement que faisait leur prunelle de mon côté, je leur disais: *J'en suis aux yeux*: cela les contrariait un peu, comme vous pouvez croire" (Vigée-Lebrun 1986: I, 39). The discussion which follows is indebted to comments made by Jane Burns and Erica Rand.

17   *Moelleuse* comes from the noun *moelle* meaning the marrow of a bone. To paint *moelleusement* literally meant to paint softly or with mellowness, but *moelleuse* had the positive connotations

of pithy, full of marrow – in other words of having substance. *Molle*, on the other hand, also meant soft, but had the connotations of slack, flabby, indolent, effeminate.

18   "On peut dire en voyant la touche mâle et ferme de ses Portraits, leurs mé-plats savans, et leurs plans de lumière de demi-teintes et d'ombre bien établis et sortiment prononcés, que Mme Guyard s'est fait homme" (*L'Impartialité au Sallon* 1783: 30).

19   *Journal de Paris* 266 (September 23, 1783): 1098: "la Nature est moins brillante, & c'est la Nature que l'on doit chercher à rendre." Also it is interesting to note that this commentator says that the *éclat* is made to please the multitude, but Madame Lebrun's talents are such that she can aspire to more.

20   "On trouve en général que le coloris des tableaux de Mme Le Brun a trop d'éclat; la nature est moins brillante et l'art qui cherche à la surpasser manque son effet" (Tourneux 1880: XIII, 440).

21   "La Peinture est ici la Dame d'atour de la beauté; elle prend soin de la parer avec tout l'art de la coquetterie la plus séduisante; mais l'art est de la cacher" (*Apelle au Sallon* 1783: 22–3).

22   This literature, moreover, only repeated the pattern set in the earliest discussion of their work published in 1774 when the two young women showed at the exhibition of the Académie de Saint–Luc. Mademoiselle Labille (Madame Guiard) was cited for a "touche très hardie et d'une couleur vraie"; her works had "verité et d'agrément." Mademoiselle Vigée (Madame Lebrun), on the other hand, composed with taste and with fire, but was in general a little mannered in her portraits of women. Her color tonalities were more brilliant and seductive than true (Passez 1971: 13).

23   For a provocative discussion of this hierarchy in the Middle Ages, see E. Jane Burns (1993) "Knowing women," part I of *Body Talk: When Women Speak in Old French Literature*.

24   "Madame Le Brun, prenant un plus noble effort s'élève jusqu'à l'Histoire. Je me garderai bien de lui conseiller, comme quelques-uns des Critiques, d'abandonner cette route; ils craignèrent qu'elle n'ait pas la force de s'y soutenir; je sais que d'ordinaire on n'accorde pas cette force à son sexe, cependant je connois nombre d'hommes qui pourroient tirer à honneur d'avoir peint *La Paix*" (*L'Impartialité* 1783: 28).

25   "Le sceptre d'Apollon semble tombé en quenouille, & c'est une femme qui emporte la palme: Je m'explique: cela ne veut pas dire qu'il y ait plus de génie dans un tableau de deux ou trois figures aux trois quarts, que dans un d'une composition vaste, de dix or douze personnages de grandeur naturelle; dans un tableau dont l'idée est simple que dans un dont le plan complexe équivaut à un poëme entier; cela signifie seulement que les ouvrages de la Minerve moderne attirent les premiers les regards du spectateur, qu'ils les rappellent sans cesse, les saissent, s'en emparent, lui arrachent ces exclamations de plaisir & d'admiration dont les artistes sont si jaloux, & communément le sceau des productions supérieures" (Bachaumont 1780–9: XXIV, 4).

26   That the *Iliad* was an important source for learned artists can be gleaned from its appearance in artists' portraits, such as Vestier's 1786 portrait of Gabriel–François Doyen (Paris, Musée du Louvre). Also, Coup de Patte specifically chastises Madame Lebrun for her use or mockery of Homer (*Le Triumvirat des Arts ou Dialogue entre un Peintre, un Musicien et un Poète* 1783: 27).

27   I thank Professor Betty Weinshenker for drawing my attention to this point. DuBos, for example, argues that in making allegories painters liked to show the brilliance of their imaginations. DuBos warns, however, that sometimes allegories are difficult to discern and do not touch the heart of the viewer (DuBos 1740: I, 198–9).

28   In the *Correspondance littéraire* this comment is attributed to Renou (Tourneux 1880: XIII, 440). It was earlier reported in the *Journal de Paris* 266 (September 23, 1783): 1097 with no name attached, and it is repeated elsewhere.

29   "Il seroit injuste d'exiger de l'estimable Artiste dont nous parlons, ces formes grandes & sublimes, qu'on ne peut acquérir par une profonde étude des chef d'oeuvres de l'antiquité. Les têtes, dans les Tableaux de Madame *le Brun*, sont très-jolies, assurément, mais ce sont de jolies têtes françoises" (Fréron 1783: 261).

30 My thinking about the imaginative identification necessary to imitation was stimulated by comments made to me by Professor Whitney Davis.

31 "L'Artiste, dit-il, auroit dû réunir le coloris de l'une à l'élégance de l'autre, pour n'en former qu'une seule; autrefois j'ai rassemblé toutes les Beautés de la Grèce et je n'ai peint que ma Venus sortant des eaux" (*Apelle au Sallon* 1783: 23).

32 "Quelques Critiques, pour diminuer la gloire de l'Artiste, disent que Madame le Brun, plus à portée qu'une autre de consulter les excéllens Modèles, n'a fait ici que les copier. Ils prétendent retrouver dans son tableau le *Guide*, le *Cortone*, *Cignani*, *Santere* &c.; mais tout cela prouve qu'elle n'en a copié aucun. Si elle a cherché à les imiter, rien n'est plus permis, & c'est même un précepte de l'Art" (*Loterie pittoresque* 1783: 23).

33 Because many writers of Salon pamphlets remain anonymous, it is sometimes difficult to know if comments were provoked by the writers' attitudes towards women, or their attitudes towards this particularly controversial woman. Exploring the interaction between attitudes towards women and political position is part of my larger project. Coup de Patte, Louis de Carmontelle, who appears as one of the most "sexist" of critics in his pronouncements about women painters was also one of the most "radical" of the critics. How many of his remarks are directed towards Lebrun because she was associated with Marie-Antoinette remains to be seen. It is noteworthy, however, that he is willing to praise her works after she stops showing history paintings at the Salon, which indicates that there is a persistent strain of anti-feminist response that does not necessarily relate to his dislike of her politics.

34 The version of the self-portrait shown in the Salon is now in a private collection. I have chosen here to illustrate the autograph copy now in London at the National Gallery of Art. This work is accessible to the reader. I have seen the two paintings, and there are no significant differences in iconography, and, for the purposes of this chapter, no significant differences in handling, composition, color, or formal structure. The version that appeared in the Salon is, however, signed and dated; the copy in London is not.

35 "Remarquez-y mille et mille défauts encore, rien ne sauroit détruit le charme de ce délicieux ouvrage. . . . J'ai vu même, à côté de cet ouvrage, des beautés d'un ordre bien supérieur, mais je n'ai point vu qui respirent davantage ce je ne sais quoi qui plaît, qui attire sans cesse les mêmes regards . . . On sent qu'il n'y a qu'une femme et une jolie femme qui puisse avoir conçu cette charmante idée, qui puisse l'avoir rendue avec une grâce si brillante et si naïve" (Tourneux 1880: XIII, 441).

36 In relating Lebrun's self-depiction to portraits of distracted artists with tousled hair and disarranged chemise, the musician's comment calls to mind works such as Largillière's portrait of Nicolas Coustou (Figure 24.11, 1710).

37 "Non. Les bras, la tête, le coeur des femmes sont privés des qualités essentielles pour suivre les hommes dans la haute région des beaux-arts. Si la nature en produisoit un capable de ce grand effort, ce seroit une monstruosité d'autant plus choquante, qu'il se trouveroit une opposition nécessaire entre son existance physique et son existence morale. Une femme qui auroit toutes les passions d'un homme, est réellement un homme impossible. Aussi le vaste champ de l'Histoire, qui n'est remplique d'objects vigoureusement passionnés est fermé pour quiconque n'y sauroit porter tous les caractères de vigueur" (*Le Triumvirate des Arts ou Dialogue entre un Peintre, un Musicien & un Poète* 1783: 27).

38 A critical point of Jones's conception of sexuality is his notion of the "deuterophallic" stage of development in which each of the two sexes is led to identify with the opposite sex to escape the threat of genital mutilation that originated in the same-sex parent. Accounts of the debate over female sexuality are intersting for the various and contradictory ways they pose the relationship among the primary players – Freud, Jones, Horney, Klein, Deutsch, Abraham. Although Rivière's essay is related to this debate, she was not a key figure in it. Her invoking of Deutsch and Jones, however, suggests that she positioned herself on the side of the debate that both Montrelay and Mitchell have labeled as essentialist or naturalist. Her essay, however, can be read through Lacan to imply that womanliness is both a biological given and a cultural construction. For further discussion of the debate over female sexuality, see Heath (1986: 44–8); Irigaray (1985b: 34–67); Montrelay (1977: 57–8); Mitchell and Rose (1985: 1–26, 86–98, 99–122).

39   This point is supported by a contemporaneous medical discourse stemming from Tissot's treatise *L'Onanisme. Dissertation sur les maladies produites par la Masturbation* (which in a tenth and considerably augmented edition was published in 1775). There Tissot associates with masturbation both the myth of the hermaphrodite and the tribade. The three are connected through abuse of the clitoris, of which tribade is one example. Most significant for my point is Tissot's discussion of women with excessively large clitorises, which could be an accident of birth or the result of their self-pollution. These women with a "half resemblance" to men he sees as the origin of the chimerical hermaphrodite, and calls them "*ces femmes imparfaites qui se sont emparées des fonctions viriles*" (Tissot, 1775: 52). He notes that one often sees "*femmes aimer des filles*" with as much ardor and as jealously as the most passionate man (Ibid.). He also cites the debauchery of Roman women as an example of this practice. One of the earliest pamphlets decrying Marie-Antoinette's tribadism (*Porte-Feuille d'un Talon Rouge* 178*: 23) will associate this practice with Roman women and will, like Tissot, cite Juvenal's satires. For a discussion of how the tribade was constructed in eighteenth-century France, see Bonnet (1981: 69–165).

40   Commentators (notably in the *Mémoires secrets* and *Correspondance Littéraire*) suggest that salon-goers found it a breach of *bienséance* to show publicly an image of the queen dressed in a garb reserved for private occasions within the palace. There is an interesting eliding of the difference between an image and the real person here.

41   A notable example is the self-portrait now in Fort Worth at the Kimball Museum.

42   That such dress did come to be associated with both Marie-Antoinette and Madame Lebrun is suggested by the events of the Diamond Necklace affair, one of the most notorious scandals associated with the queen. The lawyer for the young woman duped into impersonating Marie-Antoinette claimed that his client had no idea the costume she was wearing, a robe "*en gaule*", was identical to the one worn by the queen in a recent portrait by Lebrun. Maza has argued that one can read in the legal briefs the theme of the dangerous interchangeability of female identities (Maza, 1991: 78).

43   It is noteworthy that the *Mémoires secrets* suggest that the king forbade Marie-Antoinette from visiting Lebrun and Lebrun from coming to court without being summoned (Hautecoeur n.d.: 67).

44   "Si le trone embelli t'offre un digne modèle / Que des traits enchanteurs sont bientôt reconnus! / A l'orgueil d'Alexandre il fallait un Apelle. / C'est le Brun qu'il faut à Venus" (Miramond 1783: 3).

45   Or perhaps doubly rewritten, for the author Miramond also plays on the association of the name Lebrun – recalling the earlier court painter, Charles Le Brun, who worked for that other Alexander, Louis XIV.

46   Rivière, however, does give an example of another case that might help to overcome the issue of temporality in the masquerade. She notes that a "clever woman," a "university lecturer in an abstruse subject," chose to wear particularly feminine clothes when she lectured to her colleagues (rather than to her students). This example mentioned briefly by Rivière presents the case where the woman casts herself, at least in part, as Woman during the intellectual performance that says she is not a woman. Yet for other reasons this example would not be an appropriate analague for the case of Lebrun. Rivière also explains how this woman behaved inappropriately during these lectures: "she becomes flippant and joking, so much so that it has caused comment and rebuke." Rivière concludes that the woman has to treat the situation of displaying her masculinity as a game, as something not real, as a joke. Lebrun, I will argue, does not undercut her own self-presentation in this portrait.

47   Perhaps it is not the self-portrait, *per se*, but a whole mode of painting (a mode we know as rococo) that Pollock and Parker find "unconvincing." Do prejudices against rococo artifice, artifice gendered as "feminine," run so deep as to remain unacknowledged and at work in feminist writing? This is not to suggest that what has been gendered as feminine necessarily has anything to do with real women, only to remark on the deep suspicion of artifice that seems unexamined in much art-historical writing, including some that is sensitive to other sorts of preconceptions and constructions.

48   See, for example, the gestures for *rationes profert* and *demonstre non habere* in Bulwer's *Chirologia:*

or the Natural Language of the Hand and Chironomia: Or the Art of Manual Rhetoric (1644). Lebrun's gesture could be an example of either of these, as could the gestures made by the other artists in the examples cited above.

49 My thanks to Professor Bernadette Fort for bringing this configuration to my attention.

50 Comments by Professor Ann Bermingham suggested this line of reasoning.

51 I thank Professor Paula Radisich for suggesting to me the importance of her presentation as Rubens's wife and refer the reader to her excellent essay on Lebrun's self-portrait of 1787 (Radisich 1992). For a suggestive discussion of the relation between the lover and the beloved in terms of Titian's portraits and portrayals, see Pardo (1992: 1–5).

52 "Son grand effet réside dans les deux différentes lumières que donnent le simple jour et la lueur du soleil, ainsi les clairs sont au soleil; et ce qu'il me faut appeler les ombres, faute d'un autre mot, est le jour" (Vigée-Lebrun 1986: I, 75).

53 Other aspects of the compositional dynamics seem parallel. Rubens plays the shortened virtual line on the right side of the figure (from the downturned hat to the pointed elbow) against the extended one on the left (from the upturned hat and the drooping sleeve). Lebrun performs a similar visual maneuver, but in reverse. Now the upturned brim and the extended arm and shawl produce a long slow curve on the figure's right, where the turned-down feather and bent arm and brushes give a faster visual movement to the left.

54 "Je ne crois pas qu'aucune femme ait encore porté à un degré aussi éminent ce ton de couleur séduisant et vrai qui ne seroit pas défavoré de l'immortel *Rubens*. La *Paix ramenant l'Abondance* est un chef-d'oeuvre" (*Fréron* 1783: 259–60).

55 "Mais laissez-moi considérer les tableaux d'Histoire. Ce genre, qui n'appartient qu'au Génie créateur, pour lequel il faut que l'Artiste soit pénétré de ce feu du ciel qu'au ravi Prométhée, ce grand genre se ressuscite chez vous" (*La Morte* 1783: 8).

Bibliography

Apelle au Sallon (1783) Collection Deloynes, 288.

Bachaumont, Louis Petit de (1780–9) *Mémoires secrets pour servir à l'histoire de la république des lettres en France depuis MDCCLXII jusqu'à nos jours ou journal d'un observateur*, 36 vols., London: J. Adamson.

Baillio, Joseph (1982) *Elisabeth Louise Vigée-Lebrun*, Forth Worth, TX: Kimball Museum.

Bonnet, Marie–Jo (1981) *Un choix sans équivoque*, Paris: Editions Denoël.

Burns, E. Jane (1993) *Body Talk: When Women Speak in Old French Literature*, Philadelphia: University of Pennsylvania Press.

Butler, Judith (1990) *Gender Trouble*, New York: Routledge.

Castle, Terry (1991) "Marie Antoinette obsession," paper given at the Clark Library, Los Angeles, April.

Chadwick, Whitney (1990) *Art, Women, and Society*, London: Thames & Hudson.

Changez-moi cette tête ou Lustucru au Sallon – Dialogue entre le duc de Marlborough, un marquis françois et Lustucru (1783) Collection Deloynes, 289.

Cixous, Hélène (1983) "The laugh of the Medusa," in *The Signs Reader*, trans. Keith Cohen and Paula Cohen, Chicago: University of Chicago Press.

Clements, Candace (1992) "The Academy and the Other: les graces and le genre galant," *Eighteenth-Century Studies*, 25: 469–94.

La Critique est aisée, mais l'art est difficile (1783) Collection Deloynes, 287.

Crow, Thomas (1985) *Painters and Public Life in Eighteenth-Century France*, New Haven, CT: Yale University Press.

Derrida, J. (1976) *Of Grammatology*, trans. and intro. G. Spivak, Baltimore, MD: Johns Hopkins University Press.

—— (1987) *The Archaeology of the Frivolous*, trans. and intro. J. Leavey, Lincoln. NB: University of Nebraska Press.

DuBos, Jean–Baptiste, Abbé (1740) *Réflexions critiques sur la Poésie et sur la peinture*, Paris: Chez Pierre-Jean Mariette.

"Exposition des peintures, sculptures, dessins & gravures de MM. de l'Académie Royale, en 1783" (1783) *Mercure de France* September 20: 122–33.

"Exposition des peintures, sculptures et gravures" (1783) *Journal encyclopédique*. Collection Deloynes, 1343.

Fort, Bernadette (1989) "Voice of the public: carnivalization of salon art in pre-Revolutionary France," *Eighteenth-Century Studies* 22: 368–94.

Fréron, Elie Catherine (1783) "Observations sur les ouvrages de peinture et sculpture, exposés au Salon du Louvre, le 25 août 1783," in *L'Année littéraire*, Paris: Chez Mériot, Vol. XVI, pp. 217–67.

Freud, Sigmund (1965) "Femininity," in *New Introductory Lectures on Psychoanalysis*, ed. and trans. J. Strachey, New York: W. W. Norton.

Hautecoeur, L. (n.d.) *Madame Vigée-Lebrun*, Paris: Henri Laurens.

Heath, Stephen (1986) "Joan Riviere and the masquerade," in V. Burgin, J. Donald, and C. Kaplan (eds.) *Formations of Fantasy*, London: Methuen.

Hunt, Lynn (1984) *Politics, Culture, and Class in the French Revolution*, Berkeley, CA: University of California Press.

—— (1991) "The many bodies of Marie-Antoinette," in L. Hunt (ed.) *Eroticism and the Body Politic*, Baltimore, MD: Johns Hopkins University Press.

L'Impartialité au Sallon, dédiée à messieurs les critiques présens et à venir (1783) Collection Deloynes, 303.

Irigaray, Luce (1985a) *Speculum of the Other Woman*, trans. Gillian Gill, Ithaca, NY: Cornell University Press.

—— (1985b) *This Sex Which Is Not One*, trans. Catherine Porter and Carolyn Burke, Ithaca, NY: Cornell University Press.

Landes, Joan (1988) *Women in the Public Sphere*, Ithaca, NY: Cornell University Press.

Laqueur, Thomas (1990) *Making Sex*, Cambridge, MA: Harvard University Press.

Lauretis, Teresa de (1984) *Alice Doesn't*, Bloomington, IN: Indiana University Press.

Le Doeuff, Michèle (1987) "Women and philosophy," in T. Moi (ed.) *French Feminist Thought*, London: Blackwell.

Lichtenstein, Jacqueline, (1987) "Making up representation: the risks of femininity," *Representations* 20: 77–86.

Loterie pittoresque pour le Salon de 1783 (1783) Collection Deloynes, 291.

Marlborough au Sallon du Louvre; première édition contenant discours préliminaire, chansons, anecdotes, querelles, avis, critiques, lettre à Mlle Julie, changement de têtes, etc., etc., etc. ouvrage enrichi de figures en taille douce (1783) Collection Deloynes, 301.

Maza, Sarah (1991) "The diamond necklace affair: the case of the missing queen," in L. Hunt (ed.) *Eroticism and the Body Politic*, Baltimore, MD: Johns Hopkins University Press.

Messieurs, Ami de Tout le Monde (1783) Collection Deloynes, 295.

Miramond, M. de (1783) *Vers à Madame Le Brun de L'Académie Royale de Peinture sur les principaux ouvrages dont elle a décoré le Sallon de cette année*. Collection Deloynes, 308.

Mitchell, Juliet and Rose, Jacqueline (eds.) (1985) *Feminine Sexuality, Jacques Lacan and the école freudienne*, New York: W. W. Norton.

Momus au Sallon-Comédie-Critique en verse et en vaudeville suivie de notes critiques (1783) Collection Deloynes, 292.

Montaiglon, Anatole de (ed.) (1889) *Procès Verbaux de l'Académie Royale de Peinture et de Sculpture*, 11 vols, Paris: Charaway Frères.

Montrelay, Michèle (1977) *L'ombre et le nom. Sur la Féminité*, Paris: Editions de Minuit.

La Morte de trois mille ans au salon de 1783 (1783) Collection Deloynes, 286.

Nochlin, Linda (1971) "Why have there been no great women artists?," in V. Gornick and B. Moran (eds.) *Women in Sexist Society: Studies in Power and Powerlessness*, New York: New American Library.

Nussbaum, Felicity A. (1989) *The Autobiographical Subject. Gender and Ideology in Eighteenth-Century England*, Baltimore, MD: Johns Hopkins University Press.

Pardo, Mary (1992) "Artifice as seduction: iconological frames for Titian's *Urbino Venus*," in

James G. Turner (ed.) *Sexuality and Gender in Early Modern Europe: Institutions, Texts, Images*, Cambridge: Cambridge University Press.

Parker, R. and Pollock, G. (1981) *Old Mistresses*, New York: Pantheon.

Passez, A. M. (1971) *Adelaide Labille-Guiard*, Paris: Arts et Métiers Graphiques.

Pateman, Carole (1988) *The Sexual Contract*, Stanford, CA: Stanford University Press.

Paulson, Ronald (1975) *Emblem and Expression. Meaning in English Art of the Eighteenth Century*, Cambridge, MA: Harvard University Press.

Les Peintres volants ou Dialogue entre un françois et un anglois, sur les Tableaux exposés au Sallon du Louvre en 1783 (1783) Collection Deloynes, 297.

Porte-Feuille d'un Talon Rouge (178*) Paris.

Radisich, Paula Rea (1992) "Qui peut définer les femmes? Vigée-Lebrun's portraits of an artist," *Eighteenth-Century Studies* 25: 441–68.

Réponse à toutes les critiques sur les Tableaux du Sallon de 1783 par un frère de la Charité (1783) Collection Deloynes, 307.

Rivière, Joan (1986) "Womanliness as masquerade," in V. Burgin, J. Donald, and C. Kaplan (eds.) *Formations of Fantasy*, London: Methuen.

Rousseau, J. J. (1948) *Lettre à M. D'Alembert sur les spectacles* Geneva: Librairie Droz.

—— (1964) *Discourse on the Origins and Foundations of Inequality*, in *The First and Second Discourses* ed. Roger D. Masters, trans. Judith R. Masters and Roger D. Masters, New York: S. Martin's Press.

—— (1966) *Emile ou de l'education*, Paris: Garnier-Flammarion.

Le Sallon à l'encan. Rêve pittoresque, mêlé de Vaudevilles (1783) Collection Deloynes, 285.

Sans Quartier au Sallon avec un précis de la vie de Sans-Souci, élève de M. Raphael, des Porcherons. Histoire très véritable (1783) Collection Deloynes, 296.

Schiebinger, Londa (1989) *The Mind Has No Sex?*, Cambridge, MA: Harvard University Press.

Sheriff, Mary D. (1990) *J. H. Fragonard: Art and Eroticism* Chicago: University of Chicago Press.

Stanton, Domna (1987) "Autogynography: is the subject different?," in D. Stanton (ed.) *The Female Autograph*, Chicago: University of Chicago Press.

"Suite de la lettre sur le Salon" (1783) *Journal de Paris* 266: 1097–8.

Tissot, J. (1775) *L'Onanisme. Dissertation sur les maladies produites par la masturbation*, Toulouse: Laporte.

Tourneux, M. (ed.) (1880) *Correspondance littéraire, philosophique et critique par Grimm, Diderot, Raynal, Meister, etc.*, Paris: Garnier Frères.

Le Triumvirat des Arts ou Dialogue entre un Peintre, un Musicien & un Poète sur les Tableaux exposés au Louvre, année 1783, pour servir de continuation au Coup de Patte & à la Patte de velours (1783) Collection Deloynes, 305.

Le Véridique au Sallon (1783) Collection Deloynes, 298.

Vigée-Lebrun, Elisabeth (1986 [1827]) *Souvenirs* Paris: des femmes.

25
Elegant females and gentlemen connoisseurs
The commerce in culture and self-image in eighteenth-century England

Ann Bermingham

Education in the visual arts in the late eighteenth century generally took two forms. Women were educated in the skills of drawing and painting while men were educated in the skills of judging drawing and painting. This gender difference was institution-alized in the form of the teaching of "accomplishments" to young women and taking young men on a Grand Tour of Italy. Implicit in these pedagogical approaches was the idea that women learn by doing whereas men learn by looking. With this very rough distinction in mind I want to investigate the place of the accomplished woman and the gentleman connoisseur relative to each other at the end of the eighteenth century. I chose this historical period for two reasons: first because it is at this time that accomplishments become important social attributes for young women to possess, and second because at this time the connoisseur emerges as a figure of power and import-ance in the art world. Occupying roughly the same historical moment, social status, and cultural ground the accomplished woman and the connoisseur appear as comp-lementary rather than identical subjectivities. This chapter, then, is an attempt to map the supplementary nature of their symmetries and differences.

> The . . . two Miss Beauforts were just such young ladies as may be met with, in at least one family out of three, throughout the kingdom; they had tolerable complexions, shewy figures, an upright decided carriage, & an assured Look; – they were very accomplished & very Ignorant, their time being divided be-tween such pursuits as might attract admiration, & those Labours & Expedients of dexterous Ingenuity, by which they could dress in a stile much beyond what they ought to have afforded; they were some of the first in every change of fashion – & the object of all, was to captivate some Man of much better fortune than their own. . . . [Thus] with the hire of a Harp for one, & the purchase of some Drawing paper for the other & all the finery they could already command, they meant to be very economical, very elegant & very secluded; with the hope on Miss Beaufort's side, of praise & celebrity from all

who walked within the sound of her instrument, & on Miss Letitia's of curiosity & rapture in all who came near her while she sketched – and to Both, the consolation of meaning to be the most stylish Girls in the Place.[1]

(Austen 1982b: 421)

If the Miss Beauforts' plans to dazzle the seaside resort of Sanditon are any indication, music and art played rather prominent roles in a young lady's repertoire of elegant accomplishments. As the necessary accoutrements of style, harps and drawing paper were caught up in a discourse of fashion and femininity ordered by an economy of commodification and consumerism that constituted the bourgeois marriage market. Implied in this passage from *Sanditon* is the understanding that women in marketing themselves had to market a particular idea of culture as well. One could go further and say that in her description of the Miss Beauforts Austen suggests a virtual collapse of their consumption of culture – commodified in the form of rented musical instruments and commercial art supplies – into their commodification of themselves *as* culture. Her mapping of this culture on to the "shewy figures" of the Miss Beauforts becomes even more explicit in her description of their rooms at Sanditon. Their apartments commanded a view of the favorite lounge of all the visitors to the spa. Consequently, Austen writes:

> there c'd not have been a more favourable spot for the seclusions of the Miss Beauforts. And accordingly, long before they had suited themselves with an Instrument, or with Drawing paper, they had, by the frequency of their appearance at the low Windows upstairs, in order to close the blinds, or open the Blinds, to arrange a flower pot on the Balcony, or look at nothing through a Telescope, attracted many an eye upwards, & made many a Gazer gaze again.

(Austen 1982b: 422)

In a supplementary move, the Miss Beauforts replace art-making with an elaborate pantomime of elegant feminine poses. Their image repertoire, whether it be playing harps or looking through telescopes, conforms to those found in fashion magazines of the day (Plates 25.1 and 25.2).[2] Thus they enact a femininity already constructed by the period's commercialization of fashion. By locating art on their own eroticized, aestheticized, and marketable bodies, the Miss Beauforts sexualize, feminize, and commodify it.

The growing importance of accomplishments in the education of young women in the later eighteenth and the early nineteenth centuries has to do, in part, with changes in the customs of display associated with the marriage market. The older practice of taking young, unmarried women to spa towns like Sanditon or Bath where, in the public, processional spaces of pump rooms and assemblies, circuses and crescents, they could be looked over by eligible bachelors, was falling out of favor. In these anonymous spaces it was difficult to know whom one was meeting and whether or not they were respectable. Towns like London and Bath were perceived as sites for debauchery and for fortune-hunting; they were not therefore entirely proper places for young people to get acquainted (Nenedich 1991). (Think, for instance, of James and Catherine Morland's close call with the Thorpes at Bath in *Northanger Abbey*.) This distrust of the town coupled with the growing taste for private rather than public entertainment meant that unmarried women were increasingly intended to be seen within their domestic surroundings.[3] The accomplishment is directly tied to this new construction of the domestic space as the space of authentic subjectivity. In this sense, accomplishments should not simply be understood as ways for women with increasingly too much time on their hands to fill idle hours, but as ways for women to perform their subjectivity through certain allotted modes of artistic expression. Austen's disapproval of the Miss Beauforts betrays a discomfort with the ambiguous nature of this performance, the possibility that it might be just empty show. In Austen's account the two sisters displace true accomplishments in the "elegant" and "secluded" spaces in which they were intended to be performed with their flashy dresses and eye-catching public pantomimes.

As Austen suggests, their "femininity" is neither essential nor eternal. Animated by fashion and consumerism it is an ever-changing bricolage of images, positions, roles, and sites. To borrow Michel de Certeau's military analogy we might describe it as a tactic, for unlike a strategy it is mobilized by the absence of a proper locus of power (de Certeau 1984: 29–42). De Certeau describes the tactic as the "art of the weak" for its reactive nature derives from an inability to view the whole as a distinct objectifiable space. Thus, unlike the totalizing gaze of the Sanditon gazers, the "assured looks" of the Miss Beauforts "look at nothing at all." Deprived of a broad overview they occupy themselves with the moment-to-moment positioning of an aestheticized feminine self within the scopic regime of the spa loungers. Their mode of looking is ultimately directed back to their own self-consciously elaborated, narcissistic play of feminine masquerade. Moreover, the object of their tactical deployment of this femininity and culture is an unabashedly economic one, "to captivate some Man of much better fortune than their own." Like objects in a shop window – in this case false, or maybe we should even say faux (!), luxury objects – they invite the Sanditon gazers to buy. Thus like their stylish dresses and pretensions to music and art their posing at the window is a lure, a not so subliminal form of advertising.

An important role of accomplishments was to mitigate this brazen solicitation and vulgar gazing, and in doing so to mask women's commodity status. Accomplishments provided an occasion for women to display themselves while denying that this was in fact what was happening. Men, in turn, could look while seeming to listen, or size up a woman while appearing to be judging a drawing. Accomplishments were intended to arouse masculine desire, yet desire could now be masked and displaced as a detached aesthetic judgment. Needless to say the feminine subjectivity displayed by accomplishments was no more authentic than the Miss Beauforts' posings, it was just that its "reality effect" now depended less on notions of publicity and consumption and more on ideas of interiority and private self-expression. Accomplishments therefore did not do away with femininity as a lure, they merely denied it, and consequently they did nothing to undermine femininity's suspect status as a commercial and fabricated mode of subjectivity, they merely suppressed it. As a result the accomplished woman was a deeply ambiguous figure in eighteenth- and nineteenth-century culture for she not only continued to problematize ideas of individuality and subjectivity but she did so now within the domestic space of the home – that is, within the space reserved for the exercise of privacy and individual authenticity.

In order to describe the commodification and consumption of femininity through accomplishments, I want to make some use of psychoanalytical notions of "the gaze." That is what Freud and Lacan have described as the mode of viewing which derives pleasure from taking women as objects and subjecting them to a voyeuristic or fetishistic look[4] (Freud 1962: 22–6; Lacan 1977b: 67–119). Like the Miss Beauforts, the accomplished woman was the object of this mode of looking. My point therefore in introducing such a reading into the discussion is to describe an economy of masculine desire. In theorizing this gaze as a mode of consumption and power, I want to connect its psycho/sexual operations to those of the aesthetic and political sphere, as encoded in the activity of connoisseurship. I should make clear that I am not attempting an historical account of actual incidents of practice – documentary accounts of various individuals' drawing, music-making, and connoisseurship – but attempting to describe the social meaning of such activities. Part of my argument will be that it was the psycho/sexual ambiguities produced by situating the commodification and consumption of culture within the feminized Other that the eighteenth century found necessary both to enact, in the form of feminine accomplishments, and to transcend, in the form of masculine connoisseurship. It is important to understand that discursive bi-polarities such as normal and pathological, or masculine and feminine, are in practice always radically unstable. While a culture's construction of gender difference is always in crisis it is always and everywhere attempting to stabilize itself and to reinstate and reinscribe itself through ideological constructions and social and material practice. What I will be describing therefore is not an actual "feminization" of aesthetic culture, one that figures like the Miss Beauforts threaten to perform, but instead a tension between competing masculine and feminine engenderings of culture.

Cultural contestation in the eighteenth century *was* highly sexualized, and charges of effeminacy or female prostitution were commonly used to discredit certain cultural forms as deviant in order to validate others as proper – that is to say, as "manly" and thus worthy of true Englishmen.[5] These negative constructions of feminine subjectivity established all that this high culture was not, that is, all that it needed to oppose in order to constitute itself. Women were positioned in relation to high art culture – that is to say in, relation to all the cultural sites and practices from which they were excluded by virtue of their sex – by being positioned in relation to certain specific constructions of masculine subjectivity: the artist, the critic, the artisan, the connoisseur, to name but a few.[6] Foucault has reflected on the fact that it is the transgressive act that establishes the norm, not the other way around (Foucault 1977: 34–5). Finally then I would like to suggest that what was/is always is already at stake in the construction of feminine subjectivity as high culture's transgressive Other is not femininity but high culture. Moreover, in so far as that cultural ideal can be said to be non-feminine, what is ultimately at stake in this construction is all that can be understood to be masculine.

I Positioning the gaze

The importance of accomplishments in the construction of femininity and the positioning of women within high culture is neatly encapsulated in a portrait by George Romney of *Caroline, Viscountess Clifden and Lady Elizabeth Spencer* from the Huntington

Art Gallery in San Marino (Plate 25.3). It depicts Lady Caroline sketching her sister who is seated before her in profile playing a harp. The painting was begun in 1786 four years before Lady Elizabeth married John Spencer, son of Lord Charles Spencer, in 1790 and it was finished in 1791 one year before Lady Caroline married the Viscount Clifden. It was commissioned by the women's father, the fourth duke of Marlborough, and although it is a large canvas, over 6 feet in width, it appears to have been intended as a private image for it was not exhibited to the public until the late nineteenth century. I would like to read within the private space of the portrait and the domestic space it represents, three different subject positions: that of the accomplished woman, the artist, and the father. These positions represent three distinct exercises of the gaze all of which construct femininity as a matter of continual differentiation and deferral.

Lady Caroline is shown in a dark mulberry dress covered by a muslin apron. Her relative informality contrasts with her sister's powdered hair and white silk dress. Lady Elizabeth's greater elegance of dress is not a characterological sign intended to reflect personality differences – formality as opposed to casualness or even a younger sister's sartorial competitiveness. Rather her powdered hair like Lady Caroline's protective apron is a sign that she has been made the object of her older sister's artistic labors. Lady Caroline turns from copying an antique-looking statue of a nymph to sketching her sister from life. In academic practice drawing from the antique preceded drawing from life. Thus having copied the statue Lady Caroline is now prepared to copy her sister. Lady Elizabeth in turn becomes a version of the nymph; she is self-consciously posed as a kind of living statue for her sister to copy. The marble nymph displays her femininity as an essential sexual difference which she attempts to modestly conceal. By contrast the image of Lady Elizabeth suggests that her femininity consists in assuming certain roles: the musical sister, the accomplished woman; the elegant woman, the object of art. Lady Elizabeth's femininity does not consist of an essential sexual difference, but exists as a kind of performative subjectivity. Femininity is constructed by being set within the social order in a certain way, and within a particular relationship to high art. Whereas classical art – in the form of the statue – deals in essences, the art of accomplishments, like the art of femininity, deals in appearances. Like femininity it demands to be read as a surface of socially signifying signs: harp; dress; hair-style; deportment; etc.

The sisters' accomplishments must also be seen as distinct from Romney's art and as subsumed by it. Thus Lady Caroline's gaze gives way to the artist's, and her amateur sketching takes its secondary place within the context of the paid professional's oil painting. The portrait thus foregrounds Romney's skill that defines the sisters as amateurs, and makes their artistry both inferior and coextensive with their femininity. The portrait is as much about the difference between their genteel pastimes and his professional vocation as it is about the sisters themselves. For finally their meaning as accomplished women receives definition only in contrast to the professionalism of the male artist. It is important to note here that the accomplished woman was understood to be "artistic" but not an artist. She was not an artist because she was neither original nor a paid professional. Unlike the artist who was a creator and producer of culture, she was a consumer and reproducer of culture. The word "artistic" inscribes art on to the body and into the personality of the subject who makes art. "Artistic types" are works of art themselves, embodying art without necessarily mastering it. Hence it is not surprising that when engraved in the late nineteenth-century the portrait was said to depict Lady Caroline and Lady Elizabeth as "muses" of painting and music. As muses the women represent an abstract potential that may be brought into consciousness and into culture only through the work of an other, the artistry of a real artist.

Connoting "acquisition" the very word accomplishment suggests its consumerist character. The accomplished woman was accomplished because she had managed to purchase the artistic skill and sometimes the style of others through manuals and lessons, and not because she herself was creative. Her social standing and purchasing power thus excluded her from the economic necessity that drove professional artists to succeed. Depending, of course, on how one values this professional artistic activity, the sisters' amateurism becomes either a demonstration of their inferiority as cultural producers and/or their conspicuous leisure and freedom from the necessity to produce. Thus it cuts both ways, against their gender but in favor of their class. The word accomplishment also means "to bring to completion or perfection," and "to finish off." In a sense this was the role of the accomplished woman, to bring to perfection the artistry of others rather than to initiate new artistic forms, and in so doing to bring herself to the point of aesthetic completion. All art-making therefore is turned inwards upon this project of self-fashioning, onto the ever ongoing project of completing or even "finishing off" femininity. What Romney's portrait represents as a essential lack of essence is encoded within the accomplishment as a lack of originality and completion. The accomplished woman is thus positioned as a void that must be continually filled and objectified by art.

The portrait situates this feminine lack within the gaze of the father, the fourth duke of Marlborough, who as the patron becomes the portrait's primary beholder for it is his will and desire that Romney must satisfy. In addition to being a man of great wealth and power, the duke was also a famous collector of old master paintings. As a collector he is the perfect judge of Romney's artistry and his daughters' aestheticized femininity. Under his gaze Romney becomes a paid employee, a laborer, while his daughters become signs of their father's power and status. As Richard Leppert has noted, the accomplished woman was an object of conspicuous consumption; that is, the means whereby a family announced its economic hegemony (Leppert 1995). Thus not only is the Romney portrait an aesthetic object in the duke's collection but his accomplished daughters / muses are similarly aestheticized and objectified. Yet something more seems at work here. It is important to remember that the portrait was started when both women were still single, and that by the time it was finished one daughter was married and the other was nearly so. The portrait therefore commemorates the liminal moment between maidenhood and marriage. The sisters' display of accomplishments signals their desirability and availability and points to the time when each will be given by her father to another man – that is to say, to the moment when they will be exchanged between men. The portrait thus reflects back again upon the power of the father not only his economic status but his power to determine his daughters' worth, their status, their meaning, and their futures.

As spectators we are invited to inhabit all these viewing positions. We may imaginatively project ourselves into the roles of the sisters while also, almost simultaneously, identifying with the artist's and the father's points of view. We derive visual pleasure from the mobility of our vantage points, objectifying at one moment and narcissistically identifying at another. In addition, we are also invited to share a fourth point of view: that of the desiring subject who delights in Lady Caroline and Lady Elizabeth's display of femininity, and in the painting as the medium of this display. In the process of discriminating between each woman's appearance and her performance of her subjectivity, we also may assess and wonder at Romney's skill in sparking our interest and desire through paint. In this case, we are positioned before the painting as consumers and connoisseurs of art and feminine beauty. This mode of viewing valorizes the women as aesthetic objects while subjecting them to aesthetic judgment. Such a gaze is fetishistic in that it displaces fear of loss on to the aestheticized bodies of the women and voyeuristic in that it subjects those bodies to objectification and visual control. The sisters' essential lack – lack of essence, lack of creativity, lack of power – can be read in psychoanalytical terms as signifying castration and thus as inducing scopic mechanisms of displacement and control to circumvent the threat they represent. Their construction as lack receives definition only when they are placed in a differential relationship to certain constructions of masculinity – the artist, the father, the implied male beholder. Moreover, as accomplished women they must take their place alongside other competing constructions of femininity – the sister, the daughter, the mother, the beloved – which may or may not be compatible. It is this differential movement of feminine subjectivity that I would like to explore now in greater detail.

II   The accomplished woman

In response to the good-natured Mr. Bingley's remark that all young ladies are accomplished for "they all paint tables, cover screens and net purses," his more discriminating friend Mr. Darcy claimed to know only "half a dozen" women who "are really accomplished" (Austen 1982a: 39). Hastening to agree with him, the snobbish Miss Bingley added:

> "no one can be really esteemed accomplished, who does not greatly surpass what is usually met with. A woman must have a thorough knowledge of music, singing, drawing, dancing and the modern languages, to deserve the word; and besides all this, she must possess a certain something in her air and manner of walking, the tone of her voice, her address, and expressions, or the word will be but half deserved."
>
> "All this she must possess," added Darcy, "and to all this she must yet add something more substantial, in the improvement of her mind by extensive reading."
>
> (Austen 1982a: 39)

Elizabeth Bennet's response to all this formidable fastidiousness was to remark to Darcy, "I am no longer surprised at your knowing *only* six accomplished women. I rather wonder now at your knowing *any*" (Austen 1982a: 39). As this passage from *Pride and Prejudice* suggests, the discourse surrounding accomplishments was largely a disciplinary one. Elizabeth's remark points to the very impossibility of any woman's meeting such unreasonable expectations. The point of such a discourse could only be to make a woman look and feel inadequate and this was, of course, the jealous Miss

Bingley's objective. As a mytheme of feminine subjectivity, the accomplished woman – or as Darcy would have it, "the really accomplished" woman – was used to discipline women into a certain regime of femininity. Because it depended so much on Miss Bingley's "certain something," this ineffable "*je ne sais quoi*" made feminine accomplishment an ideal that could never be fully attained, critiqued, or transcended. Instead it operated like an ever present reproach, like a panoptic gaze trained upon the self, like a self-conscious standard of measure against which one could never quite measure up.

This internalization of the gaze through accomplishments was deeply problematic for it raised the possibility that identity arose only after the subject formed an image of itself by identifying with another's perception and expectations of it. In short, it threatened the notion of a stable subject and raised the specter of false consciousness. The self now could be seen to depend wholly on the representational systems of language and images for it could conceptualize itself only when it was mirrored back to itself from the position of another's desire. It was this possibility that the accomplished woman embodied in all its threatening ambiguity, an ambiguity moralized by Austen as the Miss Beauforts' vanity and characterized by Romney as femininity. Elizabeth Bennet's ironic response to Darcy signals her strength of character and it is this quality not her competency in music that Darcy by the end of the novel must come to recognize and embrace.

Austen's position with respect to accomplishments is quite interesting. Heroines like Elizabeth Bennet, Jane Fairfax, and Eleanor and Marianne Dashwood are truly accomplished, usually (with the exception of Eleanor) in keyboard music. Their accomplishments are not for empty show but are avenues of self-expression and, in times of heartache, comfort. They remain outside the marriage schemes that circulate throughout the novels, and when they are brought into the narratives as ways to further someone's cause – as in the case of the Miss Beauforts' drawing paper and harps, Mary Crawford's harp, Frank Churchill's purchase of a pianoforte for Jane Fairfax, or Emma's portrait of Harriet for Mr. Elton – they become sites of misunderstanding and of unpleasant, narcissistic self-promotion. As these examples suggest, accomplishments are intended to be largely private affairs rather than tools for social and erotic advancement. Austen's "truly accomplished" heroines are always virtuous and use their accomplishments for personal enrichment. Moreover, they are women of the gentry who are comfortable enough with their social standing to practice accomplishments unselfconsciously as the inevitable and "natural" expressions of their station. In a sense, this would fit with Austen's approach to her own writing which began as a pastime to amuse herself and her immediate family; an inconspicuous occupation that could be quietly slipped under the blotter on her writing table when visitors came calling. It would also fit with the purposely narrow gauge of her novels, those meticulous sketches on tiny bits of ivory that eschewed the historical and intercontinental sweep of Ann Radcliffe's gothics.

Austen's cautious and somewhat ambivalent attitude towards accomplishments suggests that the accomplished woman was in competition with other ideals of feminine subjectivity. The pursuit of accomplishments was subject to criticism by feminists, educational reformers, pietistic and Evangelical religious figures of the day. Their target was most often the numerous female boarding schools that sprang up at the end of the century. Originally these institutions taught English, arithmetic, needlework, bookkeeping, and natural history for a flat fee of about 40 to 200 guineas a year, and for about 10 to 50 guineas more a girl could be taught extras such as French, drawing, music, dancing, and writing (Miller 1982: 302–15). By the last decade of the century, these "extras" had become part of the regular curriculum supplanting more practical subjects like bookkeeping. Edward Francis Burney's satirical drawing of one such elegant establishment shows young women learning erect posture from a military man and with the aid of dumbbells, neck braces, and a tortuous traction device suspended from the ceiling (Plate 25.4). Other girls examine a fashion doll from Paris, practice fainting gracefully, and are taught the arts of dance, sculpture, painting, acting, and music from a variety of affected and flirtatious masters. Outside the window a young woman elopes beneath a sign that announces "Man Traps Set Here."[7] The argument against this "fashionable education" was that it was morally and intellectually corrupting. In her *Vindication of the Rights of Women*, Mary Wollstonecraft made the case most forcefully.

> Novels, music, poetry, and gallantry, all tend to make women the creatures of sensation, and their character is thus formed in the mould of folly during the time they are acquiring accomplishments, the only improvement they are excited, by their station in society, to acquire. This overstretched sensibility naturally relaxes the other powers of the mind, and prevents intellect from attaining that sovereignty which it ought to attain to render a rational creature useful to others, and content with its own station; for the exercise of the understanding, as life advances, is the only method pointed out by nature to calm the passions.
>
> (Wollstonecraft 1978: 152)

As Wollstonecraft's remarks about "station" suggest, accomplishments were felt to be particularly dangerous to lower-class women. Hannah More remarked that such women "got just enough [education] to laugh at their fond parents' rustic manners and vulgar language, and just enough taste to despise every girl who was not as vainly dressed as themselves" (Miller 1982: 310). Austen's observation that the Miss Beauforts "dressed in a stile much beyond what they *ought* to have afforded" is in keeping with More's censor of lower-class women attempting to ape their betters through fashion and accomplishments. In addition, Austen's remark that the Miss Beauforts were "very accomplished & very Ignorant" conforms to a growing sentiment that accomplishments were barriers to real knowledge. While a fashionable education was intended to trap husbands, the "practical education" advocated by reformers like Hannah More and Maria Edgeworth was directed to keeping husbands contented (and faithful) after marriage.

The controversy spilled over into popular women's magazines. In the advice column of the *Lady's Monthly Museum* (1799) we find this assessment of a young woman who has devoted herself to "the science of music":

> Has she no more important duties to discharge than to tickle the idle ear, and to excite the unmeaning applause? Does she reflect that she was not made to shine in any artificial accomplishment, but to qualify herself to be a wife, a

mother, an agreeable companion, and a prudent domestic manager? Though the lover may compliment her on her skill in music, – will the ears of the husband listen to her performance with the same pleasure as to her conversation sweetened with sense and good temper? – Will he not blame the misapplication of the time in a wife, which, perhaps, he commended in the mistress? And will he not, justly, think that she is more desirous to throw out lures for the praise of others, than to be useful and amiable in his eye?

(*Lady's Monthly Museum* XVII, November 1799: 357)

As this makes clear, the woman's subjectivity depended on the man's position as either her lover or husband. Once the lover becomes the husband, the accomplished woman becomes the virtual antithesis of the wife, mother, agreeable companion and, of course, "the prudent domestic manager." And the accomplishment, which before marriage was intended to signal future connubial bliss, becomes after marriage a source of domestic irritation. The accomplished woman did not sit well with other feminine ideals under construction during the period. The danger of losing the husband she had worked so hard to gain was the fate that came from transforming herself into a fashionable commodity, an insubstantial object of commercially produced desire whose unhappy destiny it was to be consumed and then discarded.

Yet despite its high moral tone, this column appeared in a magazine that regularly carried a column entitled the "School of Art" which provided information on how to decorate fire-screens, tea-trays, card tables, and the like. In addition, the *Monthly* had columns devoted to the latest taste in music, charades, and plays suitable for amateur theatricals, as well as serialized romance novels like *The Two Monks*, *Edric of the Forest* and *The Maid of San Marino*, and fashion illustrations and advice on health and beauty. The message to women was mixed to say the least; the *Monthly*, like other women's magazines, was a site of competing and contesting constructions of feminine subjectivity and desirability. Undoubtedly one of the reasons for this mixed message was that accomplishments and the kind of genteel femininity they represented provided an avenue for social advancement. For, as the Miss Beauforts understood, the deployment of fashionable dress and accomplishments were important means, virtually the only means, women had to improve their station by marrying up. Thus the commodification of femininity suffered the same social ambivalences that accompanied the changes brought about by commercial capitalism and increased consumption. The very success of fashionable education in promoting upward mobility was seen as simultaneously a natural benefit of free enterprise and a threat to the stability of the social hierarchy. Hence it provoked old arguments against luxury and emulation, arguments that after 1793 took on a decidedly anti-Jacobin tone.

The moral argument against accomplishments and the practical economic results gained by their deployment must be read therefore within the context of a larger ongoing debate about the nature of the individual subject in a commercial culture. In a society governed by economic self-interest in which one was judged not by who one *was* but by how one *appeared*, a polite and sociable exterior had important economic advantages. As Lawrence Klein has noted, the "Commercial personality conceived under the sign of consumption rather than accumulation required such qualities as the desire for pleasure and comfort, a willingness to spend, playfulness, and ambitions to emulate and display. The latter were expressed in capacities and interests concerned with the 'ornamental' aspects of life, such as taste, style, fashion, and politeness" (Klein 1995). Acquiring social skills came from manuals with titles like *The New Academy of Complements; Or the Lover's Secretary* (1715, 4th edition) and *The Queens Closet Opened* (1658, 1710); these manuals coexisted with other self-help books devoted to more useful subjects such as *The Pleasant Art of Money Catching* (1737) or – the less pleasant – *Every man his Own Vermin Killer* (c. 1771). The joining of a discourse of politeness to one of economic self-interest has psychological consequences. J. G. A. Pocock has observed that in the eighteenth century, "social morality was becoming divorced from personal morality, and from the ego's confidence in its own integrity and reality" (Pocock 1975: 465). He notes, for instance, that Rousseau's social contract was based on the assumption that "the real world of economy and polity rested on a myriad fantasy worlds maintained by private egos; and he [Rousseau] deeply disturbed his contemporaries, less by telling them that they were greedy and selfish than by telling them that they were unreal" (Pocock 1975: 465–6). The anxiety surrounding the phantasmagoria of the commercial subject that so unsettled the moral and political discourses of the period, was often displaced on to women or the feminized Other – the aristocrat, the Frenchman, the fop – that is to say, mapped on to what was perceived to be an essential lack of authentic subjectivity. It is this that we find figured in the criticisms of the accomplished woman.

When the accomplished woman was imagined as an active agent, she was seen as a morally subversive and socially disruptive force; however, when the accomplished woman was perceived as a passive object of commodity exchange, as we find her portrayed by Romney, she was valued for her elegance and refinement. Nowhere is the irresolvable dilemma caused by her exchange-value more thoroughly evoked than in a pair of etchings by Maria Cosway published in 1800 in a book entitled *The Progress of Female Virtue and the Progress of Female Dissipation* (see Plates 8.5 and 8.6). In the first, a representation of virtue, a young woman is seated in profile before a window sketching the landscape beyond; on an easel behind her is a depiction of a woman bending over a cradle. The inscription reads: "While Nature's beauties her free lines pourtray, / She knows not that she's fairer far than they." The corresponding representation of vice shows a young woman playing a harp. Unlike the sketcher who is totally focused on her sketching, the musician turns from her music straining to catch a glimpse of herself in a mirror. The inscription from Pope reads: "Her own fair Image in the glass appears, / To that she bends, to that her eye she rears." While the sketcher is lovelier than her art, the musician like the Miss Beauforts is wholly caught up in the aesthetic effect that she, not her art, is producing. While the sketcher may be read as an attempt to redeem the accomplishment as something not incompatible with individual authenticity, the musician represents its subversive aspects as an occasion for feminine masquerade.

What Cosway opposes as feminine virtue and vice, or more specifically as modesty and vanity, are, in fact, the two positions women can maintain with regard to the look. Within the terms of her opposition, this gaze remains unchallenged by the sketcher who unconsciously capitulates to its scopophilia. The issue is less clear with the musician for, like the Miss Beauforts, she openly solicits the gaze thus raising the possibility of controlling it. Her narcissism is a way of looking: in looking at herself in the mirror she becomes in the words of John Berger, both "the surveyor and the surveyed" (Berger

1972: 46). Accomplishments here become the means whereby women either virtuously ignore the gaze or narcissistically invite and internalize it. The space of the gaze emerges as a neutral place, not unlike a market, in which commodities, or in this case competing femininities, display themselves. Yet this is precisely, I would argue, the ideology of the gaze – for the space in which women are displayed is not a neutral place but one circumscribed by high culture and charged with economic and erotic significance. What the prints represent as a moral opposition between two kinds of feminine subjectivities is, in fact, the moral ambiguity of the social, psychic, and economic space they inhabit.

The binary and exclusionary operations of sexual difference are evident in Cosway's etchings. In the print of virtue the modest sketcher is by nature lovelier than any art she could possibly produce, so that her art-making is eroticized as a lack, as something to contrast to the beholder's visual access to the plenitude of her natural beauty. Absorbed in drawing nature the sketcher's gaze becomes an occasion merely to reconfirm her status as the surveyed object. The print's inscription recalls Mary Ann Doane's observation that "when a woman looks, the verb 'looks' is generally intransitive (she *looks* beautiful)" (Doane 1987: 177).[8] As the unconscious object of the gaze she is the equivalent of the landscape she sketches, and her naturalness is reified again in the image of motherhood in the painting on the easel. Reproduction is the true source and goal of feminine creativity. The sketcher's lack of artistic skill – the inability to abstract herself from nature, the nature that *is* her, in order to render it – denotes women's inability to represent nature in any way other than in their own persons or through their own sexuality. Thus, like nature – the nature she embodies – her true role is not that of artist but that of art object.

In the second print the woman watches herself in the process of making art in order to form that process into a performance for the gaze. Unlike the sketcher, the musician does not represent nature but an artificial, self-consciously constructed image of femininity. The mirror produces her as a picture, one which situates her body among other objects. The mirror's production of the self-as-image proposes that subjectivity is a matter of constructing and manipulating appearances. Unlike the transparent window which leads the eye into the deep space of the landscape beyond, the mirror creates images that refuse to be read in depth, suggesting that all consciousness is a form of self-consciousness, a self-consciousness derived from seeing oneself as a surface, and as an aestheticized arrangement of surfaces. The musician's gaze is thus pathologized as a narcissistic over-identification with the image. Just as an aside, it is worth noting Lacan's observation that in men this self-conscious, self-reflexive gaze is the basis for philosophy for it is the means whereby, according to Freud, they form the ego, whereas when employed by women this gaze traditionally signals their vanity[9] (Lacan 1977a: 93–100, 101–24 and 585–645). The temptation is to see the musician's mirror-gazing as simply a static image of feminine vanity. Nevertheless, I would suggest that in addition to providing the occasion for a self-absorbed delight in her own appearance, the mirror also figures a dynamic, proleptic state of being, for it enables the harp player to rehearse and imaginatively anticipate the effect her appearance will have on others. Like the Miss Beauforts, Cosway's musician practices her music in anticipation of "praise & celebrity" in the future. What the mirror reflects is the self-objectifying movement of feminine desire; the musician's desire to appear beautiful to herself is ultimately directed to the desiring gaze of the beholder. Thus, even while subverting it, she, like the sketcher, exists ultimately to acknowledge its presence and power. In both prints, the operation of the gaze either validates a natural lack or pathologizes an unnatural narcissism. What Cosway represents as opposites are under patriarchy really interchangeable feminine subject positions. In neither their passive nor their active roles can women escape their commodification by the gaze, for in both cases their acts of looking immediately collapse back into eroticized representations of their impotent or impertinent object status.

The narcissistic woman is a very ambiguous figure. For the more a culture organizes itself as a visual culture, and poses sexual difference as an experience of looking or being looked at, the more problematic the tactical modes of looking employed by the Miss Beauforts and Cosway's musician become, and the more they have to be morally disavowed. What is striking about the Cosway prints is that by themselves, the visual images suggest that the sketcher and the musician could, in fact, be the same woman represented at different times, in different moods, employing her accomplishments to different ends. The text works to divide the images into representations of two different kinds of femininities – the good girl and the bad girl. Visually the images underscore the moral and psychological ambiguities inherent in the practice of accomplishments and their signification, while the texts repress this ambiguity through a kind of moral essentialism.

The idea that the two women might be read as one is suggested by Cosway's own talents as an artist and a musician. Throughout her life she alternated between art and music. Known as a great beauty – one who counted Thomas Jefferson among her many male admirers – Cosway had always wanted to be a nun. She ended her life living in a convent and working as headmistress at a girls' academy she founded at Lodi. As a young woman she had trained as an artist in Italy. Married to the miniaturist and art dealer Richard Cosway, she found her considerable artistic talents were a source of jealousy to him. In a letter written at the end of her life she recalled: "had Mr. C. permitted me to rank professionally I should have made a better painter but left to myself by degrees instead of improving I lost what I had brought from Italy of my early studies" (Walker 1986: 318–19). In 1790 she gave up exhibiting for six years to devote herself to her daughter and to promoting her husband's career. During that time she practiced and excelled at the harp, the harpsichord, and the organ, on which she performed at home and in polite company. After her daughter's death she separated from Cosway, and in 1801 went to live abroad. *The Progress of Female Virtue and the Progress of Female Dissipation* was finished just before her leaving England and represents her return to the visual arts. I mention this only by way of suggesting that as a story of an accomplished woman, Cosway's life testifies to the ambiguities, instabilities, and contradictions that the role inevitably produced for women.

As both an economic necessity and a moral liability the accomplished woman figured an ambiguous system of signification that subtended all social relations in a commercial society. Her unreadability, her refusal to signify, her polysemiscity both invited and frustrated any attempt to impose stable meaning. In denying feminine masquerade by attacking the accomplished woman, writers like Hannah More were attempting to rescue femininity from its negative gender codings as the site of the inauthentic, the superficial, and the narcissistic. Yet it was a rescue that took place within the polarities established by patriarchy, for it assumed a masculinist norm, and an essentialist construction of sexuality and subjectivity. Their rescue attempts thus conformed to the reformist ambitions of the Evangelical movement which focused its own moralizing disciplinary gaze on women. To their eyes her moral ambiguity and her refusal to signify only made the necessity of policing her all the more apparent. The accomplishment thus invited the technologies of subjectivity and control that structured sexual relations within the bourgeois social and domestic sphere. Moreover, in underscoring the economic necessity for self-display the accomplishment imposed on the female subject an ego-ideal coextensive with her consumerism and commodification. In the mytheme of the accomplished woman we see the formation of the middle-class feminine subject under consumer capitalism. The real question posed by consumerism was not *who* should consume but *how* one should consume and *how much*, and the increasing sophistication in the techniques for its encouragement, direction, and control in the form of novels, magazines, fashion-plates, advertisements, catalogues, displays of merchandise, and the like indicates a growing understanding of the ways in which this consumption might be managed by managing a particular mode of subjectivity. The colonization of the subject by these images, as in the Miss Beauforts' fashion-plate posing, therefore invited the disciplinary gaze of both the reformers and the market. For her part, the accomplished woman's role was to consume art in order to be exchanged as art, and it was her very skills as a consumer – her taste and discrimination in choosing and displaying those commodities that would be an extension of her subjectivity – that in turn would determine how she was consumed.

III   The connoisseur

Writing to a friend about the Berry sisters, the novelist, antiquarian, collector, and connoisseur Horace Walpole remarked: "They are of pleasing figures; Mary the eldest, sweet, with fine dark eyes, that are very lively when she speaks, with a symmetry of face that is the more interesting from being pale. Agnes, the younger, has an agreeable sensible countenance, hardly to be called handsome, but almost. . . . [T]hey dress within the bounds of fashion, though fashionably; but without the excrescences and balconies with which modern hoydens overwhelm and barricado their persons. In short, good sense, information, simplicity and ease characterize the Berrys" (Walpole 1937–83: XXXIV, 25). Clearly Mies van der Rohe's maxim "less is more" could be applied as readily to women in Walpole's day as it might today to modern buildings. Excrescences and balconies were to be avoided in a woman as much as in one's country seat. The ease with which Walpole moves from a description of the appearance of the Berrys to architectural metaphors is I think significant and symptomatic of the connoisseur's tendency to exercise aesthetic judgment over art and feminity. As an exercise of taste and judgment it was a demonstration of sexual difference. It was a way of signifying relationships of power, a power moreover that was never secure and thus always in need of exercise, a power ultimately tied up with the establishment of masculine subjectivity through the fetishization of women. My point here will be that the connoisseur's power to aestheticize expresses a deeper need to fetishize.

In the last decade of the century there developed what can only be called a culture of connoisseurship in England. There are a number of historical reasons for this but the most obvious is the fact that as a result of the French Revolution and subsequent wars there was a breakup of many significant continental collections. The result was a radical commodification of art as a large number of works found their way to England where they were privately auctioned. For the first time, the English aristocracy and gentry had an opportunity to decorate their houses in the style of the nobility of Rome, Venice, and Paris as masterpieces like Titian's *Rape of Europa*, and *Bacchus and Ariadne*, arrived in London in an almost endless flow. Energetic dealers like William Buchanan made enormous fortunes, for as Francis Haskell has said, "Bliss indeed it was to be a collector in that dawn, but to be a dealer was very heaven" (Haskell 1976: 26–7). This was the period in which for the first time there was serious discussion about forming a National Gallery (an idea put forth by Buchanan as a scheme to sell art directly to the government) and it was the period in which important collections like those of the Angerstein, Beaumont, and Dulwich were formed. It was a tidal swell that raised all boats; for in addition to this importation of old masters, there was significant invest- ment for the first time in modern British artists. As a result of this interest in native painting an attempt was made in 1802 to found an exhibiting society called "The British School" that would rival the Royal Academy. The organization had the support of the Prince of Wales, and its patrons included important members of the nobility and wealthy amateurs. The British School floundered after one year, yet it set the stage for the founding of the British Institution in 1805. The success of the British Institution was the palpable sign that the power of the connoisseur, the collector, and the dealer was now secure. No artist had any share in its founding or its management which was wholly entrusted to a committee of subscribers who included collectors and connois- seurs such as the earl of Dartmouth, the marquis of Stafford, Lord Lowther, Charles Long, Sir George Beaumont, Sir Francis Baring and Richard Payne Knight (Whitley 1973: I, 107). As the membership indicates, the British Institution, under the veil of wartime patriotism, conceived of itself as a remedy to the Royal Academy which was considered too riddled with artistic rivalries and professional jealousies to be an impar- tial body. By excluding artists, the founders of the British Institution signaled their ability as connoisseurs and gentlemen to rise above the petty politics of professional faction in order to form impartial aesthetic judgments and guide the taste of the nation at this critical time. Thus the fate of British art was seen to lie not with its producers, but rather with its discriminating and impartial consumers.

"Impartiality" or "disinterestedness" is, of course, what Bourdieu has described in his critique of Kant's *Judgment of Taste*, as the doxa of aesthetic judgment. Kant's "disinterestedness" Bourdieu claims is implicitly class-bound for it assumes that only those who are both properly educated in the ways of reason and who are removed enough from the wants of everyday life have the ability to make aesthetic judgments free of prejudice. This gaze constructs the art-object as a self-referential entity – one whose "purposelessness" and uselessness free it from both its historical context and its commercial value. This pure mode of aesthetic perception trained on the equally pure self-referential art object he finds objectified in the art museum, where, he writes, "the aesthetic disposition becomes an institution" (Bourdieu 1984: 30). The notion of dis- interestedness was basic to eighteenth-century theories of connoisseurship and emerges as early as Jonathan Richardson's essay "The science of a connoisseur" published in

1719. "To be a connoisseur," he wrote, "a man must be as free from all kinds of prejudice as possible; he must moreover have a clear and exact way of thinking and reasoning; he must know how to take in, and manage just ideas; and throughout he must have not only a solid, but unbiased judgment" (Richardson 1969: 283–4). Richardson's point was to argue that the study of art could uplift the morals of the nation and increase its wealth by improving the arts of designing (Richardson 1969: 267). Richardson's writings on the arts were subtended by civic humanist ideals (Barrell 1986: 16–17 and 20–3). His commercial agenda to put art at the economic service of the nation was overlaid with a discourse of public service and private virtue. Accordingly, Richardson envisioned a republic of taste governed by connoisseurs, that is to say, men whose judgment would not be impaired by economic or political self-interest, and whose social class and taste would entitle them to guide both the nation and its art.

Richardson called the exercise of the broad and disinterested gaze of the connoisseur "connoissence" in order to distinguish it from the more narrow and more self-interested gaze of the older "virtuoso." As Jay Tribby has shown, the virtuoso collected curiosities from both art and nature which he ordered according to rhetorical tropes he might choose to describe them. This rhetorical troping took the form of civil conversation which was intended to display the wit, taste, and knowledge of the virtuoso (Tribby 1991). By contrast, the eighteenth-century connoisseur focused his attention on issues of quality and authenticity not on curiosity and variety, and unlike the virtuoso the connoisseur used empirical judgment based on visual evidence in order to classify the objects he collected. The connoisseur trained his eye so that he could authenticate and judge works of art on the basis of a visual taxonomy of stylistic attributes. This training of the eye had direct commercial application for it was a technical knowledge that the connoisseur shared with the artist. Nevertheless, in addition to this appreciation of the mechanical and technical side of art, the connoisseur unlike the artist was expected to have a complete grasp of art's philosophical character. This demanded a familiarity with all of culture; that is to say, with history, philosophy, rhetoric, religion, and classical literature and languages. In the eyes of the connoisseurs, artists were seen as mere mechanics, as technicians too involved in the making of art to take a broad and disinterested view of its cultural meaning and significance. This position was increasingly contested by artists who insisted that they could not paint if they did not first possess a knowledge of the liberal arts. Reynolds perhaps did the most to elevate and gentrify the status of the artist through his elegant and extremely learned *Discourses*. However, with his retirement in 1790 from the presidency of the Royal Academy and his succession by the much less elegant and much less learned Benjamin West, the status of the artist declined while the power and influence of the gentleman connoisseur rose.[10]

It almost goes without saying that the grand intellectual overview of the connoisseur could not be shared by women who were not suited by nature to reason abstractly and thus comprehend broad philosophical arguments.[11] Writing in 1799 Hannah More declared that:

> Both in composition and action they [women] excel in details; but they do not
> so much generalize their ideas as men, nor do their minds seize a great subject

with so large a grasp. . . . A woman sees the world, as it were, from a little elevation in her own garden, where she make an exact survey of home scenes, but takes not in that wider range of distant prospects which he who stands on a loftier eminence commands.

(More 1799: 127)

The survey from the garden hillock was no match for the panoramic view from the Olympian heights occupied by the connoisseur. Moreover, since women were taught to appreciate the visual arts only through copying drawings, prints, and engravings, they were placed in somewhat the same position as the artists *vis à vis* the connoisseurs, for it was through their mechanical skills not their intellectual abilities that they managed in only a partial and imperfect way to access high culture. Thus it is in the context of the rise of connoisseurship at the end of the century that the increasing stress placed on feminine accomplishments must be understood in all its exclusionary power. Women's lack of reason and originality was manifested in the accomplishment and rehearsed and reconfirmed every time they sketched, or painted, or played. The accomplished woman not only performed her femininity but her "natural" inferiority as well. Not only did her accomplishments invite the gaze, they also justified her exclusion from public life and from the connoisseur's republic of taste.

The trope of lack used to differentiate the accomplished woman from the gentleman connoisseur is symptomatic of the patriarchal subtext contained within the discourses of connoisseurship and civic humanism. I would like to conclude by mapping this discursive space inhabited by the accomplished woman as it is traversed and triangulated by the "disinterested gazes" of the connoisseur and the civic humanist, and "the gaze" as we have already described it. To do so I would like to turn briefly to something that I had previously thought of just as a quirky moment in the history of connoisseurship of the late eighteenth century but which now seems to me to deserve some attention. In 1781 Sir William Hamilton, a member of the Society of Dilettanti and a great connoisseur of Greek and Roman antiquities, wrote to Sir Joseph Banks that he had a report from a reliable source that "the cult of Priapus [is] in full vigor as in the days of the Greeks and the Romans at Isernia in Abruzzo." Hamilton visited Isernia in the hope of witnessing the festival in which wax effigies representing "male organs of generation, of various dimensions, some even the length of a palm," were offered for sale (Plate 25.5). Women were reported to carry these *ex-voti* to a church dedicated to the Saints Cosimus and Damian. There they kissed the effigies and placed them in a bowl in the vestibule while uttering dedications like "St. Cosimo, I thank you," and "Blessed Cosimo, let it be like this" (Knight 1957: 21). By the time Hamilton arrived the festival had been suppressed; however, he did manage to recover some of the wax images or "great Toes" as he called them which he personally carried to London in 1784 and deposited in the British Museum with strict instructions to "Keep Hands Off."[12]

Hamilton's letters to Sir Joseph Banks were published by the Dilettanti in 1786 along with an explanatory *Discourse on the Worship of Priapus* by another connoisseur, Richard Payne Knight. Hamilton's news was received with great interest by the Dilettanti for it confirmed theories many of the members had entertained that the origin of all religions was to be found in ancient phallic cults. According to Knight, "what more just and natural image could they find [that is, the ancients not the Dilettanti], by which to express the beneficent power of the great Creator . . ." (Knight 1957: 31). Like the modern-day women of Isernia, Knight noted that the women of antiquity also carried phallic amulets, and these he illustrated in his text. In Knight's view "so expressive a symbol, being constantly in her view, must keep her attention fixed on its natural object, and constantly remind her of the gratitude she owed the Creator, for having taken her into his service . . . and employed her as the passive instrument in his exertion of his most beneficial power" (Knight 1957: 52–3). Obviously, it does not take much to read into the account of these phallic worshipping women, a wishful fantasy of bourgeois patriarchal domesticity. Yet there is more at stake. Knight continued, "The female organs of generation were revered as symbols of the generative powers of nature or matter, as the male were of the generative powers of God" (Knight 1957: 53). The primitive phallic rites at Isernia thus appeared to confirm to the minds of connoisseurs like Hamilton and Knight, as well as other members of the Dilettanti like Charles Towneley, that religion and civilization originated in the imposition of sexual difference, a difference that constituted femininity as nature and masculinity as divine, and that associated women's creative power with procreation and men's with the artistic originality of the Creator. Moreover given the Whiggish politics of the Dilettanti, who were intrigued with antiquity for it seemed to provide an origin for their own progressively liberal and even libertarian views, the Isernia phalluses signaled the exclusively virile nature of ancient republicanism. The *ex-voti* thus conjoined the discourse of connoisseurship and civic humanism with one of patriarchy and male homosocial bonding; in doing so they demonstrated that the phallic worship of the ancients was no more ardent than that of the moderns.

It is in this context of aestheticization, commodification, and pagan patriarchy that the saga of Sir William's beloved Emma Hart, later Lady Hamilton, takes on special meaning. Emma Hart was born Emma Lyons, the daughter of a Cheshire blacksmith. Before being taken up by Sir William Hamilton's nephew, Charles Grenville, she had been the mistress of a naval officer, Captain John Willet-Payne, and a country squire, Sir Harry Fetherstonehaugh. In 1782 she wrote to Grenville announcing she was with child and pleading for his protection: "What shall I dow? Good God what shall I dow . . . I can't come to toun for want for mony. I have not a farthing to bless my self with, and I think my friends looks cooly on me. I think so. O. G. what shall I dow? What shall I dow?" (Wark 1972: 52). Grenville took her in, helped improve her manners, and introduced her to his friend the painter George Romney. Romney's obsession with the beautiful Emma is recorded in dozens of drawings and oil portraits or "fancy pictures" in which she appears in various guises such as Circe, Calypso, a Magdalen, a Wood Nymph, a Bacchante, and St. Cecilia (Hayley 1809: 115–20). "Her personal loveliness was wonderful," Allan Cunningham explains, "and in her youth she took her beauty freely to the market of art – exposing her charms without reserve" (Cunningham 1832: 113). As a second son Grenville needed to marry if he was to secure for himself a suitable income. Emma was an impediment and after failing to interest Romney in taking her off his hands he introduced her to his uncle who, at the time, was serving as ambassador to Naples. Sir William was smitten but cautious. The transaction by letters took a year with Grenville praising her beauty and her virtues and Sir William acknowledging both but fearing that "I am not a match for so much youth and beauty," and observing "it would be fine for the young English travellers to endeavour to cuckold the old gentleman their Ambassador" (Warner 1960: 82–3). In spite of these misgivings, Grenville prevailed and Emma arrived in Naples in 1786 with permission from her former protector to "go to bed with Sir William" (Warner 1960: 58).

As Sir William's mistress and later his wife, Hart became the most prized *objet d'art* in his collection. Just as she had posed for Romney, she now performed "attitudes" or *tableaux vivants* based on famous antique sculptures and wall paintings familiar to Sir William and his circle of antiquarian friends. These attitudes were a great success and were sketched from life by Frederick Rehberg and then engraved by Thomas Piroli in 1794 (Plate 25.6).[13] Reporting on one of Lady Hamilton's performances, Georgiana, duchess of Devonshire observed:

> Her appearance was more striking than I can describe or could have imagined, She was draped exactly like a Grecian statue, her chemise of white muslin was exactly in that form, her shawl in the antique manner, her fine hair flowing over her shoulders. It was a Helen, a Cassandra, an Andromache! No Grecian or Trojan princess could have had a more perfect or commanding form.
>
> (Warner 1960: 108–9)

Like most, the duchess found Hart to be "coarse and vulgar" in life yet "just and beautiful" in art (Warner 1960: 108–9). Aestheticized as art, as a Cassandra or Andromache, Hart became socially acceptable as an extension of Sir William's collection. As Goethe famously observed of Hamilton "[he] has now, after many years of devotion to the arts and the study of nature, found the acme of these delights in the person of an English girl of twenty with a beautiful face and a perfect figure. . . . The old knight idolizes her and is quite enthusiastic about everything she does. In her he has found all the antiquities, all the profiles of Sicilian coins, even the Apollo Belvedere" (Wendorf 1990: n.p.). When Hamilton finally married Hart in 1791 Horace Walpole remarked, "Sir William has actually married his gallery of statues" (Wendorf 1990: n.p.).

Emma Hart and Sir William Hamilton exemplify the complementary dynamic that by the later eighteenth century came to link the figures of the aestheticized accomplished woman to the aestheticizing gentleman connoisseur. Hart was the blank screen on which masculine desire could project itself. Like the vases, coins, and marbles in Sir William's collection she was an object of aesthetic exchange among men, a rare commodity to be shared, bartered, envied, and, when showing signs of wear, to be discarded. She existed to be consumed as pure image for when she opened her mouth to speak the illusion of refinement ended. As Romney's model or Hamilton's gallery of statues her accomplishments consisted of reenacting established images of femininity. It was her ability to impersonate these culturally validated artistic constructions of womanhood that gave her an air of politeness and that transformed her raw sexual identity as a working-class woman into something more acceptable, something ennobled by art. For, as her contemporaries reasoned, how could a truly common woman bring great art to life unless she possessed an aesthetic sensibility herself. Yet such a sensibility was not artistic originality but the ability to copy or mimic, under the tutelage of men, the genius of the past. In a stroke she both confirms woman as an aesthetic object and femininity as masquerade, conflating into one richly ambiguous figure Cosway's two images of the accomplished woman.

For all his aesthetizing and objectifying of Emma Hart, Sir William, Goethe's quixotic "old knight," emerges as a somewhat comic figure. Far from being the embodiment of an uncomplicated and "hard" masculinity, his dry aestheticism appears to undermine his virility. In exercising the gaze he risked becoming merely a passive spectator in the thrall of feminine beauty. A true libertine such as Casanova recognized this and observed of Hamilton's marriage: "a clever man marrying a young woman clever enough to bewitch him. Such a fate often overtakes a man of intelligence when he grows old. It is always a mistake to marry, but when a man's physical and mental forces are declining it is a calamity" (Warner 1960: 110). In Hamilton's case one gets the distinct impression that looking took the place of anything more active. As John Barrell has pointed out, in the eighteenth century the danger of aestheticism was understood in sexual terms; that is, as a seductive and enervating danger to masculine virtue (Barrell 1992: 75). When seen in contrast to the stern civic humanism of earlier connoisseurs like Richardson, the collecting obsessions of the Dilettanti seem almost effeminate. Hence possibly the need to construct a feminine Other that might, through the force of contrast, stiffen their masculine image. Perhaps at stake in the Dilettanti's collective gazing at antiquity was not so much castration but the very thing that the wax *malias* offered to St. Cosimus were intended to cure, a kind of infertility or impotence. The irony, of course, is that the "phallic rites" of the women of Isernia were not, as the Dilettanti hoped, simple examples of "phallic worship." Rather, the rites seem to have been instrumental in kind: a series of Christianized folk practices intended to promote virility and therefore to secure the production of feminine pleasure and motherhood in marriage.

I would like to conclude with two images by Johan Zoffany of connoisseurs and their objects (Plates 25.7 and 25.8). The first shows Charles Towneley in his study with friends from the Society of Dilettanti, including Charles Grenville, clustered around the most admired sculpture in his collection, the so-called bust of Clytie, a figure which Towneley and the others believed to be a personification of the "passive means of generation" and which was appropriately enough placed within the center of that symbol of the active male principle, the lotus flower. The other painting shows English connoisseurs in the Uffizi examining the feminine Other represented in the archetypal forms of Venus and Virgin: that is to say, as Titan's *Venus of Urbino* and the *Medici Venus*, and as a Raphael Madonna. In the back of the gallery a solitary figure stares at a marble dancing satyr, an image of the raw Dionysian creative impulse (perhaps an image of the artist), which contrasts with the connoisseur's own more refined Apollonian contemplation.[14] In both paintings the aestheticizing gaze of the connoisseur exercised on images of the Other confirms his masculinity in particular ways. In addition, in both paintings the connoisseur's gaze both masks and unmasks the work of art's commodity status and its fetishistic meaning as a sign of power and prestige.

When turned upon the accomplished woman that same gaze also acknowledged and disavowed her commodity status as an object to be exchanged in the marriage market by transforming her into a work of art. In doing so it reconfirmed the connoisseur's subjectivity and her objecthood. In this way, the accomplished woman's dangerous and potentially subversive "unreadability" was continually denied and replaced by a dialectic between completeness and lack, authenticity and inauthenticity, subject and object. Thus in mapping the accomplished woman on to the culture of the late eighteenth century we enter into what Laura Mulvey has called the "closed loop" of male sexual fantasy which, far from being about women, is about masculinity as it is structured by male castration anxiety (Mulvey 1987: 112–20). Like the "great toes" of Isernia, or the useless aesthetic object, the accomplished woman signifies castration and in doing so induces scopic and representational mechanisms of control and displacement to manage the anxiety caused by her lack of a penis.

The aestheticization of women which seems so much a part of late eighteenth- and early nineteenth-century culture went along with the domestic confinement of women and the increasing tendency to transform the home into an aestheticized space of commodity display, a space where commercial wares constructed gender identities and social positions. So even though the home was designated the space of authentic subjectivity, that subjectivity could only be expressed and represented through objects and the objectification of the self, that is through the display of commodities and through the performance of accomplishments. Along these lines it is worth remembering that this was the age that invented interior decoration, and architects/decorators like the Adam brothers and Thomas Hope made vast fortunes constructing fantasy environments of ancient Greek or Roman or Egyptian or even exotic Chinese domesticity. What better site, then, than this museum-like domestic space for the self-absorbed and self-referential feminine Other, whose conspicuous decorativeness confirmed her non-utilitarian aesthetic value and thus invited the controlling and fetishistic masculine/connoisseurial gaze. Like the aesthetic object, her very lack of usefulness signaled a value which could only be realized through exchange and consumption, a value therefore that was relative and not intrinsic, a value that depended finally on the irrational workings of masculine anxiety and desire. Thus it appears only logical that in the post-revolutionary return to order – the order of the father and the order of industrial capitalism – the domestic space should increasingly be given over to the exhibition of that ur-commodity fetish of bourgeois masculinity, the accomplished woman.

Notes

I am grateful to Nicholas Mirzoeff who read a working draft of this paper and who made helpful comments, and to Mary Sheriff, Lisa Tickner, John Barrell, John Brewer, D. A. Miller, Andrew Hemingway, and Mark Rose for their suggestions for revision.

1   I wish to thank D. A. Miller for alerting me to this passage from *Sanditon*.
2   These illustrations from Nikolaus Heideloff's *Gallery of Fashion* (1794–1802) show the increasing tendency to depict fashion figures in everyday situations. Like those found in the medieval books of hours, these pictures tell time by constructing "typical" daily events and seasonal pastimes. Unlike the books of hours, however, the daily and annual circularity of events as depicted in the fashion books is inflected with a change of dress. Days and years are differentiated one from the other not by individual acts or historical events, but by stylistic novelty. In this sense women's ability to act, to direct their own lives, or to create

their own history, is presented exclusively in terms of their ability to consume and manipulate new fashion styles. See my "The picturesque and ready-to-wear feminity" (1994).

3   Richard Leppert (1988: 102) has noted that the musical instruments that were felt to be appropriate for young women to play – harps and keyboards – were not portable and were instead domestic furniture. See also his "Social order and the domestic consumption of music: The politics of sound in the policing of gender construction in eighteenth-century England" in this collection.

4   In this passage Freud identifies scopophilia and links it to sadism. He identifies the "perversions" he describes in the *Three Essays* as masculine because men's "erotic life alone has become accessible to research. That of women – partly owing to the stunting effect of civilized conditions and partly owing to their conventional secretiveness and insincerity – is still veiled in an impenetrable obscurity" (1962: 17). In a later essay on fetishism (1927) he described the fetishistic gaze as that which simultaneously believes and disbelieves in the mother as having a penis. The child maintains this contradiction by focusing on some object or part of her body as a substitute for the penis. While taking the place of a penis this fetishized object or body part reinforces in the child a fear of castration. The mother is thus an ambivalent, one might almost say sublime, object of the child's awe and fear, a figure to be simultaneously overvalued (fetishism) and devalued (sadism). Lacan's analysis of the gaze and its relation to the construction of masculinity and feminity can be found in *The Four Fundamental Concepts of Psycho-analysis* (1977b: 67–119). For Lacan sexuality and subjectivity are matters of masquerade and are constructed in relation to the phallus. On the subject of the phallus see his "The signification of the phallus" (1977a: 281–91). Femininity is thus understood in opposition to this male sign, and is viewed differentially as "Other." On the subject of Lacan's reopening of Freud's theories of sexuality see Jacqueline Rose (1986). A classic essay on the gaze and its objectification of women in film is Laura Mulvey's "Visual pleasure and narrative cinema" (1975: 6–18). My own analysis of the accomplished woman and the connoisseur is indebted to the work of Rose and Mulvey.

5   On this subject see Barrell (1992); and essays by John Brewer, Felicity Nussbaum, and Kathleen Wilson in this collection.

6   In stressing the contingent nature of femininity and the differential operations of subjectivity, I again call on the work of Lacan (1982), as well as that of Luce Irigaray (1986) and Goran Therborn (1980). Lacan sees subjectivity as a masculine prerogative which is constituted through the denial of the feminine. Hence far from being subjects women are a mysterious unknowable Other. In a more extreme move, Irigaray sees in the formation of male subjectivity a total repudiation of the feminine and maternal foundations and a corresponding fantasy of autogenesis. Therborn has argued that ideological positions are not fixed, and that individuals take up a number of different ideological positions which they modify in different ways in the process of applying them to different situations.

7   On Burney's work see Patricia Crown (1977 and 1982).

8   For a discussion of the problem of female spectatorship by a variety of feminists and film theorists see the special issue of *Camera Obscura: A Journal of Feminism and Film Theory* (20–1, May–September 1989) entitled "The Spectatrix."

9   See Lacan on the "imaginary" (1977a: 93–100, 101–24, and 585–645). See also Shoshana Feldman (1988: 104) who quotes Lacan: "Does its empire [narcissism's] not extend as far as this reference of the philosophical tradition represented by plenitude encountered by the subject in the mode of contemplation."

10   Despite Castiglione's dictum that a knowledge of drawing was necessary for a gentleman, drawing and painting never became part of the regular curriculum (outside of the military academies) for educating young men in the eighteenth century. John Locke, whose ideas on education became orthodoxy in the eighteenth century, saw drawing and painting as too sedentary and too much of a distraction from "other more useful studies." See Ian Pears (1988: 184). In his *Treatise on Painting* (1740) George Turnbell lamented that "the Fine Arts have never had any place in Liberal Education among us" (quoted in Pears 1988: 185) As Locke saw it, the role of the gentleman was to have the necessary training in the important

subjects of history and philosophy that would allow him to appreciate pictures, but not the manual training that would enable him to actually make them. As Pears points out, while some men of the upper classes, like Sir George Beaumont, obviously did learn to draw and paint and even exhibited at the Royal Academy, they were in the minority; more common was the practice, exemplified by connoisseurs like the third earl of Shaftesbury, Lord Burlington, Richard Payne Knight, and William Beckford, of hiring an artist to execute one's design ideas.

11 In addition, few women – with the exception of some widows – had significant amounts of money at their disposal and the little money that was permitted them was restricted to purchases of clothing and trivial necessities. Most women therefore were in no financial position to buy art. See Susan Staves (1990: 131–61).

12 On this episode see Michael Clarke and Nicholas Penny (1982). For discussions of its meaning for Knight's sexuality see G. S. Rousseau (1988). On the subject of male homosocial bonding see Eve Kosofsky Sedgwick (1985).

13 Rehberg entitled his volume *Drawings Faithfully copied from Nature at Naples*. "Nature" is taken by the artist to mean Emma Hart who personifies nature's achievement of perfection. On the relationship of Hart's attitudes to contemporary theories of gesture and expression see Richard Wendorf (1990).

14 For a thorough analysis of this painting see Oliver Millar (1966).

Bibliography

Austen, Jane (1982a) *Pride and Prejudice*, Vol. II of the Oxford Illustrated Jane Austen, ed. R. W. Chapman, Oxford: Oxford University Press.
—— (1982b) *Sanditon*, in *Minor Works*, Vol. VI of the Oxford Illustrated Jane Austen, ed. R. W. Chapman, Oxford: Oxford University Press.
Barrell, John (1986) *The Political Theory of Painting from Reynolds to Hazlitt: "The Body of the Public,"* New Haven, CT: Yale University Press.
—— (1992) *The Birth of Pandora and the Division of Knowledge*, London: Macmillan.
Berger, John (1972) *Ways of Seeing*, Harmondsworth, Mx: Penguin.
Bermingham, Ann (1994) "The picturesque and ready-to-wear femininity," in *The Politics of the Picturesque*, ed. P. Gartside and S. Copley, Cambridge: Cambridge University Press.
Bourdieu, Pierre (1984) *Distinction: A Social Critique of the Judgement of Taste*, trans. Richard Nice, Cambridge, MA: Harvard University Press.
Brewer, John (1995) " 'The most polite age and the most vicious': attitudes towards culture as a commodity, 1660–1800," Chapter 18 in this volume.
Camera Obscura: A Journal of Feminism and Film Theory 20–1 (May–September 1985).
Clarke, Michael and Penny, Nicholas (eds.) (1982) *The Arrogant Connoisseur: Richard Payne Knight 1751–1824*, Manchester: Manchester University Press.
Cosway, Maria (c. 1800) *The Progress of Female Virtue and the Progress of Female Dissipation*, London: R. Ackerman.
Crown, Patricia (1977) "Edward Francis Burney: an historical study in English Romantic art," PhD dissertation, University of California, Los Angeles.
—— (1982) *Drawings by E. F. Burney in the Huntington Collection*, San Marino, CA: the Huntington Library.
Cunningham, Allan (1832) *The Lives of the Most Eminent British Painters and Sculptors and Architects*, 5 vols., London: John Murray.
De Certeau, Michel (1984) *The Practice of Everyday Life*, trans. Steven Randall, Berkeley, CA: University of California Press.
Doane, Mary Ann (1987) *The Desire to Desire: The Women's Film of the 1940's*, Bloomington and Indianapolis, IN: Indiana University Press.
Feldman, Shoshana (1988) "Lacan's psychoanalysis, or the figure in the screen," *October* 45: 97–106.

Foucault, Michel (1977) "Preface to transgression," in *Language, Counter-Memory, Practice*, trans. Donald F. Bouchard and Sherry Simon, Ithaca, NY: Cornell University Press.

Freud, Sigmund (1962) *Three Essays on Sexuality*, trans. James Strachey, New York: Basic Books.

Haskell, Francis (1976) *Rediscoveries in Art*, Ithaca, NY: Cornell University Press.

Hayley, William (1809) *The Life of George Romney*, 2 vols., London: William Mason.

Heidcloff, Nikolaus (1794–1802) *The Gallery of Fashion*, 8 vols., London: Ackerman.

Irigaray, Luce (1986) *The Speculum of the Other Woman*, Ithaca, NY: Cornell University Press.

Klein, Lawrence (1995) "Politeness for plebes: consumption and social identities in early eighteenth-century England," Chapter 19 in this volume.

Knight, Richard Payne (1957 [1786]) *A Discourse on the Worship of Priapus*, rep. in *Sexual Symbolism: A History of Phallic Worship*, ed. Ashley Montagu, New York: Julian Press.

Lacan, Jacques (1977a) *Ecrits*, trans. Alan Sheridan, New York: W. W. Norton.

—— (1977b) *The Four Fundamental Concepts of Psycho-analysis*, trans. Alan Sheridan, New York: W. W. Norton.

—— (1982) *Feminine Sexuality*, trans. Jacqueline Rose, New York: W. W. Norton.

Lady's Monthly Museum XVII (November 1799) London.

Leppert, Richard (1988) *Music and Image: Domesticity, Ideology, and Socio-Cultural Formation in Eighteenth-Century England*, Cambridge: Cambridge University Press.

—— (1995) "The domestic consumption of music: the politics of sound in the policing of gender construction in eighteenth-century England," Chapter 26 in this volume.

Millar, Oliver (1966) *Zoffany and His Tribuna*, London: Routledge & Kegan Paul.

Miller, J. (1982) "Women's education, 'self-improvement' and social mobility – a late eighteenth-century debate," *British Journal of Educational Studies* XX (October): 302–15.

More, Hannah (1799) *Strictures on the Modern System of Female Education*, London: T. Cadell and W. Davies.

Mulvey, Laura (1975) "Visual pleasure in narrative cinema," *Screen* 16: 6–18.

—— (1987) "You don't know what's happening do you Mr. Jones," in *Framing Feminism: Art and the Women's Movement*, ed. Roszika Parker and Griselda Pollock, London: Pandora.

Nenedich, Stana (1991) "Patterns of domestic consumption in Glasgow and Edinburgh," paper given at the Clark Library at the University of California, Los Angeles on May 4, 1991.

Nussbaum, Felicity A. (1995) "Polygamy, *Pamela*, and the prerogative of empire," Chapter 12 in this volume.

Pears, Ian (1988) *The Discovery of Painting: The Growth of Interest in the Arts in England, 1680–1768*, New Haven, CT: Yale University Press.

Pocock, J. G. A. (1975) *The Machiavellian Moment: Florentine Republican Thought and the Atlantic Tradition*, Princeton, NJ: Princeton University Press.

Richardson, Jonathan (1969 [1773]) *The Works of Mr. Jonathan Richardson*, Hildesheim: G. Olms.

Rose, Jacqueline (1986) *Sexuality in the Field of Vision*, London: Verso.

Rousseau, G. S. (1988) "The sorrows of Priapus: anticlericalism, homosocial desire, and Richard Payne Knight," in *Sexual Underworlds of the Enlightenment*, ed. G. S. Rosseau and Roy Porter, Chapel Hill, NC: University of North Carolina Press.

Sedgwick, Eve Kosofsky (1985) *Between Men: English Literature and Male Homosocial Desire*, New York: Columbia University Press.

Staves, Susan (1990) *Married Women's Separate Property in England, 1660–1833*, Cambridge, MA: Harvard University Press.

Tribby, Jay (1991) "Stalking civility: conversing and collecting in early modern Europe," *Rhetorica* 9 (Winter): 139–63.

Therborn, Goran (1980) *The Ideology of Power and the Power of Ideology*, New York: Schocken Books.

Walker, John (1986) "Maria Cosway: an undervalued artist," *Apollo* 123 (May): 315–20.

Walpole, Horace (1937–83) *Horace Walpole's Correspondence, 1725–1797*, ed. W. S. Lewis *et al.*, vol. XXXIV, New Haven, CT: Walpole Society.

Wark, Robert (1972) *Meet the Ladies*, San Marino, CA: the Huntington Library.

Warner, Oliver (1960) *Emma Hamilton and Sir William Hamilton*, London: Chatto & Windus.

Wendorf, Richard (1990) *Emma Hamilton's Attitudes by Frederick Rehberg*, Cambridge MA: the

26
Social order and the domestic consumption of music
The politics of sound in the policing of gender construction in eighteenth-century England

Richard Leppert

What is it that one "consumes" when one "consumes" music? What are the relationships of this consuming to the construction of personhood, that is, to identity established on the basis of nation, class, and gender? What is the function of consumption for the performer or auditor of privatized, domestic music? How ought this consumption to be philosophically theorized and morally evaluated in comparison with public music? What are the social and cultural consequences of maintaining or blurring the boundaries of musical production and consumption established between private and public, domestic and worldly, amateur and professional, English and foreign, female and male? These questions, of considerable interest to the English upper classes, were addressed by numerous writers of philosophy, aesthetics, sermons and moral tracts, educational treatises, courtesy and conduct literature, and even crop up in novels and verse.[1] The stakes involved the very possibility of Englishness, defined by and for an elite, in light of a cultural practice about which enormous anxiety existed. The appetite for music in England was great; the fear of satisfying that appetite was perhaps still greater. The issue hinged, one way or the other, on properly theorizing the nature of what was available for consumption and the conditions under which consumption might take place.

The consumption of music has to be understood in light of several interlocking, mutually mediating but inevitably dialectical and different ways of defining this category of human activity. To begin first with the obvious, "music" constitutes certain phenomena experienced as sound via the sense of hearing; and second, speaking of western high culture, "music" refers to notated "instructions" for producing such sounds. Third, and here the story becomes more complex, music is a sight, and as a visual phenomenon it is richly semantic. It is a sight in performance, thus specifically seen as an embodied and humanly interactive, hence social, practice (except when performed for the self and outside the audition of others). It is an activity subject to the gaze, not least because music was theorized, both as social practice and sonority, as possessing sensual power. It was understood to act with dangerous immediacy on the

Houghton Library.

Whitley, William T. (1973) *Art in England, 1800–1820*, 2 vols., New York: Hacker Art Books.

Wilson, Kathleen (1995) "The good, the bad, and the impotent: imperialism and the politics of identity in Georgian England," Chapter 13 in this volume.

Wollstonecraft, Mary (1978) *Vindication of the Rights of Women*, ed. Miriam Kramnick, Harmondsworth, Mx: Penguin.

sensate body. The "musical" gaze was supercharged by the potentiality of sexuality, producing an "interest" simultaneously encoded with pleasure and anxiety. Music as a sight and a sound together, inevitably united in performance prior to the advent of recording technology, cannot be fully understood except in this conjunction.

A fourth component, closely related to the third, involves a perception of music as a potential but *un*realized practice, specifically and only as a sight, one nonetheless semantically rich: musical furniture as accoutrement of domestic, private space, without specific regard to whether actually played or, if played, how often and how well. Fifth, and last, music was conceived as an abstract subject, a component of philosophical and mathematical discourses – hence part of formal and informal education – attempting to sort out the nature of all nature. Discussions ranged from attempts to articulate music's proper place in society, citing sources from ancient to modern and often turning on the question of ethics, to pseudo-scientific accounts of western musical authority based on detailed measurements of intervals and such, with acknowledged debts to ancient Greek music theory, that fetishized number as such.[2]

It is here that I will begin my effort to sort out the conflicts encountered on the question of musical consumption. That is, I will start with the abstract and move towards concrete practice. In laying out just the bare bones of these complicated issues I will restrict my comments to their implications for the English upper classes, since the story was theorized quite differently for the lower social orders.

How men and women approached music, and what it should mean to the formation of their character and identity, was strikingly different, and the subject of endlessly reiterated discussion. Men were provided scant encouragement to study music as a performed practice; instead they were invited to approach it cognitively as a "science"[3] concatenating philosophy and mathematics. Music's value for men was theoretical:

> *Music* is a *science* established on the most sublime parts of mathematical truths; its *theory* founded on the doctrine of *Proportion*; on the most *wonderful*, though the most *simple* and *few Principles*; the knowledge of which, fills the enquiring mind with the most transcendent pleasure, and admiration of the wisdom of the Creator, who "*hath filled all things with good*."[4]
>
> (Anon. *c.* 1778: 15)

Music's value in this typical account was fully appropriated in the logic of ratio, as pure abstraction, as the absence of the sound for which music might otherwise be thought to exist. John Aubrey noted that "Statics, music, fencing, architecture and bits of bridges are all reducible to the laws of geometry" (Stephens 1972: 113). To connect a mathematics of music to the geometries of civil engineering and fighting, as Aubrey does, along with many other contemporaneous writers, connects a non-sonoric "scientific" music to the exclusive male domain of state power and its politics. Two comments are required: first, that by so doing "music" justifies its existence as a masculine and mental practice (which counters an opposite view); second, it is radically utilitarian. Music's proper function is not aesthetic, nor is it valorized for its inherent internal mathematical logic as such; instead, music is useful as a means to another end in excess of itself: it is a tool for domination. But to operate ideally and most effectively in this respect, it is silent. Indeed, music's sound is a threat to the instrumentalized variety of reason, to power, and to men. Put differently, in the texts to which I am referring, musical practice as such – the actual making of music, the sonorities produced in performance – is consistently gendered: as Woman, as opposite, as enemy.

Ambivalences about music became especially serious once it was actually performed. Never less than poorly hidden from open discussion, and indeed frequently the explicit target of concern, was music's relation to the body and, by implication, the mind and soul. Music's impact on the body was explicitly organized as a moral question, which in truth operated as a convenient and somewhat abstract smoke-screen for anxieties about identities grounded on nation, class, and gender to the extent these components of identity might be located as qualities of the body. This is a far more important matter than a theorization of a "science" of music in the absence of musical sound as such, for reasons that are entirely obvious. To be sure, the formal study of musical acoustics, scale systems, harmonic relations and so forth may indeed be of some interest to some people, but hardly to many, especially if that study is ideally valorized more than musical sonority itself. To the vast majority of people having any musical interests, music on paper, so to speak, is not really music at all and is in any but small dosages profoundly boring. Musical "science" is not music. So no matter to what extent writers urged upper-class men to consume music in an abstract contemplative, non-performative, and silent act, there is little evidence to suggest that many did so, despite the enormous body of literature devoted to the topic.[5] The ideal of a wholly "intellectual" music was fundamentally unrealized, whereas, as one would expect, actual music was produced and consumed. But here I must again emphasize the extraordinary level of attention focused on performed music and its performers, and the degree to which this attention revolved explicitly around music's necessarily embodied state. To regulate music's relation to the body was of profound concern for both men and women alike, though for very different reasons. Music's danger was located in a perception that it possessed the power to destabilize virtually every social relation, notably including relations between men and women, one social class and another, England and the Continent, Europeans and racial Others, and so on.[6]

Music was recognized as a discursive practice; as such it was entirely meaningful. The difficulty ensued from the inability to stabilize and to predict its meanings with certainty, though not for want of trying. Sacred music was of course more approved than secular, yet even sacred music might be papist in its appeal, depending on what it sounded like and what it might be associated with. Secular music might be very English and masculine (Squire Western in *Tom Jones* liked his Handel, small irony, but especially his English pop tunes) (Fielding 1973: Book 4, Ch. 5, p. 128), always to the good, but native English music might also be feminine (feminizing) and textually immoral.

One always needed to keep a sharp ear for a foreign music which was commonly theorized as the sonoric agent of sedition and, if it were French or Italian, seduction (of men as well as women). This at least was the lament by xenophobes as different in period and concern as John Dennis[7] and Lord Chesterfield,[8] neither of whom could apparently conceive of Italian music or musicians separately from foppishness and sodomy, and the degenerating effects of both on anyone who came within hearing and seeing of practitioners, whether on the English stage as regards Dennis or on the Grand Tour as regards Chesterfield.

Yet for many writers, so long as music was consumed passively and in public the real issues involved were confined to an evaluation of the music heard. To hear or not to hear any music was for most not such a great issue. Everything turned on the distinction between public and private, on the one hand, and on the distinction between passive listening and active performance, on the other. Contentious debate most commonly ensued once music entered the doors of the home's private space, where a first distinction must be made between the professional musician and the amateur upper-class "homeowner."

Music enters the home, as regards music professionals, in two ways, the most common being via the music teacher hired to teach daughters the accomplishment. This practice produced an immensely complicated and conflicted discourse largely centering on threats to a daughter's virginity, and hence her father's authority, by a social inferior who in all likelihood was also a foreigner.[9] The second way professionals entered the home was as performers hired for occasions; by itself this was largely unproblematic as long as a barrier was maintained between performers and those who hired them. So long as the structured difference between production and consumption was mirrored by the structured difference between the social classes of the patron and those he hired, propriety could be maintained. The moment a personal relationship between the two was formed, however, all bets were off, which in fact sometimes occurred (Dr. Charles Burney being an especially famous example).[10] Ultimately, the professional musician was a laborer, fraternizing with whom carried social risk. Quite apart from the myriad difficulties of the particular type of music in question, whether sacred or secular, English or foreign, and so on, there was, then, the matter of who was making the sounds.

Yet the issue is not settled once professionals are kept out of domestic surroundings. The question of amateur performers demanded theorization. If the performer were a woman, public performance as an amateur was extraordinarily difficult in that public "display" directly challenged the very identity of the category of "woman": it was public, not domestic; active not passive; it attracted attention away from her father or husband; it opened up large questions as to who was managing the domestic economy while she performed, and so on.[11]

Musical education for women was generally accepted as a requisite of class position, and typically began during childhood. But whereas an ideal musical education for men was theoretical, that for women was largely practical, aimed at producing performance abilities on keyboard instruments, in particular. Yet the very thing a woman was expected to learn, namely how to perform, was the subject of intense anxiety, centering first on the question of privacy but involving much more besides. Not only was a woman's performance invariably to be given in private company, among family and friends, but she was further cautioned to treat it "Carelessly like a Diversion, and not with Study and Solemnity, as if it was a Business, or yourself overmuch Affected with it" (Anon. 1701: 48–9). Ironically – and impossibly – the common social ideal demanded that her performance of music be accomplished with the utmost metaphorical and literal passivity. To be sure, the anxiety immanent in injunctions of this sort clearly suggests that women by no means universally agreed to the limits defined for them, but that could not have been for lack of awareness about what was expected of them. Erasmus Darwin, among many others, thus unambiguously recommended that a woman literally restrict the development of her talents in effect so as not to compete with her husband in the public eye:

> It is perhaps more desirable, that young ladies should play, sing, and dance, only so well as to amuse themselves and their friends, than to practice those arts in so eminent a degree as to astonish the public; because a great apparent attention to trivial accomplishments is liable to give suspicion, that more valuable acquisitions have been neglected.[12]

(Darwin 1798: 13)

(By contrast, if the performer were a man, his very identity was at risk precisely as regards that component of his identity most central to himself and all other men who might view him, his sexuality. Indeed, the discussions about male upper-class music-making are legion and virtually none offers unambiguous encouragement. Very few judge the practice as, at best, anything more than a waste of time; the few who grudgingly allow music, and the fewer still who defend it, invariably authorize it only as a leisure exercise, a passing fancy to which no great importance should be attached.[13])

The delight and gratification received in making music depend absolutely on the difference of sonority from its opposite, silence, and the signification of silence. Yet music's pleasures are more than the experience of sound as such. When we consume music we consume as well a sight – embodied, active, and situated, all of which mediate musical meanings. The result is the consumption and simultaneous production of identity. As regards the question of the sight of music, writers of the period commonly urge the man who would be a musician to practice his art "at his private recreation" – a tacit acknowledgment of shame. The sight of men making music was derogatively described with considerable consistency. As Chesterfield put it: piping or fiddling [his words] "puts a gentleman in a very frivolous, contemptible light" (Stanhope 1926: I, 170).

The domestic production, hence consumption, of music – specifically if problematically sanctioned for upper-class girls and women – was placed among the so-called "accomplishments" that made females fit for the marriage market and thereafter fit reflectors of their husbands' station. The function of the accomplishments within the domestic economy was principally one of containment. Erasmus Darwin, among a lengthy list of other writers on the subject, captured this succinctly. The accomplishments serve "the purpose of relieving each other [!]; and of producing by such means an uninterrupted cheerfulness of mind; which is the principal charm, that fits us for society, and the great source of earthly happiness."[14] That is, the accomplishments' purpose is to keep women content by their number and variety, allowing them to turn from one to another so as to avoid boredom. The tacit corollary is that women ought to engage in nothing important enough to render them a danger to men, either by the temptation to interfere in men's affairs or by the activation of their sexuality outside tightly prescribed limits. Indeed, one of the great fears about music as regards women was its impact on their sexuality. Many writers expressed the concern that musical education specifically encouraged females to act beyond the bounds of the modesty and deference expected of their sex.[15] Indeed, the potential effects of music on girls and women were theorized as profound:

> Our Music [lamented one writer] has become so totally changed. It is not now sought as a repose for the mind after its fatigues, but to support its *Tumults*, – not to impress the *Delights* of *calm reason*, or prevail on us to *listen* to the *charmer*; but she must leave the purity of her *own Nature*, and by divesting herself of *Simplicity*, force us to *admire*, not *feel*, and yield to *astonishment* and *absurdity*, instead of *chaste Beauty* and delight.
>
> (Anon. *c.* 1778: 6)

The split between mind and body, between reason and emotion, and between men and women is both inscribed and sanctioned in this passage. The fear of music in women is a fear of female eruption, of tumult and not calmness, of she who ceases to charm us, who in effect de-naturalizes herself, losing her simplicity, becoming complex, admirable (!) and – more than a vision of loveliness – more like a man. The argument depends on a preconceived musical ideal. Since music and women are conflated in eighteenth-century English culture, since art, that is, is fundamentally feminized, it follows that music like women should be simple ("natural"); music is understood to be of the body – feelings – not of the mind, though in its simplicity it might appeal to the mind for just this (throw-away) quality. The writer continues: "Let our daughters . . . [not] ever attempt any thing but *select pieces* of *familiar, easy, simple* construction, such as may delight the *ear* of their friends, and contribute to improve their own *Hearts* by directing its influence to the proper object" (Anon. *c.* 1778: 13–14).

Leisured women had a lot of time on their hands and men must see to it that this time was spent appropriately. For men time was a developmental parameter, lived socially; for women time was non-developmental, lived familially. Activities viewed as non-developmental and expressive of stationary time, such as music, were peripheral to men's lives and fundamentally improper for them to engage in. But for females such activities were considered *by men* appropriate and important, as delineators both of gender difference and of gender hierarchy. Music helped produce an ideologically correct species of woman; in the eyes of men music accordingly contributed to social stability by keeping women in the place that men had assigned them.

A well-bred woman who took music seriously constituted a threat to social boundaries. Accordingly, most courtesy and conduct literature charged women to view music as but a trivial pursuit, like virtually everything else they did apart from bearing and raising children. The trivialization of women's activities, to men and women alike, was an essential component in maintaining the status quo based on gender hierarchy. Now, clearly, it can be argued that music nonetheless created a compensatory space for women condemned to live within these contradictory parameters, a space in which a woman engaged in a private action for her own pleasure, as such an assertion of her own agency, however circumscribed. Yet music under these circumstances was a compensation whose negative dialectics were constantly reasserted. There was no escaping the functional reality of her music-making, namely as a means of demonstrating her accomplishment as something that reflected credit not on her but on her husband, together with the contradictory requirement that she had to restrain any acknowledgment of musical devotion (her attachment to music for her own sake, that is) and also to hide – or limit the development of – her talents, almost as if they were family secrets. (I will return to this at the end.)

I have argued for an understanding of music in relation to its sound and sight taken together, mediated by "philosophies" about music enjoying contemporaneous currency. The only effective way we can link sound and sight as experienced and understood in this past society is by reference to music as a subject in visual art, painting in particular, though of course we so do at the ironic expense of musical sonority as such. I stress painting because of all visual discursive media of the eighteenth century it was easily the most important. Its prestige was enormous by comparison with drawings or prints – relatively large sums of money were spent on commissions, especially so weighed against the earnings of ordinary workers (though to be sure there was no established sense of a unified and uniformly paid working class prior to the industrial revolution). The discursive stakes of painting were recognized and non-controversial as such, one sign of which was the high degree of conventionality established as the sanctioned mode of expression. (Conventions serve as the grammar and syntax of any practice, and hence work as devices of cultural stabilization and internalized self-discipline. Indeed, when conventions are violated the destabilizing effects of the gesture have commonly been loudly debated, whatever the discursive practice.)

By means of introducing this topic, there is one thing more of considerable importance. The musical images which interest me were displayed in the home. Accordingly, they replicated in paint the very setting of which they were a part. Thus the painted musical subject formed a double inscription; it was a two-dimensional sign, enjoying spatial privilege on domestic walls, of a three-dimensional sign that likely resided in the same spatial enclosure (actual musical instruments as "furniture") and of the practices that may or may not have occurred within and on that sign (actual musical performance). The intentionality inherent in choosing musical props for paintings should not be downplayed; it is necessarily the result of a recognition of music's importance as a signifier of identity.

The signifying function of domestic music consumption in visual representation can be examined in a variety of topoi, especially single and group portraits. But I want to begin with pictorial ephemera, namely, the fashion plate (Plate 26.1). Artist-illustrators like Robert Dighton produced these images, intended for reproduction, as information sources on current seasonal fashions for wealthy women. The pictorial emphasis, as one would expect, is on the dresses, but the semantic valorization of the gowns themselves is inevitably established not only by the surroundings in which the begowned model is placed but also by the narrative that these surroundings (objects and "events") imply. By their very nature, fashion plates are *about* consumption: they are to be visually consumed in an act producing desire and prior to another, more material act of consumption, buying. And in many such plates, music is incorporated as the sign of identification and valorization of the (consuming) woman, a composite of feminization established both visually and, by implication, sonorically.

The correspondence is profound between Robert Dighton's fashion plate and Johan Zoffany's elaborately decorative portrait of the Armstrong sisters (Plate 26.2), though several decades separate the two images. The state of excess in the latter image is especially striking, for the aging sisters are profoundly overdressed, as though immobilized by drapery that virtually renders their bodily presence irrelevant, their plain faces an unfortunate distraction from their finery. Their music-making provides the visual excuse – and apology – for their immobility. Music aestheticizes the social condition it simultaneously masks. In fact, the two women do not make music, nor do they even promise to do so. Instead music is an impossible and silent icon, here of consumption, all the more excessive by its literal absence: musically speaking, what are they doing? The English guitarist appears to play, but her sister with book in lap, apparently a singer, shows no hint of breaking into song. Nor does she accompany her sister on the two-manual harpsichord. Instead, she sits as if she were helping her sister to tune, but surely not so given the high octave string she engages. Nor do the women address each other, as would be necessary for an ensemble to occur.

All this is more interesting in light of the fact that Zoffany himself was not only a music lover but a musician. He knew how to paint musicians. Yet this image has nothing to do with music, in the most literal sense, though everything to do with it as regards what underwrites musical consumption in English domestic life. The picture is a lie masquerading as truth, but dialectically one in which, ironically, the lie *is* the truth of music's relation to women and gender construction. Music's present absence in the guise of musical props anchors the Armstrong sisters' identities at the same moment that the role of music in the lives of women like them binds them into inferiority. Music has a very important role to play, but its sonorities as such are but accompaniment to the nonsonoric structures the music helps ensure: music, the sonoric medium, in English private life serves as a tool which, by its consumption, silences.

One sort of family group picture that enjoyed considerable currency in eighteenth-century England, the so-called conversation piece, commonly incorporated music in pictorially notable ways, usually in indoor settings (such as the one by Zoffany of the Armstrong sisters; also (Plate 26.3) or, less commonly, outdoors (Plate 26.4), but in either case set in elaborate surroundings that establish the expenditure of considerable monetary sums on finery and furnishings. At this juncture I only want to make a few points about these images, by no means exhausting what is interesting and significant about them. The first (Plate 26.3), attributed to the painter Henry Pickering, is characteristic for the incorporation of a large two-manual harpsichord as the principal piece of domestic furniture at which, also characteristic, a young woman sits to play, though judging from her hand position on the keyboard – extremely relaxed – one has doubts as to the musical event. What needs to be asked is: Why this instrument?

To answer this question something needs to be said about the politics of consumption in mid-century England in relation to the conversation picture. These images were in fact commissioned by families economically located through the full range of the upper classes. Despite their typically modest size (this one is 50 × 40 inches) conversation pictures were ordered up by newly wealthy parvenus seeking visually to represent their newfound status via idealizations that seemingly provided an excuse to believe in established pedigree. But members of the landed and secure aristocracy commissioned them as well.[16] It is not easy to detect stylistic differences in the representations intended for one group or another. Nonetheless, the small size of these images made them especially suitable to the more modestly sized houses (not to say small) of the newly wealthy. Among this group, musical props like double-manual harpsichords, like the elaborately framed and large paintings within the painting (ironically, dimensionally very different from the little conversation pictures in which they were included!), were of course signs of wealth, refined taste, and accomplishment.

Large double-manual harpsichords which occupy considerable compositional space loom in importance within the closed world of the picture frame in ways that do not necessarily translate into reality. That is, their purpose may have relatively little to do with familial musical tastes and practices as such. Whether this is so in any given instance is nearly always impossible to say, unless a great deal is known about the sitters, which is seldom the case. But what we can know, for example, as regards the harpsichord represented in Pickering's painting, is that its presence plays off the long-lived pictorial and textual conventions from Plato onward that associate music, or certain kinds of music, with a non-musical metaphorical harmony that is at once cultural, social, familial, wealth-based, and prestigious. This *signifiance* is encoded without regard to whether any music was ever made on the instrument here used as prop – as I have shown elsewhere, it is an established fact that once musically trained and even accomplished girls became women and married they commonly closed up their harpsichords more or less for good.[17]

One other detail requires comment, the sitters' hand gestures. It is crucial to realize that the iconic value of the image centers around the women and their *purported* musicality. The painting's three women are literally framed by men, the father on the right and a son, perhaps, on the left, both of whom gesture elaborately, and unnaturally, towards the women, so as to draw our attention to them. Such gesturing in fact reduces the status of the women as people, hence diminishes them in relation to the men – the gesture is arguably almost rude; at the same time it increases the women's status as signs which in turn reflect on the men. The women are decorative in every possible way: as musicians (the mother holds a music book in her lap in such a way to allow her other daughter to look on and sing to the harpsichord's accompaniment), as elaborately, fashionably dressed consumers of familial wealth, and as doers of nothing. It is anything but accidental, indeed convention virtually demands, that the painter place in the seated daughter's lap a bouquet of flowers and a comb. Her role is her beauty. She is decorative, like the flowers in vases on the wall. And is it any wonder that no one of the sitters appears to be having any pleasure from this gathering – the faces are entirely typical for the genre – their seriousness, to put the best light on it, confirming the stakes of the representation? But this is only to acknowledge that conversation pieces are rarely celebrations; they are fundamentally aestheticized, domesticated polemics which, ideally, the visual consumer of the image will internalize.

A Frenchified conversation picture by Joseph Nollekens (Plate 26.4), typical of a number of other examples he produced,[18] repeats everything contained in the image attributed to Pickering though with a fundamental difference. In this instance architecture and Continental landscape take over, with music nonetheless incorporated via the small harpsichord and the classical musical scene in relief on the large urn. It seems to me that the very decorativeness, falseness, and, indeed, preposterousness of the image articulate a more aristocratic lineage. The painting seems to record real people, but in a setting that cannot make up its mind between Arcadia and the Roman Forum. And its unabashed French flavor likewise suggests a family very certain about its position – in politics nonetheless likely more Whig than Tory! – for to valorize the Continental carried risk of censure usually formulated around a suspected lack of patriotism; only the well-established could be expected to buck this dynamic. But what of the music?

As a literal event it makes no sense; people did not characteristically tote harpsichords outdoors; it disturbed the tuning, the sound was diminished by the open acoustical setting, and, in any case, what would otherwise be the point of it? Indeed, Nollekens produced a conceit sufficiently compelling to master the apparent disadvantage of the "event" making no sense. I would argue that senselessness may be just the point, one deeply informing certain kinds of consumption including music. The act of moving the music outdoors tacitly argues for music's inconsequentiality, but hence its value. It is a nothingness – non-material, non-productive – and thereby a sign of status. The production–consumption of nothing argues better than anything else for the sumptuary degree of wealth, status and power available to this family.

Once again it is no accident that, even with this group of highly privileged sitters, there is no joy, no pleasure registered. This is not to say, as I suggested earlier, that music is registered in an anti-emotional, rationalized exercise, so much as it is a sign of grim-faced harmony. Not for nothing is allusion made to Apollonian classicism, via the lyre on the urn. Taken as a whole, the scene is Plato's utopia calmly realized. Nonetheless, the social harmony thus enacted, under whose "protection" the arts flourish, demands that one's guard never be let down. The paterfamilias may gesture towards his fake garden – its design borrowed from Versailles – thereby making sure we notice, but the gesture itself argues that the visual feast we are invited to consume, including whatever musical echoes may be incorporated, is not quite so secure as one might hope.

The wind blows hard, so the Boucher-like tree at the center informs us, but its force is blocked by the fortress portico of the great house. The sky, quite English, is at once sunny and storm-threatened. There is much to be kept at bay. What then is the man's gesture? In fact, it is an odd one. For he does not precisely ask us to look on to the scene behind him, as I first suggested; if that were the case we might expect a hand gesture of palm upwards, like Pickering's in the preceding image. Oddly, Nollekens's sitter makes a gesture more characteristic of one that "asks" for silence; but if this is so, who or what is silenced? Is it the wind, the ancient sign of change? Is it control over nature itself that his incongruous move articulates? (The gesture is fully characteristic of those described in many contemporaneous manuals on body carriage and taught by dancing masters designed to establish visually and publicly one's social position – to articulate via grace, its radical opposite: power.[19]) Whether he or his daughter's music – she a reflection of his power – can still the metaphorical winds (as Orpheus charmed the animals) remains an open question.

What is clear is that his gesture incorporates our own consumption of the painting's look, just as within the painting its every person is in turn defined by the sonoric harmonies the harpsichord purports to deliver. The consumption of the image by the viewer, and the consumption of the metaphorical sonorities by the painting's sitters, alike seek to overdetermine human identities for the simple but essential reason that their and our identities will determine the social order. The final irony of musical consumption in eighteenth-century England – from which we can in fact generalize well beyond its shores and that century – is that it was a feminine and feminized practice which served as the visual metaphor for the possibility of tranquility and of nurture in a culture that constructed the feminine, and the women condemned to live within the confines of that construction, as other, as enemy, and as threat – as well as the beloved. And in this light there can be little wonder at the ironic fact that the most perfect music was not that heard or that practiced, but that painted, or that the women in paintings consistently fulfill roles not in their own interests but in that of their men in whose image they are, ideally at least, to be created. I have no way of knowing whether the women in Nollekens's or Zoffany's paintings were as severe as they are represented; I do have some idea as to why they were painted in such a manner, whose interests it served, and whose anxieties it might have assuaged. There is very little to suggest that English attitudes towards actual music were very different from English attitudes towards real women, especially since the two were so conflated, and this fact determines why the consumption of the proper look of both, in a culture of the gaze, was of the most fundamental importance.

But I hesitate to end on this grim note, and indeed were I to do so I would have neglected to acknowledge the existence of another sort of visual representation that mediates the account so far provided. I want to turn briefly to drawing, and away from painting, for to do so allows for a change in both the social "rules" and visual codes governing representation. Drawing allows representation of that which in painting is unrepresentable. The issue hinges on the differing functions of drawing and painting governed by the important difference between the private and the (semi)public.

A painting, even when hanging in a house, was never a totally private image, though its purpose, in the terms I have discussed, first and foremost served familial interests. The homes of the elite were invariably traversed by many people, notably people sharing the approximate status of the residents. Paintings were important for what they projected about their owners to these viewers, ranging from the accomplishment of their aesthetic tastes to their wealth to, not least, what they held dear. But drawings were different. Some of the upper classes collected them; a few even produced them. By no means all drawings, in other words, were preliminary studies for paintings and hence intended principally for artists' eyes only – the nineteenth-century taste for water-colors is of course an especially dramatic example though it is less important a phenomenon for the eighteenth century and for the subject-matter I am considering. To protect drawings, and to store them efficiently, they were kept in drawers or cartons, from which they could be taken at will to be looked at, shared, passed around. Compared with paintings they not only carried a lesser burden of prestige, they also remained less bound to the demands and expectations for outwardly projected ideological correctness. In other words, the representational gap between ideology and practice (not terribly wide so far as I can determine), and between ideology and desire (often very wide indeed), could be narrowed if not closed in this medium.

What can be more readily represented in drawings, less so or not at all in paintings, is a music for "purposeless" pleasure (Plate 26.5),[20] where a woman performs for herself, where producer and consumer become one, and where the only intrusion into this momentarily pleasured space is the natural antipathy between a cat and dog, rendered charming. If we realize that the image is by Lady Burlington, possibly sketching herself, the issue I am driving at becomes clearer. The drawing represents a woman's projection of her own musical activity. As such, it refuses to acknowledge male-prescribed functions of music for women, except for one which it cannot avoid, namely, the advantage music brought to men as a devourer of women's extensive leisure time, a device for keeping women out of men's affairs. This aside, it cannot be denied that in the instance represented here a woman's pleasure is her own; and it is a pleasure embued with symbolic agency. The sign Lady Burlington employs is the dog which, despite the provocation about to be delivered by the cat, sits up to listen to the tune, perhaps to dance. In the history of western visual representation, dogs are male (invariably so in seventeenth-century marriage portraits, for example, where they stand in as metaphors of *fides*, fidelity),[21] whereas by contrast cats are commonly gendered female (as is of course their libidinous temperament, no accident). Lady Burlington, in other words, through her music exercises a power over a male stand-in for her husband; she calls the tune. (That she might desire to do so would hardly be surprising given the well-known preference of her husband, Richard Boyle, 3rd earl of Burlington, for the company of men, notably including George Frideric Handel.)

Lady Burlington's sketch of these two animals is visually striking, and quite out of keeping with conventional representation. The dog, for centuries heavily embued with the familial symbolism of male control, here appears both ineffectual and even silly, whereas the crouching cat, close to the musician, hence to be associated with her, prepares to take on her musically transfixed and immobilized, physically larger opposite. If this makes sense, then I must amend my comment about Lady Burlington's musician's pleasure: her playing is not wholly purposeless, but is as well an expression of desire, almost certainly forever sublimated and deferred, to live her own life.

Drawings make clear, where paintings seldom do, that women's pleasure could be mutual, hence social. It might even occur outdoors, hence be subject to others' view (Plate 26.6). More unusual, drawing allows the representation of the same sociability among men (Plate 26.7), but in closed-in settings which emphasize the absence of observers and which – nearly invariably – hint of the comic, as though even in a drawing the musicians' guilt and shame about their musical proclivities needed to be paid for by acknowledging – or pretending to – the limitations of their seriousness. The musically passionate Pepys, who could appropriately stand in for practically any eighteenth-century male amateur in this respect, acknowledged "being fearful of being too much taken with musique" (Hufstader 1968: 448).

Perhaps the most affecting imagery of this sort occurs in the few drawings that both preserve and valorize music in family groups, where affection and sociability inter-mingle in both the practice of music and the metaphorical charge of harmony represen-tationally projected (Plate 26.8 and 26.9). In the first of these a mother cradles her child and the father looks closely on, while in front of them, in the center foreground, two young children play at tea, and on the left two older daughters sing and play the harpsichord, watched by a brother. At the rear by the hearth another man looks on, but as something of a witness or even an intruder, perhaps an acquaintance, perhaps the eldest son, already spatially separated and set to live on his own. In the second drawing, the situation is much the same except that the ages are advanced; the parents are now grandparents and old. In both there is a warmth and an affection that is extraordinarily rare in contemporaneous paintings, whose purpose largely disallowed the valorization or representation of affectional relations as such, and which required tight control over practices like music that possessed potential for exceeding conven-tionally appropriate ideological boundaries.

The social danger such drawings articulate is triply contained, by the limited pres-tige accorded to drawings (and these are hardly by major artists), by their inaccessi-bility to viewing, and finally by their size. Each of the drawings I have so far discussed is tiny, the largest being 11 × 17 inches, the smallest less than 9 × 7. Size matters; size means. The paintings discussed earlier are many times larger than these drawings. Their size is discursively emphatic by comparison, and this rhetorical quality is only increased by the medium of oil paint itself (its ability to manifest color, texture, quality of light, etc.). If paintings shout, drawings whisper. The practices and tastes these drawings represent, whether of affection or music, are unofficial – as any ideal and intended viewer from the period would unquestionably have understood. The values projected *cannot* be "stated" publicly, insofar as they valorize a radically oppositional formula for both identity and subjectivity upon which to base and sustain both nation and class. Specifically, they organize intersubjectivity on a model marked by the culture as feminine, hence as degraded.

The rare drawings I have considered thus far exist in the company of a still more radical – and final – sort: images of non-familial groups, adult women and men together and in private quarters for the purpose of making music (Plates 26.10 and 26.11).[22] These minuscule images (each roughly 6 × 7 inches) are, however, quite different from each other. The first is perhaps about what we might expect; a man sits at a keyboard (though fundamentally a woman's instrument), possibly accompanying a singing woman, towards whom others look and listen. One visual element is striking. The music acts as a gravitational pull on everyone present. The left side is heavy with dark, fast pen strokes delineating the musician(s) and immediate audience. The right side, distinctly lighter in tone and pen stroke, shows two women in very different stance. The one more towards the center is set at greater depth from the figures at the left, but she seems drawn towards them and unquestionably gives the music her attention. The woman farthest to the right is slightly ghostly, lighter, still further removed. But her profile accounts for her attentiveness. More to the point, both women are visually pulled towards the music, their visual lightness overwhelmed by the concentration of lines to the left. As viewers, our eyes complete the task they themselves cannot accomplish, frozen as they are in time: our eyes make the shift from them towards the source of sonority. Something is happening here compositionally that seldom occurs in paintings: the experiential power of music is visually activated; its action on the body is both acknowledged and celebrated.

If this is so, it is still more the case in the second drawing, thought to be the work of the musicianly Zoffany (Plate 26.11). This drawing loses something as regards the reality of musical practice (the woman's standing position at the keyboard, and her hand position on the keys, are both preposterous) in order to gain something else. In my judgment the gain is that which I suggested for the prior drawing, celebration via a musical pleasure that momentarily suspends gender relations, where men and women come together and do so in a setting where a woman literally stands up to men and by so doing equalizes the normal relation of lead-part to accompaniment. The male flautist here sits, though he has the tune; his partner who "merely" fills in at the keyboard stands – and in a pose that is strikingly, purposefully unnatural. She is an icon of difference. Little wonder that her female friend at her side smiles as she prepares to turn the page, or that the standing men opposite her seem uncertain how to react. Four men are included. Two of them help form a circle with the women; both may also be musicians, but the sketch is unclear. Their pleasure, judging from their faces, is evident from the concentration they give to their practice. The other two men are compositionally outside this closed circle; further recessed; they stand apart even from each other. But they share a stare and a bit of a frown – I am uncertain that their look is one of concentration; it appears not to be one of pleasure. Whatever else, they pass judgment and, I think, acknowledge the real trouble that this ensemble must cause. Here are production and consumption which not only admit their own practice, but which also acknowledge the ideological and practical implications of difference: an altered relation of men to women and women to men – not one where women overtake men, become men so to speak, but something far more dangerous: women as men's joyful equals. The rampant misogyny of the English in the eighteenth century sought to convince men that usurpation as such by women of men's position was impossible, risible. It was the possibility of equality that defined misogyny's project. Domination was never at issue; sharing was.[23]

Such music both as practice and sonority momentarily enacts unity of mind and body, man and woman. Its consumption is simultaneously a production of utopian desire for wholeness. But this is a dangerous valorization, one that must be rejected at the same moment it is embraced. The rage for and against music never fails to preserve this ironic dialectic as the insurance policy for the depth of reaction music enacts. This is the price of its pleasure. The solace that music genuinely provides at once protests and condemns the disharmonious relations its sonorities momentarily displace. When Zoffany's musicians and listeners leave off, just as when we depart the concert hall and head for the parking lot, they reclaim the truth which they sought in music to dispel. But the music itself does not lie – even if it is a music of untruth, the worst sort of music, the most debased drivel – music cannot help encoding by its very nature the distinction between its own sonorities and the other sounds in life that we seek by means of music to drown out. Music *is* the utopian promise, though as such our culture has consistently sought not merely to control it but to marginalize its practice, since its utopian promise can never be fully and effectively marshalled against itself. Nonetheless, music is commonly asked to play the role of liar, to make us find in it – and hence be satisfied with – what we cannot have in excess of music's nothingness. Still, music plays its role of liar poorly, for no matter what it might "say" to our minds, it cannot disguise to our bodies: that most bodies exist in some state of unwilling bondage which music reminds us of by inviting us to move.

In moving towards my conclusion, I want to say something more about pleasure, to suggest that the appeal of music to men and women alike in this culture was sometimes sufficiently strong to overcome the most stringent restrictions, if not outright prohibitions, relating to its production and consumption. It must be kept in mind that music's pleasure was, and is, in part accounted for by its semantic slipperiness. That is, music remains a discourse that can manifest its compliance to the social order in the very act of disclaiming and ironicizing the said compliance. Music's "ability" to deny what it claims – which could be theorized as a lack, and disingenuously articulated as music's triviality – was already very well understood in the eighteenth century. Music's perniciousness was located in its semantic excesses: paradoxically, its literal quality of nothingness, confirmed by its immeasurability. Thus in a world soon to be made subject to classificatory scientisms, where what counted was what could be quantified, it is not surprising that one group would seek to account for music as non-mysterious and measurable, via an account of its numbers and ratios, or that another group, proto-

Romantics, would valorize music precisely because such measurements were so utterly meaningless to music's experiential power.[24]

To return to the question with which I opened: "What is it that one 'consumes' when one 'consumes' music?" The answer – or that part of the answer that interests me here – might go something like the following. One consumes pleasure, wherein pleasure as a category of human experience is at once "disinterested" and "interested." By disinterested I mean that music's pleasure is produced in part by aural stimulations which in turn trigger physiological and emotional responses that result in some sense, inevitably temporary, of well-being. This pleasure is embodied; it may be simultaneously of body and mind and as such the sonoric simulacrum of an organic totality absent from an otherwise fractured reality. Nonetheless, music's organicism can be imagined only to the extent that it is lost as soon as it is gained, inevitably lost the moment sound ceases. By "interested" I mean that music's pleasures, just described, are never totally innocent, never produced or experienced solely as autonomous reaction ("disinterested"). This says no more than that any discursive practice must give meaning to and gain meaning from not only its own practice and result (in this case, sonority proper) but also from the larger system of discursive and semantic practices of which it is never more than a part.

Pleasure by its very nature comes with strings attached. In a culture of scarcity, even among those for whom scarcity is not more than a theoretical possibility, pleasure by definition is understood to be an unstable and exceptional category of human experience. This is because pleasure is not solely dependent upon material excess – financial means do not guarantee access to pleasure. Pleasure is an uncommodified commodity; its consumption incorporates loss at the moment of gain. This partly accounts for the desire that pleasure produces, to the extent that we understand by desire that which we have not (even in the moment of having). Pleasure in our culture is always on loan, and repayment is invariably demanded.

Even when most semantically drained, as in the abstract projection "pleasure for pleasure's sake" – as such, an ideology but not a lived reality – pleasure remains semantically rich. Pleasure is experiential; it involves consciousness and intentionality. Even when, as is often the case, it locates itself outside the mind by a nonetheless mental conception of its escape from the bounds of rationalization, pleasure's contingency is not only a matter of physical–emotional sensing but also the mental awareness of the difference it allows, momentarily, from the mental (or, better, the rationalized). The desire for pleasure of whatever kind is embodied. But the embodiment I refer to is the sort possible only by conceiving embodiment as a (wished-for) totality of body and mind.

Music is a repeatedly inscribing marker. Its "repetitions," the result of music as an embodied sound and sight, serve as sensory over-determinations of every semantic value it produces. Indeed, therein lie much of music's power and pleasure: whatever it might mean, it means repeatedly – whether referring to the replaying of a piece of music over some interval of time, or referring instead to the internal repetitions in all music but especially obvious in formal procedures like dance forms or theme and variations. Repetition inscribes reassurance and predictability. As such it is the sonoric–visual simulacrum of contentment, the *promesse de bonheur* which Stendhal described as art and which the Frankfurt school took up in its account of the utopian moment in culture.[25] What I mean is that music, like dance with which it is closely associated, both visually and sonorically enacts a stylized and aestheticized order which human beings valorize highly, especially in light of its abundant opposite, chaos or disorder: noise.[26]

Among contemporaneous eighteenth-century discursive practices only theater works somewhat similarly to music to the extent that it acts in time and produces its effects through both sight and sound. But theater works differently, if not necessarily less effectively. This is so because theater never escapes words or the demands that words as such make on the mind in theoretical absence of the body – even pantomime narrates via language, through language's very absence and retranslation into gesture sufficiently exaggerated to re-create the grammar and syntax of the told story. With music – even, perhaps especially, texted music – words' affects are by contrast degraded by music's acoustic transliteration. Expressing the same thought conversely, all that music adds to words is in effect taken *from* words. Whether in song, cantata, opera or oratorio, etc., text depends utterly on sonority at the same time that sonority robs text of its word-driven sign value. (This is not to deny, however, the highly self-conscious attempts by some composers – Debussy, for example – to subvert the text–music relation I am describing.) To be sure, words still mean when paired with music, but music takes nearly full charge of them. In a paradoxical manner, texted music acts in discursive excess of words by inscribing the effects of words and music together on the mind and body together, but in a hierarchy opposite to that culturally sanctioned: the body excels. Music betrays the very paucity of the words it sets, or, rather it makes emphatic the severe limitations of a reason that valorizes a rationality divorced from embodiment. Reason's poverty is unmasked. (And it can be no accident that wordless music rises in importance in western history, apart from the special and important exception of dance, which by definition privileges the body's relation to music over that of the mind by itself, at the precise moment in early modernity that language itself is more and more systematically institutionalized as the bureaucratic tool of would-be corporate and state power, beginning with the slow rise of the literate classes from the ranks of monastic clergy, and ending in the modern boardroom.) This says no less than that music's ultimate pleasure lies in its greatest threat, at least to a society defined by the goals of instrumentalized rationalism. Music's pleasure is the temporary "realignment" of body with mind, though in prevailing accounts of that pleasure, extant well before the eighteenth century but still largely current in the 1700s, its action was theorized less as a realignment than a usurpation. That is to say that what music offered – its *promesse de bonheur* of a momentary peace between body and mind – was not a gift particularly appreciated.

Thus spoke Philip Stubbes, the English pamphleteer born about 1555, in *The Anatomie of Abuses* (1583) a virulent attack on the manners, customs and amusements of the period, though there is little original in his diatribe:

> I Say of Musicke as Plato, Aristotle, Galen, and many others have said of it; that it is very il for yung heds, for a certeine kind of nice, smoothe sweetnes in alluring the auditorie to niceness, effeminancie, pusillanimitie, & lothsomnes of life, so as it may not improperly be compared to a sweet electuarie of honie, or rather to honie it-self; for as honie and such like sweet things, received into the

> stomack, dooth delight at the first, but afterward they make the stomack so
> quasie, nice and weake, that it is not able to admit meat of hard digesture:
> So sweet Musick at the first delighteth the eares, but afterward corrupteth and
> depraveth the minde. . . .
>
> But being uscd in publique assemblies and private conventicles, as direc-
> tories to filthie dauncing, thorow the sweet harmonie & smoothe melodie
> therof, it estraungeth the mind, stireth up filthie lust, womannisheth the
> minde, ravisheth the hart, enflameth concupisence, and bringeth in
> uncleannes.

> (Stubbes 1877–82: I, 169–70)

It should not be lost on us that Stubbes's metaphor of music's action is literally one of
consumption, involving food (honey) that acts as a poison on the body (stomach). But
his concern is with music's attack, via its entrance through the ears, on the mind
("yung heds," "corrupteth and depraveth the minde"), which is overwhelmed and
degraded by the awakening of sexuality, and by the concurrent loss of gender identity
marked by difference (music makes the man "womanish"). The words inscribe
pollution ("bringeth in uncleannes") and, oddly, rape ("ravisheth the hart"). Music is
pleasure at a high price. But what is most interesting is the sense that music is
something which when consumed consumes in turn. Its danger lies in its being internalized: it infects us; it eats us out from within.

Jeremy Collier's account of music in his 1697 conduct book argued for a music
"rightly order'd" which exalts the mind, calms the passions and affords pleasure; the
pleasure he acknowledges is explicitly anti-corporeal (indeed, he had in mind a simple
devotional music). Yet he feared music of all kinds because of the alterations it affected
on the listener; he hinted of its anarchic powers. Music

> Raises, and Falls, and Counterchanges the Passions at an unaccountable Rate.
> It Charms and Transports, Ruffles and Becalms, and Governs with an almost
> arbitrary Authority. There is scarcely any Constitution so heavy, or any
> Reason so well fortified, as to be absolutely proof against it.

> (Collier 1697: 21)

In the end Collier lumped secular and devotional music together and implied that it
might be best to do without both:

> Yet to have our Passions lye at the Mercy of a little Minstrelsy; to be Fiddled
> out of our Reason and Sobriety. . . . If we were proof against the charming of
> Sounds; or could we have the Satisfaction without the Danger; or raise our
> Minds to what pitch we pleas'd by the Strength of *Thinking*, it would be a
> nobler Instance of Power and Perfection. But such an Independency is not to
> be expected in this World, therefore we must manage wisely and be contented.

> (Collier 1697: 24–5)

Thus music is "danger" articulated as anti-thought; it activates the enemy within, the
body. Music activates the corporeal passions which in turn destroy reason. It is not
accidental that Collier's metaphors locate music's dangers very close to the body via
sexuality, or that he thinks of music as a feminine entity ("charming" in English culture

is invariably a female characteristic) whose mission is to unman men ("strength" in English culture is invariably male). Music at its highest degree of abstraction, as is sometimes, for example, associated – quite mistakenly – with Beethoven's late string quartets – never exceeds the body by its appeal to the mind. Music is inevitably of the body, though whether as guest or a virus cannot be decided as a general principle in the culture under consideration.[27]

Notes

1   For a detailed discussion of these sources see R. Leppert, *Music and Image* (1988: Chs. 2–3 in particular).
2   I have discussed the ideological underpinnings and sociocultural implications of a treatise on the mathematics of sound by John Keeble, *The Theory of Harmonics: or, an Illustration of the Grecian Harmonica* (1784), and its relation to Rameau's music theory, in R. Leppert, "Music, domestic life and cultural chauvinism: images of British subjects at home in India" (1987: 71–8).
3   See, for example, Henry Curson, *The Theory of Sciences Illustrated* (1702: 129–31).
4   Anon., *Euterpe: or, Remarks on the Use and Abuse of Music, as a Part of Modern Education* (c. 1778: 15). Cf. the very similar views on music, order, and morality expressed by John Dennis in "Advancement and reformation of poetry" (1939–43a: I, 336).
5   See J. Kassler, *The Science of Music in Britain, 1714–1830* (1979).
6   See R. Leppert, "Imagery, musical confrontation and cultural difference in early 18th-century London" (1986: 323–45).
7   See J. Dennis, *An Essay on Opera's after the Italian Manner* . . . (1939–43b: I, 382–93, 520–4); and Leppert, "Imagery, musical confrontation, cultural difference" (1986: 337–8).
8   P. Stanhope, *Letters to his Son by the Earl of Chesterfield* (1926: I, 170, letter 68, dated April 19 [O.S.], 1749). In another letter (1926: I, 186, letter 73, dated June 22 [O.S.], 1749) of similar vein he cites the musical proclivities of the Italians as direct proof of the country's decline.
9   See Leppert, *Music and Image* (1988: 56–66); and R. Leppert, "Music teachers of upper-class amateur musicians in eighteenth-century England" (1985: 133–58).
10 See P. Scholes, *The Great Doctor Burney* (1948).
11 For a famous example of a father's attempting to prevent a public musical performance by his daughter, the case of Ann Ford, see Leppert, *Music and Image* (1988: 40–2).
12 E. Darwin, *A Plan for the Conduct of Female Education* (1798: 13). The book appeared in Derby and London editions in 1797. In spite of the fact that the author was male, the work is formated as a series of letters from a mother to her daughter. For more information on the author and the text, see Kassler, *Science of Music* (1979: I, 263–4). Cf. Anon., *Euterpe* (c. 1778: 18); Anon., *The Polite Lady* (1769: 24); and H. Chapone, *Letters on Improvement of the Mind.* (1818–19: 193): "it is but seldom that a private person has leisure or application enough to gain any high degree of excellence in [music]; and your own partial family are perhaps the only persons who would not much rather be entertained by the performance of a professor than by yours: but, with regard to yourself, it is of great consequence to have the power of filling up agreeably those intervals of time, which too often hang heavily on the hands of a woman, if her lot be cast in a retired situation." (This book was first published in 1773, with four additional editions in Great Britain by 1783; it was published in American editions as late as 1834.)
13 See Leppert, *Music and Image* (1988: 16–27, 107–46).
14 Darwin, *Conduct of Female Education* (1798: 125). For a detailed treatment of this general issue see Leppert, *Music and Image* (1988: 29–45).
15 See, for example, W. Darrell, *A Gentleman Instructed in the Conduct of a Virtuous and Happy Life* (1704: 129).

16 See on this point E. D'Oench, *The Conversation Piece* (1980: 21–2).

17 See further Leppert, *Music and Image* (1988: 43–5).

18 See Ibid.: 201–4, for a discussion of a similar painting by Nollekens (Figure 93) and additional information about the artist.

19 See further Ibid.: 99–105.

20 For other examples, see Ibid.: 159–61, Figures 63–4, both by artist Paul Sandby. For another drawing by Lady Burlington from the same album but of a radically different sort, see Ibid.: 192–3, Figure 86.

21 See R. Leppert, "Music as a sight in the production of music's meaning" (1991: 69–88).

22 Cf. a well-known drawing of similar sort by Thomas Gainsborough reproduced in J. Hayes, *The Drawings of Thomas Gainsborough* (1971: no. 47).

23 Little wonder that when Zoffany took up in paint the subject of music and sociability what he projected in this drawing is present only as the most distant – dangerous – reflection. For example, see Leppert, *Music and Image* (1988: 91–2, Figure 25).

24 Romanticist aesthetics attempted to locate art in a "disinterested" autonomous realm separate from a lived and mundane reality viewed as debased. The ideal music, best able to lay apparent claim to autonomy, was non-texted, non-programatic instrumental music (that is, music at its most abstract), never previously in western history valorized so highly. Adorno pointed out that the plea for musical autonomy is not only ideology (which he used in the narrow sense of "false consciousness") but also unrealizable (art is incapable of being removed from lived social reality). But he argued that the ideology of aesthetic autonomy nonetheless incorporated a truth at its deepest core. By nature of its demand to find in art something better than mundane reality, romantic aesthetics implicitly acknowledged the inadequacy of the social reality from which escape was sought through art. See further Adorno, *Introduction to the Sociology of Music* (1976); and especially his *Aesthetic Theory* (1984), though the translation of the latter is notoriously unreliable. Regarding pertinent primary sources, see two excellent anthologies: P. Le Huray and J. Day (eds.) *Music and Aesthetics in the Eighteenth and Early-Nineteenth Centuries* (1981); and E. Lippman (ed.) *Musical Aesthetics: A Historical Reader* (1986–90).

25 See further F. Jameson, *Late Marxism: Adorno, or, the Persistence of the Dialectic* (1990: 146–7); and H. Marcuse, "The affirmative character of culture" (1968: 115).

26 J. Attali, *Noise: The Political Economy of Music* (1985) is the best theoretical account of the music–noise continuum as a metaphor for and herald of social structure and political organization.

27 This raises an important issue to which I can only point – to deal adequately with its complexity demands a separate project – namely, the consumer's ability to produce his or her own meanings for what is consumed. One consumes meanings in consuming music, opening oneself, willingly or not, to the complicated processes of internalization and naturalization by which cultural and social identities are forged and then maintained. Saying this does not establish whether the identities forged are necessarily those of the dominant in the society and culture, but it does indicate that internationalization and naturalization processes always act in relation to the dominant, even if specifically to oppose them. And this fact was lost on no one philosophizing on music's relation to society in the eighteenth century. Indeed, every sort of written record I have alluded to acknowledges, either implicitly or explicitly, that these are the stakes involved.

Yet when people "consume" meanings their role is by no means entirely or even primarily passive. This is because consumption is inevitably always already production as well. Consumption, whether reading a novel or making or listening to music, involves an ongoing process of assessment: "re-reading." In the sense given to this term by postmodern cultural theory, the act of consumption is in part one of the re-production of meanings, which as such are never identical to the "original" model. In other words, consumption is a component part of human agency. To consume in part means to decide to consume (more so in history predating mass culture). Nonetheless, no reading is Archimedean; the force of sanctioned or preferred readings, established via the institutions of the socially dominant (state, church, education, etc.), cannot be eliminated or even easily rendered marginal except over enormous spans of time (if at all) precisely because these readings are internalized into the gestures and practices of every discursive act prior to their ever being challenged.

Bibliography

Adorno, T. (1976) *Introduction to the Sociology of Music*, trans. E. Ashton, New York: Continuum.

—— (1984) *Aesthetic Theory*, ed. G. Adorno and R. Tiedemann, trans. C. Lenhardt, London and New York: Routledge & Kegan Paul.

Anon. (1701) *The Whole Duty of a Woman, or a Guide to the Female Sex. From the Age of Sixteen to Sixty*, 3rd edn., London.

Anon. (1769) *The Polite Lady; or, a Course of Female Education*, 2nd edn., corrected, London.

Anon. (*c.* 1778) *Euterpe; or, Remarks on the Use and Abuse of Music, as a Part of Modern Education*, London.

Attali, J. (1985) *Noise: The Political Economy of Music*, trans. B. Massumi, Minneapolis, MN: University of Minnesota Press.

Chapone, H. (1818–19) *Letters on Improvement of the Mind, Addressed to a Young Lady*, 2 vols. in 1, Hagerstown, MD.

Collier, J. (1697) *Essays upon Several Moral Subjects. In Two Parts*. 2nd. edn., corrected and enlarged, London.

Curson, H. (1702) *The Theory of Sciences Illustrated; or the Grounds and Principles of the Seven Liberal Arts*, London.

Darrell, W. (1704) *A Gentleman Instructed in the Conduct of a Virtuous and Happy Life*, London.

Darwin, E. (1798) *A Plan for the Conduct of Female Education, in Boarding Schools, Private Families, and Public Seminaries*, Philadelphia, PA.

Dennis, J. (1939–43a) "Advancement and reformation of poetry," in E. Hooker (ed.) *The Critical Works of John Dennis*, 2 vols., Baltimore, MD: Johns Hopkins University Press.

—— (1939–43b) *An Essay on Opera's after the Italian Manner, Which are about to be Establish'd on the English Stage: With Some Reflections on the Damage Which They May Bring to the Publick*, in E. Hooker (ed.) *The Critical Works of John Dennis*, 2 vols., Baltimore, MD: Johns Hopkins University Press.

D'Oench, E. (1980) *The Conversation Piece: Arthur Devis and his Contemporaries*, New Haven, CT: Yale Center for British Art.

Fielding, H. (1973) *Tom Jones*, ed. Sheridan Baker, New York: Norton.

Hayes, J. (1971) *The Drawings of Thomas Gainsborough*, New Haven, CT: Yale University Press.

Hufstader, A. (1968) "Samuel Pepys, inquisitive amateur," *Musical Quarterly* 54: 437–61.

Jameson, F. (1990) *Late Marxism: Adorno, or, the Persistence of the Dialectic*, London: Verso.

Kassler, J. (1979) *The Science of Music in Britain, 1714–1830: A Catalogue of Writings, Lectures and Inventions*, 2 vols., New York: Garland.

Keeble, J. (1784) *The Theory of Harmonics: or, an Illustration of the Grecian Harmonica*, London.

Le Huray, P. and Day, J. (eds.) (1981) *Music and Aesthetics in the Eighteenth and Early-Nineteenth Centuries*, Cambridge: Cambridge University Press.

Leppert, R. (1985) "Music teachers of upper-class amateur musicians in eighteenth-century England," in A. Atlas (ed.) *Music in the Classic Period: Essays in Honor of Barry S. Brook*, New York: Pendragon, pp. 133–58.

—— (1986) "Imagery, musical confrontation and cultural difference in early 18th-century London," *Early Music* 14, 3: 323–45.

—— (1987) "Music, domestic life and cultural chauvinism: images of British subjects at home in India," in R. Leppert and S. McClary (eds.) *Music and Society: The Politics of Composition. Performance and Reception*, Cambridge: Cambridge University Press, pp. 63–104.

—— (1988) *Music and Image: Domesticity. Ideology & Socio-Cultural Formation in Eighteenth-Century England*, Cambridge: Cambridge University Press.

—— (1991) "Music as a sight in the production of music's meaning," in J. Kassler (ed.) *Metaphor: A Musical Dimension*, Sydney: Currency Press, pp. 69–88.

Lippman, E. (ed.) (1986–90) *Musical Aesthetics: A Historical Reader*, 3 vols, New York: Pendragon.

Marcuse, H. (1968) "The affirmative character of culture," in *Negations: Essays in Critical Theory*, trans. J. Shapiro, Boston, MA: Beacon.

Scholes, P. (1948) *The Great Doctor Burney: His life his Travels, his Works, his Family and his Friends*, 2 vols., Oxford: Oxford University Press.

Stanhope, P. (1926) *Letters to his Son by the Earl of Chesterfield on the Fine Art of Becoming a Man of the World and a Gentleman*, ed. O. Leigh, 2 vols., London: Navarre Society.

Stephens, J. (ed.) (1972) *Aubrey on Education: A Hitherto Unpublished Manuscript by the Author of "Brief Lives"*, London and Boston, MA: Routledge & Kegan Paul.

Stubbes, P. (1877–92) *Philip Stubbes's Anatomy of Abuses in England in Shakespeare's Youth. A. D. 1583*, ed. F. Furnivall, 2 vols., London: New Shakespeare Society.

Index